JUDGE YOURSELF
BEFORE JUDGEMENT DAY

AK MD ABDUL HAYE

ISBN: 000-0-000000-0 (Paperback)

ISBN: 000-0-000000-0 (Hardcover)

Front cover image by Artist.

Book design by Designer.

First printing edition 2025

Publisher

Address, City,

Edited by

Muhammed Mujeebur Rahman

Barrister of the Hon'ble Society of Lincoln's Inn

Printed By

Contents

The Journey Back Home:.. i

A Quest for Purity and Divine Truth i

Judge Yourself Before Judgment Day ii

Your Soul, Your Spark! iii

Acknowledgements.. v

Preface... vi

Introduction.. viii

From Editor's Desk:... xi

Chapter 1 Power of Journey.. 1

Chapter 2 8

Chapter 3 22

Chapter 4 45

Chapter 5 118

Chapter 6 206

Chapter 7 247

Chapter 8 277

Chapter 9 326

Chapter 10 352

Chapter 11 358

Chapter 12 428

Chapter 13 468

Chapter 14 504

Chapter 15 521

Chapter 16 549

Chapter 17 581

QUR'ANIC VERSE INDEX... 603

KJV BIBLE VERSE INDEX 617

CONTENTS SOURCING INDEX.. 621

References.. 636

The Journey Back Home:

"Thereof (the earth) We created you, and into it We shall return you, and from it We shall bring you out once again." — **Surah Ta-Ha 20:55**

"I will give them a heart to know Me, for I am the Lord; and they will be My people, and I will be their God, for they will return to Me with their whole heart." — **Jeremiah 24:7**

Verse Concepts

A Quest for Purity and Divine Truth

We all enter this world with a pure soul, carrying a unique purpose and guided by a higher power. Our time here is limited, and just as we came from a sacred origin, we must one day return to it. But the journey home is not without its challenges, and the path to success is filled with questions that we often overlook.

How do we measure the purity of our souls? Have we truly followed the divine guidance set for us? What will our answer be when asked about our identity—who we are and what we stand for? These are the essential questions that must be confronted if we hope to enter our eternal home in Heaven rather than face the terrifying prospect of failure.

The journey towards the ultimate destination requires deep reflection and unwavering resolve. Along the way, we must confront obstacles, recognise our weaknesses, and purify ourselves in preparation for the final test that follows—the Day of Judgement. This is a path of wisdom and self-awareness, where no one can take our steps for us.

Are you ready to face the truth about your own soul? Are you walking the straight path?

This book serves as a guide for those seeking clarity, courage, and success on the journey back to their heavenly home. The answers are within, but the questions must be asked.

Is it straight, or have you veered,
From the truth, from what is revered?

Have you searched for the keys to the gate,
Where heaven waits, and love radiates?
Why have you not, why do you delay,
In seeking light to guide your way?

On Judgment Day, love and compassion will stand,
Justice and honesty will take your hand.
But selfishness, greed, and cruelty too,
Will bear witness against you.

So think again, no matter how you pray,
No matter how often you go and stay,
In sacred rooms, in pilgrimage high,
You must still answer to the sky.

The Supreme Court awaits, no hiding now,
Will you be ruined or will you bow
To the light that leads beyond the strife—
The journey toward eternal life?

Acknowledgements

Firstly, I express my gratitude to Allah SWT, whose immense mercy and grace made this journey possible.

I am deeply grateful to Barrister Muhammad Mujeebur Rahman, Barrister of the Hon'ble Society of Lincoln's Inn and former Judge of the Bangladesh Judiciary, for dedicating his valuable time over the past year to meticulously reviewing this text and offering insightful suggestions, which have greatly contributed to its transformation into a book.

I would also like to extend my special thanks to Professor Dr Syed Azizur Rahman of the University of Sharjah, United Arab Emirates; Md Zakaria, Associate Professor of Islamic History and Culture at the University of Dhaka and PhD researcher at Royal Holloway, University of London; Dr Mahmudur Rahman, Ophthalmologist, London; and the former Chairman, Mr Abdul Hannan Tarofdar, of Somers Town Mosque, Central London, for their invaluable feedback and support during the review process.

Finally, I would like to express my heartfelt gratitude to my wife, Nasreen Ahmed, MPhil, and my two daughters, whose unwavering support during those incredibly challenging times allowed me to stay focused on my work despite the panic and chaos of the Covid-19 pandemic surrounding us. Their strength and encouragement were nothing short of miraculous, and I cannot find words adequate enough to convey my appreciation or repay their kindness.

In view of this, I hereby declare that I fully and unconditionally transfer all rights to the book *Judge Yourself Before Judgement Day* to my dear wife, Mrs Nasreen Ahmed, with no reservations.

Preface.

By the boundless favour of Allah (SWT), I made the decision to write this book on 24 March 2019, a Sunday, during the 17th of Rajab, 1440. It followed a prolonged debate with my inner self, yet I was eventually overcome by my abilities and mental strength, enabling me to embark on this writing journey.

The idea to write a book was sparked when a group of my friends expressed their desire to visit the city of Darussalam, the fifth heaven, and search for their eternal home within it. Initially, their idea seemed absurd to me, but it became even more intriguing when, one evening, they entrusted me with the task of collecting navigation materials to serve as a guide for our journey. Although this journey was essentially a spiritual one, comprising a sequential series of profound practices leading to heaven, the realisation struck me that this book could serve as a blessed implementation of that aspiration.

As human beings, irrespective of our religious affiliations, we can reach our ultimate destination of *heaven* by sincerely engaging with the text of the final book of divine guidance, following its teachings with courage and sacrifice.

This book has been thoughtfully crafted to facilitate precise and periodic self-examination, providing insights into one's spiritual state and the consequences of their actions. Hence, the title of this book is

"Judge yourself before judgement day"

The necessity of a pre-test has also been narrated by Umar ibn al-Khattab (PBUH), the second Khalifa of the Muslims, in one of his famous speeches:

احكموا على أنفسكم قبل أن يحكم عليكم ، وقيّموا أنفسكم قبل أن

تقيّموا ، واستعدوا لأعظم التحقيق (أي يوم القيامة)

"Judge yourselves before you are judged. Evaluate yourselves before you are evaluated, and be ready for the greatest investigation—that is, the Day of Judgement."

Wise is the one who continually assesses himself and performs good deeds for the life after death.

Foolish is the one who follows his desires and entertains very high hopes from Allah. *(Tirmidhi).*

I have endeavoured to simplify the task as much as possible, emphasising the areas that require attention while progressing towards our final destination. Within this book, I strive to convey a clear message to those who may be indifferent or less focused on practising their faith or searching for the true path.

Qur'anic verses are sourced from **Sharif.org** and **Alquranbd.com**. English translations are provided from *The Noble Quran* by renowned scholars Dr Muhammad Muhsin Khan, Dr Muhammad Taqi-ud-Din Al-Hilali, PhD, and Yusuf Ali. Bible verses are taken from **King James Version (KJV).**

I must mention the challenges I encountered when initially embarking on this work. With the sudden onset of the COVID-19 pandemic, all avenues were closed, making it difficult to reach out to scholars, utilise libraries, or seek advice from my usual sources. However, despite the odds, I did not lose hope, and by the grace of the Almighty, I persevered. Now, in June 2023, during the months of Dhul-Qa'dah to Dhul-Hijjah 1444, my work is finally complete and has been sent for scholarly review. I am unsure when I will receive approval and be able to publish it. Though I have put in my utmost sincerity to ensure its accuracy, I would greatly appreciate any suggestions from discerning readers if any errors are found.

I am older in years, but I hesitate to call myself "retired." I still work as a freelance technical analyst in the financial markets, where I also authored a specialised book titled *CFDs: The Art of Currency Trading.* In addition to my professional work, I dedicate much of my time to voluntary consulting and social service, often working late into the night, seven days a week. This routine has become a way of life for me. The idea of fully retiring feels like an unnecessary burden on others, leaving me without purpose. I consider it a true miracle and a direct blessing from Almighty Allah (SWT) that I continue to enjoy such good health.

However, I humbly request all my well-wishers, readers, and friends to remember me in their prayers, seeking Allah's (SWT) mercy and strength for me to continue doing good in this world until my last moment.

M.A. Haye

akm.haye@gmail.com

Introduction

First of all, thanks to Allah, the Almighty, who granted me the opportunity, endurance, and ability to start this journey and gave me the strength and patience to continue this learning process, which has no end.

"The Qur'an is not meant for any particular sect; it is the only scripture that claims to be a book of guidance for all mankind, regardless of their race, ethnicity, or religious affiliation on this earth."

The book *Judge Yourself Before the Day of Judgement* simplifies the complex teachings found in religious texts, making it easier for everyday people to understand how to lead a righteous (*Momin*) life and navigate their journey safely. It offers guidance on how to prepare for the Day of Judgement and ease the ultimate test at the end of life's path.

In major religious traditions, judgement plays a central role. The Bible, Torah, and Qur'an each convey that one day, we will be held accountable for our actions and judged based on what we have done. Aside from the Qur'an, the Bible states:

"For we must all appear before the judgment seat of Christ; that every one may receive the things done in his body, according to that he hath done, whether it be good or bad." (2 Corinthians 5:10)

Similarly, in the Torah, it says:

"And I saw the dead, small and great, stand before God; and the books were opened: and another book was opened, which is the book of life: and the dead were judged out of those things which were written in the books, according to their works." (Revelation 20:12)

This book, *Judge Yourself Before the Day of Judgement*, is a call to action for all who believe in these teachings. It invites travellers to take a hard look at themselves and honestly assess their own lives, asking difficult questions about their beliefs, behaviours, and relationships.

Travellers also search for answers to fundamental questions: Who am I? Why am I here? What is the purpose of this life? What happens when my journey ends? Finding these answers helps build self-awareness, leading us to explore how to prepare ourselves for the final judgement that awaits us all.

In the Bible, final judgement will take place at the end of time, when God will judge all people according to their deeds. In the Torah, the concept of judgement is central to Jewish belief, as the righteous are rewarded and the wicked are punished. Finally, in the Qur'an, the Day of Judgement is described as a time when all of humanity will be held accountable for their actions, and justice will be served.

However, the question still lingers: how do we perceive and judge ourselves, particularly in light of the ongoing search for meaning? In today's society, it is all too common to be influenced by the expectations and opinions of others. We often measure our worth through external markers such as social standing or financial success, rather than the depth of our character.

This book encourages readers to pause and reflect on their own lives before embarking on a journey into an unfamiliar realm, where ultimately, everyone will face judgement.

Drawing on the wisdom of the Bible, the Torah, and the Qur'an, *Judge Yourself Before the Day of Judgement* illuminates the areas of concern that may cause the hearts of true seekers to tremble with fear and search for the path to enlightenment. But this book also offers practical advice and spiritual guidance, encouraging self-examination and the cultivation of virtues such as compassion, humility, and gratitude—helping travellers prepare for the final judgement that awaits us all.

The book narrates the journey of a group of individuals who pack their belongings and set out for the heavenly city of **Darus Salaam**, seeking to meet their Lord, Allah (SWT). Their ultimate goal is to reach this divine city, where they hope to find their eternal home.

This story highlights key areas of concern and serves as an example, helping us reflect on our thoughts and awareness. It emphasises the need to continuously assess our current situation in order to address any challenges that may obstruct travellers' journeys.

A lack of awareness about whether the journey is on the right path can result in failure. This book serves as a navigator, designed to cultivate mindfulness—guiding readers on how to step onto this path and remain righteous as they travel towards the Celestial City and the City of Heaven.

In the Qur'an, Allah has prescribed a straight path for humanity to follow in order to attain success in this life and the next:

"Guide us to the straight path—the path of those whom You have favoured, not of those who have earned [Your] anger or of those who are astray." (Qur'an 1:6-7)

In the Torah, it is said that Moses implored the Israelites to choose life and follow the commandments of God:

"See, I have set before thee this day life and good, and death and evil; In that I command thee this day to love the Lord thy God, to walk in his ways, and to keep his commandments and his statutes and his judgments, that thou mayest live and multiply: and the Lord thy God shall bless thee in the land whither thou goest to possess it." (Deuteronomy 30:15-16)

Readers will find many clues about what it takes to find a path that is narrow but straight—hard to follow, yet leading to eternal life and God's blessings.

FINALLY

With its accessible style and compelling insights, *Judge Yourself Before the Day of Judgement* is sure to resonate with readers of all faiths and backgrounds.

Whether simply seeking to live a more purposeful life or hoping to deepen their spiritual journey and cultivate a stronger connection to divine revelation, readers must search for what the Almighty, our Lord, has said in His final revealed book, the Qur'an.

Allah revealed the Qur'an through Prophet Muhammad ﷺ and declared that it is a guidance for all who are present in this world today and for those who will come until the end of time. Therefore, all of humanity must come under the umbrella of the Qur'anic instructions. This is the final scripture, and Prophet Muhammad ﷺ is the last prophet—not for a particular community or for Muslims alone, but for all mankind. The Qur'an covers all previous verses revealed by God in the Old Testament.

Anyone unfamiliar with the Qur'an will not be lost, but will feel a sense of familiarity when reciting and searching for the truth in order to become a believer.

The Qur'an is the only scripture that claims to be a book of guidance for all mankind. Below are some of the many verses where God addresses the people of the world:

> "Alif. Lam. Ra. (This is) a Scripture which We have revealed unto thee (Muhammad ﷺ) that thereby thou mayst bring forth mankind from darkness unto light, by the permission of their Lord, unto the path of the Mighty, the Owner of Praise." *(Qur'an 14:1 - Surah Ibrahim, Pickthall)*

> "O mankind! Verily, there has come to you a convincing proof (Prophet Muhammad ﷺ) from your Lord, and We sent down to you a manifest light (this Qur'an)." *(Qur'an 4:174 - Surah An-Nisaa, Dr M. Muhsin Khan / Dr M. Taqi-ud-Din Al-Hilali)*

> "O mankind! There has come to you good advice from your Lord (i.e. the Qur'an, ordering all that is good and forbidding all that is evil), and a healing for that (disease of ignorance, doubt, hypocrisy, and differences) in your breasts—a guidance and a mercy (explaining lawful and unlawful things) for the believers." *(Qur'an 10:57 - Surah Yunus, Dr M. Muhsin Khan / Dr M. Taqi-ud-Din Al-Hilali)*

These verses allow us to conclude that the Qur'an is the final and complete revelation from God to mankind, and that its message is universal and timeless.

The Torah, Bible, and other sacred texts from the same divine source consistently offer practical guidance, urging readers to nurture virtues like love, compassion, and forgiveness while steering clear of vices such as greed, envy, and pride. Through its deep wisdom and straightforward analysis, *Judge Yourself Before the Day of Judgement* resonates with those who take their faith to heart and seek to ensure they are ready to stand before God on the Day of Judgement.

From Editor's Desk:

Alhamdulillahi Rabbil A'lamin. At the very outset, I would like to express my utmost gratitude and exaltation to the Omnipotent and Omniscient **Allah** SWT, who has enabled me to undertake such a daunting task—to edit this seminal work on such an important topic covering both worlds, highlighting Eternal Salvation and Bliss for those who truly deserve it by being sincere in each and every action.

I praise the Only Lord, seek His helping hand on every occasion to make it successful and beneficial for both worlds, seek His forgiveness so that we may be raised before Him in a condition He loves most, and seek His refuge from the evils of ourselves and from the evil of our actions. I firmly believe that whomever **Allah** SWT guides, none can lead astray, and whomever **Allah** SWT leads astray, none can guide.

I testify unequivocally that none has the right to be worshipped but **Allah** SWT alone, having no partners whatsoever, and I testify that Muhammad (peace be upon him) is His slave and final Messenger, after whom there remains no chance for any human being to claim prophethood.

This seminal book, entitled *Judge Yourself Before Judgment Day*, deals with some of the most important topics, highlighting ways to be well-prepared for Supreme Success by the will of the Only True Lord, **Allah** SWT. It contains numerous references from the Glorious Qur'an, which is the compilation of the very words of **Allah** SWT, and from the sayings, actions, and approvals of the Last Messenger of **Allah** SWT, who is widely known as **Rahmah** (a blessing) for the entire humanity, irrespective of creed, caste, colour, or religion [21:107], and **Uswatun Hasanah** (a followable role model) for all of humanity [33:21]. He was a teacher who imparted the best lessons from **Kalamullah** (the words of **Allah** SWT), a **Nadhir** (warner) who awakened us to the severe punishment of **Allah** SWT if we do not follow his teachings, a **Mubashshir** (giver of glad tidings) to those who follow the teachings of the Qur'an and Ahadith, and **Huda** (a guide) who showed the correct, easy, and simple path to enter Jannatul Firdaus.

Judge Yourself Before Judgment Day is a book that calls for deep self-reflection, moral accountability, and spiritual awareness. In a world full of distractions, where self-examination is often neglected, this book serves as a reminder that every action, intention, and decision carries weight—not only in this life but in the hereafter.

The central theme of this book is personal accountability. It urges readers to engage in honest introspection, evaluating their deeds, intentions, and character before they stand before the ultimate Judge, **Allah** SWT, for the final determination of whether they will be blessed or wretched. By doing so, one can strive for a life of righteousness, humility, and sincere repentance, rather than facing regret when it is too late.

Drawing from timeless wisdom, religious teachings, and real-life examples, *Judge Yourself Before Judgment Day* is not meant to instill fear but to inspire change. It is a call to awaken the conscience, correct one's course, and seek forgiveness while the opportunity still exists.

As you journey through these pages, approach them with an open heart. Reflect on the message, implement the lessons, and use this book as a tool for self-improvement. May it serve as a source of guidance, motivation, and ultimately, salvation.

What if you had the chance to evaluate your life before facing the ultimate judgment? Would you live differently? Would you make better choices? *Judge Yourself Before Judgment Day* is not just a book—it's a wake-up call. It challenges you to take an honest look at your actions, intentions, and beliefs before it's too late.

In a world where self-reflection is often overshadowed by daily distractions, this book urges you to pause and assess your spiritual and moral standing. Are you truly prepared for what comes after this life? By holding yourself accountable now, you can make meaningful changes, seek forgiveness, and strive for a life of purpose and righteousness.

Filled with timeless wisdom, thought-provoking insights, and practical guidance, *Judge Yourself Before Judgment Day* is a powerful tool for personal transformation. It's not about fear—it's about empowerment. The opportunity to change is in your hands today, but one day, that chance will be gone.

Don't wait until it's too late. Start your journey of self-examination now. Let this book guide you toward a life of sincerity, repentance, and ultimate success.

I pray to the Almighty **Allah** SWT to guide all of us to read this book, learn its teachings, and apply them in our practical lives by inviting people toward **Al-Ma'ruf** (righteous and good deeds) and forbidding them from committing any **Munkar** (indecent and reprehensible actions), so that we may be pleased with our Lord and He may be pleased with us, granting us entry into His Jannah forever. May **Allah** SWT accept our sincere intentions and help us put them into action solely for His satisfaction, following the ways taught, shown, and practised by our beloved Prophet **Muhammad Mustafa Ahmed Mustafa**, peace be upon him. **Ameen. Thumma Ameen.**

Muhammad Mujeebur Rahman
Public Access Barrister & Head of the Chambers
Acumen Barristers' Chambers
243a Whitechapel Road
2nd Floor
London E1 1DB
M: 07540660593
E: judgenbarrister@gmail.com

JUDGE YOURSELF
BEFORE JUDGEMENT DAY

بِسْمِ ٱللَّهِ ٱلرَّحْمَـٰنِ ٱلرَّحِيمِ

Chapter 1 Power of Journey

Oath We Take:

➢ We believe in Allah, His angels, His Book, and His messengers.

➢ We make no distinction between one of His messengers and another.

➢ We Muslims believe in what has been revealed to our Prophet from his Lord.

From now on, we Muslims will obey, listen, stand firm for righteousness, and seek forgiveness from our Lord until the end of our journey.

"The Messenger has believed in what was revealed to him from his Lord, and so have the believers. They all believe in Allah, His angels, His books, and His messengers. 'We make no distinction between any of His messengers.' And they say, 'We hear and obey. We seek Your forgiveness, our Lord. And to You is the final destination.'"

— Qur'an (2:285)

Regardless of whether they are believers or non-believers, if they decide to join the journey, they must revert and swear by heart:

There is no god but Allah, and Muhammad is His messenger.

لا إله إلا الله محمد رسول الله

(lā ʾilāha ʾillallāh, Muḥammad rasūlu-llāh)

1

Make The Journey Successful

To successfully end the journey, one must successfully pass the final test.

✌ ✌ ✌

To successfully pass the test, one must successfully seek knowledge.

✌ ✌ ✌

Successfully acquiring knowledge makes you a true believer.

✌ ✌ ✌

Successful believers can successfully face the judgment.

✌ ✌ ✌

All success leads to the joyous end of a difficult journey.

OUR PROPHET (ﷺ) says:

Seeking knowledge in different ways:

> ➤ *Time:* "Seek knowledge from the cradle to the grave."
> ➤ *Place:* "Seek knowledge even if it is as far as China."
> ➤ *Gender:* "Seeking knowledge is a duty of every Muslim."

Abu Huraira, a companion of Prophet Muhammad (ﷺ), is reported to have said:

The Messenger of Allah said, "The wise saying is the lost property of the believer, so wherever he finds it, he has a right to it."

— (Source: Sunan At-Tirmidhi)

Warning

- A Philosophical songwriter & singer Bob Dylan wrote:

"The Times They Are A-Changin'

Come gather 'round people

Wherever you roam

And admit that the waters

Around you have grown

And accept it that soon

You'll be drenched to the bone

If your time to you is worth saving'

Then you better start swimming' or you'll sink like a stone

For the times they are a-changin' ……."

"They rejected him, but We delivered him and those with him in the Ark, and We made them inherit the earth, while We overwhelmed in the flood those who rejected Our signs. Then see what was the end of those who were warned but heeded not!" - *(Surah Yunus 10:73)*

- **NASA is Monitoring Sea Level Rise**

Earth's global sea levels are rising—and at an accelerating rate. Ocean waters are expanding as they absorb massive amounts of heat trapped by greenhouse gases in Earth's atmosphere. Glaciers and ice sheets are adding hundreds of gigatonnes of meltwater into the oceans each year. The land surface along the coasts is also shifting, affecting relative sea level rise. People are feeling the impacts, as seemingly small increments of sea level rise become significant problems along coastlines worldwide.

قَالَ يَا قَوْمِ إِنِّي لَكُمْ نَذِيرٌ مُّبِينٌ

- *He said: "O my People! **I am to you a Warner, clear and open**:*

(Surah Nuh 71:28)

The world will be caught by surprise at the Second Coming, despite the Bible's many warnings—repeated by preachers throughout the centuries—that this event will bring judgment for the ungodly. If Jesus' warnings before His Second Coming are ignored, then surely Noah's warnings were also disregarded by his people before the flood.

- **Matthew 24:38** – *" For as in the days that were before the flood they were eating and drinking, marrying and giving in marriage, until the day that Noah entered into the ark."*

- **Matthew 24:39** – *" And knew not until the flood came, and took them all away; so shall also the coming of the Son of man be."* ([1])

https://versebyverseministry.org/bible-answers/did-noah-warn-the-world-about-the-coming-flood

---

[1] https://versebyverseministry.org/bible-answers/did-noah-warn-the-world-about-the-coming-floo

3

- The Qur'an reminds us that Allah cares for us by creating our world with the ozone layer to protect us from ultraviolet (UV) radiation, which can harm us and other organisms. However, Allah already knows that humans, in their greed, will destroy the ozone layer. This serves as a reminder that we must protect Allah's creation in order to protect ourselves as well.
- **"And We made the sky a protected ceiling, but they, from its signs, are turning away."** - *(Qur'an 21:32, Surah Al-Anbiyaa)*
- Allah has chosen and created humans to preside over the earth. The Qur'an, similar to the Bible, alludes to a stewardship role for humans through their title as **khalifahs** (guardians) over all of the earth. It is, therefore, our responsibility to fulfil this role that Allah has entrusted to us, and this can be achieved through the safeguarding of the environment.
- **"Remember when your Lord said to the angels, 'I am going to place a successive human authority on earth.'"** - *(Qur'an 2:30)* [2]Surah Al-Baqara

This Is What The LORD Says:

- **"See how the waters are rising in the north; they will become an overflowing torrent. They will overflow the land and everything in it—the towns and those who live in them. The people will cry out; all who dwell in the land will wail."** *(*[3]*)*

Humanity—not one agency, not one country, not one continent, but humanity—has been monitoring global sea levels from space with exquisite accuracy for more than 28 years.

—Michael Freilich, 1954–2020 ([4])

Greed

The story of Prophet Noah (PBUH) narrates that a great flood was a divine intervention and punishment for those who rejected the signs or disobeyed Allah. God had no intention of destroying the entire world.

A subjective explanation cannot draw a direct link between global sea level rise due to human activities and God's wrath. We are destroying the world. It is the result of human greed, not God's wrath or punishment.

Sea level rise is primarily attributed to natural processes such as the thermal expansion of seawater and the melting of ice caps and glaciers. These changes are

---

[2] https://themuslimvibe.com/faith-islam/7-verses-from-the-quran-on-the-environment
[3] https://biblehub.com/jeremiah/47-2.htm
[4] *https://climate.nasa.gov/news/3030/rising-waters/*

influenced by factors such as climate change, which is largely driven by human activities such as fossil fuel burning and deforestation. The greed behind such actions will one day turn the world into an ocean—for which we cannot blame the Creator, only ourselves.

"May Allah protect us and our future generations from acts of greed that are beyond our control."

***

Journey with Enlightened Souls

When devoted individuals embark on a demanding and arduous journey toward their ultimate destination, it is a path we are presently preparing for. In this profound moment, we shall refrain from debating matters of Madhhab, be it Hanbali, Maleki, Hanafi, or delving into Sufism. Instead, our quest lies in the pursuit of wisdom that illuminates the heart and uplifts us on this expedition.

The following lines have been curated from the book *The Secret of Secrets*, originally penned by Abd al-Qadir al-Jilani (1077–1166) and presented in English for the first time by Shaykh Tosun Bayrak al-Jerrahi al-Halveti.

The Messenger of Allah says:

"My companions are like the stars in the sky. Whichever of them you follow, you will find the true path."

The Prophet also said:

"The sleep of the wise is more worthy than the worship of the ignorant."

The wise are those who have acquired the knowledge of the truth that has no letters, no sound. That knowledge is received through the continuous repetition of the divine Name of Unity with the secret tongue. The wise are those whose core is turned into divine light by the light of unity.

Allah speaks through His Prophet and says:

"Man is My secret, and I am his secret. The inner knowledge of the spiritual essence (ilm al-batin) is a secret of My secrets. Only I put this into the heart of My good servant, and none may know his state other than Me."

And:

"I am as My servant knows Me. When he seeks Me and remembers Me, I am with him. If he seeks Me inwardly, I seek him with My Essence. If he remembers and mentions Me in good company, I remember and declare him as My good servant in better company."

5

While our grasp of these philosophical concepts may be limited and sometimes perplexing in their practical application during travel, it remains valuable to explore simple ways to enhance our experience while travelling.

Allah Mentioned In The Quran:

الَّذِينَ آمَنُوا وَتَطْمَئِنُّ قُلُوبُهُم بِذِكْرِ اللَّهِ ۗ أَلَا بِذِكْرِ اللَّهِ تَطْمَئِنُّ الْقُلُوبُ

Those who believe (in the Oneness of Allah – Islamic Monotheism) and whose hearts find rest in the remembrance of Allah—verily, in the remembrance of Allah do hearts find rest. (Surah Ar-Ra'd 13:28)

The verse above teaches us that inner reflection, through practices like Zikr, can gradually illuminate our souls, elevating us to a dignified state and guiding us towards Allah's pleasure.

Zikr involves silently and continuously reciting phrases like la ilaha ill'Allah, any of the Ninety-Nine Names of Allah, or expressing beautiful praises for Allah deep within our hearts. It is a deeply personal and private form of prayer that remains hidden from others.

Zikr (inner) can have a profound impact on our spiritual well-being when practised in accordance with the strict principles of Sharia and Islamic jurisprudence, as outlined in the Quran and Sunnah. This practice involves controlling our tongues and actions, exercising self-discipline, and maintaining constant mindfulness of our behaviour. The Quran offers clear guidance and assurance for those chosen by Allah to embark on this journey of enlightenment.

اللَّهُ لِنُورِهِ مَن يَشَاءُ ۚ وَيَضْرِبُ اللَّهُ الْأَمْثَالَ لِلنَّاسِ ۗ وَاللَّهُ بِكُلِّ شَيْءٍ عَلِيم

***

اللَّهُ نُورُ السَّمَاوَاتِ وَالْأَرْضِ ۚ مَثَلُ نُورِهِ كَمِشْكَاةٍ فِيهَا مِصْبَاحٌ ۖ الْمِصْبَاحُ فِي زُجَاجَةٍ ۖ الزُّجَاجَةُ كَأَنَّهَا كَوْكَبٌ دُرِّيٌّ يُوقَدُ مِن شَجَرَةٍ مُّبَارَكَةٍ زَيْتُونَةٍ لَّا شَرْقِيَّةٍ وَلَا غَرْبِيَّةٍ يَكَادُ زَيْتُهَا يُضِيءُ وَلَوْ لَمْ تَمْسَسْهُ نَارٌ ۚ نُّورٌ عَلَىٰ نُورٍ ۗ يَهْدِي اللَّهُ لِنُورِهِ مَن يَشَاءُ ۚ وَيَضْرِبُ اللَّهُ الْأَمْثَالَ لِلنَّاسِ ۗ وَاللَّهُ بِكُلِّ شَيْءٍ عَلِيمٌ

Allah is the Light of the heavens and the earth. The parable of His Light is as (if there were) a niche, and within it a lamp. The lamp is in glass, the glass as if it were a brilliant star, lit from a blessed tree—an olive—neither of the east (i.e. it does not receive sunlight only in the morning) nor of the west (i.e. it does not receive sunlight only in the afternoon, but it is exposed to the sun all day long). Its oil would almost glow forth by itself, though no fire touched it. Light upon Light! Allah guides to His Light whom He wills. And Allah sets forth parables for mankind, and Allah is All-Knowing of everything. - (Surah An-Nur 24:35)

وَلَا تَدْعُ مَعَ اللَّهِ إِلَٰهًا آخَرَ ۘ لَا إِلَٰهَ إِلَّا هُوَ ۚ كُلُّ شَيْءٍ هَالِكٌ إِلَّا وَجْهَهُ ۚ لَهُ الْحُكْمُ وَإِلَيْهِ تُرْجَعُونَ

And do not invoke any other ilah (god) alongside Allah. La ilaha illa Huwa (none has the right to be worshipped but He). Everything will perish except His Face. His is the Decision, and to Him you (all) shall return. (Surah Al-Qasas 28:88)

وَإِذِ اعْتَزَلْتُمُوهُمْ وَمَا يَعْبُدُونَ إِلَّا اللَّهَ فَأْوُوا إِلَى الْكَهْفِ يَنشُرْ لَكُمْ رَبُّكُم مِّن رَّحْمَتِهِ وَيُهَيِّئْ لَكُم مِّنْ أَمْرِكُم مِّرْفَقًا

(The young men said to one another): - "And when you withdraw from them and from that which they worship, except Allah, then seek refuge in the cave. Your Lord will open a way for you from His mercy and will make your affair easy (i.e. will provide for your needs, such as sustenance and shelter)." - (Surah Al-Kahf 18:16)

***

For a journey, a valid visa is required.

Be prepared to obtain an entry visa.

A visa may be denied or even revoked midway through the journey.

***

"He grants Hikmah to whom He pleases, and he to whom Hikmah is granted is indeed given abundant good. But none will remember (or receive admonition) except men of understanding."

269. Al-Baqarah

***

"Is it sufficient that Allah bestowed upon us reason to govern our minds, knowledge of the world around us, and the freedom to act as we please? Undoubtedly, each of these assets is essential for leading a fulfilling life."

$$\text{بِسْمِ اللَّهِ الرَّحْمَـٰنِ الرَّحِيمِ}$$

Chapter 2

Abu Huraira reported that Allah's Messenger (Peace Be Upon Him) said: "In Paradise, there is a tree under whose shadow a rider can travel for a hundred years."

Book Number: 6784

📖📖📖📖📖📖

A Journey To Celestial City

It tells the story of a group of people embarking on a journey to meet their Lord, Allah (SWT), in the city of *Dar al-Salam*. They seek to complete their journey in *Jannatul Firdaus*, where their permanent home is located.

This city was created by the Almighty before the creation of mankind, and this ethereal place will never end. Their entry into this city is possible because Allah (SWT) repeatedly says:

$$\text{لَهُمْ دَارُ السَّلَامِ عِندَ رَبِّهِمْ ۖ وَهُوَ وَلِيُّهُم بِمَا كَانُوا يَعْمَلُونَ}$$

For them will be a home of peace in the presence of their Lord. He will be their friend because they practised righteousness. - (Surah Al-An'am 6:127)

$$\text{وَاللَّهُ يَدْعُو إِلَىٰ دَارِ السَّلَامِ وَيَهْدِي مَن يَشَاءُ إِلَىٰ صِرَاطٍ مُّسْتَقِيمٍ}$$

Allah calls to the home of peace (i.e. Paradise, by accepting Allah's religion of Islamic Monotheism, doing righteous good deeds, and abstaining from polytheism and evil deeds) and guides whom He wills to a Straight Path. - (Surah Yunus 10:25)

After the Judgement, the believers will be admitted to Dar al-Salam, where they will live eternally in the presence of Allah SWT.

Allah says that we will enter Paradise by His grace and mercy as a result of His justice. The fate of every child of Adam (PBUH) will be determined by his good deeds.

Allah says:-

$$\text{فَلَا تَعْلَمُ نَفْسٌ مَّا أُخْفِيَ لَهُم مِّن قُرَّةِ أَعْيُنٍ جَزَاءً بِمَا كَانُوا يَعْمَلُونَ}$$

No person knows what is kept hidden for them of joy as a reward for what they used to do. - (Surah As-Sajda 32:17)

Now, those people are engaged in seeking the path of their Lord—the path He has commanded His creation to follow if they wish to succeed.

Our Prophet Mohammed ﷺ also confirmed: "There is a Straight Path, which he left us on one end of, and the other end is in Paradise. To its right and left are paths branching off, on which stand people summoning those who pass by. Whoever takes to those paths will end up in Hell. Only those who remain on the Path will enter Paradise and meet their Lord."

This fact is established in the Qur'an, where Allah says:

وُجُوهٌ يَوْمَئِذٍ نَّاضِرَةٌ // إِلَىٰ رَبِّهَا نَاظِرَةٌ

Some faces, that Day, will beam (in brightness and beauty),

Looking towards their Lord. - (Surah Al-Qiyamah 75:22-23)

The journey towards meeting the Lord can be challenging because many distractions and temptations can derail one's progress. These distractions come in various forms, such as material possessions, worldly pleasures, or negative emotions like anger, jealousy, and greed.

Not only that, but inner obstacles can also make the journey extremely difficult. These may include negative thought patterns, limiting beliefs, or unresolved issues.

Overcoming these distractions requires deep commitment to inner work, such as mindfulness, meditation, and following a spiritual path, along with a willingness to sacrifice anything that hinders progress. One of the most challenging aspects of this journey is surrendering the ego. The ego is the part of us that seeks control, dominance, and self-preservation at all costs.

Letting go of the ego's desires and attachments to justice, peace, and harmony can be difficult, but it is essential for spiritual growth and progress on the journey.

Allah says:

إِنَّ الَّذِينَ قَالُوا رَبُّنَا اللَّهُ ثُمَّ اسْتَقَامُوا تَتَنَزَّلُ عَلَيْهِمُ الْمَلَائِكَةُ أَلَّا تَخَافُوا وَلَا تَحْزَنُوا وَأَبْشِرُوا بِالْجَنَّةِ الَّتِي كُنتُمْ تُوعَدُونَ

Verily, those who say, "Our Lord is Allah (Alone)," and then they remain steadfast (Istaqamu), on them the angels will descend (at the time of their death), saying:

"Fear not, nor grieve! But receive the glad tidings of Paradise, which you have been promised." - (Surah Fussilat [Ha-Mim] 41:30)

And Allah also says:

9

وَسَارِعُوا إِلَىٰ مَغْفِرَةٍ مِّن رَّبِّكُمْ وَجَنَّةٍ عَرْضُهَا السَّمَاوَاتُ وَالْأَرْضُ أُعِدَّتْ لِلْمُتَّقِينَ

And march forth on the path that leads to forgiveness from your Lord, and to Paradise, as vast as the heavens and the earth, prepared for Al-Muttaqun (the pious – see V.2:2), prepared for the righteous.

(Surah Aal-e-Imran 3:133)

Rumi (Mawlana Jalal al-Din Muhammad Rumi), a renowned Persian poet and theologian of the 13th century, lifted the veil in his poetry, illuminating our journey. He wrote:

"I said: What about my eyes?

God said: Keep them on the road.

I said: What about my passion?

God said: Keep it burning.

I said: What about my heart?

God said: Tell me what you hold inside it.

I said: Pain and sorrow.

He said: Stay with it. The wound is the place

where the Light enters you."

Then He said:

"Don't run away from grief, O soul.

Look for the remedy inside the pain,

Because the rose came from the thorn,

And the ruby came from a stone.

There is a candle in your heart, ready to be kindled.

There is a void in your soul, ready to be filled.

You feel it, don't you?"

The purification of the soul is also a vital aspect of the spiritual journey in seeking closeness to Allah. The Qur'an emphasises the importance of purifying one's soul and character in numerous verses, such as:

قَدْ أَفْلَحَ مَن زَكَّاهَا

"Truly, he succeeds who purifies it."

(Surah Ash-Shams 91:9)

That is, the one who obeys and performs all that Allah has commanded, by following the true faith of Islamic Monotheism and doing righteous good deeds.

However, this journey is a personal path of self-discovery for a group of people. Spiritual journeys often involve questioning one's beliefs and values, exploring simpler ways of thinking and being. This journey may include confronting and healing past mistakes, developing a deeper connection with one's inner self, and finding inner peace and strength.

It can be a challenging and sometimes uncomfortable process, as it requires confronting one's fears, making sacrifices, and facing vulnerabilities. However, the rewards can be transformative and life-changing, leading to greater understanding, compassion, and a deeper connection with righteousness. This journey contains guidance and teachings that help individuals embark on a spiritual path, including:

> *Seeking Knowledge*

> *Worship and Prayer*

> *Practising Good Deeds*

> *Reflecting on the Qur'an* – The Qur'an is a source of guidance and wisdom for Muslims. Allah says in the Qur'an:

> *"We have certainly sent down to you the Book for mankind in truth. So, whoever is guided..."*

> *(Qur'an 39:27)*

> *Striving for Self-Improvement* – Based on verse *13:11*, where Allah says:

> *"Indeed, Allah will not change the condition of a people until they change what is in themselves."*

Finally

In spiritual traditions, facing tests and suffering on one's journey is seen as a necessary part of transformation. These challenges can take many forms—physical, emotional, or mental difficulties—and can be both internal and external. This concept is mentioned in several places in the Qur'an. One of the most significant verses on this topic is found in **Surah Al-Baqarah, verse 214**, where it says:

أَمْ حَسِبْتُمْ أَن تَدْخُلُوا الْجَنَّةَ وَلَمَّا يَأْتِكُم مَّثَلُ الَّذِينَ خَلَوْا مِن قَبْلِكُم ۖ مَّسَّتْهُمُ الْبَأْسَاءُ وَالضَّرَّاءُ وَزُلْزِلُوا حَتَّىٰ يَقُولَ الرَّسُولُ وَالَّذِينَ آمَنُوا مَعَهُ مَتَىٰ نَصْرُ اللَّهِ ۗ أَلَا إِنَّ نَصْرَ اللَّهِ قَرِيبٌ

"Or do you think that you shall enter the Garden (of bliss) without such trials as came to those who passed away before you? They encountered suffering and adversity and were so shaken in spirit that even the Messenger and those of faith

11

who were with him cried: 'When will the help of Allah come?' Ah! Verily, the help of Allah is always near."

This verse suggests that enduring tests and hardships is a necessary part of the journey towards Paradise or spiritual success. It also highlights that even the prophets and their followers were not exempt from trials and tribulations in their lives.

In another verse, **Surah Al-Ankabut 29:2-3**, *Allah says:*

أَحَسِبَ النَّاسُ أَن يُتْرَكُوا أَن يَقُولُوا آمَنَّا وَهُمْ لَا يُفْتَنُونَ

وَلَقَدْ فَتَنَّا الَّذِينَ مِن قَبْلِهِمْ ۖ فَلَيَعْلَمَنَّ اللَّهُ الَّذِينَ صَدَقُوا وَلَيَعْلَمَنَّ الْكَاذِبِينَ

2. Do people think that they will be left alone because they say, "We believe," and will not be tested?

3. And We indeed tested those who were before them. And Allah will certainly make it known (the truth of) those who are true and will certainly make it known (the falsehood of) those who are liars, (although Allah knows all that before putting them to the test).

This verse emphasises the inevitability of tests and trials for those who believe and highlights that these tests serve to distinguish the true believers from the false ones.

Overall, the Quran teaches that tests and hardships are an integral part of the spiritual journey and that they serve to purify and strengthen the believers' faith. However, it also emphasises that Allah is merciful and compassionate towards His believers and that He is always near to help and support them through their struggles.

In Conclusion

The journey towards meeting the Lord is not an easy one, but it is deeply rewarding for those who are firmly committed to it. As stated earlier, this requires overcoming distractions, internal obstacles, doubts, and ego. However, with devotion, discipline, and perseverance, it is possible to gain experience and progress on the divine path.

In this book, we can embark on a self-examination of our strength as seekers of truth, which can help generate deeper thinking and foster a connection with the divine or spiritual realm.

The First Step on This Journey

Tests and Our Accountability

Trials and challenges are an inherent part of life, acting as keys that determine our success or failure in achieving our goals. These experiences are not mere philosophical musings but inevitable realities that shape us. They provide opportunities to grow, learn, and cultivate resilience. How we choose to respond to these trials ultimately determines the outcome of our endeavours, whether they are personal, professional, financial, emotional, or physical in nature. By adopting a positive attitude, learning valuable lessons from our failures, and persevering in the face of adversity, we can overcome obstacles and reach our desired outcomes.

The life of believers is also seen as a time of trial or testing, where individuals are given the opportunity to demonstrate their faith, loyalty, or moral character. The result of this test determines one's destiny or spiritual position in the next life.

Metaphorically, life is a never-ending journey of self-discovery, exploration, and transformation. We are constantly faced with new situations, choices, and experiences that shape our character and determine the course of our lives. Life is an ongoing process of learning and evolution. Every experience, whether positive or negative, provides lessons and insights that contribute to personal and collective growth. The challenges we face help us gain knowledge, skills, and understanding.

From an existential perspective, life can be seen as a series of challenges and choices that test our ability to find meaning and create our own purpose in an otherwise uncertain and potentially meaningless world. How individuals respond to these challenges shapes their personal growth and development.

The journey of exploration begins early in life when a child takes their first tentative steps, reaches towards an object, and successfully grasps it. This marks their initial exploration of the complex and rapidly changing world around them. As children grow into adults, they gain a deeper understanding of life's trials and the realities they will inevitably face. It is during this period that they begin to prepare themselves for the challenges ahead.

Integrity, self-motivation, exemplary behaviour, tolerance, humanity, and knowledge become guiding principles that motivate individuals to become influential contributors to society. The value of this education and character can be demonstrated through academic testing.

Each person has a unique set of skills, experiences, and ways of thinking that set them apart from others. Even identical twins, who share the same genetic makeup, exhibit distinct personalities and interests. The skills and mindset needed to navigate life successfully also vary depending on the situation and environment in which a person finds themselves.

For example, people living in rural areas may need to acquire skills in agriculture and animal husbandry to thrive, while those in urban environments may require skills in technology and finance. Similarly, individuals in developed countries may have different perspectives and priorities from those in developing countries.

Furthermore, a professor's expertise can significantly influence their students due to the extensive knowledge gained through dedicated study of a specific topic. Likewise, an academically uneducated yet highly skilled fisherman can contribute to the greater good by undertaking the dangerous task of deep-sea fishing. Thus, both formal education and acquired knowledge play important roles in enhancing individual skills and collectively contributing to human welfare.

In society, we often find uneducated people showing unwavering loyalty to educated individuals who exploit them for personal gain, taking advantage of their innocence and trust. This phenomenon manifests itself in various domains, including the workplace, politics, and even personal relationships. One possible explanation for this dynamic is that uneducated individuals may lack the necessary knowledge and critical thinking skills to recognise when they are being used or manipulated.

It is important to recognise that education alone does not guarantee moral behaviour or ethical values. Education and wisdom are distinct concepts, and having knowledge does not automatically ensure responsible and just actions. True enlightenment and the tendency to act ethically stem from wisdom, which goes beyond mere education and encompasses a deeper understanding of oneself and the world.

As Allah (SWT) Says In The Quran:

أَمَّنْ هُوَ قَانِتٌ آنَاءَ اللَّيْلِ سَاجِدًا وَقَائِمًا يَحْذَرُ الْآخِرَةَ وَيَرْجُو رَحْمَةَ رَبِّهِ ۗ قُلْ هَلْ يَسْتَوِي الَّذِينَ يَعْلَمُونَ وَالَّذِينَ لَا يَعْلَمُونَ ۗ إِنَّمَا يَتَذَكَّرُ أُولُو الْأَلْبَابِ

...″Are those who have knowledge equal to those who do not have knowledge?″ (Az-Zumar, 39:9)

Muhammad ﷺ, the last prophet of humanity, did not receive education from any institution. Instead, Allah (SWT) endowed him with divine knowledge and wisdom, benefiting mankind through his guidance.

Accountability is an integral aspect of our lives that cannot be avoided. It is a two-way process where everyone is accountable to each other. Parents are responsible for their children, husbands for their wives, teachers for their students, and vice versa. Sometimes, this accountability is so authoritative that it instils fear in people's minds. This fear overrides other negative emotions such as jealousy, violence, selfishness, and competition, which can lead them astray from their normal lives.

In the book No More Excuses by Sam Silverstein, accountability is described as the foundation of all meaningful human achievements. Some people question how God can be good considering the issues in the world. However, it is not God who created these issues—we did. We make choices every day and must live with the consequences. Even when we make the wrong choices, God works to bring goodness into our lives. Catherine Pulsifer emphasises that blaming others or external factors does not solve problems; it only makes people defensive. Personal accountability transcends age and experience. We must take responsibility for all outcomes, positive or negative, without making excuses or shifting blame onto others or external factors (Kory Livingstone).

Ultimately, we will be held accountable in this world and on the Day of Judgement. Life is a temporary assignment, filled with trials, accountability, tests of faith, and challenges. We must face these multifaceted challenges at every step of life while seeking the right path on our unique journey towards Al-Sirat Al-Mustaqim. It is on the Day of Judgement that we will encounter the final trial and meet the Almighty. This is the true meaning of life in this world.

The American Baptist author Richard Duane Warren said:

"When you understand that life is a test, you realise that nothing is insignificant in your life. Even the smallest incident has significance for your character development. Every day is an important day, and every second is a growth opportunity to deepen your character, to demonstrate love, or to depend on God... All of them have eternal implications" (Warren, 43).

In addition, if the sincere seeker revisits verses 2 and 3 of Surah Al-Ankabut, it will provide further solace and clarity as they continue their journey. However, we find the same message in the Bible, which states:

Life is a test. Words like trials, temptations, refining, and testing occur more than 200 times.

Allah ﷻ tested Abraham by asking him to offer his son Isaac... Adam and Eve failed their test... We are always being tested. Allah (SWT) constantly watches one's response to people, problems, success, conflict, illness, disappointment, and even the weather! He even watches the simplest actions, such as when you open a door for others" (Warren, 42-43).

This perspective is deeply life-giving because it makes sense—God wants to see who we really are, and our character is revealed through suffering. The concept of trials or challenges in life exists in many religions and philosophies.

Finding one's purpose in life is a deeply personal journey, often shaped by challenges such as financial hardships, illness, or personal losses. These trials are considered part of Allah's divine plan, designed to test how individuals respond to difficulties and whether they remain steadfast in their faith and obedience to Allah (SWT).

In Buddhism, the concept of dukkha refers to the idea that life is inherently unsatisfactory and that one must face challenges to overcome suffering and find inner peace. In Hinduism, the concept of karma suggests that our actions in this life determine our fate in the next, and that overcoming challenges is essential for achieving spiritual enlightenment.

Through these tests, believers are given the opportunity to demonstrate their trust in Allah (SWT) and their willingness to submit to His will, even in times of hardship. However, these tests and trials are not punishments but rather opportunities for growth and spiritual development. A believer's soul must face these trials with patience, perseverance, and trust in Allah (SWT).

Allah (SWT) has revealed many verses in which He confirms:

وَلَنَبْلُوَنَّكُم بِشَيْءٍ مِّنَ الْخَوْفِ وَالْجُوعِ وَنَقْصٍ مِّنَ الْأَمْوَالِ وَالْأَنفُسِ وَالثَّمَرَاتِ ۗ وَبَشِّرِ الصَّابِرِينَ

"Be sure We shall test you with something of fear and hunger, some loss in goods or lives or the fruits (of your toil), but give glad tidings to those who patiently persevere." (Al-Baqara, 2:155)

In Surah Al-Anbiyaa' (21:35)

كُلُّ نَفْسٍ ذَائِقَةُ الْمَوْتِ ۗ وَنَبْلُوكُم بِالشَّرِّ وَالْخَيْرِ فِتْنَةً ۖ وَإِلَيْنَا تُرْجَعُونَ

"Every soul shall have a taste of death: and We test you by evil and by good by way of trial. To Us must ye return." (Al-Anbiyaa, 21:35)

Allah (SWT) says:

الَّذِي خَلَقَ الْمَوْتَ وَالْحَيَاةَ لِيَبْلُوَكُمْ أَيُّكُمْ أَحْسَنُ عَمَلًا ۚ وَهُوَ الْعَزِيزُ الْغَفُورُ

"Who has created death and life, that He may test you as to which of you is best in deed. And He is the All-Mighty, the Oft-Forgiving." (Al-Mulk, 67:2)

OR

أَمْ حَسِبْتُمْ أَن تَدْخُلُوا الْجَنَّةَ وَلَمَّا يَعْلَمِ اللَّهُ الَّذِينَ جَاهَدُوا مِنكُمْ وَيَعْلَمَ الصَّابِرِينَ

"Do you think that you will enter Paradise before Allah tests those of you who fought (in His cause) and also tests those who are steadfast?" (Surah Al-Imran, 3:142)

Allah reminded us again:

"You shall certainly be tried and tested in your wealth and properties and in your personal selves." (Surah Al-Imran, 3:186)

"Do men think that they will be left alone on saying, 'We believe,' and that they will not be tested?

We did test those before them, and Allah will certainly know those who are true from those who are false."

Allah reminded us:

أَمْ حَسِبَ الَّذِينَ يَعْمَلُونَ السَّيِّئَاتِ أَن يَسْبِقُونَا ۚ سَاءَ مَا يَحْكُمُونَ

"Or do those who do evil deeds think that they can outstrip Us (i.e. escape Our punishment)? Evil is that which they judge!" (Surah Al-Ankabut, 29:4)

On the Day of Judgment, it is believed that Allah (SWT) will assess individuals by evaluating their deeds, weighing the balance of their good and bad actions. This test aims to determine whether individuals, regardless of their religious affiliation, have led a righteous life in accordance with Islamic principles. Based on the outcome, they will either attain different levels of Heaven or face punishment in Hell.

Our Prophet (ﷺ) said:

"The extent of the reward will be in accordance with the extent of the trial. If Allah loves a people, He tries them, and whoever is content will have contentment, and whoever is angry will have anger." [Tirmidhi]

We know that Salah is an act of worship, Zakat is an act of worship, Ruku is an act of worship, and Sujood is an act of worship. Reading the Qur'an is also an act of worship. However, we should also recognise that enduring hardships, sorrows, and difficulties is a test and a form of worship of Allah.

If we deeply consider the meaning of the following verse, all confusion will be removed from our hearts. Allah (SWT) says:

وَمِنَ النَّاسِ مَن يَعْبُدُ اللَّهَ عَلَىٰ حَرْفٍ ۖ فَإِنْ أَصَابَهُ خَيْرٌ اطْمَأَنَّ بِهِ ۖ وَإِنْ أَصَابَتْهُ فِتْنَةٌ انقَلَبَ عَلَىٰ
وَجْهِهِ خَسِرَ الدُّنْيَا وَالْآخِرَةَ ۚ ذَٰلِكَ هُوَ الْخُسْرَانُ الْمُبِينُ

"And among mankind is he who worships Allah as it were, upon the very edge (i.e. in doubt); if good befalls him, he is content therewith, but if a trial befalls him, he turns back on his face (i.e. reverts to disbelief after embracing Islam). He loses both this world and the Hereafter. That is the evident loss." (Surah Al-Hajj, 22:11)

As narrated by Tirmidhi and Ibn Majah:

(This is the Hadith that we started with) – The Prophet (ﷺ) said:

"The greater the trial or difficulty, the greater the reward. When Allah loves a person, He will test them. So, he who is pleased, then Allah will be pleased with him. And he who is displeased, then Allah will be displeased with him." (Sahaba's name not clear)

As narrated by Tirmidhi and Ibn Majah, the Prophet (ﷺ) also said:

"As long as people are in good health, good shape, and good condition, they remain covered. You do not know their true character because they are in a favourable situation. However, when a trial, difficulty, or hardship comes upon

17

them, their reality is revealed. The believer (Mu'min) will turn to his faith (Iman), while the hypocrite will turn to his hypocrisy." **Index** [5]

Let us now explore the process of embracing the *Deen* (Islamic way of life) and adhering to Allah's guidance with confidence, ensuring that we are truly fulfilling the prerequisites to continue our journey on the righteous path.

Our primary focus should be on self-assessment. We need to ensure that we fulfil all the requirements to become sincere *Mu'mins* (believers), as this is the fundamental condition for obtaining a valid entry visa to the straight path.

Merely being born into a Muslim family does not automatically qualify us as true believers. Any doubts or uncertainties can be resolved through introspection. We may identify ourselves as Muslims due to our familial background, but we cannot claim the status of a believer (*Mu'min*) until we undergo a personal transformation and truly embody the principles of belief.

Here, I would like to share my experience about a Muslim family, as described above:

"A close friend of mine invited me to a Muslim family's home for an important business meeting. Each member of the family was highly educated and respected within the community. It happened to be the month of Ramadan. Upon our arrival, we realised that there was less than half an hour remaining until the fast was to be broken. However, our host immediately initiated the discussion without taking into account the proximity of the fast-breaking time. It was only when my friend reminded him that the time was nearing that he realised his oversight. The host felt embarrassed by the lack of formal arrangements made for breaking the fast, but they quickly improvised to accommodate us. Unfortunately, they also forgot to provide mats for the evening prayers. Witnessing such incidents did not surprise me, as I have encountered numerous well-established Muslims who seem to be disconnected from their religious practices."

On the contrary, we have observed a divergence among many young individuals from Muslim families who engage in religious practices that do not align with the traditions followed by their parents, teachers, or neighbours. They refer to themselves as *"practising Muslims."* This often leads to conflicts between these young men and women and their elders, as they grapple with upholding the Islamic way of life and worshipping Allah Almighty.

In society, there exists a distinct subset of young Muslims who typically perceive and embrace *jihad* as a tranquil, introspective, and personal spiritual journey. Over time, *jihad* has developed a diverse range of interpretations and practices that persist even today.

---

[5] https://abdurrahman.org/2014/01/08/greater-hardship-greater-reward/

The Quran's teachings concerning war and *jihad* are intricately intertwined with the imperative of generosity and compassion for the less fortunate. It is evident that numerous young individuals who embark on the path of *jihad* often channel their energy towards constructive and innovative endeavours. They are driven by a noble cause, encouraging Muslims to defend the oppressed—regardless of gender or age—and strive to establish a just society with the ultimate goal of serving humanity for the sake of Allah (SWT).

It is clearly visible that these young *jihadists* do not distinguish between Muslims and non-Muslims when it comes to establishing peace or engaging in warfare. They restlessly sacrifice their youth for the sake of peace in society.

These efforts encompass endeavours such as striving to deepen one's faith and pursuing personal growth, both of which can be regarded as forms of *jihad*.

Allah (SWT) says:

"Let those (believers) who sell the life of this world for the Hereafter fight in the Cause of Allah, and whoever fights in the Cause of Allah and is killed or attains victory, We shall bestow on him a great reward." (4:74, Surah An-Nisaa)

However, it is crucial to acknowledge that, in certain instances, we can observe strong viewpoints—often regardless of the Quran's specific delineations—pertaining to political, economic, or social issues.

There also exists another group of Muslims who, as mentioned earlier, do not prioritise their obligatory daily religious duties. However, they actively participate in religious festivals and ceremonies. It is also observed that they enjoy organising lavish *Iftar* parties, despite not fasting for the majority of them.

Nevertheless, it is important to note that these individuals are not inherently bad people. Many of them are well-educated and contribute their talents and knowledge to various fields for the betterment of the nation. Typically, they are financially well-off and engage in philanthropic activities such as donating to orphanages, assisting in the construction of mosques and schools, and supporting charities.

While these actions are commendable, they primarily serve as a means of personal gain rather than genuine internal supplication, as prescribed by Allah.

Allah (SWT) says in a verse:

اعْلَمُوا أَنَّمَا الْحَيَاةُ الدُّنْيَا لَعِبٌ وَلَهْوٌ وَزِينَةٌ وَتَفَاخُرٌ بَيْنَكُمْ وَتَكَاثُرٌ فِي الْأَمْوَالِ وَالْأَوْلَادِ ۖ كَمَثَلِ غَيْثٍ أَعْجَبَ الْكُفَّارَ نَبَاتُهُ ثُمَّ يَهِيجُ فَتَرَاهُ مُصْفَرًّا ثُمَّ يَكُونُ حُطَامًا ۖ وَفِي الْآخِرَةِ عَذَابٌ شَدِيدٌ وَمَغْفِرَةٌ مِّنَ اللَّهِ وَرِضْوَانٌ ۚ وَمَا الْحَيَاةُ الدُّنْيَا إِلَّا مَتَاعُ الْغُرُورِ

1. *"Know that the life of this world is only play and amusement, pomp and mutual boasting among you, and rivalry in respect of wealth and children—like vegetation after rain, whose growth delights the tiller; then it withers,*

and you see it turning yellow, before it becomes dry straw. But in the Hereafter, there is severe torment (for the disbelievers and evildoers), and forgiveness from Allah and His good pleasure (for the believers and righteous). Whereas the life of this world is nothing but a deceiving enjoyment." (57:20, Al-Hadid)

In addition, we should acknowledge and appreciate another vital group of individuals who play a significant role in society and consistently guide our religious lives. These individuals are our imams, who oversee the operations of mosques and teach in religious institutions. From the moment we enter this world, they call the Azan, and when we depart, they conduct the Janazah prayer, regardless of the strength of our faith.

However, it is not uncommon to witness diverse perspectives, thoughts, and actions among Muslim youth and our elders within society. Sunni Muslims follow various schools of jurisprudence, such as Hanafi, Maliki, Shafi'i, and Hanbali. More broadly, Muslims can be categorised into two groups: Sunni and Shia. The Shia community also encompasses numerous different schools of thought. However, delving into this subject requires a separate and extensive study.

When embarking on a journey, it is crucial to embrace compassion as a fundamental aspect of one's character. Criticism becomes an opportunity to cultivate tolerance, manage anger, patiently listen to alternative viewpoints, and exert control over challenging situations that may arise, transforming the environment from a battlefield into a harmonious space. Possessing these essential qualities sets believers apart from others.

In the Quran, a verse defines this as:

الَّذِينَ يُنفِقُونَ فِي السَّرَّاءِ وَالضَّرَّاءِ وَالْكَاظِمِينَ الْغَيْظَ وَالْعَافِينَ عَنِ النَّاسِ ۗ وَاللَّهُ يُحِبُّ الْمُحْسِنِينَ

- *Those who spend (freely), whether in prosperity or in adversity, who restrain anger and pardon all men – for Allah loves those who do good. (3:134, Surah Al-Imran)*

The true Muslim does not limit his compassion only to his family, children, relatives, and friends but extends it to all people. This aligns with the teachings of the Prophet 纖, which encompass all of humanity and make compassion a condition of faith. As Abu Musa al-Ash'ari (RadiyAllahu Anhu) narrated from the Prophet Muhammad 纖:

"You will not believe until you have compassion towards one another."

(Reported by Bukhari in *Al-Adab Al-Mufrad.*)

Each of the Quran's 114 chapters, except for the 9th, begins with the words:

"In the name of ALLAH, the Merciful, the Compassionate."

These qualities form the foundation of true compassion—those who control their anger, pardon others, and do good are the ones whom Allah loves. This is the first step in preparing ourselves with the necessary qualities to truly understand ourselves and continue searching for a safe path towards our ultimate destination: *Darus-Salam* and, ultimately, *Jannatul Firdaus*.

In the same way, the entire human race is searching for the path leading to Paradise, even though their jurisprudence may differ.

To conclude this discussion, let us recall this verse:

$$\text{لَّذِي خَلَقَ الْمَوْتَ وَالْحَيَاةَ لِيَبْلُوَكُمْ أَيُّكُمْ أَحْسَنُ عَمَلًا ۚ وَهُوَ الْعَزِيزُ الْغَفُورُ}$$

"Who has created death and life, that He may test you to see which of you is best in deed. And He is the All-Mighty, the Oft-Forgiving." - (67:2, Al-Mulk)

بِسْمِ ٱللَّهِ ٱلرَّحْمَـٰنِ ٱلرَّحِيمِ

Chapter 3

Say, O Muhammad ﷺ, "This is my way; I invite unto Allah (i.e. to the Oneness of Allah – Islamic Monotheism) with sure knowledge— I and whosoever follows me with sure knowledge."

(Surah Yusuf 12:108, Dr M. Muhsin Khan / Dr M. Taqi-ud-Din Al-Hilali)

📖📖📖📖📖📖

Preparation

Planning and preparation are crucial aspects of any journey, but the specific nature of these activities depends on the characteristics of the trip. For instance, if the journey involves exploring unknown territories, traversing air, sea, and mountains, and visiting different countries, the planning and preparation required will be significantly different from that of a leisurely holiday aimed at relaxation and stress-free experiences.

Preparing for an expedition to an unfamiliar location and embarking on an exploration can be both exhilarating and adventurous. Although you may lack detailed information about the destination, there are several general steps to undertake in order to prepare for such a journey. These steps include:

1. **Gathering information about the region or country you will be visiting:** Learn about local customs, culture, climate, and any necessary safety precautions. This knowledge will serve as a foundation for your trip.

2. **Packing essentials:** Understand the nature of the journey and pack accordingly. Consider the specific equipment and gear required for your exploration, taking into account factors such as terrain, weather conditions, and planned activities.

3. **Arranging necessary travel documents:** Ensure that you have a valid passport for the entire duration of your trip. If required, obtain the necessary visas or permits well in advance to avoid any last-minute complications.

4. **Travel insurance:** Consider acquiring travel insurance to safeguard against any unforeseen circumstances or emergencies that may arise during your journey. This will provide you with peace of mind and financial protection.

5. **Necessary medicines:** If you have any specific medical needs or require regular medications, make sure to bring an ample supply with you. Research the availability of medical facilities and pharmacies at your destination, and carry any relevant prescriptions or documentation.

6. **Staying connected:** Research options for staying connected during and after your trip. Depending on the location, you may need to arrange for mobile data or Wi-Fi services. Additionally, consider bringing necessary equipment such as chargers, adapters, or portable power banks.

To adequately prepare for an unfamiliar destination, it's important to maintain a flexible and open mind, embracing new experiences along the way—whether you're embarking on an exploration of the unknown or looking for a peaceful holiday getaway. All of this pertains to worldly matters.

However, the journey we are preparing for is distinct in nature. It is a unidirectional expedition encompassing both physical and spiritual aspects, presenting formidable challenges throughout its entirety. It also entails embarking on an exhilarating spiritual path that remains largely unknown, necessitating thorough planning and preparation akin to a worldly travel itinerary.

This spiritual journey is replete with personal growth, profound wisdom, and an intimate sense of connection that only righteous individuals can confidently engage with, relying on guiding principles to advance towards the ultimate destination. Nevertheless, when contemplating the concept of a perpetual journey, we come to comprehend that meticulous planning and financial considerations hold minimal significance.

Eternal travel transcends the pursuit of earthly comforts and pleasures. Rather, it embodies a profound essence far beyond the realm of fantastical imaginings, intimately tied to the purity of one's soul. However, for those determined to explore the path of an unknown spiritual journey, which can be an exciting and transformative experience, some initial suggestions and preparation are essential before embarking on the journey.

1. **Self-Reflection:** Begin by engaging in self-reflection and exploring your intentions for embarking on this journey. What are you seeking? What do you hope to learn or achieve? Understanding your motivations will provide a solid foundation for your spiritual exploration.

2. **Research and Study:** Read books, attend lectures, and explore philosophies. Gain knowledge from the Holy Qur'an and the teachings of Prophet Muhammad ﷺ to strengthen your belief and understanding of spiritual paths. This will broaden your perspective and help shape your own beliefs and approach.

3. **Cultivate Openness:** Approach your spiritual journey with an open mind and heart. Let go of preconceived notions and be willing to explore new ideas and experiences. Embrace the possibility of change and growth, allowing yourself to be transformed by the journey.

4. **Develop Mindfulness:** Cultivate mindfulness through practices such as meditation. These practices help develop present-moment awareness and create space for inner stillness and reflection. Mindfulness can deepen your connection with your inner self and facilitate a more profound spiritual experience.

5. **Seek Guidance:** Consider finding a mentor, spiritual teacher, or guide who can offer support and direction along your journey. They can provide insights, answer questions, and offer valuable perspectives that enhance your understanding and progress.

6. **Create Rituals and Practices:** Establish rituals or daily practices that align with your spiritual path. These could include prayer, meditation, journaling, or engaging in specific activities that hold spiritual significance to you. Consistency in these practices can help maintain focus and cultivate a deeper connection to the Divine.

7. **Connect with Nature:** Spend time in nature and connect with its beauty and wisdom. Whether it's taking walks in the forest, sitting by the ocean, or watching a sunset, nature can provide profound insights and a sense of connectedness with the larger universe.

8. **Embrace Solitude and Silence:** Allocate regular periods of solitude and silence to reflect and connect with your inner self. This could involve retreating to a quiet space, engaging in silent meditation, or going on a solo journey. These moments of solitude can foster introspection and clarity.

9. **Practice Gratitude:** Cultivate an attitude of gratitude for the blessings in your life. Expressing gratitude regularly helps shift your focus towards the positive aspects of your journey and enhances your overall spiritual experience.

10. **Trust the Process:** Remember that a spiritual journey is unique to each individual, and there is no right or wrong way to navigate it. Trust yourself and the process, and have faith that the path will unfold before you as you progress.

Embrace the unknown, stay open to the possibilities, and be patient with yourself as you embark on your spiritual journey. It will be filled with growth, wisdom, and a deep sense of connection. These aspects have the potential to guide your transformation towards a virtuous state or a superior level, granting you entry onto the straight path that leads to the culmination of this material realm.

At the outset, it is essential for each individual in this travelling group to introduce themselves and embark on a process of self-reflection and self-evaluation, affirming their worthiness to join this spiritual journey. Each step of this profound expedition must align with the principles laid out by divine law and the teachings of the esteemed Prophet Muhammad ﷺ.

Allah (SWT) declared:

"I will be accountable on the Day of Judgement, and no one will come forward to help me."

الْيَوْمَ تُجْزَىٰ كُلُّ نَفْسٍ بِمَا كَسَبَتْ ۚ لَا ظُلْمَ الْيَوْمَ ۚ إِنَّ اللَّهَ سَرِيعُ الْحِسَابِ

That Day will every soul be required for what it earned; no injustice will there be that Day, for Allah is swift in taking account. (Surah Al-Mu'min 40:17)

As stated in the Bible:

"So then every one of us shall give account of himself to God."

(Romans 14:12, KJV)

Understanding Our True Identity

Our sense of identity is shaped by various factors, including our upbringing, cultural background, heritage, and philosophical or spiritual beliefs. These elements manifest through our actions, values, contributions, and personality traits, influencing how we perceive ourselves and our role in the world.

For instance, being a father, mother, husband, wife, businessperson, or politician may define aspects of our identity, but it is the quality of our engagement in these roles that truly matters. Whether we are regarded as good or bad parents, honest or dishonest politicians, these evaluations significantly impact our personal lives, and their effects may endure until the end of our journey.

However, **our worldly identity holds no value before Allah**. We cannot establish our identity by referencing others; rather, our sole identity before Allah should be as a **Mu'min** (believer). We can say:

"O Allah, I am Your faithful, righteous servant."

(أنا عبدك البار الأمين)

This represents the most fundamental form of identification. While there may be deeper levels of identity, for the purposes of our discussion, we will focus on this foundational understanding of the individual.

The Condition of the Heart

Only a believer with a pure heart can stand before Allah. Allah (SWT) says:

$$\text{يَوْمَ لَا يَنفَعُ مَالٌ وَلَا بَنُونَ إِلَّا مَنْ أَتَى اللَّهَ بِقَلْبٍ سَلِيمٍ}$$

A Day when neither wealth nor children will be of any benefit, except for he who comes to Allah with a pure heart. (Surah Ash-Shu'ara 26:88-89)

This means that our journey to meet the Almighty depends on the purification of our hearts in this life.

In another chapter, we will explore the process of self-purification extensively. For now, let us focus on its significance and the steps we should take to achieve it.

Spiritual Identity vs Worldly Identity

Within society or even within our own families, we may possess a unique identity. However, it is within ourselves that the true essence of who we are resides. Our inner soul holds this profound truth. Recognising and embracing this reality allows us to embark on a journey of spiritual growth.

However, without a pure soul, our spiritual journey cannot truly commence.

Embarking on a spiritual journey is akin to embarking on a physical journey. Just as we require a passport, visa, and money for travel, these concepts serve as metaphors in the realm of spirituality. Using the example of passports and visas, we can better understand the barriers that hinder our progress and why it is necessary to address them.

Every individual, whether born into the faith or having reverted (converted), is considered a passport holder in this context. However, merely possessing a passport does not automatically grant eligibility to travel the straight path. One must demonstrate faith and sincerity as a believer to obtain an entry visa, allowing them to continue their journey along the right path. This process requires self-assessment and introspection.

The Reality of Supplication and Commitment

Many mistakenly believe that external supplication alone is sufficient to reach our spiritual destination. However, when we examine the comprehensive list of obligations that must be fulfilled concurrently, we realise the challenges of qualifying for the straight path.

It demands:

1. **The courage to make sacrifices.**

2. **The determination to adhere to divine guidelines.**

3. **Personal transformation into a righteous individual.**

We must remember the oath we took:

"From now on, we Muslims will obey, listen, stand firm for righteousness, and ask forgiveness from our Lord until the end of our journey." (Surah Al-Baqarah 2:285)

Our progress halts when we lack awareness of our personal circumstances that validate our righteousness. Therefore, it is crucial for each of us to introspect and ask:

"Am I genuinely a righteous person? Do I possess a pure heart and soul that truly define a believer?"

The responses to these questions reside within us, and only we can provide the authentic answers.

However, Allah (SWT) has made it clear through the verses that without a pure heart, there is no chance of becoming a true believer. If one is not a believer, there is no chance of walking the straight path that leads to Allah.

As Allah says:

$$قَدْ أَفْلَحَ مَن زَكَّاهَا وَقَدْ خَابَ مَن دَسَّاهَا$$

He has succeeded who purifies the soul, and he has failed who corrupts the soul. (Surah Ash-Shams 91:9-10)

Proving Our Worthiness for the Journey

Hence, each traveller must demonstrate their worthiness for a visa to embark on the straight path. This may lead many to wonder:

"Are my acts of performing the five daily prayers, fasting, giving zakat, and undertaking the Hajj pilgrimage sufficient to attain entry into heaven or to meet Allah?"

The answer lies within the individual. Outward prayers hold value only when accompanied by genuine and sincere inner prayers that cleanse the soul.

When both external and internal devotion align, a person undergoes a profound transformation into a true believer. And it is these believers whom Allah desires to embrace.

The Ultimate Goal: A Purified Heart

To achieve success in the Hereafter, our evaluative thinking must encompass our heart, soul, and mind. The profound verses emphasise that purification of the heart and soul during our earthly existence is paramount and serves as a gateway to the Hereafter.

From birth, every individual embarks on a journey towards the culmination of this life. It is intriguing to observe how many individuals tread the righteous path designated by Allah (SWT), which serves as a direct route leading to paradise for believers.

We find the same message in the Bible:

For this is he that was spoken of by the prophet Esaias, saying, The voice of one crying in the wilderness, Prepare ye the way of the Lord, make his paths straight. Matthew 3:3 (KJV)

"Watch the path of your feet, and all your ways will be established.

Ponder the path of thy feet, and let all thy ways be established. Turn not to the right hand nor to the left: remove thy foot from evil. **Proverbs 4:26-27** (KJV)[6]

"Blessed are the pure in heart: for they shall see God." Matthew 5:8 (KJV)[7]

Therefore, there is no doubt among us that, in order to gain permission to walk the straight path, one must first purify the soul.

In our journey as a cohesive travelling group, we rely on the navigator—a fusion of knowledge, wisdom, and courage. These elements serve as our protectors, expertly guiding us along the path to achieve ultimate success.

Now, let us delve into the concept of the soul. The soul can be understood as an intangible essence within our bodies, intimately connected to a higher power such as Allah (SWT). It is important to note that every individual possesses a soul, regardless of their religious beliefs. The soul serves as the driving force within the body, akin to a driver manoeuvring a vehicle. It is often referred to as the spirit, atma, or nafs, and its presence infuses life into the physical form. Various religious and philosophical traditions share the notion that the soul is a celestial entity—a non-material spark unique to each living being.

وَلَا أُقْسِمُ بِالنَّفْسِ اللَّوَّامَةِ

"And I do call to witness the self-reproaching spirit (Eschew Evil)." (75:2, Surah Al-Qiyamah)

When a body is given a soul, life begins. And when the soul leaves the body, life ends, bringing about death.

The Qur'an identifies different levels of *nafs* (the self or soul). The following verses explain why a believer must give utmost attention to these levels in order to achieve success:

ارْجِعِي إِلَىٰ رَبِّكِ رَاضِيَةً مَّرْضِيَّةً

---

[6] Source: https://bible.knowing-jesus.com/topics/Straight-Paths
[7] https://www.openbible.info/topics/a_pure_heart

28

"Come back thou to thy Lord—well pleased (thyself), and well-pleasing unto Him." (89:28, Surah Al-Fajr)

Another verse states:

وَمَا أُبَرِّئُ نَفْسِي ۚ إِنَّ النَّفْسَ لَأَمَّارَةٌ بِالسُّوءِ إِلَّا مَا رَحِمَ رَبِّي ۚ إِنَّ رَبِّي غَفُورٌ رَّحِيمٌ

"Nor do I absolve my own self (of blame): the (human) soul is certainly prone to evil, unless my Lord bestows His Mercy. Surely, my Lord is Oft-Forgiving, Most Merciful." (12:53, Surah Yusuf)

The word *nafs* is used in various ways in the Qur'an, all of which refer to a soul within a body, over which Allah Almighty has given man a degree of control, reform, and change. The word *nafs* (or soul) is also used to indicate one's own self. An example of this is found in the following verse:

وَاذْكُر رَّبَّكَ فِي نَفْسِكَ تَضَرُّعًا وَخِيفَةً وَدُونَ الْجَهْرِ مِنَ الْقَوْلِ بِالْغُدُوِّ وَالْآصَالِ وَلَا تَكُن مِّنَ الْغَافِلِينَ

"And remember your Lord by your tongue and within yourself, humbly and with fear, without loudness in words, in the mornings and in the afternoons, and be not of those who are neglectful." (7:205, Surah Al-A'raf)

The *nafs* also refers to a specific part of the self that harbours desires and appetites; some refer to it as the *ego*. It encompasses anger, passion, lust, and desire—sometimes called the *carnal self* or *carnal soul*. However, *nafs* is distinct from *ruh*, which is an entirely different matter. Though associated with *nafs*, the *ruh* does not play a significant role in our quest for purification of the soul.[8][9]

Allah (SWT) says:

وَيَسْأَلُونَكَ عَنِ الرُّوحِ ۖ قُلِ الرُّوحُ مِنْ أَمْرِ رَبِّي وَمَا أُوتِيتُم مِّنَ الْعِلْمِ إِلَّا قَلِيلًا

"They ask you [O Muhammad (SAWS)] concerning the Ruh (soul). Say: 'It is one of the things, the knowledge of which is only with my Lord. And of knowledge, you (mankind) have been given very little.'" (Qur'an 17:85, Surah Al-Israa)

Therefore, we should refrain from excessive curiosity and questioning about the *ruh*. Most Islamic scholars are also discouraged from wasting time on this subject. Our primary purpose is to understand the heart, *nafs* (soul), and spirit so that we may act according to the instructions of Allah (SWT).

The Noble Qur'an describes three different types of *nafs*, as mentioned below:

---

[8] http://al-qiyamah.org/ruh_of_allah_al_isra.htm
[9] (IbnKathir (Ibn Kathīr was a highly influential scholar during the Mamluk era in Syria. Born: 1301, Busra, Syria an expert on tafsir and faqīh, he wrote several books, including a fourteen-volume universal history. Wikipedia)

1. The Soul Which Commands (*Nafs-e-Ammara*)

This refers to a state in which we are subjugated by our desires, listening to and following their commands. It represents the part of us that craves material possessions and sensual pleasures. Various verses in the Holy Qur'an describe the existence of this kind of *nafs*, which inclines towards sin. It is considered lower than animals because animals act according to their natural instincts, whereas humans are expected to exercise self-control.

وَمَا أُبَرِّئُ نَفْسِي ۚ إِنَّ النَّفْسَ لَأَمَّارَةٌ بِالسُّوءِ إِلَّا مَا رَحِمَ رَبِّي ۚ إِنَّ رَبِّي غَفُورٌ رَّحِيمٌ

"And I free not myself (from blame). Verily, the (human) self is inclined to evil, except when my Lord bestows His Mercy (upon whom He wills). Verily, my Lord is Oft-Forgiving, Most Merciful." (12:53, Surah Yusuf)

2. The Soul That Blames (*Nafs-e-Lawwama*)

The word *lawwama* is derived from *lom*, meaning "to reproach." At this stage, the *nafs* reaches a level of self-awareness where, if it commits a sin, the conscience awakens and criticises the wrongdoing. This stage signifies an awareness of one's imperfections and a sincere aspiration for self-improvement, inspired by the heart.

وَلَا أُقْسِمُ بِالنَّفْسِ اللَّوَّامَةِ

"And I swear by the self-reproaching person (a believer)." (75:2, Surah Al-Qiyamah)

3. The Soul at Peace (*Nafs-e-Mutmainnah*)

This refers to the serene, contented soul that has attained tranquillity. At this stage, the *nafs* reaches certainty and stability, ensuring that it neither collapses nor regresses. It has full conviction in its spiritual journey and its eventual meeting with the Lord. While it may still commit faults, it remains steadfast in its faith, knowing that it will not backslide.

يَا أَيَّتُهَا النَّفْسُ الْمُطْمَئِنَّةُ

ارْجِعِي إِلَىٰ رَبِّكِ رَاضِيَةً مَّرْضِيَّةً

(It will be said to the pious :)

"O (you) the one in (complete) rest and satisfaction!

Come back to your Lord, well-pleased (yourself) and well-pleasing unto Him!" (89:27-28, Surah Al-Fajr)[10]

This stage is the ultimate purpose of life: to attain complete contentment with Allah (SWT).

---

[10] http://www.ezsoftech.com/akram/nafs.asp

It involves abstaining from knowingly committing any sins and finding joy in performing righteous deeds. It was at this moment that the soul was addressed on the day of Ashura when Imam Hussain (AS) lowered his sword and heard the voice proclaiming:

"O satisfied soul! Return to your Lord, well-pleased and pleasing to Him." *(Different scholars' findings)*[11]

Self-Purification

The following verses refer to self-purification:

Allah (SWT) says (we are repeating the verse again):

قَدْ أَفْلَحَ مَن زَكَّاهَا

"Indeed, he has succeeded who purifies his own self (i.e. obeys and performs all that Allah has ordered, by following the true faith of Islamic monotheism and by doing righteous good deeds)." (91:9) Surah Ash-Shams[12]

He who purifies his soul through obeying Allah and who purifies it from sins and immoral behaviour. Self-purification is about clearing away all the tarnish of the baser self, with all its ugliness and evil, and replacing it with good morals and noble manners.

Quranic Guidance on Self-Purification:

قَدْ أَفْلَحَ مَن تَزَكَّىٰ

وَذَكَرَ اسْمَ رَبِّهِ فَصَلَّىٰ

1.   *"Indeed, whosoever purifies himself (by avoiding polytheism and accepting Islamic Monotheism) shall achieve success." (87:14) Surah Al-A'la*

"And remembers (glorifies) the Name of his Lord (worships none but Allah), and prays (five compulsory prayers and Nawafil additional prayers)." (87:15) Surah Al-A'la

وَنَفْسٍ وَمَا سَوَّاهَا

فَأَلْهَمَهَا فُجُورَهَا وَتَقْوَاهَا

1.   *"And by Nafs (Adam or a person or a soul, etc.), and Him Who perfected him in proportion; Then He showed him what is wrong for him and what is right for him." (91:7–8) Surah Ash-Shams*

---

[11] http://www.ezsoftech.com/akram/nafs.asp
[12] Ibn Kathīr was a highly influential scholar during the Mamluk era in Syria. Born: 1301, Busra, Syria an expert on tafsir and faqīh, he wrote several books, including a fourteen-volume universal history. Wikipedia)

قَدْ أَفْلَحَ مَن زَكَّاهَا

وَقَدْ خَابَ مَن دَسَّاهَا

2. *"Indeed, he succeeded who purifies his own self (i.e. obeys and performs all that Allah has ordered, by following the true Faith of Islamic Monotheism and by doing righteous good deeds)." (91:9) Surah Ash-Shams*

"And indeed, he fails who corrupts his own self (i.e. disobeys what Allah has ordered by rejecting the true Faith of Islamic Monotheism or by following polytheism, etc., or by committing evil and wicked deeds)." (91:10) Surah Ash-Shams

We must now carefully examine our character, heart, and spirit, and evaluate how much we have corrupted these three precious elements. In the Holy Quran, Allah (SWT) states:

الَّذِينَ آمَنُوا وَتَطْمَئِنُّ قُلُوبُهُم بِذِكْرِ اللَّهِ ۗ أَلَا بِذِكْرِ اللَّهِ تَطْمَئِنُّ الْقُلُوبُ

1. *"Those who believe (in the Oneness of Allah – Islamic Monotheism), and whose hearts find rest in the remembrance of Allah, verily, in the remembrance of Allah do hearts find rest." (13:28) Surah ar-Ra'd*

If we desire peace in our hearts and purity in our souls, we should remember Allah Almighty sincerely. However, we must reflect on the condition of our hearts. Even if our hearts are burdened with sin, we can still find solace by seeking repentance and repairing our ways.

It is unfortunate that within the Muslim community, numerous individuals are engaged in external acts of worship, yet simultaneously commit sinful deeds such as illegal land acquisition, bribery, murder, accumulating wealth through forbidden means, and many other unspeakable sins. Such a heart cannot attain purity until it is mended and rectified.

Allah (SWT) said:

لَّيْسَ الْبِرَّ أَن تُوَلُّوا وُجُوهَكُمْ قِبَلَ الْمَشْرِقِ وَالْمَغْرِبِ وَلَٰكِنَّ الْبِرَّ مَنْ آمَنَ بِاللَّهِ وَالْيَوْمِ الْآخِرِ وَالْمَلَائِكَةِ وَالْكِتَابِ وَالنَّبِيِّينَ وَآتَى الْمَالَ عَلَىٰ حُبِّهِ ذَوِي الْقُرْبَىٰ وَالْيَتَامَىٰ وَالْمَسَاكِينَ وَابْنَ السَّبِيلِ وَالسَّائِلِينَ وَفِي الرِّقَابِ وَأَقَامَ الصَّلَاةَ وَآتَى الزَّكَاةَ وَالْمُوفُونَ بِعَهْدِهِمْ إِذَا عَاهَدُوا ۖ وَالصَّابِرِينَ فِي الْبَأْسَاءِ وَالضَّرَّاءِ وَحِينَ الْبَأْسِ ۗ أُولَٰئِكَ الَّذِينَ صَدَقُوا ۖ وَأُولَٰئِكَ هُمُ الْمُتَّقُونَ

1. *"It is not Al-Birr (piety, righteousness, and each and every act of obedience to Allah, etc.) that you turn your faces towards east and west (in prayers); but Al-Birr is (the quality of) the one who believes in Allah, the Last Day, the Angels, the Book, the Prophets, and gives his wealth, in spite of love for it, to the kinsfolk, to the orphans, and to the poor, and to the wayfarer, and to those who ask, and to set slaves free, performs As-Salat (Iqamat-as-Salat), and gives the Zakat, and who fulfil their covenant when they make*

32

it, and who are patient in extreme poverty, illness, and at the time of fighting (during battles). Such are the people of truth, and they are the pious." (2:177) Surah Al-Baqarah

The Prophet (SAW) said:

"Nothing is heavier on the believer's Scale on the Day of Judgement than good character." (Tirmidhi)

From the above saying, we can conclude that on the Day of Judgement, a person's good character and pure heart will matter. In another hadith, 'Abu Huraira narrated that the Messenger of Allah (PBUH) said:

"Allah does not look at your figures, nor at your attire, but He looks at your hearts and accomplishments." (Sahih Muslim)[13]

We have already explained that obligatory prayers alone are not enough to please Allah. Obligatory duties are a part of the purification process and a means of pleasing Allah.

Allah (SWT) says:

اتْلُ مَا أُوحِيَ إِلَيْكَ مِنَ الْكِتَابِ وَأَقِمِ الصَّلَاةَ ۖ إِنَّ الصَّلَاةَ تَنْهَىٰ عَنِ الْفَحْشَاءِ وَالْمُنكَرِ ۗ وَلَذِكْرُ اللَّهِ أَكْبَرُ ۗ وَاللَّهُ يَعْلَمُ مَا تَصْنَعُونَ

1. *"Recite what is sent of the Book by inspiration to thee, and establish regular Prayer: for Prayer restrains from shameful and unjust deeds; and remembrance of Allah is the greatest (thing in life) without doubt. And Allah knows the (deeds) that ye do." (29:45) Surah Al-Ankabut*

Allah (SWT) then says in Surah Ash-Shu'ara:

يَوْمَ لَا يَنفَعُ مَالٌ وَلَا بَنُونَ

إِلَّا مَنْ أَتَى اللَّهَ بِقَلْبٍ سَلِيمٍ

1. *"The Day whereon neither wealth nor sons will avail, except him who brings to Allah a clean heart (clean from Shirk (polytheism) and Nifaq (hypocrisy))." (26:88–89) Surah Ash-Shu'ara*

Our Difficulty in Purifying the Heart

Being righteous and having a pure heart is a formidable challenge for various reasons. The primary obstacle arises from the malevolent force known as "Satan," who possesses a divine power that is exceedingly difficult to overcome. However,

---

[13] http://www.quranreading.com/blog/purification-of-the-heart-and-soul-in-islam-tips-from-quran-and-sunnah/

by embracing the determination to control one's heart and being willing to make sacrifices, it becomes possible to attain righteousness.

While we have previously defined the concept of the soul, it is important to differentiate between the spiritual heart (Qalb) and the visible heart. The soul is a force that exists within the biological heart. The heart serves as the abode of both virtuous and wicked qualities. To avoid confusion, it is crucial to understand that the physical heart, a muscular organ about the size of a fist located slightly to the left of the breastbone, is responsible for pumping blood throughout the body, supplying oxygen, nutrients, and removing waste products like carbon dioxide. However, the spiritual heart, which is connected to the soul, is distinct from the physical heart. It possesses its own intelligence and influences the thoughts of the brain. Moreover, it has the ability to absorb physical energy, control knowledge, and interact with the brain and the body.

Our main focus lies on the spiritual heart, which Allah (SWT) has cautioned all His Prophets about and instructed His followers to safeguard. It is the primary target of Satan's attacks. The spiritual heart serves as the chamber where emotions and desires originate, propelling the will of individuals towards action.

The old scripture, the Bible, also says that the heart is the spiritual organ that drives man's behaviour.[14]

Verse 26: "A new heart also will I give you, and a new spirit will I put within you: and I will take away the stony heart out of your flesh, and I will give you an heart of flesh." Ezekiel 36:26 (KJV).

The heart is the starting place for spiritual life because of what the Bible says about God's actions toward the human heart. In order to get people to desire what He desires, God must:

"I will take away the stony heart out of your flesh, and I will give you an heart of flesh" Ezekiel 36:26 (KJV).

Prophet Jesus said that sins like evil thoughts, sexual immorality, theft, murder, adultery, greed, malice, deceit, lewdness, envy, slander, arrogance, and foolishness actually originate in the heart of man Mark 7:21-23 (KJV).

"21 For from within, out of the heart of men, proceed evil thoughts, adulteries, fornications, murders,

22 Thefts, covetousness, wickedness, deceit, lasciviousness, an evil eye, blasphemy, pride, foolishness:

23 All these evil things come from within, and defile the man." Mark 7:21-23 (KJV). (Index 11)

---

[14] http://quranproject.org/The-human-heart-in-the-glorious-Quran-481-d

God is faithful to forgive us and cleanse us from everything that our new hearts are not proud of. If we don't come into the light and admit that we have sinned, there is no possible healing (John 1:5-10).

Spiritual life also begins in the heart, and it begins with God. God is a Saviour at heart. He wants people to be saved and to delight in knowing the truth and in knowing Him. When our hearts are afraid of condemnation, we can be comforted by the fact that:

"Trust in the Lord with all thine heart; and lean not unto thine own understanding" (Proverbs 3:5 KJV). (Index 12) Source

In the following verses of the Holy Quran, we find that it is the heart where true knowledge, guidance, and awareness are hidden:

$$إِنَّ فِي ذَٰلِكَ لَذِكْرَىٰ لِمَن كَانَ لَهُ قَلْبٌ أَوْ أَلْقَى السَّمْعَ وَهُوَ شَهِيدٌ$$

1. "Verily, in this is a Message for anyone who has a heart and understanding, or who gives ear and earnestly witnesses (the truth)." (50:37) Surah Qaf

$$فِي قُلُوبِهِم مَّرَضٌ فَزَادَهُمُ اللَّهُ مَرَضًا ۖ وَلَهُمْ عَذَابٌ أَلِيمٌ بِمَا كَانُوا يَكْذِبُونَ$$

2. "In their hearts is a disease; and Allah has increased their disease: and grievous is the penalty they incur, because they are false (to themselves)." (2:10) Surah Al-Baqara

3. Allah SWT has raised the question:

$$أَفَلَا يَتَدَبَّرُونَ الْقُرْآنَ أَمْ عَلَىٰ قُلُوبٍ أَقْفَالُهَا$$

4. "Do they not then think deeply in the Qur'an, or are their hearts locked up (from understanding it)?" (47:24) Surah Muhammad

Think carefully about what Allah SWT says:

$$كَلَّا ۖ بَلْ ۜ رَانَ عَلَىٰ قُلُوبِهِم مَّا كَانُوا يَكْسِبُونَ$$

"By no means! But on their hearts is the stain of (the ill) which they do!" (83:14) Surah Al-Mutaffifeen

Verily, when the servant commits a sin, a black spot appears in his heart. If he repents from it, his heart is polished clean. However, if he persists in the sin, the spot will continue to increase. This is the statement of Allah, and Allah (SWT) also shows us the way out of these difficulties. Recite this verse deep inside your heart:

$$رَبَّنَا لَا تُزِغْ قُلُوبَنَا بَعْدَ إِذْ هَدَيْتَنَا وَهَبْ لَنَا مِن لَّدُنكَ رَحْمَةً ۚ إِنَّكَ أَنتَ الْوَهَّابُ$$

"Our Lord! Let not our hearts deviate (from the truth) after You have guided us, and grant us mercy from You. Truly, You are the Bestower." (3:8) Surah Al-Imran

Explanation:

Our Lord! Let not our hearts deviate (from the truth) after You have guided us. Meaning: "Do not deviate our hearts from the guidance after You have allowed them to acquire it. Do not make us like those who have wickedness in their hearts, those who follow the Mutashabih in the Qur'an. Rather, make us remain firmly on Your straight path and true religion."

Mutashabih: meaning has been described in the Qur'an (Al-i'Imran 3:7 and others) as allegorical verses (Mutashabih); those in whose hearts there is malformation follow parts of it which are allegorical, seeking to mislead and seeking to give their own interpretation. As mentioned, this is the work of the evil force (devil). Allah (SWT) says:

هُوَ الَّذِي أَنزَلَ عَلَيْكَ الْكِتَابَ مِنْهُ آيَاتٌ مُّحْكَمَاتٌ هُنَّ أُمُّ الْكِتَابِ وَأُخَرُ مُتَشَابِهَاتٌ ۖ فَأَمَّا الَّذِينَ فِي قُلُوبِهِمْ زَيْغٌ فَيَتَّبِعُونَ مَا تَشَابَهَ مِنْهُ ابْتِغَاءَ الْفِتْنَةِ وَابْتِغَاءَ تَأْوِيلِهِ ۗ وَمَا يَعْلَمُ تَأْوِيلَهُ إِلَّا اللَّهُ ۗ وَالرَّاسِخُونَ فِي الْعِلْمِ يَقُولُونَ آمَنَّا بِهِ كُلٌّ مِّنْ عِندِ رَبِّنَا ۗ وَمَا يَذَّكَّرُ إِلَّا أُولُو الْأَلْبَابِ

"It is He Who has sent down to you (Muhammad ﷺ) the Book (this Qur'an). In it are Verses that are entirely clear, they are the foundations of the Book [and those are the Verses of Al-Ahkam (commandments, etc.), Al-Fara'id (obligatory duties), and Al-Hudud (legal laws for the punishment of thieves, adulterers, etc.)]; and others not entirely clear. So as for those in whose hearts there is a deviation (from the truth) they follow that which is not entirely clear thereof, seeking Al-Fitnah (polytheism and trials, etc.), and seeking for its hidden meanings, but none knows its hidden meanings save Allah. And those who are firmly grounded in knowledge say: "We believe in it; the whole of it (clear and unclear Verses) are from our Lord." And none receives admonition except men of understanding. (Tafsir At-Tabari) (3:7) Surah Al-Imran[15]

The evidence above and below confirm that the purification of the soul and protection of the heart are essential components of perseverance, enabling one to confidently claim to be on the straight path.

Allah purifies His Messenger's heart

Allah cleansed His Messenger's heart. Allah (SWT) says in Surah Al-Sharh:

أَلَمْ نَشْرَحْ لَكَ صَدْرَكَ

"Have We not opened your breast" (94:1) Surah Al-Sharh

---

[15] (Muhkam and Mutashabih meaning is known only to Allah although many scholars given their own views such as "We believe in whatever our Lord means to say."' Muhkam can be translated as "decisive and Mutashabih as "allegorical")

Allah cleansed His Messenger's heart. Allah (SWT) continues in Surah Al-Sharh, verses 1-4:

$$ أَلَمْ نَشْرَحْ لَكَ صَدْرَكَ $$

"Have We not expanded for you your breast?"

Then Allah (SWT) continues to explain its effect in the following verses of the same Surah:

$$ وَوَضَعْنَا عَنكَ وِزْرَكَ $$

$$ الَّذِي أَنقَضَ ظَهْرَكَ $$

"And We removed from you your burden, which weighed down your back." **(94:2-3)**

First, when He ﷺ was a boy, Allah (SWT) opened the heart of the Messenger ﷺ of Allah and made it clear that there was no place for satanic activity in it. The Messenger ﷺ was designed and equipped with a heart capable of performing his magnificent work as the Messenger ﷺ of Allah.

How Many Times Was The Prophet Muhammad's ﷺ Blessed Chest Opened And Why?

The splitting of the blessed chest took place four times.

Mawlānā Shāh 'Abdul 'Azeez Muhaddith Dehlwi (may Allah shower him with mercy) mentions in the commentary of Sūrah al-Inshirāh, and 'Allāmah 'Abdul Mustafā A'azamī (may Allah shower him with mercy) mentions in his book *Seerat-e-Mustafā*, that the noble chest of the Prophet Muhammad ﷺ was split four times and filled with light [Nūr] and wisdom.

1. The first time occurred when He ﷺ was at the home of Sayyidatunā Haleemah (may Allah be pleased with her). The wisdom behind this was to protect the noble Prophet ﷺ from the whispers and thoughts that affect children, which incline them toward playing and mischief.

2. The second time took place at the age of ten, so that He ﷺ would not be affected by the mischievous desires of adolescence.

3. The third occasion of the splitting of the blessed chest of the Noble Messenger ﷺ occurred in the cave of Hirā. It was filled with the light of tranquillity so that He ﷺ could bear the mighty and immense weight of the revelation of Allah.

4. The fourth time the blessed chest of the Holy Prophet ﷺ was split and filled with treasures of light [Nūr] and wisdom was on the Night of Mi'rāj (Ascension), so that his blessed heart may become vast and capacious

enough to bear the Divine vision of Allah (Most High) and the Majestic Grandeur of the Divine Speech.[16]

Purification First Or Knowledge First

1. Both elements are equally important, but the gravity of self-purification is so significant that Allah (SWT) purifies His Messenger first and then teaches him wisdom.

2. Allah (SWT) also mentions that acquiring knowledge (wisdom) before purification is extremely harmful.

3. If we analyse the following verses, we will see that Allah Ta'ala first emphasised purifying the heart before acquiring knowledge. The verse says:

هُوَ الَّذِي بَعَثَ فِي الْأُمِّيِّينَ رَسُولًا مِّنْهُمْ يَتْلُو عَلَيْهِمْ آيَاتِهِ وَيُزَكِّيهِمْ وَيُعَلِّمُهُمُ الْكِتَابَ وَالْحِكْمَةَ وَإِن كَانُوا مِن قَبْلُ لَفِي ضَلَالٍ مُّبِينٍ

"He it is Who sent among the unlettered ones a Messenger (Muhammad ﷺ) from among themselves, reciting to them His Verses, purifying them (from the filth of disbelief and polytheism), and teaching them the Book (this Qur'an, Islamic laws and Islamic jurisprudence) and Al-Hikmah (As-Sunnah: legal ways, orders, acts of worship, etc. of Prophet Muhammad ﷺ). And verily, they had been before in manifest error." (62:2, Al-Jumu'a)

كَمَا أَرْسَلْنَا فِيكُمْ رَسُولًا مِّنكُمْ يَتْلُو عَلَيْكُمْ آيَاتِنَا وَيُزَكِّيكُمْ وَيُعَلِّمُكُمُ الْكِتَابَ وَالْحِكْمَةَ وَيُعَلِّمُكُم مَّا لَمْ تَكُونُوا تَعْلَمُونَ

"Similarly, (to complete My Blessings on you) We have sent among you a Messenger (Muhammad ﷺ) of your own, reciting to you Our Verses (the Qur'an) and sanctifying you, and teaching you the Book (the Qur'an) and the Hikmah (i.e. Sunnah, Islamic laws and Fiqh – jurisprudence), and teaching you that which you used not to know." (2:151, Al-Baqara)

An Example:

When Allah (SWT) became annoyed with the actions of our Prophet Muhammad ﷺ in an incident mentioned below, Allah the Almighty says:

"When the blind came to him, he frowned and turned away. And what could you say? He came here to be holy (he probably was) to receive advice. You are present to him, who is responsible enough, even though he is free, it is not your concern. And the one who came to you with great interest and fear, you were reluctant about him."

---

[16] [Mirāt ul-Manājīh, vol 1, pg 110] and Answered by Mufti Qasim Zia al-Qadri Translated by Zameer Ahmed. https://www.seekerspath.co.uk/

This is indeed a reminder in Surah Abasa (80:1-11):

1. The Prophet (ﷺ) frowned and turned away,

2. Because there came to him the blind man (i.e. 'Abdullah bin Umm-Maktum, who came to the Prophet (ﷺ) while he was preaching to one or some of the Quraysh chiefs).

3. But what could tell you that perhaps he might become pure (from sins)?

4. Or that he might receive admonition, and that the admonition might profit him?

5. As for him who thinks himself self-sufficient,

6. To him you attend;

7. What does it matter to you if he will not become pure (from disbelief, you are only a Messenger, your duty is to convey the Message of Allah)?

8. But as to him who came to you running,

9. And is afraid (of Allah and His Punishment),

10. Of him you are neglectful and divert your attention to another,

11. Nay, (do not do like this), indeed it (these Verses of this Qur'an) are an admonition.

In this surah, Allah reminds His Messenger ﷺ because he turned away from a blind man who came to seek knowledge so that he might be purified. The Messenger turned away from him because he was busy with those whom he thought were more important and significant for the religion of Islam; i.e. his attempt to invite Quraysh leaders, hoping that they and the Arab tribes who followed them might accept Islam and revert to it. What was this serious matter that deserved Allah's, the Almighty, blame of His beloved Messenger?

Further Exploration:

Before wrapping up this chapter of our preparation, it might prove beneficial to explore a few additional verses along with the hadith for our purpose. Allah (SWT) says:

1. Thus it is [what has been mentioned in the above said Verses (27, 28, 29, 30, 31) is an obligation that mankind owes to Allah]. And whosoever honours the Symbols of Allah, then it is truly from the piety of the heart. (22:32, Surah Al-Hajj)

2. O you who believe! Answer Allah (by obeying Him) and (His) Messenger when he (ﷺ) calls you to that which will give you life, and know that Allah comes in between a person and his heart (i.e. He prevents an evil person

39

from deciding anything). And verily to Him you shall (all) be gathered. (08:24, Al-Anfal)

3. And keep yourself (O Muhammad ﷺ) patiently with those who call on their Lord (i.e. your companions who remember their Lord with glorification, praising in prayers, etc., and other righteous deeds) morning and afternoon, seeking His Face, and let not your eyes overlook them, desiring the pomp and glitter of the life of the world; and obey not him whose heart We have made heedless of Our Remembrance, one who follows his own lusts and whose affair (deeds) has been lost. (18:28, Al-Kahf)

The verses above offer potent guidance directly from Allah (SWT) on cleansing our hearts. Allah emphasises the significance of morning and afternoon as prime moments for remembering Him, glorifying Him, and patiently repeating the phrase "La Ilaha Illallah" alongside all His servants, irrespective of their wealth, strength, or status.

This method stands out as one of the finest paths to attain purity of heart. In this context, "weak" refers to individuals who haven't yet gained significant esteem among the esteemed circles of the powerful Quraysh. It's crucial to incorporate the two hadiths linked with the verse into our practices.

It was said that this was revealed about the nobles of Quraysh when they asked the Prophet ﷺ to sit with them alone and not bring his weak companions with him, such as Bilal, Ammar, Suhayb, Khabbab, and Ibn Masud. They wanted him to sit with them alone, but Allah forbade Him from doing that and said:

"And turn not away those who invoke their Lord, morning and afternoon, seeking His Face. You are accountable for them in nothing, and they are accountable for you in nothing, that you may turn them away, and thus become of the Zalimun (unjust)." (6:52, Al-An'am)[17]

With an unyielding thirst for knowledge and an insatiable curiosity to decipher the divine mysteries that steer us toward our destined paths, we embark on a diligent quest. Each page we turn becomes a stepping stone, guiding us closer to the enlightenment we seek. Let us forge ahead in our reading, optimistic that it will illuminate the way to our desired destination.

---

[17] Abū al-Ḥusayn 'Asākir ad-Dīn Muslim ibn al-Ḥajjāj ibn Muslim ibn Ward ibn Kawshādh al-Qushayrī an-Naysābūrī or Muslim Nayshāpūrī commonly known as Imam Muslim, was an Islamic scholar from the city of Nishapur (early Khorasan and present day Iran), particularly known as a muhaddith (scholar of hadith). His hadith collection, known as Sahih Muslim, is one of the six major hadith collections in Sunni Islam and is regarded as one of the two most authentic (sahih) collections, alongside Sahih al-Bukhari. From Wikipedia, the free encyclopedia

Following are some general guidelines that may be helpful:

1. **Repentance**: Acknowledge any wrongdoings or sins you have committed and sincerely seek forgiveness from Allah. This involves a deep sense of remorse and a commitment to avoid repeating the same mistakes in the future.

2. **Prayer and meditation**: Regular prayer and meditation can help you connect with a higher power and gain spiritual strength. This can involve reciting specific prayers, reading religious texts, or simply sitting in silence and focusing on your breath.

3. **Fasting**: Fasting is a way to discipline the body and focus on spiritual goals. If one observes the true conditions of fasting, it can form a secret bridge between external prayer and internal prayer. The combination of both can purify the soul.

4. **Charity and good deeds**: Helping others is a key component of many religions, and actively seeking opportunities to do good can help purify the soul and strengthen your connection to a higher power.

5. **Education**: Studying the teachings of your religion and seeking guidance from religious leaders can help you deepen your understanding of spiritual principles and develop a more meaningful relationship with Allah (SWT).

At the end, Allah (SWT) says:

إِلَّا مَنْ أَتَى اللَّهَ بِقَلْبٍ سَلِيمٍ وَأُزْلِفَتِ الْجَنَّةُ لِلْمُتَّقِينَ

"Except him who brings to Allah a clean heart [clean from Shirk (polytheism) and Nifaq (hypocrisy)]. And Paradise will be brought near to the Muttaqun (pious – see V. 2:2)." (26:89-90, Surah Ash-Shu'araa)

Allah (SWT) also guided us, saying:

وَإِمَّا يَنزَغَنَّكَ مِنَ الشَّيْطَانِ نَزْغٌ فَاسْتَعِذْ بِاللَّهِ ۚ إِنَّهُ سَمِيعٌ عَلِيمٌ

"And if an evil whisper comes to you from Shaitan (Satan), then seek refuge with Allah. Verily, He is All-Hearer, All-Knower." (7:200, Surah Al-A'raf)

A Beautiful Story: *Conference of the Birds*

Conference of the Birds is a story based on a Persian epic philosophical poem by the poet Farid-ud-Din Attar, from the twelfth century. This story offers a wide-open space for thought and helps you find your inner self.

The hoopoe is the first bird introduced in *The Conference of the Birds*. Heaven has sent him to lead the other birds in their quest for a king. The hoopoe is a prophet, trusted by Allah, who has travelled the world. The birds of the world all gather together to name twelve other types of birds, including the ringdove, the parrot, the partridge, the hawk, and the goldfinch. They seek to find the legendary Simorgh, who can correct all the wrongs of mankind by leading them.

The hoopoe takes charge of the quest to find the Simorgh and wants his fellow birds to accompany him to find their rightful king. He tells them outright that the quest is long and dangerous, as they must pass over *The Seven Valleys* to reach their destination. Though many birds make excuses, such as the faults of infatuation, religious delusion, frivolous attachments, avarice, pride, ambition, misguided longing, materialism, false humility, and others, all the birds begin the spiritual journey.

They face many challenges, where human flaws in each bird are revealed and described in detail, preventing mankind from growing. Many birds die during the journey or fall victim to the human weaknesses that are being portrayed to them.

The birds travel through the seven valleys of search, love, perception, freedom and isolation, unity, wonder, and finally, poverty and emptiness. However, at the end, only thirty birds reach the door of Simorgh, where they later learn that they themselves are idols of God – their own characteristics have been lost. There is only one God.

Each valley teaches a different moral:

1. In the Valley of the Quest, the book undergoes a hundred difficulties and trials. After one has been tested and become free, one learns in the Valley of Love that love has nothing to do with reason.

2. The Valley of Understanding teaches that knowledge is temporary, but understanding endures. Overcoming faults and weaknesses brings the seeker closer to the goal.

3. In the Valley of Independence and Detachment, one has no desire to possess nor any wish to discover. To cross this difficult valley, one must be roused from apathy and renounce inner and outer attachments so that one can become self-sufficient.

4. In the Valley of Unity, the hoopoe announces that although you may see many beings, in reality, there is only one, which is complete in its unity. As long as you are separate, good and evil will arise; but when you lose yourself in the divine essence, they will be transcended by love. When unity is achieved, one forgets all and forgets oneself in the Valley of Astonishment and Bewilderment.

5. The hoopoe declares that the last valley, of deprivation and death, is almost impossible to describe. In the immensity of the divine ocean, the patterns of the present world and the future world dissolve. As you realise that the individual self does not really exist, the drop becomes part of the great ocean forever in peace.

The analogy of moths seeking the flame is used. Out of thousands of birds, only thirty reach the end of the journey. When the light of lights is manifested and they are at peace, they become aware that the Simorgh is them. They begin a new life in the Simorgh and contemplate the inner world.

Simorgh, it turns out, means thirty birds; but if forty or fifty had arrived, it would have been the same. By annihilating themselves gloriously in the Simorgh, they find themselves in joy, learn the secrets, and receive immortality. So long as you do not realise your nothingness and do not renounce your self-pride, vanity, and self-love, you will not reach the heights of immortality.

أَلَمْ تَرَ أَنَّ اللَّهَ يُسَبِّحُ لَهُ مَن فِي السَّمَاوَاتِ وَالْأَرْضِ وَالطَّيْرُ صَافَّاتٍ ۖ كُلٌّ قَدْ عَلِمَ صَلَاتَهُ وَتَسْبِيحَهُ ۗ وَاللَّهُ عَلِيمٌ بِمَا يَفْعَلُونَ

"See you not (O Muhammad ﷺ) that Allah, He it is Whom glorify whosoever is in the heavens and the earth, and the birds with wings outspread (in their flight). Of each one He (Allah) knows indeed his Salat (prayer) and his glorification, [or everyone knows his Salat (prayer) and his glorification], and Allah is All-Aware of what they do." (24:41, Surah An-Nur)

Attar concludes with the advice that if you want to find the sea of your soul, die for all your old life and then remain silent.

Conclusion

The Seven Valleys in The Conference of the Birds represent the path of the soul on a spiritual journey, finding its way from this world to the realm of Allah. By the end of the seventh valley, 30 birds remain; they are taken to the home of the Simorgh, where they gaze into a lake. All 30 birds are able to see the Simorgh in their own reflections. Since these birds had been able to make it past all the tests put forth by the seven valleys, the Simorgh was now within all of them. Thus, their physical journey to the Simorgh's abode represents the journey of being metaphorically illuminated. Each valley represents a fear or guilt that may hinder one from acquiring the mentioned knowledge.

The ending of the poem is also connected with the Sufi teachings: according to Sufism, God is formless and is not any type of entity, but instead exists within all of worldly creations. (1)

Readers unacquainted with the writings of Sufis could have no better introduction than Attar's Manteq at-Tair (The Conference of the Birds), where the seven valleys traversed by the birds of the quest are: Search, Love, Mystic Apprehension, Detachment/Independence, Unity, Bewilderment, and Fulfilment in Annihilation. The purpose of the discipline is to achieve purification. The aspirant must purify his nafs, i.e. his personality-self, from its inclination to shahawat, that is, the thoughts and desires of the natural man, and substitute these with love

43

(mahabba); then he must be cast into the flames of passion (ishq) to emerge in the state of union (wusla) with the transmutation of self. (2)[18]

However, there is really no end to preparing for a spiritual journey. Although it may seem daunting to embark on a journey without a clear end or conclusion, the beauty of a spiritual journey lies in the process itself.

It is a personal preparation and ongoing exploration where the journey involves learning, growth, and self-improvement that help deepen our spiritual understanding and enrich our faith and life. Still, progressing on this spiritual journey is very challenging, no matter how wise you are. You may get lost or derailed during the journey by an invisible, powerful enemy who can block you from the path and disqualify you from righteous status, even though you think you are on the right path. When a person loses control in a moment of weakness, Satan can find an opportunity to take over and control your soul and your journey.

As individuals, we can be called upon to resist such influences through spiritual discipline, wisdom, and faith. Allah did not leave us empty-handed in this battle. Our weapon is the divine power of the Qur'an, along with the teachings of Prophet Muhammad ﷺ, but it is up to us whether we will be spiritual warriors or not.

However, let's move on to another chapter to continue our journey.

---

[18] https://www.gradesaver.com/the-conference-of-the-birds/study-guide/summary 2
http://traditionalhikma.com/wp-content/uploads/2015/06/Conference-of-the-Birds-by-Faridudin-Attar.pdf//Source: collection from the following sights
http://www.poemhunter.com/poem/conference-of-the-birds/

بِسْمِ ٱللَّهِ ٱلرَّحْمَـٰنِ ٱلرَّحِيمِ

Chapter 4

Jabir reported: I heard Allah's Messenger (peace be upon him) say:

"The throne of Iblis is upon the ocean, and he sends detachments (to different parts) in order to put people to trial. The most important figure in his eyes is the one who is most notorious in sowing the seed of dissension."

Book 39, Number 6754:

Translation of Sahih Muslim, Book 39.

📖📖📖📖📖📖

Satan and Our Defence

In order to set foot upon the righteous journey, an individual must harbour a soul untainted by impurities, as this is the singular prerequisite to professing faith and securing passage onto this path. There exists no alternative route to reach the destination of this righteous journey. The undeniable truth is that your supplications and inner purification must align harmoniously in order to confidently progress. Many of our companions are still grappling with the profound process of wholly transforming themselves into devout believers.

For a common Muslim, the transformation into a true believer proves to be an arduous task, as Satan vehemently opposes it at every turn. However, if one is resolute in defying Satan's influence, it becomes imperative to identify the specific instances, locations, and methods through which he infiltrates our hearts and minds, compelling us to act in accordance with his desires.

Every human being is born with certain inherent qualities, which gradually manifest in their daily lives. Satan is well aware of these characteristics and adeptly exploits them to contaminate human hearts and minds, coercing individuals to comply with his whims and wishes. These elements include:

- Hypocrisy
- Backbiting
- Patience
- Anger
- Envy

- Greed
- Jealousy

Humans are inherently bound to exhibit certain behaviours, as they are comprised of various human elements instilled by Allah (SWT). Despite the Quran's instructions being easy to recite, adhering to them can be challenging due to the interference of malevolent forces of divine origin. Concurrently, we understand from verse six in Surah Fatir that purification of our hearts and souls is indispensable for attaining success. Allah (SWT) has warned His servants on earth to beware of Satan:

إِنَّ الشَّيْطَانَ لَكُمْ عَدُوٌّ فَاتَّخِذُوهُ عَدُوًّا ۚ إِنَّمَا يَدْعُو حِزْبَهُ لِيَكُونُوا مِنْ أَصْحَابِ السَّعِيرِ

"Surely, Shaitan (Satan) is an enemy to you, so take (treat) him as an enemy. He only invites his Hizb (followers) that they may become the dwellers of the blazing Fire."

35/6 Fatir

Satan not only obstructs our adherence to Allah's commands but also ensures that we recognise our inability to hold him accountable on the Day of Judgment for his influence upon us in this worldly realm.

"It was Allah Who gave you a promise of Truth: (1) I too promised, (2) But I failed in my promise to you. I had no authority over you except to call you, but ye listened to me: then reproach not me, but reproach your own souls. I cannot listen to your cries, nor can ye listen to mine. I reject your former act in associating me with Allah. For wrongdoers, there must be a grievous penalty."

Satan will mock us by pushing the burden back onto us. He would say:

وَقَالَ الشَّيْطَانُ لَمَّا قُضِيَ الْأَمْرُ إِنَّ اللَّهَ وَعَدَكُمْ وَعْدَ الْحَقِّ وَوَعَدتُّكُمْ فَأَخْلَفْتُكُمْ ۖ وَمَا كَانَ لِيَ عَلَيْكُم مِّن سُلْطَانٍ إِلَّا أَن دَعَوْتُكُمْ فَاسْتَجَبْتُمْ لِي ۖ فَلَا تَلُومُونِي وَلُومُوا أَنفُسَكُم ۖ مَّا أَنَا بِمُصْرِخِكُمْ وَمَا أَنتُم بِمُصْرِخِيَّ ۖ إِنِّي كَفَرْتُ بِمَا أَشْرَكْتُمُونِ مِن قَبْلُ ۗ إِنَّ الظَّالِمِينَ لَهُمْ عَذَابٌ أَلِيمٌ

"…And Shaitan (Satan) will say when the matter has been decided:

"Verily, Allah promised you a promise of truth. And I too promised you, but I betrayed you. I had no authority over you except that I called you, so you responded to me. So blame me not, but blame yourselves. I cannot help you, nor can you help me. I deny your former act in associating me (Satan) as a partner with Allah (by obeying me in the life of the world). Verily, there is a painful torment for the Zalimun (polytheists and wrongdoers, etc.)."

14/22 Surah Ibrahim

In the verse cited, Satan has unveiled the truth of Allah and his position in such a clear manner that on the Day of Judgment, we will not find ourselves devoid of any space to present counterarguments. Nevertheless, even Satan acknowledges that he cannot elude retribution, yet his intention is to lure us into damnation alongside him. This is the vow he has made to Allah (SWT), and Allah (SWT) has accepted his pledge with certain conditions, understanding that He cannot compel those who fortify themselves against Satan's influence and safeguard their hearts and souls from his corrupting grasp. Those are the believers.

Allah says in the Quran:

قَالَ فَبِعِزَّتِكَ لَأُغْوِيَنَّهُمْ أَجْمَعِينَ"

"إِلَّا عِبَادَكَ مِنْهُمُ الْمُخْلَصِينَ"

Iblis (Satan) said: "By Your Might, then I will surely mislead them all,

"Except Your chosen slaves amongst them (faithful, obedient, true believers of Islamic Monotheism)."

38 / 82-83 Surah Sad

Allah SWT accepts His challenge and replies to Him as follows:

قَالَ فَالْحَقُّ وَالْحَقَّ أَقُولُ

لَأَمْلَأَنَّ جَهَنَّمَ مِنْكَ وَمِمَّنْ تَبِعَكَ مِنْهُمْ أَجْمَعِينَ

(Allah) said: "The Truth is, and the Truth I say,

That I will fill Hell with you [Iblis (Satan)] and those of them (mankind) that follow you, together."

38/84,85 Surah Sad

The angry argument between Allah (SWT) and Satan does not end here. He continues:

قَالَ فَبِمَا أَغْوَيْتَنِي لَأَقْعُدَنَّ لَهُمْ صِرَاطَكَ الْمُسْتَقِيمَ

(Iblis) said: "Because You have sent me astray, surely I will sit in wait against them (human beings) on Your Straight Path."

7/16 Surah Al-Araf

ثُمَّ لَآتِيَنَّهُم مِّن بَيْنِ أَيْدِيهِمْ وَمِنْ خَلْفِهِمْ وَعَنْ أَيْمَانِهِمْ وَعَن شَمَائِلِهِمْ ۖ وَلَا تَجِدُ أَكْثَرَهُمْ شَاكِرِينَ

Then I will come to them from before them and behind them, from their right and from their left, and You will not find most of them as thankful ones (i.e., they will not be dutiful to You).

7/17 Surah Al-Araf

The intense confrontations and trials between Allah and Satan stemmed from Satan's frustration following his expulsion from Heaven by Allah (SWT) due to his disobedience to divine commands.

We will delve deeper into the play's portrayal of Satan's actions towards Adam and Eve following his expulsion from Heaven. However, our primary focus at present is to dissect the dialogues between Allah (SWT) and Satan, where Satan adamantly vows to corrupt us, lead us astray from the righteous path, and drag us into Hell alongside him. This becomes even more chilling when he receives Allah's (SWT) consent to manipulate His human creation as he pleases, except for those who remain steadfast in their faith.

Throughout this journey, it's vital to consider the present conditions, especially if we're grappling with adverse influences. If an individual is still struggling to comprehend their situation, it is crucial to continue reading and explore different stages, as this will facilitate the discovery of one's authentic self.

Another significant aspect to contemplate is the gravity of the Day of Judgement, during which Satan's deceitful schemes might jeopardise our journey, as he unequivocally disavows any accountability or culpability on that day. Simultaneously, Allah (SWT) instructs us to steer clear of Satan's enticements while journeying. Hence, it is imperative for members of our travel group to heed Allah's SWT admonition, conscientiously evaluate their circumstances, and take appropriate measures to cleanse and purify themselves.

Satan, also known as Iblis and by other names in various religious texts, is depicted as possessing divine intelligence, making it exceptionally challenging for individuals to resist his influence, regardless of their intelligence. In the following chapter, we delve into how he holds humanity hostage and exerts control over the world. However, it is through the guidance of Allah (SWT) that only true believers, endowed with unwavering willpower and inner strength, can defy Satan's powers, which he received from the Almighty.

In order to develop our inner strength and build a forte within the heart and soul, we must strictly consider the rule of Allah and the teachings of our Prophet Muhammad ﷺ. Allah says:

الشَّيْطَانُ يَعِدُكُمُ الْفَقْرَ وَيَأْمُرُكُم بِالْفَحْشَاءِ ۖ وَاللَّهُ يَعِدُكُم مَّغْفِرَةً مِّنْهُ وَفَضْلًا ۗ وَاللَّهُ وَاسِعٌ عَلِيمٌ

Shaitan (Satan) threatens you with poverty and orders you to commit Fahsha (evil deeds, illegal sexual intercourse, sins etc.); whereas Allah promises you forgiveness from Himself and bounty, and Allah is All-Sufficient for His creatures' needs, All-Knower.

2/268 Al-Baqara

There awaits a free one-way ticket straight to Jahannam, reserved in Shaitan's company, for those who follow his way. We should consider all the situations; despite all our prayers, can we be saved from the conspiracy of the powerful Satan when Allah (SWT) warned every prophet about Satan when they came to this earth to deliver the word of Allah, aiming to refrain from sin?

Satan tried to mislead the Messenger of Allah, our Prophet Muhammad (ﷺ). For this reason, Allah (SWT) said to His messenger, "If you feel any disturbance from Satan, seek refuge in Allah." Allah says:

وَإِمَّا يَنزَغَنَّكَ مِنَ الشَّيْطَانِ نَزْغٌ فَاسْتَعِذْ بِاللَّهِ ۚ إِنَّهُ هُوَ السَّمِيعُ الْعَلِيمُ

And if an evil whisper from Shaitan (Satan) tries to turn you away (O Muhammad) (from doing good, etc.), then seek refuge in Allah. Verily, He is the All-Hearer, the All-Knower.

41/36 Surah Ha-Mim

We see in the Torah and the Bible that Allah (SWT) warned them about Satan and his evil deeds, which would cause them trouble. Many scholars of that time were also concerned and thought about saving the human soul from Satan.

Russian Hesychasm:

The Spirituality of Nil Sorskij

Devil Had Driven Out Man

Should Show Supreme Heroism

In Fighting The Devil In His Interior

In The Depths Of His Soul.

Guard The Mind Into Your Heart

Keep The Heart Silent

Look Into The Depth Of The Heart

Enclose The Mind And Heart

Bring The Mind Under Control

Gather The Mind Into Your Heart

Contain The Mind In The Heart

Free Of All Imaginings

The Monk's First Concern Is To Destroy

The Source Of Bad Thoughts By Battling Always

Against The Passions.

When He Reaches This Stage Through

Purifying The Heart Of All Imaginations,

He Acquires Apatheia.

When The Monk Is "Dispassion,"

Then He Can Occupy His Mind And Heart

With The Continual Presence Of[19]

*****

The Fall of Lucifer (Devil)

12 "How you are fallen from heaven,

O Lucifer, son of the morning!

How you are cut down to the ground,

You who weakened the nations!

13 For you have said in your heart:

'I will ascend into heaven,

I will exalt my throne above the stars of God;

I will also sit on the mount of the congregation

On the farthest sides of the north;

14 I will ascend above the heights of the clouds,

I will be like the Most High."[20]

*****

Ananias and Sapphira (Acts 5:3)

...Then Peter said, "Ananias, how is it that Satan has so filled your heart that you have lied to the Holy Spirit and have kept for yourself some of the money you received for the land?"[21]

---

[19] Nil Sorsky (Russian: Нил Сорский, also Nilus of Sora and Nil Sorski; birth name: Nikolai Maikov (Russian: Николай Майков) (c. 1433–1508) became a leader of a tendency in the medieval Russian Orthodox Church known as the Non-possessors (nestyazhateli) which opposed ecclesiastic landownership.[1] The Russian Orthodox Church venerates Nil Sorsky as a saint, marking his feast day on the anniversary of his repose on May 7.[2]
https://en.wikipedia.org/wiki/Nilus_of_Sora
[20] Index 17 https://biblia.com/bible/nkjv/isaiah/14/12-14
[21] (Index 14) https://biblia.com/bible/esv/acts/5/3

What does Acts 5:3 mean?

Ananias—not the man whom Saul met with after his encounter with Jesus (Acts 9:10–19)—had presented some of the proceeds from the sale of a piece of land to the apostles for the care of the church members. Unfortunately, it seems that he had vowed to God that he would donate all the money, but he decided to bring only part of it (Acts 5:1–2). While he was within his rights to give as much as he wished, he had already committed to giving it all. By going back on his word, and more so by lying about it to the congregation, he "kept back" or embezzled part of the donation. He took that which rightfully belonged to God.

(Follow the web link below to read the full story.)[22]

*****

James 4:7–8

Submit yourselves therefore to God. Resist the devil, and he will flee from you. Come near to God, and He will come near to you. Wash your hands, you sinners, and purify your hearts, you double-minded.[23].

*****

1 Peter 5:8–9

Be alert and of sober mind. Your enemy the devil prowls around like a roaring lion, looking for someone to devour. Resist him, standing firm in the faith, because you know that the family of believers throughout the world is undergoing the same kind of sufferings.[24]

And 'Umar ibn Abdul Aziz (PBUH) said,

"The best jihad is the jihad against desires."

Whispers and his relentless attempts to exploit evil influences are another internal war against the devil. Even the smallest holes in our mental fortresses can easily spread into the shallows, allowing enemy troops to attack the fortresses of our hearts.

Islamic scholar Ibn al-Jawzi (Index 19) says[25]

Indeed, Iblis (Satan) only enters people to the extent that he is able. His ability to do so is increased or decreased according to the degree of their mindfulness, their negligence, their ignorance, and their deeds. Know that the heart is like a

---

[22] https://www.bibleref.com/Acts/5/Acts-5-3.html

[23] Index15 https://www.biblegateway.com/

[24] Index 16 https://www.biblegateway.com/

[25] (Ibn al-Jawzi (d. 597 H/1201 AD) was a Baghdadi storyteller, preacher, and prolific Islamic scholar associated with the Hanbali school of jurisprudential thought. He is well known for his exegeses of the Qur'an and Hadith, including his famous compendium, Al-Tahqiq.)

fortress. Upon that fortress are walls, and the walls have gates, with chambers inside where the mind resides. The angels often visit that fortress. Beside it are siege towers, where desires and devils frequently occupy them, with none to stop them. War is declared between the inhabitants of the fortress and those of the siege towers. The devils continuously circle around the fortress, seeking the negligence of the guards and passage into some of its chambers. Thus, the guards should be aware of all the gates of the fortress, upon which its protection depends.

Consider this a clarion call to awaken from our slumber. We often dismiss the threat posed by evil forces, comfortably cocooned within the fabric of our everyday lives. Satan operates not by overt disruption, but through insidious infiltration of our innermost being. Stealthily, he penetrates the fortress of our mind, then the sanctuary of our heart, and ultimately taints the very essence of our soul, corrupting it with his malevolence.

Once he gains dominion over our thoughts and emotions, we become unwitting subjects to his dark influence, bound by chains of servitude, regardless of our worldly status – be it power, wealth, wisdom, or piety. Shockingly, his enslavement is embraced with pride by many, even within the folds of religious communities, oblivious to the insidious nature of his machinations.

This is a clandestine warfare, an unseen battle where Satan flaunts his prowess before the Almighty, boasting of his control and corruption over the divine creation.

Whispers and his relentless attempts to exploit evil influences are another internal war waged by the devil. Even the smallest holes in our mental fortresses can easily spread into the shallows, allowing enemy troops to attack the fortresses of our hearts.

Insinuating whispers commit immoral acts, which come from three directions by Satan's forces: first, the nafs (or self), which is inclined to evil; second, the devils among the jinn (demons); and third, the devils among mankind.

Allah says, describing the first source, which is the nafs:

وَلَقَدْ خَلَقْنَا الْإِنسَانَ وَنَعْلَمُ مَا تُوَسْوِسُ بِهِ نَفْسُهُ ۖ وَنَحْنُ أَقْرَبُ إِلَيْهِ مِنْ حَبْلِ الْوَرِيدِ

"And indeed, We have created man, and We know what his ownself whispers to him. And We are nearer to him than his jugular vein (by Our Knowledge)." (50:16 Qaf)

Allah (SWT) says, describing the second source, which is the devils among the jinn (interpretation of the meaning):

فَوَسْوَسَ إِلَيْهِ الشَّيْطَانُ قَالَ يَا آدَمُ هَلْ أَدُلُّكَ عَلَىٰ شَجَرَةِ الْخُلْدِ وَمُلْكٍ لَّا يَبْلَىٰ

"Then Shaitan (Satan) whispered to him, saying: 'O Adam! Shall I lead you to the Tree of Eternity and to a kingdom that will never waste away?'" (20:120 Ta-Ha)

And Allah says, describing the third source, which is the devils among mankind (interpretation of the meaning):

Say: "I seek refuge with (Allah), the Lord of mankind,

The King of mankind,

The Ilah (God) of mankind,

From the evil of the whisperer (devil who whispers evil in the hearts of men) who withdraws (from his whispering in one's heart after one remembers Allah),

Who whispers in the breasts of mankind,

Of jinns and men." (114:1-6 Al-Naas) [26]

For the sake of discussion, we can set the following headlines, though, just a glimpse cannot compare to the continuous havoc and horror unfolding every minute. For the sake of discussion, we can set the following headings, although only a glimpse cannot compare with the constant disaster and horror that occurs every minute. This is a particularly ominous event that stands out, where Satan cunningly displays his power. Usually, every human being is accustomed to these kinds of incidents happening every day and finds nothing to look back on or worry about because common people know that they have no power to do anything, even though they understand it well.

In this sacred month (April 2022), in a holy place where spiritual leaders and thousands of worshippers from various faiths unite in devotion to the same God, Satan has managed to cloud our inner vision, knowledge, wisdom, and patience. It is a shameful surrender of all worshippers to the very entity responsible for defiling our souls. We must recognise that this defilement is in no way a grace or favour from Allah (SWT).

This is the month of Ramadan, Sha'ban 1443, and April 2022. I am still working on my writing in this book. On the 15th of this month, for the first time in decades, multiple monotheistic religions came together as closely as they do in Jerusalem. The festivals of Passover, the Friday Prayer, and the Easter celebrations coincidentally took place in Jerusalem. The outskirts of Jerusalem's Old City literally vibrate with various religious pilgrims each year.

This Ramadan (2022) is no exception. The devil becomes more active when Passover, Ramadan, and Easter festivals come together for the first time in three

---

[26] Index 20 So these waswas may come from the jinn or from the sons of Adam (human beings). https://islamqa.info/en/answers/39684/sources-of-waswas-and-accountability

decades, and thousands of believers gather in the holy city of Jerusalem to pray to the same God. However, whatever the cause of the disturbance, clashes erupted at the scene just shortly before dawn on a Friday morning. The skies above Jerusalem became shrouded in tear gas as a tumultuous scene unfolded at the Holy Place. Worshippers found themselves caught in a bitter clash, fuelled by anger, violence, and a thirst for revenge. This chaotic outburst included incidents such as stone throwing and even acts of murder. It was as if Satan himself orchestrated this dark spectacle, deceiving those who had gathered for worship, regardless of their esteemed scholarly status. In an audacious challenge to the teachings of the Holy Scriptures, he dared to obstruct their path. It is undeniable that this event represents a resounding triumph for Satan, a fact that cannot be denied.

Muslims go to the Al-Aqsa Mosque, known as the Temple Mount mosque. Jews pray at the Wailing Wall, considered one of the holiest places for Jews to pray, as well as a site sacred to them as the holy of holies—Jewish tradition's spiritual junction of Heaven and Earth, the axis mundi. This place is so pure and sanctified that only particular people are allowed to enter for prayer.

Passover (or Pesach in Hebrew), the story of Exodus, is one of the most important festivals in the Jewish year. It is a spring festival that begins on the 15th day of Nisan, the first month of the Jewish calendar. Jews remember how their ancestors left slavery behind when they were led out of Egypt by Moses. Passover is celebrated with a series of rituals, each symbolising a different part of the story, which is also mentioned in the Holy Qur'an.

In short, one day, however, Moses receives a command from Allah (SWT) to return to Egypt and free his kin from bondage, according to the Hebrew Bible. Along with his brother Aaron, Moses approaches the reigning Pharaoh (who is unnamed in the biblical version of the story) several times, explaining that his people need a three-day holiday to celebrate a festival to their Hebrew God.

When the Pharaoh refuses, God unleashes plagues on the Egyptians, including turning the Nile River red with blood, diseased livestock, boils, hailstorms, and three days of darkness, culminating in the slaying of every firstborn son by an avenging angel. The Israelites, however, mark the doorframes of their homes with lamb's blood so that the angel of death will recognise and "pass over" each Jewish household.

According to the Hebrew Bible, the Jews—now numbering in the hundreds of thousands—then trek through the Sinai desert for 40 tumultuous years before finally reaching their ancestral home in Canaan, later known as the Land of Israel.[27]

---

[27] (Index20a)
https://www.history.com/topics/holidays/passover
https://www.bbc.co.uk/bitesize/topics/znwhfg8/articles/zn22382

Christians worldwide have celebrated Easter for centuries as the day of Jesus Christ's resurrection, of course, in the city of Jerusalem, Israel, as written in the New Testament of the Christian Bible. According to the Gospel of John in the New Testament, Mary Magdalene came to the tomb where Jesus was buried and found it empty. An angel told her that Jesus had risen. It says in the Bible:

"After the Sabbath, at dawn on the first day of the week, Mary Magdalene and the other Mary went to look at the tomb.

2 There was a violent earthquake, for an angel of the Lord came down from heaven and, going to the tomb, rolled back the stone and sat on it.

3 His appearance was like lightning, and his clothes were white as snow.

4 The guards were so afraid of him that they shook and became like dead men.

5 The angel said to the women, 'Do not be afraid, for I know that you are looking for Jesus, who was crucified.

6 He is not here; he has risen, just as he said. Come and see the place where he lay.

7 Then go quickly and tell his disciples: 'He has risen from the dead and is going ahead of you into Galilee. There you will see him.' Now I have told you.'" [28]

Ramadan is a much-revered and blessed month for Muslims. This is the month in which they get the opportunity to teach fear of Allah (taqwa) by refraining from violence, anger, envy, greed, lust, angry or sarcastic retorts, gossip, and other negative behaviours. It is a time for striving to get along with each other better than usual, with a particular focus on the purification of the soul.

Allah (SWT) ordered Moses (PBUH) to fast as a means of purification for thirty days, and then added ten more days. After the fast was completed, Moses was ready to once again communicate with Allah (SWT). As mentioned in Surah Al-A'raf (7:142):

وَوَاعَدْنَا مُوسَىٰ ثَلَاثِينَ لَيْلَةً وَأَتْمَمْنَاهَا بِعَشْرٍ فَتَمَّ مِيقَاتُ رَبِّهِ أَرْبَعِينَ لَيْلَةً ۚ وَقَالَ مُوسَىٰ لِأَخِيهِ هَارُونَ اخْلُفْنِي فِي قَوْمِي وَأَصْلِحْ وَلَا تَتَّبِعْ سَبِيلَ الْمُفْسِدِينَ

And We appointed for Musa (Moses) thirty nights and added (to the period) ten (more), and he completed the term appointed by his Lord of forty nights. And Musa (Moses) said to his brother Harun (Aaron): "Replace me among my people, act in

---

[28] Index 20 b https://www.biblegateway.com/passage/?search=Matthew+28&version=NIV
Sabbath Definition & Meaning - Merriam-Websterhttps://www.merriam-webster.com › dictionary › Sabbath
: a day of the week that is regularly observed as a day of rest and worship Jews observe the Sabbath from Friday evening to Saturday evening. More from Merriam- ...
https://www.biblegateway.com/passage/?search=Matthew+28&version=NIV

the right way (by ordering the people to obey Allah and to worship Him alone) and follow not the way of the Mufsidun (mischief-makers)."

Although fasting aims to purify the soul, my keen observation reveals a troubling trend: violence frequently intensifies during the month of Ramadan, leading to chaos and bloodshed that contradicts the essence of the teachings found in the Holy Quran.

It is perplexing to comprehend the motives behind those individuals who are willing to sacrifice their own lives or the lives of others in such cruel manners. My understanding may not fully grasp their purpose or gain, but Allah (SWT) says in the Quran:

يَا أَيُّهَا الَّذِينَ آمَنُوا لَا تَأْكُلُوا أَمْوَالَكُم بَيْنَكُم بِالْبَاطِلِ إِلَّا أَن تَكُونَ تِجَارَةً عَن تَرَاضٍ مِّنكُمْ ۚ وَلَا تَقْتُلُوا أَنفُسَكُمْ ۚ إِنَّ اللَّهَ كَانَ بِكُمْ رَحِيمًا

O you who believe! Eat not up your property among yourselves unjustly except it be a trade by mutual consent. And do not kill yourselves (nor kill one another). Surely, Allah is Most Merciful to you. (4:29, Surah An-Nisaa)

I have collected numerous examples for our research. These examples will help us derive our own conclusions regarding the importance of the guidance provided in the Holy Quran.

For instance, explosions occurred during the Islamic holy month of Ramadan, just two days after blasts tore through a high school in a predominantly Shiite Hazara area of the capital, Kabul, killing at least six.[29]

16 April 2022

In Sweden, unrest has been reported in several towns for the third consecutive day since Quran burnings caused riots over the Easter weekend.[30]

A bomb attack on a Sunni mosque in the city of Kunduz, Afghanistan, has killed 33 people and injured 43 others, including children, officials say.[31] "Forty-one civilians, mainly women and children, were killed, and 22 others were wounded in air strikes by Pakistani forces near the Durand Line in Khost province," Shabir Ahmad Osmani, director of information and culture in Khost, told AFP on Sunday.[32]

---

[29] Index 20 e Index 20 e https://www.france24.com/en/asia-pacific/20220421-deadly-attacks-target-shiites-in-afghanistan-is-group-claims-mosque-blast

[30] Index 20 f Index 20f https://www.aljazeera.com/news/2022/4/20/sweden-believes-foreign-actors-behind-riots-over-quran-burning

[31] . Index 20g Index 20g https://www.bbc.co.uk/news/world-asia-61191643

[32] Index 20h . Index 20h https://www.aljazeera.com/news/2022/4/17/afghanistan-death-toll-in-pakistan-strikes-rises-to-47-official

6 Apr 2022

At least six people have been wounded in a grenade blast at a mosque in a densely populated area of the Afghan capital, Kabul, police said, minutes after worshippers had offered midday prayers. [33]

The above conversation prompts us to reassess our own circumstances and take proactive steps to steer clear of the negative influences along our journey. Despite this, we will persist in our reading endeavours, confident that they will provide us with additional insights to develop effective safeguards.

Allah (SWT) instructed His messenger, our Prophet Mohammed ﷺ, to remind us of how to build fortresses around our minds, hearts, and souls, and to guard carefully against the attacks of Satan. Allah says to His messenger:

وَقُل لِّعِبَادِي يَقُولُوا الَّتِي هِيَ أَحْسَنُ ۚ إِنَّ الشَّيْطَانَ يَنزَغُ بَيْنَهُمْ ۚ إِنَّ الشَّيْطَانَ كَانَ لِلْإِنسَانِ عَدُوًّا مُّبِينًا

And say to My slaves (i.e. the true believers of Islamic Monotheism) that they should (only) say those words that are the best. (Because) Shaitan (Satan) verily sows disagreements among them. Surely, Shaitan (Satan) is to man a plain enemy.

17:53 Surah Israel

Allah (SWT) also reminds us:

وَلَقَدْ أَضَلَّ مِنكُمْ جِبِلًّا كَثِيرًا ۖ أَفَلَمْ تَكُونُوا تَعْقِلُونَ

And indeed he (Satan) did lead astray a great multitude of you. Did you not, then, understand?

36:62 Surah Ya-Sin

Sufyan al-Thawri said: [34]

"The most courageous of people are the strictest in controlling their desires." The most important fight in this world is not against other people, but against our own desires and the devils who manipulate them. This is the way we can come close to purification.

The Bible says in the verses: Romans 1:28-32 KJV:

28 And even as they did not like to retain God in their knowledge, God gave them over to a reprobate mind, to do those things which are not convenient;

---

[33] Index 20k Index 20k https://www.aljazeera.com/news/2022/4/6/afghanistan-kabul-grenade-mosque-attack-leaves-six-wounded

[34] Index18) Index 18 (Abu Abdullah Sufyan ibn Said ibn Masruq al-Thawri was a Tābiʿ al-Tābiʿīn Islamic scholar and jurist, founder of the Thawri madhhab. He was also a great hadith compiler. Wikipedia)

29 Being filled with all unrighteousness, fornication, wickedness, covetousness, maliciousness; full of envy, murder, debate, deceit, malignity; whisperers,

30 Backbiters, haters of God, despiteful, proud, boasters, inventors of evil things, disobedient to parents,

31 Without understanding, covenantbreakers, without natural affection, implacable, unmerciful:

32 Who knowing the judgment of God, that they which commit such things are worthy of death, not only do the same, but have pleasure in them that do them.

Romans 1:28-32 KJV

The Messenger of Allah (ﷺ) declared:

"Wise is the man who reminds himself constantly of the accountability on the Day of Resurrection and so works hard for the life succeeding death."

Simultaneously, we can keep in mind what Allah (SWT) says:

وَإِمَّا يَنزَغَنَّكَ مِنَ الشَّيْطَانِ نَزْغٌ فَاسْتَعِذْ بِاللَّهِ ۚ إِنَّهُ سَمِيعٌ عَلِيمٌ

And if an evil whisper comes to you from Shaitan (Satan), then seek refuge with Allah. Verily, He is All-Hearer, All-Knower.

7:200 Surah Al-A'raf

The preceding lines serve as a guideline for safeguarding the heart, yet it's crucial to recognise that Satan is keenly observant of our every action, thought, and intention. He adeptly manipulates these to sway us towards his desires through subtle persuasion and insidious whispers. His threat is profoundly menacing, surpassing what many may not conceive.

It was narrated by Safiyyah bint Huyayy (may Allah be pleased with her) that our Prophet (ﷺ) said:

"The Shaitan flows through man like blood." (al-Bukhari, 3281; and Muslim, 2175)

Shaikh Ibn Baaz (may Allah have mercy upon him) was asked:

"If someone intends to do something good, does the Shaitan come to know and try to divert him from it?"

He replied:

"Every person has a devil and an angel with him, as the Prophet (ﷺ) said: 'There is no one who does not have a companion from among the jinn and a companion from among the angels.'"

They asked: *"Even you, O Messenger of Allah?"*

He said: *"Even me, but Allah helped me with him and he became Muslim (that is: 'and I am safe from him'), so he only enjoins me to do that which is good."*[35]

Drawing from the aforementioned hadith, it becomes evident that each individual is accompanied by both angelic and demonic companions. Through adherence to Allah's (SWT) guidance and observance of His religion, believers overcome the influence of their demonic companions. They diminish the devil's power to the point where it cannot deter them from virtuous acts or lead them astray, except as Allah (SWT) decrees.

Again, the transgressor unwittingly empowers their inner demon through their sinful and malevolent actions, until it gains enough strength to lead them further astray, urging them to embrace falsehood. Eventually, it gains such influence that it prevents them from engaging in virtuous deeds.[36]

Who Can Attain High Status While Travelling On The Straight Path?

Achieving a greater level of success on the journey requires a greater level of knowledge and wisdom, which can be identified as follows:

- Muslim
- Mu'min
- Ihsan

The understanding of these three categories in a Muslim's life is commonly familiar.

Level One: Muslim

At this level, we are all submissive to Allah and His Messenger ﷺ, fulfilling the basics of the five daily prayers, fasting, charity, the Hajj pilgrimage, and all other religious activities that are the primary outer actions of all Muslims as an obligatory duty. However, we would not be considered a true believer at this level because the heart can still be corrupted by Satan's influence. The purified soul may be absent, or the heart may act as a hypocrite.

Level Two: Mu'min

At the second level of a Muslim, his perception of faith becomes more mature, and he performs his internal activities as well as external ones, making him a true Mu'min (believer). His inner actions and beliefs have entered the heart at a deeper spiritual level that will not be interrupted by Satan's influence. He has firm belief in Allah, the Angels, the books of Revelation, the Messengers, and the unseen, such as the Day of Judgement, Paradise, and Hell.

---

[35] https://www.arabnews.pk/news/480921
[36] Index 21 Index 21 https://www.arabnews.com/news/474041

The combination of external activities and inner action (Iman), along with the purification of the Nafs, describes the complete Mu'min. The term Mu'min is the preferred term used in the Qur'an to describe monotheistic believers.

Allah (SWT) says:

قَالَتِ الْأَعْرَابُ آمَنَّا ۖ قُل لَّمْ تُؤْمِنُوا وَلَٰكِن قُولُوا أَسْلَمْنَا وَلَمَّا يَدْخُلِ الْإِيمَانُ فِي قُلُوبِكُمْ ۖ وَإِن تُطِيعُوا اللَّهَ وَرَسُولَهُ لَا يَلِتْكُم مِّنْ أَعْمَالِكُمْ شَيْئًا ۚ إِنَّ اللَّهَ غَفُورٌ رَّحِيمٌ

The Bedouins say, "We believe." Say, "You do not believe, but say, 'We have surrendered (in Islam),' for faith has not yet entered your hearts. But if you obey Allah and His Messenger (ﷺ), He will not decrease anything in reward for your deeds. Verily, Allah is Oft-Forgiving, Most Merciful." (49/14 Surah Al-Hujurat)

Level Three: Ihsan

This stage is the highest level of maturity for a Mu'min. At this stage, a Mu'min has reached the level of Ihsan. The depth of inner Iman and ibadah, and outer action such as control of greed, restraining anger, justice, love for others, kindness to parents and family—all reflect a remarkable beauty, *Muhsin* in Arabic. Satan cannot enter to defile his heart because he is constantly receiving favour and protection from Allah (SWT).

When one practises Ihsan with a heart full of love for Allah, as a result, his whole being goes through a transformation that makes him worthy of Allah's love, as the Qur'an says:

وَأَنفِقُوا فِي سَبِيلِ اللَّهِ وَلَا تُلْقُوا بِأَيْدِيكُمْ إِلَى التَّهْلُكَةِ ۛ وَأَحْسِنُوا ۛ إِنَّ اللَّهَ يُحِبُّ الْمُحْسِنِينَ

And spend in the Cause of Allah (i.e. Jihad of all kinds, etc.), and do not throw yourselves into destruction (by not spending your wealth in the Cause of Allah), and do good. Truly, Allah loves Al-Muhsinun (the good-doers). (2/195 Surah Al-Baqara)

الَّذِينَ يُنفِقُونَ فِي السَّرَّاءِ وَالضَّرَّاءِ وَالْكَاظِمِينَ الْغَيْظَ وَالْعَافِينَ عَنِ النَّاسِ ۗ وَاللَّهُ يُحِبُّ الْمُحْسِنِينَ

Those who spend [in Allah's Cause – deeds of charity, alms, etc.] in prosperity and in adversity, who repress anger, and who pardon men; verily, Allah loves Al-Muhsinun (the good-doers). (3/134 Surah Al-Imran)

إِنَّ اللَّهَ يَأْمُرُ بِالْعَدْلِ وَالْإِحْسَانِ وَإِيتَاءِ ذِي الْقُرْبَىٰ وَيَنْهَىٰ عَنِ الْفَحْشَاءِ وَالْمُنكَرِ وَالْبَغْيِ ۚ يَعِظُكُمْ لَعَلَّكُمْ تَذَكَّرُونَ

Verily, Allah enjoins Al-Adl (i.e. justice and worshipping none but Allah Alone – Islamic Monotheism) and Al-Ihsan [i.e. to be patient in performing your duties to Allah, totally for Allah's sake and in accordance with the Sunnah (legal ways) of the Prophet ﷺ in a perfect manner], and giving (help) to kith and kin (i.e., all that Allah has ordered you to give them, e.g., wealth, visiting, looking after them, or any other kind of help, etc.); and forbids Al-Fahsha' (i.e. all evil deeds, e.g. illegal sexual acts, disobedience of parents, polytheism, to tell lies, to give false witness, to kill a life without right, etc.), and Al-Munkar (i.e. all that is prohibited by Islamic law: polytheism of every kind, disbelief and every kind of evil deeds, etc.), and Al-Baghy (i.e. all kinds of oppression), He admonishes you, that you may take heed. (16/90 Surah An-Nahl)

وَوَصَّيْنَا الْإِنسَانَ بِوَالِدَيْهِ إِحْسَانًا ۖ حَمَلَتْهُ أُمُّهُ كُرْهًا وَوَضَعَتْهُ كُرْهًا ۖ وَحَمْلُهُ وَفِصَالُهُ ثَلَاثُونَ شَهْرًا ۚ حَتَّىٰ إِذَا بَلَغَ أَشُدَّهُ وَبَلَغَ أَرْبَعِينَ سَنَةً قَالَ رَبِّ أَوْزِعْنِي أَنْ أَشْكُرَ نِعْمَتَكَ الَّتِي أَنْعَمْتَ عَلَيَّ وَعَلَىٰ وَالِدَيَّ وَأَنْ أَعْمَلَ صَالِحًا تَرْضَاهُ وَأَصْلِحْ لِي فِي ذُرِّيَّتِي ۖ إِنِّي تُبْتُ إِلَيْكَ وَإِنِّي مِنَ الْمُسْلِمِينَ

And We have enjoined on man to be dutiful and kind to his parents. His mother bears him with hardship, and she brings him forth with hardship, and the bearing of him, and the weaning of him is thirty (30) months. Till when he attains full strength and reaches forty years, he says: "My Lord! Grant me the power and ability that I may be grateful for Your Favour which You have bestowed upon me and upon my parents, and that I may do righteous good deeds, such as please You, and make my offspring good. Truly, I have turned to You in repentance, and truly, I am one of the Muslims (submitting to Your Will)." (46/15 Surah Al-Ahqaf)

If one of our companions is worried about his past, then the following verse should also be considered:

لَيْسَ عَلَى الَّذِينَ آمَنُوا وَعَمِلُوا الصَّالِحَاتِ جُنَاحٌ فِيمَا طَعِمُوا إِذَا مَا اتَّقَوا وَّآمَنُوا وَعَمِلُوا الصَّالِحَاتِ ثُمَّ اتَّقَوا وَّآمَنُوا ثُمَّ اتَّقَوا وَّأَحْسَنُوا ۗ وَاللَّهُ يُحِبُّ الْمُحْسِنِينَ

Those who believe and do righteous good deeds, there is no sin on them for what they ate (in the past), if they fear Allah (by keeping away from His forbidden things), and believe and do righteous good deeds, and again fear Allah and believe, and once again fear Allah and do good deeds with Ihsan (perfection). And Allah loves the good-doers. (5/93 Surah Al-Maidah)

Jesus (PBUH) said when they asked him:

"On one occasion, an expert in the law stood up to test Jesus.

'Teacher,' he asked, 'what must I do to inherit eternal life?'

'What is written in the Law?' he replied. 'How do you read it?'

He answered, 'Love the Lord your God with all your heart, with all your soul, with all your strength, and with all your mind'; and, 'Love your neighbour as yourself.'

"Thou hast answered right: this do, and thou shalt live." (Luke 10:25-28 KJV)

Once, the Prophet (ﷺ) was asked, "What is Ihsan?" Our Prophet (ﷺ) replied:

"Ihsan is to worship Allah as though you see Him, and if you cannot see Him, then indeed He sees you."[37]

Many Muslims sincerely believe that their knowledge suffices and that their actions exemplify the highest level of faith. However, there is concern that this sincerity may be at odds with their limited knowledge or wisdom, leaving them vulnerable to manipulation by Satan and leading them astray.

For example, if we analyse the content of a story collected in a prominent Bangla newspaper, *Dainik Prothom Alo*, published on 20 August 2020, the gist of the story can be titled: "Absolutely 'Playing with Fire'". Locals called it a "fire play" between the two sides. There had been four fires in a month centred on the financial account of a mosque in the village. The two parties were blaming each other for this.

The dispute began when the president of the mosque committee refused to disclose the income and expenditure account, as demanded by the locals, including a retired school teacher who led the opposition. The two warring parties blamed each other, and anger developed. A complaint was lodged against the president of the mosque committee and his brother. Since the complaint, fires have been reported one after another, taking place at night in and around the houses of the two warring parties. Locals called it a "fire play" between the two sides.

In total, there have been four fires in a month, all centred around the financial account of the mosque. They continued to blame each other for these incidents. Finally, state officials intervened to settle the dispute regarding the mosque's financial affairs. [38]

The above story reflects that their hearts are mixed with the following elements:

(A) Pride

(B) Evil

(C) Guilt game

(D) Lack of patience

(E) Hypocrisy

In this case, according to the verses we read earlier, can we claim ourselves to be true believers? This is the game of Satan with common Muslims, and we must understand this.

---

[37] Index 22 https://www.deccanherald.com/content/71956/practice-ihsan-all-walks-life.html
[38] (Al-Ghazali was a Persian philosopher who was one of the most prominent and influential Muslim philosophers, theologians, jurists, and mystics, of Sunni Islam. Died: 19 December 1111, Tous, Iran Wikipedia) Index 23, (Index 24)

The following unique advice from the philosopher Abu Hamid al-Ghazzali is appropriate to quote here for every Muslim to learn to appeal against his opponent:

"As for beneficial deeds, it is to be a judge over envy. For everything that envy brings to the court of sayings and deeds, he should oblige himself to do its opposite. If envy compels him to disparage the envied, then he should oblige his tongue to praise him and commend him. If envy compels him to be arrogant towards him, then he should require himself to be humble before him and apologise to him... These are the cures for envy and they are very beneficial, although they are very bitter for the heart. Rather, the benefit is in bitter medicine."

Jihad

At the outset, I outlined several prerequisites for attaining the purity of heart, among which jealousy stands as a significant barrier. True success is best achieved through jihad—the earnest struggle against malevolence, fortified by unwavering faith. The ultimate form of jihad lies in the inner battle against satanic thoughts, ideas, feelings, and emotions, all aimed at purifying the heart to stand before the Almighty Allah (SWT) in purity.

The internal struggle, known as jihad, unfolds within the depths of our hearts in defiance of Iblis. Despite Iblis' relentless opposition, our unwavering resolve, sacrifices, and the aid of Allah are our sole prospects for vanquishing this foe. As Satan senses our allegiance to the virtuous path, he retreats in frustration, yet his forces persistently prowl, seeking opportunities to infiltrate our spirits once more and subjugate us. His divine prowess renders this task effortless. Satan and his minions, resembling serpents and lions, lie in ambush, ready to strike during moments of vulnerability. Hence, it is imperative to erect a formidable fortress to shield our souls.

Hypocrisy

The word "hypocrite" is rooted in the Greek word *hypocrites*, which means, "stage actor, pretender, and dissembler." So, think of a hypocrite as a person who pretends to be a certain way but really acts and believes the total opposite.

إِنَّ الْمُنَافِقِينَ فِي الدَّرْكِ الْأَسْفَلِ مِنَ النَّارِ وَلَن تَجِدَ لَهُمْ نَصِيرًا

Verily, the hypocrites will be in the lowest depths (grade) of the Fire; no helper will you find for them.

— Surah An-Nisaa 4:145

A hadith says:

Jabir reported that Allah's Messenger (may peace be upon him) came back from a journey, and as he was near Medina, there was such a violent gale that the mountain seemed to be pressed. Allah's Messenger ﷺ said, "This wind has perhaps

63

been made to blow for the death of a hypocrite," and as he reached Medina, a notorious hypocrite from amongst the hypocrites had died.

— Book 38, Number 6694 [39]

Hadith on Hypocrisy: Three signs of a hypocrite, even if he is Muslim Abu Huraira reported:

The Messenger of Allah ﷺ said,

"Among the signs of a hypocrite are three, even if he fasts and prays and claims to be a Muslim:

- When he speaks, he lies.
- When he gives a promise, he breaks it.
- When he is trusted, he betrays."
- *Source: Ṣaḥīḥ al-Bukhārī 33, Ṣaḥīḥ Muslim 59*

A hypocrite, also known as *Munafiq* or *Nifaq* in Arabic, is a person whose internal thoughts starkly contrast with their outward appearance, exhibiting two-faced behaviour. Such individuals articulate beliefs with their tongue that they do not genuinely hold in their hearts. This phenomenon is not confined to Islam or any specific religion; rather, it permeates various sectors, including politics, business, and even within familial and social circles. The influence of hypocrisy establishes a pervasive dominance in society, eroding trust, genuine love, affection, and respect.

Typically, as explained earlier, hypocrites are well-educated, intelligent individuals who hold significant positions in the state, contribute to the economy, serve in legislatures, adjudicate as judges, or even hold religious roles. Despite their achievements, these individuals often lose sight of their humanity, morality, and divine grace. Why does this occur? Satan incessantly seeks to recruit individuals to his cause, often targeting the intelligent and smart among us, whispering promises of a bright future or other enticing rewards. Many succumb to his traps, forfeiting their moral compass and spiritual grounding. However, there are exceptions—those who remain vigilant against such dangers from an early age or swiftly confront them with courage once they recognise the insidious forces at play.

Read Al-Munafiqun verse 63:1:

إِذَا جَاءَكَ الْمُنَافِقُونَ قَالُوا نَشْهَدُ إِنَّكَ لَرَسُولُ اللَّهِ ۗ وَاللَّهُ يَعْلَمُ إِنَّكَ لَرَسُولُهُ وَاللَّهُ يَشْهَدُ إِنَّ الْمُنَافِقِينَ لَكَاذِبُونَ

---

[39] Index26 ndex 26 ttps://www.iium.edu.my/deed/hadith/muslim/038_smt.html

"When the hypocrites come to you (O Muhammad ﷺ), they say: 'We bear witness that you are indeed the Messenger of Allah.' Allah knows that you are indeed His Messenger, and Allah bears witness that the hypocrites are indeed liars."

The Prophet Muhammad ﷺ identified the hypocrites as the most perilous adversaries of Islam. He went as far as stating that they were the sole enemies of Islam. Below is an excerpt from his speech:

"I have never been frightened of any nation conquering Islam. I only worry about one group of people: the unbelievers who pretend to be Muslim, the two-faced hypocrites. They are with you in their words, but they would never take a step with you."[10]

The Prophet of Islam's best student, the Commander of the Faithful (a), said the following regarding the hypocrites:

"I warn you about the hypocrites. They are misguided and they misguide as well. They have appeared in society in different colours and with different faces. Their speech is eloquent, profitable, and even a cure for pain. But their actions are like incurable diseases."[11] [40]

Muslims should be aware that they conceal their malevolent deeds by participating in religious rituals (refer to verse 63:4, Al-Munafiqun).

وَإِذَا رَأَيْتَهُمْ تُعْجِبُكَ أَجْسَامُهُمْ ۖ وَإِن يَقُولُوا تَسْمَعْ لِقَوْلِهِمْ ۖ كَأَنَّهُمْ خُشُبٌ مُّسَنَّدَةٌ ۖ يَحْسَبُونَ كُلَّ صَيْحَةٍ عَلَيْهِمْ ۚ هُمُ الْعَدُوُّ فَاحْذَرْهُمْ ۚ قَاتَلَهُمُ اللَّهُ ۖ أَنَّىٰ يُؤْفَكُونَ

"And when you look at them, their bodies please you; and when they speak, you listen to their words. They are as blocks of wood propped up. They think that every cry is against them. They are the enemies, so beware of them. May Allah curse them! How are they denying (or deviating from) the Right Path?" (Verse 63:4, Al-Munafiqun)

Because of the historical circumstances surrounding this verse, we cannot take the appealing appearance of the hypocrites as a general principle. Perhaps the meaning of the sentence,

"When you look at them, their exteriors please you,"

is that the hypocrites hide their true faces in front of the believers.

The serene demeanour hypocrites exhibit would surely earn admiration from anyone, embodying a sense of peace and tranquillity. Believers regard them as exemplars of righteousness. This possibility might be closer to the actual meaning

---

[40] Index 27 Index 27
http://www.islamicstudiesresources.com/uploads/1/9/8/1/19819855/story_of_prpht_dawud_prosyst3ms.pdf

65

of the verse than what other commentators have mentioned. According to this view, a broad principle emerges: hypocrites conceal their true nature behind a facade, seeking acceptance among believers, yet harbouring malicious intentions. Despite their outward calm, they are not hesitant to speak their minds when required. [41]

Matthew 23:13-15 (KJV):

13 But woe unto you, scribes and Pharisees, hypocrites! for ye shut up the kingdom of heaven against men: for ye neither go in yourselves, neither suffer ye them that are entering to go in.

14 Woe unto you, scribes and Pharisees, hypocrites! for ye devour widows' houses, and for a pretence make long prayer: therefore ye shall receive the greater damnation.

15 Woe unto you, scribes and Pharisees, hypocrites! for ye compass sea and land to make one proselyte, and when he is made, ye make him twofold more the child of hell than yourselves.

A Jewish proverb said that if hypocrites were divided into ten parties, nine of them would be found in Jerusalem, and one in the rest of the world.

Narrated 'Abdullah bin 'Amr:

The Prophet (ﷺ) said, "Whoever has the following four (characteristics) will be a pure hypocrite, and whoever has one of the following four characteristics will have one characteristic of hypocrisy unless and until he gives it up:

1. Whenever he is entrusted, he betrays.

2. Whenever he speaks, he tells a lie.

3. Whenever he makes a covenant, he proves treacherous.

4. Whenever he quarrels, he behaves in a very imprudent, evil and insulting manner."[42]

When an individual forfeits their sincerity and credibility within society, they essentially become hypocritical, rendering their good deeds devoid of value in the eyes of Allah. Such individuals become susceptible to the influence of Satan's temptations, spreading seeds of discord within the community. It is not uncommon to encounter individuals in society, particularly among Muslims, who offer praise in one's presence but readily criticise behind their back. Furthermore, they have no

---

[41] Index 27A Bible in Hypocrite

[42] Index 28

Reference : Sahih al-Bukhari 34 In-book reference : Book 2, Hadith 27 USC-MSA web (English) reference : Vol. 1, Book 2, Hadith 34

copiedhttps://www.islamweb.org/en/article/170841/hypocrisy-is-internal-destruction.

https://sunnah.com/bukhari:34

qualms about resorting to falsehoods for personal gain, revealing their hypocritical nature through their actions.

It is essential to recognise that any challenges or trials within our family or personal lives are part of Allah's will. Doubting this may indicate a hypocritical mindset. Allah tests us, and these trials may manifest as difficult or intricate problems, where immediate relief might not be apparent even with prayers for guidance. During such trying times, Satan may whisper temptations, urging us to seek alternative solutions. If our faith in Allah wavers, Satan can exploit our vulnerabilities, leading us towards hypocrisy. Hence, it is crucial to remain vigilant and not succumb to Satan's traps during these tests of faith.

The following verse confirms this:

وَمَا كَانَ لَهُ عَلَيْهِم مِّن سُلْطَانٍ إِلَّا لِنَعْلَمَ مَن يُؤْمِنُ بِالْآخِرَةِ مِمَّنْ هُوَ مِنْهَا فِي شَكٍّ ۗ وَرَبُّكَ عَلَىٰ كُلِّ شَيْءٍ حَفِيظٌ

"And he (Iblis – Satan) had no authority over them, except that We might test him who believes in the Hereafter from him who is in doubt about it. And your Lord is a Hafiz over everything. (All-Knower of everything i.e. He keeps a record of each and every person regarding deeds, and then He will reward them accordingly)." (34:21 Saba)

Our expeditionary group needs to carefully examine the chosen verses below and promptly assess whether any of us discern any shortcomings in this aspect, where Allah's disapproval and anger are unmistakably evident:

Satan plants seeds of doubt in their hearts, yet those who firmly believe in Allah with unwavering certainty never waver in their faith, seeking refuge in Allah from such uncertainties. Conversely, the hypocrite harbours doubts regarding faith. It is Satan, their chosen companion and guide, who installs these uncertainties within them.

Satan said:

وَلَأُضِلَّنَّهُمْ وَلَأُمَنِّيَنَّهُمْ وَلَآمُرَنَّهُمْ فَلَيُبَتِّكُنَّ آذَانَ الْأَنْعَامِ وَلَآمُرَنَّهُمْ فَلَيُغَيِّرُنَّ خَلْقَ اللَّهِ ۚ وَمَن يَتَّخِذِ الشَّيْطَانَ وَلِيًّا مِّن دُونِ اللَّهِ فَقَدْ خَسِرَ خُسْرَانًا مُّبِينًا

"Verily, I will mislead them, and surely, I will arouse in them false desires; and certainly, I will order them to slit the ears of cattle, and indeed I will order them to change the nature created by Allah." And whoever takes Shaitan (Satan) as a Wali (protector or helper) instead of Allah, has surely suffered a manifest loss." (4:119 An-Nisa')

The following verses we can link to this topic in our thinking:

1.

يَا أَيُّهَا الَّذِينَ آمَنُوا لَا تُبْطِلُوا صَدَقَاتِكُم بِالْمَنِّ وَالْأَذَىٰ كَالَّذِي يُنفِقُ مَالَهُ رِئَاءَ النَّاسِ وَلَا يُؤْمِنُ بِاللَّهِ وَالْيَوْمِ الْآخِرِ ۖ فَمَثَلُهُ كَمَثَلِ صَفْوَانٍ عَلَيْهِ تُرَابٌ فَأَصَابَهُ وَابِلٌ فَتَرَكَهُ صَلْدًا ۖ لَّا يَقْدِرُونَ عَلَىٰ شَيْءٍ مِّمَّا كَسَبُوا ۗ وَاللَّهُ لَا يَهْدِي الْقَوْمَ الْكَافِرِينَ

"O you who believe! Do not render in vain your Sadaqah (charity) by reminders of your generosity or by injury, like him who spends his wealth to be seen of men, and he does not believe in Allah, nor in the Last Day. His likeness is the likeness of a smooth rock on which is a little dust; on it falls heavy rain which leaves it bare. They are not able to do anything with what they have earned. And Allah does not guide the disbelieving people." (2:264 Al-Baqara)

2.

أَرَأَيْتَ الَّذِي يُكَذِّبُ بِالدِّينِ

فَذَٰلِكَ الَّذِي يَدُعُّ الْيَتِيمَ

وَلَا يَحُضُّ عَلَىٰ طَعَامِ الْمِسْكِينِ

فَوَيْلٌ لِّلْمُصَلِّينَ

الَّذِينَ هُمْ عَن صَلَاتِهِمْ سَاهُونَ

الَّذِينَ هُمْ يُرَاءُونَ

وَيَمْنَعُونَ الْمَاعُونَ

"Have you seen him who denies the Recompense?

That is he who repulses the orphan (harshly),

And urges not the feeding of AlMiskin (the poor),

So woe unto those performers of Salat (prayers) (hypocrites),

Who delay their Salat (prayer) from their stated fixed times,

Those who do good deeds only to be seen (of men),

And refuse Al-Ma'un (small kindnesses e.g. salt, sugar, water, etc.)." (107:1-7 Surah Al-Ma'un)

3.

إِنَّ الْمُنَافِقِينَ يُخَادِعُونَ اللَّهَ وَهُوَ خَادِعُهُمْ وَإِذَا قَامُوا إِلَى الصَّلَاةِ قَامُوا كُسَالَىٰ يُرَاءُونَ النَّاسَ وَلَا يَذْكُرُونَ اللَّهَ إِلَّا قَلِيلًا

"Verily, the hypocrites seek to deceive Allah, but it is He Who deceives them. And when they stand up for As-Salat (the prayer), they stand with laziness and to be seen of men, and they do not remember Allah but little." (4:142 An-Nisa)

There's no lack of such individuals in our society, but those within our group must introspect their circumstances and rectify any inconsistencies or contradictions with the verses.

Allah SWT has confirmed the fate of such people in this verse:

أُولَٰئِكَ الَّذِينَ كَفَرُوا بِآيَاتِ رَبِّهِمْ وَلِقَائِهِ فَحَبِطَتْ أَعْمَالُهُمْ فَلَا نُقِيمُ لَهُمْ يَوْمَ الْقِيَامَةِ وَزْنًا

"They are those who deny the Ayat (proofs, evidences, verses, lessons, signs, revelations, etc.) of their Lord and the Meeting with Him (in the Hereafter). So their works are in vain, and on the Day of Resurrection, We shall not give them any weight." (18:105 Al-Kahf)

Allah (SWT) also points out the nature of hypocrites in the following few verses in Surah Al-Baqara:

وَمِنَ النَّاسِ مَن يَقُولُ آمَنَّا بِاللَّهِ وَبِالْيَوْمِ الْآخِرِ وَمَا هُم بِمُؤْمِنِينَ

يُخَادِعُونَ اللَّهَ وَالَّذِينَ آمَنُوا وَمَا يَخْدَعُونَ إِلَّا أَنفُسَهُمْ وَمَا يَشْعُرُونَ

"Of the people, there are some who say: 'We believe in Allah and the Last Day;' but they do not (really) believe." (2:8 Al-Baqara)

"Fain would they deceive Allah and those who believe, but they only deceive themselves, and realise (it) not." (2:9 Al-Baqara)

وَإِذَا لَقُوا الَّذِينَ آمَنُوا قَالُوا آمَنَّا وَإِذَا خَلَوْا إِلَىٰ شَيَاطِينِهِمْ قَالُوا إِنَّا مَعَكُمْ إِنَّمَا نَحْنُ مُسْتَهْزِئُونَ

"When they meet those who believe, they say: 'We believe'; but when they are alone with their evil ones, they say: 'We are really with you: We (were) only jesting.'" (2:14 Al-Baqara)

As the verse continues:

فِي قُلُوبِهِم مَّرَضٌ فَزَادَهُمُ اللَّهُ مَرَضًا ۖ وَلَهُمْ عَذَابٌ أَلِيمٌ بِمَا كَانُوا يَكْذِبُونَ

"In their hearts is a disease; and Allah has increased their disease: And grievous is the penalty they (incur), because they are false (to themselves)." (2:10 Al-Baqara)

وَإِذَا قِيلَ لَهُمْ لَا تُفْسِدُوا فِي الْأَرْضِ قَالُوا إِنَّمَا نَحْنُ مُصْلِحُونَ

"When it is said to them: 'Make not mischief on the earth,' they say: 'Why, we only want to make peace!'" (2:11 Al-Baqara)

أَلَا إِنَّهُمْ هُمُ الْمُفْسِدُونَ وَلَٰكِن لَّا يَشْعُرُونَ

"Of a surety, they are the ones who make mischief, but they realise (it) not." (2:12 Al-Baqara)

In this verse, Allah reminds us again:

اسْتَحْوَذَ عَلَيْهِمُ الشَّيْطَانُ فَأَنسَاهُمْ ذِكْرَ اللَّهِ ۚ أُولَٰئِكَ حِزْبُ الشَّيْطَانِ ۚ أَلَا إِنَّ حِزْبَ الشَّيْطَانِ هُمُ الْخَاسِرُونَ

69

"Shaitan (Satan) has overtaken them. So he has made them forget the remembrance of Allah. They are the party of Shaitan (Satan). Verily, it is the party of Shaitan (Satan) that will be the losers!" (58:19 Al-Mujadila)

They cause corruption on earth through both their speech and their actions. Regarding this, Allah the Almighty says (what means):

الَّذِينَ يَلْمِزُونَ الْمُطَّوِّعِينَ مِنَ الْمُؤْمِنِينَ فِي الصَّدَقَاتِ وَالَّذِينَ لَا يَجِدُونَ إِلَّا جُهْدَهُمْ فَيَسْخَرُونَ مِنْهُمْ ۙ سَخِرَ اللَّهُ مِنْهُمْ وَلَهُمْ عَذَابٌ أَلِيمٌ

"Those who criticize the contributors among the believers concerning [their] charities and [criticize] the ones who find nothing [to spend] except their effort, so they ridicule them - Allah will ridicule them, and they will have a painful punishment."

(Quran 9:79, At-Taubah)

We are accustomed to reciting the Qur'an and knowing its verses by heart. However, this time, let us approach selected verses not just for recitation, but for meticulous scrutiny, ensuring our actions align with the divine message. I urge each member of our group embarking on the journey towards Darussalam to introspect, assess themselves, rectify any discrepancies, and strive to embody the essence of true believers as guided by Allah (SWT).

Backbiting

We find ourselves confronting yet another battle against malevolent forces. Though the complete defeat of evil may elude us, we possess the capability to shield our hearts and souls from its onslaught. By fortifying our defences and maintaining vigilance, we can resist succumbing to the influence of darkness. Having achieved this, our focus turns to safeguarding every entry point to our hearts, preventing Satan from breaching our inner sanctum.

Engaging in backbiting, which entails disclosing someone's personal matters in their absence or without their consent, is a harmful act. Whether one speaks falsely or praises the person, discussing someone behind their back can lead to misunderstandings and foster animosity between individuals. Satan targets such behaviour, as he seeks to perpetuate these sinful activities and hinder spiritual growth.

Backbiting is considered a grave sin across humanity. Even before the advent of Islam, Allah (SWT) prohibited backbiting. References to this prohibition can be found in various religious texts, including the Torah, the Bible, and, of course, the Holy Quran.

Backbiting is also a form of self-jihad that requires us to exercise control over our own wisdom and judgment.

70

Abu Huraira narrated that Allah's Messenger, Prophet Muhammad (P.B.U.H), said:

"Backbiting is when you talk about a person behind their back (and not in front of them) in a manner they would not like."

The companions asked, *"What if we mention things that are actually true about that person?"*

Prophet Muhammad (P.B.U.H) replied:

"If those things are actually true about the person, then you have still backbitten them. And if those things are not true, then you have slandered them."

Individuals who openly engage in wrongdoing should be constructively criticised in public, and if feasible, their harmful actions should be brought to light. However, resorting to gossip or backbiting is not permissible. There are instances where it may be necessary to show disdain towards certain individuals.

The Prophet (P.B.U.H) states the following regarding this issue:

*"It is not haram to backbite three groups of people:

- A person who is not ashamed of committing a sin openly;

- An oppressive administrator;

- A person who introduces bid'ah (innovation) into the religion."*

- *"If the subject of backbiting is an open and unashamed sinner who is not troubled by evil, but instead takes pride in the sins they commit and finds pleasure in their wrongdoing..."*

- (Jamiu's-Saghir, Hadith No: 3516)[43]

The following words come from Allah (SWT) regarding backbiting. It is essential for us to seize this opportunity to reflect upon our own circumstances and take appropriate action.

Allah (SWT) says about backbiting:

وَيْلٌ لِّكُلِّ هُمَزَةٍ لُّمَزَةٍ

"Woe to every slanderer and backbiter."

(Quran 104:1, Al-Humaza)

إِذْ تَلَقَّوْنَهُ بِأَلْسِنَتِكُمْ وَتَقُولُونَ بِأَفْوَاهِكُم مَّا لَيْسَ لَكُم بِهِ عِلْمٌ وَتَحْسَبُونَهُ هَيِّنًا وَهُوَ عِندَ اللَّهِ عَظِيمٌ

---

[43] Index 30 Jamiu's-Saghir, Hadis No: 8525. https://questionsonislam.com/question/what-are-types-backbiting-why-and-what-extent-backbiting-bad

71

"When you were propagating it with your tongues, and uttering with your mouths that of which you had no knowledge, you counted it a little thing, while with Allah it was very great."

(Quran 24:15, An-Nur)

يَا أَيُّهَا الَّذِينَ آمَنُوا اجْتَنِبُوا كَثِيرًا مِّنَ الظَّنِّ إِنَّ بَعْضَ الظَّنِّ إِثْمٌ ۖ وَلَا تَجَسَّسُوا وَلَا يَغْتَب بَّعْضُكُم بَعْضًا ۚ أَيُحِبُّ أَحَدُكُمْ أَن يَأْكُلَ لَحْمَ أَخِيهِ مَيْتًا فَكَرِهْتُمُوهُ ۚ وَاتَّقُوا اللَّهَ ۚ إِنَّ اللَّهَ تَوَّابٌ رَّحِيمٌ

"O you who believe! Avoid much suspicion, indeed some suspicion is a sin. And spy not, neither backbite one another. Would one of you like to eat the flesh of his dead brother? You would hate it (so hate backbiting). And fear Allah. Verily, Allah is the One Who accepts repentance, Most Merciful."

(Quran 49:12, Surah Al-Hujuraat)

Now let us see what Allah told His servants about backbiting before the advent of our Prophet Muhammad ﷺ:

In Judaism, backbiting is considered a severe sin.

Backbiting or tale-bearing is to slander someone in their absence — to bite them behind their back. Originally, backbiting referred to an unsporting attack from the rear in the blood sport of bear-baiting.

Backbiting is considered a sin. The Baha'i leaders condemned it as the worst of sins, as it destroyed the 'life of the soul' and provoked divine wrath.[44]

What the Bible says:

Psalms 15:1-3 (KJV):

1 Lord, who shall abide in thy tabernacle? who shall dwell in thy holy hill?

2 He that walketh uprightly, and worketh righteousness, and speaketh the truth in his heart.

3 He that backbiteth not with his tongue, nor doeth evil to his neighbour, nor taketh up a reproach against his neighbour.

James 1:26 (KJV):

If any man among you seem to be religious, and bridleth not his tongue, but deceiveth his own heart, this man's religion is vain.

James 3:8 (KJV):

But the tongue can no man tame; it is an unruly evil, full of deadly poison.

---

[44] Index 31 [2] Webb B. Garrison (2007), "To Backbite", Why You Say It, Read Books, p. 166, ISBN 9781406776195

James 3:6 (KJV):

And the tongue is a fire, a world of iniquity: so is the tongue among our members, that it defileth the whole body, and setteth on fire the course of nature; and it is set on fire of hell.

The message gleaned from the preceding text provides us with sufficient guidance to comprehend the necessary steps for attaining eligibility to acquire a visa and embark on the correct trajectory. It is evident that we must fulfil certain prerequisites in order to obtain authorisation on our journey towards Heaven.

To ensure a successful journey, every traveller must prioritise the personal task of acknowledging their participation in backbiting and remain vigilant in eliminating this habit, regardless of their intentions. It's crucial to recognise that breaking the habit of backbiting isn't simple, as it serves as a lucrative tool for Satan to hinder our efforts to please Allah. We must always remember that Satan relentlessly pursues our souls, so we must diligently guard ourselves to prevent his influence from infiltrating our inner selves.

Jealousy (Hasad)

In this segment, we encounter yet another hurdle in the journey of purifying our soul and heart: envy. While we have previously delved into topics like hypocrisy and backsliding, jealousy stands distinct from these vices. Every human being is born with these complex negative elements that create emotions in the mind.

When a baby cries, it could be hungry, tired, hot or, as new research suggests, jealous. Babies can show signs of jealousy when they're as young as three months old, new Canadian research has found, which contradicts theories that it takes two years for humans to first experience the emotion. Researchers at York University's psychology department found that babies have negative reactions when their mother's attention is diverted by another person.

Jealousy, along with embarrassment, pride, and guilt, are so-called non-basic emotions. The team, led by Professor Maria Legerstee, studied babies who were three, six, and nine months old. Legerstee's findings will appear in a book to be published next fall entitled *Handbook of Jealousy: Theories, Principles and Multidisciplinary Approaches*, which researchers have long thought only developed during the second year of life because they are too complex for infants' basic cognitive abilities.[45]

We have all, to some extent, experienced jealousy among our brothers and sisters during our teenage years for various reasons, such as disparities in parental affection. Jealousy between siblings, which can sometimes escalate into violence,

---

[45] Index 32 https://www.ctvnews.ca/babies-get-jealous-before-they-can-even-crawl-study-1.335347

is most common in families. This is the second stage of jealousy experienced in the early part of our lives.

As we transition into adulthood and embark on practical life, we encounter numerous challenges in our careers, personal lives, and businesses. We may come across competitors who are perceived as superior, triggering feelings of jealousy within us. These emotions give rise to a sense of greed and envy, accompanied by the development of anxiety and fear of potential threats. In some cases, these negative emotions can even lead to self-destructive behaviour. However, it's important to recognise that jealousy is not merely a standalone emotion; it's a complex amalgamation of various sentiments, such as violence, greed, lust for power, desire for vengeance, fervent passion, anxiety, and fear. Under its sway, lives can be torn asunder, manipulated by the insidious influence of darker forces.

Allah (SWT) reminds us once again of Satan. He says:

يَا بَنِي آدَمَ لَا يَفْتِنَنَّكُمُ الشَّيْطَانُ كَمَا أَخْرَجَ أَبَوَيْكُم مِّنَ الْجَنَّةِ يَنزِعُ عَنْهُمَا لِبَاسَهُمَا لِيُرِيَهُمَا سَوْآتِهِمَا إِنَّهُ يَرَاكُمْ هُوَ وَقَبِيلُهُ مِنْ حَيْثُ لَا تَرَوْنَهُمْ إِنَّا جَعَلْنَا الشَّيَاطِينَ أَوْلِيَاءَ لِلَّذِينَ لَا يُؤْمِنُونَ

"Children of Adam! Let not Shaitan (Satan) deceive you, as he got your parents [Adam and Hawwa (Eve)] out of Paradise, stripping them of their raiments, to show them their private parts. Verily, he and Qabiluhu (his soldiers from the jinn or his tribe) see you from where you cannot see them. Verily, We made the Shayatin (devils) Auliya' (protectors and helpers) for those who believe not."

(Sura 7:27, Al-A'raf)

In this passage, Allah (SWT) elucidates the perilous influence of Iblis, cautioning humanity (the children of Adam) to remain vigilant against his schemes. Iblis's wrath, envy, pride, and hostility led to the expulsion of the progenitor of mankind, Adam (PBUH), from Paradise, plunging him into turmoil and hardship. Additionally, Iblis's actions resulted in the exposure of Adam's private parts, which had previously been concealed from him.

It is, in fact, a manifestation of deep hatred (from Satan to Adam and mankind). Allah has expressed His wrath and envy against the Father of mankind in similar verses:

وَإِذْ قُلْنَا لِلْمَلَائِكَةِ اسْجُدُوا لِآدَمَ فَسَجَدُوا إِلَّا إِبْلِيسَ كَانَ مِنَ الْجِنِّ فَفَسَقَ عَنْ أَمْرِ رَبِّهِ أَفَتَتَّخِذُونَهُ وَذُرِّيَّتَهُ أَوْلِيَاءَ مِن دُونِي وَهُمْ لَكُمْ عَدُوٌّ بِئْسَ لِلظَّالِمِينَ بَدَلًا

"And (remember) when We said to the angels, 'Prostrate to Adam.' So they prostrated, except Iblis (Satan). He was one of the jinn; he disobeyed the command of his Lord. Will you then take him (Iblis) and his offspring as protectors and helpers rather than Me, while they are enemies to you? What an evil exchange for the Zalimun (polytheists, and wrong-doers, etc.)!"

74

(Sura 18:50, Al-Kahf)

The inhabitants of Earth are aware that Iblis harboured such intense anger and jealousy towards Adam (peace be upon him) that he outright defied the command of Almighty Allah. He said to Allah (SWT):

قَالَ أَرَأَيْتَكَ هَـٰذَا الَّذِي كَرَّمْتَ عَلَيَّ لَئِنْ أَخَّرْتَنِ إِلَىٰ يَوْمِ الْقِيَامَةِ لَأَحْتَنِكَنَّ ذُرِّيَّتَهُ إِلَّا قَلِيلًا

Iblis (Satan) said: "See? This one whom You have honoured above me, if You give me respite (keep me alive) to the Day of Resurrection, I will surely seize and mislead his offspring (by sending them astray), all but a few!"

(Sura 17:62, Surah Israel)

As it is well understood, the animosity of Iblis, upon whom be the curse of Allah, traces back to the time of Adam's creation. When Allah commanded the angels to bow before Adam, all complied except for Iblis, who, consumed by arrogance, defiantly refused to submit to him. He said in a tone indicating contempt: "Shall I prostrate myself to one whom You created from clay?" According to another Ayah, we find:

قَالَ مَا مَنَعَكَ أَلَّا تَسْجُدَ إِذْ أَمَرْتُكَ قَالَ أَنَا خَيْرٌ مِّنْهُ خَلَقْتَنِي مِن نَّارٍ وَخَلَقْتَهُ مِن طِينٍ

(Allah) said: "What prevented you (O Iblis) from prostrating when I commanded you?" Iblis said: "I am better than him (Adam). You created me from fire, and him You created from clay."

(Sura 7:12, Al-A'raf)

Considering the aforementioned realities, it proves to be an arduous endeavour to maintain clarity in our hearts, free from the grip of greed, anger, passion, and jealousy. Nevertheless, we should remain hopeful and resolute in safeguarding our hearts against the corrupting influences of Satan's malevolent forces. This can be achieved through seeking the assistance of Allah (SWT) and following the teachings of our prophets (ﷺ).

It's crucial to recognise that Satan lacks the direct power to compel individuals into committing evil deeds. However, he can entice or orchestrate circumstances that tempt people into acting recklessly without weighing the repercussions.

Jealousy, a conspicuous force, led to Satan's expulsion from heaven by Allah due to his envious actions. Now, he is engaged with full force in fulfilling the divine mission of leading humanity to damnation. A potent Psalm from the Old Testament aptly depicts jealousy, revealing its true nature. The psalm says:

Song of Solomon 8:6 (KJV):

Set me as a seal upon thine heart, as a seal upon thine arm: for love is strong as death; jealousy is cruel as the grave: the coals thereof are coals of fire, which hath a most vehement flame.

James 3:14-15 (KJV):

14 But if ye have bitter envying and strife in your hearts, glory not, and lie not against the truth.

15 This wisdom descendeth not from above, but is earthly, sensual, devilish.

James 3:16 (KJV):

For where envying and strife is, there is confusion and every evil work.

Job 5:2 (KJV):

For wrath killeth the foolish man, and envy slayeth the silly one.

Proverbs 23:17-18 (KJV):

17 Let not thine heart envy sinners: but be thou in the fear of the Lord all the day long.

18 For surely there is an end; and thine expectation shall not be cut off.

The first sin to be committed on earth was also jealousy, which caused one of the two sons of Adam to kill the other.[46]

Our Prophet (ﷺ) said:

"Do not be jealous of each other, do not boycott each other, do not hate each other, do not contrive against each other. Be all of you brothers to each other, O Servants of Allah." (Dawood 41:14)

Azazel and Jealousy

Satan, formerly known in Hebrew as Azazel, is referred to in Arabic as عَبَازِيل (Azazel). He exposes evil and temptation and is known as the deceiver who leads humanity astray. However, Iblis is the real name of Azazel, which belongs to Jewish tradition, and Allah (SWT) granted him power.

The Arabic word *jinn* comes from the verb *'Jannah'*, which literally means "to hide or conceal." The jinn are supernatural beings created by Almighty Allah who live on earth invisibly, possessing the same free will as mankind. The existence of the jinn, who are made from smokeless flame of fire, is mentioned in the Quran in the following verses:

---

[46] . Index 34 http://www.gsalam.net/jealousy/

وَلَقَدْ خَلَقْنَا الْإِنسَانَ مِن صَلْصَالٍ مِّنْ حَمَإٍ مَّسْنُونٍ

وَالْجَانَّ خَلَقْنَاهُ مِن قَبْلُ مِن نَّارِ السَّمُومِ

"And indeed, We created man from sounding clay of altered black smooth mud.

And the jinn, We created aforetime from the smokeless flame of fire."

(Sura 15:26-27, Al-Hijr)

This is also confirmed in Sura 55:15, Ar-Rahman:

وَخَلَقَ الْجَانَّ مِن مَّارِجٍ مِّن نَّارٍ

"And He created the jinn from a smokeless flame of fire."

Our Prophet ﷺ also said, *"The angels were created from light and the jinn from smokeless fire."* (Sahih Muslim)

The jinn live in a parallel world to humans, and since they reside in a different dimension, the flow of time is different for them. Consequently, the lifespan of jinn is far longer than that of humans. It is said that they live for around 1,000 to 1,500 years. Ibn Jawi [R] narrates from the book *As-Safwa* that, in one place, he saw an old jinn praying facing the Baitullah. He was wearing a fur coat. Hazrat Sohal (RA) said, "I greeted him after the prayer, and he replied and said, 'Are you not surprised to see the splendour of this fur coat? I have been wearing this dress for 700 years. I met Prophet Isa (PBUH) in this dress. Then I met Muhammad (ﷺ) wearing this dress. I am one of the jinn about whom Surah Jinn has been revealed."[47].

The lives of jinn are very similar to those of humans; they eat, drink, marry, have children, and are even instructed and guided in the same way as humans. We can clearly understand this statement by the following verse from Surah Al-An'am:

يَا مَعْشَرَ الْجِنِّ وَالْإِنسِ أَلَمْ يَأْتِكُمْ رُسُلٌ مِّنكُمْ يَقُصُّونَ عَلَيْكُمْ آيَاتِي وَيُنذِرُونَكُمْ لِقَاءَ يَوْمِكُمْ هَٰذَا ۚ

قَالُوا شَهِدْنَا عَلَىٰ أَنفُسِنَا ۖ وَغَرَّتْهُمُ الْحَيَاةُ الدُّنْيَا وَشَهِدُوا عَلَىٰ أَنفُسِهِمْ أَنَّهُمْ كَانُوا كَافِرِينَ

"O assembly of jinn and mankind! Did not there come to you messengers from amongst you, reciting unto you My verses and warning you of the meeting of this Day of yours?" They will say: "We bear witness against ourselves." It was the life of this world that deceived them. And they will bear witness against themselves that they were disbelievers.

(Surah 6:130, Al-An'am)

This verse illustrates that messengers were sent not only to guide humans but also to guide both humans and jinn. Among the jinn, there exist both believers and unbelievers. The unbelievers are referred to as "Satan." Iblis, who was a jinn, became an unbeliever when Allah commanded him to prostrate before Hazrat

---

[47] Source: Tafsir from the Quran

Adam (A.S), but he refused and was expelled from heaven. Hence, we now call him Satan because of his disbelief.

Jinn possess the ability to perceive us, while we, as humans, are unable to see them. The believers among the jinn attempt to lead us astray and divert us from the remembrance of Allah. Allah has already made us aware of this in Surah Al-Araf, verse 27. Allah says:

يَا بَنِي آدَمَ لَا يَفْتِنَنَّكُمُ الشَّيْطَانُ كَمَا أَخْرَجَ أَبَوَيْكُم مِّنَ الْجَنَّةِ يَنزِعُ عَنْهُمَا لِبَاسَهُمَا لِيُرِيَهُمَا سَوْآتِهِمَا ۗ إِنَّهُ يَرَاكُمْ هُوَ وَقَبِيلُهُ مِنْ حَيْثُ لَا تَرَوْنَهُمْ ۗ إِنَّا جَعَلْنَا الشَّيَاطِينَ أَوْلِيَاءَ لِلَّذِينَ لَا يُؤْمِنُونَ

"Children of Adam! Let not Shaitan (Satan) deceive you, as he got your parents [Adam and Hawwa (Eve)] out of Paradise, stripping them of their raiments, to show them their private parts. Verily, he and his tribe (Qabiluhu) see you from where you cannot see them. Verily, We made the Shayatin (devils) Auliya' (protectors and helpers) for those who believe not." (Surah 7:27, Al-Araf) [48]

The primary characteristic of the Devil, besides hubris, is that he has no power other than the ability to cast evil suggestions into the hearts of men, women, and jinn. Although the Qur'an does mention appointing jinn to assist those who are far from Allah (SWT), it also states: "We made the evil ones friends (only) to those without faith." Azazel was an angel of single-minded devotion, but despite his high position, he received the curse of Allah (SWT) and became a tool of darkness and misguidance for refusing to bow before Adam at the command of the Almighty.

Although he had been created from smokeless fire, whereas the angels had been created from light, Iblis is described as an archangel—the leader and teacher of the other angels, and a keeper of heaven. At the same time, he was the closest to the Throne of Allah. Allah gave him authority over the lower heavens and the earth.

Iblis is also considered the leader of those angels who battled the earthly jinn. Therefore, Iblis and his army drove the jinn to the edge of the world, to Mount Qaf. Knowing of the corruption of the former earthen inhabitants, Iblis protested when he was instructed to prostrate himself before the new earthen inhabitant, Adam. He assumed that the angels, who praise Allah's glory day and night, were superior compared to the mud-made humans and their bodily flaws. He even regarded himself as superior to the other angels, since he was one of those created from fire. However, he was degraded by Allah for his arrogance.

On the other hand, since he, unlike the other jinn, was pious, the angels were impressed by his nobility, and Iblis was allowed to join the company of angels and elevated to their rank. However, although he had the outer appearance of an angel, he was still a jinn in essence, and thus was able to choose when the angels and Iblis

---

[48] Index 34 a https://www.quranexplorer.com/blog/Education-In-The-Light-Of-Sunnah-And-Qura'an/Reality-of-Jinn-accordin-to-the-Quran-and-Hadith

were commanded to prostrate themselves before Adam. Iblis, abusing his free will, disobeyed the command of Allah. Iblis considered himself superior because of his physical nature, constituted of fire and not clay. Allah (SWT) sentenced Iblis to hell forever, but granted him a favour for his former worship: to take revenge on humans by attempting to mislead them until the Day of Judgment.

In some interpretations, Iblis is associated with light that misleads people. Hasan of Basra was quoted as saying:[49]

"If Iblis were to reveal his light to mankind, they would worship him as God."[77]

Additionally, based on Iblis' role as keeper of heaven and ruler of earth, Ayn al-Quzat Hamadani stated that:

Iblis represents the "dark light" of the earthen world, standing in opposition to the Muhammadan Light, which represents the heavens.

Quzat Hamadani relates his interpretation of Iblis' light to the shahada:

Accordingly, people whose service to God is merely superficial are trapped within the circle of la ilaha (the first part of the shahada, meaning "there is no God"), worshipping their nafs rather than Allah.

Only those who are worthy of leaving this circle can pass Iblis and enter the circle of illa-Allah, the Divine presence.[50]

Keeper of Paradise

Serpent and Peacock

Although the serpent is not mentioned in the Quran, Quranic commentaries, as well as the Stories of the Prophets, include the serpent, which was borrowed from Gnostic and Jewish oral traditions circulating in the Arabian Peninsula.

Iblis attempted to infiltrate Adam's dwelling, yet the celestial sentry steadfastly barred his entry. Undeterred, Iblis concocted a scheme to outsmart the guards. He approached a peacock and told it that all creatures would die and the beauty of the peacock would be ruined. However, Iblis promised eternal life to every living being if granted the fruit of eternity. So, the peacock convinced the serpent to take Iblis in its mouth and carry him to the garden, where Iblis spoke through the serpent to Adam and Eve, tricking them into eating from the forbidden tree.[51]

---

[49] Index 35 Hasan of Basra was a Sunni Islamic ulama, nicknamed as Abi Sayeed, born two years before the end of the era of the second Caliph Umar. The mausoleum is located ...

[50] Index 36 From Wikipedia, the free encyclopaedia

[51] Index 37 https://slife.org/iblis/ Reference code: slife.org

Satan Manipulates Women's Minds to Establish His Authority

Women are the Devil's Gateway

What Allah says in the Quran:

إِن يَدْعُونَ مِن دُونِهِ إِلَّا إِنَاثًا وَإِن يَدْعُونَ إِلَّا شَيْطَانًا مَّرِيدًا

لَّعَنَهُ اللَّهُ ۘ وَقَالَ لَأَتَّخِذَنَّ مِنْ عِبَادِكَ نَصِيبًا مَّفْرُوضًا

117 "They (all those who worship others than Allah) invoke nothing but female deities besides Him (Allah), and they invoke nothing but Shaitan (Satan), a persistent rebel!"

118 Allah cursed him. And he [Shaitan (Satan)] said: "I will take an appointed portion of your slaves."

(Surah An-Nisaa, 4/117-118)

He was so arrogant and fierce that he did not hesitate to declare:

وَلَأُضِلَّنَّهُمْ وَلَأُمَنِّيَنَّهُمْ وَلَآمُرَنَّهُمْ فَلَيُبَتِّكُنَّ آذَانَ الْأَنْعَامِ وَلَآمُرَنَّهُمْ فَلَيُغَيِّرُنَّ خَلْقَ اللَّهِ ۚ وَمَن يَتَّخِذِ الشَّيْطَانَ وَلِيًّا مِّن دُونِ اللَّهِ فَقَدْ خَسِرَ خُسْرَانًا مُّبِينًا

"I will mislead them, and I will create in them false desires; I will order them to slit the ears of cattle, and to deface the (fair) nature created by Allah."

And at that moment, Allah declared:

Whoever, forsaking Allah, takes Satan for a friend, has surely suffered a loss that is manifest. (4/119)

Is it Only Women's Fault That They Are Accountable for Any Mischief?

No, because Satan can easily influence anyone to do wrong. Women can protect themselves from Satan's influence if they are cautious. Often, women are blamed for many wrongdoings, but we should realise that we can't blame them alone. As partners, we share responsibility, and there is a missing element we fail to recognise and address before trouble arises.

We tend to blame Eve for all the trouble, but it's important to understand that Allah (SWT) allows Satan to play a role. This drama continues, and it will reach its conclusion on Judgment Day.[52]

---

[52] Index 38 https://www.mtholyoke.edu/projects/lrc/arabic/women_deceit/p13_p36.html

Adam and Eve

When Allah housed Adam in heaven and then created Eve from Adam's rib, He forbade them from eating the fruit of certain trees. However, they did eat, and it was Eve who started first.

Al-Kalbi reported the story as follows:[53]

Iblis was jealous of Adam and Eve being in heaven. May Allah curse him. He was exiled to earth and wanted to enter heaven to trick Adam and Eve, to tempt both of them with wicked suggestions so that they would eat the fruit of the tree. He begged every animal to let him hide inside it so that, when that animal crossed the gates of heaven, Iblis would find an easy pass. All animals declined, except for the snake. The snake was the most beautiful animal in heaven, with many colours. It resembled a camel and walked on four legs. Iblis was able to convince the snake, and thus he was able to enter inside it and settle in its head. Once the snake passed through the gates of heaven, Iblis came out and began to call on Adam and Eve.

He asked:

"Hey, what was Allah's order to you? What did He prohibit you from doing in heaven?"

They said:

"He ordered us to eat all kinds of fruit from all kinds of trees, except this one tree."

He said:

"He only did that so that you will not be able to be like angels. When you become like angels, you will know what is right and what is wrong. You will be eternal. You will never die. The first one to eat will be the dominant."

Then Satan began to whisper suggestions to them, bringing openly before their minds all their shame that was hidden from them (before).

He said:

فَوَسْوَسَ لَهُمَا الشَّيْطَانُ لِيُبْدِيَ لَهُمَا مَا وُورِيَ عَنْهُمَا مِن سَوْآتِهِمَا وَقَالَ مَا نَهَاكُمَا رَبُّكُمَا عَنْ هَـٰذِهِ الشَّجَرَةِ إِلَّا أَن تَكُونَا مَلَكَيْنِ أَوْ تَكُونَا مِنَ الْخَالِدِينَ

---

[53] Index 39 Hisham ibn al-Kalbi, also known as Ibn al-Kalbi was an Arab historian. His full name Abu al-Mundhir Hisham bin Muhammed bin al-Sa'ib bin Bishr al-Kalbi. Dihyah bin Khalifah al-Kalbi (Arabic: دِحْيَة ٱبْن خَلِيفَة ٱلْكَلْبِيّ, Dihyah al-Kalbīy), sometimes spelled Dahyah, was the envoy who delivered the Muslim prophet Muhammad's message to the Roman Emperor Heraclius According to Muhammad's wife Aisha, he saw Jibril twice "in the form that he was created" and on other occasions as a man resembling Dihyah ibn Khalifah al-Kalbi, an extraordinarily handsome disciple of Muhammad. From Wikipedia, the free encyclopaedia

$$\text{وَقَاسَمَهُمَا إِنِّي لَكُمَا لَمِنَ النَّاصِحِينَ}$$

20 Then Shaitan (Satan) whispered suggestions to them both in order to uncover that which was hidden from them of their private parts (before); he said: "Your Lord did not forbid you this tree, save that you should become angels or become of the immortals."

21 And he [Shaitan (Satan)] swore by Allah to them both (saying): "Verily, I am one of the sincere well-wishers for you both."

(7/20-21, Al-A'raaf)

Iblis, may Allah curse him, lied in that regard. However, Eve rushed to the tree.

Eve said:

"All right, take this!"

Adam said:

"Woe unto you! Don't you know that Allah has forbidden us from eating its fruit and promised us punishment if we do?"

She said:

"But He is Most Merciful!"

She ate a little and gave some to Adam. He ate too. When the fruit reached their bellies, their clothes began to disappear. Their clothing was only light.

Allah (SWT) said:

$$\text{فَدَلَّاهُمَا بِغُرُورٍ فَلَمَّا ذَاقَا الشَّجَرَةَ بَدَتْ لَهُمَا سَوْآتُهُمَا وَطَفِقَا يَخْصِفَانِ عَلَيْهِمَا مِن وَرَقِ الْجَنَّةِ وَنَادَاهُمَا رَبُّهُمَا أَلَمْ أَنْهَكُمَا عَن تِلْكُمَا الشَّجَرَةِ وَأَقُل لَّكُمَا إِنَّ الشَّيْطَانَ لَكُمَا عَدُوٌّ مُبِينٌ}$$

"So he misled them with deception. Then when they tasted of the tree, that which was hidden from them of their shame (private parts) became manifest to them and they began to stick together the leaves of Paradise over themselves (in order to cover their shame). And their Lord called out to them (saying): 'Did I not forbid you that tree and tell you: Verily, Shaitan (Satan) is an open enemy unto you?'" *(7/22, Al-A'raaf)*

Ibn 'Abbaas said:

When Adam entered heaven, he was dressed in light, had a garland of gold and rubies, and two bracelets of small and big pearls. When they tasted the fruit from the tree, they lost their clothes, and their private parts were exposed. So they began to collect leaves to cover themselves.

In His Interpretations Of The Qur'an, Al-Imam Al-Qushairi Said:

"There was no place more honourable than heaven, and there was no man with better manners other than Adam. There was no advice more elegant than that of Allah, and there was no one with stronger determination other than Adam. However, when Allah's decree was ordered, no one could object to it. At the time when Adam was in heaven, he was extremely well, but when the problem started, the gate of blessings was shut off, and the gate of ordeal became wide open. That took place because Adam obeyed what Eve had suggested. Adam was carried by angels, and they bent down to him. He had around his waist the belt of being close to Allah, and around his neck the necklace of sycophancy. Nobody was higher than him in rank, and none was closer to his supremacy. Allah kept calling upon him continuously by saying: 'Oh, Adam! Oh, Adam!' Now, Allah had taken away his clothes, and with that, He took his happiness. He changed his place and confused his time."

In his book, *Aqaa'iq al-Haqaa'iq*, Abu Najim Rukn al-Diin (40) was quoted as saying:

"When Allah created Adam, He brought him to heaven. The angel Radwan and the gatekeeper received Adam and gave him the keys to all heavens. Allah said to Adam,

'Oh, Adam! This is the eternal house where one would not get bored with one's wives. It is a property that cannot be transferred. Look at these respectable blessings. But, by the way, there is a tempting issue. Don't you two ever come close to this tree! If you go closer, it will be the reason for your misfortune.'"

Adam sat on the bed of his kingdom, looking up at the throne and reciting the greatness of his Creator. Allah gently and kindly took a rib from Adam's left side. Adam did not feel any pain. Allah created Eve from that rib. Great is He who has created everything perfect. Heaven was illuminated by Eve's shining face. She had 600 braids and wore 70 garments of different colours. They were transparent, allowing the colour of each garment to be seen. These 70 garments were not heavy; they were like standing in the shade of a tree—certainly, one would not feel the weight of that tree. Eve was adorned with all kinds of jewellery and precious stones that no one could describe accurately.

Adam turned around and found that Eve was sitting next to him on his bed. Her light was brighter than that of the moon. She was surrounded by 4,000 virgins of Paradise. If you looked at one of them, you would give up on the moon and the sun. Each of them was nothing but a single light in comparison to Eve, who resembled the sun.

Adam asked:

"My Creator, what is this?"

Allah said:

"Oh, Adam, I created her from you, and she is yours."

Adam said:

"But she is sitting far from me."

Allah said:

"Until you pay her dowry."

Adam said:

"All the garments and the precious stones that you have offered me are her dowry!"

Allah said:

"Oh, Adam, her dowry is more superior and expensive than all that. Look at the throne!"

Adam looked at the throne and saw a phrase written in light:

"No God but Allah, Mohammed is the messenger of Allah."

Allah (SWT) said:

"Pray once for this messenger, and that equals the dowry of your wife, Eve. Furthermore, I will make it for your offspring: each one of them who offers his prayers for Him among the Muslims, I promise 70 virgins of Paradise. I have made the prayers for this prophet of mercy equal the dowry for those 70 virgins of Paradise."

When Adam offered his prayers for Mohammed, Allah made Adam closer to Him, chose him, and sealed his marriage to Eve. Allah ordered the tree of blessing to shower Adam with pearls and said to him,

"My servant, I have married you off to my slave girl."

Adam looked at the side of the bed and noticed a wheat plant, which he did not like. He ordered the bed to fly away, and the bed flew over pastures and gardens for a thousand years. When it landed, Adam noticed that the wheat plant was still there. Though he was afraid of leaving again, he ordered his bed to take off, and it flew for another thousand years. When it stopped, the wheat plant was still there. Adam ordered the bed to take off 70 times. Every time the bed stopped, Adam noticed that the wheat plant was still standing in its place. Finally, the wheat plant said to him:

"Forgiveness is granted, and I am attached to you forever."

Adam said:

"Oh God, You forbade me, but You put the tree next to my bed. Where do I get the power to resist fate? You put it next to me and left its temptation in my heart. You judged that I would have no option. What can I do in my present situation?"

The voice came to him and said:

"While it is true that I put the plant next to your bed, it is also equally true that I have promised you forgiveness whenever and wherever you commit a mistake."

Adam continued his attempts to protect himself by avoiding the tree. However, Satan tempted him, and he committed the sin. When the taste of the fruit reached his mouth, his heavenly clothes disappeared. When Adam's hand reached the tree that the Angel Radwan had planted, Radwan screamed:

"My God, Adam has disobeyed!" The Paradise echoed, "Adam has disobeyed!" and the heavens repeated, "Adam has disobeyed!" The call reached the earth, and the earth echoed the same call. Allah said:

"Be quiet! Yes, it is true that Adam has disobeyed, but it is Satan's fault."

Adam began to run and turned his head right and left out of fear. Even the trees began to avoid him because of just one mistake. What would be the condition of someone who had filled his page with 70 years of recorded sins without even a single good act? What would this man do on the Day of Judgement? How could he taste the water of the river in Paradise? All kinds of good people would avoid him, like the trees. He would be exiled, away from those who knew the truth, and would be exposed to all people. He would not find anyone to comfort him.

It was reported that Adam began to look around and offer his apologies, then started running, filled with fear. He was told that there was no place for him where he could offer his apologies. He had to go somewhere else. When Adam left heaven, a black cloud took over him. He cried and showed humility. Angel Jibra'il said,

"Oh Adam, don't be frightened. The Most Gracious light will guide you."

Adam turned around to Eve and asked:

"Where should we go? Now that we are leaving Paradise, where should we get water?"

Eve said:

"I will follow you wherever you go and will listen to whatever you say forever."

Angel Jibra'il separated them and said:

"This is a route that you are not allowed to take a companion. All of you should leave now: I mean both of you—Adam and Eve, Iblis, the snake, and the peacock."

Adam cried, and his tears, which fell on the mountainside, became wheat and cloves. Those that fell on fields that were not tilted became salt. His tears, which fell in the valleys, became medicinal plants and herbs—these were signs of someone who feared Allah. When Eve cried, her tears that fell in the desert region of Arabia became henna, and those that fell in the sea became beautiful pearls for her daughters to wear and be valued. When Iblis, may Allah curse him, cried, his tears, which fell on the prairies, became ghouls and desert demons appearing in ever-varying shapes. Those tears that fell on islands became satins, and those that fell in the sea became crocodiles and crayfish. When the snake cried, her tears that fell on the ground became scorpions, and those that fell on the salty land became fire ants. When the peacock cried, his tears that fell on the island became coffee trees, and those that fell on trees and dates became worms. Those that fell in the sea became carnelian.

Finally, the snake ended on top of the mountain, Iblis came down accompanied by jealousy, Adam came down accompanied by deep regret, and was destined to be worried and confused for the rest of his life. It was also mentioned that when Adam and Eve came down from Paradise, they did not know where to go. Adam turned to Eve and said, in tears:

"You see, Eve, what you have done to yourself and to me! You caused us to be kicked out of Paradise and leave the neighbourhood of our Master. You assisted Iblis, and that hurt both of us."

Eve said:

"Oh Adam, it was destined for both of us."

Adam said:

"You are right! There is neither power nor means without the assistance of Allah."

Abu al-Faraj Ibn al-Jawzi said:

"It was Eve who ate first from the tree, and she tempted Adam to eat as well. That was the reason why he was kicked out of Paradise. This agrees with what the fourth Well-guided Caliph, al-Imam Ali Ibn Abi Taalib (PBUH), had said:

'Beware, even when you are in the company of the best of women.'"

Abu al-Faraj Ibn al-Jawzi (PBUH) was also quoted as saying that when Adam disobeyed, he heard a voice while he was grieving. The voice said:

"Why are you grieving? Was this my reward for asking the angels to bow down to you, for making you reside in My paradise, for marrying My slave-girl off to you? Surely, it was a bad reward. You disobeyed Me, and therefore, you do not fit to be near Me nor live in My house. You all leave My paradise! It was Iblis who caused all this trouble for you. I made him My enemy because of you, and you obeyed and followed his advice!"

Adam heard that, and his cry and regret became even stronger. He heard the voice again, which said:

"Why are you crying and regretting? Certainly, your situation has become more complicated and out of your control."

Adam said:

"I swear by Your power that I am not regretting for being kicked out of paradise. My regret is for being separated from You and being far away from You."

The voice said:

"Your crying will last for a long time. When you settle down on earth, you will miss paradise. When you become acquainted with someone else, you will realise your true loss."

Then the voice recited a few lines of poetry:

"You will remember me when you try someone else,

You will learn that I was your treasure.

Your cry on earth will be long,

And you will realise that your opinion was truly a defect."

"Get out of here!"

Adam turned to Eve and asked in tears:

"Oh Eve, where should we go now? Where should we go?"

It was reported that Allah pointed to two angels to show both Adam and Eve the door and expel them from His sight because they had disobeyed Him. Both Adam and Eve cried. The angels asked them to get ready. Angel Jibra'il approached Adam and removed the crown from his head. Angel Mikaa'il removed the wreath from Adam's forehead. While the other two angels were conducting their assignment, Allah asked:

"Oh Adam, what kind of a neighbour was I to you?"

Adam said:

"My Master, You were the best."

Allah said:

"Get out of here! You disobeyed Me."

Adam's clothes fell off, and his private parts were exposed. Adam looked at them and started to run, hiding behind trees. He picked a branch and covered himself with it.

Allah asked:

"Are you running away from Me?"

Adam responded:

"No, my Master. I am simply ashamed!"

Allah said:

"You all get out of here! Adam, you disobeyed and broke My command."

The angels asked:

"Oh, Our Master, You talk to someone who disobeyed You?"

Allah responded:

"Oh, My Angels, if I do not talk to My disobedient slave, who should I talk to? It is in the nature of human beings that they get mad and stop talking if someone disobeys them. In My case, if My slave disobeys Me and comes back and says 'My God!' I will respond 'Yes, My slave.' If he expresses regret and asks for My forgiveness, I will grant him that. I will respond to his repentance."

"Now, take them out!" The angels began to push Adam and Eve's backs.

Then the winds came and carried them down to earth. Adam landed on top of a mountain in the valley of Sarandiib, near India (also known as Serendip, Arabic Sarandīb, the name for the island of Sri Lanka). Eve landed on the sea beach near Jeddah in Arabia. Iblis landed in Bisaan in Palestine, and the snake landed in Asphahan in Iran. It was said that when the snake lost its limbs, it claimed that it would not care and would crawl on the ground the same way a whale swims in the water. It was reported that it even dared to talk while losing its limbs, and as a result, its tongue was split off. Therefore, it was unable to talk after that, but the snake did not lose its ability to hear.

All of them were expelled from the nearness of God in heaven. They were all exiled, scattered, and confused.

From one side, one of them (Iblis) would shout, "Lord, I swear by Your Greatness that I will tempt all of them." From the other side, another voice would say, "Our Lord! We indeed did ourselves much harm." Allah would say to the first one, "Go, you have My curse until the Day of Judgment!" To the couple, He would say, "Now that you have expressed your regret, you will have My forgiveness. But everyone should leave paradise, though."

Every time Adam recalled paradise, he would pass out. So, Allah sent him an angel who touched his heart with his hand, reduced his anxiety, and helped him recover. When Adam landed on a mountain near India, he was able to hear the angels' prayers and was close enough to smell the fragrance of heaven. Therefore, Allah sent the angel Jibriil, who put his hand on top of Adam's head and pushed it down. Adam became much shorter, to the point that he would no longer be able to hear the prayers nor smell heaven's fragrance. Adam cried, and Jibriil came once again and asked:

"Oh Adam, what made you cry?"

Adam said:

"I used to enjoy listening to the angels' prayers and smelling the heaven's fragrance. Now, I cannot do either!"

Jibriil said:

"This is the punishment for disobedience and lack of gratitude to the One Who loved you."

Nothing can describe Adam's condition better than these lines of poetry:

"I have been standing at the door for a long time,

Every time I shoot for reaching them, they ignore me.

I deserve to be shunned off, but You made me think that

A communion in love is possible.

I deserve not such a communion,

But listen to what I say so that You have mercy on me.

Open up to me and I promise not to disobey again.

If I do, then You can part company with me."

Calamities became Adam's share, and problems came to him from every side. He suffered from hot weather as well as cold conditions. He endured insect stings and animal bites. He cried, and Jibriil came down to him and asked:

"What are you crying for now?"

Adam said:

"I came out from the house of comfort and ended up in the house of difficulties and suffering."

Jibriil said:

"Oh Adam, how quickly you have forgotten Allah's warning to you:

'So let him not get you both out of the Garden, so that you land in misery.'"

Adam recalled the past and groaned for missing those days. He asked:

"Oh Jibriil, what can I do?"

Jibriil said:

"Cry a lot in regret!"

Adam asked:

"Would He restore my conditions back if I do?"

Jibriil said:

"Yes. Your Lord likes those who cry out of their fear of Him."

Adam sat on top of that mountain and cried for the next hundred years. Clover and medicinal herbs grew all over the valley. That is why herbal medicine always comes from India. The deer ate those herbs and developed musk in their stomachs. Cows ate those herbs and developed ambergris in their stomachs. The whole world was filled with a pleasant fragrance.

Adam asked:

"Oh Jibriil, what is this pleasant fragrance?"

Jibriil said:

"This is the fragrance of the tears of the disobedient."

While Adam cried in India, Eve herself was crying on the shores of the sea near Jeddah. He did not know where she was, and neither did she know where he was. Finally, Allah inspired Adam to walk towards the holy land. Jibriil came down and showed Adam the way to the holy land.

Jibriil then came to Eve and asked:

"What makes you cry?"

Eve said:

"I miss Adam."

So, Jibriil showed her how to get to the holy land.

Both Adam and Eve began to walk towards the holy land. Eventually, they met on the top of Mount Arafat.

{Mount Arafat or Mount Arafah (Arabic: جبل عرفات, transliterated Jabal 'Arafāt) is a granite hill east of Mecca, in the plain of Arafat. Arafat is a plain about 20 km (12 miles) southeast of Mecca. Mount Arafat reaches about 70 m (230 ft) in height and is also known as the Mount of Mercy (Jabal ar-Rahmah). According to Islamic

tradition, the hill is the place where the Islamic prophet Muhammad stood and delivered the Farewell Sermon to the Muslims who had accompanied him for the Hajj towards the end of his life.}—from Wikipedia.

When Adam and Eve met, they recognised each other. That is how the mountain got its name. Soon, they complained to Allah about their bodies' nakedness. Allah sent them a number of rams. Eve collected some wool and knitted garments that had a rough texture. The coarseness of their clothes reminded them of the beautiful days in paradise, and they both cried.

In the morning, the angels were standing by, bowing and attending to Adam's and Eve's needs. They were the same angels who had led them out of Paradise that afternoon. In the morning, Adam and Eve had enjoyed eating fresh fruits from the trees in paradise, but now, in the afternoon, they lacked even a bite. In the morning, Adam was sitting on his bed, happy and content, and now, in the afternoon, he was sitting on top of a mountain, crying. In the morning, he had seventy transparent garments, and in the afternoon, he was putting pieces of wool together to cover his private parts.

In another account, it was said that when the wind had landed Adam on top of Sarandiib Mountain near India, Adam cried for his sin. He cried so much that his tears formed pools in the valley.

The eagle took a sip from one pool and came to Adam and said:

"Oh Adam, I have never tasted fresh water like your tears. Why are you crying?"

Adam said:

"I cry because of my sins and disobedience to my Lord."

He told the eagle his story in all its details.

The eagle said:

"Oh Adam, I am speechless! I cannot believe what you have done. Allah created you with His own hands, married you off to Eve, His slave girl, gave you residence in paradise, and made His angels bow down to you. He gave you many things that none before you had been blessed with, and you go and disobey Him? How could you dare to disobey Him? You have committed a great sin. I wish I had not tasted your tears and mixed them with my blood and flesh!"

The eagle's words fell harshly on Adam's ears, even worse than his original sin. Allah made the eagle pronounce, "Allah is my witness, Adam, that I will never taste any plant again."

The eagle lived until the time of Prophet Solomon. When all the birds paid a visit to Solomon, he asked them, and the eagle moved forward and said:

91

"Peace be upon you, the King of the World! I have never seen a king who has a greater kingdom than yours. I was in the company of your father, Adam. I consoled him when he used to cry, to the point that I drank his tears. I was the first to know of his arrival on earth, and I was with him when Allah granted him His forgiveness. Adam had told me that, at some point in time, birds will bow down to some of Adam's own offspring. He told me to give his greetings when I had the chance to meet that grandchild of his. Now, that I have delivered his message to you, Prophet of Allah, you should hire me. I have extensive knowledge of mountains and caves. I have also heard him reciting a great verse that my tongue kept repeating."

اللَّهُ لَا إِلَٰهَ إِلَّا هُوَ ۚ لَيَجْمَعَنَّكُمْ إِلَىٰ يَوْمِ الْقِيَامَةِ لَا رَيْبَ فِيهِ ۗ وَمَنْ أَصْدَقُ مِنَ اللَّهِ حَدِيثًا

"Allah! La ilaha illa Huwa (none has the right to be worshipped but He). Surely, He will gather you together on the Day of Resurrection, about which there is no doubt. And who is truer in statement than Allah?"—4/87 Al-Nisaa'

There is no doubt about that. Both the eagle and Solomon prayed to Allah at that moment. When the eagle looked up, Solomon made him the king of birds.

It was also reported that a sparrow landed in front of Solomon and greeted him in three languages: the language of Adam, Noah, and Abraham. It said:

"Oh Prophet of Allah! I am the one whom Noah had chosen and carried with him on his ark. All the sparrows in the world are my offspring. I am telling you that Adam, peace be upon him, had said to me, 'You sparrow, you and your offspring will be blessed. You will meet one of my grandchildren whose kingdom is like mine. Allah will make birds, wild animals, lions, and jinn obey his orders. When you meet him, give him my regards.' You, Prophet of Allah, let me tell you of a chapter that only your father Abraham had heard. So I came to him and was able to win his trust. He taught me that chapter. Do you wish to hear it?"

Solomon said:

"Sure."

The sparrow recited:

In the name of Allah,

Most Gracious, Most Merciful.

Praise to Allah,

The Cherisher and Sustainer

of the Worlds;

Most Gracious, Most Merciful;

Master of the Day of Judgment.

You do we worship,

And Your aid we seek.

Show us the straight way,

The way of those whom

You have bestowed Your Grace,

Those whose (portion)

Is not wrath,

And who go not astray.

—Al-Faatiha

The sparrow extended its voice when it said the word "Amen!" The sparrow bent down in prayer, and so did Solomon. That kind of sparrow is the black one, which people call "the sparrows of paradise."

Solomon then spoke to the raven. The raven said:

"Oh Prophet of Allah! Allah has favoured you above all of Adam's offspring. He taught you things that you had never known before. God's blessings on you are unlimited. Oh Prophet of Allah, I want you to know that my colour was originally white, but it turned black when I heard the infidels say:

وَقَالُوا اتَّخَذَ اللَّهُ وَلَدًا ۗ سُبْحَانَهُ ۖ بَل لَّهُ مَا فِي السَّمَاوَاتِ وَالْأَرْضِ ۖ كُلٌّ لَّهُ قَانِتُونَ

"Allah has begotten a son."

—2/116 Al-Baqarah

My colour was changed because of what they said. I met your father, Adam, who prayed for me to have a long life. I heard your father recite a verse from his books, and all the spiritual angels nodded in agreement.

The verse said:

كُلُّ نَفْسٍ بِمَا كَسَبَتْ رَهِينَةٌ

"Every person is a pledge for what he has earned."

(74:38, Al-Muddaththir)

A few hours following Adam's landing on earth, he was reported to have felt an internal pain. Jibriil was still with him, so he asked:

"What is the matter?"

Adam said:

"I feel I am shaking and lack strength. I don't think I can even worship like this. I feel a sensation like ants creeping between my skin and flesh."

Jibriil said:

"Oh! That is something called 'hunger'."

Adam asked:

"How can I get rid of it?"

Jibriil said:

"By Allah's will, I will show you how."

Jibriil disappeared for an hour and then returned with two bay oxen, some equipment, a hammer, and a blower. He placed everything in front of Adam and then disappeared for another hour. When he came back this time, he brought with him a spark from Hell. He placed it in Adam's hand, but the spark flew away and fell into the sea.

Jibriil extended his hand, grabbed the spark, and gave it back to Adam again. Seven times the spark flew away, and seven times Jibriil brought it back. That is why Prophet Muhammad (ﷺ) said:

"Compared to the fire of Hell, this fire of yours is only one portion out of seventy."

When Jibriil returned the spark for the seventh time, it said:

"Oh, Adam! I will not feed you, and on the Day of Judgment, I will take revenge on any of your children who have disobeyed Allah."

Jibriil said to Adam:

"It will not obey you, but you must keep it, for it has many benefits for you and your children."

Thus, Adam placed the fire inside the stones and iron. That is why Allah said:

$$\text{أَفَرَأَيْتُمُ النَّارَ الَّتِي تُورُونَ}$$

"Tell Me! The fire which you kindle."

(56:71, Surah Al-Waqi'a)

After showing Adam how to make a plough out of iron, Jibriil brought three wheat seeds and said:

"Okay, Adam! Two seeds for you and one for Eve."

That is why, in Islamic inheritance, men receive twice the share of women. Each seed weighed approximately 3.12 grams.

Adam asked:

"What do I do with them?"

Jibriil said:

"Take them! You were expelled from Paradise because of them. They will satisfy your hunger and sustain you. They will help you and your children survive hardships and trials."

Jibriil instructed Adam to break pieces of wood, place them around the two oxen, and plough the ground. Adam was the first to plough! The oxen cried from the hard labour, remembering the ease of their life in Paradise. When their tears hit the ground, they turned into peas, which then began to grow. When the peas grew, they produced lentils.

Adam broke the three wheat seeds into small pieces to increase their number and scattered them across his field. Soon, the wheat plants began to grow.

It was said that at some point, Adam struck one of the oxen. The ox asked:

"Oh Adam, why did you hit me?"

Adam said:

"Because you disobeyed me."

The ox said:

"Did anyone hit you in Paradise when you disobeyed Allah and ate from the forbidden tree?"

Adam felt ashamed and said to Allah:

"You see, Lord! Even animals blame me and remind me of my sin."

In response to Adam's complaint, Allah made all animals mute from that moment onward.

As soon as the wheat plants began to grow, Adam asked Jibriil if he could eat them. Jibriil responded that Adam had to wait until they grew spikes. When the spikes appeared, Adam asked again. Jibriil told him to wait until they were fully grown.

A few weeks later, Adam asked if it was time to eat, but Jibriil told him that he must first harvest them. When Adam finished his harvest, he and Eve sat down to eat, but Jibriil told them that they needed to step over the ears to separate the seeds. They did so and thought it was finally time to eat.

Jibriil then instructed them to grind and sift the wheat next. Adam followed these steps and spread the bran across his field. Barley plants then began to grow.

Jibriil showed Adam how to make dough from the flour. He instructed him to dig a hole in the ground, collect dry branches, place them inside the hole, and start a fire. He then showed him how to spread the dough over the fire to make bread.

When that was done, Adam asked if it was time to eat, but Jibriil told him to wait until the bread had cooled.

Finally, Adam was able to eat, but he began to cry.

Jibriil asked:

"Oh Adam, all this labour just for making bread?"

Jibriil said:

"This is what Allah has destined for you for eternity. Remember what He said:"

فَقُلْنَا يَا آدَمُ إِنَّ هَٰذَا عَدُوٌّ لَّكَ وَلِزَوْجِكَ فَلَا يُخْرِجَنَّكُمَا مِنَ الْجَنَّةِ فَتَشْقَىٰ

"Then We said: 'O Adam! Verily, this is an enemy to you and to your wife. So let him not get you both out of Paradise, so that you be distressed in misery.'"

(20:117, Taaha)

In his book Al-Mawrid al-'Athb, Ibn al-Jawzi said: [54]

Adam once met with Iblis and said:

"You kept coming after me until I was expelled from the Garden to this place, where there is hard work, treachery, and suffering."

Iblis replied:

"Talking about the past is like leaving wax in the sun. If you believe that I caused you to be expelled, who do you think caused me to be expelled?"

However, Abu al-Najm Rukn al-Din reported in his book entitled 'Aqā'iq al-Ḥaqā'iq [55]

---

[54] 41 Imam Ibn al-Jawzī A depiction of Baghdad from 1808, taken from the print collection in Travels in Asia and Africa, etc. (ed. J. P. Berjew, British Library); Ibn al-Jawzī spent his entire life in this city in the twelfth-century Jurisconsult, Preacher, Traditionist; Abd al-Raḥmān b. 'Alī b. Muḥammad Abu 'l-Farash b. al-Jawzī,[6] often referred to as Ibn al-Jawzī (Arabic: ابن الجوزي, Ibn al-Jawzī; ca. 1116 – 16 June 1201) for short, or reverentially as Imam Ibn al-Jawzī by some Sunni Muslims, was an Arab Muslim jurisconsult, preacher, orator, heresiographer, traditionist, historian, judge, Shaykh of Islam, Orator of Kings and Princes, Imam of the Hanbalites Venerated in Sunni Islam, but particularly in the Hanbali school of jurisprudenceMajor shrine Green Cement Tomb at Baghdad, Iraq From Wikipedia, the free encyclopedia

[55] Index 42 Rukn al-dīn Maḥmūd ibn Muḥammad al-Malāḥimī al-Khuwārazmī (died 19 October 1141) was a Khwārazmian Islamic theologian of the Muʿtazilī and Ḥanafī schools.[1] He wrote six

When Adam and Eve lost their clothes, their private parts were exposed. As a result, their nakedness became a source of shame. Adam and Eve ran to the trees for cover, but all the trees moved away from them except the fig tree, which stopped and allowed them to collect its leaves to cover themselves.

The other trees were surprised and asked the fig tree why it had done that. The fig tree replied:

"I learned from the Lord how to be generous. He never stopped talking about Adam. I believe that honouring Adam by mentioning his name was more important than my leaves."

The fig tree was then told that it would be honoured by Muslims, who would swear by it, as mentioned in the Qur'an:

بِّسْمِ اللَّهِ الرَّحْمَٰنِ الرَّحِيمِ وَالتِّينِ وَالزَّيْتُونِ

"By the Fig and the Olive." *(At-Tin 95:1)*

This is how Allah honoured something for helping an individual He had blamed. Imagine the honour He will bestow on someone who helps an individual He has chosen.

When Adam landed on earth covered with fig leaves, the wild animals came to greet him. The deer was the first to arrive. Adam took a piece of fig leaf and fed it to the deer, which then became musk. When the deer returned to the other animals and told them of Adam's generosity, they all rushed to meet him. Adam fed them with fig leaves, but they did not turn into musk. They complained to him, asking why the deer was different. Adam did not have an answer, so he turned to Jibriil for an explanation.

Jibriil said:

"The deer came to greet you and received your blessings. The other animals came, but they had their own motivations."

Both Mujahid and Ibn 'Abbas reported that:

---

works known by title, but of these only one is completely preserved and two partially; the rest are lost.[2] Ibn al-Malāḥimī was a staunch opponent of metaphysics. He saw in the teachings of Ibn Sīnā a dilution of Islam's prophetic character. Christianity, in his view, was the paradigm of a religion of divine revelation and prophecy compromised by Greek philosophy. He wrote a compendium of the Mu'tazilī theology of al-Baṣrī, The Reliable Book on the Principles of Religion,[a] but only the first section and part of another have been preserved. He wrote an abridged version of his compendium, The Excellent Book on the Principles of Religion,[b] completed in December 1137. This work survives complete.[3] In it he mentions two other works[c] of his that are not known to have been preserved.[2] Between 1137 and 1141, he completed a third book,

Adam entered Paradise on a Friday, just before the afternoon. He was expelled just before sunset. Therefore, he stayed in Heaven for eighty-three years. They also said that after Adam landed on earth, Allah inspired him to take a pilgrimage to His house in Mecca and spend a week performing all the rituals to seek His forgiveness.

Allah sent Jibriil to guide Adam to Mecca. When Adam arrived and his eyes captured the sight of the ancient house, they filled with tears. He spent a whole week crying while circumambulating it. He waded through his own tears, stood on Mount 'Arafat, then on Mount Mina, where he threw the stones and performed the rituals.

He returned to Mecca to complete his pilgrimage. Once he had finished, the angels met him there and wished that Allah would accept his pilgrimage. They also told him that they had been circumambulating the ancient house two thousand years before his creation.

Adam performed the pilgrimage seventy times, travelling all the way from India to Mecca and Mount 'Arafat.[56]

Patience

Our journey continues, full of challenges, yet with determination to overcome all adversities, obstacles, and resistance by the grace of Allah (SWT). It is a challenging task to guard yourself as Al-Muttaqun during this journey.

Allah (SWT) says:

وَاسْتَعِينُوا بِالصَّبْرِ وَالصَّلَاةِ ۚ وَإِنَّهَا لَكَبِيرَةٌ إِلَّا عَلَى الْخَاشِعِينَ

"And seek help in patience and As-Salat (the prayer), and truly it is extremely heavy and hard except for Al-Khashi'un [i.e. the true believers in Allah—those who

---

[56] Index 43 He was one of the leading Qur'anic commentators and a translator of the generation after that of the Prophet Muhammad and his Companions. He is the first to compile a written exegesis of the Qur'an, in which he stated "It is not permissible for one who holds faith in Allah and the Day of Judgment to speak on the Qur'an without learning classical Arabic."[citation needed] He is said to have studied under Amir al-Mu'minin 'Ali ibn Abi Talib until his martyrdom. At that point, he began to study under Ibn Abbas, a companion of the Prophet known as the father of Qur'anic exegesis. Mujahid ibn Jabr was known to be willing to go to great lengths to discover the true meaning of a verse in the Qur'an, and was considered to be a well-travelled man.[3] However, there is no evidence he ever journeyed outside of the Arabian Peninsula.[citation needed] https://en.wikipedia.org/wiki/Mujahid_ibn_Jabr
Index 44 Abd Allah ibn Abbas, also known simply as Ibn Abbas, was one of the cousins of the Islamic Prophet Muhammad and he is considered to be the greatest mufassir of Qur'an. He was the son of Abbas ibn Abd al-Muttalib, an uncle of the Muhammad, and a nephew of Maymunah bint al-Harith, who later became Muhammad's wife. WikipediaBorn: 619 AD, Mecca, Saudi Arabia Died: 687 AD, Taif, Saudi Arabia Place of burial: Al-Baqi', Medina, Saudi Arabia

obey Allah with full submission, fear much from His punishment, and believe in His promise (Paradise, etc.) and in His warnings (Hell, etc.)]." *(Al-Baqarah 2:45)*

Again, in the following verse, Allah (SWT) calls only the believers who have purified their inner selves and tells them:

يَا أَيُّهَا الَّذِينَ آمَنُوا اصْبِرُوا وَصَابِرُوا وَرَابِطُوا وَاتَّقُوا اللَّهَ لَعَلَّكُمْ تُفْلِحُونَ

"O you who believe! Endure and be more patient (than your enemy), and guard your territory by stationing army units permanently at the places from where the enemy can attack you, and fear Allah, so that you may be successful." *(Aal-e-Imran 3:200)*

Allah (SWT) also reminds us in the following verse that our supplications have no value unless we are truthful. I refer to this important verse many times as a reminder.

Allah (SWT) says:

لَّيْسَ الْبِرَّ أَن تُوَلُّوا وُجُوهَكُمْ قِبَلَ الْمَشْرِقِ وَالْمَغْرِبِ وَلَكِنَّ الْبِرَّ مَنْ آمَنَ بِاللَّهِ وَالْيَوْمِ الْآخِرِ وَالْمَلَائِكَةِ وَالْكِتَابِ وَالنَّبِيِّينَ وَآتَى الْمَالَ عَلَىٰ حُبِّهِ ذَوِي الْقُرْبَىٰ وَالْيَتَامَىٰ وَالْمَسَاكِينَ وَابْنَ السَّبِيلِ وَالسَّائِلِينَ وَفِي الرِّقَابِ وَأَقَامَ الصَّلَاةَ وَآتَى الزَّكَاةَ وَالْمُوفُونَ بِعَهْدِهِمْ إِذَا عَاهَدُوا ۖ وَالصَّابِرِينَ فِي الْبَأْسَاءِ وَالضَّرَّاءِ وَحِينَ الْبَأْسِ ۗ أُولَٰئِكَ الَّذِينَ صَدَقُوا ۖ وَأُولَٰئِكَ هُمُ الْمُتَّقُونَ

"It is not Al-Birr (piety, righteousness, and each and every act of obedience to Allah) that you turn your faces towards the east or the west (in prayers); but Al-Birr is (the quality of) the one who believes in Allah, the Last Day, the Angels, the Book, and the Prophets, and gives his wealth—despite his love for it—to his kinsfolk, the orphans, the poor, the wayfarer, and those who ask, and to set slaves free; performs As-Salat (Iqamat-as-Salat), and gives Zakat; and those who fulfil their covenant when they make it, and who are As-Sabirin (the patient ones) in extreme poverty and ailment (disease) and at the time of battle. Such are the people of the truth, and they are Al-Muttaqun (the pious)." *(Al-Baqarah 2:177)*

However, those who are still interested in joining this journey but believe that the straight path does not qualify for a full visa should consider the above verse along with verses 183 and 2 of Surah Al-Baqarah. Patience is another important brick that can be laid.

Allah (SWT) says:

قُلْ يَا عِبَادِ الَّذِينَ آمَنُوا اتَّقُوا رَبَّكُمْ ۚ لِلَّذِينَ أَحْسَنُوا فِي هَٰذِهِ الدُّنْيَا حَسَنَةٌ ۗ وَأَرْضُ اللَّهِ وَاسِعَةٌ ۗ إِنَّمَا يُوَفَّى الصَّابِرُونَ أَجْرَهُم بِغَيْرِ حِسَابٍ

"Say (O Muhammad ﷺ): 'O My slaves who believe (in the Oneness of Allah, Islamic Monotheism), be afraid of your Lord (Allah) and keep your duty to Him. Good is (the reward) for those who do good in this world, and Allah's earth is spacious (so if you cannot worship Allah in one place, then go to another)! Only those who are patient shall receive their rewards in full, without reckoning.'" *(Az-Zumar 39:10)*

The word patience appears in every religious scripture as well as in many literary works, emphasising its significance. It is also known as Sabr, which means self-discipline of the soul. Sabr is defined as tolerance of any unpleasant circumstance, the ability to withstand provocation without responding in anger or annoyance, and steadfastness in times of hardship—especially when faced with long-term difficulties. [57]

Patience

"To have sabr means that one's common sense and religious motives are stronger than his whims and desires."

"When a man's patience is stronger than his whims and desires, then he is like an angel; but when his whims and desires are stronger than his patience, then he is like a devil. If his desire for food, drink, and physical relations is stronger than his patience, then he is no better than an animal. Lying, cheating, and self-admiration are his most common traits, and his reason is held prisoner by Satan, who directs it to serve evil purposes. The main cause of his sorry fate is that he ran out of patience."

Patience is most commonly defined as the capacity to accept or tolerate delay, trouble, or suffering without getting angry or upset. In other words, patience is essentially "waiting with grace."

The Greek concept of patience endurance involved an inner strength of soul that could withstand hardships, achieved through disciplined schooling of the will. In contrast, the Hebrew Scriptures describe patience endurance as outwardly directed—towards God. It reflects a confident waiting until God intervenes. The Psalmist exhorts us to "wait upon the Lord" (see Psalm 33:20; 37:7).

Christianity

In Christianity, patience is considered one of the most valuable virtues of life.

James 5:7 (KJV):

Be patient therefore, brethren, unto the coming of the Lord. Behold, the husbandman waiteth for the precious fruit of the earth, and hath long patience for it, until he receives the early and latter rain.

---

[57] A scholar Ibn al-Qayyim wrote,(index 45) Index 45 Ibn Qayyim al-Jawziyya (29 January 1292–15 September 1350 CE / 691 AH–751 AH son of the principal Imam Ibn al-Qayyim regarded as "one of the most important thinkers. https://en.wikipedia.org/wiki/Ibn_Qayyim_al-Jawziyya https://www.muslimink.com/islam/faith/what-sabr-really-means/

Psalm 33:20 (KJV):

Our soul waiteth for the Lord: he is our help and our shield.

Psalm 37:7 (KJV):

Rest in the Lord, and wait patiently for him: fret not thyself because of him who prospereth in his way, because of the man who bringeth wicked devices to pass.

Judaism

In the Hebrew Torah, patience is referred to in several proverbs, such as:

Proverbs 14:29 (KJV):

He that is slow to wrath is of great understanding: but he that is hasty of spirit exalteth folly.

Proverbs 15:18 (KJV):

A wrathful man stirreth up strife: but he that is slow to anger appeaseth strife.

Ecclesiastes 7:8-9 (KJV):

8 Better is the end of a thing than the beginning thereof: and the patient in spirit is better than the proud in spirit.

9 Be not hasty in thy spirit to be angry: for anger resteth in the bosom of fools.

The broader meaning of patience is the ability to stand up against sin and challenge all kinds of evil, corruption, decay, oppression, and injustice on the path to perfection.

Obstacles arise from two sources:

1. Internal barriers – These include love, competition, and material commitments.

2. External barriers – These include corrupt administrations and the power of enemies.

In such situations, our choice is either to embark on this dangerous path and move forward with determination or to wait patiently for the day and turn towards the help of Allah (SWT).

An ancient writer once said that the key to Roman success was their "policy and patience." By patience, the author meant the Roman quality of persistence in the pursuit of victory—never making peace in defeat. [58]

---

[58] (Index 46) https://spectrummagazine.org/article/sabbath-school/2010/01/24/meaning-patience

In the Quran, Allah says:

وَكَأَيِّن مِّن نَّبِيٍّ قَاتَلَ مَعَهُ رِبِّيُّونَ كَثِيرٌ فَمَا وَهَنُوا لِمَا أَصَابَهُمْ فِي سَبِيلِ اللَّهِ وَمَا ضَعُفُوا وَمَا اسْتَكَانُوا ۗ وَاللَّهُ يُحِبُّ الصَّابِرِينَ

(3:146 Al 'Imraan)

"And many a Prophet (i.e. many from amongst the Prophets) fought (in Allah's Cause), and along with him (fought) large bands of religiously learned men. But they never lost heart for that which did befall them in Allah's Way, nor did they weaken nor degrade themselves. And Allah loves As-Sabirin (the patient ones, etc.)." *(3:146 Al 'Imraan)*

We should recall the verse from Surah Al-Baqara (2:177) where Allah tells us to stay firm and wait patiently in any difficult time that may come in life, such as:

- Any hardship,
- Great pain,
- Adversity,
- Panic,
- Financial difficulty,
- Loss of a loved one.

A hadith supports this type of patience:

"Accepted patience is the one you show the first time you face a calamity, or patience is against the first blow of calamity."

The verse also reminds us of our responsibility towards orphans, the needy, regular charities, and patiently performing prayers and all other religious obligations with a pure heart.

At the same time, we must remember what Allah is telling us and how He has tested His chosen people with fear, hunger, some loss of wealth, life, and long physical suffering which they patiently endured. We should seek Allah's blessings, guidance, and mercy, saying firmly: "We belong to Allah, and to Him is our return."

Here, we can recite again the verse where Allah reminds us:

وَلَنَبْلُوَنَّكُم بِشَيْءٍ مِّنَ الْخَوْفِ وَالْجُوعِ وَنَقْصٍ مِّنَ الْأَمْوَالِ وَالْأَنفُسِ وَالثَّمَرَاتِ ۗ وَبَشِّرِ الصَّابِرِينَ

Be sure we shall test you with something of fear and hunger, some loss in goods or lives or the fruits (of your toil), but give glad tidings to those who patiently persevere. (2:155 Al-Baqara)

The following verses provide clearer guidance on cultivating self-correction, a crucial element in becoming true Muttaqun, which is essential for passing the test on our journey:

1. وَلَا تَسْتَوِي الْحَسَنَةُ وَلَا السَّيِّئَةُ ۚ ادْفَعْ بِالَّتِي هِيَ أَحْسَنُ فَإِذَا الَّذِي بَيْنَكَ وَبَيْنَهُ عَدَاوَةٌ كَأَنَّهُ وَلِيٌّ حَمِيمٌ

The good deed and the evil deed cannot be equal. Repel (the evil) with one which is better (i.e. Allah ordered the faithful believers to be patient at the time of anger, and to excuse those who treat them badly), then verily, he, between whom and you there was enmity, (will become) as though he was a close friend. (41:34)

2. وَمَا يُلَقَّاهَا إِلَّا الَّذِينَ صَبَرُوا وَمَا يُلَقَّاهَا إِلَّا ذُو حَظٍّ عَظِيمٍ

But none is granted it (the above quality) except those who are patient, and none is granted it except the owner of the great portion (of the happiness in the Hereafter, i.e., Paradise, and in this world, of high moral character). (41:35 Surah Ha-Mim)

3. وَأَطِيعُوا اللَّهَ وَرَسُولَهُ وَلَا تَنَازَعُوا فَتَفْشَلُوا وَتَذْهَبَ رِيحُكُمْ ۖ وَاصْبِرُوا ۚ إِنَّ اللَّهَ مَعَ الصَّابِرِينَ

And obey Allah and His Messenger, and do not dispute (with one another) lest you lose courage and your strength depart, and be patient. Surely, Allah is with those who are As-Sabirin (the patient ones, etc.). (8:46 Surah Al-Anfal)

4. وَإِنْ عَاقَبْتُمْ فَعَاقِبُوا بِمِثْلِ مَا عُوقِبْتُمْ بِهِ ۖ وَلَئِنْ صَبَرْتُمْ لَهُوَ خَيْرٌ لِلصَّابِرِينَ

And if you punish (your enemy, O you believers in the Oneness of Allah), then punish them with the like of that with which you were afflicted. But if you endure patiently, verily, it is better for As-Sabirin (the patient ones, etc.). (16:126 Surah An-Nahl)

5. إِنْ تَمْسَسْكُمْ حَسَنَةٌ تَسُؤْهُمْ وَإِنْ تُصِبْكُمْ سَيِّئَةٌ يَفْرَحُوا بِهَا ۖ وَإِنْ تَصْبِرُوا وَتَتَّقُوا لَا يَضُرُّكُمْ كَيْدُهُمْ شَيْئًا ۗ إِنَّ اللَّهَ بِمَا يَعْمَلُونَ مُحِيطٌ

If a good befalls you, it grieves them, but if some evil overtakes you, they rejoice at it. But if you remain patient and become Al-Muttaqun (the pious), not the least harm will their cunning do to you. Surely, Allah surrounds all that they do. (3:120 Al-Imran)

Members of our group travelling on the straight path rejoice in the good news from Allah (SWT), declared that the victory of attaining Jannah and escape from Hell awaits the righteous. This announcement is reserved for those who obey the verse that says, "Verily, today I have rewarded them for their patience; they are the successful."

He says:

إِنِّي جَزَيْتُهُمُ الْيَوْمَ بِمَا صَبَرُوا أَنَّهُمْ هُمُ الْفَائِزُونَ

"Verily, I have rewarded them this Day for their patience; they are indeed the ones that are successful." (23:111 Al-Muminun)

6. قَالُوا أَإِنَّكَ لَأَنْتَ يُوسُفُ ۖ قَالَ أَنَا يُوسُفُ وَهَٰذَا أَخِي ۖ قَدْ مَنَّ اللَّهُ عَلَيْنَا ۖ إِنَّهُ مَن يَتَّقِ وَيَصْبِرْ فَإِنَّ اللَّهَ لَا يُضِيعُ أَجْرَ الْمُحْسِنِينَ

They said: "Are you indeed Yusuf (Joseph)?" He said: "I am Yusuf (Joseph), and this is my brother (Benjamin). Allah has indeed been gracious to us. Verily, he who fears Allah with obedience to Him (by abstaining from sins and evil deeds, and by performing righteous good deeds), and is patient, then surely, Allah makes not the reward of the Muhsinun (good-doers) to be lost." (12:90 Surah Yusuf)

7. وَقَالَ الَّذِينَ أُوتُوا الْعِلْمَ وَيْلَكُمْ ثَوَابُ اللَّهِ خَيْرٌ لِّمَنْ آمَنَ وَعَمِلَ صَالِحًا وَلَا يُلَقَّاهَا إِلَّا الصَّابِرُونَ

But those who had been given (religious) knowledge said: "Woe to you! The reward of Allah (in the Hereafter) is better for those who believe and do righteous good deeds, and this none shall attain except those who are patient (in following the truth)." (28:80 Al-Qasas)

Allah SWT has made patience like a horse that never gets tired, an army that can never be defeated, and a strong fortress that can never be breached. Patience and victory are twin brothers, for victory comes with patience, relief comes with distress, and ease comes with hardship. Patience is of more help to the one who has it than men, as it helps without any need for equipment or numbers, and its relationship to victory is like that of the head to the body.

8. يَا أَيُّهَا الَّذِينَ آمَنُوا اسْتَعِينُوا بِالصَّبْرِ وَالصَّلَاةِ ۚ إِنَّ اللَّهَ مَعَ الصَّابِرِينَ

O you who believe! Seek help in patience and As-Salat (the prayer). Truly, Allah is with As-Sabirin (the patient ones, etc.). (2:153)

9. قُلْ يَا عِبَادِ الَّذِينَ آمَنُوا اتَّقُوا رَبَّكُمْ ۚ لِلَّذِينَ أَحْسَنُوا فِي هَٰذِهِ الدُّنْيَا حَسَنَةٌ ۗ وَأَرْضُ اللَّهِ وَاسِعَةٌ ۗ إِنَّمَا يُوَفَّى الصَّابِرُونَ أَجْرَهُم بِغَيْرِ حِسَابٍ

Say (O Muhammad ﷺ): "O My slaves who believe (in the Oneness of Allah Islamic Monotheism), be afraid of your Lord (Allah) and keep your duty to Him. Good is (the reward) for those who do good in this world, and Allah's earth is spacious (so if you cannot worship Allah at one place, then go to another)! Only those who are patient shall receive their rewards in full, without reckoning." (39:10 Surah Az-Zumar)

10. إِلَّا الَّذِينَ صَبَرُوا وَعَمِلُوا الصَّالِحَاتِ أُولَٰئِكَ لَهُم مَّغْفِرَةٌ وَأَجْرٌ كَبِيرٌ

Except those who show patience and do righteous good deeds; for them there will be forgiveness and a great reward (Paradise). [11:11] Surah Hood

Allah SWT tells us that patience and forgiveness are among the things recommended by Allah, and those who heed this will never lose, as Allah (SWT) says:

11   وَلَمَن صَبَرَ وَغَفَرَ إِنَّ ذَٰلِكَ لَمِنْ عَزْمِ الْأُمُورِ

And verily, whosoever shows patience and forgives, that would truly be from the things recommended by Allah. [42:43] Surah Ash-Shura

Allah commanded His Messenger to wait patiently for His decision and told him that his patience is only from Him, and by virtue of patience, all calamities become easy, as He said:

12   وَاصْبِرْ لِحُكْمِ رَبِّكَ فَإِنَّكَ بِأَعْيُنِنَا ۖ وَسَبِّحْ بِحَمْدِ رَبِّكَ حِينَ تَقُومُ

So wait patiently (O Muhammad ﷺ) for the decision of your Lord, for verily, you are under Our Eyes, and glorify the praises of your Lord when you get up from sleep. [52:48] Surah At-Tur

13   رَبُّ السَّمَاوَاتِ وَالْأَرْضِ وَمَا بَيْنَهُمَا فَاعْبُدْهُ وَاصْطَبِرْ لِعِبَادَتِهِ ۚ هَلْ تَعْلَمُ لَهُ سَمِيًّا

The Lord of the heavens and the earth, and all that is between them; so worship Him (Alone) and be constant and patient in His worship. Do you know of any who is similar to Him? (Of course, none is comparable or equal to Him, and He has no partner). [19:65] Surah Maryam

Allah SWT has chosen the people of patience and gratitude to benefit from His signs and be distinguished by this great good fortune. He says in His Holy Book:

We Sent Musa (PBUH) With Our Signs

14   وَلَقَدْ أَرْسَلْنَا مُوسَىٰ بِآيَاتِنَا أَنْ أَخْرِجْ قَوْمَكَ مِنَ الظُّلُمَاتِ إِلَى النُّورِ وَذَكِّرْهُم بِأَيَّامِ اللَّهِ ۚ إِنَّ فِي ذَٰلِكَ لَآيَاتٍ لِّكُلِّ صَبَّارٍ شَكُورٍ

And indeed We sent Musa (Moses) with Our Ayat (signs, proofs, and evidences) saying: "Bring out your people from darkness into light, and make them remember the annals of Allah. Truly, therein are signs for every patient, thankful person." [14:5] Surah Ibrahim

With regard to the hadeeth which speaks of the virtue of patience, they include the following:

Al-Bukhari (1496) and Muslim (1053) narrated that Abu Sa'eed al-Khudri (may Allah be pleased with him) said:

The Messenger of Allah (ﷺ) said: "…whoever is patient, Allah will bestow patience upon him, and no one is ever given anything better and more generous than patience."

And Muslim (918) narrated that Umm Salamah (may Allah be pleased with her) said:

I heard the Messenger of Allah (S) say: "There is no Muslim who is stricken with a calamity and says what Allah has enjoined – 'Verily, to Allah we belong and to Him is our return. O Allah, reward me for my affliction and compensate me with something better' – but Allah will compensate him with something better."

'Umar ibn 'Abd al-'Azeez (may Allah be pleased with him) said:

Allah has not bestowed any blessing upon His slaves, then taken it away and replaced it with patience, but what He has compensated them with is better than what He has taken away. And Allah knows best.[59]

"One who adopts patience will never be deprived of success, though it may take a long time to reach him."

Prophet Ayyub (PBUH) is the ideal example of the afflicted believer who remained patient and faithful to His Lord. His name is mentioned many times in the Quran. He was a Syrian resident and a wealthy man with vast land, farms, cattle, gold, and many children. However, at the age of seventy-five, he fell ill, according to scholars. The illness was so severe that historians recorded not a single part of his body was free from disease, except his tongue and heart, which he used to remember Allah (SWT). He lost his children and his whole family, except for his wife, who remained loyal to him. It was recorded that his illness lasted for different lengths of time—some said three years, others said eight years. But despite this suffering and the loss of everything, Prophet Ayyub patiently sought the help of his Lord because he understood the inner meaning of verse 155 from Surah Al-Baqara, as we mentioned earlier, where Allah (SWT) says:

وَلَنَبْلُوَنَّكُم بِشَيْءٍ مِّنَ الْخَوْفِ وَالْجُوعِ وَنَقْصٍ مِّنَ الْأَمْوَالِ وَالْأَنفُسِ وَالثَّمَرَاتِ ۗ وَبَشِّرِ الصَّابِرِينَ

"And certainly, We shall test you with something of fear, hunger, loss of wealth, lives, and fruits, but give glad tidings to As-Sabirin (the patient ones, etc.)." *[2:155]*

There is a very important Hadith we should keep in mind. It says:

The companion Sa`d ibn Abi Waqqas asked... [60]

"O Messenger of Allah, which of the people are most sorely tested?"

He said, "The Prophets, then the next best and the next best. A man will be tested in accordance with his level of religious commitment. If his religious commitment is strong, he will be tested more severely, and if his religious commitment is weak, he will be tested in accordance with his religious commitment. Calamity will keep befalling a person until he walks on the earth with no sin on him."

---

[59] (Index 47) https://islamqa.info/en/answers/35869/the-virtue-of-patience
[60] Index 49) https://saudigazette.com.sa/article/529006

The idea is that when we face challenges and respond patiently, our faith and character become stronger. Our faith becomes stronger because ideally it will help us engage in more worship, seeking the help of Allah. And our character becomes stronger, enabling us to handle the struggles of life.

Surah Al-Asr is the 103rd surah in the Quran. This surah provides us with a clear direction on how we manage our day and success in this life and the Hereafter. There are only four verses in this surah, but each verse carries a vast message that many scholars of Islam have written pages to explain for our benefit. The last verse tells us about **PATIENTS (SABR)** as salvation, which gives perseverance and enjoins it upon one another.

Now, let's redirect our attention to another barrier hindering our ability to become genuine believers, and that is **"anger."**

Anger And Envy

Anger is a disease of the soul. Satan uses this tool to prevent one from becoming a true believer. Rather, he whispers incessantly to weaken the faith.

Allah (SWT) says in the Holy Quran:

الَّذِينَ يُنفِقُونَ فِي السَّرَّاءِ وَالضَّرَّاءِ وَالْكَاظِمِينَ الْغَيْظَ وَالْعَافِينَ عَنِ النَّاسِ ۗ وَاللَّهُ يُحِبُّ الْمُحْسِنِينَ

"Those who spend [in Allah's Cause – deeds of charity, alms, etc.] in prosperity and in adversity, who repress anger, and who pardon men; verily, Allah loves Al-Muhsinun (the good-doers)." [3:134 Al-Imran]

The above verses of the Qur'an give us the message to refrain from evil elements like the wrath of character. However, this only applies to those who have the right mind and are able to judge right and wrong and control anger, resentment, malice, and envy. As we know, many people in every society are suffering from various mental illnesses, of which anger is one of them. Many mental illnesses are not usually visible to a person until they disclose their situation, and this is why people misunderstand their behaviour, such as at work, at home, or in the community.

As we focus on anger, for our understanding, we want to briefly define and discuss this mental illness and how it affects the pain in someone's life.

What is Anger?

Anger is a fundamental part of the human natural response, an emotional state that can range in intensity from happiness, sadness, anxiety, disgust, or hostility. It can vary widely from person to person depending on their personal circumstances.

Experiences of anger can range from mild annoyance to frustration, misbehaviour, criticism, or not getting what they want, all of which can be potential causes of anger.

There are different types of anger disorders. Identifying what kind of anger a person is feeling and learning how to deal with problems can improve physical and mental health. Below, we will discuss the most common types of anger disorders.

Uncontrolled Anger

Uncontrolled anger can quickly become problematic. While short-term anger can be effective, long-term or uncontrolled anger can cause significant problems, both personally and professionally. Uncontrolled anger may manifest differently from one person to another. Some may quietly think about and focus on what makes them angry, while others may become easily angered and exhibit aggressive or violent behaviour.

Intermittent Explosive Disorder

A person with intermittent explosive disorder (IED) (also known as "volatile" anger) experiences repeated episodes of aggressive, impulsive, or violent behaviour. Their angry response may seem out of proportion to the situation. IED episodes usually last less than 30 minutes, and they may occur suddenly or without any warning. People with the disorder may feel irritable and angry most of the time. Some common behaviours associated with IED include:

- Temper tantrums
- Fighting
- Physical violence
- Throwing things

It can be very frustrating when we feel that someone has wronged us or should apologise, but the person does not admit it. For some, it is difficult to move forward. Holding on to unresolved feelings can lead to feelings of hatred or bitterness. This may result in being "stuck" or hardened in anger. Anger can be classified into different medical terms, e.g.

Chronic Anger Vengeful Anger [61] Bipolar Disorder may cause Anger?[62]

Depression

Anger can be a symptom of depression. Depression is characterised by prolonged feelings of sadness and a loss of interest lasting at least two weeks. Individuals who are depressed may experience anger that is suppressed. People who are depressed may also show symptoms of anger that manifest as:

---

[61] index 51 Source: katemangostar via freepik.com
[62] Index 52 Source: pixabay.com

- Irritability
- Thoughts of harming others or oneself
- Suicidal ideations

However, many of us may be suffering from a mental illness that has been under treatment for many years and, Allah's will, can be cured through long-term therapy under expert supervision. In this circumstance, we only have one choice: to seek Allah's help. Allah says in the Holy Quran:

"Call on Me, and I will answer."

وَقَالَ رَبُّكُمُ ادْعُونِي أَسْتَجِبْ لَكُمْ ۚ إِنَّ الَّذِينَ يَسْتَكْبِرُونَ عَنْ عِبَادَتِي سَيَدْخُلُونَ جَهَنَّمَ دَاخِرِينَ

And your Lord said: "Invoke Me, [i.e. believe in My Oneness (Islamic Monotheism)] (and ask Me for anything) I will respond to your (invocation). Verily, those who scorn My worship [i.e. do not invoke Me, and do not believe in My Oneness (Islamic Monotheism)] they will surely enter Hell in humiliation!" [40:60 Al-Mu'min]

Allah (SWT) also says:

وَنُنَزِّلُ مِنَ الْقُرْآنِ مَا هُوَ شِفَاءٌ وَرَحْمَةٌ لِّلْمُؤْمِنِينَ ۙ وَلَا يَزِيدُ الظَّالِمِينَ إِلَّا خَسَارًا

And We send down from the Qur'an that which is a healing and a mercy to those who believe (in Islamic Monotheism and act on it), and it increases the Zalimun (polytheists and wrong-doers) nothing but loss. [17:82 Surah Israel]

"Seek Me, and I shall respond." These are the words of Allah, and they hold true. Through Allah's grace, those afflicted can discover a path to alleviate their mental disorder.

It's crucial for individuals to maintain a calm demeanour to nurture purity within. Often, individuals are unfairly branded as 'angry' due to their tendency to display anger when they see fit, sometimes even leveraging it for personal gain. However, it's worth noting that such behaviour is often influenced by negative forces (Satan). Those who manipulate anger as a tool for deceit are guided by harmful influences. Conversely, in the Qur'an, Allah (SWT) emphasises the virtue of restraining anger, expressing love for those who embody this restraint.

The verse below, emphasising the importance of self-correction and staying on the righteous path, is essential for individuals to self-examine and correct their actions accordingly. Members can also strive towards spiritual growth and adherence to righteous principles. This verse serves as a guiding light, urging individuals to constantly evaluate themselves and make the necessary adjustments to align their moral compass with the straight path.

Malice, Envy, or Jealousy is the fuel of integrated anger that can be linked to greed or activities that make others angry. Envy is an evil disease of the heart that leads to foul conduct and bad behaviour. It leads to animosity, thinking evil of the intentions of others, backbiting, talebearing, lying, and the abandonment of other Muslims. It may lead its possessor to inflict physical harm on the person whom he envies and can even lead to murder. It is considered to be among the most dangerous and destructive of internal diseases and is the most destructive to a person's religion and worldly life. The Messenger of Allah (SAW) said:

"Do not envy one another; do not hate one another; do not turn your back on one another (in discontent); (but) be slaves of Allah as brothers." [Al-Bukhari & Muslim][63]

The greatest harm from envy comes to the envier, who, with one's displeasure with Allah's decree, attains a great loss to oneself.

Al-Mubarrad, a great philologist, recited the following lines:

The eye of the envier always sees scandal,

Bringing out faults and hiding the good.

He meets you cheerfully, with a smiling face,

While his heart conceals his true feelings.

The envier's enmity comes without provocation,

Yet he accepts no excuses while he attacks.[64]

In Describing Envy, New York Times Author Natalie Angier Writes:

"Envy may help keep us in line, making us so desperate to look good that we take the high road and start to act good, too. We struggle with our private envy, our longing for more esteem than we command, and the struggle only sharpens the painful contrast between the imagined perfection of the envied adversary that we have enshrined on an imaginary throne, and the defective merchandise that is ourselves. If you desire glory, you may envy Napoleon," Bertrand Russell said. "But Napoleon envied Caesar, Caesar envied Alexander, and Alexander, I daresay, envied Hercules, who never existed." If envy is a tax levied by civilisation, it is one that everyone must pay."

Allah (SWT) mentions in the Quran the envy of the disbelievers, the hypocrites, and people in general. Speaking about the disbelievers, Allah says:

---

[63] (Index 53) https://www.islamweb.net/en/article/88951/the-dangers-of-envy
[64] (Index 54) Article source: http:/www.islamweb.net/emainpage/

وَدَّ كَثِيرٌ مِّنْ أَهْلِ الْكِتَابِ لَوْ يَرُدُّونَكُم مِّن بَعْدِ إِيمَانِكُمْ كُفَّارًا حَسَدًا مِّنْ عِندِ أَنفُسِهِم مِّن بَعْدِ مَا تَبَيَّنَ لَهُمُ الْحَقُّ ۖ فَاعْفُوا وَاصْفَحُوا حَتَّىٰ يَأْتِيَ اللَّهُ بِأَمْرِهِ ۗ إِنَّ اللَّهَ عَلَىٰ كُلِّ شَيْءٍ قَدِيرٌ

Many of the people of the Scripture (Jews and Christians) wish that they could turn you away as disbelievers after you have believed, out of envy from their own selves, even after the truth (that Muhammad Peace be upon him is Allah's Messenger) has become manifest unto them. But forgive and overlook, till Allah brings His Command. Verily, Allah is Able to do all things. (2/109 Al-Baqara)

Allah also says:

أَمْ يَحْسُدُونَ النَّاسَ عَلَىٰ مَا آتَاهُمُ اللَّهُ مِن فَضْلِهِ ۖ فَقَدْ آتَيْنَا آلَ إِبْرَاهِيمَ الْكِتَابَ وَالْحِكْمَةَ وَآتَيْنَاهُم مُّلْكًا عَظِيمًا

Or do they envy men (Muhammad ﷺ and his followers) for what Allah has given them of His Bounty? Then We had already given the family of Ibrahim (Abraham) the Book and Al-Hikmah (As-Sunnah – Divine Inspiration to those Prophets not written in the form of a book), and conferred upon them a great kingdom. (4/54 An-Nisaa)

When we delve into the teachings of both the Torah and the Bible, a common message resonates: the importance of managing our anger and purging ourselves of envy and malice, thereby sanctifying the heart. Allah (SWT) said in the Quran:

وَلَا تُجَادِلُوا أَهْلَ الْكِتَابِ إِلَّا بِالَّتِي هِيَ أَحْسَنُ إِلَّا الَّذِينَ ظَلَمُوا مِنْهُمْ ۖ وَقُولُوا آمَنَّا بِالَّذِي أُنزِلَ إِلَيْنَا وَأُنزِلَ إِلَيْكُمْ وَإِلَٰهُنَا وَإِلَٰهُكُمْ وَاحِدٌ وَنَحْنُ لَهُ مُسْلِمُونَ

And argue not with the people of the Scripture (Jews and Christians), unless it be in (a way) that is better (with good words and in a good manner, inviting them to Islamic Monotheism with His Verses), except with such of them as do wrong, and say (to them): "We believe in that which has been revealed to us and revealed to you; our Ilah (God) and your Ilah (God) is One (i.e. Allah), and to Him we have submitted (as Muslims)." (29/46 Al-Ankabut)

The preceding verse offers another valuable insight, urging us to exercise caution and emphasising the importance of showing respect, refraining from inciting anger, or getting embroiled in disputes over scriptures meant for others. Instead, it encourages us to broaden our knowledge, which in turn can bolster our faith. Similarly, in the subsequent verse, Allah admonishes us to be mindful of the robustness of our faith. Allah (SWT) says:

وَمَن يَبْتَغِ غَيْرَ الْإِسْلَامِ دِينًا فَلَن يُقْبَلَ مِنْهُ وَهُوَ فِي الْآخِرَةِ مِنَ الْخَاسِرِينَ

And whoever seeks a religion other than Islam, it will never be accepted of him, and in the Hereafter, he will be one of the losers. (3/85 Al-Imran)

It does not mean to seek a religion other than Islam, but rather to utilise other sources as references to bolster our faith within Islam. Now, let's look at how the Bible and the Torah talk about anger and how Satan plays with these elements.

The Bible Says:

Envy is a deadly sin, destroying our capacity to enjoy life. We're always feeling robbed, cheated, defrauded. We experience our own life as lacking, and emptiness.

The Psalmist confesses the sin of envy:

I was envious of the arrogant;

I saw the prosperity of the wicked.

For they have no pain;

Their bodies are sound and sleek.

They are not in trouble as others are;

They are not plagued like other people.

Therefore pride is their necklace;

Violence covers them as a garment.

Their eyes swell out with fatness;

Their heart overflows with follies.

They scoff and speak with malice;

Loftily they threaten oppression.

They set their tongues against heaven,

And their tongues range over the earth.

Therefore, the people turn and praise them,

And find no fault in them....

Such are the wicked;

Always at ease, they increase in riches.

All in vain I have kept my heart clean

And washed my hands in innocence. (Psalm 73:3-13, NRSV)

Devil Controls Our Anger

In your anger, do not sin. "Be angry and do not sin; do not let the sun go down on your anger, and give no opportunity to the devil" (Eph. 4:26-27).

Anger is not a sin in itself; uncontrolled anger quickly leads to injustice. Honour requires self-control to express anger in a respectful way. Anger does not always lead to sin. In Ephesians 4:26 mentioned above, it says "Be angry and do not sin." This phrase may seem confusing, but when we look at the surrounding verses, the meaning becomes clearer. Ephesians 4:25–32 beautifully expresses how a believer and righteous person should lead his life by controlling anger. Prophet (PBUH) Jesus says:

"Therefore, having put away falsehood, let each one of you speak the truth with his neighbour, for we are members one of another. Be angry and do not sin; do not let the sun go down on your anger, and give no opportunity to the devil. Let the thief no longer steal, but rather let him labour, doing honest work with his own hands, so that he may have something to share with anyone in need. Let no corrupting talk come out of your mouths, but only such as is good for building up, as fits the occasion, that it may give grace to those who hear. And do not grieve the Holy Spirit of God, by whom you were sealed for the day of redemption. Let all bitterness and wrath and anger and clamour and slander be put away from you, along with all malice. Be kind to one another, tender-hearted, forgiving one another, as God in Christ forgave you."

In the Psalm (mentioned above), Ephesians 4:26 says, "In anger, do not sin." What does it mean? It describes as though God is slow to anger, yet the Bible frequently describes God as having anger. His anger is always righteous, just as Romans 1:18 says:

"For the wrath of God is revealed from heaven against all ungodliness and unrighteousness of men, who by their unrighteousness suppress the truth."

(Holman Christian Standard Bible) [65]

God's anger is sparked by disobedience and unrighteousness. If we allow unrighteous anger to linger within our own hearts, it will suppress the truth, giving the Devil a foothold.

God expresses the extraordinary level of anger in the case of the Golden Calf. Prophet Moses (PBHH) was told by God that He would destroy the people, saying, "Now, let me alone, that my wrath may be kindled against them, and I may destroy them" (Exodus 32:10-14). [66]

10 "Now leave me alone so that my anger may burn against them and that I may destroy them. Then I will make you into a great nation."

11 But Moses sought the favour of the Lord his God. "Lord," he said, "why should your anger burn against your people, whom you brought out of Egypt with great power and a mighty hand?

---

[65] Index 56 https://biblehub.com/romans/1-18.htm
[66] (Index 57) https://www.biblegateway.com/passage/?search=Exodus+32%3A10-14&version=NIV

12 Why should the Egyptians say, 'It was with evil intent that he brought them out, to kill them in the mountains and to wipe them off the face of the earth'? Turn from your fierce anger; relent and do not bring disaster on your people.

13 Remember your servants Abraham, Isaac, and Israel, to whom you swore by your own self: 'I will make your descendants as numerous as the stars in the sky, and I will give your descendants all this land I promised them, and it will be their inheritance forever.'"

14 Then the Lord relented and did not bring on His people the disaster He had threatened.

God Expresses Anger, As Described:

Then the LORD's anger burned against Moses, and He said,

"What about your brother, Aaron the Levite? I know he can speak well. He is already on his way to meet you, and he will be glad to see you. You shall speak to him and put words in his mouth; I will help both of you speak and will teach you what to do." (Exodus 4:14-15 NIV) [67]

The Background Of The Story, As Described Both In The Bible And In The Quran, Is As Follows:

When Prophet Moses (PBUH) freed the people from the slavery of the dictatorial ruler, King Pharaoh, they were completely dependent on him. They thought Moses (PBUH) was their God, just as they had previously thought Pharaoh was their God. However, when Moses (PBUH) was absent for a long time, they became worried and frightened. They gathered around Aaron (Harun) and expressed their concerns, demanding a physical representation of a deity, as they said, "As for this Moses (PBUH), the man who brought us out of the land of Egypt, we do not know what has become of him."

Aaron showed no leadership. Instead, he told them to bring the golden ornaments they had, such as earrings, necklaces, etc. The people brought these to Aaron, and he made a molten calf. They then said, "These are your gods, O Israel, who brought you up out of the land of Egypt." When Aaron saw this, he built an altar before the calf and made a proclamation, saying, "Tomorrow is a feast to the Lord." (Exodus 32:1-5, 9).

The Golden Calf

This story is narrated in the Psalms and in Exodus 32:1-5 in the Bible as follows:

1. When the people saw that Moses (PBUH) was so long in coming down from the mountain, they gathered around Aaron and said, "Come, make us gods

---

[67] (Index 58) https://www.ligonier.org/learn/devotionals/anger-sin-and-the-devil/

who will go before us. As for this fellow Moses who brought us up out of Egypt, we don't know what has happened to him."

2. Aaron answered them, "Take off the gold earrings that your wives, your sons, and your daughters are wearing, and bring them to me."

3. So all the people took off their earrings and brought them to Aaron.

4. He took what they handed him and made it into an idol cast in the shape of a calf, fashioning it with a tool. Then they said, "These are your gods, Israel, who brought you up out of Egypt."

5. When Aaron saw this, he built an altar in front of the calf and announced, "Tomorrow there will be a festival to the Lord."

6. So the next day, the people rose early, sacrificed burnt offerings, and presented fellowship offerings. Afterward, they sat down to eat and drink, and got up to indulge in revelry.

7. Then the Lord said to Moses, "Go down, because your people, whom you brought up out of Egypt, have become corrupt.

8. They have been quick to turn away from what I commanded them and have made themselves an idol cast in the shape of a calf. They have bowed down to it, sacrificed to it, and have said, 'These are your gods, Israel, who brought you up out of Egypt.'

9. I have seen these people," the Lord said to Moses, "and they are a stiff-necked people.

10. Now leave me alone so that my anger may burn against them and that I may destroy them. Then I will make you into a great nation."[68]

Why is Aaron unwilling or unable to assist the Israelites in managing Moses's (PBUH) absence while preventing them from succumbing to their idolatrous desires? Despite holding the position of High Priest, Aaron exhibits a deficiency in leadership, which can be attributed to various factors. The text suggests that he may have feared that refusing the people's demands would result in his own demise (Exodus 32:22). Additionally, Aaron (PBUH) lacked substantial leadership experience, as Moses (PBUH) had assigned him limited independent responsibilities.

In Verse 20:90, Aaron (PBUH) Had Said To Them Even Before Moses's Return:

"My people, you have fallen into error because of the calf. Surely your Lord is Most Compassionate; so follow me and obey my command." (20:91)

---

[68] (Index 59) https://www.biblegateway.com/passage/?search=Exodus+32&version=NIV

But they answered:

"By no means shall we cease to worship it until Moses returns to us."

In the following verses in the Quran, Surah Ta-Ha, 20:83-89, we find Allah's anger towards Prophet Musa (PBUH) and Aaron (PBUH):

When Moses was up on the Mount, Allah said:

1. **83** "And what made you hasten from your people, O Musa (Moses)?"

2. **84** "He replied: 'They are close on my footsteps, and I hastened to You, O my Lord, that You might be pleased.'"

3. **85** (Allah) said: "Verily, We have tried your people in your absence, and As-Samiri has led them astray."

4. **86** Then Musa (Moses) returned to his people in a state of anger and sorrow. He said: "O my people! Did not your Lord promise you a fair promise? Did the promise seem long in coming? Or did you desire that wrath should descend from your Lord on you, so you broke your promise to me (i.e., disbelieving in Allah and worshipping the calf)?"

5. **87** They said: "We broke not the promise to you of our own will, but we were made to carry the weight of the ornaments of the [Pharaoh's] people, then we cast them (into the fire), and that was what As-Samiri suggested."

6. **88** Then he took out (of the fire) for them a statue of a calf which seemed to low. They said: "This is your ilah (god), and the ilah (god) of Musa (Moses), but [Musa (Moses)] has forgotten (his god)."

7. **89** "Did they not see that it could not return them a word (for answer), and that it had no power either to harm them or to do them good?"

And then in Surah Al-A'raf, 7:148, it says:

148 "And the people of Musa (Moses) made, in his absence, out of their ornaments, the image of a calf (for worship). It had a sound (as if it was mooing). Did they not see that it could neither speak to them nor guide them to the way? They took it for worship and they were Zalimun (wrong-doers)."

The story continues in Surah Al-Baqarah, 2:51, 92, and 54:

1. **51** "And (remember) when We appointed for Musa (Moses) forty nights, and (in his absence) you took the calf (for worship), and you were Zalimun (polytheists and wrong-doers)."

2. **92** "And indeed, Musa (Moses) came to you with clear proofs, yet you worshipped the calf after he left, and you were Zalimun (polytheists and wrong-doers)."

3. **54** "And (remember) when Musa (Moses) said to his people: 'O my people! Verily, you have wronged yourselves by worshipping the calf. So turn in repentance to your Creator and kill yourselves (the innocent among you killing the wrong-doers), that will be better for you with your Lord.' Then He accepted your repentance. Truly, He is the One Who accepts repentance, the Most Merciful."

Then again, Surah Al-A'raf 7 continues with the following verses:

150 "And when Musa (Moses) returned to his people, angry and grieved, he said: 'What an evil thing is that which you have done (i.e., worshipping the calf) during my absence. Did you hasten and go ahead as regards the matter of your Lord (you left His worship)?' And he threw down the Tablets and seized his brother by (the hair of) his head and dragged him towards him. Harun (Aaron) said: 'O son of my mother! Indeed the people judged me weak and were about to kill me, so make not the enemies rejoice over me, nor put me amongst the people who are Zalimun (wrong-doers).'"

149 "And when they regretted and saw that they had gone astray, they (repented and) said: 'If our Lord does not have mercy upon us and forgive us, we shall certainly be of the losers.'"

At the end of the story, Surah Al-A'raf concludes in verse **151**:

151 "Musa (Moses) said: 'O my Lord! Forgive me and my brother, and make us enter into Your Mercy, for You are the Most Merciful of those who show mercy.'"

Conclusion

Here, we identify that "anger" can also be an element that creates obstruction. We must judge ourselves based on the information presented, as we know that, in the end, we will be accountable (in fact, only I alone) and no one else.

To address anger, James presents a beautiful idiom in James 1:19/20: *"Slow to speak, slow to anger; for the anger of man does not produce the righteousness of God."*

Many small, unnoticed actions can lead us astray. Satan is actively working to obstruct our path. This reading has stirred questions in my mind about how I am preparing to address these challenges and face the final test at the crossroads before entering the next phase of my obligatory journey. It is certainly challenging to reflect on oneself.

Be patient, keep exploring, and strive to discover where you truly belong. Until we identify our true enemy—one who possesses divine intelligence and dominates this world under his command—it will be impossible to defend ourselves against his control. This critical understanding will be discussed in the next chapter.

Chapter 5

Now is the judgment of this world;

Verily, I will mislead them, and surely, I will arouse in them false desires; and certainly, I will order them to slit the ears of cattle, and indeed I will order them to change the nature created by Allah.

And whoever takes Shaitan (Satan) as a Wali (protector or helper) instead of Allah has surely suffered a manifest loss.

— *The Qur'an, 4:19*

Now the ruler of this world will be cast out. And I, if I am lifted up from the earth, will draw all peoples to Myself.'

— *John 12:31-32*

"The shaitan flows through man like blood."

— *(Al-Bukhari, 3281; and Muslim, 2175)*

📖📖📖📖📖📖📖

Living in the Dark Occupied World

Life on Earth Before Adam

(Qur'an 2:31)

وَعَلَّمَ آدَمَ الْأَسْمَاءَ كُلَّهَا ثُمَّ عَرَضَهُمْ عَلَى الْمَلَائِكَةِ فَقَالَ أَنْبِئُونِي بِأَسْمَاءِ هَـٰؤُلَاءِ إِن كُنتُمْ صَادِقِينَ

And He taught Adam all the names (of everything); then He showed them to the angels and said, "Tell Me the names of these if you are truthful."

There is nothing in the Qur'an or Sunnah (prophetic teachings) to indicate that there were any people living on Earth before Adam (peace be upon him). However, verse 2:30 states:

وَإِذْ قَالَ رَبُّكَ لِلْمَلَائِكَةِ إِنِّي جَاعِلٌ فِي الْأَرْضِ خَلِيفَةً ۖ قَالُوا أَتَجْعَلُ فِيهَا مَن يُفْسِدُ فِيهَا وَيَسْفِكُ الدِّمَاءَ وَنَحْنُ نُسَبِّحُ بِحَمْدِكَ وَنُقَدِّسُ لَكَ ۖ قَالَ إِنِّي أَعْلَمُ مَا لَا تَعْلَمُونَ

"I am about to place a vicegerent in the earth."

The Arabic word used for "vicegerent" is *khalifa*, which denotes a successor.

And (remember) when your Lord said to the angels: "Verily, I am going to place (mankind) generations after generations on earth." They said: "Will You place therein those who will make mischief therein and shed blood, while we glorify You with praises and thanks (Exalted be You above all that they associate with You as partners) and sanctify You?" He (Allah) said: "I know that which you do not know."

— Surah Al-Baqarah, 2:30

However, Al-'Allamah at-Tahir ibn 'Ashoor said in *at-Tahreer wa't-Tanweer*: Many scholars say that the Jinn were created before Adam (pbuh), and before them, a creature named *Hin* and *Bin* lived on this Earth. Due to their wickedness, they are called *At-Tamam wa* and were defeated by the Jinn. *Hin* is part of the "circle of time," which belongs to the period before the creation of mankind. The following circle starts with Adam and ends with Muhammad ﷺ, marking the period in which humans now live.

According to Ibn Kathir, the *Hin* are associated with the Jinn who shed blood on Earth before mankind, which led the angels to question God's command to keep Adam as *Khalifa*. In his book *Al-Bidaya wa'n-Nihaya*, he describes how *Hin* and *Bin* were destroyed by the Jinn so that they could live on Earth. According to some accounts, the *Hin* supported the angels, led by Iblis, during a battle against the earthen Jinn, who caused disaster on the world. Tabari explained that the *Hin* are created from the fire of *samum* (poisonous fire), which is mentioned in the Qur'an, verse 27 of Surah Al-Hijr:

$$وَالْجَانَّ خَلَقْنَاهُ مِن قَبْلُ مِن نَّارِ السَّمُومِ$$

"And the Jinn We created before from the fire of Samum."

— Surah Al-Hijr, 15:27

The regular Jinn are created from *marij min nar* (smokeless flame), as mentioned in the Qur'an, Surah Ar-Rahman (55:15):

$$وَخَلَقَ الْجَانَّ مِن مَّارِجٍ مِّن نَّارٍ$$

"And He created the Jinn from a smokeless flame of fire."

— Surah Ar-Rahman, 55:15

The *Hin* are also said to have supported the angels, led by Iblis, during a battle against the earthen Jinn, who brought disaster to the world. According to the opinions of Qur'an commentators among the Sahabah (companions) and Tabi'een (successors), the Earth was inhabited by the Jinn, whom Allah, may He be exalted, created from fire. Most of the Mufassirun, including At-Tabari, narrated in Tafseer from Ibn 'Abbas (may Allah be pleased with him) that he said:

"The first ones to dwell on Earth were the Jinn, and they caused mischief therein, shedding blood and killing one another."

119

It was narrated from Ar-Rabee' ibn Anas that he said:

"Allah (SWT) created the angels on Wednesday, and He created the Jinn on Thursday. He created Adam on Friday. Then some of the Jinn disbelieved, and the angels used to come down to Earth to fight them, resulting in bloodshed and corruption on Earth."

Another opinion is that there was no one on Earth, Jinn or otherwise, before Adam (peace be upon him).

However, the Bible does mention the existence of other creatures before Adam and Eve. In the Book of Genesis:

20 And God said, Let the waters bring forth abundantly the moving creature that hath life, and fowl that may fly above the earth in the open firmament of heaven.

21 And God created great whales, and every living creature that moveth, which the waters brought forth abundantly, after their kind, and every winged fowl after his kind: and God saw that it was good.

— Genesis 1:20-21 (KJV)

24 And God said, Let the earth bring forth the living creature after his kind, cattle, and creeping thing, and beast of the earth after his kind: and it was so.

25 And God made the beast of the earth after his kind, and cattle after their kind, and every thing that creepeth upon the earth after his kind: and God saw that it was good.

Genesis 1:24–25 (KJV)

However, the Bible does not provide detailed descriptions of these creatures, so it's difficult to say exactly what they looked like or what their characteristics were.

The First Man and Woman

Adam ("man of earth") was the name of the first human being whom God formed out of soil taken from all parts of the Earth. Then, God created the first woman, Eve, to be Adam's wife. God blessed Adam and Eve, saying: "Be fruitful and multiply, cultivate the earth, and control it. Rule over the fish of the sea, and over the birds of the air, and over every living thing that moves on the earth!"

Christian Views

"And the Lord God formed man of the dust of the ground, and breathed into his nostrils the breath of life; and man became a living soul."

— Genesis 2:7 (KJV)

Then God said:

"And the Lord God said, it is not good that the man should be alone; I will make him a help meet for him."

— Genesis 2:18 (KJV)

Thus, God created the first woman, Eve, according to the Book of Genesis, from the rib of Adam. However, the Qur'an does not support the view that Eve was created from Adam's rib but instead states:

يَا أَيُّهَا النَّاسُ اتَّقُوا رَبَّكُمُ الَّذِي خَلَقَكُم مِّن نَّفْسٍ وَاحِدَةٍ وَخَلَقَ مِنْهَا زَوْجَهَا وَبَثَّ مِنْهُمَا رِجَالًا كَثِيرًا وَنِسَاءً ۚ وَاتَّقُوا اللَّهَ الَّذِي تَسَاءَلُونَ بِهِ وَالْأَرْحَامَ ۚ إِنَّ اللَّهَ كَانَ عَلَيْكُمْ رَقِيبًا

"O mankind! Reverence your Guardian-Lord, who created you from a single soul, and created from it its mate, and scattered (like seeds) countless men and women. Reverence Allah, through whom ye demand your mutual (rights), and (reverence) the wombs (that bore you): for Allah ever watches over you."

— Surah An-Nisaa, 4:1

The intention behind the words is not to suggest that woman was fashioned from the physical body of man, but rather to emphasise that she is of the same human species, endowed with identical abilities and inclinations, as delineated in the Holy Qur'an.

The Earth is Satan's Kingdom

God reveals that there was a great angel, Lucifer, who rebelled against Him:

"12 How art thou fallen from heaven, O Lucifer, son of the morning! how art thou cut down to the ground, which didst weaken the nations!

13 For thou hast said in thine heart, I will ascend into heaven, I will exalt my throne above the stars of God: I will sit also upon the mount of the congregation, in the sides of the north:

14 I will ascend above the heights of the clouds; I will be like the most High.'"

— *Isaiah 14:12–14 (KJV)*

Here, God explains that Lucifer had a throne, representing a position of leadership and authority. He rose from somewhere below to try to overthrow God, but was "cut down to the ground."

"I beheld Satan as lightning fall from heaven." He said.

— *Luke 10:18 (KJV)*

Lucifer, who became Satan (meaning *Adversary*) at his rebellion, was cast down from heaven—to the Earth!

The Book of Job records God asking Satan:

"Whence comest thou?"

Satan's reply was:

"From going to and fro in the earth, and from walking up and down in it."

— *Job 1:7 (KJV)).index 60*

"I beheld Satan as lightning fall from heaven," He said (Luke 10:18). Lucifer, who became Satan (meaning Adversary) at his rebellion, was cast down from heaven—to the earth! The earth is Satan's realm. The book of Job records God asking Satan, "Whence comest thou?" Satan's reply was, "From going to and fro in the earth, and from walking up and down in it." (Job 1:7).[69]

From the moment he descended from Heaven alongside Adam and Eve, Satan embarked on his mission of intrigue and deception—a mission that would persist until the Earth's final days. His first target was the two sons of Adam and Eve, and he achieved success in his endeavour. Thus, we have traced the origin of mankind's first sin on this Earth.

We should note that killing is the ultimate goal of his every action. Since then, Satan has taken over the whole world under his control—rule over the fish of the sea, the birds of the air, and every living creature that moves on the ground—which God gifted and said:

"Be fruitful and increase in number; fill the earth and subdue it for mankind."

(Genesis 1:26–28, emphasis mine)

Let us now see what Satan has done to the two sons of Adam, the consequences of which mankind is suffering—and will continue to suffer—until the end of this world.

The story is reported in the Qur'an when Allah SWT said:

وَاتْلُ عَلَيْهِمْ نَبَأَ ابْنَيْ آدَمَ بِالْحَقِّ إِذْ قَرَّبَا قُرْبَانًا فَتُقُبِّلَ مِنْ أَحَدِهِمَا وَلَمْ يُتَقَبَّلْ مِنَ الْآخَرِ قَالَ لَأَقْتُلَنَّكَ ۖ قَالَ إِنَّمَا يَتَقَبَّلُ اللَّهُ مِنَ الْمُتَّقِينَ

"And (O Muhammad ﷺ) recite to them (the Jews) the story of the two sons of Adam [Habil (Abel) and Qabil (Cain)] in truth: when each offered a sacrifice (to Allah), it was accepted from the one but not from the other. The latter said to the former: 'I will surely kill you.' The former said: 'Verily, Allah accepts only from those who are Al-Muttaqun (the pious – see V.2:2).'"

(Surah Al-Ma'idah 5:27)

---

[69] Index 60 https://www.somaliwave.com/index.php?threads/life-on-earth-before-adam.10026/
https://islamicinfodotcom.wordpress.com/2017/01/01/first-blog-post/
http://victoryforabraham.blogspot.com/2011/11/was-adam-first-man-on-earth-both-quran.htm

Ibn 'Abbaas was quoted to have said that Eve used to give birth to twins—always a boy and a girl. She gave birth five hundred times. The first twin was Cain and his sister Iqliima. After two years, she gave birth to Abel and his sister Leoda.

When they became teenagers, Allah ordered Adam to marry off Cain's sister to Abel, and Abel's sister to Cain. Abel agreed to such an arrangement, but Cain refused to marry Leoda. He would not agree that his sister Iqliima—more attractive than Leoda—should marry Abel.

Adam suggested that each of the boys should offer a sacrifice. The one whose sacrifice was accepted would marry Iqliima. Abel took a fat heifer, milk, and butter from the best of his sheep, while Cain took the worst grain spikes from his farm. They headed to the top of the mountain.

On the way, Cain said to himself that he would not care if Allah SWT accepted his sacrifice or not—Abel would never marry Iqliima. On the other hand, Abel said to himself that he would be satisfied with Allah's SWT satisfaction and would accept His verdict.

A fire came down from Heaven and accepted Abel's sacrifice. They went down the mountain, each going his own way. A few hours later, Cain approached his brother while he was attending his sheep. He told Abel that he would kill him:

"Behold! They each presented a sacrifice to Allah SWT. It was accepted from one, but not from the other. Said the latter: 'Be sure I will slay you.'

'Surely,' said the former, 'Allah does accept of the sacrifice of those who are righteous.'"

Cain was a farmer and Abel a herder. So, Cain gathered and offered some grain spikes, and Abel picked out one of his fat rams. A fire came down from Heaven, took the ram, and left the grain spikes behind. Cain was filled with jealousy and said that he would kill his brother.

Abel contented himself by saying that Allah SWT had accepted the sacrifice of the one who was righteous. People said that Allah had accepted Abel's sacrifice to glorify him, while Allah SWT had rejected Cain's sacrifice to express His disdain.

When choosing to give a sacrifice, one must be careful that it should be something worthwhile and dear to the one who offers it. The Qur'an said:

$$\text{لَن تَنَالُوا الْبِرَّ حَتَّىٰ تُنفِقُوا مِمَّا تُحِبُّونَ ۚ وَمَا تُنفِقُوا مِن شَيْءٍ فَإِنَّ اللَّهَ بِهِ عَلِيمٌ}$$

"By no means shall ye attain righteousness unless ye give (freely) of that which ye love; and whatever ye give, of a truth Allah knoweth it well."

(Surah Al-Imran 3:92)

Cain had all the bad characteristics—ungratefulness towards his father, jealousy of his brother, trivialising sacrifice, and paying no attention to punishment on the Day of Judgement. Therefore, Cain became an infidel.

Cain came to his brother and said, "I am going to kill you."

Abel replied, "If you would extend your hand in order to kill me, I would not extend mine. I am fearful of the Lord of the Worlds. I will submit, be patient, and will not object."

Resisting someone's attempt to commit murder was forbidden at that time. Abel was told that he truly feared Allah and would not do anything that was forbidden. While Abel was sleeping, his brother approached and smashed his head with a large stone. The Qur'an said:

$$فَطَوَّعَتْ لَهُ نَفْسُهُ قَتْلَ أَخِيهِ فَقَتَلَهُ فَأَصْبَحَ مِنَ الْخَاسِرِينَ$$

"So the Nafs (self) of the other (latter one) encouraged him and made fair-seeming to him the murder of his brother; he murdered him and became one of the losers."

(Surah Al-Ma'idah 5:30)

This means that Cain's jealous soul led him to commit such an act without fear or thought of any consequences.

Qatada ibn al-Nu'man said that Cain's jealous soul "tempted" him to commit murder.

Mujaahid said that Cain was "encouraged," while Abu 'Ubaida said that he was "supported."

However, Ibn Yahya said that Cain was merely responding to his jealous soul.

Al-Kalbi said that Cain was led—or made bold—to commit his act.

So, he killed his brother and became a loser—meaning that he would lose this world and the Hereafter. He made his father angry, killed his brother, and earned Allah's wrath. So, he headed to Hell.

Another narration says Cain did not know how to kill. Therefore, Iblis came to him in the form of a bird. That bird took another bird, cut off its head, placed it between two stones, and crushed it. Iblis' purpose was to show Cain how to kill his brother.

Cain had decided to kill his brother. He took off and found Abel sleeping in the shade of the mountain while his sheep were grazing. Cain took a stone and struck Abel's head hard with it. Thus, Abel was the first victim of murder on Earth.

The Prophet Muhammad ﷺ said that no soul should be victimised by aggression.

Ibn 'Abbaas said that Adam was in Makkah when Cain killed his brother, Abel. Trees began to bear thorns, fruits turned sour, water became bitter, and the Earth's surface grew dusty. Adam travelled to India, repeating the following stanza of Arabic poetry:

The Earth and its inhabitants have changed

The face of the Earth is dusty

Every taste and colour is changed

All beautiful faces are no longer so

How come I have not shed heavy tears

For Abel who is now resting in his tomb

I will spend the rest of my life in grief

I will not have a moment of rest

He said that wild animals once trusted Adam's two sons. However, after the murder, they became shy of humans. The wind blew up, and the atmosphere darkened. Adam was performing his pilgrimage when he noticed this and said to Jibriil, "What is going on?"

Jibriil replied:

"This is a result of your son's misfortune. Cain has killed his brother, Abel."

Adam cried and never laughed for the next hundred years. It was also said that he did not touch Eve after that crime. Ibn 'Abbaas added that when Cain killed his brother, he did not know what to do with the body. Allah SWT sent a raven that began to dig and move dirt around to show Cain how to bury his brother's decomposed body.

A raven killed another raven and began to cover it with dirt. Ibn 'Abbaas said that a raven came to the corpse of a dead one and began to cover it with soil.

Al-Hasan said that Allah SWT sent a raven that began to dig the dirt with its beak, and therefore Cain got the idea of burying his brother's corpse. Only Allah SWT knows the truth.

Cain said to himself, "Woe to me! I am not even as smart as a raven." That indicated that Cain was sad and regretted his action.

Iblis asked Cain:

Do you know why your brother's sacrifice was accepted?

Cain said:

No.

Iblis said:

Well, he worshipped fire, and that is why the fire consumed his sacrifice. You need to kneel down to fire.

Cain kneeled down and therefore became the first human to worship fire.

Mohammed Ibn Ali al-Tarmathy (Muhammad ibn al-Hanafiyya, also known as Muhammad al-Akbar, was born in Medina around AD 633—though some say during Umar's era—the third of Ali's sons. He was called Ibn al-Hanafiyya after his mother, Khawla bint Ja'far. She was known as Hanafiyya, "the Hanafi woman", after her tribe Banu Hanifa. *Source: Wikipedia, the free encyclopaedia*) said that Cain was created from the power of a seed from the fruit that Adam ate from the forbidden tree. That is why the boy was born corrupt. He fathered Ya'juuj and Ma'juuj, who would needlessly fill the world with sins before it came to its end. Cain would be in Hell forever, together with Iblis.

The people of Hell would say:

وَقَالَ الَّذِينَ كَفَرُوا رَبَّنَا أَرِنَا اللَّذَيْنِ أَضَلَّانَا مِنَ الْجِنِّ وَالْإِنسِ نَجْعَلْهُمَا تَحْتَ أَقْدَامِنَا لِيَكُونَا مِنَ الْأَسْفَلِينَ

"And the unbelievers will say, 'Our Lord! Show us those among Jinns and men who misled us. We shall crush them beneath our feet so that they become the vilest.'"

41:29 – Fussilat / Ha-Mim

What they meant by saying "the Jinns" was Iblis, may Allah curse him. By "men" they meant Cain, who was jealous and would be in Hell forever. This account was reported in the interpretations of al-Imaam al-Nasfi. *Index 60*

https://www.ligonier.org/learn/devotionals/depth-our-sin

Through his deception of Adam and Eve, and their subsequent submission to Satan's authority, the devil gained power over the earth. This prompts a crucial inquiry we must confront before progressing: **How did Satan gain the power to stand in heaven and show his pride before God?**

The battle for the salvation of human souls has been ongoing for centuries. Under Satan's dominion, the entire world system has become a construct influenced by malevolent spiritual forces far beyond the comprehension of our human minds. As described in the Book of Revelation by John, these dark spiritual entities have been intricately involved in shaping cultures and influencing rulers, with the aim of eradicating humanity's belief in a loving Creator God who cherishes His greatest creation—mankind.[70] Index 62

---

[70] *Index 62*   *https://www.groupbiblestudy.com/engrevelation/13.-war-in-heaven-and-on-earth?*

In this modern age, all kinds of unimaginable things have become prevalent in the world. From pierced tongues to pierced spirits, sex, drugs, and rock and roll—everything all at once—we see man becoming the most devoted servant of God, while at the same time becoming the devoted slave of his desires.

Prophet Yahya (PBUH) said:

"That Satan has so structured his evil forces [to] control the whole world."

As an example, we can compare this to Hitler's top men who formed the Nazi Party before World War II—those who sat with Hitler and took steps to dominate most of Europe.

Satan promised the Almighty that he would defile the people of this world. Prior to the unveiling of the Qur'an, God cautioned every follower through His earlier sacred texts—the Zubur, the Torah, and the Bible—to beware of Satan. Let me cite a passage from the Old Testament to elucidate how the adversary, Satan, asserts his dominion over humanity.

In the Psalm, **Colossians 1:13–14 (KJV)** says:

13 Who hath delivered us from the power of darkness, and hath translated us into the kingdom of his dear Son:

14 In whom we have redemption through his blood, even the forgiveness of sins.

Prophet 'Isa (PBUH) said:

"And ye shall know the truth, and the truth shall make you free." (John 8:32 KJV)

And in the Qur'an, Allah SWT reminded all mankind and said:

نَزَّلَ عَلَيْكَ الْكِتَابَ بِالْحَقِّ مُصَدِّقًا لِّمَا بَيْنَ يَدَيْهِ وَأَنزَلَ التَّوْرَاةَ وَالْإِنجِيلَ

It is He Who has sent down the Book (the Qur'an) to you (Muhammad ﷺ) with truth, confirming what came before it. And He sent down the Taurat (Torah) and the Injeel (Gospel).

3:3 – Surah Al-'Imran

Keith Thomas, in his Bible studies, has clearly described how this world is operating under Satan. He wrote:

"We see this world is commanded under the chain of authority. It speaks of an evil spirit that is given permission, capability, right, and authority to act."

Using the analogy of Hitler's men, this would be like his generals directing the field of battle—men who were given commands from above and exercised that authority on the battlefield. These evil spirits take their orders from those that are high in Satan's chain of command. They exert their power by instilling fear of death and domination through sin and the ignorance of Satan's ways.

Referring to the Psalm, **Matthew 8:9-11 (KJV)** says:

9 I am a man under authority, having soldiers under me: and I say to this man, Go, and he goeth; and to another, Come, and he cometh; and to my servant, Do this, and he doeth it.

10 When Jesus heard it, he marvelled, and said to them that followed, Verily I say unto you, I have not found so great faith, no, not in Israel.

11 And I say unto you, That many shall come from the east and west, and shall sit down with Abraham, and Isaac, and Jacob, in the kingdom of heaven.[71]

Satan is blinding people's minds and directing the powers of this dark world. The blind cannot see other blind, and this is our concern: how can we fight against unseen spiritual forces?

To counteract Satan's hold, we must grasp the invisible mechanisms by which these malevolent energies operate. By shedding light on the ways in which wickedness infiltrates our hearts and minds, we can begin to resist and break free from its clutches. It is crucial to exemplify the pervasive influence of evil and how it steers us towards immorality, enabling us to save ourselves from its grip.

Out of concern, a school principal expressed this idea more eloquently in a letter he sent out on the first day of the school year. He wrote:

Dear Teacher,

I am a survivor of a concentration camp. My eyes saw what no man should witness:

Gas chambers built by learned engineers.

Children poisoned by educated physicians.

Infants killed by trained nurses.

Women and babies shot and burned by high school and college graduates.

So, I am suspicious of education.

---

[71] Keith Thomas Email: keiththomas@groupbiblestudy.com Website: www.groupbiblestudy.com [1] http://www.artofwarquotes.com [2] Edited by Michael Green, 1500 Illustrations for Biblical Preaching, Published in 1982 by Baker Book House, Grand Rapids, Mich. Page 121.

My request is: help your students become human. Your efforts must never produce learned monsters, skilled psychopaths, educated Eichmanns (Adolf Eichmann).

Reading, writing, and arithmetic are important only if they serve to make our children more human..[72] *Index 64*

When World War I broke out, the War Ministry in London, England, sent a coded message to one of the British outposts in an inaccessible area of British-controlled Africa, saying:

"War declared, arrest all enemy aliens in your district."

The prompt reply came back:

"Have arrested ten Germans, six Belgians, four Frenchmen, two Italians, three Austrians, and an American. Please advise immediately who we are at war with."

In this study, if we closely observe how Satan and demonic forces intensify warfare, we may lose our minds and make no effort to identify the real enemy or what plans he intends to implement.

In the book *The Art of War*, written by Sun Tzu—an ancient Chinese military treatise from roughly the 5th century BC (*Wikipedia, the free encyclopaedia*)—he said:

"If you know your enemy and you know yourself, you need not fear the results of a hundred battles.

If you know yourself but not the enemy, for every victory gained you will also suffer a defeat.

If you know neither the enemy nor yourself, you will sink in every battle."

Allah (SWT) also tells us what to do to protect ourselves from Satan in the following verse—4:76, Surah An-Nisaa—where He says:

الَّذِينَ آمَنُوا يُقَاتِلُونَ فِي سَبِيلِ اللَّهِ ۖ وَالَّذِينَ كَفَرُوا يُقَاتِلُونَ فِي سَبِيلِ الطَّاغُوتِ فَقَاتِلُوا أَوْلِيَاءَ الشَّيْطَانِ ۚ إِنَّ كَيْدَ الشَّيْطَانِ كَانَ ضَعِيفًا

"Those who believe, fight in the cause of Allah, and those who disbelieve, fight in the cause of Taghut (Satan, etc.). So fight against the allies of Shaitan (Satan); ever feeble indeed is the plot of Shaitan." (4:76, Surah An-Nisaa)

In the previous chapter, we explored the crucial matter of safeguarding ourselves from the influence of Satan as we journey towards our ultimate

---

[72] https://www.facinghistory.org/holocaust-human-behavior/education-and-future

destination. However, regrettably, many individuals still fail to grasp the gravity of this issue. Their indifference risks rendering all their endeavours futile.

It is imperative to recognise that since the time of Hazrat Adam (A.S), humanity has been under the sway of Satan, effectively making us his subjects. Yet, alarmingly, the vast majority of people remain oblivious to this fundamental truth—save for a small minority (the true believers). This ignorance persists despite the repeated admonitions found in every scripture, including the final revelation, the Qur'an.

Allah has endowed Satan with divine permission to manipulate humanity according to his whims, with only a select few possessing the insight to perceive the ultimate consequences. Tragically, Satan's influence extends even to the highest echelons of human intellect—scholars, religious leaders, and adherents of all faiths. His mastery of deception is so profound that no example can adequately encapsulate its breadth.

Nevertheless, certain instances from our own time serve as stark reminders of his dominance and prowess, showcasing his unparalleled ability to manipulate events to his advantage. This manipulation has been witnessed throughout history, persists today, and will continue until the culmination of this world.

It is a sobering realisation that no force on Earth can thwart his machinations, and each of his deeds inevitably becomes a part of our collective history. The examples presented here demand patient analysis, illuminating Satan's methods in complex problems, mischievous schemes, and ultimately shifting the burden, consequences, suffering, and blame onto our shoulders to achieve his goals.

Such scrutiny leaves no room for doubt regarding his authority over the hearts and minds of humanity. Indeed, it prompts introspection, compelling us to assess the extent to which we unwittingly immerse ourselves in his domain.

For those who are inclined, let us revisit the verse once more, examining it through this lens of understanding and awareness:

اللَّهُ وَلِيُّ الَّذِينَ آمَنُوا يُخْرِجُهُم مِّنَ الظُّلُمَاتِ إِلَى النُّورِ ۖ وَالَّذِينَ كَفَرُوا أَوْلِيَاؤُهُمُ الطَّاغُوتُ يُخْرِجُونَهُم مِّنَ النُّورِ إِلَى الظُّلُمَاتِ ۗ أُولَٰئِكَ أَصْحَابُ النَّارِ ۖ هُمْ فِيهَا خَالِدُونَ

"Allah is the Wali (Protector or Guardian) of those who believe. He brings them out from darkness into light. But as for those who disbelieve, their Auliya (supporters and helpers) are Taghut [false deities and false leaders, etc.]; they bring them out from light into darkness. Those are the dwellers of the Fire, and they will abide therein forever." (2:257)

COVID-19 and Our Thinking

As I pen down these thoughts, our world is gripped by a profoundly unsettling lockdown. Across the globe, a growing number of individuals have begun to perceive the coronavirus not merely as a natural phenomenon but as a manifestation of sinister influences. It is seen as a global crisis that prompts profound questions about the essence of humanity and the reasons behind such catastrophes—even while we live in a universe ordained by Allah (SWT), where all things exist in relation to Him.

However, it is important to note that Allah is always aware of our suffering. In these challenging times, we witness an increasing number of individuals turning to God for help, strengthening their faith, and fostering a deeper connection with Him. This adversity becomes an opportunity for people to develop a more profound relationship with God and to become more resilient against the influence of Satan.

In the midst of this self-made disaster, people find themselves drawing closer to God, uncovering His loving purposes—even though they may initially be disguised.

Allah (SWT) declared in Surah Al-Isra (The Journey by Night), Ayah 17:82:

وَنُنَزِّلُ مِنَ الْقُرْآنِ مَا هُوَ شِفَاءٌ وَرَحْمَةٌ لِّلْمُؤْمِنِينَ ۙ وَلَا يَزِيدُ الظَّالِمِينَ إِلَّا خَسَارًا

"And We send down from the Qur'an that which is a healing and a mercy to those who believe (in Islamic Monotheism and act on it), and it increases the Zalimun (polytheists and wrongdoers) in nothing but loss." (17:82)

Our occupied Earth has experienced many grave epidemics and plagues before—killing people on a massive scale and altering the course of human history. Now, in the twenty-first century, we are confronted with the virus "corona," similar in nature to what our ancestors faced.

As of August 2020, the current world population stands at 7.8 billion, according to the most recent United Nations estimates—and all are vulnerable to this virus. The World Health Organization warns that this novel coronavirus, officially named COVID-19, is a global pandemic. The word pandemic comes from the Greek word meaning "everybody"—pan meaning "everyone," and demos, meaning "population.".

Viruses, though not classified as living organisms, are incredibly abundant biological entities that rely on host cells for replication. They exist as the most prevalent entities on Earth. A virus cannot sustain itself independently and requires a host for survival over an extended period.

Eradicating viruses presents a significant challenge due to the absence of a definitive cure; however, vaccination serves as an effective means of prevention. Viruses manifest in two primary forms: epidemic and pandemic. Epidemic viruses typically remain localised to specific regions, while pandemic strains can rapidly spread across entire countries or even globally, as seen in current events.

Scientists worldwide are diligently working to develop defences against these elusive pathogens, striving to safeguard the global population against their threats. We are sure that Allah (SWT) will soon be gracious to us and help us obtain effective vaccines to protect us from such diseases.

At this moment, the world's economy stands still. People remain hidden in their homes, and religious establishments lie closed. Across the globe, millions have perished, with the death toll continuing to rise. Uncertainty shrouds our future; we remain unaware of what lies ahead. This unprecedented lockdown has brought modern civilisation to a halt, leaving us uncertain as to when normalcy will return. The magnitude of this crisis surpasses even that of a nuclear attack.

The global Muslim community has not witnessed the suspension of Friday prayers on such a scale since the time of Prophet Muhammad ﷺ. Many Muslim scholars and academics speculate that the deadly coronavirus initially emerged in China. Some interpret this as divine retribution—a manifestation of Allah's will—punishing the Chinese for their alleged mistreatment of the Uighur Muslims in western China.

Some individuals label the coronavirus as a "soldier of Allah (SWT)," sent to chastise both the Western world and Muslims. They argue that Allah (SWT) is displeased with humanity, particularly Muslims, due to their disobedience.

A cleric from Tunisia remarked, *"Allah has many soldiers, including both angels and viruses."* Similarly, Othman Khamis, a Sunni religious scholar from Kuwait, shared on his YouTube channel that this isn't the first instance of Allah's retribution. He cited the story of Nimrod, whom Allah punished with a mosquito, and the ten plagues unleashed upon the Egyptians.

Thus, the coronavirus serves as another admonition or warning from Allah (SWT) to humanity. [73]*Index 65*

Scholars and theologians from various faiths have been actively engaged in addressing a fundamental query:

"If God is inherently good and merciful, why does the coronavirus exist?"

This question carries profound significance for us, as it unveils our existential quandary in the face of suffering. Understanding the true reason behind why the Almighty seemingly inflicts such cruelty upon humanity on Earth remains pivotal to our defence.

Allah (SWT) provides illumination to the entire human community and elucidates His stance through the following two verses:

Allah (SWT) says:

---

[73] https://www.tearfund.org/en/2020/03/decoding_coronavirus

وَلَوْ يُؤَاخِذُ اللَّهُ النَّاسَ بِمَا كَسَبُوا مَا تَرَكَ عَلَىٰ ظَهْرِهَا مِن دَابَّةٍ وَلَـٰكِن يُؤَخِّرُهُمْ إِلَىٰ أَجَلٍ مُّسَمًّى ۖ فَإِذَا جَاءَ أَجَلُهُمْ فَإِنَّ اللَّهَ كَانَ بِعِبَادِهِ بَصِيرًا

And if Allah were to punish men for that which they earned, He would not leave a moving (living) creature on the surface of the earth, but He gives them respite to an appointed term, and when their term comes, then verily, Allah is Ever All-Seer of His slaves. (35:45, Surah Fatir)

Another verse states:

فَكَأَيِّن مِّن قَرْيَةٍ أَهْلَكْنَاهَا وَهِيَ ظَالِمَةٌ فَهِيَ خَاوِيَةٌ عَلَىٰ عُرُوشِهَا وَبِئْرٍ مُّعَطَّلَةٍ وَقَصْرٍ مَّشِيدٍ

And many a township have We destroyed while it was given to wrongdoing, so that it lies in ruins (to this day), and (many) a deserted well and lofty castles! (22:45, Al-Hajj)

The aforementioned verses provide some clarity, yet further contemplation is required to reach a definitive conclusion. Throughout history, it has been demonstrated that Allah (SWT) intervenes and administers collective punishment—either on a local or larger scale—when human society transgresses boundaries and indulges in sin under the influence of Satan. It is evident that whenever such punishment is meted out by Allah (SWT), it is proportionately minimal compared to the magnitude of our transgressions.

This action may serve as a mere warning to humanity, rather than a true punishment. The only exception occurs when Allah's wrath befalls an entire nation due to their persistent indulgence in extreme levels of sin, despite repeated warnings from His messengers. This outcome is what Satan desires and considers a success.

Throughout the course of history, spanning from the time of Prophet Adam (PBUH) to the present day, Lucifer has wielded pervasive control over the world. Employing a combination of overt and covert methods, Lucifer's strategies continually adapt to circumstances. He expertly manipulates individuals, enticing them to embrace a path fixated on amassing wealth, acquiring power, and pursuing hedonistic pleasures.

In this analysis, we shall explore how Lucifer cunningly manipulates the forces of the invisible. By gaining an understanding of these techniques, we can cultivate awareness of the inherent dangers that permeate our existence on Earth. Consequently, we must take all possible measures to protect our souls and ensure their purity so that we may be prepared for the coming Day of Judgement.

It has already begun to show visible signs of Satan's game, as he has played before. China blames the United States for spreading the virus in their country, and the United States strongly denies the allegations. The United States, in turn, blames China for developing this deadly virus in their laboratories. In Europe, especially

133

Germany, there are also accusations against China. But no country has any concrete evidence to justify their claims.

Newspapers and electronic media publish incriminating stories that help open new fronts of hate and conflict. Satan drives very influential leaders to carry out his plan and, in the end, declares victory over us.

Whenever there was a major epidemic, there were always many heroes and heroines fighting disease and saving lives. Unfortunately, every time, there were also those who engaged in ugly blame games.

When a typhus epidemic broke out in Britain in 1847, Irish immigrants were targeted for transmitting the "Irish Fever", which led to racial, religious or political discrimination, stigmatisation, and persecution. This scenario still exists, as we see some populist politicians using the pandemic as a political tool—blaming others.

Speaking to broadcaster TV2000 (an Italy-based network that carries Roman Catholic-themed programming and is owned by the Italian Episcopal Conference), the Pontiff said:

"I'm convinced that one must never converse with Satan – if you do that, you'll be lost.

He's more intelligent than us, and he'll turn you upside down, he'll make your head spin.

He always pretends to be polite – he does it with priests, with bishops. That's how he enters your mind.

But it ends badly if you don't realise what is happening in time. We should tell him, 'Go away'.

He is evil, he's not like mist. He's not a diffuse thing, he is a person."

Pope Francis warned: *The Devil is REAL: Satan is more intelligent than mortals*, insisting the devil is a real person who uses dark powers to "enter the minds" of mortals.

In the New Testament, Satan is also described as a force of evil. He tempts Jesus to abandon his mission:

"And saith unto him, all these things will I give thee, if thou wilt fall down and worship me." (Matthew 4:9 KJV)

He is portrayed as a hunter of souls. The First Epistle of Peter warns:

"Be sober, be vigilant; because your adversary the devil, as a roaring lion, walketh about, seeking whom he may devour." (1 Peter 5:8 KJV)

Europe Faced a Dark Period

The history of epidemics has indeed challenged the notion that outbreaks only bring unity. On the contrary, they have often led to blame and discrimination against certain groups—such as foreigners, minorities, or marginalised communities. This was especially true when the causes and cures of diseases were unknown, and people relied on superstition and misconception to explain the spread of illness.

Plagues and epidemics have ravaged humanity throughout its existence. Nothing has killed more human beings than vicious infectious diseases caused by bacteria and viruses. [74] Index 107

For example, between the 14th and 18th centuries, the Black Death caused more than 200 million deaths in Eurasia and North Africa. Peaking in Europe from 1347 to 1352 CE, it was the most infamous plague outbreak of the mediaeval world—unprecedented and unequalled until the 1918–1919 CE flu pandemic in the modern age.

The cause of the plague was unknown and, in accordance with the general understanding of the Middle Ages, was attributed to supernatural forces and, primarily, the will or wrath of God.

Italian historian Agnolo di Tura recorded his experience from Siena, where the plague arrived in May 1348:

Father abandoned child, wife, husband, one brother another; for this illness seemed to strike through the breath and sight. And so they died. And none could be found to bury the dead for money or friendship. Members of a household brought their dead to a ditch as best they could, without a priest, ... great pits were dug and piled deep with the multitude of dead. And they died by the hundreds both day and night ... And as soon as those ditches were filled, more were dug ... And I, Agnolo di Tura ... buried my five children with my own hands. And there were also those who were so sparsely covered with earth that the dogs dragged them forth and devoured many bodies throughout the city. There was no one who wept for any death, for all awaited death. And so many died that all believed it was the end of the world. [103]

In Europe, the Black Death, famine, and war established a widespread fear of the devil, and his influence grew, as evidenced by an explosion of witch hunts. Unlike necromancers, whom the Church viewed differently, it was believed that the devil actively sought out women as his partners. Witches were thought to sign pacts and engage in evil acts on his behalf.

---

[74] Index 107 https://www.ncbi.nlm.nih.gov/pmc/articles/PMC4422154/

People were no longer seen as merely deceived by Satan, but as being in active collusion with him against God. By this point in European history, the devil no longer sat passively. Taking on an active role, Satan was perceived as present in the world—stealing souls and recruiting people to do his bidding.[75] *Index 108*

During the Black Death, Jewish people were attacked and killed throughout Europe because they were blamed for the outbreak. Satan began to play the game of guilt, defiling minds by targeting Christians. Christians started to hate the Jews, which eventually led to mass murder, as many Christians believed that Jews were responsible for spreading the disease and deliberately poisoning wells.

At that time, the official Church policy was to protect Jews, since Jesus was born into the Jewish race. However, in practice—and under the influence of Satan—Jews became the target of Christian loathing. As the plague swept across Europe in the mid-14th century, annihilating nearly half the population, people had little scientific understanding of the disease and were desperate for an explanation.

The first massacres directly related to the plague took place in April 1348 in Toulon, Provence (Toulon is a port city on southern France's Mediterranean coast), where the Jewish quarter was sacked and forty Jews were murdered in their homes. The next occurred in Barcelona.

In 1349, massacres and persecution spread across Europe, including the Erfurt massacre, the Basel massacre, and massacres in Aragon and Flanders.[7][8] Two thousand Jews were burnt alive on 14 February 1349 in the "Valentine's Day" Strasbourg massacre—even though the plague had not yet reached the city. Christian residents of Strasbourg sifted through and collected the valuable possessions of Jews who had not been consumed by the fires.

In the spring of 1349, the Jewish community in Frankfurt am Main was annihilated (Am Main means "Frankfurt on the Main", the city's full name). This was followed by the destruction of Jewish communities in Mainz (a German city on the Rhine River) and Cologne.

The 3,000-strong Jewish population of Mainz initially defended themselves and managed to hold off the Christian attackers. However, in the end, the Christians overwhelmed the Jewish ghetto and killed all of its inhabitants..[76] *Index 109*

Cats Blamed for the Black Plague

Ironically, when the deadly plague first arrived in the 13th century, cats became scapegoats. The belief spread that God had abandoned humans; thus, religious

---

[75] Index 108 https://www.nationalgeographic.com/history/magazine/2018/09-10/history-devil-medieval-art-middle-ages
[76] 109 https://en.wikipedia.org/wiki/Persecution_of_Jews_during_the_Black_Death

leaders needed a way to curb the people's loss of faith, which threatened the Church's profit and authority. They needed to blame Satan for the plague. As physical evidence of Satan's presence, cats were singled out as agents of the devil, "vessels of evil," carrying death and sickness with them wherever they went. [77]Index 110

The wave of anti-cat sentiment swept through Europe, with religious leaders labelling cats as evil and "diabolical." In southern France, the "First Inquisition" was created by religious courts to combat heresy and witchcraft. At the same time, cats began to be considered suspicious animals because of their independent nature and their ability to survive in extraordinary circumstances. Gradually, they became associated with witches and witchcraft. The population began to fear cats, associating them with satanic and demonic characteristics.

The first step to condemn the "evil" black cats was taken by Pope Gregory IX, who, in his Bull *Vox in Rama* in the early thirteenth century, stated that:

"The evil black cat had fallen from the clouds, bringing unhappiness to man."

This is how medieval citizens began to believe that it was safer to exterminate cats, especially the black ones. However, the various superstitions and ecclesiastical decisions meant that, with the passage of time, there was almost widespread killing of cats in many parts of Europe. Several sources indicate that the number of cats killed was approximately 200,000. The result of this extermination was the rapid proliferation of rodents, particularly the "black rat," which was found to be the main transmitter of the deadly Black Plague. Elderly women who kept cats were especially vulnerable to charges of witchcraft. Of all those accused of witchcraft in Europe during the Middle Ages, 80% were women, and the charge almost always ended in the woman's death. Although the most popular image is of an alleged witch burning at the stake, it was far more common to tie the condemned witch in a sack with her cat and throw both into a river. *(Index 111)*

The third plague pandemic was a major bubonic plague pandemic that began in Yunnan, China, in 1855 during the fifth year of the Xianfeng Emperor of the Qing dynasty. This episode of the bubonic plague spread to all inhabited continents and ultimately led to more than 12 million deaths in India and China, with about 10 million killed in India alone. According to the World Health Organisation, the pandemic was considered active until 1960. The plague spread further, also caused by disputes between Han Chinese and Hui Muslim miners in the early 1850s, which erupted into a violent uprising known as the Panthay Rebellion. This led to further displacements due to troop movements and refugee migrations. [78] Index 112

---

[77] 110 https://sites.stedwards.edu/comm2399-eflores9/2012/11/01/black-death/
[78] 112 https://en.wikipedia.org/wiki/Third_plague_pandemic

Devil's Blame Game

Who Was to Blame?

The Black Death was blamed on evil humours carried in the air or earthquakes releasing poisonous fumes. In Europe, the Jews were blamed for poisoning the wells (an explanation which was impossible in England due to Edward I's expulsion of the Jews in 1290); and of course, it was also blamed on sin.

If I am asked what is the cause of pestilence, what is its physical cause, and by what means can someone save himself from it, I answer to the first question that sin is the cause. To the second question, I say that it arises from the sea, as the evangelist says:

"There shall be signs in the sun and in the moon and in the stars; and upon the earth distress of nations, by reason of the confusion of the roaring of the sea and of the waves."

For the devil, by the power committed to him when the seas rise up high, is voiding his poison, sending it forth to be added to the poison in the air, and that air spreads gradually from place to place and enters man through the ears, eyes, nose, mouth, pores and other orifices. Then, if the man has a strong constitution, nature can expel the poison through ulcers, and if the ulcers putrefy, are strangled and fully run their course, the patient will be saved, as can be clearly seen. But if the poison should be stronger than his nature, so that his constitution cannot prevail against it, then the poison instantly lays siege to the heart and the patient dies within a short time, without the relief that comes from the formation of ulcers. (Anon. BL Sloane MS 965, folio 144.)

Sin or Prayer?

Bishop Edendon of Winchester issued an edict throughout his diocese, known as the 'Voice in Rama' speech because of its opening line, which once again graphically underlines this conflict in understanding:

A voice in Rama has been heard, and much lamentation and mourning has echoed throughout the world... We report with anguish the serious news which has come to our ears, that this cruel plague has now begun a similarly savage attack upon the coastal areas of England. We are struck by terror lest (may God avert it!) this brutal disease should rage in any part of our city or diocese. Although God often strikes us, to test our patience and justly punish our sins, it is not in the power of man to understand the divine will. But it is to be feared that the most likely explanation is that human sensuality - that fire which blazed up as a result of Adam's sin - has now plumbed greater depths of evil, producing a multitude of sins which have provoked the divine anger, by a just judgement, to this revenge. — Bishop Edendon

(Rama: This is a reference to Matthew 2:18: *"A voice in Rama was heard, lamentation and great mourning; Rachel bewailing her children, and would not be comforted, because they are not."* It refers to the Massacre of the Innocents. Half of Hampshire's population died.)

Dr Mike Ibeji is a Roman military historian who was an associate producer on Simon Schama's *A History of Britain*. [79] *Index 113*

Disease should rage in any part of our city or diocese. Although God often strikes us to test our patience or justly punish our sins, it is not in the power of man to understand the divine will. But it is to be feared that the most likely explanation is that human sensuality — that fire which blazed up as a result of Adam's sin — has now plumbed greater depths of evil, producing a multitude of sins which have provoked the divine anger, by a just judgement, to this revenge, says Bishop Edendon.

Satan has become a force of evil.

He tempts Jesus to abandon his mission: Satan told Jesus:

"All these I will give you, if you will fall down and worship me" (Matthew 4:9).

He is described as a hunter of souls: The First Epistle of Peter warns:

"Be sober, be vigilant; because your adversary the devil, as a roaring lion, walketh about, seeking whom he may devour." (1 Peter 5:8 KJV).[80] *Index 114*

The Temptation of Jesus - Matthew 4:8-10 (KJV)

8 Again, the devil taketh him up into an exceeding high mountain, and sheweth him all the kingdoms of the world, and the glory of them;

9 And saith unto him, All these things will I give thee, if thou wilt fall down and worship me.

10 Then saith Jesus unto him, Get thee hence, Satan: for it is written, Thou shalt worship the Lord thy God, and him only shalt thou serve.[81] **Index 115**

14 And no marvel; for Satan himself is transformed into an angel of light.. 2 Corinthians 11:14 (KJV)

Darkness and light are metaphors for evil and good. If anyone sees an angel of light, it will automatically seem to be a good being, for the correlation of evil with darkness, and of good with light, is a powerful archetype in human history. In the Bible, light is a spiritual metaphor for truth and God's unchanging nature.

---

[79] 113 http://www.bbc.co.uk/history/british/middle_ages/blackdisease_01.shtml
[80] *Index 114 https://www.ancient.eu/article/1387/cats-in-the-middle-ages/*
[81] Index 115 https://biblehub.com/matthew/4-9.htm

Who only hath immortality, dwelling in the light (1 Timothy 6:16 KJV), and hath shined in our hearts, to give the light of the knowledge of the glory of God in the face of Jesus Christ (2 Corinthians 4:6 KJV).[82] *Index 116*

How can we discern which light is of God and which light is of Satan? Our minds and hearts are easily confused by conflicting messages. How can we make sure we are on the right path?

(Psalm 119 KJV) says, "Thy word is a lamp unto my feet, and a light unto my path" (Psalm 105), and "The entrance of thy words giveth light; it giveth understanding unto the simple." (Psalm 130).

The words of God have power. Just as God's voice spoke physical light into existence, it can speak spiritual light into our hearts. Exposure to His voice – in His Word – will help us recognise the difference between the good light of God and that which is counterfeit.

Satan presents sin to us as something pleasing and beautiful to be desired, and he presents false teaching as enlightening and life-changing. The people of Israel had been seeking truth by consulting mediums, deceived by Satan's lie. In Isaiah 8:20–22 (KJV) says:

"20 To the law and to the testimony: if they speak not according to this word, it is because there is no light in them.

21 And they shall pass through it, hardly bestead and hungry: and it shall come to pass, that when they shall be hungry, they shall fret themselves, and curse their king and their God, and look upward.

22 And they shall look unto the earth; and behold trouble and darkness, dimness of anguish; and they shall be driven to darkness."

Darkness is a result of attempting to find truth without the Word of God. [83]

Now let's look at the Qur'an, which repeatedly warns us to protect ourselves from Satan if we want to succeed on the Day of Judgment:

Surah Al-Baqara 2:168

يَا أَيُّهَا النَّاسُ كُلُوا مِمَّا فِي الْأَرْضِ حَلَالًا طَيِّبًا وَلَا تَتَّبِعُوا خُطُوَاتِ الشَّيْطَانِ ۚ إِنَّهُ لَكُمْ عَدُوٌّ مُّبِينٌ

"O people! Eat of what is on earth, lawful and good; and do not follow the footsteps of the evil one, for he is to you an avowed enemy."

---

[82] *Index 116 https://biblia.com/bible/esv/psalm/119/130*
[83] https://www.gotquestions.org/angel-of-light.html

Surah Al-Baqara 2:268

الشَّيْطَانُ يَعِدُكُمُ الْفَقْرَ وَيَأْمُرُكُم بِالْفَحْشَاءِ ۖ وَاللَّهُ يَعِدُكُم مَّغْفِرَةً مِّنْهُ وَفَضْلًا ۗ وَاللَّهُ وَاسِعٌ عَلِيمٌ

"The evil one threatens you with poverty and bids you to conduct unseemly. Allah promises you His forgiveness and bounties. And Allah cares for all and He knows all things."

Surah Al-A'raf 7:200

وَإِمَّا يَنزَغَنَّكَ مِنَ الشَّيْطَانِ نَزْغٌ فَاسْتَعِذْ بِاللَّهِ ۚ إِنَّهُ سَمِيعٌ عَلِيمٌ

"And if an evil whisper comes to you from Shaitan (Satan), then seek refuge with Allah. Verily, He is All-Hearer, All-Knower."

Surah Al-Imran 3:155

إِنَّ الَّذِينَ تَوَلَّوْا مِنكُمْ يَوْمَ الْتَقَى الْجَمْعَانِ إِنَّمَا اسْتَزَلَّهُمُ الشَّيْطَانُ بِبَعْضِ مَا كَسَبُوا ۖ وَلَقَدْ عَفَا اللَّهُ عَنْهُمْ ۗ إِنَّ اللَّهَ غَفُورٌ حَلِيمٌ

"Those of you who turned back on the day the two hosts met (i.e., the battle of Uhud), it was Shaitan (Satan) who caused them to backslide (run away from the battlefield) because of some (sins) they had earned. But Allah, indeed, has forgiven them. Surely, Allah is Oft-Forgiving, Most Forbearing."

Surah An-Nisa 4:76

الَّذِينَ آمَنُوا يُقَاتِلُونَ فِي سَبِيلِ اللَّهِ ۖ وَالَّذِينَ كَفَرُوا يُقَاتِلُونَ فِي سَبِيلِ الطَّاغُوتِ فَقَاتِلُوا أَوْلِيَاءَ الشَّيْطَانِ ۖ إِنَّ كَيْدَ الشَّيْطَانِ كَانَ ضَعِيفًا

"Those who believe fight in the Cause of Allah, and those who disbelieve fight in the cause of Taghut (Satan, etc.). So fight you against the friends of Shaitan (Satan); Ever feeble indeed is the plot of Shaitan (Satan)."

Surah An-Nisa 4:120

يَعِدُهُمْ وَيُمَنِّيهِمْ ۖ وَمَا يَعِدُهُمُ الشَّيْطَانُ إِلَّا غُرُورًا

"Satan makes them promises, and creates in them false desires; but Satan's promises are nothing but deception."

Surah Al-An'am 6:68

وَإِذَا رَأَيْتَ الَّذِينَ يَخُوضُونَ فِي آيَاتِنَا فَأَعْرِضْ عَنْهُمْ حَتَّىٰ يَخُوضُوا فِي حَدِيثٍ غَيْرِهِ ۚ وَإِمَّا يُنسِيَنَّكَ الشَّيْطَانُ فَلَا تَقْعُدْ بَعْدَ الذِّكْرَىٰ مَعَ الْقَوْمِ الظَّالِمِينَ

"And when you (Muhammad ﷺ) see those who engage in a false conversation about Our Verses (of the Qur'an) by mocking at them, stay away from them till they turn to another topic. And if Shaitan (Satan) causes you to forget, then after the remembrance sit not you in the company of those people who are the Zalimun (polytheists and wrong-doers, etc.)."

Surah Al-Hajj 22:52

وَمَا أَرْسَلْنَا مِن قَبْلِكَ مِن رَّسُولٍ وَلَا نَبِيٍّ إِلَّا إِذَا تَمَنَّىٰ أَلْقَى الشَّيْطَانُ فِي أُمْنِيَّتِهِ فَيَنسَخُ اللَّهُ مَا يُلْقِي الشَّيْطَانُ ثُمَّ يُحْكِمُ اللَّهُ آيَاتِهِ ۗ وَاللَّهُ عَلِيمٌ حَكِيمٌ

"Never did We send a Messenger or a Prophet before you, but when he did recite the revelation or narrated or spoke, Shaitan (Satan) threw (some falsehood) in it. But Allah abolishes that which Shaitan (Satan) throws in. Then Allah establishes His Revelations. And Allah is All-Knower, All-Wise." [84] *Index 117*

Devil's Plot and Our Patience

Catastrophes, such as the current COVID-19 pandemic, may befall the Earth for various reasons. Allah, regardless of our faith, may test our collective and individual patience. He has tested the devotion of His beloved prophets in the past by subjecting them to severe difficulties. Such calamities can serve as an opportunity for true believers to demonstrate their patience and gratitude towards Allah (SWT).

I am quoting a few verses from the Qur'an below where Allah (SWT) emphasises the importance of patience when we face problems:

Surah Al-Ma'arij 70:3

مِّنَ اللَّهِ ذِي الْمَعَارِجِ

(A Penalty) from Allah, Lord of the Ways of Ascent.

Surah Al-Ma'arij 70:4

تَعْرُجُ الْمَلَائِكَةُ وَالرُّوحُ إِلَيْهِ فِي يَوْمٍ كَانَ مِقْدَارُهُ خَمْسِينَ أَلْفَ سَنَةٍ

"The angels and the Ruh [Jibrael (Gabriel)] ascend to Him in a Day the measure whereof is fifty thousand years."

---

[84] Index 117 https://www.answering-islam.org/Silas/satan.htm

Surah Al-Ma'arij 70:5

فَاصْبِرْ صَبْرًا جَمِيلًا

"So be patient (O Muhammad ﷺ), with a good patience."

Allah (SWT) also says:

Surah Al-Baqarah 2:45

وَاسْتَعِينُوا بِالصَّبْرِ وَالصَّلَاةِ ۚ وَإِنَّهَا لَكَبِيرَةٌ إِلَّا عَلَى الْخَاشِعِينَ

"And seek help in patience and As-Salat (the prayer), and truly it is extremely heavy and hard except for Al-Khashi'un [i.e. the true believers in Allah – those who obey Allah with full submission, fear much from His Punishment, and believe in His Promise (Paradise, etc.) and in His Warnings (Hell, etc.)."

As devoted believers, it is imperative for us to internalise the essence of these verses within our hearts. Doing so can provide solace in times of losing our loved ones and alleviate the prolonged suffering caused by the devastating impact of the COVID-19 pandemic. This affliction has impacted humanity as a whole, indiscriminately affecting believers, non-believers, and individuals of diverse faiths. However, Allah (SWT) has not forsaken them; His messages and guidance continue to shine brightly. Only those who are true believers and possess knowledge can truly comprehend the workings of Allah (SWT).

Let us look at what Allah (SWT) says about His previous prophets during similar difficulties. Here, I quote a few Psalms about patience mentioned in the Old Testament:

Philippians 4:6 (KJV)

Be careful for nothing; but in everything by prayer and supplication with thanksgiving let your requests be made known unto God.

Psalm 37:7 (KJV)

Rest in the Lord, and wait patiently for him: fret not thyself because of him who prospereth in his way, because of the man who bringeth wicked devices to pass.

Psalm 37:8 (KJV)

Cease from anger, and forsake wrath: fret not thyself in any wise to do evil.

Psalm 37:9 (KJV)

For evildoers shall be cut off: but those that wait upon the Lord, they shall inherit the earth.

Ephesians 4:2 (KJV)

"Be completely humble and gentle; be patient, always be humble and gentle. Be patient with each other, making allowance for each other's faults because of your love."

Ephesians 4:2 (KJV)

"With all lowliness and meekness, with longsuffering, forbearing one another in love; with all humility and gentleness, with patience, bearing with one another in love."[85]

Before exploring the second reason, it's crucial to underscore occasions where Allah (SWT), in His wisdom, placed His beloved Prophets in difficult circumstances to test their patience. By contemplating these instances, we can extract valuable lessons on navigating challenges with resilience and earnestly seeking Allah's aid to overcome them. It's a frequent occurrence for us to grow impatient when confronted with adversity, hastily pursuing solutions without acknowledging the potential influence of Satan. We must remember that Satan seeks to manipulate the minds of believers and strives to undermine our faith.

As Muslims (believers), when confronted with the trials and tests of life, we should adhere closely to the guidance of the Qur'an and the teachings of the Prophet Muhammad ﷺ in order to effectively navigate moments of hardship. The following points encapsulate some key guidance relevant to this matter.

It was narrated from Abu Hurayrah (may Allah be pleased with him) that the Prophet ﷺ said:

"The strong believer is better and more beloved to Allah than the weak believer, although both are good. Strive to do that which will benefit you and seek the help of Allah, and do not feel helpless. If anything befalls you, do not say 'If only I had done (such and such), the such and such would have happened,' rather say: 'Allah has decreed and what He wills He does,' for 'if only' opens the door to the work of Satan." (Muslim, 2664).

Ibn al-Qayyim (may Allah have mercy on him) said:

This Hadith includes several important principles of faith, including the following: "Do not feel helpless." Feeling helpless is contrary to striving for that which will benefit him, and it is contrary to seeking the help of Allah (SWT). The one who strives for that which will benefit him and seeks the help of Allah is the opposite of the one who feels helpless. So, this is telling him, before what has been decreed happens, of that which is one of the greatest means of attaining it, which

---

[85] https://www.biblestudytools.com/topical-verses/patience-bible-verses/

is striving for it whilst seeking the help of the One in Whose hand is control of all things, from Whom they come and to Whom they will return.

If he does not attain what was not decreed for him, then he may feel either of two things:

Helplessness, which opens the door to the work of Satan. So, his sense of helplessness leads him to say "if only," but there is nothing good in saying "if only" in this case. Rather, that opens the door to blame, panic, discontentment, regret, and grief— all of which are the work of Satan.

The Prophet Muhammad ﷺ forbade us to open the door to his works in this manner and told us to adopt the following:

The second option, which is looking at the divine decree and bearing it in mind. For if it was decreed for him, it would never have missed him, and no one could have prevented him from attaining it. Hence, he said:

"If anything befalls you, do not say 'If only I had done (such and such), the such and such would have happened,' rather say: 'Allah has decreed and what He wills He does,'" and he taught him that which will benefit him in either case, whether he gets what he wanted or not. Hence, this hadith is one which a person can never do without. (Shifa Al-Aleel, 37-38)

As highlighted in the mentioned hadith, steadfast faith is the pillar that uplifts us. In moments of wavering belief, turning to the Qur'an serves as a reminder that only through Allah (SWT) can we find liberation from our trials. Allah (SWT) says again in the Qur'an:

Surah Al-Imran 3:160

إِن يَنصُرْكُمُ اللَّهُ فَلَا غَالِبَ لَكُمْ ۖ وَإِن يَخْذُلْكُمْ فَمَن ذَا الَّذِي يَنصُرُكُم مِّن بَعْدِهِ ۗ وَعَلَى اللَّهِ فَلْيَتَوَكَّلِ الْمُؤْمِنُونَ

"If Allah helps you, none can overcome you; and if He forsakes you, who is there after Him that can help you? And in Allah (Alone) let believers put their trust." (Qur'an, 3/160, Al-Imran)

As part of that verse, we should, therefore, recognise that "Allah does what He wills."

Allah (SWT) tells us in the Qur'an:

Surah Al-Baqarah 2:64

ثُمَّ تَوَلَّيْتُم مِّن بَعْدِ ذَٰلِكَ ۖ فَلَوْلَا فَضْلُ اللَّهِ عَلَيْكُمْ وَرَحْمَتُهُ لَكُنتُم مِّنَ الْخَاسِرِينَ

"Then after that you turned away. Had it not been for the Grace and Mercy of Allah upon you, indeed you would have been among the losers."

After all the above examples, still, those who question why a benevolent and merciful God would allow the existence of something as devastating as the coronavirus should ponder deeply upon the following verse. It is through this reflection that truth seekers may find the answers they seek and come to a deeper understanding of faith. Allah (SWT) in the Qur'an:

Surah Al-Hud 11:3

وَأَنِ اسْتَغْفِرُوا رَبَّكُمْ ثُمَّ تُوبُوا إِلَيْهِ يُمَتِّعْكُم مَّتَاعًا حَسَنًا إِلَىٰ أَجَلٍ مُّسَمًّى وَيُؤْتِ كُلَّ ذِي فَضْلٍ فَضْلَهُ ۖ وَإِن تَوَلَّوْا فَإِنِّي أَخَافُ عَلَيْكُمْ عَذَابَ يَوْمٍ كَبِيرٍ

"And (commanding you): 'Seek the forgiveness of your Lord, and turn to Him in repentance, that He may grant you good enjoyment, for a term appointed, and bestow His abounding Grace to every owner of grace (i.e. the one who helps and serves the needy and deserving, physically and with his wealth, and even with good words). But if you turn away, then I fear for you the torment of a Great Day (i.e. the Day of Resurrection).'"

We know from the story of Prophet Yunus (peace be upon him) when he was swallowed by a whale. Out of His mercy, Allah (SWT) finally relieved him of that calamity. Allah (SWT) tells us in the Qur'an:

Surah As-Saffaat 37:143-144

فَلَوْلَا أَنَّهُ كَانَ مِنَ الْمُسَبِّحِينَ // لَلَبِثَ فِي بَطْنِهِ إِلَىٰ يَوْمٍ يُبْعَثُونَ

"Had he not been of them who glorify Allah, he would have indeed remained inside its belly (the fish) till the Day of Resurrection."[86] *Index 66*

Likewise, we observe that Allah (SWT) has challenged the endurance of His other revered prophets through diverse hardships. In the account of Surah Yusuf within the Qur'an, we encounter the comprehensive tale of Prophet Yusuf and how Allah (SWT) safeguarded him from all those arduous trials.

The Miracle: Allah Saves Ibrahim From The Fire

Prophet Ibrahim rejected the worship of idols as their god. Ibrahim (AS) once asked his father, Azar:

"How can you worship what does not see or hear, or do you any good?"

In reply, his father became very angry and said, "Do you deny the gods of our people?" and asked him to get out of his sight. Ibrahim left his father, as he did not want to live with a father who worshipped idols. He also asked the people of the town:

---

[86] *116 https://biblia.com/bible/esv/psalm/119/130*

146

"What are you worshipping? Do these idols hear when you call them? Can they help you or hurt you?"

The people would reply, "It is the way of our forefathers."

Despite all efforts failing to convince Ibrahim to accept idols as gods, his father, the priests, and the king of Babylon, Nimrud, decided to burn Ibrahim to death.

Surah Al-Anbiyaa 21:68

قَالُوا حَرِّقُوهُ وَانصُرُوا آلِهَتَكُمْ إِن كُنتُمْ فَاعِلِينَ

"They said: 'Burn him and help your aliha (gods), if you will be doing.'" (21:68, Al-Anbiyaa)

The news spread quickly throughout the Kingdom, and people came from all places to watch the execution. A huge pit was dug, and a large quantity of wood was piled up. Then the biggest fire people had ever witnessed was lit. The flames were so high that even the birds could not fly over it for fear of being burnt themselves. Ibrahim's hands and feet were chained, and he was ready to be thrown into the fire. During this time, Angel Jibril came to him and said:

"O Ibrahim! Is there anything you wish for?"

Ibrahim could have asked to be saved from the fire or to be taken away, but he replied:

"Allah is sufficient for me, He is the best disposer of my affairs."

The catapult was released, and Ibrahim was thrown into the fire. Allah (SWT) then gave an order to the fire:

Surah Al-Anbiyaa 21:69

قُلْنَا يَا نَارُ كُونِي بَرْدًا وَسَلَامًا عَلَىٰ إِبْرَاهِيمَ

"O Fire! Be thou cool, and (a means of) safety for Ibrahim!" (21:69, Al-Anbiyaa)

A miracle occurred: the fire obeyed and burned only his chains. Ibrahim came out of it as if he were coming out of a garden—peaceful, his face illuminated, and not a trace of smoke on his clothes. People watched in shock and exclaimed:

"Amazing! Ibrahim's Allah has saved him from the fire!"

Allah (SWT) helped him through such a difficult situation because of his strong trust and patience.[87] *Index 67*

---

[87] 116 https://biblia.com/bible/esv/psalm/119/130

Genesis Rabbah (38:11)

(Nimrod) said to (Abram): "You are merely piling words; we should bow to none other than the fire. I shall therefore cast you into it, and let your God to whom you bow come and save you from it!" (38:11)

A powerful example is found in the story of Prophet Ayoub, who remained patient and faithful to his Lord until he was honourably rewarded. Allah (SWT) mentioned in the following verse in Surah Al-Anbiyaa:

Surah Al-Anbiyaa 21:83-85

وَأَيُّوبَ إِذْ نَادَىٰ رَبَّهُ أَنِّي مَسَّنِيَ الضُّرُّ وَأَنتَ أَرْحَمُ الرَّاحِمِينَ

"And Ayoub (Job) when he cried to his Lord: 'Verily, distress has seized me, and You are the Most Merciful of all those who show mercy.'"

فَاسْتَجَبْنَا لَهُ فَكَشَفْنَا مَا بِهِ مِن ضُرٍّ ۖ وَآتَيْنَاهُ أَهْلَهُ وَمِثْلَهُم مَّعَهُمْ رَحْمَةً مِّنْ عِندِنَا وَذِكْرَىٰ لِلْعَابِدِينَ

"So We answered his call, and We removed the distress that was on him, and We restored his family to him (that he had lost), and the like thereof along with them, as a mercy from Ourselves and a Reminder for all who worship Us."

وَإِسْمَاعِيلَ وَإِدْرِيسَ وَذَا الْكِفْلِ ۖ كُلٌّ مِّنَ الصَّابِرِينَ

"And (remember) Isma'il (Ishmael), and Idris (Enoch), and Dhul-Kifl (Isaiah), all were from among As-Sabirin (the patient ones, etc.)."

The story goes on:

Ibn Kathir [88] A historian narrates that the Prophet Ayub (Job) (peace be upon him) was a rich man who owned all kinds of wealth, such as cattle, sheep, servants, and vast property in a place called Hooran. He had many children and families as well. The Qur'an describes Job as a righteous servant of Allah (SWT) who endured long periods of suffering and continued to lose all his wealth when he was struck by a disease. Allah (SWT) wanted to test the patience of His Prophet. However, it is clear that Job never lost faith in Allah and prayed to Him continuously to alleviate his suffering.

This is the devil's plot, planned to keep him away from the grace of Allah (SWT) by making him a disbeliever. When it was confirmed by the angels that Ayub was chosen as a prophet of the Almighty, Satan was allowed to exercise his full power over Job, dealing with serious illness and suffering, as well as corrupt practices. Accordingly, Satan came to Job as an old man and advised him that Allah

---

[88] (1300 – 1373), Ibn Kathīr from Syria at 1300-1373 was a highly influential historian, scholar and expert on tafsir also wrote 14 volume of universal history)

did not reward Job for praying for his work and not wasting time. However, Job became angry and did not accept his advice.

Abu Jafar Al-Tabari, an early ninth-century Qur'anic interpreter, gives this account of Job's troubles:

"Satan rushes back and forth from heaven to earth. He resorts to various ruses and disguises. He causes female breasts to grow on Job's chest and warts the size of sheep's buttocks." (Kassis, p. 267, 22)

Some Islamic accounts suggest that this is a sign of his patience, while others say it was a signal of repentance that gave Iblis full power over Ayub, except for his tongue. Others say it was his tongue and his heart that stayed free of the Evil One. A number of Muslim exegetes claim that Iblis blew into Ayub's nostrils, causing an inflammation of the body and filling it with worms. His body became so defiled that Ayub was forced to take refuge in an isolated place. [89]

Satan did not easily give up. He then tried to create distance between Job and his wife. Job's wife could not bear the pain and suffering any longer, but her faith in Allah (SWT) remained intact. She insisted that Job pray to Allah (SWT) to remove the suffering, but Job got angry with his wife and told her that the suffering had been for a short period of time. He also told her that she would be punished with 100 strokes for her complaining. However, when Satan failed to corrupt Job and realised that Job was determined to patiently wait for Allah's mercy, he gave up.

Job cried to Allah (SWT), saying:

وَأَيُّوبَ إِذْ نَادَىٰ رَبَّهُ أَنِّي مَسَّنِيَ الضُّرُّ وَأَنتَ أَرْحَمُ الرَّاحِمِينَ ¬

"Truly, distress has seized me, but Thou art the Most Merciful of those that are merciful." (21/83 Al-Anbiyaa)

After Job was cured, as mentioned in the above verse, Allah (SWT) revealed another verse, ordering him to punish his wife 100 times with grass to fulfil his promise. The verse says:

وَخُذْ بِيَدِكَ ضِغْثًا فَاضْرِب بِّهِ وَلَا تَحْنَثْ ۗ إِنَّا وَجَدْنَاهُ صَابِرًا ۚ نِّعْمَ الْعَبْدُ ۖ إِنَّهُ أَوَّابٌ ¬

"And take in your hand a bundle of thin grass and strike therewith (your wife), and break not your oath. Truly! We found him patient. How excellent (a) slave! Verily, he was ever oft-returning in repentance (to Us)!" (38/44 Surah Sad)

Hazrat Ayub was the most beloved person to Allah, and his test was so harsh and cruel in our eyes that it could measure the physical pain beyond his heart and wounds, which are beyond our knowledge. His wealth gradually dwindled, and he

---

[89] [23See Falzan Rahman, Major Themes of the Qu'ran (Chicago: University of Chicago Press, 1980].

149

fell into misery, losing family members as well. Satan may have acted through Job's wife, Rahma. It was Allah's test, and Job passed the test, resisting Satan's desperate attempt to divert him from Allah's path. Eventually, Allah's grace fell upon him. He recovered in the water mentioned in the verse. Job's wounds were healed by the rising of a holy stream, which was seen when Allah instructed the Prophet to strike the ground with his feet.

As test-takers, it's crucial to remember that whenever we face trials from Allah, no matter how challenging they may seem, Satan will try to interfere. We must remain steadfast and seek Allah's guidance and support.[90] *Index 68*

Divine Warning Navigating Your Inner Depths

Our quest is to cleanse our souls and reject the influence of Satan, striving to return from darkness to light by steadfastly holding onto our faith. However, we must be aware that Satan, as the ruler of this world, will make our journey difficult because he wants to mark us as sinners, as revealed many times in Psalm 12:3, 4, and 9, and in many verses of the Qur'an that we discussed earlier.

While it may appear repetitive to delve into the same subject repeatedly, it holds value for those earnestly seeking to ensure they tread the path of truth during their ongoing journey. This expedition is intricate and delicate, necessitating a continuous search for clues with each step, illuminating the soul and facilitating progress.

Allah (SWT) has revealed many verses in the Qur'an about how Satan corrupts the soul and mind, and advises every human being to take all possible measures to protect themselves from Satan's evil influence. We should note the following verses carefully:

Allah (SWT) says:

هُوَ الَّذِي يُنَزِّلُ عَلَىٰ عَبْدِهِ آيَاتٍ بَيِّنَاتٍ لِّيُخْرِجَكُم مِّنَ الظُّلُمَاتِ إِلَى النُّورِ ۚ وَإِنَّ اللَّهَ بِكُمْ لَرَءُوفٌ رَّحِيمٌ

"It is He Who sends down manifest Ayat (proofs, evidences, verses, lessons, signs, revelations, etc.) to His slave (Muhammad ﷺ) that He may bring you out from darkness into light. And verily, Allah is to you full of kindness, Most Merciful." (Verse 57/9, Al-Hadid)

يَا أَيُّهَا الَّذِينَ آمَنُوا ادْخُلُوا فِي السِّلْمِ كَافَّةً وَلَا تَتَّبِعُوا خُطُوَاتِ الشَّيْطَانِ ۚ إِنَّهُ لَكُمْ عَدُوٌّ مُّبِينٌ

"O you who believe! Enter perfectly into Islam (by obeying all the rules and regulations of the Islamic religion) and follow not the footsteps of Shaitan (Satan). Verily, he is to you a plain enemy." (Verse 2/208, Al-Baqara)

---

[90] Index 68 https://bibleinterp.arizona.edu/articles/Vicchio_Image_Ayyub

يَا أَيُّهَا الَّذِينَ آمَنُوا لَا تَتَّبِعُوا خُطُوَاتِ الشَّيْطَانِ ۚ وَمَن يَتَّبِعْ خُطُوَاتِ الشَّيْطَانِ فَإِنَّهُ يَأْمُرُ بِالْفَحْشَاءِ وَالْمُنكَرِ ۚ وَلَوْلَا فَضْلُ اللَّهِ عَلَيْكُمْ وَرَحْمَتُهُ مَا زَكَىٰ مِنكُم مِّنْ أَحَدٍ أَبَدًا وَلَٰكِنَّ اللَّهَ يُزَكِّي مَن يَشَاءُ ۗ وَاللَّهُ سَمِيعٌ عَلِيمٌ

"O you who believe! Follow not the footsteps of Shaitan (Satan). And whosoever follows the footsteps of Shaitan (Satan), then verily he commands Al-Fahsha' [i.e. to commit indecency (illegal sexual intercourse, etc.)], and Al-Munkar [disbelief and polytheism (i.e. to do evil and wicked deeds; to speak or to do what is forbidden in Islam, etc.)]. And had it not been for the Grace of Allah and His Mercy on you, not one of you would ever have been pure from sins. But Allah purifies (guides to Islam) whom He wills, and Allah is All-Hearer, All-Knower." (24/21, An-Nur)

Allah (SWT) has issued warnings not only through the Qur'an but also in the ancient scriptures revealed to the people of their time. These warnings serve to safeguard their souls from the onslaught of Satan, whose primary objective is to lead them towards the fiery torment of Hell.

Abdullah ibn Umar ibn al-Khattab (c. 610–693 CE), a companion of the Islamic prophet Muhammad ﷺ and son of the second Caliph Umar, and a prominent authority in hadith and law, said: While on the Ark, [Prophet] Nooh ('pbuh) noticed an old man whom he did not recognise. Nooh inquired:

'What brought you here?'

He replied: 'I came to strike the hearts of your followers, so their hearts become with me, while their bodies with you.'

Nooh responded: 'Leave, O enemy of Allah.'

Iblis said: 'There are five things that cause people to become destroyed (deviated). I will inform you of three and not of the other two. It was revealed to Nooh that he needed not know the three, but that he should inquire about the two.'

Iblis said: 'The two that are certain to work are: envy: I was cursed because of my envy, and became a stoned devil.

And the second is eagerness (to have more): The entire paradise was made permissible to Adam ('alayhis-salam). I got what I wanted from him because of his eagerness.' [91]

Khurasan in 678/79–681 said, "While [Prophet] Musa ('PBUH) was in a gathering, Iblis came wearing a hooded cap that changed colours. When the devil came nearer, he took off the cap, set it down, and approached Musa, saying:

---

[91] Ibn Abee al-Dunya in Maka'd al-Shaytaan , 65/ 44. the Book – The Devil's Deceptions (Talbis Iblis): By Imam Abu'l Faraj Ibn Al Jawzi, Dar as-sunnah Publishers. Page 74

'Peace be upon you.'

Musa replied, 'Who are you?'

He said, 'I am Iblis.'

Musa responded, 'No greetings from Allah to you. What brought you here?'

The devil said, 'I came to greet you because of your high godly status.'

Musa said, 'What have I seen you wearing?'

Iblis replied, 'I use it (the cape) to capture the hearts of the sons of Adam.'

Musa asked, 'What is it that if a human does will enable you to take him over?' He replied, 'If he becomes fond of himself and considers his (good) deeds plentiful.' I warn you of three things:

- First, never be alone with a woman who is not lawful to you. Because whenever someone does so, I personally accompany him and use her to seduce him.

- Second, never promise Allah something unless you fulfil your promise. Whenever someone promises Allah something, I personally accompany him to prevent him from fulfilling his promise.

- Third, never take an amount of money to give to charity unless you make sure you give it to that charity. Whenever someone takes an amount of money to give to charity, I personally accompany him to persuade him not to give it.

Then Iblis walked away, saying: 'Woe to me, thrice! I have taught [Prophet] Musa what to warn the sons of Adam about.'

Ibn Abi al-Dunya in Maka'd al-Shaitan, 11/47.

Al-Ḥasan al-Baṣrī, known to his generation as an eloquent preacher, a paragon of the truly pious Muslim, and an outspoken critic of the political rulers of the Umayyad dynasty (661–750), said:

'There used to be a tree that was being worshipped instead of Allah.' A man went to the tree with the intention of cutting it down. The devil came to him in human form and asked:

'What are you aiming to do?'

The man replied, 'I wish to cut down this tree that is being worshipped in place of Allah.'

The devil said, 'You are not worshipping it. So what harm is there if others are worshipping it?'

The man responded, 'I will cut it down.'

The devil said, 'Let me suggest something better for you. Do not cut it down, and you shall find two dinars every morning under your pillow.'

The man replied, 'Who would guarantee me this?'

The devil said, 'I would.'

The following day, the man saw two dinars under his pillow. But the next day, he did not see the money again, as expected. So he again went to cut down the tree.

The devil came to him in his true shape and asked him, 'What do you wish to do?'

He replied, 'I want to cut down that tree because it is being worshipped in place of Allah.'

The devil responded, 'You lie. You have no power to do so.'

The man continued walking, but the devil threw him down, began choking him, and said, 'Do you know who I am? I am the devil. Initially, you were angry for Allah's sake, so I had no power over you. I deceived you with the two dinar promise. Later, you became angry for the sake of the two dinars, so I was able to overpower you.*Ibn Abi al-Dunya in Maka'd al-Shaitan, 79/60.*

The aforementioned verses and hadiths serve as a reminder to the descendants of Adam, cautioning them about the perilous influence of Satan, the fallen Jinn, whose destructive power can lead us astray from the righteous path. It is crucial for us to acknowledge the significance of fortifying our minds and aiding the salvation of souls in order to safeguard our hearts and thoughts. In this dark world, numerous individuals deny or remain oblivious to the existence of the unseen devil, and they are unwilling to contemplate the malevolent spirits that submerge them in a sea of sin, eroding their faith.

An author wrote in his article, "If I Were the Devil." The first thing I would do would be to deny my own existence.

Every religion teaches that without faith and belief, it is impossible to please Allah.

In the Qur'an, it says:

إِنَّ الَّذِينَ آمَنُوا وَالَّذِينَ هَادُوا وَالنَّصَارَىٰ وَالصَّابِئِينَ مَنْ آمَنَ بِاللَّهِ وَالْيَوْمِ الْآخِرِ وَعَمِلَ ¬
صَالِحًا فَلَهُمْ أَجْرُهُمْ عِندَ رَبِّهِمْ وَلَا خَوْفٌ عَلَيْهِمْ وَلَا هُمْ يَحْزَنُونَ

"Verily! Those who believe and those who are Jews, Christians, and Sabians, whoever believes in Allah and the Last Day and does righteous good deeds shall have their reward with their Lord. On them shall be no fear, nor shall they grieve." (2/62, Al-Baqara)

In the Bible, **Hebrews 11:6 (KJV) says:**

153

"But without faith it is impossible to please him: for he that cometh to God must believe that he is, and that he is a rewarder of them that diligently seek him."

The following poem, by an unknown author, vividly describes the devil's attitude of denial:

The Devil

Men don't believe in a devil now, as their fathers used to do.

They've opened the door to the broadest creed to let his majesty through.

There isn't a print of his cloven feet or a fiery dart from his bow

To be found on earth or anywhere, for the world has voted it so.

But who is mixing the fatal draught that kills both heart and brain,

And loads the earth each passing year with ten hundred thousand slain?

Who blights the bloom of the land today with the fiery breath of hell?

If the devil isn't or never was – won't somebody please rise and tell?

Who does the steps of the toiling saint and digs the pits for his feet?

Who sows the tares in the field of time when God is sowing pure wheat,

But the devil is voted just not to be – and of course the thing is true.

But who is doing the kind of work the devil is supposed to do?

Won't somebody step to the front right now – and immediately begin to show

How the frauds and the crimes of the day spring up – for surely we want to know!

The devil was fairly voted out – and of course, the devil's gone –

But simply folk would like to know, who carries his business on?

Our Hope

According to Ibn al-Jawzi (d. 597 H):

Indeed, Iblis (Satan) only enters people to the extent he is able. His ability to do so is increased or decreased according to the degree of their mindfulness, negligence, ignorance, and deeds. Know that the heart is like a fortress. Upon that fortress are walls, and the walls have gates, and in it are chambers in which the mind resides. The angels often visit that fortress. To its side are siege towers, in which are desires and devils frequently occupying them, with none to stop them. War is declared between the inhabitants of the fortress and the inhabitants of the siege towers. The devils continuously circle around the fortress, seeking the negligence of the guards and passage into some of its chambers. Thus, the guards should know all of the gates of the fortress, upon which its protection depends.

Refusing to believe in the devil is part of his strategy, as it allows one to eventually realise that it is beneficial for them. However, it is important to acknowledge that although Satan wields divine power and authority over the human mind, he is still a being within the universe and lacks omnipotence and omniscience.[92]

He is not a creator. While the devil possesses an extensive amount of knowledge surpassing human capacity, he remains completely ignorant of many things known by the most humble and even uneducated believers. He has no control over Allah's love, mercy, grace, and forgiveness. The devil is unaware of the future and lacks knowledge of all the secrets of the past. His power holds no value for those who genuinely believe in Allah, and this assurance is repeatedly emphasised in the Qur'an and the Old Testament. He cannot control the word of Allah, nor can he drag the soul of a believer to hell. However, the devil does not sit idle. His agenda is to lead this world as a field marshal under his authority and drag all the children of Adam to the fires of hell. The soul cannot be controlled so much by weak faith, where Satan attacks, and these attacks go deeper than the way he defeated Adam and Eve.

Our only hope is that when Allah (SWT) controls the mind, Satan cannot lead the believer astray. That demonic influence can only be prevented if "we will know the truth, and the truth will set us free" (John 8:32) from the devil's prison. Otherwise, everything else is under the control of Satan, and he directs the system of this material dark world. He is an intelligent, knowledgeable creature in the universe and possesses great organisational ability, which was proven when he convinced one-third of heaven's angels to march with him. It will be the devil who will organise and lead the last rebellion against Allah (SWT).

It was the devil who systematically subjected the Old Testament patriarch Prophet Ayyub (Job) to fiery trials in an attempt to break him (see Job 1–2).

In our modern era, we find ourselves witnessing a recurring pattern reminiscent of ancient times. Despite our awareness of the truth, we often choose to overlook it, leading to a failure in establishing justice. Our indifference stems from an overwhelming force that controls us, rendering us powerless to alter our course. Regardless of our wisdom, education, or strength, we are bound to perpetuate the

---

[92] (Omnipotence means that God is in total control of himself and his creation. Omniscience means that he is the ultimate criterion of truth and falsity, so that his ideas are always true. Omnipresence means that since God's power and knowledge extend to all parts of his creation, he himself is present everywhere. Together they define God's lordship, and they yield a rich understanding of creation, providence, and salvation.
https://www.thegospelcoalition.org/essay/omnipotence-omniscience-omnipresence-god)

existing system. A stark illustration of this predicament can be observed when we engage with mainstream media, be it through television or newspapers. Instead of being confronted with honesty, we are bombarded with falsehoods, conspiracy theories, oppressive occupations, opposition fuelled by vengeance, hunger, the plight of immigrants, societal divisions, and ultimately, the horrors of war and plunder. These cruel and unjust acts seem to pervade our world, perpetuated by the powerful elite who hold positions of authority.

Allah (SWT) says:

فِي قُلُوبِهِم مَّرَضٌ فَزَادَهُمُ اللَّهُ مَرَضًا ۖ وَلَهُمْ عَذَابٌ أَلِيمٌ بِمَا كَانُوا يَكْذِبُونَ

"In their hearts is a disease (of doubt and hypocrisy) and Allah has increased their disease. A painful torment is theirs because they used to tell lies." (Qur'an 2:10, Al-Baqara)

Hypocrites lie and tell lies for their own benefit, although lies can never lead to good. Satan uses lies as an element to mislead others and create the illusion of continuing success, blocking their judgment. This can lead to serious immorality and consequences, taking them far from the direction of the Almighty. Allah (SWT) has highlighted this fact in the following verses of the Qur'an:

وَإِن تُطِعْ أَكْثَرَ مَن فِي الْأَرْضِ يُضِلُّوكَ عَن سَبِيلِ اللَّهِ ۚ إِن يَتَّبِعُونَ إِلَّا الظَّنَّ وَإِنْ هُمْ إِلَّا يَخْرُصُونَ

"And if you obey most of those on earth, they will mislead you far away from Allah's Path. They follow nothing but conjectures, and they do nothing but lie." (Qur'an 6:116, Surat al-An`am)

Satan's traits, which lead people astray from the path of truth, always point out to man—no matter how intelligent he may be—leading them to sin by becoming disobedient, rebellious, ill-tempered, aggressive, insane, and arrogant. Allah (SWT) tells us about him:

قَالَ فَاهْبِطْ مِنْهَا فَمَا يَكُونُ لَكَ أَنْ تَتَكَبَّرَ فِيهَا فَاخْرُجْ إِنَّكَ مِنَ الصَّاغِرِينَ

(Allah) said: "(O Iblis) get down from this (Paradise), it is not for you to be arrogant here. Get out, for you are of those humiliated and disgraced." (Qur'an 7:13, Surat al-A`raf)

Allah (SWT) also advises His servants, saying:

يَا أَيُّهَا الَّذِينَ آمَنُوا إِن جَاءَكُمْ فَاسِقٌ بِنَبَإٍ فَتَبَيَّنُوا أَن تُصِيبُوا قَوْمًا بِجَهَالَةٍ فَتُصْبِحُوا عَلَىٰ مَا فَعَلْتُمْ نَادِمِينَ

"O you who believe! If a rebellious evil person comes to you with news, verify it, lest you harm people in ignorance, and afterwards you become regretful for what you have done." (Qur'an 49:6, Surah Al-Hujurat)

However, it is permissible to lie if one cannot avoid danger in a particularly difficult situation. That danger may concern one's own life or someone else's,

156

honour, or property. In some cases, it becomes mandatory to lie or take false oaths to avoid immediate risk to life. Similarly, if someone deposits something in your possession and someone else wants to occupy it, it is your duty to protect what has been entrusted to you, even if you have to resort to lies or take false oaths. Other than these exceptions, lying is not permissible. The truthful are most beloved by Allah (SWT). Allah mentioned in the Qur'an:

يَا أَيُّهَا الَّذِينَ آمَنُوا اتَّقُوا اللَّهَ وَكُونُوا مَعَ الصَّادِقِينَ

"O you who believe! Be afraid of Allah, and be with those who are true (in words and deeds)." (Qur'an 9:119, Surah At-Taubah)

Prophet (PBUH) said:

"I enjoin you to be truthful, for truthfulness leads to righteousness, and righteousness leads to Paradise. A man may continue to tell the truth and endeavour to be truthful until he is recorded with Allah as a speaker of truth. And beware of lying, for lying leads to wickedness, and wickedness leads to Hell. A man may continue to tell lies and endeavour to tell lies until he is recorded with Allah as a liar." (Narrated by Sahih Bukhari: 6094 and Sahih Muslim: 2607)

Now Let Us Find Out: What Does God Teach Other Than Muslim Believe About Lying in the Bible?

Satan, known as the enemy of our souls, is a master of deception. He consistently spreads lies and manipulates individuals, causing them to believe in falsehoods and rely on his authority. It is crucial for us to recognise Satan's remarkable organisational skills and comprehend the magnitude of his influence.

Lying is listed as a sin in the Ten Commandments:

Exodus 20:16 (KJV)

Thou shalt not bear false witness against thy neighbour..

Throughout history, lying has been universally regarded as an act of sin. This belief was reinforced by the condemnation of the serpent's deceit in the Garden of Eden (Genesis 3) and the subsequent divine judgement upon it. Another notable instance is when Abraham (PBUH) falsely claimed that Sarah was his sister instead of his wife, jeopardising their relationship. However, divine intervention saved them from the consequences, but it was still acknowledged as morally wrong (Genesis 12:18–20 KJV):

18 And Pharaoh called Abram and said, What is this that thou hast done unto me? why didst thou not tell me that she was thy wife?

19 Why saidst thou, She is my sister? so I might have taken her to me to wife: now therefore behold thy wife, take her, and go thy way.

20 And Pharaoh commanded his men concerning him: and they sent him away, and his wife, and all that he had.

The devil, the father of lies.

Secondly, lying is ultimately the work of the devil. Jesus taught:

John 8:44 (KJV)

"Ye are of your father the devil, and the lusts of your father ye will do. He was a murderer from the beginning, and abode not in the truth, because there is no truth in him. When he speaketh a lie, he speaketh of his own: for he is a liar, and the father of it."

Lying without repentance and forgiveness leads to "the second death" described in Revelation, which says:

Revelation 21:8 (KJV)

But the fearful, and unbelieving, and the abominable, and murderers, and whoremongers, and sorcerers, and idolaters, and all liars, shall have their part in the lake which burneth with fire and brimstone: which is the second death..[93]
Index 69

The Devil's Drama That Shakes the World

قَالَ رَبِّ بِمَا أَغْوَيْتَنِي لَأُزَيِّنَنَّ لَهُمْ فِي الْأَرْضِ وَلَأُغْوِيَنَّهُمْ أَجْمَعِينَ

Iblis (Satan) said: "O my Lord! Because You misled me, I shall indeed adorn the path of error for them (mankind) on the earth, and I shall mislead them all." — Qur'an 15:39

On 11 September 2001, a tragic event unfolded as hijacked planes crashed into the Twin Towers in New York, Northern Virginia, and Pennsylvania. This devastating act claimed the lives of over 3,000 individuals from various backgrounds and beliefs. It was an attack that shook humanity, leaving us grappling with the unimaginable capacity for evil that exists in our world, and unveiling the devil's first stage performance of this century.

The repercussions and detrimental impacts of this event continue to shape our future, surpassing our comprehension as human beings. We are faced with the stark realisation that our ability to grasp the extent of its consequences is limited, underscoring the profound and lasting effects it will have on our lives.

The devil exposed himself, and through this attack, he demonstrated his power and dominance. The image of the devil in the smoke rising from the Twin Towers was framed by CNN and other renowned photographers, published in newspapers

---

[93] Index 69 https://www.myjewishlearning.com/article/truth-and-lies-in-the-jewish-tradition/ https://www.islamicfinder.org/news/the-status-of-a-liar-in-islam/

and broadcast on TV screens, making a significant impact on the general public during that difficult moment. (Here, the perception and dissemination by the general public hold significance, rather than the actual reality.)

George W. Bush's address that night included the words:

"Today our nation saw evil."

From the depths of fiery chaos emerged the visage of Satan himself, bearing witness to his hand in the relentless destruction. Yet, amidst this dramatic spectacle, we, as believers, find no surprise. For we are aware that today or tomorrow, the unimaginable will unfold—driven by the arrogance, vengeance, racial domination, hate, enmity, and injustice that taint the existence of humankind on this earthly realm.

These multifaceted expressions of evil stand as clear indicators of Satan's reign over this world, pointing us towards Al-Qiyamah. The Almighty Allah (SWT) has graciously revealed a potent verse, urging all of humanity to reflect deeply upon the necessary actions required to evade the seductive allure of Satan's influence:

اللّهُ سُبْحَانَهُ وَتَعَالَى

يَا بَنِي آدَمَ لَا يَفْتِنَنَّكُمُ الشَّيْطَانُ كَمَا أَخْرَجَ أَبَوَيْكُم مِّنَ الْجَنَّةِ يَنزِعُ عَنْهُمَا لِبَاسَهُمَا لِيُرِيَهُمَا سَوْآتِهِمَا ۗ إِنَّهُ يَرَاكُمْ هُوَ وَقَبِيلُهُ مِنْ حَيْثُ لَا تَرَوْنَهُمْ ۗ إِنَّا جَعَلْنَا الشَّيَاطِينَ أَوْلِيَاءَ لِلَّذِينَ لَا يُؤْمِنُونَ

O Children of Adam! Let not Shaitan (Satan) deceive you, as he got your parents [Adam and Hawwa (Eve)] out of Paradise, stripping them of their garments to show them their private parts. Verily, he and Qabiluhu (his soldiers from the jinn or his tribe) see you from where you cannot see them. Verily, We made the Shayatin (devils) allies for those who believe not.

— Surah Al-A'raf, 7:27

In another verse, Surah Al-An'am (6:142), Allah (SWT) advises the sons of Adam not to follow the footsteps of Shaitan (Satan), saying:

"Surely he is your open enemy."

Not only that, Allah SWT reminded His human creation on earth to be cautious in advance and not to deny the release of this clear warning in the Hereafter. Allah says in the Holy Qur'an:

43:36–39 — Surah Az-Zukhruf:

وَمَن يَعْشُ عَن ذِكْرِ الرَّحْمَٰنِ نُقَيِّضْ لَهُ شَيْطَانًا فَهُوَ لَهُ قَرِينٌ

وَإِنَّهُمْ لَيَصُدُّونَهُمْ عَنِ السَّبِيلِ وَيَحْسَبُونَ أَنَّهُم مُّهْتَدُونَ

حَتَّىٰ إِذَا جَاءَنَا قَالَ يَا لَيْتَ بَيْنِي وَبَيْنَكَ بُعْدَ الْمَشْرِقَيْنِ فَبِئْسَ الْقَرِينُ

وَلَن يَنفَعَكُمُ الْيَوْمَ إِذ ظَّلَمْتُمْ أَنَّكُمْ فِي الْعَذَابِ مُشْتَرِكُونَ

36. And whosoever turns away (blinds himself) from the remembrance of the Most Beneficent (Allah)—We appoint for him a Shaitan (Satan, devil) to be a Qarin (an intimate companion) to him.

37. And verily, they (Satans) hinder them from the Path (of Allah), but they think that they are guided aright!

38. Till, when (such a one) comes to Us, he says to his Qarin (devil companion), "Would that there were between me and you the distance of the two easts!" What a terrible companion indeed!

39. It will not profit you this Day, as you did wrong, and you will both share in the punishment.

This signifies that those who persist in killing, butchering, and causing carnage—without acknowledging His grace and mercy in this significant declaration—will inevitably face the eternal flames.

By examining the events of 9/11 and connecting them to the aforementioned messages, one can gain insight into the workings of evil forces. This analysis sheds light on the extent of Satan's influence and how people are drawn to his destructive agenda, displaying their strength and engaging in theatrics on the global stage under Satan's guidance. This dramatic spectacle also serves as a catalyst for alternative thinking and encourages individuals to rediscover the right path.

However, amidst the narrative of this tragic drama, the opposing side—the main protagonist—proclaims their intention to identify and punish all the criminals involved, vowing to create a safer world. Yet, this declaration lacks the power to bring about true peace. Satan may allow such actions to occur on his terms, but he never permits authorities to fully comprehend how an individual's anger can fester over time and erupt in such a catastrophic manner, shaking the foundations of global power.

Satan finds comfort in such declarations, as he understands that eliminating criminals through violence will only breed further hostility, vengeance, and bloodshed. Though the victims perceive the identified individuals as wrongdoers, Satan's vast global following views them as warriors, actively or indirectly endorsing their cause. This perspective amplifies the potential for increased conflict and perpetuates a cycle of violence.

Here we can refer to some of the comments and findings published by **RAND**, a well-known institution. It stated:

The Effects of 9/11 and the War on Terror

"It raises the question: did September 11 bring about a quantum change in Muslim attitudes? A common view among our interlocutors is that September 11 opened a new era in the United States and Europe, but not in the Muslim world. As an Egyptian interlocutor told us, September 11 was an American event whose consequences America has visited upon Muslims."

"Most Muslims were horrified by the death and destruction wreaked by the September 11 attacks, but many—particularly in the Arab world—found some satisfaction in the idea that America's nose had been bloodied and that the United States had felt some of the pain that they believed had been inflicted on Muslims. So condemnation of the attacks was common but conditional."

The public Arab reaction to the attacks usually included some combination of the following:

- Satisfaction that the United States tasted what it had allegedly dished out to the Arab world (and poorer countries globally) for years.

- Condemnation of the attacks as criminal and anti-Islamic but seen as a natural result of U.S. foreign policy, which was primarily to blame.

- Spreading of conspiracy theories asserting the attacks were the work of American domestic extremists, the U.S. government, or Israel's Mossad intelligence service.

- Rejection of claims that the perpetrators were Arab or Muslim, based on the belief that Muslims would not commit mass murder, or that the operation was too complex to have been executed by their own.

— RAND Report, Page 94/567, Index 70

After 11 September, Indian Muslims increasingly began to identify with their counterparts internationally. The response of the Muslim community directly following the attacks was largely one of sympathy for the U.S. victims, but Indian Muslims were firmly against the war in Afghanistan.

RAND also found the opinions of eminent individuals who do not support the actions Satan has incited. He destroyed the Twin Towers and now deploys others on many fronts in retaliatory killing missions—ignoring the opinions of the broader global community.[94]

According to Adil Mehdi, "Even before the war began in Afghanistan, the majority of people did consider America as a force antagonistic to Islam and did

---

[94] Adil Abdul-Mahdi al-Muntafiki (Arabic: عادل عبد المهدي المنتفكي, born 1 January 1942) is an Iraqi politician who served as Prime Minister of Iraq from October 2018 until May 2020. Abdul-Mahdi is an economist and was one of the vice presidents of Iraq from 2005 to 2011.

not regret the attack on WTC, though they carefully refrained from speaking in public in support of it." (p. 46)

The fundamentalist Muslim leader Shahi Imam of Jama Masjid, Syed Ahmad Bukhari, went further in his remarks against the United States. He called the war against Afghanistan a war against Islam and stated his support for Osama bin Laden. (p. 47) The Shahi Imam is well known for issuing inflammatory statements, however, and thus he does not necessarily represent the sentiments of the majority of Indian Muslims. (The Muslim, p. 316)

World After 9/11

George W. Bush's address that night included the words:

"Today our nation saw evil."

True—but since World War II, Satan has been constantly working to find his chosen actors to stage another equally cruel, clinging script, so that the people of the world would see another dilemma, lose the value of humanity, and turn themselves into enemies of each other.

The intricate backdrop of the tragic 9/11 plot is masterfully crafted. An influential force manipulates individuals, skilfully influencing their thoughts and gradually involving them in intricate and sensitive religious and geopolitical matters. This process leads to the emergence of conflicts, heightened emotions, insults, authoritarianism, and degradation—all of which are meticulously monitored by this influential force.

The parties involved, unknowingly under its sway, find themselves unable to think positively. Instead, their initial hostility transforms into arrogance, division, and a strong inclination for vengeance, which we now witness as the opening act of this dramatic stage.

Let us reflect on the ongoing conflict between al-Qaeda, led by Osama bin Laden, and the United States, which intensified following the bombing of the embassy in Nairobi, Kenya, in 1988.

On 7 August 1988, a bomb exploded in front of the American Embassy in Nairobi, Kenya, and at about the same time in Dar es Salaam, Tanzania. The United States embassies were bombed, killing more than 200 people and wounding thousands. [95] Index 71

---

[95] Index71 Wikipedia/ https://www.fbi.gov/history/famous-cases/east-african-embassy-bombings

East African Embassy Bombings

The attacks were part of a planned campaign that was gaining momentum. In 1996, bin Laden called on his followers to "start a guerrilla war against American forces and expel infidels from the Arabian Peninsula."

Bin Laden, having established the newly formed al-Qaeda after 1989—first in Sudan and later in Afghanistan—began orchestrating acts of terror with increasing precision and scale.[96]Index 72

An interview with Time Magazine in December 1998 recorded the following statements from Osama bin Laden:

Are you responsible for the bomb attacks on the two American embassies in Africa?

He said:

"The International Islamic Front for Jihad against the U.S. and Israel has, by the grace of God, issued a crystal-clear fatwah calling on the Islamic nation to carry on jihad [holy war] aimed at liberating holy sites. The nation of Muhammad has responded to this appeal. If the instigation for jihad against the Jews and the Americans in order to liberate al-Aqsa Mosque and the Holy Ka'aba [Islamic shrines in Jerusalem and Saudi Arabia] is considered a crime, then let history be a witness that I am a criminal. Our job is to instigate and, by the grace of God, we did that, and certain people responded to this instigation."

In response to another enquiry about the "US expectation" from him, he replied:

"Any thief or criminal or robber who enters another country in order to steal should expect to be exposed to murder at any time. For the American forces to expect anything from me personally reflects a very narrow perception. Thousands of millions of Muslims are angry. The Americans should expect reactions from the Muslim world that are proportionate to the injustice they inflict."

He also said:

"Acquiring weapons for the defence of Muslims is a religious duty. If I have indeed acquired these weapons, then I thank God for enabling me to do so. And if I seek to acquire these weapons, I am carrying out a duty. It would be a sin for Muslims not to try to possess the weapons that would prevent the infidels from inflicting harm on Muslims."

When asked about his intention to accrue chemical weapons, and for his comment on America—then the world's only superpower—having labelled him Public Enemy Number One, he responded:

---

[96] https://aoav.org.uk/2021/the-devils-face-the-suicide-attacks-on-9-11-remembered/

"Hostility toward America is a religious duty, and we hope to be rewarded for it by God. To call us Enemy No. 1 or 2 does not hurt us. Osama bin Laden is confident that the Islamic nation will carry out its duty. I am confident that Muslims will be able to end the legend of the so-called superpower that is America."

Similarly, in another interview conducted by ABC News on 24 December 1998, reporter John [last name not provided] recorded that bin Laden said he wanted to:

"Put to rest"

...speculation that he had been hurt or killed in the U.S. retaliatory missile strikes in Afghanistan and Sudan.

He denied being behind the bombings of the U.S. embassies in East Africa, but described two of the suspects—whom he said he knew—as "two men whom we respect and hold in the highest esteem."

Bin Laden stated in his fatwah:

"We are confident that the Muslim nation would rid Islamic countries of the Americans and the Jews."

He also did not deny charges that he tried to develop chemical and nuclear weapons:

"If I seek to acquire such weapons, this is a religious duty. How we use them is up to us."

As televised on ABC News, bin Laden reiterated his intention to "put to rest" speculation about his death or injury in the missile strikes on Afghanistan and Sudan.[97]

This bombing and the subsequent interviews appear to justify such cruelty, indicating that Satan has already begun quietly exercising his agenda through two parties he has chosen to act out his evil script. The general audience witnesses the suffering of many innocent people in the first stage of this drama.

At this point, believers may recall verse 15:39 in the Qur'an, as mentioned earlier, where Allah says:

"Iblis (Satan) said: 'O my Lord! Because You misled me, I shall indeed adorn the path of error for them (mankind) on the earth, and I shall mislead them all.'"

It is a warning that this kind of drama will continue until the last day of this world.

---

[97] Indedx 74   https://www.pbs.org/wgbh/pages/frontline/shows/binladen/who/edicts.html web site copyright 1995-2014 WGBH educational foundation.

Muslims engaged in acts of violence and terrorism believe that killing is justified in order to protect Islam and establish justice. However, it is important to note that this perspective does not represent the beliefs of the majority of Muslims worldwide. These individuals are often influenced by the destructive teachings of extremist ideologies, which can be likened to the commands of Satan.

Engaging in a blame game and pointing fingers is a common response that only fuels animosity and hostility. Unfortunately, finding meaningful common ground to change course and bring peace to society becomes exceedingly difficult, as the influence of the devil prevents rational thought and reconciliation. This holds true regardless of the wisdom or power of any given leader.

The devil delights in orchestrating a sinister game in which he manipulates the minds of influential individuals, exploiting their authority to foster a culture of arrogance, power, domination, and mistrust. His ultimate goal is to exacerbate existing conflicts, perpetuating a cycle of violence and division with which we are all too familiar.

In contrast to the above, the following verses from the Qur'an and Hadith can guide believers, even in the most complex disagreements—including religious issues—towards respectful discussion, contribution of opinions, and just conclusions.

This principle aligns with the general rule in the Qur'an that Muslims can and should maintain good relations with peaceful non-Muslims. Allah SWT said:

لَّا يَنْهَاكُمُ اللَّهُ عَنِ الَّذِينَ لَمْ يُقَاتِلُوكُمْ فِي الدِّينِ وَلَمْ يُخْرِجُوكُم مِّن دِيَارِكُمْ أَن تَبَرُّوهُمْ وَتُقْسِطُوا إِلَيْهِمْ ۚ إِنَّ اللَّهَ يُحِبُّ الْمُقْسِطِينَ

Allah does not forbid you to deal justly and kindly with those who fought not against you on account of religion and did not drive you out of your homes. Verily, Allah loves those who deal with equity.

Surat al-Mumtahanah 60:8

Ibn Umar (PBUH) reported: When the Messenger of Allah ﷺ was victorious at the Battle of Khaybar, he intended to expel the Jews from there. However, they asked if they could remain on condition that they work the land and receive half of its fruits. The Prophet said:

نُقِرُّكُمْ بِهَا عَلَى ذَلِكَ مَا شِئْنْ

"We will allow you to remain upon that as long as we wish."

Source: Ṣaḥīḥ Muslim 1551, Grade: Sahih.

In the Qur'an, Allah SWT Says:

فَمَنِ اعْتَدَىٰ عَلَيْكُمْ فَاعْتَدُوا عَلَيْهِ بِمِثْلِ مَا اعْتَدَىٰ عَلَيْكُمْ ۚ وَاتَّقُوا اللَّهَ وَاعْلَمُوا أَنَّ اللَّهَ مَعَ الْمُتَّقِينَ

165

…Then whoever transgresses the prohibition against you, you transgress likewise against him. And fear Allah, and know that Allah is with Al-Muttaqun (the pious – see V.2:2).

Surat al-Baqarah 2:194

This verse permits legal retaliation, but it also warns believers to fear Allah, as humans have a tendency, in their thirst for revenge, to go beyond what is legally allowed.

Al-Qurtubi commented on this verse, writing:

"Whoever oppresses you, then you may take your rights from him according to the measure of his oppression. Whoever abuses you, then you may respond similarly. Whoever takes from your honour, then you may take from his honour. But do not transgress against his parents or his sons or his relatives. It is not your right to lie against him if he has lied against you. Indeed, an act of sinful disobedience cannot be met with further disobedience."

Source: Tafsīr al-Qurṭubī 2:194

And Ibn al-ʿArabi commented:

"Rather, it is not for you to lie against him even if he lies against you, for a sinful act of disobedience cannot be met with further disobedience."

Source: Aḥkām al-Qurʾān 1/159

Likewise, treacherous behaviour is sinful in itself and is not an appropriate response to being the victim of treachery, because treachery is always sinful in every case.

Abu Huraira reported:

The Messenger of Allah ﷺ said:

"Do not be treacherous to the one who betrays you."

Source: Sunan al-Tirmidhī 1264, Grade: Sahih

This principle also extends to the prohibition of killing civilians, including women and children. The Prophet ﷺ explicitly condemned the killing of individuals such as workers, servants, monks, women, children, and any noncombatants who do not pose a threat during times of war.

Abdullah ibn Umar reported:

166

A woman was found killed in one of the battles of the Messenger of Allah ﷺ, so the Prophet condemned the killing of women and children.[98]

9/11 Commission Report

Reflecting Satan's Power

Upon examining the 9/11 Commission Report, which can be found on the website, we encounter a wealth of information and perplexity. It sheds light on how even the most powerful nation in the world can feel powerless and struggle to find effective ways to combat malevolence.

Various methods, such as killing, waterboarding, torture, and possession, have been explored, but none have yielded satisfactory results. While physical elimination is possible, eradicating the "mind" is unequivocally impossible. To attain genuine peace, it is imperative to discover common ground and reconcile differences with a compassionate approach aimed at establishing lasting harmony. This is the sole path to permanently rid ourselves of malevolent thinking.

Achieving this objective requires unwavering determination to overcome satanic forces and embrace a mindset diametrically opposed to the sentiments expressed by President Bush on page 219 of the report, where he conveyed his concerns.

The report says:

Rice and others recalled the president saying,

"I am tired of swatting at flies."

The president reportedly also said, **"I am tired of playing defence. I want to play offence. I want to take the fight to the terrorists."**

President Bush explained to us that he had become impatient. He apparently had heard proposals for rolling back al-Qaeda but felt that catching terrorists one by one or even cell by cell was not an approach likely to succeed in the long run. At the same time, he said, he understood that policy had to be developed slowly so that diplomacy and financial military measures could mesh with one another.[99]

Definition of Terrorism

To the best of my knowledge, the United Nations member states have yet to reach a definitive consensus on the definition of "terrorism" and the appropriate internationally accepted course of action. However, individual countries have the

---

[98] Source: Ṣaḥīḥ al-Bukhārī 3014, Grade: Muttafaqun AlayhiThe meaning of the term: 'muttafaqun 'alayh' (agreed upon) https://hadithanswers.com › When the Hadith Masters use this term, it means that the Hadith in question is found in both books; Sahih Bukhari & Sahih Muslim, on the authority of the same Sahabi (radiyallahu'anhu) even if there exists variation in the wording.
[99] Index 75 https://www.9-11commission.gov/report/911Report.pdf)

ability to establish their own definitions of terrorism. For instance, Israel views Palestinian fighters as terrorists, while among Palestinians, they are regarded as freedom fighters, engaged in a struggle for liberation, the return of their occupied lands, and the establishment of justice. The United States and its allies staunchly support Israel, regardless of perceived injustices. Consequently, Palestinians and Muslims perceive the United States and its allies as supporting terrorism and endorsing injustice.

The United States' number one enemy, terrorist Osama bin Laden, described **"good and bad terrorism"**. He says, **"Terrorism can be commendable, and it can be reprehensible."**[100]

Nevertheless, Satan cunningly exploits the term "terrorism" or "terrorist" as a potent weapon to sow chaos among nations and incite discord within communities. Regrettably, we witness instances where individuals who identify as Muslims commit acts of violence, such as bombing mosques and taking the lives of fellow Muslims. Even though Islam itself does not endorse such killings, these tragic events occur due to Satan's insidious efforts to manipulate and corrupt minds, ultimately aiming to annihilate the essence of humanity.

We see the same word used in the *9/11 Commission Report*, on page 47, and on page 49, where the report continues, saying:

"Islam (a word that literally means 'surrender to the will of God') arose in Arabia with what Muslims believe are a series of revelations to the Prophet Mohammed from the one and only God, the God of Abraham and of Jesus. These revelations, conveyed by the angel Gabriel, are recorded in the Qur'an. Muslims believe that these revelations, given to the greatest and last of a chain of prophets stretching from Abraham through Jesus, complete God's message to humanity. The Hadith, which recount Mohammed's sayings and deeds as recorded by his contemporaries, are another fundamental source. A third key element is the Sharia, the code of law derived from the Qur'an and the Hadith…"

And on page 54, it states:

Bin Laden's Historical Opportunity

"Most Muslims prefer a peaceful and inclusive vision of their faith, not the violent sectarianism of Bin Laden. Among Arabs, Bin Laden's followers are commonly nicknamed *takfiri*, or 'those who define other Muslims as unbelievers,' because of their readiness to demonise and murder those with whom they disagree. Beyond the theology lies the simple human fact that most Muslims, like most other human beings, are repelled by mass murder and barbarism, whatever their justification.

---

[100] Index 76 https://jmvh.org/wp-content/uploads/2013/06/Definition-of-Terrorism.pdf

'All Americans must recognise that the face of terror is not the true face of Islam,' President Bush observed. 'Islam is a faith that brings comfort to a billion people around the world. It's a faith that has made brothers and sisters of every race. It's a faith based upon love, not hate.'

Yet as political, social, and economic problems created flammable societies, Bin Laden used Islam's most extreme, fundamentalist traditions as his match. All these elements—including religion—combined in an explosive compound."

On page 363, the report continues:

"Islam is not the enemy. It is not synonymous with terror. Nor does Islam teach terror. America and its friends oppose a perversion of Islam, not the great world faith itself. Lives guided by religious faith, including literal beliefs in Holy Scriptures, are common to every religion, and represent no threat to us."

On page 367, the commission gives its recommendation as follows:

"The U.S. government must identify and prioritise actual or potential terrorist sanctuaries. For each, it should have a realistic strategy to keep possible terrorists insecure and on the run, using all elements of national power. We should reach out, listen to, and work with other countries that can help."

Now, the devil is once again actively present and busy guiding his chosen players for the second part of the drama, which will soon be unveiled under the title *Enduring Freedom*—a thrilling action intended as a platform to destroy the Al Qaeda incubator in Afghanistan.

"When President Bush argued that the new war went beyond Bin Laden:

'Our war on terror begins with al Qaeda, but it does not end there,' he said. 'It will not end until every terrorist group of global reach has been found, stopped, and defeated.'

The President had a message for the Pentagon:

'The hour is coming when America will act, and you will make us proud.'

He also had a message for those outside the United States:

'This is civilisation's fight,' he said. 'We ask every nation to join us.'"

President Bush approved military plans to attack Afghanistan in meetings with Central Command's General Franks and other advisers on September 21 and October 2. Originally titled *Infinite Justice*, the operation's code name was changed—to avoid offending Muslims who associate the concept of infinite justice with God alone—to the operational name still used for missions in Afghanistan: *Enduring Freedom*. (Page 337)

The Commission Report Describes Afghanistan As Follows:

"Afghanistan was the incubator for al Qaeda and for the 9/11 attacks. In the autumn of 2001, the U.S.-led international coalition and its Afghan allies toppled the Taliban and ended the regime's protection of al Qaeda. Notable progress has been made. International cooperation has been strong, with a clear UN mandate and a NATO-led peacekeeping force (the International Security Assistance Force, or ISAF). More than 10,000 American soldiers are deployed today in Afghanistan, joined by soldiers from NATO allies and Muslim states. A central government has been established in Kabul, with a democratic constitution, new currency, and a new army." (Page 369)

When examining the influence of evil forces, it is important to assess the consequences of the invasions of Iraq and Afghanistan in order to ascertain the extent to which they accomplished their intended goals and to identify those who suffered humiliation as a result. The presence of Satan in these conflicts is evident, as he manipulates and perpetuates the ongoing turmoil according to his own agenda. A thorough examination of the Bible can provide further insight into this matter.

- God still grants Satan some authority in this world, which means that his power is not yet completely broken—except in one area: his power of death. *(Hebrews 2:14–15)*

- Since instigating evil on Earth, Satan has been called the "prince", "god", or "ruler" of this world. *(John 14:30; cf. John 12:31; 16:11; 2 Thessalonians 2:9–12)*. He is the enemy of God and truth, and he does everything he can to tempt individuals.

- He "leads the whole world astray" *(Revelation 12:9)*. Satan accomplishes this by various means, including appealing to man's pride *(1 Timothy 3:6; 1 Corinthians 4:6)* and interfering with the transmission of truth *(Matthew 13:18–22, 38–39)*.

Following the attack on the Twin Towers, the American ruling class veered off course and succumbed to a desperate desire for vengeance. Counsellors lost their ability to think rationally, and their extensive knowledge failed to provide wise guidance. They either disregarded the possibility of alternative actions that could benefit humanity in the long run or were hesitant to consider such alternatives.

In the initial stages, prior to the invasions of Afghanistan and Iraq, Secretary of Defence Donald Rumsfeld sought advice from his advisers on how to halt the ongoing proliferation of Islamist terrorism.

He asked:

12.3 Prevent The Continued Growth Of Islamist Terrorism

"……..Defence Secretary Donald Rumsfeld asked his advisers: Are we capturing, killing or deterring and dissuading more terrorists every day than the madrassas and the radical clerics are recruiting, training and deploying against us? Does the US need to fashion a broad, integrated plan to stop the next generation of terrorists? The US is putting relatively little effort into a long-range plan, but we are putting a great deal of effort into trying to stop terrorists. The cost-benefit ratio is against us! Our cost is billions against the terrorists' costs of millions."

These are the right questions. Our answer is that we need short-term action on a long-range strategy—one that invigorates our foreign policy with the attention that the President and Congress have given to the military and intelligence parts of the conflict against Islamist terrorism. *(Page 374)*

Defining The Threat

"It is further fed by grievances stressed by Bin Laden and widely felt throughout the Muslim world—against the U.S. military presence in the Middle East, policies perceived as anti-Arab and anti-Muslim, and support of Israel. Bin Laden and Islamist terrorists mean exactly what they say: to them America is the font of all evil, the 'head of the snake', and it must be converted or destroyed.

It is not a position with which Americans can bargain or negotiate. With it, there is no common ground—not even respect for life—on which to begin a dialogue. It can only be destroyed or utterly isolated.

Because the Muslim world has fallen behind the West politically, economically, and militarily for the past three centuries—and because few tolerant or secular Muslim democracies provide alternative models for the future—Bin Laden's message finds receptive ears. It has attracted active support from thousands of disaffected young Muslims and resonates powerfully with a far larger number who do not actively support his methods." *(Page 362, continued)*

In Afghanistan

Anger and revenge are prominent aspects of Satan's dominion tools, which become evident in the second part of the play. During this episode, the United States showcases its power, strength, and arrogance. However, it falls short in demonstrating the harmonious blend of wisdom, exceptional leadership, and compassion, as Satan impedes their ability to think in such a manner.

The actor of 9/11, Osama Bin Laden, and his followers' home, Afghanistan, was invaded in October 2001 to eradicate them from the face of the Earth, with the declaration:

"It can only be destroyed."

But in 20 years of military operations—spending more than $2 trillion (USD), as referenced by President Biden based on a recent study by Brown University, which includes interest on debt used to finance the war—success remains questionable. (That war was not against any country, but solely to destroy one person and his followers.)

The study found that the costs of the war (and future commitments) in Afghanistan from 2001 to 2022 amount to **$2.3 trillion**. The **UK** and **Germany**— who had the largest numbers of troops in Afghanistan after the US—spent an estimated **$30 billion** and **$19 billion**, respectively, over the course of the war.

Despite pulling out nearly all their troops, the **US and NATO** have promised a total of **$4 billion a year** until 2024 to fund Afghanistan's own forces, according to an audit report dated 3 September 2021, cited by the **BBC**.[101] The story does not end there. What about the human cost?

Since the hunt for Osama bin Laden and the destruction of his network began, the United States and its allies have suffered significant losses. There have been more than 3,500 coalition deaths, of which over 2,300 were US soldiers. UK troops have lost more than 450 personnel. A further 20,660 US soldiers have been injured in action. However, these casualty figures are dwarfed by the loss of life among Afghan security forces and civilians.

President Ghani stated in 2019 that more than 45,000 members of the Afghan security forces had been killed since he took office five years earlier. Research conducted by Brown University in 2019 estimated the total loss of life among Afghanistan's national military and police to be more than 64,100 since the war began in October 2001.

According to the United Nations Assistance Mission in Afghanistan (UNAMA), nearly 111,000 civilians have been killed or injured since it began systematically recording civilian casualties in 2009.[102]

In the end, the report concluded that the growth of domestic threats, combined with the spread of groups with affiliations or affinities to al-Qaeda and ISIL, and further destabilisation in Afghanistan, ensures that—despite two decades of consistent efforts to combat them since 9/11—attacks on the US, whatever form they take, remain a continuing concern.

"It's hard to look at the world today from the United States and feel any sense of safety, security or any kind of contentment," said Hoffman. "Unfortunately, I

---

[101] Index 77 https://www.bbc.co.uk/news/world-47391821
[102] Index 78 https://www.bbc.co.uk/news/world-47391821 Reality Check

think the sad truth and the irony is, we're less safe, given the multiplicity of threats to the United States today."

This is called the power of the devil.[103]

A Big Lie

Dominate Iraq War

Our nation saw evil,

The very worst of human nature.

"O children of Adam. Let not Shaitan deceive you"

يَا بَنِي آدَمَ لَا يَفْتِنَنَّكُمُ الشَّيْطَانُ كَمَا أَخْرَجَ أَبَوَيْكُم مِّنَ الْجَنَّةِ يَنزِعُ عَنْهُمَا لِبَاسَهُمَا لِيُرِيَهُمَا سَوْآتِهِمَا ۗ إِنَّهُ يَرَاكُمْ هُوَ وَقَبِيلُهُ مِنْ حَيْثُ لَا تَرَوْنَهُمْ ۗ إِنَّا جَعَلْنَا الشَّيَاطِينَ أَوْلِيَاءَ لِلَّذِينَ لَا يُؤْمِنُونَ

Children of Adam! Let not Shaitan (Satan) deceive you, as he got your parents [Adam and Hawwa (Eve)] out of Paradise, stripping them of their raiments, to show them their private parts. Verily, he and Qabiluhu (his soldiers from the jinns or his tribe) see you from where you cannot see them. Verily, We made the Shayatin (devils) Auliya' (protectors and helpers) for those who believe not.

— Quran 7:27, Surah Al-A'raf

Lying is part of the devil's character.

He said, "When he speaketh a lie, he speaketh of his own: for he is a liar, and the father of it."

— John 8:44

Lying is Satan's primary weapon against us all. He uses this tactic to confuse us, leave us hopeless, and twist God's Word. He wants us to doubt the goodness of God. The Bible says Satan's followers will end up being deceived — and deceiving others (2 Timothy 3:13).

Third Episode Of The Drama

"A Grand Deception"

Lucifer, having successfully orchestrated the second act of the theatrical spectacle, now takes centre stage to deliver a brief overview of the upcoming third act to the assembled cast. The title of this chapter is *"A GRAND DECEPTION,"* a complex narrative that intertwines with the tragic events of 9/11 and the subsequent commission report 10.3.

---

[103] Index 79   Source: al Jazeera

173

In this act, referred to as *"PHASE TWO,"* Lucifer aims to reveal the insidious methods he employs to seduce the minds of influential leaders, entangling them in the destructive grip of warfare.

This part of the commission report says:

10.3 "Phase Two" And The Question Of Iraq

"………Iraq had been an enemy of the United States for 11 years, and was the only place in the world where the United States was engaged in ongoing combat operations. As a former pilot, the President was struck by the apparent sophistication of the operation and some of the piloting, especially Hangout's high-speed dive into the Pentagon. He told us he recalled Iraqi support for Palestinian suicide terrorists as well. Speculating about other possible states that could be involved, the President told us he also thought about Iran."

— Page 334

On 20 September, President Bush met with British Prime Minister Tony Blair, and the two leaders discussed the global conflict ahead. When Blair asked about Iraq, the President replied that Iraq was not the immediate problem. Some members of his administration, he commented, had expressed a different view, but he was the one responsible for making the decisions.

— Page 336/585

At one point during the meeting, when Satan watches over them, he hatches a vicious conspiracy in their minds:

"This is your enemy's breeding ground. Destroy them."

Lucifer, known as Satan, derives pleasure from igniting flames. Having successfully caused destruction in Afghanistan, he now plans to embark on another deadly mission in the chosen territory of Iraq. His intention is to demonstrate to the Almighty God how he can oppress humanity by manipulating a group of proud and highly educated individuals from the elite class, whom he regards as tools.

The involvement of the British Government, led by Prime Minister Tony Blair, in Iraq is believed to be swayed by malevolent forces. These forces cloud the judgement of the vast majority of well-educated individuals who occupy positions of power in legislative bodies. Satan directs his "fiery darts" toward their hearts and minds, implanting false, sacrilegious, and malevolent thoughts about others. It fuels suspicion and an insatiable craving to indulge in sinful acts, all under the misguided notion that it is the path to achieving global harmony.

Faith is a defensive weapon that protects from Satan's fiery darts.

Faith serves as a protective shield, guarding us against the flaming arrows of Satan. If we fail to extinguish these arrows through faith, they have the power to

174

ignite a destructive fire within us, leading us astray from God's will. Since we cannot predict when Satan will launch his attacks, it is crucial that we consistently rely on faith and wield the shield of faith as our defence.

The question arises amidst the war in Iraq: was the conflict truly necessary? Can the tyrannical ruler of Iraq truly pose a threat to our safety, or is this villain capable of disrupting world peace?

We were informed of an imminent attack and urged not to passively hope for the best, but rather to eliminate this individual in order to safeguard our lives from the looming danger posed by the Iraqi regime. This grave concern has once again been validated on the floor of the Commons. Examining the dossier, it was stated that Iraq had the capability to deploy chemical or biological weapons within a mere 45 minutes of receiving the order. However, it's important to note that this claim pertained to battlefield weapons and not strategic ones with the capability to strike Cyprus.

On 5 February 2003, Colin Powell, the U.S. Secretary of State, delivered a significant speech to the United Nations. However, this speech turned out to be highly consequential and filled with misleading information. Despite being aware that the talking points provided to him were either misleading or outright false, Powell proceeded to present the United States' case for the invasion of Iraq, alleging the country's possession of weapons of mass destruction.

This speech marked a major stain on Powell's reputation, as he later referred to it as a *"blot"* on his record. Despite claiming to present "facts and conclusions based on solid intelligence," Powell knowingly deceived the UN by asserting that Iraq possessed biological weapons.[104]

The belief held by the US Secretary of State is subject to questioning, as no belief can negate the eventual judgement on the Day of Reckoning. Powell, being the highest-ranking official globally, knowingly delivered a speech before the highest court of the world, filled with statements lacking truth, solely to gain support from member states through deceit and temporary success. However, has he ever contemplated how Satan manipulated him for his own agenda, and pondered the potential consequences for him in this earthly realm and the Hereafter? *(Of course, if he believes in the Hereafter and is finally judged.)*

This is precisely what Satan aims to achieve with every individual. He relentlessly engages in the business of deceit and the destruction of humanity. His intent is not to set you free, but to hold you captive. He harbours no desire for you, your family, or your descendants to embrace a life following God.

---

[104] Index 80 Index 80 https://www.history.com/this-day-in-history/secretary-of-state-colin-powell-speaks-at-un-invasion-of-iraq

He wants you to doubt God and His goodness:

"He was a murderer from the beginning, not holding to the truth, for there is no truth in him.

When he lies, he speaks his native language, for he is a liar and the father of lies."[105]

Let's return to our previous discussion, which centres on an excerpt from Peter Oborne's book titled *Not the Chilcot Report*. Peter Oborne, the former chief political commentator of *The Daily Telegraph,* sheds light on Tony Blair's deceptive actions that led the UK into war.

According to Oborne, the defining catastrophe of the post-Cold War era occurred in 2003, when the invasion of Iraq triggered the disintegration of the Middle East's state system. In his book, Oborne meticulously examines how evidence was manipulated and laws were twisted in 2002 and 2003 to justify a war aimed at regime change. The government altered facts to align with its determination to participate in the US invasion; parliamentary scrutiny of the evidence fell short, the intelligence services were compromised, and the media succumbed to sensationalism.

In his book *The Rise of Political Lying,* he says:

"Tracing the history of political falsehood back to its earliest days, but focusing specifically on the exponential rise of the phenomenon during the Major and Blair governments, Peter Oborne demonstrates that the truth has become an increasingly slippery concept in recent years.

From woolly pronouncements that are designed merely to obfuscate to outright and blatant lies whose intention is to deceive, the political lie is never far from the surface. And its prevalence has led to a catastrophic decline in trust, at a time when people are more politicised than ever."[106]

On 19 March 2003, just after explosions began to rock Baghdad, Iraq's capital, U.S. President George W. Bush announced in a televised address:

"At this hour, American and coalition forces are in the early stages of military operations to disarm Iraq, to free its people and to defend the world from grave danger."

---

[105] Index 81 http://folcc.org/satan-is-a-liar-three-common-lies-he-tells-believers-and-how-to-overcome/
[106] Index 82 says Not-Chilcot-Report-Peter-Oborne/dp/1784977969 and
https://www.middleeasteye.net/big-story/howtony-blair-lied-parliament-fulfil-his-war-promise-bush

President Bush and his advisers constructed a significant portion of their argument for war based on the belief that Iraq, governed by Dictator Saddam Hussein, either possessed or was actively developing weapons of mass destruction.[107]

The word mentioned above is associated with evil. Neither G.W. Bush nor anyone of such status can consciously justify or declare such a harmful falsehood. At the time, they and their associates may have been influenced by negative forces and acted according to their own intentions.

In religious texts, the devil is depicted as a deceptive entity who deceives the entire world. Referred to as the Red Dragon, Satan, or Lucifer in the Bible, this being is described as a powerful, intelligent Jinn with multiple heads, horns, crowns, and a large tail capable of casting stars from the sky to the earth, along with his fallen angels (Revelation 12:9). It is alleged that this entity revealed its presence through fire and smoke when Flight 175 crashed into the south side of the Twin Towers. It is believed that, at that moment, it influenced the hearts, souls, and minds of the ruling party members, holding them captive until its objectives were fulfilled. Consequently, every word they uttered or thought they had is believed to have been influenced by Lucifer rather than originating from themselves.

Speculation arose from a speech given by George W. Bush on that fateful night, in which he stated: *"Today our nation saw evil, the very worst of human nature."* Some individuals interpreted this as evidence of Lucifer's presence.

The "Mission Accomplished"

This notion was reinforced when President Bush made a triumphant declaration on 1 May 2003 aboard the aircraft carrier *USS Abraham Lincoln*, stating that the mission in Iraq had been accomplished, marking the conclusion of significant combat operations. However, unbeknownst to George W. Bush, the source of this pride was not his own but rather the pride of Satan—Lucifer.

President Bush's announcement may be linked to the Project for the New American Century (PNAC), a contentious neoconservative think tank that promoted U.S. global dominance. Their views strongly influenced George W. Bush, particularly in shaping the decision to prioritise military intervention in Iraq and Afghanistan over diplomacy or waiting for conflicts to escalate. This, however, resulted in significant instability in the region, created a power vacuum, and contributed to the rise of extremist groups such as ISIS.

---

[107] Index 83 https://www.history.com/this-day-in-history/war-in-iraq-begins

Following the so-called successful completion of the mission, the devil assigned President Bush and his associates the responsibility of putting an end to the remaining skirmishes and killings in the country.[108]

The U.S. Lost The Iraq War

The article presented below was authored by Dr Daniel Larison, a prominent writer associated with *The American Conservative* (TAC), a reputable publication. Dr Larison's work has also been featured in renowned platforms such as *The New York Times Book Review*, *Dallas Morning News*, *World Politics Review*, and *Politico Magazine*.

He wrote:

This is just pitiful. Bush loyalists will believe whatever they want to believe, but their self-serving spin has to be rejected for what it is. The Iraq war may not have been "the worst foreign policy decision in U.S. history," as Will claimed, but it ranks among the four or five worst blunders in the annals of the United States. It was an unnecessary war, it had nothing to do with securing the U.S. or its allies, and it has manifestly made the region less stable and secure than it was before the invasion.

The U.S. paid an appalling price in thousands of lost lives, tens of thousands wounded, and trillions of dollars wasted on a fool's errand to "disarm" a government that had been disarmed years earlier. American soldiers were sacrificed year after year in the name of creating a democratic government in Iraq, only to usher in a sectarian, semi-authoritarian regime whose abusive misrule helped to create the current conflict. Along the way, millions of Iraqis were displaced internally or forced into exile, over a hundred thousand died, and most of the rest have been living in a failed state for more than ten years.

The U.S. lost that war by any reasonable measure, in that it threw away thousands of American lives and more than a hundred thousand Iraqi lives for the sake of creating a wrecked, impoverished country ruled by sectarian thugs. The "surge" served the purpose of allowing American politicians to pretend that this hadn't happened, in order to extricate American forces from the debacle sooner rather than later.

Daniel Bolger made a related point in his assessment of the failed wars in Iraq and Afghanistan:

"The surge in Iraq did not 'win' anything. It bought time. It allowed us to kill some more bad guys and feel better about ourselves. But in the end, shackled to a corrupt, sectarian government in Baghdad and hobbled by our fellow Americans' unwillingness to commit to a fight lasting decades, the surge just forestalled today's

---

[108] Index 84https://www.cfr.org/timeline/iraq-war

stalemate. To the extent that the 'surge' ever 'worked', it provided Americans with an excuse to leave the country that our government helped to ruin, and created just enough of an illusion of stability to permit walking away from the disaster that Bush and his allies caused."

Bush will never own up to his responsibility for this disaster, and apparently neither will many of his supporters. That is their failure. No one else has to share in it.

Maybe it would be "interesting" for Will to give a more complete accounting of when and how he came to be so disgusted with the Iraq war, but it would be even better if dead-ender Iraq war supporters such as Wehner stopped offering laughable apologies for the worst foreign policy failure of the last generation.[109]

Satan's Victory Celebration

The Legacy of Torture

In the Devilish Way

In Abu Ghraib:

This conflict does not belong to the United States; it belongs to the forces of evil. It is a war that originates from lies and thrives on lies. The authority of deception, Satan himself, is the only one capable of declaring the mission accomplished, and no one else. He has manipulated and triumphed over this war. Revealing his true nature, he severed his victory by converting your soldiers into his spirits and exploiting them for his own purposes.

Satan chose his dwelling place in Abu Ghraib prison, where the entire military system acted in a profoundly wicked manner. Major General Antonio M. Taguba's report, a fifty-three-page document not intended for public release, obtained by *The New Yorker*, portrayed the institutional failures of the Army prison system in a devastating manner. The report disclosed that between October and December of 2003, there were numerous instances of "sadistic, blatant, and wanton criminal abuses" at Abu Ghraib.[110]

"America is the friend of all Iraqi people." This is a sign of friendship when the Iraqis were humiliated in a way that is hard to describe. Horrific dehumanisation of Muslims, especially in the Arab world or in any culture, is unacceptable. Homosexual acts are against Islamic law, and it is insulting for men to be naked in front of other men, Bernard Haykel, a professor of Middle Eastern studies at New York University, explained. "Being put on top of each other and forced to

---

[109] Index 85 https://www.theamericanconservative.com/larison/the-u-s-lost-the-iraq-war
[110] Index 86 www.newyorker.com/magazine/2004/05/10/torture-at-abu-ghraib

masturbate, being naked in front of each other—it's all a form of torture," Haykel said.

The U.S. Official Finding Report was published in May 2004 under the title *Taguba Report on the Abuse of Prisoners in Abu Ghraib Prison*, and Major General Antonio Taguba conducted a formal military investigation into prison abuse. From Wikipedia, the free encyclopaedia.

Major General Antonio Taguba identified the so-called "bad apples" and prosecuted them to restore the dignity and value of the United States of America. Only 11 military personnel were convicted of their crimes, and all others, as per Taguba's findings, were described as very fresh and good apples, torturing the prisoners under the corporate contractors who were running the prison. President Bush responded, saying:

"Under the dictator, prisons like Abu Ghraib were symbols of death and torture. That same prison became a symbol of disgraceful conduct by a few American troops who dishonoured our country under the US. It is simply 'disgraceful conduct.'"

Taguba's report listed some of the wrongdoings:

- Breaking chemical lights and pouring the phosphoric liquid on detainees;
- Pouring cold water on naked detainees;
- Beating detainees with a broom handle and a chair;
- Threatening male detainees with rape;
- Allowing a military police guard to stitch the wound of a detainee who was injured after being slammed against the wall in his cell;
- Sodomising a detainee with a chemical light and perhaps a broomstick;
- Using military working dogs to frighten and intimidate detainees with threats of attack, and in one instance actually biting a detainee.[111]

Taguba added the discovery of extremely graphic photographic evidence. Photographs and videos taken by the soldiers as the abuses were happening were not included in his report, Taguba said, because of their "extremely sensitive nature."

The photographs—several of which were broadcast on CBS's 60 Minutes 2 show—depict naked Iraqi prisoners who are forced to assume humiliating poses. The photographs tell it all. In one, Private Lynndie England, a cigarette dangling from her mouth, is giving a jaunty thumbs-up sign and pointing at the genitals of a young Iraqi, who is naked except for a sandbag over his head, as he masturbates.

---

[111] Index 87 https://www.newyorker.com/magazine/2004/05/10/torture-at-abu-ghraib

Three other hooded and naked Iraqi prisoners are shown, hands reflexively crossed over their genitals. A fifth prisoner has his hands at his sides. In another, England stands arm in arm with Specialist Graner; both are grinning and giving the thumbs-up behind a cluster of perhaps seven naked Iraqis, knees bent, piled clumsily on top of each other in a pyramid. There is another photograph of a cluster of naked prisoners, again piled in a pyramid. Near them stands Graner, smiling, his arms crossed; a woman soldier stands in front of him, bending over, and she, too, is smiling. Then, there is another cluster of hooded bodies, with a female soldier standing in front, taking photographs. Yet another photograph shows a kneeling, naked, unhooded male prisoner, head momentarily turned away from the camera, posed to make it appear that he is performing oral sex on another male prisoner, who is naked and hooded.

The images are indelible: Groups of prisoners, naked except for hoods covering their heads, are piled on top of one another; soldiers grin and give thumbs-up to the camera; one holds a naked prisoner on a leash. In the most infamous photo, a hooded man balances on a cardboard box, arms outstretched, electrical wires attached to his hands.

All the identified officers are now facing prosecution in Iraq, on charges that include conspiracy, dereliction of duty, cruelty toward prisoners, maltreatment, assault, and indecent acts. A seventh suspect, Private Lynndie England, was reassigned to Fort Bragg, North Carolina, after becoming pregnant.[112]

The shared endeavour mentioned above is a commemoration of the triumph of darkness. The individuals currently residing within this confinement have been ensnared by malevolent entities, compelled to engage in wicked and abominable deeds as per their command. Lucifer possesses an intimate understanding of human psychology, adeptly manipulating their thoughts and actions to suit his own agenda. Although the Abu Ghraib prison was officially shuttered in 2014, its horrifying imprint continues to haunt the collective consciousness.

Conclusion:

The events of 9/11 are an exceptional and daunting challenge that surpasses the capabilities of any superpower. It represents a diabolical conflict that cannot be resolved through conventional methods, as the forces of evil have already infiltrated minds and are determined to exploit our power and resources, sowing discord among us. Upon closer examination of the intricate political and military actions

---

[112] Index 88 https://www.newyorker.com/magazine/2004/05/10/torture-at-abu-ghraib
https://truthout.org/articles/seeking-corporate-accountability-for-crimes-at-abu-ghraib/
https://www.aljazeera.com/opinions/2017/10/1/abu-ghraib-the-legacy-of-torture-in-the-war-on-terror
https://www.newyorker.com/magazine/2004/05/10/torture-at-abu-ghraib
https://www.newyorker.com/magazine/2004/05/10/torture-at-abu-ghraib

undertaken in the aftermath of 9/11, it becomes evident that, even after two decades of relentless efforts, the results remain futile.

However, Bin Laden is an individual and cannot be equated with a nation or an organisation. Even if he were to make a statement, it would not hold significant weight for the United States to consider it seriously. Rather than attempting to find a middle ground or a way to understand his intentions, they chose to stand resolute against Bin Laden. Pride, arrogance, and a desire for power clouded their judgment, preventing world leaders from considering alternative perspectives.[113]

In the Qur'an, where Allah (SWT) says:

اسْتَحْوَذَ عَلَيْهِمُ الشَّيْطَانُ فَأَنسَاهُمْ ذِكْرَ اللَّهِ ۚ أُولَٰئِكَ حِزْبُ الشَّيْطَانِ ۚ أَلَا إِنَّ حِزْبَ الشَّيْطَانِ هُمُ الْخَاسِرُونَ ¬

Shaitan (Satan) has overtaken them. So he has made them forget the remembrance of Allah. They are the party of Shaitan (Satan). Verily, it is the party of Shaitan (Satan) that will be the losers! (58:19, Surah Al-Mujadila)

The Bible has the same message in 2 Corinthians 4:4 (KJV), which says:

"In whom the god of this world hath blinded the minds of them which believe not, lest the light of the glorious gospel of Christ, who is the image of God, should shine unto them."

In Islam, it is strictly forbidden to kill, terrorise, or torture innocent people under any circumstances. Even in the face of attacks targeting Islam, specific rules are in place to ensure the protection of innocent individuals from suffering. If someone commits the crime of murder in the name of Islam, engages in mass killings through suicide, or terrorises innocent souls to establish their faith in Islam, such actions are unequivocally wrong and attributed to the influence of Satan.

The same message applies to other beliefs about refraining from killing innocent people.

In Surah An-Nisa, Allah (SWT) says in verse 76:

الَّذِينَ آمَنُوا يُقَاتِلُونَ فِي سَبِيلِ اللَّهِ ۖ وَالَّذِينَ كَفَرُوا يُقَاتِلُونَ فِي سَبِيلِ الطَّاغُوتِ فَقَاتِلُوا أَوْلِيَاءَ ¬
الشَّيْطَانِ ۖ إِنَّ كَيْدَ الشَّيْطَانِ كَانَ ضَعِيفًا

Those who believe, fight in the cause of Allah, and those who disbelieve, fight in the cause of Taghut (Satan, etc.). So fight you against the friends of Shaitan (Satan); ever feeble indeed is the plot of Shaitan (Satan). (4:76, Surah An-Nisa)

Ephesians 6:12 mentions that God said that Satan will always be the enemy of mankind. It follows that the people who are on Satan's side will be engaged in a

---

[113] Index 89 https://www.aljazeera.com/news/2004/5/25/iraqis-dismiss-bushs-abu-ghraib-plan

perpetual war with God's elect, and we are engaged in a very real battle between good and evil.

As ordinary individuals, we encounter grave calamities resulting from the interconnections between climate change, poverty, conflict, suffering, forest fires, volcanoes, earthquakes, floods, and landslides. Moreover, the additional burdens of human migration, refugee crises, and chronic youth depression exacerbate the misery we face, all of which are man-made. These forces are governed by a higher power, and no inhabitant of our planet can evade this truth unless we join together in pursuit of redemption and are guided by sincerity and a virtuous spirit.

The Devil's Diary is Full:

Arab Spring and the Crying of People

In 2011, a powerful wave of resistance emerged, as people worldwide united against a group of oppressive leaders who were controlling humanity under a regime known as the Iron Fist. This significant movement, referred to as "the Arab Spring," rapidly spread throughout the Middle East, aiming to overthrow their rulers. The protests against these leaders gained momentum, where individuals identified them as viruses and took to the streets, engaging in protests, demonstrations, and even armed revolts to remove them from power.

The oppressive rulers were warned by Satan that if they were to concede to the people's demands for just rights and a fair governance system, they would permanently lose their authority. Consequently, those leaders resolved to annihilate the rebellion by employing ruthless measures. The Arab Spring initially ignited in Tunisia and swiftly extended its influence to Egypt, Yemen, Bahrain, Libya, and Syria, spreading across these nations within a matter of weeks. Over time, the movement continued to gain traction, reaching countries such as Morocco, Algeria, Iraq, Lebanon, Iran, Jordan, Kuwait, Oman, and Sudan.

The following summary, based on Amnesty International's observations, highlights the outcomes of the movement against these oppressive satanic forces:

1. **Tunisia**: The Arab Spring originated in Tunisia, resulting in the removal of the long-standing oppressive ruler.

2. **Egypt**: Massive protests led to the resignation of the autocratic leader, bringing hope for a more just future.

3. **Yemen**: The uprising against the oppressive regime led to a prolonged conflict, causing immense suffering for the people.

4. **Bahrain**: Protests demanding democratic reforms faced violent suppression from the authorities, leading to ongoing unrest.

5. **Libya**: The movement against the oppressive ruler escalated into a full-scale armed conflict, resulting in significant instability and humanitarian crises.

6. **Syria**: The Syrian people's calls for change were met with brutal repression, leading to a devastating and protracted civil war.

The Arab Spring movement, driven by the desire for justice and freedom, had a profound impact on the region. While some nations witnessed notable progress and positive change, others endured prolonged conflicts and suffering, highlighting the complex and multifaceted nature of such transformative movements.[114]

Quranic guidance is totally ignored.

Genocide-like activities can be seen as a sinister manifestation of evil that has influenced the minds of numerous rulers throughout history. The term "genocide" refers to the act of deliberately killing a particular group of people. However, the question arises: who are the targets of this killing? Shockingly, it is often one's own people, driven by the destructive forces of racial and religious divisions. Regardless of how our lawmakers define genocide or the extent of killings according to the law, it is evident that the laws of our society cannot fully prevent mass killings.

Such atrocities have occurred in the past, continue to happen in the present, and unfortunately, are likely to recur in the future. This is because those responsible for perpetrating such heinous acts are not truly human; they embody a malevolent force controlled by the influence of Satan, akin to dangerous and infectious viruses.

From a Religious Perspective:

What does the Hebrew Bible say?

"The earth was corrupt in God's sight, and the earth was filled with violence."

Genesis 49:5-7 (KJV)

5 Simeon and Levi are brethren; instruments of cruelty are in their habitations.

6 O my soul, come not thou into their secret; unto their assembly, mine honour, be not thou united: for in their anger they slew a man, and in their selfwill they digged down a wall.

7 Cursed be their anger, for it was fierce; and their wrath, for it was cruel: I will divide them in Jacob, and scatter them in Israel.[115]

In the Qur'an, it says:

إِنَّمَا الْمُؤْمِنُونَ إِخْوَةٌ فَأَصْلِحُوا بَيْنَ أَخَوَيْكُمْ ۚ وَاتَّقُوا اللَّهَ لَعَلَّكُمْ تُرْحَمُونَ ¬

---

[114] Index 90https://www.amnesty.org/en/latest/campaigns/2016/01/arab-spring-five-years-on/
[115] https://www.biblegateway.com/

¬ *The believers are nothing else than brothers (in the Islamic religion). So make reconciliation between your brothers, and fear Allah, that you may receive mercy.* (49:10, Surah Al-Hujurat)

In another verse, mentioned below, Muslims need to emphasise and explain more broadly when considering resolving any major contentious issue among believers. The verse says:

$$\text{وَإِن طَائِفَتَانِ مِنَ الْمُؤْمِنِينَ اقْتَتَلُوا فَأَصْلِحُوا بَيْنَهُمَا ۖ فَإِن بَغَتْ إِحْدَاهُمَا عَلَى الْأُخْرَىٰ فَقَاتِلُوا الَّتِي تَبْغِي حَتَّىٰ تَفِيءَ إِلَىٰ أَمْرِ اللَّهِ ۚ فَإِن فَاءَتْ فَأَصْلِحُوا بَيْنَهُمَا بِالْعَدْلِ وَأَقْسِطُوا ۖ إِنَّ اللَّهَ يُحِبُّ الْمُقْسِطِينَ} ¬$$

¬ *And if two parties or groups among the believers fall to fighting, then make peace between them both. But if one of them rebels against the other, then fight against the one that rebels until it complies with the command of Allah; then if it complies, make reconciliation between them justly, and be equitable. Verily! Allah loves those who are equitable.* (49:9, Surah Al-Hujurat)

Then Allah (SWT) states:

$$\text{وَلَا تُصَعِّرْ خَدَّكَ لِلنَّاسِ وَلَا تَمْشِ فِي الْأَرْضِ مَرَحًا ۖ إِنَّ اللَّهَ لَا يُحِبُّ كُلَّ مُخْتَالٍ فَخُورٍ} ¬$$

¬ *"And turn not your face away from men with pride, nor walk in insolence through the earth. Verily, Allah does not like each arrogant boaster."* (31:18, Surah Luqman)

However, Satan actively opposes the idea of obeying Allah's (SWT) command to peacefully resolve disputes, whether they occur within our own homes, among individuals, political parties, or even between nations. His influence extends to all levels of conflict, and he manipulates people into pursuing his agenda. One of his primary objectives is to instigate violence and cause harm through human actions. It is important to note that Muslims are not exempt from falling victim to his conspiracy. Satan works diligently to erase from their minds the guidance provided by Allah (SWT) on how to handle such challenges.

His tactics involve deliberately sparking controversies and manipulating individuals to the point where matters become so convoluted that they may result in acts of revenge, ultimately culminating in a verdict where both sides of the disputes suffer defeat, while he emerges victorious in the case.

Satan is Victorious

1. Muslim vs Muslim

Game of Satan

Here we see that those who killed people were all Muslims, and they killed thousands of Muslim worshippers and Muslim security forces in the name of reforming Islam.

185

On 9 January 1980, 63 rebels were publicly beheaded in the squares of eight Saudi cities (Buraidah, Dammam, Mecca, Medina, Riyadh, Abha, Ha'il, and Tabuk). According to Sandra Mackey, the locations "were carefully chosen not only to give maximum exposure but also to reach other potential nests of discontent."[116]

Al-Masjid Al-Haram in Mecca was attacked on November 20, 1979, by Islamic militants, on the first day of the month of Muharram in the Islamic year 1400. The mosque was seized by an armed group, which killed hundreds of worshippers and took others hostage with the intention of overthrowing the House of Saud. One of the extremist insurgents announced that the Mahdi (the redeemer of Islam) had arrived and was among them — their leader, Mohammed Abdullah al-Qahtani. This sinful seizure of Allah's House shocked every Muslim on Earth. It took two weeks to flush out the militants and restore the mosque's normal function, costing the lives of hundreds of militants, worshippers, and security forces.

This attack was orchestrated by Juhayman al-Qahtani, one of the prominent members of Najd, and his brother-in-law, Mohammed Abdullah al-Qahtani, whom they declared to be the Mahdi. They proclaimed that the Day of Judgment was near. To justify their actions, they carefully chose Mohammed Abdullah al-Qahtani as the Mahdi. The date of the seizure was strategically set for November 20, 1979, which marked the first day of the Islamic calendar year, 1400. According to hadith, this is the day the reformer (mujaddid) of Islam would appear physically on Earth.

It ended as follows: Al-Qahtani was killed during the recapture of the mosque, but Juhayman and 67 of his fellow rebels survived the assault and were captured. "All the surviving males" were tried in secret. They were not shown leniency. The king secured a fatwa from the Council of Senior Scholars, which found the defendants guilty of seven crimes: violating the sanctity of the Masjid al-Haram (the Grand Mosque); violating the sanctity of the month of Muharram; killing fellow Muslims; disobeying legitimate authorities; suspending prayer at the Masjid al-Haram; erring in identifying the Mahdi; and exploiting the innocent for criminal acts.[117]

2. Pakistan: Muslims Are All Brothers

Now, let's see how a Muslim country became engaged in killing among itself. Pakistan is a great Muslim country, which consists of two parts: East and West Pakistan. Since its creation, with its capital in West Pakistan, East Pakistan was dominated and suppressed by West Pakistan. From the very beginning, the West conspired against East Pakistan in every possible way and enforced unjust laws

---

[116] Index 91 https://military.wikia.org/wiki/Grand_Mosque_seizure
[117] Index 92 https://military.wikia.org/wiki/Grand_Mosque_seizure

upon it. The East was extremely dissatisfied and angry at the behaviour of West Pakistani politicians and government policymakers.

Both parts of the country's population are 95% Muslim in principle, and according to the teachings of the Qur'an and Sunnah, the ruling leaders should treat the citizens of both parts of the country equally. But in reality, what we have seen is that three million East Pakistani Muslim brothers were killed to quell their anger, and the Muslim citizens of East Pakistan were taught how to deal with their (then) older brothers.

On 13 June 1971, an article in the UK's *Sunday Times* exposed the brutality of Pakistan's suppression of the Bangladeshi uprising. Written by Anthony Mascarenhas, a Pakistani reporter, and printed in the *Sunday Times*, it exposed for the first time the scale of the Pakistan Army's brutal campaign to suppress its breakaway eastern province in 1971.

Nobody knows exactly how many people were killed, but certainly, a huge number of people lost their lives. Independent researchers think that between 300,000 and 500,000 died, while the Bangladesh government puts the figure at three million.

Satan dictated the leaders who unanimously committed the sin and evil decision to kill their East Pakistani Muslim brothers. He entered their minds and blocked their morality, humanity, Islamic teachings, and the teachings of their parents.

If those Muslim leaders had had strong faith, belief, and pure hearts, their decision would have been different. Today, we might read a different story of Pakistan, where both parties could have moved forward with more strength and success. But, in the end, who won in that game?

The simple answer is **Satan**.

Because they lost East Pakistan, which is now Bangladesh, they also hanged one of their own prominent leaders. Thousands of their soldiers surrendered to the enemy state.

All the people who were involved in architecting and operating this genocide are individual losers, because they were all Muslims by faith, and therefore, they are individually accountable to justify their actions on Judgment Day.

3. World War II

Satan played a major role in the Second World War, the deadliest military conflict in modern history. An estimated total of 70–85 million people perished, which was about 3% of the world population in 1940 (estimated at 2.3 billion). He (Satan) sowed satanic seeds when drafting the terms of the Treaty of Versailles, which became the root cause of World War II, following the First World War that ended in 1918. The deal was nothing more than a breeding ground for the devil's virus, which captured the minds of a few world leaders at the time.

They did not leave any room to consider peace in the future, to defuse the anger (temporary insanity) caused by this agreement. According to Michael Newberg, Professor of History at the U.S. Army War College and author of *The Treaty of Versailles: A Concise History* (2017), he says:

"I'm not one of those people who believes the treaty made the Second World War inevitable, but I think you could argue that it made Europe a less stable place."[118]

Here, we must open the Book of the Almighty and find out what instructions we have been given, without following the methods of practice.

يَا أَيُّهَا الَّذِينَ آمَنُوا كُونُوا قَوَّامِينَ لِلَّهِ شُهَدَاءَ بِالْقِسْطِ ۖ وَلَا يَجْرِمَنَّكُمْ شَنَآنُ قَوْمٍ عَلَىٰ أَلَّا تَعْدِلُوا ۚ اعْدِلُوا هُوَ أَقْرَبُ لِلتَّقْوَىٰ ۖ وَاتَّقُوا اللَّهَ ۚ إِنَّ اللَّهَ خَبِيرٌ بِمَا تَعْمَلُونَ

You who believe! Stand out firmly for Allah and be just witnesses, and let not the enmity and hatred of others make you avoid justice. Be just: that is nearer to piety, and fear Allah. Verily, Allah is Well-Acquainted with what you do. (5/8 Al-Maidah)

And in the Holy Book of all other believers, God says:

And in that day, I will make a covenant for them with the beasts of the field, and with the fowls of heaven, and with the creeping things of the ground. And I will break the bow and the sword and the battle out of the earth, and will make them lie down safely. (Hosea 2:18)

And I will cut off the chariot from Ephraim, and the horse from Jerusalem, and the battle bow shall be cut off. And he shall speak peace unto the heathen, and his dominion shall be from sea even to sea, and from the river even to the ends of the earth. (Zechariah 9:10)

4. The Ugly Conflict: Bosnia

Look at the ugly conflict in Bosnia. We can see that a few people were personally responsible for killing around 8,000 Muslims in the Srebrenica massacre in 1995. Historians have compared this massacre to the horrors of World War II.

Muslims were banned from conducting their religious activities, and all Muslim institutions, Islamic schools, and Dervish religious practices were abolished. *(Note: Islam does not believe in such forms of Dervish worship.)* "Dervish" refers to Sufi Whirling Dervishes. Sufism, the mystical branch of Islam, emphasises universal love and peace.

---

[118] Index 93 https://www.history.com/news/treaty-of-versailles-world-war-ii-german-guilt-effects

Satan was obsessed with the human virus and began to ruthlessly kill ordinary innocent people at the behest of his superiors. However, in the end, we can conclude that Satan was the winner. Milosevic and Radovan Karadžić, along with their allies, were charged with genocide and crimes against humanity.

Mr Milosevic died in prison in 2006, and Mr Karadžić was sentenced to 40 years in prison. When the decision was appealed in 1999, a UN Tribunal extended his sentence to life in prison.[119]

5. Sudanese Civil War

The Sudanese Civil War was man-made, orchestrated by Satan, and made so complicated that Allah (SWT) eventually rained down His wrath upon them. Satan celebrates human misery, but the whole world is stunned by its horrible consequences.

If they had followed the guidance of the Qur'an, they would have eventually found the path to the middle ground, but Satan would never allow them to follow that path.

The civil war in Sudan was reignited in 1983 when the military regime tried to impose Sharia Law as part of its overall policy to "Islamicise" all of Sudan, ignoring the opinions of Christians.

The background of the Sudan conflict turned into a civil war that began in 1955, due to political and economic grievances between the predominantly Arab Muslim north and the predominantly African Christian and animist south. However, later, the Islamic government of Khartoum publicly admitted that there was no possibility of ending the war militarily.

In the face of such genocide, what have they accomplished? They have acquired a burden of "guilt" and fostered hatred within their community, making them accountable to Allah on the Day of Judgment. Now, let us examine the repercussions of the civil war:

"1.9 Million Dead from Sudan's Civil War; More Than 70,000 Estimated Deaths in 1998, Report"

This is the headline of the U.S. Committee for Refugees, originally published on 10 December 1998, which says:

---

[119] Index 94 https://www.britannica.com/biography/Biljana-Plavsic
https://www.britannica.com/biography/Biljana-Plavsic
https://www.independent.co.uk/news/world/europe/karadzic-and-the-largest-mass-murder-in-europe-since-wwii-874039.html
https://www.britannica.com/place/Banja-Luka
https://www.theatlantic.com/photo/2012/04/20-years-since-the-bosnian-war/100278/

It is believed that at least one out of every five southern Sudanese has died because of the 15-year civil war, and more than 80 percent of southern Sudan's estimated 5 million population have been displaced at some point since 1983. Some 4 million Sudanese are internally displaced—more than any other country on earth—and nearly 350,000 are refugees in six neighbouring countries. The death toll is much harder to quantify accurately due to many reasons, but the U.S. Committee for Refugees' 1993 study includes estimates of war-related deaths in central Sudan's remote Nuba Mountain area, where more than 100,000 to 200,000 people are believed to have perished because of the conflict.[120]

A 'silent' famine spreads death in South Sudan, causing widespread death. As international aid workers reached Irol, situated across the Nile from Bor, a heartbreaking scene unfolded before them. Thirty individuals lay motionless in the town, while the remaining women, children, and elderly struggled to survive, their emaciated bodies a haunting reflection of the imminent threat of starvation.

"They've been in the bush, just eating the leaves from the trees mainly,"

The emerging dimension of the misery in southern Sudan has prompted U.S. officials to call it the world's "most silent" famine, a looming crisis, according to an international agency.

"Southern Sudan has become one of the world's darkest humanitarian nightmares,"

While numerous emergency relief agencies, such as the UN's food arm, work tirelessly to prevent and protect humanity, it is unfortunate that there are also certain disguised organisations that perpetuate conflict and suffering, ultimately benefiting from such situations. In the following verses, Allah (SWT) reiterates the message to all of humanity, emphasising its universality rather than being specific to any particular believer community.

In the Qur'an, Allah (SWT) tells us:

مِنْ أَجْلِ ذَٰلِكَ كَتَبْنَا عَلَىٰ بَنِي إِسْرَائِيلَ أَنَّهُ مَن قَتَلَ نَفْسًا بِغَيْرِ نَفْسٍ أَوْ فَسَادٍ فِي الْأَرْضِ فَكَأَنَّمَا قَتَلَ النَّاسَ جَمِيعًا وَمَنْ أَحْيَاهَا فَكَأَنَّمَا أَحْيَا النَّاسَ جَمِيعًا ۚ وَلَقَدْ جَاءَتْهُمْ رُسُلُنَا بِالْبَيِّنَاتِ ثُمَّ إِنَّ كَثِيرًا مِّنْهُم بَعْدَ ذَٰلِكَ فِي الْأَرْضِ لَمُسْرِفُونَ

And do not kill anyone which Allah has forbidden, except for a just cause. And whoever is killed (intentionally with hostility and oppression, and not by mistake), We have given his heir the authority (to demand Qisas, Law of Equality in punishment, or to forgive, or to take Diya [blood money]). But let him not exceed

---

[120] Index 96 https://reliefweb.int/report/sudan/19-million-dead-sudans-civil-war-more-70000-deaths-1998-report-estimates Source US Committee for Refugees and Immigrants

limits in the matter of taking life (i.e., he should not kill except the killer only). Verily, he is helped [by the Islamic law]. 17/33 Surah Al-Isra

Because of that, We ordained for the Children of Israel that if anyone killed a person not in retaliation of murder, or to spread mischief in the land – it would be as if he killed all mankind, and if anyone saved a life, it would be as if he saved the life of all mankind. And indeed, there came to them Our Messengers with clear proofs, evidences, and signs, even then after that many of them continued to exceed the limits (e.g. by doing oppression unjustly and exceeding beyond the limits set by Allah by committing major sins) in the land! 5/32 Surah Al-Maidah

The Bible Also Says:

- **Isaiah 58:10 (KJV)** "And if thou draw out thy soul to the hungry, and satisfy the afflicted soul; then shall thy light rise in obscurity, and thy darkness be as the noonday."

- **Matthew 14:16 (KJV)** "But Jesus said unto them, They need not depart; give ye them to eat."

- **Romans 12:20 (KJV)** "Therefore if thine enemy hunger, feed him; if he thirst, give him drink."

In Islamic teachings, Allah SWT grants permission to engage in warfare when certain conditions arise, including widespread unrest, oppression, a lack of justice, and a decline in faith in Allah. During such circumstances, the struggle may continue until the divine law of Allah is reinstated, which is confirmed in the verse where Allah SWT says:

وَقَاتِلُوهُمْ حَتَّىٰ لَا تَكُونَ فِتْنَةٌ وَيَكُونَ الدِّينُ لِلَّهِ ۖ فَإِنِ انتَهَوْا فَلَا عُدْوَانَ إِلَّا عَلَى الظَّالِمِينَ

And fight them until there is no more Fitnah (disbelief and worshipping of others along with Allah) and (all and every kind of) worship is for Allah (Alone). But if they cease, let there be no transgression except against Az-Zalimun (the polytheists, and wrong-doers, etc.). 2/193

This verse is self-evident in its recognition of inherent dignity for all human beings without qualification of any kind.

The Qur'an commentator, Shihab al-Din al-Alusi, an Arabic scholar of Baghdad, Iraq, who died in 1854 and was best known for writing *Ruh Al-Ma'ani*, a Tafsir of the Qur'an, wrote that:

"Everyone and all members of the human race, including the pious and the sinner, are endowed with dignity, nobility, and honour, which cannot be made exclusive to any particular group or class of people."

Let me recount a heart-wrenching incident that unfolded during the war and famine in Sudan in 1993—an event that left a profound mark on the world's

191

conscience. Kevin Carter, a South African photojournalist, captured a haunting photograph that would echo through history. In the image, a frail child is seen crawling toward a United Nations food camp, approximately one kilometer away, while a vulture lurks ominously in the background, waiting. Tragically, Carter took the photograph but left without ensuring the child's safety.

Three months later, overwhelmed by depression and haunted by the gravity of his experiences, Carter took his own life. In an interview prior to his death, when asked what he had done after capturing the image, it became clear that he was tormented by guilt—perhaps realizing the heavy moral burden of documenting suffering without intervening.

Although the photograph succeeded in drawing global attention to the humanitarian crisis ravaging Sudan, Carter faced sharp criticism. Many accused him of exploiting the child's suffering for personal gain, with some going as far as calling him the "real vulture" in hateful letters. While some photojournalists might have dismissed such backlash, Carter internalized the condemnation deeply, fueling his anguish and self-doubt.

Upon returning from New York, Carter wrote: "Depressed... without a phone... rent money... child support money... loan money... money!!! ... Vivid memories of murder and corpses, anger and pain haunt me... hungry or injured children, murderers, often police, murderous executioners..." The weight of these memories became unbearable, culminating in his tragic suicide.

In his final note—a desperate, fragmented attempt at autobiography, confession, and explanation—Carter poured out his nightmares and dark visions. His diary contained a moving prayer that reads:

"Dear God, I promise I will never waste my food, no matter how bad it may taste or how full I may be. I pray that He will protect this little boy, guide him, and deliver him from his misery. I pray that we will become more sensitive to the suffering around us and not be blinded by our own selfish nature and interests."

Killing Is Not A Solution

Killing has no end. Our modern civilisation cannot stop killing. The Devil came along with us on this earth with the agenda from the Almighty to destroy us using His mighty power. He will come to you and corrupt and control your brain. On one occasion, the great Communist leader of China, Chairman Mao, said:

"Killing became the mark of a true revolutionary. The more ferocious the better. Don't you think? The more people you kill, the more revolutionary you are."

The act of taking lives is a tool employed by malevolent forces to enforce ideological theories or political strategies. Engaging in mass extermination, whether targeting entire populations or specific groups based on ethnicity, religion, or other affiliations, fails to contribute any genuine value to humanity, leadership, or the preservation of dignity and honour passed down through generations.

Satan Knows The Strategy

This malevolent strategy is known to Satan, who understands that once killing is set in motion, absolute control falls into its hands, rendering earthly powers powerless to intervene. Peace negotiations and similar endeavours prove ineffective in the face of this malevolence, as it continually introduces new, unimaginable means to perpetuate sinful atrocities and sacrifice countless lives in pursuit of its leaders' agenda. [121]

Allah (SWT) says:

ظَهَرَ الْفَسَادُ فِي الْبَرِّ وَالْبَحْرِ بِمَا كَسَبَتْ أَيْدِي النَّاسِ لِيُذِيقَهُم بَعْضَ الَّذِي عَمِلُوا لَعَلَّهُمْ يَرْجِعُونَ ¬

---

[121] https://www.soundvision.com/article/does-god-really-command-muslims-to-kill-non-muslims
97https://www.justice.gov/sites/default/files/eoir/legacy/2013/11/07/ISSUES_PAPER_CHRONO LOGY-OF-EVENTS-APRIL-1993-APRIL-1995.pdf)

وَمِنَ النَّاسِ مَن يُعْجِبُكَ قَوْلُهُ فِي الْحَيَاةِ الدُّنْيَا وَيُشْهِدُ اللَّهَ عَلَىٰ مَا فِي قَلْبِهِ وَهُوَ أَلَدُّ الْخِصَامِ ۔

وَإِذَا تَوَلَّىٰ سَعَىٰ فِي الْأَرْضِ لِيُفْسِدَ فِيهَا وَيُهْلِكَ الْحَرْثَ وَالنَّسْلَ ۚ وَاللَّهُ لَا يُحِبُّ الْفَسَادَ ۔

Evil (sins and disobedience of Allah, etc.) has appeared on land and sea because of what the hands of men have earned (by oppression and evil deeds, etc.), that Allah may make them taste a part of that which they have done, in order that they may return (by repenting to Allah, and begging His Pardon). — 30/41 Surah ar-Rum

And of mankind, there is he whose speech may please you (O Muhammad ﷺ), in this worldly life, and he calls Allah to witness as to that which is in his heart, yet he is the most quarrelsome of the opponents. — 2/204 Surah al-Baqarah

And when he turns away (from you "O Muhammad ﷺ"), his effort in the land is to make mischief therein and to destroy the crops and the cattle, and Allah likes not mischief. — 2/205 Surah al-Baqarah

Satan Builds His Own Sect

Same-sex marriage is a matter of civil law, not religious doctrine. It means they disregard verses of the Qur'an and the Bible, indicating a rejection of the teachings of religion. From a religious perspective, some believe that Satan has significant influence over same-sex marriage, popularising this marriage and legalising it as civil law worldwide, despite strong opposition from Christian and Muslim clerics.

The decision to legalise same-sex marriage is made by governments and lawmakers, and it does not necessarily imply a disregard for religious doctrine or beliefs. Satan encourages you to accept same-sex marriage. In the United States, marriage is a legal institution that is governed by secular laws and regulations, which means that religious institutions are not required to perform or recognise same-sex marriages if it goes against their beliefs. However, many people and organisations believe that denying same-sex couples the right to marry is a form of discrimination and a violation of the basic human rights of LGBTQ+ individuals, including the right to marry.

Many liberal and progressive branches of Christianity, Judaism, and Buddhism now allow and perform same-sex marriages. The United Church of Christ, for instance, has been performing same-sex marriages since 2005 by virtue of the Civil Partnership Act 2004, and the Episcopal Church, the Presbyterian Church (USA), and the Evangelical Lutheran Church in America are among the other Christian denominations that have also embraced marriage equality.

"Marriage is the bedrock of our society, and now, irrespective of sexuality, everyone in British society can make that commitment," said the UK Women and Equalities Minister. "It is a wonderful achievement, and whilst this legislation may be about marriage, its impact is so much wider. Making marriage available to all couples demonstrates our society's respect for all individuals, regardless of their sexuality. It demonstrates the importance we attach to being able to live freely. It says so much about the society that we are and the society that we want to live in. This is a historic moment that will resonate in many people's lives. I am proud that we have made it happen, and I look forward to the first same-sex wedding by next summer."[122]

In 2011, the United Nations Human Rights Council passed its first resolution recognising LGBT rights, after which the Office of the United Nations High Commissioner for Human Rights issued a report documenting violations of the rights of LGBT people, including hate crimes, criminalisation of homosexual activity, and discrimination. Following the issuance of the report, the United Nations urged all countries that had not yet done so to enact laws protecting basic LGBT rights.[123]

Moreover, the question of whether same-sex marriage is a sin or not is a matter of interpretation and belief within each religious tradition. There are many people of faith who believe that love is love and that same-sex relationships can be holy and blessed. Ultimately, whether or not to recognise same-sex marriage is a matter of civil law and personal beliefs, and it is up to each individual and community to decide what is right for them. It is important to respect the diversity of religious beliefs and to work towards creating a society that values equality, dignity, and compassion for all.

By contrast, many countries effectively impose the death penalty on consensual same-sex sexual acts. For example, Iran, Saudi Arabia, Yemen, Afghanistan, Pakistan, Qatar, the United Arab Emirates, Iraq, and a few other countries.

Ultimately, whether or not an individual or group chooses to believe in a religion and follow its teachings is a personal choice, and it is not for others to command or judge. Therefore, the legal recognition by a nation of same-sex marriage has no bearing on one's beliefs or choices.

This is a sin and absolute Satan's victory.

God Warns The Children Of Adam

Allah (SWT) says in the Qur'an:

1. وَلُوطًا إِذْ قَالَ لِقَوْمِهِ أَتَأْتُونَ الْفَاحِشَةَ مَا سَبَقَكُم بِهَا مِنْ أَحَدٍ مِّنَ الْعَالَمِينَ

---

[122] Index 98 https://www.gov.uk/government/news/same-sex-marriage-becomes-law#
[123] Index 99 https://en.wikipedia.org/wiki/LGBT_rights_by_country_or_territory

"And (remember) Lout (Lot), when he said to his people: 'Do you commit the worst sin such as none preceding you has committed in the 'Alamin (mankind and jinn)?'" (7:80 Surah Al-A'raf)

أَئِنَّكُمْ لَتَأْتُونَ الرِّجَالَ شَهْوَةً مِّن دُونِ النِّسَاءِ ۚ بَلْ أَنتُمْ قَوْمٌ تَجْهَلُونَ .2

"Do you approach men in your lusts rather than women? Nay, but you are a people who behave senselessly." (27:55 Surah An-Naml)

وَلَمَّا جَاءَتْ رُسُلُنَا لُوطًا سِيءَ بِهِمْ وَضَاقَ بِهِمْ ذَرْعًا وَقَالَ هَٰذَا يَوْمٌ عَصِيبٌ .3

"And when Our Messengers came to Lout (Lot), he was grieved on their account and felt himself straitened for them (lest the town people should approach them to commit sodomy with them). He said: 'This is a distressful day.'" (11:77 Surah Hud)

(NOTE: Lot was powerless to protect the young boys, but they revealed to him that they were indeed Angels sent by Allah (SWT) to punish the people for their transgressions.)

Same-Sex Marriage and Torah

1. **Exodus 20:13-15 (KJV) says:**

   13 Thou shalt not kill.

   14 Thou shalt not commit adultery.

   15 Thou shalt not steal.

So, Moses asked the angels whether there was jealousy among them and whether the Evil tempter was among them.

2. **Chapters 18 and 20 of Leviticus form part of the Holiness Code:**

   Leviticus 20:13 (KJV)

   If a man also lie with mankind, as he lieth with a woman, both of them have committed an abomination: they shall surely be put to death; their blood shall be upon them.

3. **Leviticus 18:22 (KJV)**

   "Thou shalt not lie with mankind, as with womankind: it is abomination..."

4. **Romans 1:26-27 (KJV)**

   26 For this cause God gave them up unto vile affections: for even their women did change the natural use into that which is against nature:

   27 And likewise also the men, leaving the natural use of the woman, burned in their lust one toward another; men with men working that which is

unseemly, and receiving in themselves that recompence of their error which was meet.

5. **Genesis 1:27-28 (KJV):**

27 So God created man in his own image, in the image of God created he him; male and female created he them.

28 And God blessed them, and God said unto them, Be fruitful, and multiply, and replenish the earth, and subdue it: and have dominion over the fish of the sea, and over the fowl of the air, and over every living thing that moveth upon the earth.

6. **Matthew 19:4-6 (KJV)**

4 And he answered and said unto them, Have ye not read, that he which made them at the beginning made them male and female,

5 And said, For this cause shall a man leave father and mother, and shall cleave to his wife: and they twain shall be one flesh? wherefore they are no more twain, but one flesh.

6 Wherefore what therefore God hath joined together, let not man put asunder.

7. **Jude 7 (KJV)**

" Even as Sodom and Gomorrha, and the cities about them in like manner, giving themselves over to fornication, and going after strange flesh, are set forth for an example, suffering the vengeance of eternal fire."[124]

8. **1 Corinthians 6:9-10 (KJV)**

9 Know ye not that the unrighteous shall not inherit the kingdom of God? Be not deceived: neither fornicators, nor idolaters, nor adulterers, nor effeminate, nor abusers of themselves with mankind,

10 Nor thieves, nor covetous, nor drunkards, nor revilers, nor extortioners, shall inherit the kingdom of God.

Genesis 18:32 Says:

When Abraham learned of God's plan to destroy the cities of Sodom and Gomorrah, he asked God if He would spare them if He could find fifty innocent, godly people. God reassured Abraham that if He found fifty righteous people, He would spare the city for their sake. Abraham then asked about progressively smaller numbers, down to ten people, as God answered.

---

[124] Index 100 https://www.gospelherald.com/articles/56293/20150629/top-bible-verses-about-homosexuality-used-in-gay-marriage-debate.htm?

For a similar account, following the verses of the Holy Qur'an revealed in the time of Prophet Abraham (peace be upon him), it is written:

يَا إِبْرَاهِيمُ أَعْرِضْ عَنْ هَذَا إِنَّهُ قَدْ جَاءَ أَمْرُ رَبِّكَ وَإِنَّهُمْ آتِيهِمْ عَذَابٌ غَيْرُ مَرْدُودٍ

فَلَمَّا جَاءَ أَمْرُنَا جَعَلْنَا عَالِيَهَا سَافِلَهَا وَأَمْطَرْنَا عَلَيْهَا حِجَارَةً مِّن سِجِّيلٍ مَّنضُودٍ

Translation:

"O Ibrahim (Abraham)! Forsake this. Indeed, the Commandment of your Lord has gone forth. Verily, there will come a torment for them which cannot be turned back." (11:76, Surah Hud)

"The People of Lut and the city which was turned upside down: 'When Our Decree was issued, We turned (the cities) upside down, and rained down on them brimstones, hard as baked clay, spread, layer on layer.'" (11:82, Surah Hud)

The statement "turning (the cities) upside down" implies that the region was totally destroyed by a violent earthquake. After leaving Ibrahim's company, the angels, who were sent as messengers, came to Lut. Not having met the messengers before, Lut first became anxious, but then calmed down after talking to them.

When Our messengers came to Lut, he was grieved on their account and felt himself powerless (to protect) them. He said:

"This is a distressful day." (Surah Hud: 77)

Prophet Lut then addressed the issue of homosexuality and informed them that it was indeed an immoral practice. He said:

"Do you approach males among the worlds, and leave those whom your Lord has created for you as your wives? Nay, you are a people of transgressing!"

Prophet Lut then informed his people that he would never agree to be a part of such a practice and warned them of a severe punishment from Allah. He said:

"I am indeed of those who disapprove with severe anger and fury of your action (of sodomy)."

The men and women of Sodom became very angry at Lut's speech. They began to discuss amongst each other, planning to drive Lut away from their city. They then warned Prophet Lut:

"If you cease not, O Lut! Verily, you will be one of those who are driven out!"

Prophet Lut became distressed. After years and years of inviting people to Islam, not one person in Sodom had entered the fold of Islam. The only Muslim household in Sodom was Lut's house, and not all its occupants were Muslims—

Lut and his daughters were steadfast in their religion, but his wife continued to be among the non-believers. So Prophet Lut raised his hands to the heavens and prayed:

"My Lord, support me against the corrupting people. My Lord, save me and my family from what they do."

Meanwhile, Allah SWT sent three angels, including Angel Jibreel, disguised as men to Prophet Ibrahim's house as guests. Ibrahim, who failed to recognise the angels, prepared a grand feast for his guests. But his guests refused the meals offered to them. Prophet Ibrahim became fearful; he asked:

"Who are you?"

The angels replied:

"Do not be afraid! We are the angels of Allah. We have been sent to the people of Lut and we have been sent to give you glad tidings of a son possessing much knowledge and wisdom."

Prophet Ibrahim knew that Allah's punishment for the people of Sodom was near. He immediately feared for his nephew, Lut; he said to the angels:

"Indeed, within it is Lut."

The angels replied:

"We are more knowing of who is within it."

They reassured Ibrahim that Lut would be saved. The angels then proceeded towards Sodom disguised as handsome young men. The daughter of Lut, a believer, witnessed the handsome men entering the city and frantically ran to her father and informed him of the three men. Prophet Lut approached the men and welcomed them into the city of Sodom. He knew too well of the fate that would befall the young men at the hands of the men of Sodom, so he intended to convince the men to leave the city for their own safety. However, Prophet Lut was too embarrassed to ask the guests to leave, so he guided them to his home, ensuring that none saw the three handsome men.

Lut's wife, a nonbeliever, saw the men as they entered her house, together with her husband, Lut. She hurried to the men of the city and informed them that Lut had three attractive, young men in his house. The men rejoiced at the news and slowly gathered outside the house of Lut and began pounding on his door.

Lut shouted:

"Do not disgrace me concerning my guests. Is there not among you a man of reason?"

Growing restless, the men shouted back:

"Have we not forbidden you from [hosting] people?"

The whole nation of Sodom had now gathered at Lut's doorstep. They grew impatient by the minute and began breaking down his door. Feeling agitated, Lut called out to his people:

"These [the girls of the nation] are my daughters [to marry lawfully] if you must act so."

The men responded:

"You have already known that we have no interest in your daughters; and indeed, you know what we want."

Prophet Lut became helpless against the corrupt people.

"If only I had against you some power or could take refuge in a strong power," he thought.

The three men then spoke up:

"O Lut, indeed we are angels of your Lord; [therefore] they will never reach you."

Angel Jibreel then stepped out of Lut's house and struck the men, causing all men to lose their eyesight. Shocked and enraged, the men shouted:

"What's this magic that just hit us? Where did this come from? O Lut! You are the one behind this. You will see what we will do to you tomorrow."

The blind men then returned to their homes, plotting to destroy Lut the following day.

Allah SWT commanded Lut:

"Set out with your family during a portion of the night and let not any among you look back, except your wife. Indeed, she will be struck by that which strikes them. Indeed, their appointment is [for] the morning. Is not the morning near?"

As instructed, Prophet Lut, together with his daughters, left Sodom during the night. (11:81, Surah Hud)

As the morning dawned, a loud, piercing cry ensued through the city that shook the occupants with great pain and fear. Jibreel then grabbed the nation from the edge of his wing, raised them high up, twisted the land, and crashed it to the ground. Allah SWT then caused the skies to rain down stones of hard clay, each stone inscribed with the name of a transgressor for whom it was intended, ending the vain lives of the occupants of Sodom.

Prophet Lut, who left Sodom with his daughters, returned to his uncle, Prophet Ibrahim. Together with Ibrahim, Lut continued to spread the message of Allah till his death.

Today, the Dead Sea lies at the site of the corrupt city of Sodom, and remains as a powerful reminder of Allah's wrath against the people of Prophet Lut. Allah, the Exalted, says in the Holy Qur'an:

"Surely! In this are signs for those who see. And verily! They (the cities) are right on the highroad (from Mecca to Syria, i.e. the place where the Dead Sea is now). Surely! Therein is indeed a sign for the believers." (11:75-77, Surah Al-Hijr) [125]

The Story of God's Wrath

After leaving Abraham, Allah's angels arrived at the gates of Sodom and Gomorrah, where they were greeted by the gatekeeper, Lot. He pleaded with the angels to join him in his house so that he could wash their feet and serve them meals. The angels agreed and went to the house of Lot. Lot, a foreigner to the realm of Sodom, had not succumbed to the lustful, degenerate sins rampant in the city.

One of the most prevalent sins in Sodom was homosexuality, with men engaging in sexual relations with other men and boys. Sodom is where we get the term "sodomy" and "sodomites," named after this widespread sin of the town. After the angels entered the home of Lot, the men of the city surrounded Lot's house. According to **Genesis 19:5 (KJV)**

"And they called unto Lot, and said unto him, Where are the men which came in to thee this night? bring them out unto us, that we may know them."

Lot pleaded with the crowd to reconsider, even offering his two virgin daughters in place of the two visiting men, whose angelic identity was apparently unknown to the lustful Sodomites.

"Get out of our way," they replied. (Genesis 19:9 KJV)

"Stand back," they said. **"This one fellow came in to sojourn, and he will needs be a judge: now will we deal worse with thee than with them."** And they pressed sore upon the man, even Lot, and came near to break the door. (Genesis 19:9 KJV)

As the crowd moved to break down the door, the men inside pulled Lot back inside and shut the door. As Genesis 19:11-13 states:

"Then they struck the men who were at the door of the house, young and old, with blindness so that they could not find the door. The two men said to Lot, 'Do you have anyone else here—sons-in-law, sons, daughters, or anyone

---

[125] Index 102   https://myislam.org/story-of-prophet-lut/

else in the city who belongs to you? Get them out of here, because we are going to destroy this place. The outcry to the LORD against its people is so great that he has sent us to destroy it.'"

After Lot was unable to convince his sons-in-law to leave the city, he fled Sodom with his wife and two daughters, encouraged by the two angels that the Lord would look after them. The angels first told Lot to flee to the mountains, but Lot requested that his family go to a nearby city, named Zoar, to ensure their survival.

The Bible describes the destruction of Sodom and Gomorrah in Genesis 19:23-29, stating:

"By the time Lot reached Zoar, the sun had risen over the land. Then the LORD rained down burning sulphur on Sodom and Gomorrah—from the LORD out of the heavens. Thus he overthrew those cities and the entire plain, destroying all those living in the cities—and also the vegetation in the land. But Lot's wife looked back, and she became a pillar of salt. Early the next morning, Abraham got up and returned to the place where he had stood before the LORD. He looked down toward Sodom and Gomorrah, toward all the land of the plain, and he saw dense smoke rising from the land, like smoke from a furnace. So when God destroyed the cities of the plain, he remembered Abraham, and he brought Lot out of the catastrophe that overthrew the cities where Lot had lived."

According to Bible commentaries, such as the NIV Zondervan Study Bible, Lot's wife was turned into a pillar of salt because she looked back, **"for disobeying the instruction not to look back. Her action suggests that she identified with the people of Sodom. Her failure to flee God's punishment becomes a vivid warning to others (Luke 17:32)."**[126]

Now the story of Sodom and Gomorrah serves as a lesson on the consequences of sin and the wrath of God.

Pompeii Had a Similar End

The destruction of Pompeii came through the eruption of the volcano Vesuvius. It happened in the 1st century CE. In Italy, Vesuvius has been called the "cautious mountain" that destroyed Pompeii.

---

[126] Index 103 https://www.christianity.com/wiki/sin/why-did-god-destroy-sodom-and-gomorrah-story-of-sin-in-the-bible.html

According to historians, around noon on 24 August, 79 CE, a huge eruption from Mount Vesuvius rained down volcanic debris on the city of Pompeii. For centuries, Pompeii lay under its ashes, completely preserving the ruins.

The Qur'an tells us in the following verses that there is no change in Allah's laws:

"They swore their strongest oaths by Allah that if a warner came to them, they would follow his guidance better than any (other) of the Peoples: But when a warner came to them, it has only increased their flight (from righteousness),"

Surah Fatir 35:42

وَأَقْسَمُوا بِاللَّهِ جَهْدَ أَيْمَانِهِمْ لَئِن جَاءَهُمْ نَذِيرٌ لَّيَكُونُنَّ أَهْدَىٰ مِنْ إِحْدَى الْأُمَمِ ۖ فَلَمَّا جَاءَهُمْ نَذِيرٌ مَّا زَادَهُمْ إِلَّا نُفُورًا

اسْتِكْبَارًا فِي الْأَرْضِ وَمَكْرَ السَّيِّئِ ۚ وَلَا يَحِيقُ الْمَكْرُ السَّيِّئُ إِلَّا بِأَهْلِهِ ۚ فَهَلْ يَنظُرُونَ إِلَّا سُنَّتَ الْأَوَّلِينَ ۚ فَلَن تَجِدَ لِسُنَّتِ اللَّهِ تَبْدِيلًا ۖ وَلَن تَجِدَ لِسُنَّتِ اللَّهِ تَحْوِيلًا

"And they swore by Allah their most binding oath, that if a warner came to them, they would be more guided than any of the nations (before them). Yet when a warner (Muhammad ﷺ) came to them, it increased in them nothing but flight (from the truth)."

Surah Fatir 35:42

"(They took to flight because of their) arrogance in the land and their plotting of evil. But the evil plot encompasses only him who makes it. Then, can they expect anything else but the Sunnah (way of dealing) of the peoples of old? So no change will you find in Allah's Sunnah (way of dealing), and no turning off will you find in Allah's Sunnah (way of dealing)."

Surah Fatir 35:43

"No change will be found in Allah's way (rules)."

Everybody who stands against His laws and rebels against Him is subject to the same divine law. Pompeii, the symbol of the degeneration of the Roman Empire, was also involved in sexual perversity. Its end was similar to that of the people of Lut.

This aspect of the event shows that the disappearance of Pompeii was similar to the destructive events mentioned in the Qur'an, because the Qur'an particularly points to *sudden annihilation* while relating these events.

For example, the "inhabitants of the city" described in Surah Ya-Sin all died at once in a single moment. The situation is described in verse 29 of the surah:

إِن كَانَتْ إِلَّا صَيْحَةً وَاحِدَةً فَإِذَا هُمْ خَامِدُونَ

"It was but one Saihah (shout, etc.), and lo! They (all) were silent (dead – destroyed)."

Surah Ya-Sin 36:29

The same moral decay is at work—not just in Capri and Italy, but around the world—urging people not to learn from the horrors of the past. This is called Satan's power.

In the 31st verse of *Surat al-Qamar* (54), it is made even clearer when Allah (SWT) says:

إِنَّا أَرْسَلْنَا عَلَيْهِمْ صَيْحَةً وَاحِدَةً فَكَانُوا كَهَشِيمِ الْمُحْتَظِرِ

"Verily, We sent against them a single Saihah (torment – awful cry, etc.), and they became like the dry stubble of a fold-builder." *Surat al-Qamar 54:31*
[127]

The Almighty Allah (SWT) does not want to see homosexual activity in His world, as has already been proven by His actions, as mentioned above. Yet the representatives of the people—the legislatures of many powerful nations—have been ignoring the will of God. They are also disregarding the advice of scholars and priests. Not only that, the United Nations Human Rights Council has even encouraged other countries to legalise this sinful same-sex marriage.

Satan loves to keep the Almighty angry with His ungrateful people, and he feels proud when Allah (SWT) sends punishment upon us. Our suffering is the success of the devil.

---

[127] Index 104 https://www.britannica.com/place/Pompeii
https://sunnahonline.com/library/purification-of-the-soul/212-fate-of-pompeii

Finally

As we embark on our journey following the straight path towards a challenging destination, we must remain vigilant—for at any moment, a traveller can be disqualified and lose their righteous status in this perilous and possessed world.

In this chapter, we have explored a few instances that serve as typical examples of the past and present horrors we encounter in our time. These examples, though just drops in the vast ocean of wickedness, serve to illustrate the magnitude of the issues at hand.

While these issues are familiar to everyone in our travelling group, it is on this occasion that reading about them will instil fear within hearts and souls, leading to a realisation of the importance of safeguarding the heart and mind against the invasive forces of the devil.

In Our Lifetime:

We will witness increasingly perilous and thrilling events orchestrated by individuals who, driven by arrogance, will defy both the laws of the civilised world and the sacred teachings of divine scriptures.

This suggests that the forces of darkness are deliberately influencing and guiding certain people, compelling them to act in alignment with their will, leaving them powerless to resist.

Let's take the journey to the next level.

بِسْمِ ٱللَّهِ ٱلرَّحْمَـٰنِ ٱلرَّحِيمِ

Chapter 6

Al-Nawwas ibn Sam'an reported:

The Messenger of Allah ﷺ said:

"O people! Enter the straight path altogether and do not divert to the side!"

A caller is placed above the path, and when anyone intends to open those doors in the slightest, he says:

"Woe to you! Do not open it, or else you will enter it!"

The path is Islam, the curtains are the limits of Allah, and the open doors are the prohibitions of Allah. The caller at the head of the path is the Book of Allah, and the caller above the path is an admonition from Allah in the heart of every Muslim (believer).

Source: Musnad Aḥmad 17634

📖📖📖📖📖📖📖

Straight Path

Part 1

يَا أَيُّهَا النَّاسُ قَدْ جَاءَتْكُم مَّوْعِظَةٌ مِّن رَّبِّكُمْ وَشِفَاءٌ لِّمَا فِي الصُّدُورِ وَهُدًى وَرَحْمَةٌ لِّلْمُؤْمِنِينَ

O mankind! There hath come to you a direction from your Lord and a healing for the (diseases) in your hearts—and for those who believe, a guidance and a Mercy. **10:57 Yunus**

Those fortunate members of our travel group who are able to continue their journey on the straight path, having left all luggage behind, have certainly been blessed. When our only objective is to avoid the plots of Satan and successfully reach the spiritual station at the end of the path, we must review and deeply understand the above verse, as well as this one, where Allah SWT says:

وَاكْتُبْ لَنَا فِي هَـٰذِهِ الدُّنْيَا حَسَنَةً وَفِي الْآخِرَةِ إِنَّا هُدْنَا إِلَيْكَ ۚ قَالَ عَذَابِي أُصِيبُ بِهِ مَنْ أَشَاءُ ۖ وَرَحْمَتِي وَسِعَتْ كُلَّ شَيْءٍ ۚ فَسَأَكْتُبُهَا لِلَّذِينَ يَتَّقُونَ وَيُؤْتُونَ الزَّكَاةَ وَالَّذِينَ هُم بِآيَاتِنَا يُؤْمِنُونَ

And ordain for us good in this world, and in the Hereafter. Certainly, we have turned unto You." He said: (As to) My Punishment, I afflict therewith whom I will, and My Mercy embraces all things. That (Mercy) I shall ordain for those who are the Muttaqun (pious – see V.2:2), and give Zakat; and those who believe in Our Ayat (proofs, evidences, verses, lessons, signs and revelations, etc.).

7:156 Surah Al-A'raf

However, there are still many among us who have not yet been fortunate enough to embark on the straight path or fully grasp its significance. It is crucial for them to shift their focus towards comprehending the nature of this path. Without finding the correct route, our journey may conclude in an undesirable destination, regardless of the qualities we possess or the intensity of our supplications.

What is the straight path? And what are the entry requirements?

In our previous discussion, we addressed these questions and their answers. However, it is important to reiterate the significance of complying with all the necessary requirements to stay on the right track towards the desired destination.

Before we proceed further, it is crucial to attentively read the aforementioned verse and sincerely attempt to comprehend the message that Allah SWT has conveyed to all of His human creation—specifically to the believers. Now, let's assess our individual circumstances and reflect upon our alignment with the straight path.

God has revealed the same message in His previous scriptures, as seen in:

Proverbs 4:25–27 (KJV)

- 25 Let thine eyes look right on, and let thine eyelids look straight before thee.
- 26 Ponder the path of thy feet, and let all thy ways be established.
- 27 Turn not to the right hand nor to the left: remove thy foot from evil.

Muslims possess a profound comprehension of the Qur'an and its lessons. Yet, encountering recurring verses delivering the same message serves as a potent call for self-reflection. As we scrutinise our deeds in the context of these verses, our inner beings are inevitably stirred. Let's delve into a collection of verses wherein Allah (SWT) directs us towards the righteous path and illuminates the steps essential for a successful journey.

1.

وَأَنَّ هَذَا صِرَاطِي مُسْتَقِيمًا فَاتَّبِعُوهُ ۖ وَلَا تَتَّبِعُوا السُّبُلَ فَتَفَرَّقَ بِكُمْ عَن سَبِيلِهِ ۚ ذَٰلِكُمْ وَصَّاكُم بِهِ لَعَلَّكُمْ تَتَّقُونَ

Verily, this is My way, leading straight: follow it. Follow not (other) paths; they will scatter you about from His (great) path. Thus doth He command you, that ye may be righteous.

207

6:153 Al-An'am

- Verily, this is My way
- Leading straight
- Follow it
- Follow not (other) paths
- They will scatter you about from His (great) path
- Thus doth He command you
- That ye may be righteous

2.

إِنِّي تَوَكَّلْتُ عَلَى اللَّهِ رَبِّي وَرَبِّكُم ۚ مَّا مِن دَابَّةٍ إِلَّا هُوَ آخِذٌ بِنَاصِيَتِهَا ۚ إِنَّ رَبِّي عَلَىٰ صِرَاطٍ مُّسْتَقِيمٍ

"I put my trust in Allah, my Lord and your Lord! There is not a moving creature but He hath grasp of its forelock. Verily, it is my Lord that is on a straight Path." **11:56 Surah Hud**

While the verse mentioned above appears simple to comprehend, its application in real life presents significant challenges. The seductive influence of the devil's whispers is incredibly potent, making it arduous to discern the righteous path. Only those individuals who possess unwavering determination to overcome the devil manage to uncover compelling insights and stay on the right track.

However, the devil does not relinquish easily. When he fails to conquer an individual, he resorts to inciting contentious disputes among believers—often centring around the interpretation of the Qur'an, Hadith, or similar matters. These disputes serve as breeding grounds for animosity and hostility, ultimately leading to the devil's triumph.

Our understanding is limited, and we strive to expand our knowledge through various means such as attending seminars, lectures, and seeking guidance from scholars. Additionally, we fulfil our religious obligations. However, it is important to recognise that there are many things we continue to engage in that are considered forbidden or go against the advice of Allah (SWT). These actions render us ineligible to remain on the righteous path, despite fulfilling our religious duties.

For instance, even if we fulfil our religious obligations, if we fail to uphold our promises and others perceive us as lacking in faithfulness, it is sufficient to deem us ineligible for the straight path.

Nevertheless, within the aforementioned verses lies a powerful formula for success in both this world and the Hereafter. To validate our understanding and acceptance of this formula, we can refer to the acknowledgement of our Prophet ﷺ regarding the truth contained in this verse as a source of success.

Our Prophet ﷺ Says:

Abū Abdur-Raḥmān, what is the Straight Path?' He replied, "The Messenger ﷺ (sall Allāhu 'alayhi wa sallam) left us upon the nearest end of the line and its other end is in Paradise. To its left and right are roads on which there are men who invite those who pass by them, saying, 'Come this way! Come this way!' Whoever is lured by them to those paths will end up in Hellfire, and whoever remains steadfast upon the great path will end up in Paradise."

Then Ibn Mas'ūd recited the verse 6:153 as mentioned above. [128]

Imam Khomeini says with regard to *Sirat* (the straight path):

"Presently we are on the *Sirat al-Mustaqeem*; it is the same path, one end of which is in this world and the other in the Hereafter, and we are walking on this *Sirat al-Mustaqeem*.

The curtain which is raised at that time is the path of Hell (*Sirat Jahannam*), which passes through Hell; that is, it engulfs the fire of Hell—it passes through the middle of this place. You have to cross it from here. The world is of the same kind. Corruption is that same fire which has surrounded you; you have to cross this same corruption in such a way that you cross it safely." (Index 01)

And he says:

"All of us are on the straight path, and it crosses over Hell. Its reality will be exposed in that world. One is on a journey (wayfaring), or is on the straight path which ends at Paradise or higher, or on a deviated path to the left or the right—both of which end at Hell."

He also says:

"The path that is stretched over Hell—if you walk straight in this world, you will be rejected from that path straight away: the inward Hell of this world. If you walk straight on this path and do not deviate to the left or the right, you will cross the *Sirat* bridge of this world directly. But you must not turn left or right; if you turn to the left, there is Hell, and if you turn to the right, it is Hell." (1A)

There are no multiple straight paths. The critical point is that whenever Almighty Allah (SWT) refers to *Sirat al-Mustaqeem* in the Holy Qur'an, it is always in the singular. In other words, there are no two straight paths. Allah says in the latter part of the verse mentioned earlier—Surah Hud (11:56):

"I put my trust in Allah, my Lord and your Lord! There is not a moving creature but He has grasp of its forelock. Verily, it is my Lord that is on a straight Path."

---

[128] Index 6 (IbnKathir (Ibn Kathīr was a highly influential scholar during the Mamluk era in Syria. Born: 1301, Busra, Syria an expert on tafsir and faqīh, he wrote several books, including a fourteen-volume universal history. Wikipedia)

Different explanations have also been given by many scholars. Even though there are many side roads available for walking, ultimately these multiple paths meet the one main highway which goes towards Him—without any detours, twists, or turns to the left or right—with the guaranteed destination being Allah (SWT). Their explanation is as follows:

"Very interesting is the fact that the Holy Qur'an also uses another term to describe the 'path'. *Sirat al-Mustaqeem* is one term used to describe the journey to Almighty Allah (SWT), and another term used for this journey is *Sabeel*. An example is the reference to *fi sabeelillah*."

There are many examples in the Holy Qur'an where *Sabeel* is used in the plural form—i.e., *subul* (paths). Leading commentators of the Holy Qur'an from the 20th century, such as Allama Tabataba'i and Ayatollah Mutahhari, explain that *subul* refers to the side roads (byways), and although these byways may be many, they eventually meet the main highway.

If we aim to incorporate this mindset into our ongoing discussion, it implies that we may hold varying perspectives on the specific journey and progression towards Almighty Allah (SWT). We can adopt diverse approaches, and this diversity is not detrimental. In fact, it is perfectly acceptable, because ultimately, these divergences in detail will lead us to the same overarching destination.

So, the path referred to in *Sirat al-Mustaqeem* is the only one true path, but there are different routes that lead to it. This is where diversity of understanding and approaches in detail is acceptable, as long as they all lead to the singular, principal straight path referred to by *Sirat al-Mustaqeem*. (2) ALLAH KNOWS BEST.

As believers, it is not our place to engage in arguments or disputes regarding others' thoughts or philosophies, as stated earlier. Instead, our focus should be on wholeheartedly adhering to the guidance provided by Allah (SWT). However, if someone is uncertain about an alternative path and seeks clarity, it is beneficial to revisit the verse mentioned earlier, which serves as a reminder and helps alleviate confusion.

The Verse Says:

"Verily, this is My way, leading straight: follow it. Follow not (other) paths: they will scatter you away from His (great) path: thus does He command you, that you may be righteous."—6:153, Surah Al-An'am

In this verse, Allah (SWT) guides us not to follow multiple paths that deviate us from the straight path. Therefore, we must follow the divine guidance accordingly if we are to achieve success.

210

Now, removing all confusion, we conclude from this discussion that the path of salvation is only one. That is the path we are continually asking Almighty Allah (SWT) to guide us towards. Allah (SWT) says in the following verses:

ذَٰلِكَ الْكِتَابُ لَا رَيْبَ ۛ فِيهِ ۛ هُدًى لِّلْمُتَّقِينَ

This is the Book; in it is guidance sure, without doubt, for those who fear Allah.

—2:2, Surah Al-Baqara

قُلْ إِنَّنِي هَدَانِي رَبِّي إِلَىٰ صِرَاطٍ مُّسْتَقِيمٍ دِينًا قِيَمًا مِّلَّةَ إِبْرَاهِيمَ حَنِيفًا ۚ وَمَا كَانَ مِنَ الْمُشْرِكِينَ

Say (O Muhammad ﷺ): "Truly, my Lord has guided me to a Straight Path, a right religion, the religion of Ibrahim (Abraham), Hanifa [i.e., true Islamic Monotheism—to believe in One God (Allah), i.e., to worship none but Allah alone], and he was not of the polytheists."

162. Say (O Muhammad ﷺ):

"Verily, my Salat (prayer), my sacrifice, my living, and my dying are for Allah, the Lord of the 'Alamin (mankind, jinns, and all that exists)."

(Surah Al-An'am 6:161–162)

Let us break down the verse to understand what Allah (SWT) says:

➢ *"Verily, my Lord hath guided me to a way that is straight, a religion of right—*

➢ *The path trodden by Abraham, true in faith—*

➢ *And he (certainly) joined not gods with Allah.*

➢ *"Truly, my prayer and my service of sacrifice, my life and my death, are (all) for Allah, the Cherisher of the worlds."*

In the light of this verse, we can differentiate between two types of guidance from Allah (SWT): Divine Guidance and Religious Guidance.

Divine Guidance refers to the innate human intelligence bestowed by Allah (SWT), which enables one to distinguish between good and bad, right and wrong, gain and loss, felicity and wretchedness, virtue and vice, and so on. It is, in essence, the inner messenger within a person.

Religious Guidance refers to the revelation sent by Allah (SWT) through prophets (ﷺ), Divine Books, and legislation to guide mankind towards righteousness in both this world and the next. When one follows this guidance sincerely, they become worthy of receiving the blessings of the Hereafter. This state is achieved through the development of the soul—acquiring knowledge, practising good habits, and nurturing commendable moral qualities. In doing so, a person may attain happiness in both worlds, through the infinite grace of Allah.

211

*In another significant verse, Allah (SWT) categorises the ranks among us,
giving us the opportunity to choose the rank we wish to attain through our deeds:*

وَمَن يُطِعِ اللَّهَ وَالرَّسُولَ فَأُولَٰئِكَ مَعَ الَّذِينَ أَنْعَمَ اللَّهُ عَلَيْهِم مِّنَ النَّبِيِّينَ وَالصِّدِّيقِينَ وَالشُّهَدَاءِ
وَالصَّالِحِينَ ۚ وَحَسُنَ أُولَٰئِكَ رَفِيقًا

**"All who obey Allah and the Messenger are in the company of those on whom
is the Grace of Allah—the Prophets (who teach), the Sincere (lovers of Truth),
the Witnesses (who testify), and the Righteous (who do good). Ah! What a
beautiful fellowship!"**

(Surah An-Nisaa 4:69)

*One narration behind the revelation of this verse comes from a hadith in which
Aishah (RA) reported:*

A man came to the Messenger of Allah ﷺ and said:

**"O Messenger of Allah, you are more beloved to me than my own self, my
wife, and my children. Whenever I remember you while at home, I cannot rest
until I come to see you. But when I remember my death and yours, I realise that
when you enter the Garden, you will be raised among the Prophets, and I fear
that even if I am granted Paradise, I will not be able to see you."**

*The Prophet ﷺ did not respond until Jibreel (peace be upon him) descended
with this verse, clarifying that attaining the companionship of the Prophet requires
fulfilling the ranks defined: Siddiqeen, Shuhadaa, and Saliheen.*

Let Us Define These Ranks Briefly:

Siddiqeen – The Sincere And Truthful

*These are individuals whose hearts are purified and who are utterly sincere in
their devotion to Allah (SWT). Their truthfulness manifests in both their words and
deeds, and their intentions are solely for the sake of Allah. Imam Raghib notes that
the highest among them are the Prophets ﷺ, who are supported by Divine power.
Regarding such people, Allah (SWT) says in Surah An-Najm 53:11–14:*

مَا كَذَبَ الْفُؤَادُ مَا رَأَىٰ

أَفَتُمَارُونَهُ عَلَىٰ مَا يَرَىٰ

وَلَقَدْ رَآهُ نَزْلَةً أُخْرَىٰ

عِندَ سِدْرَةِ الْمُنتَهَىٰ

"The (Prophet's) heart did not deny what he saw.

Will you then dispute with him about what he saw [during the Mi'raj]?

And indeed, he saw him (Jibreel) again at a second descent,

212

Near Sidrat-ul-Muntaha (the Lote Tree of the Utmost Boundary)."

Shuhadaa – The Witnesses

These are those who bear witness to the Truth in the most trying circumstances—sometimes under threat to their lives or livelihoods. They stand for Islam and work for the welfare of others, even if it means sacrificing all they have to protect innocence and promote justice.

Saliheen – The Righteous

These are those who consistently perform good deeds: praying, fasting, giving charity, visiting the sick, aiding orphans, remembering Allah, reciting the Qur'an, and devoting their limbs to the service of the Creator and His creation. As stated in Surah Al-Kahf 18:30:

إِنَّ الَّذِينَ آمَنُوا وَعَمِلُوا الصَّالِحَاتِ إِنَّا لَا نُضِيعُ أَجْرَ مَنْ أَحْسَنَ عَمَلًا

"Verily, as for those who believe and do righteous deeds, certainly, We shall not suffer to be lost the reward of anyone who does righteous deeds in the most perfect manner."

Nonetheless, we must also consider other crucial aspects that affect our journey, including internal weaknesses, fears, frustrations, and spiritual deprivation. Addressing these issues helps us build confidence and maintain a steady path.

In this regard, Surah Fatir (35) offers essential guidance. Allah (SWT) reminds us:

إِنَّ الشَّيْطَانَ لَكُمْ عَدُوٌّ فَاتَّخِذُوهُ عَدُوًّا ۚ إِنَّمَا يَدْعُو حِزْبَهُ لِيَكُونُوا مِنْ أَصْحَابِ السَّعِيرِ

"Surely, Shaitan (Satan) is an enemy to you, so treat him as such. He only invites his followers to become dwellers of the blazing Fire." (Surah Fatir 35:6)

This is also why Surah Al-Fatihah is considered the essence of the Qur'an. It was revealed as a comprehensive guide for the welfare of humanity, earning it the title Ummul Qur'an (The Mother of the Qur'an). Every word of this Surah holds deep meaning and must be carefully analysed for us to receive proper guidance and achieve true success.

Anyway, Let's Get Back To Finding The Straight Path.

اهْدِنَا الصِّرَاطَ الْمُسْتَقِيمَ

Show Us The Straight Way,

(Surah Al-Fatihah, 1:6)

صِرَاطَ الَّذِينَ أَنْعَمْتَ عَلَيْهِمْ غَيْرِ الْمَغْضُوبِ عَلَيْهِمْ وَلَا الضَّالِّينَ

213

The way of those on whom Thou hast bestowed Thy Grace, not those who earn Thine anger, nor those who go astray.

(Surah Al-Fatihah, 1:7)

It is important for us to recognise the individuals whom Allah (SWT) has blessed and seek their guidance in order to follow in their footsteps. These fortunate individuals include knowledgeable scholars and Imams (*Ma'rifat*) who receive divine grace from Almighty Allah (SWT). They possess the ability to direct us towards the correct path.

It is crucial to distinguish between receiving guidance and consistently staying on the right path, as they are separate matters. To safeguard both, it is essential to fervently pray to Allah Ta'ala, requesting His guidance: **"Guide us to the right path"** and to protect us from straying from it.

Mowlana Syed Aftab Haider of Ahlul Bait (a.s) Masjid, Ottery, Cape Town, delivered a valuable discourse on seeking guidance from Allah (SWT), which helps us build the confidence to stay on the right path. In his speech, Mowlana said:

"On this basis, when we say *Ih dinas-siratal mustaqeem*, we are asking Almighty Allah (SWT) to keep guiding us on the right path throughout this journey of progressing towards perfection. As pointed out at the beginning of this discussion, the reference to the right path is not a frozen reality.

The right path has different levels, for which we need to keep climbing the ladder of *Sirat-al-Mustaqeem* to attain. People like us are probably at the bottom rung of this ladder! But those who are on the very high steps of this ladder also keep climbing to even higher levels on this *Sirat-al-Mustaqeem*. Hence, *Ih dinas-siratal mustaqeem* means that we are asking Almighty Allah (SWT) to keep us climbing this ladder on the journey towards Him.

May Almighty Allah (SWT) enlighten us with the help of people of this divine path, with connection and commitment to the leaders of this path, to evolve, strive and progress towards His absolute perfection, Insha'Allah." (5)

Allah (SWT) Warned Us, Saying:

يَا أَيُّهَا الْإِنسَانُ إِنَّكَ كَادِحٌ إِلَىٰ رَبِّكَ كَدْحًا فَمُلَاقِيهِ

"O man! Verily, you are returning towards your Lord with your deeds and actions (good or bad), a sure returning, so you will meet (i.e. the results of your deeds)."

(Surah Al-Inshiqaq, 84:6)

It is an undeniable truth that individuals in this world, irrespective of caste or religion, cannot encounter God without enduring hardship. We too are not exempt from this reality.

The majority of Muslims hold the belief that fulfilling all obligatory religious duties is sufficient to be considered a virtuous Muslim. However, it is crucial to recognise that true faith requires one to remain steadfast on the righteous path in order to attain success in the ultimate judgement. This book serves as a constant reminder to travellers on this journey about the significance of adhering to the straight path.

Many hypocrites in society may pray better than ordinary Muslims. So, can they be eligible to follow the straight path? We can say no, because Allah (SWT) says:

بَشِّرِ الْمُنَافِقِينَ بِأَنَّ لَهُمْ عَذَابًا أَلِيمًا

"Give to the hypocrites the tidings that there is for them a painful torment."

(Surah An-Nisaa, 4:138)

Journey Through The Straight Path

This journey of our essence entails navigating with care; reckless driving could veer us off course. Beyond the clear path lies a myriad of tempting detours that lead us astray. While we speed along life's bustling thoroughfare, our concern for the destination of our souls often remains neglected.

Just as road signs guide us on our physical journey, there are numerous warning indicators on our spiritual path. These signs serve as constant reminders to steer carefully in the correct direction, lest we find ourselves diverted to an undesirable destination, akin to Hell.

Sometimes, even careful travellers cannot avoid mistakes—it's a natural part of the journey. What matters most is recognising and rectifying those missteps promptly. The best way to detect errors is to examine your own *nafs* (self). Should this self-evaluation reveal shortcomings, and if one is determined to realign with the correct path, immediate action is essential.

Self-Test

For the purpose of self-reflection, here is a compilation of selected verses that Allah (SWT) has directed us to follow. It is important to note that if any verse does not pertain to an individual's lifestyle, they may skip it and proceed to the next.

Please use a pen or pencil to mark a check (✓) in the box if you have obeyed Allah's command according to a particular verse, or mark (✗) if you have ignored or disregarded that instruction. Afterward, tally the total number of checkmarks and crosses to enable your spirit to evaluate the outcome and predict possible results. Based on this assessment, you can determine what steps you feel are necessary to correct the situation.

Identify One's Strengths and Weaknesses

Positive Answer: Tick ✔ | Otherwise: Tick ✗

What Allah SWT has commanded us – and what we're doing:

بِسْمِ اللَّهِ الرَّحْمَٰنِ الرَّحِيمِ

In the name of Allah, the Most Gracious, the Most Merciful

01

2:168 – Surah Al-Baqara

يَا أَيُّهَا النَّاسُ كُلُوا مِمَّا فِي الْأَرْضِ حَلَالًا طَيِّبًا وَلَا تَتَّبِعُوا خُطُوَاتِ الشَّيْطَانِ ۚ إِنَّهُ لَكُمْ عَدُوٌّ مُبِينٌ

O mankind! Eat of that which is lawful and good on the earth, and follow not the footsteps of Shaitan (Satan). Verily, he is to you an open enemy.

➢ O ye people! Eat of what is on earth—lawful and good;

➢ Do not follow the footsteps of the Evil One,

➢ For he is to you an avowed enemy.

Answer: ……../……../……./

02

11:85 – Surah Hud

وَيَا قَوْمِ أَوْفُوا الْمِكْيَالَ وَالْمِيزَانَ بِالْقِسْطِ ۚ وَلَا تَبْخَسُوا النَّاسَ أَشْيَاءَهُمْ وَلَا تَعْثَوْا فِي الْأَرْضِ مُفْسِدِينَ

And O my people! Give full measure and weight in justice, and reduce not the things that are due to the people. Do not commit mischief in the land, causing corruption.

Answer: ……………/…………….

03

2:183 – Surah Al-Baqara

يَا أَيُّهَا الَّذِينَ آمَنُوا كُتِبَ عَلَيْكُمُ الصِّيَامُ كَمَا كُتِبَ عَلَى الَّذِينَ مِن قَبْلِكُمْ لَعَلَّكُمْ تَتَّقُونَ

O ye who believe! Fasting is prescribed to you as it was prescribed to those before you, that ye may learn self-restraint.

Answer: …………/……….

04

4:58 – Surah An-Nisa'

وَإِذَا حَكَمْتُم بَيْنَ النَّاسِ أَن تَحْكُمُوا بِالْعَدْلِ ۚ إِنَّ اللَّهَ ۚ إِنَّ اللَّهَ يَأْمُرُكُمْ أَن تُؤَدُّوا الْأَمَانَاتِ إِلَىٰ أَهْلِهَا
نِعِمَّا يَعِظُكُم بِهِ ۚ إِنَّ اللَّهَ كَانَ سَمِيعًا بَصِيرًا

Verily! Allah commands that you should render back the trusts to whom they are due, and that when you judge between people, you judge with justice. Verily, how excellent is the teaching which He gives you! Truly, Allah is Ever All-Hearer, All-Seer.

➢ Allah doth command you:

➢ Render back your trusts to those to whom they are due;

➢ When ye judge between man and man,

➢ Judge with justice.

If applicable, identify your situation.

Answer: ……………/…………./…………../

05

4:10 – Surah An-Nisa'

إِنَّمَا يَأْكُلُونَ فِي بُطُونِهِمْ نَارًا ۖ وَسَيَصْلَوْنَ سَعِيرًا إِنَّ الَّذِينَ يَأْكُلُونَ أَمْوَالَ الْيَتَامَىٰ ظُلْمًا

Verily, those who unjustly eat up the property of orphans, eat only fire into their bellies, and they will be burnt in the blazing Fire!

Answer: …………/…………/

06

2:177 – Surah Al-Baqara

۞ لَّيْسَ الْبِرَّ أَن تُوَلُّوا وُجُوهَكُمْ قِبَلَ الْمَشْرِقِ وَالْمَغْرِبِ وَلَٰكِنَّ الْبِرَّ مَنْ آمَنَ بِاللَّهِ وَالْيَوْمِ الْآخِرِ
وَالْمَلَائِكَةِ وَالْكِتَابِ وَالنَّبِيِّينَ وَآتَى الْمَالَ عَلَىٰ حُبِّهِ ذَوِي الْقُرْبَىٰ وَالْيَتَامَىٰ وَالْمَسَاكِينَ وَابْنَ
السَّبِيلِ وَالسَّائِلِينَ وَفِي الرِّقَابِ وَأَقَامَ الصَّلَاةَ وَآتَى الزَّكَاةَ وَالْمُوفُونَ بِعَهْدِهِمْ إِذَا عَاهَدُوا ۖ
وَالصَّابِرِينَ فِي الْبَأْسَاءِ وَالضَّرَّاءِ وَحِينَ الْبَأْسِ ۗ أُولَٰئِكَ الَّذِينَ صَدَقُوا ۖ وَأُولَٰئِكَ هُمُ الْمُتَّقُونَ

It is not righteousness that ye turn your faces towards East or West; but it is righteousness to believe in Allah and the Last Day, the Angels, the Book, and the Messengers; to spend of your substance, out of love for Him, for your kin, for orphans, for the needy, for the wayfarer, for those who ask, and for the ransom of slaves; to be steadfast in prayer, and practise regular charity; to fulfil the contracts you have made; and to be firm and patient in pain (or suffering), adversity, and throughout all periods of panic. Such are the people of truth, the Allah-fearing.

217

➤ It is not righteousness to turn your faces towards East or West;

➤ But righteousness is to believe in Allah, the Last Day, the Angels, the Book, and the Messengers;

➤ To spend of your substance, out of love for Him: for your kin, orphans, the needy, the wayfarer, and those who ask;

➤ For the ransom of slaves; to be steadfast in prayer;

➤ And to practise regular charity; to fulfil the contracts made;

➤ And to be firm and patient in pain, adversity, and during times of distress.

Such are the people of truth—the Allah-fearing.

Identify the area of your situation.

Answer: …….../…………../…………../………../………../………..

07

17:26 – Surah Al-Isra'

وَلَا تُبَذِّرْ تَبْذِيرًا وَآتِ ذَا الْقُرْبَىٰ حَقَّهُ وَالْمِسْكِينَ وَابْنَ السَّبِيلِ

And give to the kindred his due, and to the poor and the wayfarer. But do not spend wastefully (your wealth) in the manner of a spendthrift.

Answer: ………../…………

08

2:278 – Surah Al-Baqara

وَذَرُوا مَا بَقِيَ مِنَ الرِّبَا إِن كُنتُم مُّؤْمِنِينَ يَا أَيُّهَا الَّذِينَ آمَنُوا اتَّقُوا اللَّهَ

O you who believe! Fear Allah and give up what remains (due to you) from usury (Riba), if you are (truly) believers.

Answer: …………/………….../………….../

09

2:238 – Surah Al-Baqara

وَالصَّلَاةِ الْوُسْطَىٰ وَقُومُوا لِلَّهِ قَانِتِينَ حَافِظُوا عَلَى الصَّلَوَاتِ

Guard strictly (the five obligatory) prayers, especially the middle prayer ('Asr). And stand before Allah in devotion.

Answer: ……………../………….

218

10

17:35 – Surah Al-Isra'

إِذَا كِلْتُمْ وَزِنُوا بِالْقِسْطَاسِ الْمُسْتَقِيمِ ۚ ذَٰلِكَ خَيْرٌ وَأَحْسَنُ تَأْوِيلًا وَأَوْفُوا الْكَيْلَ

Give full measure when you measure, and weigh with a balance that is straight. That is best and most advantageous in the end.

➢ Give full measure when ye measure,

➢ And weigh with a balance,

➢ That is straight.

Answer: ……………../…………

11

4:2 – Surah An-Nisa'

وَلَا تَتَبَدَّلُوا الْخَبِيثَ بِالطَّيِّبِ ۖ وَلَا تَأْكُلُوا أَمْوَالَهُمْ إِلَىٰ أَمْوَالِكُمْ ۚ إِنَّهُ وَآتُوا الْيَتَامَىٰ أَمْوَالَهُمْ كَانَ حُوبًا كَبِيرًا

And give the orphans their property, and do not substitute (your) worthless things for (their) good ones; and do not consume their property by adding it to your own. Surely, this is a great sin.

Answer: ………….../…………../…………/

12

2:264 – Surah Al-Baqara

أَيُّهَا الَّذِينَ آمَنُوا لَا تُبْطِلُوا صَدَقَاتِكُم بِالْمَنِّ وَالْأَذَىٰ كَالَّذِي يُنفِقُ مَالَهُ رِئَاءَ النَّاسِ وَلَا يُؤْمِنُ بِاللَّهِ وَالْيَوْمِ الْآخِرِ ۖ فَمَثَلُهُ كَمَثَلِ صَفْوَانٍ عَلَيْهِ تُرَابٌ فَأَصَابَهُ وَابِلٌ فَتَرَكَهُ صَلْدًا ۖ لَّا يَقْدِرُونَ عَلَىٰ شَيْءٍ مِّمَّا كَسَبُوا ۗ وَاللَّهُ لَا يَهْدِي الْقَوْمَ الْكَافِرِينَ

O ye who believe! Cancel not your charity by reminders of generosity or by injury—like those who spend their wealth to be seen of men but believe neither in Allah nor the Last Day. They are like a rock with a thin layer of soil; when heavy rain falls on it, it leaves it bare. They will gain nothing from their deeds. And Allah guides not those who reject faith.

➢ O ye who believe!

➢ Cancel not your charity by reminders of generosity,

➢ Or by injury—like those who spend their substance to be seen of men,

➢ But believe neither in Allah nor in the Last Day.

> They will be able to do nothing with what they have earned.

> And Allah guides not those who reject faith.

Identify the area of your situation

Answer: ………/………/………../………../………/………/

13

3:130 – Surah Aal-e-Imran

أَضْعَافًا مُضَاعَفَةً ۖ وَاتَّقُوا اللَّهَ لَعَلَّكُمْ تُفْلِحُونَ يَا أَيُّهَا الَّذِينَ آمَنُوا لَا تَأْكُلُوا الرِّبَا

O ye who believe! Eat not usury, doubled and multiplied, but fear Allah that you may be successful.

> O ye who believe!

> Devour not usury,

> Doubled and multiplied;

> But fear Allah.

Answer: ………/………/……../

14

4:36 – Surah An-Nisa'

وَاعْبُدُوا اللَّهَ وَلَا تُشْرِكُوا بِهِ شَيْئًا ۖ وَبِالْوَالِدَيْنِ إِحْسَانًا وَبِذِي الْقُرْبَىٰ وَالْيَتَامَىٰ وَالْمَسَاكِينِ وَالْجَارِ ذِي الْقُرْبَىٰ وَالْجَارِ الْجُنُبِ وَالصَّاحِبِ بِالْجَنبِ وَابْنِ السَّبِيلِ وَمَا مَلَكَتْ أَيْمَانُكُمْ ۗ إِنَّ اللَّهَ لَا يُحِبُّ مَن كَانَ مُخْتَالًا فَخُورً

Worship Allah and do not associate anything with Him; and be kind to parents, relatives, orphans, the needy, the near neighbour, the distant neighbour, the companion by your side, the wayfarer, and those whom your right hands possess. Truly, Allah does not like the proud and boastful.

> And do good—to parents,

> Kinsfolk, orphans, those in need, neighbours.

Identify your situation

Answer: …………../……………

15

2/254 Surah Al-Baqara

يَا أَيُّهَا الَّذِينَ آمَنُوا أَنفِقُوا مِمَّا رَزَقْنَاكُم مِّن قَبْلِ أَن يَأْتِيَ يَوْمٌ لَّا بَيْعٌ فِيهِ وَلَا خُلَّةٌ وَلَا شَفَاعَةٌ وَالْكَافِرُونَ هُمُ الظَّالِمُونَ

O you who believe! Spend of that with which We have provided for you, before a Day comes when there will be no bargaining, nor friendship, nor intercession. And it is the disbelievers who are the Zalimun (wrongdoers, etc.).

Identify the area of your situation:

Answer: …………/…………

16

2/188 Surah Al-Baqara

وَلَا تَأْكُلُوا أَمْوَالَكُم بَيْنَكُم بِالْبَاطِلِ وَتُدْلُوا بِهَا إِلَى الْحُكَّامِ لِتَأْكُلُوا فَرِيقًا مِّنْ أَمْوَالِ النَّاسِ بِالْإِثْمِ وَأَنتُمْ تَعْلَمُونَ

And eat not up one another's property unjustly (in any illegal way, e.g. stealing, robbing, deceiving, etc.), nor give bribery to the rulers (judges before presenting your cases), that you may knowingly eat up a part of the property of others sinfully.

Identify the area of your situation:

➤ *Do not consume your property among yourselves in vanity.*

➤ *Nor use it as bait for the judges.*

➤ *With intent to consume wrongfully and knowingly a portion of other people's property.*

Answer: …………/…………/………

17

16/90 Surah An-Nahl

إِنَّ اللَّهَ يَأْمُرُ بِالْعَدْلِ وَالْإِحْسَانِ وَإِيتَاءِ ذِي الْقُرْبَىٰ وَيَنْهَىٰ عَنِ الْفَحْشَاءِ وَالْمُنكَرِ وَالْبَغْيِ يَعِظُكُمْ لَعَلَّكُمْ تَذَكَّرُونَ

Verily, Allah enjoins Al-Adl (i.e. justice and worshipping none but Allah alone – Islamic Monotheism), and Al-Ihsan [i.e. to be patient in performing your duties to Allah, totally for Allah's sake and in accordance with the Sunnah (legal ways) of the Prophet in a perfect manner], and giving (help) to kith.

Your Answer: *………/………*

18

85/10 Surah Al-Burooj

إِنَّ الَّذِينَ فَتَنُوا الْمُؤْمِنِينَ وَالْمُؤْمِنَاتِ ثُمَّ لَمْ يَتُوبُوا فَلَهُمْ عَذَابُ جَهَنَّمَ وَلَهُمْ عَذَابُ الْحَرِيقِ

Verily, those who put believing men and women to trial (by torturing and burning them), and then do not turn in repentance to Allah, will face the torment of Hell, and the punishment of the burning Fire.

Answer: ……/………

19

2/43 Surah Al-Baqarah

وَأَقِيمُوا الصَّلَاةَ وَآتُوا الزَّكَاةَ وَارْكَعُوا مَعَ الرَّاكِعِينَ

And perform As-Salat (Iqamat-as-Salat), and give Zakat, and Irka' (i.e. bow down or submit yourselves with obedience to Allah) along with Ar-Raki'un.

Answer: ……/………/…………

20

17/37 Surah Al-Isra

وَلَا تَمْشِ فِي الْأَرْضِ مَرَحًا ۖ إِنَّكَ لَن تَخْرِقَ الْأَرْضَ وَلَن تَبْلُغَ الْجِبَالَ طُولًا

And walk not on the earth with conceit and arrogance. Verily, you can neither rend nor penetrate the earth, nor can you attain a stature like the mountains in height.

Identify your situation:

Answer: …………/…………

21

17/23 Surah Al-Isra

وَقَضَىٰ رَبُّكَ أَلَّا تَعْبُدُوا إِلَّا إِيَّاهُ وَبِالْوَالِدَيْنِ إِحْسَانًا ۚ إِمَّا يَبْلُغَنَّ عِندَكَ الْكِبَرَ أَحَدُهُمَا أَوْ كِلَاهُمَا فَلَا تَقُل لَّهُمَا أُفٍّ وَلَا تَنْهَرْهُمَا وَقُل لَّهُمَا قَوْلًا كَرِيمًا

And your Lord has decreed that you worship none but Him. And that you be dutiful to your parents. If one or both of them attain old age during your lifetime, say not to them a word of disrespect, nor shout at them, but address them with honour.

➢ *Be kind to parents.*

➢ *Whether one or both of them attain old age in your lifetime,*

➢ *Say not to them a word of contempt, nor repel them, but address them with honour.*

Answer: …………/…………

22

42/42 Surah Ash-Shurah

إِنَّمَا السَّبِيلُ عَلَى الَّذِينَ يَظْلِمُونَ النَّاسَ وَيَبْغُونَ فِي الْأَرْضِ بِغَيْرِ الْحَقِّ ۚ أُولَٰئِكَ لَهُمْ عَذَابٌ أَلِيمٌ

The blame is only against those who oppress people and wrong them, and insolently transgress beyond bounds throughout the land, defying what is right and just. For such, there will be a grievous penalty.

➢ *The blame is only against those*

➢ *Who oppress people and commit wrongdoing*

➢ *And insolently transgress across the land*

➢ *Defying right and justice*

Answer: …………/………

23

17/36 Surah Al-Isra

وَلَا تَقْفُ مَا لَيْسَ لَكَ بِهِ عِلْمٌ ۚ إِنَّ السَّمْعَ وَالْبَصَرَ وَالْفُؤَادَ كُلُّ أُولَٰئِكَ كَانَ عَنْهُ مَسْئُولًا

And follow not (O man – i.e. say not, do not, or witness not, etc.) that of which you have no knowledge (e.g. claiming "I have seen," while in fact you have not seen, or "I have heard," when you have not heard). Verily! The hearing, the sight, and the heart – all of these shall be questioned (by Allah).

Answer: …………/………..

Your genuine essence or a hidden perspective can be illuminated through the cumulative responses, provided you genuinely value the alternative aspects of the journey. Consider this your preliminary examination. The final judgment lies within your grasp, waiting to be delivered once you successfully accomplish all the remaining assessments within this book.

Part II

The Quality Of Being On The Right Track

Attain Success On The Day Of Judgment

This step marks the second phase of the examination. It's crucial to take your age into account as you delve into the verses. These selected verses are part of the "Test to Stay on the Right Path," where Allah (SWT) illuminates the correct path for us and offers guidance on how to attain it.

These verses are familiar to many of us, but often we fail to appreciate the importance of adhering to Allah SWT's commands and unintentionally or carelessly stray from the right path. Tests serve as a means of raising awareness and instilling a sense of accountability for the Day of Judgment.

In this section, we will explore additional selected verses that directly impact our daily lives. These verses serve as a connection point, guiding us to regulate our actions with utmost priority when following the righteous path.

Here, travellers on this path have an opportunity to assess their adherence to the guidelines laid out in these verses, allowing them to reaffirm their confidence. It also provides a chance to rectify any anticipated negative consequences.

As mentioned previously, many of us recite the Qur'an solely for the purpose of recitation, aiming to receive rewards for every letter uttered. While this is commendable, it is important to acknowledge that a significant number of readers fail to implement the teachings due to a lack of comprehension.

Therefore, understanding the verses of the Qur'an becomes crucial for those seeking to tread the straight path as sincere believers.

Allah (SWT) says:

لَقَدْ أَنزَلْنَا إِلَيْكُمْ كِتَابًا فِيهِ ذِكْرُكُمْ ۖ أَفَلَا تَعْقِلُونَ

Indeed, We have sent down for you (O mankind) a Book (the Qur'an) in which there is Dhikrukum (your Reminder or an honour for you — i.e. honour for the one who follows the teaching of the Qur'an and acts on its orders). Will you not then understand? (21:10, Al-Anbiyaa)

يَا أَيُّهَا النَّاسُ قَدْ جَاءَتْكُم مَّوْعِظَةٌ مِّن رَّبِّكُمْ وَشِفَاءٌ لِّمَا فِي الصُّدُورِ وَهُدًى وَرَحْمَةٌ لِّلْمُؤْمِنِينَ

O mankind! There has come to you a good advice from your Lord (i.e. the Qur'an, ordering all that is good and forbidding all that is evil), and a healing for that (disease of ignorance, doubt, hypocrisy and differences, etc.) in your breasts — a guidance and a mercy (explaining lawful and unlawful things, etc.) for the believers. (10:57, Surah Yunus)

The verses above express that the Qur'an is the paramount and conclusive compass for our life's path. Let's now examine the following verses as a form of evaluation. If the examination reveals unsatisfactory outcomes, it may lead us to recognise deficiencies within the assessment, thus highlighting issues that require attention.

Let The Assessment Begin:

Based on the following verses, identify your own (self) situation that will directly affect your righteous status.

1.

قَوْلٌ مَّعْرُوفٌ وَمَغْفِرَةٌ خَيْرٌ مِّن صَدَقَةٍ يَتْبَعُهَا أَذًى ۗ وَاللَّهُ غَنِيٌّ حَلِيمٌ

Kind words and forgiveness of faults are better than Sadaqah (charity) followed by injury. And Allah is Rich (Free of all wants), and He is Most-Forbearing. (2:263, Al-Baqarah)

Example: In each quoted verse, ask yourself where you stand (soul), and the answer may come to you in many ways, e.g.:

➢ Yes, I know and act accordingly.

➢ Yes, I know but I am not practising.

➢ No, I have not noticed this verse before and will correct myself now.

Identify Your Situation

2.

وَمَن يَكْسِبْ خَطِيئَةً أَوْ إِثْمًا ثُمَّ يَرْمِ بِهِ بَرِيئًا فَقَدِ احْتَمَلَ بُهْتَانًا وَإِثْمًا مُبِينًا

And whoever earns a fault or a sin and then throws it onto someone innocent, he has indeed burdened himself with falsehood and a manifest sin. (4:112, An-Nisaa)

3.

إِنَّ الَّذِينَ يَشْتَرُونَ بِعَهْدِ اللَّهِ وَأَيْمَانِهِمْ ثَمَنًا قَلِيلًا أُولَئِكَ لَا خَلَاقَ لَهُمْ فِي الْآخِرَةِ وَلَا يُكَلِّمُهُمُ اللَّهُ وَلَا يَنظُرُ إِلَيْهِمْ يَوْمَ الْقِيَامَةِ وَلَا يُزَكِّيهِمْ وَلَهُمْ عَذَابٌ أَلِيمٌ

Verily, those who purchase a small gain at the cost of Allah's Covenant and their oaths, they shall have no portion in the Hereafter (Paradise). Neither will Allah speak to them, nor look at them on the Day of Resurrection, nor will He purify them, and they shall have a painful torment. (3:77, Al-Imran)

4.

قُل لَّا يَسْتَوِي الْخَبِيثُ وَالطَّيِّبُ وَلَوْ أَعْجَبَكَ كَثْرَةُ الْخَبِيثِ فَاتَّقُوا اللَّهَ يَا أُولِي الْأَلْبَابِ لَعَلَّكُمْ تُفْلِحُونَ

Say (O Muhammad ﷺ): "Not equal are Al-Khabith (all that is evil and bad) and At-Tayyib (all that is good)... So fear Allah much... in order that you may be successful." (5:100, Al-Maidah)

5.

قُلْ إِنَّمَا حَرَّمَ رَبِّيَ الْفَوَاحِشَ مَا ظَهَرَ مِنْهَا وَمَا بَطَنَ وَالْإِثْمَ وَالْبَغْيَ بِغَيْرِ الْحَقِّ وَأَن تُشْرِكُوا بِاللَّهِ مَا لَمْ يُنَزِّلْ بِهِ سُلْطَانًا وَأَن تَقُولُوا عَلَى اللَّهِ مَا لَا تَعْلَمُونَ

Say (O Muhammad ﷺ): "Indeed, the things my Lord has forbidden are Al-Fawahish (great evil sins)... and saying things about Allah of which you have no knowledge." (7:33, Al-A'raf)

Identify Your Situation

6.

الَّذِينَ يَسْتَحِبُّونَ الْحَيَاةَ الدُّنْيَا عَلَى الْآخِرَةِ وَيَصُدُّونَ عَن سَبِيلِ اللَّهِ وَيَبْغُونَهَا عِوَجًا ۚ أُولَٰئِكَ فِي ضَلَالٍ بَعِيدٍ

Those who prefer the life of this world instead of the Hereafter, and hinder (men) from the Path of Allah... They are far astray. (14:3, Ibrahim)

7.

وَمِنَ النَّاسِ مَن يَعْبُدُ اللَّهَ عَلَىٰ حَرْفٍ ۖ فَإِنْ أَصَابَهُ خَيْرٌ اطْمَأَنَّ بِهِ ۖ وَإِنْ أَصَابَتْهُ فِتْنَةٌ انقَلَبَ عَلَىٰ وَجْهِهِ خَسِرَ الدُّنْيَا وَالْآخِرَةَ ۚ ذَٰلِكَ هُوَ الْخُسْرَانُ الْمُبِينُ

And among mankind is he who worships Allah as it were, upon the very edge... He loses both this world and the Hereafter. That is the evident loss. (22:11, Al-Hajj)

8.

فَإِذَا مَسَّ الْإِنسَانَ ضُرٌّ دَعَانَا ثُمَّ إِذَا خَوَّلْنَاهُ نِعْمَةً مِّنَّا قَالَ إِنَّمَا أُوتِيتُهُ عَلَىٰ عِلْمٍ ۚ بَلْ هِيَ فِتْنَةٌ وَلَٰكِنَّ أَكْثَرَهُمْ لَا يَعْلَمُونَ

When harm touches man, he calls to Us... but when We change it into a favour, he says: "Only because of knowledge I obtained it." Nay, it is only a trial... (39:49, Az-Zumar)

9.

مَّن يُطِعِ الرَّسُولَ فَقَدْ أَطَاعَ اللَّهَ ۖ وَمَن تَوَلَّىٰ فَمَا أَرْسَلْنَاكَ عَلَيْهِمْ حَفِيظًا

He who obeys the Messenger (Muhammad ﷺ) has indeed obeyed Allah... (4:80, An-Nisaa)

10.

وَمِنَ النَّاسِ مَن يَشْتَرِي لَهْوَ الْحَدِيثِ لِيُضِلَّ عَن سَبِيلِ اللَّهِ بِغَيْرِ عِلْمٍ وَيَتَّخِذَهَا هُزُوًا ۚ أُولَٰئِكَ لَهُمْ عَذَابٌ مُّهِينٌ

But among men are those who purchase idle tales... to mislead (others) from the Path of Allah... For such there will be a humiliating penalty. (31:6, Luqman)

Identify Your Situation

11.

وَلَا تَكُونُوا كَالَّذِينَ نَسُوا اللَّهَ فَأَنسَاهُمْ أَنفُسَهُمْ ۚ أُولَٰئِكَ هُمُ الْفَاسِقُونَ

And be not like those who forgot Allah (i.e. became disobedient), and He caused them to forget their own selves... (59:19, Al-Hashr)

12

وَلَا تُطِعْ كُلَّ حَلَّافٍ مَّهِينٍ

And obey not everyone who swears much, and is considered worthless.

68:10 – Al-Qalam

13

مَنَّاعٍ لِّلْخَيْرِ مُعْتَدٍ أَثِيمٍ

Hinderer of the good, transgressor, sinful.

68:12 – Al-Qalam

Identify Your Situation

14

وَمَا آتَيْتُم مِّن رِّبًا لِّيَرْبُوَ فِي أَمْوَالِ النَّاسِ فَلَا يَرْبُو عِندَ اللَّهِ ۖ وَمَا آتَيْتُم مِّن زَكَاةٍ تُرِيدُونَ وَجْهَ اللَّهِ فَأُولَٰئِكَ هُمُ الْمُضْعِفُونَ

And that which you give in gift (to others), in order that it may increase (your wealth by expecting to get a better one in return) from other people's property, has no increase with Allah. But that which you give in Zakat, seeking Allah's Countenance – it is they who will receive a manifold increase.

30:39 – Ar-Rum

15

وَمَنْ أَظْلَمُ مِمَّن ذُكِّرَ بِآيَاتِ رَبِّهِ ثُمَّ أَعْرَضَ عَنْهَا ۚ إِنَّا مِنَ الْمُجْرِمِينَ مُنتَقِمُونَ

And who does more wrong than he who is reminded of the Ayat (proofs, evidences, verses, lessons, signs, revelations, etc.) of his Lord, then turns away from them? Verily, We shall exact retribution from the Mujrimun (criminals, disbelievers, polytheists, sinners, etc.).

32:22 – As-Sajda

16

كَمَثَلِ الشَّيْطَانِ إِذْ قَالَ لِلْإِنْسَانِ اكْفُرْ فَلَمَّا كَفَرَ قَالَ إِنِّي بَرِيءٌ مِنْكَ إِنِّي أَخَافُ اللَّهَ رَبَّ الْعَالَمِينَ

(Their allies deceived them) like Shaitan (Satan), when he says to man: "Disbelieve in Allah." But when (man) disbelieves, Shaitan says: "I am free of you. I fear Allah, the Lord of the 'Alamin (mankind, jinn and all that exists)."

59:16 – Al-Hashr

17

إِنَّمَا التَّوْبَةُ عَلَى اللَّهِ لِلَّذِينَ يَعْمَلُونَ السُّوءَ بِجَهَالَةٍ ثُمَّ يَتُوبُونَ مِن قَرِيبٍ فَأُولَٰئِكَ يَتُوبُ اللَّهُ عَلَيْهِمْ ۗ وَكَانَ اللَّهُ عَلِيمًا حَكِيمًا

Allah accepts only the repentance of those who do evil in ignorance and foolishness and repent soon afterwards; it is they to whom Allah will forgive. And Allah is Ever All-Knower, All-Wise.

4:17 – An-Nisaa

Identify Your Situation

18

لَّا يُحِبُّ اللَّهُ الْجَهْرَ بِالسُّوءِ مِنَ الْقَوْلِ إِلَّا مَن ظُلِمَ ۚ وَكَانَ اللَّهُ سَمِيعًا عَلِيمًا

Allah does not like that evil should be uttered in public, except by him who has been wronged. And Allah is Ever All-Hearer, All-Knower.

4:148 – An-Nisaa

19

رِجَالٌ لَّا تُلْهِيهِمْ تِجَارَةٌ وَلَا بَيْعٌ عَن ذِكْرِ اللَّهِ وَإِقَامِ الصَّلَاةِ وَإِيتَاءِ الزَّكَاةِ ۙ يَخَافُونَ يَوْمًا تَتَقَلَّبُ فِيهِ الْقُلُوبُ وَالْأَبْصَارُ

Men whom neither trade nor sale distracts from the remembrance of Allah (with heart and tongue), nor from performing As-Salat (Iqamat-as-Salat), nor from

giving the Zakat. They fear a Day when hearts and eyes will be overturned (from the horror of the torment of the Day of Resurrection).

24:37 – An-Nur

20

وَالَّذِينَ إِذَا فَعَلُوا فَاحِشَةً أَوْ ظَلَمُوا أَنفُسَهُمْ ذَكَرُوا اللَّهَ فَاسْتَغْفَرُوا لِذُنُوبِهِمْ وَمَن يَغْفِرُ الذُّنُوبَ إِلَّا اللَّهُ وَلَمْ يُصِرُّوا عَلَىٰ مَا فَعَلُوا وَهُمْ يَعْلَمُونَ

And those who, when they have committed Fahishah (illegal sexual intercourse, etc.) or wronged themselves with evil, remember Allah and ask forgiveness for their sins – and none can forgive sins but Allah – and do not persist in what (wrong) they have done while they know.

3:135 – Al-i'Imran

21

وَيْلٌ لِّكُلِّ هُمَزَةٍ لُّمَزَةٍ

Woe to every slanderer and backbiter.

104:1 – Al-Humaza

Identify Your Situation

22

هَمَّازٍ مَّشَّاءٍ بِنَمِيمٍ

A slanderer, going about with calumnies.

68:11 – Al-Qalam

23

بَلَىٰ مَنْ أَوْفَىٰ بِعَهْدِهِ وَاتَّقَىٰ فَإِنَّ اللَّهَ يُحِبُّ الْمُتَّقِينَ

Nay. Those that keep their plighted faith and act aright – verily Allah loves those who act aright.

3:76 – Al-i'Imran

24

وَمَنْ أَرَادَ الْآخِرَةَ وَسَعَىٰ لَهَا سَعْيَهَا وَهُوَ مُؤْمِنٌ فَأُولَٰئِكَ كَانَ سَعْيُهُم مَّشْكُورًا

And whoever desires the Hereafter and strives for it with the necessary effort due for it (i.e. does righteous deeds of Allah's obedience) while he is a believer (in the Oneness of Allah – Islamic Monotheism), then such are the ones whose striving shall be appreciated, thanked, and rewarded (by Allah).

17:19 – Al-Isra

Part III – The Messages of Being A True Believer

In this segment, we continue to delve into pinpointing the areas that propel us forward on our journey. This process aligns with our path of spiritual growth and our commitment to Allah (SWT), as He desires to populate Heaven solely with true believers.

Mere participation in rituals like prayer, fasting, Hajj, and Zakat is not enough, as even hypocrites can engage in these acts. Reflecting on our recent self-assessment may stir up internal challenges such as complexity, anxiety, and self-doubt. However, overcoming these hurdles and fostering confidence through our sincere quest for devotion is vital. Allah (SWT) says:

قَدْ أَفْلَحَ مَن تَزَكَّىٰ

But those will prosper who purify themselves.

87:14 – Surah Al-A'la

This is the third segment of divine guidance (verses) we are examining for assessment. These chosen verses shed light on areas we may have previously overlooked, offering both education and prompting introspection. By contemplating and embodying the teachings within, we strive towards becoming truly righteous.

Let the assessment begin.

17:9 – Al-Isra

إِنَّ هَٰذَا الْقُرْآنَ يَهْدِي لِلَّتِي هِيَ أَقْوَمُ وَيُبَشِّرُ الْمُؤْمِنِينَ الَّذِينَ يَعْمَلُونَ الصَّالِحَاتِ أَنَّ لَهُمْ أَجْرًا كَبِيرًا

Verily, this Qur'an guides to that which is most just and right and gives glad tidings to the believers (in the Oneness of Allah and His Messenger, Muhammad ﷺ etc.), who work deeds of righteousness, that they shall have a great reward (Paradise).

16:32 – An-Nahl

الَّذِينَ تَتَوَفَّاهُمُ الْمَلَائِكَةُ طَيِّبِينَ ۙ يَقُولُونَ سَلَامٌ عَلَيْكُمُ ادْخُلُوا الْجَنَّةَ بِمَا كُنتُمْ تَعْمَلُونَ

Those whose lives the angels take while they are in a pious state (i.e. pure from all evil, and worshipping none but Allah Alone), saying to them: "Salamun 'Alaikum (peace be upon you), enter Paradise because of the good you used to do (in the world)."

35:06 Fatir

إِنَّ الشَّيْطَانَ لَكُمْ عَدُوٌّ فَاتَّخِذُوهُ عَدُوًّا ۚ إِنَّمَا يَدْعُو حِزْبَهُ لِيَكُونُوا مِنْ أَصْحَابِ السَّعِيرِ

Surely, Shaitan (Satan) is an enemy to you, so take (treat) him as an enemy. He only invites his Hizb (followers) so that they may become the dwellers of the blazing Fire.

2:62 Al-Baqara

إِنَّ الَّذِينَ آمَنُوا وَالَّذِينَ هَادُوا وَالنَّصَارَىٰ وَالصَّابِئِينَ مَنْ آمَنَ بِاللَّهِ وَالْيَوْمِ الْآخِرِ وَعَمِلَ صَالِحًا فَلَهُمْ أَجْرُهُمْ عِندَ رَبِّهِمْ وَلَا خَوْفٌ عَلَيْهِمْ وَلَا هُمْ يَحْزَنُونَ

Verily! Those who believe, and those who are Jews, Christians and Sabians—whoever believes in Allah and the Last Day and does righteous good deeds—shall have their reward with their Lord. On them shall be no fear, nor shall they grieve.

5:9 Al-Maidah

وَعَدَ اللَّهُ الَّذِينَ آمَنُوا وَعَمِلُوا الصَّالِحَاتِ ۙ لَهُم مَّغْفِرَةٌ وَأَجْرٌ عَظِيمٌ

Allah has promised those who believe (in the Oneness of Allah – Islamic Monotheism) and do deeds of righteousness, that for them there is forgiveness and a great reward (i.e., Paradise).

6:82 Al-An'am

الَّذِينَ آمَنُوا وَلَمْ يَلْبِسُوا إِيمَانَهُم بِظُلْمٍ أُولَٰئِكَ لَهُمُ الْأَمْنُ وَهُم مُّهْتَدُونَ

It is those who believe (in the Oneness of Allah and worship none but Him alone), and confuse not their belief with Zulm (wrong, i.e., by worshipping others besides Allah), for them only there is security, and they are the guided.

30:45 Ar-Rum

لِيَجْزِيَ الَّذِينَ آمَنُوا وَعَمِلُوا الصَّالِحَاتِ مِن فَضْلِهِ ۚ إِنَّهُ لَا يُحِبُّ الْكَافِرِينَ

That He may reward those who believe (in the Oneness of Allah – Islamic Monotheism), and do righteous good deeds, out of His bounty. Verily, He does not love the disbelievers.

41:08 Ha-Mim

إِنَّ الَّذِينَ آمَنُوا وَعَمِلُوا الصَّالِحَاتِ لَهُمْ أَجْرٌ غَيْرُ مَمْنُونٍ

Truly, those who believe (in the Oneness of Allah – Islamic Monotheism, and in His Messenger Muhammad ﷺ) and do righteous good deeds, for them will be an endless reward that will never cease (i.e., Paradise).

29:02 Al-Ankabut

أَحَسِبَ النَّاسُ أَن يُتْرَكُوا أَن يَقُولُوا آمَنَّا وَهُمْ لَا يُفْتَنُونَ

Do people think that they will be left alone because they say, "We believe," and will not be tested?

32:19 As-Sajda

أَمَّا الَّذِينَ آمَنُوا وَعَمِلُوا الصَّالِحَاتِ فَلَهُمْ جَنَّاتُ الْمَأْوَىٰ نُزُلًا بِمَا كَانُوا يَعْمَلُونَ

As for those who believe (in the Oneness of Allah – Islamic Monotheism) and do righteous good deeds, for them are Gardens (Paradise) as an entertainment, for what they used to do.

31:08 Luqman

إِنَّ الَّذِينَ آمَنُوا وَعَمِلُوا الصَّالِحَاتِ لَهُمْ جَنَّاتُ النَّعِيمِ

Verily, those who believe (in Islamic Monotheism) and do righteous good deeds—for them are Gardens of Delight (Paradise).

52:21 Surah At-Tur

وَالَّذِينَ آمَنُوا وَاتَّبَعَتْهُمْ ذُرِّيَّتُهُم بِإِيمَانٍ أَلْحَقْنَا بِهِمْ ذُرِّيَّتَهُمْ وَمَا أَلَتْنَاهُم مِّنْ عَمَلِهِم مِّن شَيْءٍ ۚ كُلُّ امْرِئٍ بِمَا كَسَبَ رَهِينٌ

And those who believe, and whose offspring follow them in Faith—to them shall We join their offspring, and We shall not reduce (the reward of) their deeds in anything. Every person is a pledge for that which he has earned.

3:118 Al-i 'Imran

يَا أَيُّهَا الَّذِينَ آمَنُوا لَا تَتَّخِذُوا بِطَانَةً مِّن دُونِكُمْ لَا يَأْلُونَكُمْ خَبَالًا وَدُّوا مَا عَنِتُّمْ قَدْ بَدَتِ الْبَغْضَاءُ مِنْ أَفْوَاهِهِمْ وَمَا تُخْفِي صُدُورُهُمْ أَكْبَرُ ۚ قَدْ بَيَّنَّا لَكُمُ الْآيَاتِ ۖ إِن كُنتُمْ تَعْقِلُونَ

O you who believe! Take not as your *Bitanah* (advisors, consultants, protectors, helpers, friends, etc.) those outside your religion (pagans, Jews, Christians, and hypocrites), since they will not fail to do their best to corrupt you. They desire to harm you severely. Hatred has already appeared from their mouths, but what their breasts conceal is far worse. Indeed, We have made plain to you the Ayat (proofs, evidences, verses) if you understand.

Ye who believe! Take not into your intimacy those outside your ranks:

– They will not fail to corrupt you.

– They only desire your ruin.

– Rank hatred has already appeared from their mouths.

– What their hearts conceal is far worse.

– We have made plain to you the Signs, if ye have wisdom.

16:30 An-Nahl

وَقِيلَ لِلَّذِينَ اتَّقَوْا مَاذَا أَنزَلَ رَبُّكُمْ ۚ قَالُوا خَيْرًا ۗ لِّلَّذِينَ أَحْسَنُوا فِي هَٰذِهِ الدُّنْيَا حَسَنَةٌ ۚ وَلَدَارُ الْآخِرَةِ خَيْرٌ ۚ وَلَنِعْمَ دَارُ الْمُتَّقِينَ

And (when) it is said to those who are the *Muttaqun* (pious – see V.2:2), "What is it that your Lord has sent down?" They say: "That which is good." For those who do good in this world, there is good, and the home of the Hereafter will be better. And excellent indeed will be the home (i.e., Paradise) of the *Muttaqun*.

16:97 An-Nahl

مَنْ عَمِلَ صَالِحًا مِّن ذَكَرٍ أَوْ أُنثَىٰ وَهُوَ مُؤْمِنٌ فَلَنُحْيِيَنَّهُ حَيَاةً طَيِّبَةً ۖ وَلَنَجْزِيَنَّهُمْ أَجْرَهُم بِأَحْسَنِ مَا كَانُوا يَعْمَلُونَ

Whoever works righteousness, whether male or female, while he (or she) is a true believer (of Islamic Monotheism)—verily, to him We will give a good life (in this world with respect, contentment and lawful provision), and We shall certainly pay them a reward in proportion to the best of what they used to do (i.e., Paradise in the Hereafter).

– Whoever works righteousness,

– Man or woman, and has Faith,

– Verily, to him will We give a new life,

– A life that is good and pure,

– And We will bestow on such their reward,

– According to the best of their actions.

14:27 Ibrahim

يُثَبِّتُ اللَّهُ الَّذِينَ آمَنُوا بِالْقَوْلِ الثَّابِتِ فِي الْحَيَاةِ الدُّنْيَا وَفِي الْآخِرَةِ ۖ وَيُضِلُّ اللَّهُ الظَّالِمِينَ ۚ وَيَفْعَلُ اللَّهُ مَا يَشَاءُ

Allah will keep firm those who believe, with the word that stands firm in this world (i.e., they will continue to worship Allah Alone and none else), and in the Hereafter. And Allah will cause to go astray those who are *Zalimun* (polytheists and wrong-doers, etc.), and Allah does what He wills.

20:112 Ta-Ha

وَمَن يَعْمَلْ مِنَ الصَّالِحَاتِ وَهُوَ مُؤْمِنٌ فَلَا يَخَافُ ظُلْمًا وَلَا هَضْمًا

And he who works deeds of righteousness, while he is a believer (in Islamic Monotheism), then he will have no fear of injustice nor of any curtailment (of his reward).

48:04 Al-Fath

هُوَ الَّذِي أَنزَلَ السَّكِينَةَ فِي قُلُوبِ الْمُؤْمِنِينَ لِيَزْدَادُوا إِيمَانًا مَّعَ إِيمَانِهِمْ ۗ وَلِلَّهِ جُنُودُ السَّمَاوَاتِ وَالْأَرْضِ ۚ وَكَانَ اللَّهُ عَلِيمًا حَكِيمًا

He it is Who sent down *As-Sakinah* (calmness and tranquillity) into the hearts of the believers, that they may grow more in faith along with their present faith. And to Allah belong the hosts of the heavens and the earth, and Allah is Ever All-Knowing, All-Wise.

40:40 Al-Mu'min

۞ مَنْ عَمِلَ سَيِّئَةً فَلَا يُجْزَىٰ إِلَّا مِثْلَهَا ۖ وَمَنْ عَمِلَ صَالِحًا مِّن ذَكَرٍ أَوْ أُنثَىٰ وَهُوَ مُؤْمِنٌ فَأُولَٰئِكَ يَدْخُلُونَ الْجَنَّةَ يُرْزَقُونَ فِيهَا بِغَيْرِ حِسَابٍ

"Whosoever does an evil deed will not be requited except the like thereof; and whosoever does a righteous deed, whether male or female, and is a true believer (in the Oneness of Allah)—such will enter Paradise, where they will be provided therein (with all things in abundance) without limit.

66:06 At-Tahrim

يَا أَيُّهَا الَّذِينَ آمَنُوا قُوا أَنفُسَكُمْ وَأَهْلِيكُمْ نَارًا وَقُودُهَا النَّاسُ وَالْحِجَارَةُ عَلَيْهَا مَلَائِكَةٌ غِلَاظٌ شِدَادٌ لَّا يَعْصُونَ اللَّهَ مَا أَمَرَهُمْ وَيَفْعَلُونَ مَا يُؤْمَرُونَ

O you who believe! Ward off from yourselves and your families a Fire (Hell) whose fuel is men and stones, over which are appointed angels, stern and severe, who disobey not the Commands they receive from Allah, but do that which they are commanded.

4:111 An-Nisaa

وَمَن يَكْسِبْ إِثْمًا فَإِنَّمَا يَكْسِبُهُ عَلَىٰ نَفْسِهِ ۚ وَكَانَ اللَّهُ عَلِيمًا حَكِيمًا

And whoever earns sin, he earns it only against himself. And Allah is Ever All-Knowing, All-Wise.

3:131 Al-i 'Imran

وَاتَّقُوا النَّارَ الَّتِي أُعِدَّتْ لِلْكَافِرِينَ

And fear the Fire which is prepared for the disbelievers.

16:128 An-Nahl

نَّ اللَّهَ مَعَ الَّذِينَ اتَّقَوا وَّالَّذِينَ هُم مُّحْسِنُونَ

Truly, Allah is with those who fear Him (keep their duty unto Him), and those who are *Muhsinun* (good-doers – see the footnote of V.9:120).

35:10 Fatir

ـَن كَانَ يُرِيدُ الْعِزَّةَ فَلِلَّهِ الْعِزَّةُ جَمِيعًا ۚ إِلَيْهِ يَصْعَدُ الْكَلِمُ الطَّيِّبُ وَالْعَمَلُ الصَّالِحُ يَرْفَعُهُ ۚ وَالَّذِينَ يَمْكُرُونَ السَّيِّئَاتِ لَهُمْ عَذَابٌ شَدِيدٌ ۖ وَمَكْرُ أُولَـٰئِكَ هُوَ يَبُو

Whosoever desires honour, power and glory, then to Allah belong all honour, power and glory. [And one can attain honour, power and glory only by obeying and worshipping Allah (Alone)]. To Him ascend all goodly words, and righteous deeds exalt it. But those who plot evils—theirs will be severe torment. And the plotting of such will perish.

2:220 – Al-Baqara

ـِي الدُّنْيَا وَالْآخِرَةِ ۗ وَيَسْأَلُونَكَ عَنِ الْيَتَامَىٰ ۖ قُلْ إِصْلَاحٌ لَّهُمْ خَيْرٌ ۖ وَإِن تُخَالِطُوهُمْ فَإِخْوَانُكُمْ ۚ وَاللَّهُ يَعْلَمُ الْمُفْسِدَ مِنَ الْمُصْلِحِ ۚ وَلَوْ شَاءَ اللَّهُ لَأَعْنَتَكُمْ ۚ إِنَّ اللَّهَ عَزِيزٌ حَكِيمٌ

In (to) this worldly life and in the Hereafter. And they ask you concerning orphans. Say: -

""The best thing is to work honestly with their property, and if you mix your affairs with theirs, then they are your brothers. And Allah knows him who means mischief (e.g. to swallow their property) from him who means good (e.g. to safeguard their property). And if Allah had wished, He could have put you into difficulties. Truly, Allah is All-Mighty, All-Wise."

41:49 – Ha-Mim

لَّا يَسْأَمُ الْإِنسَانُ مِن دُعَاءِ الْخَيْرِ وَإِن مَّسَّهُ الشَّرُّ فَيَئُوسٌ قَنُوطٌ

Man (the disbeliever) does not get tired of asking for good (things from Allah), but if evil touches him, then he gives up all hope and is lost in despair.

39:7 – Az-Zumar

إِن تَكْفُرُوا فَإِنَّ اللَّهَ غَنِيٌّ عَنكُمْ ۖ وَلَا يَرْضَىٰ لِعِبَادِهِ الْكُفْرَ ۖ وَإِن تَشْكُرُوا يَرْضَهُ لَكُمْ ۗ وَلَا تَزِرُ وَازِرَةٌ وِزْرَ أُخْرَىٰ ۗ ثُمَّ إِلَىٰ رَبِّكُم مَّرْجِعُكُمْ فَيُنَبِّئُكُم بِمَا كُنتُمْ تَعْمَلُونَ ۚ إِنَّهُ عَلِيمٌ بِذَاتِ الصُّدُورِ

If you disbelieve, then verily, Allah is not in need of you. He does not like disbelief for His slaves. And if you are grateful (by being believers), He is pleased with you. No bearer of burdens shall bear the burden of another. Then to your Lord is your return, so He will inform you of what you used to do. Verily, He is the All-Knower of that which is in (men's) breasts.

2:149 – Al-Baqara

وَمِنْ حَيْثُ خَرَجْتَ فَوَلِّ وَجْهَكَ شَطْرَ الْمَسْجِدِ الْحَرَامِ ۖ وَإِنَّهُ لَلْحَقُّ مِن رَّبِّكَ ۗ وَمَا اللَّهُ بِغَافِلٍ عَمَّا تَعْمَلُونَ

And from wherever you start forth (for prayers), turn your face in the direction of Al-Masjid-al-Haram (at Makkah); that is indeed the truth from your Lord. And Allah is not unaware of what you do.

2:261 – Al-Baqara

مَّثَلُ الَّذِينَ يُنفِقُونَ أَمْوَالَهُمْ فِي سَبِيلِ اللَّهِ كَمَثَلِ حَبَّةٍ أَنبَتَتْ سَبْعَ سَنَابِلَ فِي كُلِّ سُنبُلَةٍ مِّائَةُ حَبَّةٍ ۗ وَاللَّهُ يُضَاعِفُ لِمَن يَشَاءُ ۗ وَاللَّهُ وَاسِعٌ عَلِيمٌ

The likeness of those who spend their wealth in the Way of Allah is as the likeness of a grain (of corn); it grows seven ears, and each ear has a hundred grains. Allah gives manifold increase to whom He pleases. And Allah is All-Sufficient for His creatures' needs, All-Knower.

2:123 – Al-Baqara

وَاتَّقُوا يَوْمًا لَّا تَجْزِي نَفْسٌ عَن نَّفْسٍ شَيْئًا وَلَا يُقْبَلُ مِنْهَا عَدْلٌ وَلَا تَنفَعُهَا شَفَاعَةٌ وَلَا هُمْ يُنصَرُونَ

And fear the Day (of Judgement) when no person shall avail another, nor shall compensation be accepted from him, nor shall intercession be of use to him, nor shall they be helped.

22:67 – Al-Hajj

لِّكُلِّ أُمَّةٍ جَعَلْنَا مَنسَكًا هُمْ نَاسِكُوهُ ۖ فَلَا يُنَازِعُنَّكَ فِي الْأَمْرِ ۚ وَادْعُ إِلَىٰ رَبِّكَ ۖ إِنَّكَ لَعَلَىٰ هُدًى مُّسْتَقِيمٍ

For every nation, We have ordained religious ceremonies [e.g. the slaughtering of the beast of cattle during the three days of stay at Mina (Makkah) during Hajj (pilgrimage)] which they must follow. So let them (pagans) not dispute with you on the matter (i.e. eating cattle slaughtered in the name of Allah versus those which die naturally). But invite them to your Lord. Verily! You (O Muhammad ﷺ) are indeed on the (true) straight guidance (i.e. the true religion of Islamic Monotheism).

64:11 – At-Taghabun

مَا أَصَابَ مِن مُّصِيبَةٍ إِلَّا بِإِذْنِ اللَّهِ ۗ وَمَن يُؤْمِن بِاللَّهِ يَهْدِ قَلْبَهُ ۚ وَاللَّهُ بِكُلِّ شَيْءٍ عَلِيمٌ

No calamity befalls, except by the Leave [i.e. decision and Qadar (Divine Preordainment)] of Allah. And whosoever believes in Allah, He guides his heart [to the true Faith with certainty, i.e. that what has befallen him was already written for him by Allah]. And Allah is the All-Knower of everything.

35:5 – Fatir

يَا أَيُّهَا النَّاسُ إِنَّ وَعْدَ اللَّهِ حَقٌّ ۖ فَلَا تَغُرَّنَّكُمُ الْحَيَاةُ الدُّنْيَا ۖ وَلَا يَغُرَّنَّكُم بِاللَّهِ الْغَرُورُ

O mankind! Verily, the Promise of Allah is true. So let not this present life deceive you, and let not the chief deceiver (Satan) deceive you about Allah.

47:1 – Muhammad

الَّذِينَ كَفَرُوا وَصَدُّوا عَن سَبِيلِ اللَّهِ أَضَلَّ أَعْمَالَهُمْ

Those who disbelieve [in the Oneness of Allah and in the Message of Prophet Muhammad ﷺ], and hinder (men) from the Path of Allah (Islamic Monotheism), He will render their deeds vain.

40:7 – Al-Mu'min

لَّذِينَ يَحْمِلُونَ الْعَرْشَ وَمَنْ حَوْلَهُ يُسَبِّحُونَ بِحَمْدِ رَبِّهِمْ وَيُؤْمِنُونَ بِهِ وَيَسْتَغْفِرُونَ لِلَّذِينَ آمَنُوا رَبَّنَا وَسِعْتَ كُلَّ شَيْءٍ رَّحْمَةً وَعِلْمًا فَاغْفِرْ لِلَّذِينَ تَابُوا وَاتَّبَعُوا سَبِيلَكَ وَقِهِمْ عَذَابَ الْجَحِيمِ

Those (angels) who bear the Throne (of Allah) and those around it glorify the praises of their Lord, and believe in Him, and ask forgiveness for those who believe (in the Oneness of Allah), saying: "Our Lord! You encompass all things in mercy and knowledge, so forgive those who repent and follow Your Way, and save them from the torment of the blazing Fire."

29:58 – Al-Ankabut

وَالَّذِينَ آمَنُوا وَعَمِلُوا الصَّالِحَاتِ لَنُبَوِّئَنَّهُم مِّنَ الْجَنَّةِ غُرَفًا تَجْرِي مِن تَحْتِهَا الْأَنْهَارُ خَالِدِينَ فِيهَا ۚ نِعْمَ أَجْرُ الْعَامِلِينَ

And those who believe (in the Oneness of Allah – Islamic Monotheism) and do righteous good deeds, to them We shall surely give lofty dwellings in Paradise, underneath which rivers flow, to live therein forever. Excellent is the reward of the workers.

30:36 – Ar-Rum

وَإِذَا أَذَقْنَا النَّاسَ رَحْمَةً فَرِحُوا بِهَا ۖ وَإِن تُصِبْهُمْ سَيِّئَةٌ بِمَا قَدَّمَتْ أَيْدِيهِمْ إِذَا هُمْ يَقْنَطُون

And when We cause mankind to taste of mercy, they rejoice in it; but when some evil afflicts them because of (the evil deeds and sins) that their (own) hands have sent forth, lo! they are in despair.

3:135 – Al-i'Imran

وَالَّذِينَ إِذَا فَعَلُوا فَاحِشَةً أَوْ ظَلَمُوا أَنفُسَهُمْ ذَكَرُوا اللَّهَ فَاسْتَغْفَرُوا لِذُنُوبِهِمْ وَمَن يَغْفِرُ الذُّنُوبَ إِلَّا اللَّهُ وَلَمْ يُصِرُّوا عَلَىٰ مَا فَعَلُوا وَهُمْ يَعْلَمُونَ

And those who, when they have committed Fahishah (illegal sexual intercourse, etc.) or wronged themselves with evil, remember Allah and ask forgiveness for their sins – and none can forgive sins but Allah – and do not persist in what (wrong) they have done, while they know.

29:69 – Al-Ankabut

وَالَّذِينَ جَاهَدُوا فِينَا لَنَهْدِيَنَّهُمْ سُبُلَنَا ۚ وَإِنَّ اللَّهَ لَمَعَ الْمُحْسِنِينَ

As for those who strive hard in Us (Our Cause), We will surely guide them to Our Paths (i.e. Allah's Religion – Islamic Monotheism). And verily, Allah is with the Muhsinun (good-doers)."

7:158 – Al-A'raf

قُلْ يَا أَيُّهَا النَّاسُ إِنِّي رَسُولُ اللَّهِ إِلَيْكُمْ جَمِيعًا الَّذِي لَهُ مُلْكُ السَّمَاوَاتِ وَالْأَرْضِ ۖ لَا إِلَٰهَ إِلَّا هُوَ يُحْيِي وَيُمِيتُ ۖ فَآمِنُوا بِاللَّهِ وَرَسُولِهِ النَّبِيِّ الْأُمِّيِّ الَّذِي يُؤْمِنُ بِاللَّهِ وَكَلِمَاتِهِ وَاتَّبِعُوهُ لَعَلَّكُمْ تَهْتَدُونَ

Say (O Muhammad ﷺ): "O mankind! Verily, I am sent to you all as the Messenger of Allah – to Whom belongs the dominion of the heavens and the earth. *La ilaha illa Huwa* (none has the right to be worshipped but He); it is He Who gives life and causes death. So believe in Allah and His Messenger (Muhammad ﷺ), the Prophet who can neither read nor write (i.e. Muhammad ﷺ), who believes in Allah and His Words [(this Qur'an), the Taurat (Torah), the Injeel (Gospel), and also Allah's Word: "Be!" – and he was, i.e. 'Isa (Jesus), son of Maryam (Mary)], and follow him so that you may be guided."

4:47 – An-Nisa

يَا أَيُّهَا الَّذِينَ أُوتُوا الْكِتَابَ آمِنُوا بِمَا نَزَّلْنَا مُصَدِّقًا لِمَا مَعَكُم مِّن قَبْلِ أَن نَّطْمِسَ وُجُوهًا فَنَرُدَّهَا عَلَىٰ أَدْبَارِهَا أَوْ نَلْعَنَهُمْ كَمَا لَعَنَّا أَصْحَابَ السَّبْتِ ۚ وَكَانَ أَمْرُ اللَّهِ مَفْعُولًا

O you who have been given the Scripture (Jews and Christians)! Believe in what We have revealed (to Muhammad ﷺ), confirming what is (already) with you, before We efface faces (by making them like the backs of necks—without nose, mouth, eyes, etc.) and turn them backwards, or curse them as We cursed the Sabbath-breakers. And the Commandment of Allah is always executed.

2:219 – Al-Baqara

يَسْأَلُونَكَ عَنِ الْخَمْرِ وَالْمَيْسِرِ ۖ قُلْ فِيهِمَا إِثْمٌ كَبِيرٌ وَمَنَافِعُ لِلنَّاسِ وَإِثْمُهُمَا أَكْبَرُ مِن نَّفْعِهِمَا ۗ وَيَسْأَلُونَكَ مَاذَا يُنفِقُونَ قُلِ الْعَفْوَ ۗ كَذَٰلِكَ يُبَيِّنُ اللَّهُ لَكُمُ الْآيَاتِ لَعَلَّكُمْ تَتَفَكَّرُونَ

They ask you (O Muhammad ﷺ) concerning alcoholic drink and gambling. Say:

"In them is a great sin, and (some) benefit for men, but the sin of them is greater than their benefit."

And they ask you what they ought to spend. Say: "That which is beyond your needs."

Thus Allah makes clear to you His Laws, in order that you may give thought.

50:17–18 – Qaf

إِذْ يَتَلَقَّى الْمُتَلَقِّيَانِ عَنِ الْيَمِينِ وَعَنِ الشِّمَالِ قَعِيدٌ

مَّا يَلْفِظُ مِن قَوْلٍ إِلَّا لَدَيْهِ رَقِيبٌ عَتِيدٌ

(Remember!) that the two receivers (recording angels) receive (each human being after he or she has attained the age of puberty), one sitting on the right and one on the left (to note his or her actions).

3:103 – Al-i'Imran

وَاعْتَصِمُوا بِحَبْلِ اللَّهِ جَمِيعًا وَلَا تَفَرَّقُوا ۚ وَاذْكُرُوا نِعْمَتَ اللَّهِ عَلَيْكُمْ إِذْ كُنتُمْ أَعْدَاءً فَأَلَّفَ بَيْنَ قُلُوبِكُمْ فَأَصْبَحْتُم بِنِعْمَتِهِ إِخْوَانًا وَكُنتُمْ عَلَىٰ شَفَا حُفْرَةٍ مِّنَ النَّارِ فَأَنقَذَكُم مِّنْهَا ۗ كَذَٰلِكَ يُبَيِّنُ اللَّهُ لَكُمْ آيَاتِهِ لَعَلَّكُمْ تَهْتَدُونَ

And hold fast, all of you together, to the Rope of Allah (i.e. this Qur'an), and be not divided among yourselves, and remember Allah's favour upon you. For you were enemies one to another, but He joined your hearts together, so that by His grace, you became brethren (in Islamic Faith); and you were on the brink of a pit of Fire, and He saved you from it.

Thus Allah makes His Ayat (proofs, evidences, verses, lessons, signs, revelations, etc.) clear to you, that you may be guided.

Part IV

Do I Know Now Where The Straight Path Is?

Or

Am I Still Looking For A Guide To Take Me There?

هْدِنَا الصِّرَاطَ الْمُسْتَقِيمَ

Guide us to the Straight Path

Attaining virtues that reflect our inner purity, knowledge, and good deeds requires thorough preparation for the journey—guided by Allah (SWT) and the teachings of Prophet Muhammad ﷺ.

Self-examination serves as the initial step, allowing us to gauge the extent of our spiritual development—an ongoing process of acquiring knowledge, inner resilience, and spiritual purification that validates our journey.

As we embark on the fourth stage of our quest for the straight path, it is imperative that we truly seek it. Despite reciting Surah Al-Fatiha, beseeching *"Guide us to the Straight Path"* at least seventeen times a day during *Salah* (the five daily prayers), we must honestly ask ourselves:

Are we actively pursuing this path?

Our Prophet ﷺ said,

"I have left you upon a clear path; its clarity is the same by night or day. No one deviates from it after me but that he will be ruined."

(Source: Al-'Irbad ibn Sariyah reported. *Sunan Ibn Mājah* 44)

Let us now seek the straight path and potential guidance from what Allah (SWT) says about our pursuit of the straight path:

Surah al-Baqarah

كَانَ النَّاسُ أُمَّةً وَاحِدَةً فَبَعَثَ اللَّهُ النَّبِيِّينَ مُبَشِّرِينَ وَمُنذِرِينَ وَأَنزَلَ مَعَهُمُ الْكِتَابَ بِالْحَقِّ لِيَحْكُمَ بَيْنَ النَّاسِ فِيمَا اخْتَلَفُوا فِيهِ ۚ وَمَا اخْتَلَفَ فِيهِ إِلَّا الَّذِينَ أُوتُوهُ مِن بَعْدِ مَا جَاءَتْهُمُ الْبَيِّنَاتُ بَغْيًا بَيْنَهُمْ ۖ فَهَدَى اللَّهُ الَّذِينَ آمَنُوا لِمَا اخْتَلَفُوا فِيهِ مِنَ الْحَقِّ بِإِذْنِهِ ۗ وَاللَّهُ يَهْدِي مَن يَشَاءُ إِلَىٰ صِرَاطٍ مُّسْتَقِيمٍ

Mankind were one community and Allah sent Prophets with glad tidings and warnings, and with them He sent the Scripture in truth to judge between people in matters wherein they differed. And only those to whom (the Scripture) was given differed concerning it after clear proofs had come unto them through hatred, one to another. Then Allah by His Leave guided those who believed to the truth of that wherein they differed. And Allah guides whom He wills to a Straight Path.

(2:213, *Surah al-Baqarah*)

Surah al-Mā'idah

سُبُلَ السَّلَامِ وَيُخْرِجُهُم مِّنَ الظُّلُمَاتِ إِلَى النُّورِ بِإِذْنِهِ وَيَهْدِيهِمْ يَهْدِي بِهِ اللَّهُ مَنِ اتَّبَعَ رِضْوَانَهُ إِلَىٰ صِرَاطٍ مُّسْتَقِيمٍ

Wherewith Allah guides all those who seek His Good Pleasure to ways of peace, and He brings them out of darkness by His Will unto light and guides them to a Straight Way (Islamic Monotheism).

(5:16, *Surah al-Mā'idah*)

Surah Yūnus

وَيَهْدِي مَن يَشَاءُ إِلَىٰ صِرَاطٍ مُّسْتَقِيمٍ وَاللَّهُ يَدْعُو إِلَىٰ دَارِ السَّلَامِ

Allah calls to the home of peace (i.e. Paradise, by accepting Allah's religion of Islamic Monotheism and by doing righteous good deeds and abstaining from polytheism and evil deeds) and guides whom He wills to a Straight Path.

(10:25, *Surah Yūnus*)

Surah Āl-'Imrān

فَاعْبُدُوهُ هَٰذَا صِرَاطٌ مُّسْتَقِيمٌ إِنَّ اللَّهَ رَبِّي وَرَبُّكُمْ

Truly! Allah is my Lord and your Lord, so worship Him (Alone). This is the Straight Path.

(3:51, *Surah Āl-'Imrān*)

Surah al-Baqarah

مَا وَلَّاهُمْ عَن قِبْلَتِهِمُ الَّتِي كَانُوا عَلَيْهَا قُل لِّلَّهِ الْمَشْرِقُ وَالْمَغْرِبُ سَيَقُولُ السُّفَهَاءُ مِنَ النَّاسِ يَهْدِي مَن يَشَاءُ إِلَىٰ صِرَاطٍ مُّسْتَقِيمٍ

The fools (pagans, hypocrites, and Jews) among the people will say, "What has turned them (Muslims) from their Qiblah [prayer direction (towards Jerusalem)] to which they were used to face in prayer." Say (O Muhammad ﷺ), "To Allah belong both, east and the west. He guides whom He wills to a Straight Way."

(2:142, *Surah al-Baqarah*)

Surah al-Naḥl

أَحَدُهُمَا أَبْكَمُ لَا يَقْدِرُ عَلَىٰ شَيْءٍ وَهُوَ كَلٌّ عَلَىٰ مَوْلَاهُ أَيْنَمَا يُوَجِّههُّ وَضَرَبَ اللَّهُ مَثَلًا رَّجُلَيْنِ لَا يَأْتِ بِخَيْرٍ هَلْ يَسْتَوِي هُوَ وَمَن يَأْمُرُ بِالْعَدْلِ وَهُوَ عَلَىٰ صِرَاطٍ مُّسْتَقِيمٍ

And Allah puts forward (another) example of two men, one of them dumb, who has no power over anything (disbeliever), and he is a burden to his master, whichever way he directs him, he brings no good. Is such a man equal to one (believer in the Islamic Monotheism) who commands justice, and is himself on a Straight Path?

(16:76, Surah al-Naḥl)

اجْتَبَاهُ وَهَدَاهُ إِلَىٰ صِرَاطٍ مُّسْتَقِيمٍ شَاكِرًا لِّأَنْعُمِهِ

(He was) thankful for His (Allah's) Graces. He (Allah) chose him (as an intimate friend) and guided him to a Straight Path (Islamic Monotheism, neither Judaism nor Christianity).

(16:121, Surah al-Naḥl)

Surah Maryam

فَاعْبُدُوهُ ۚ هَٰذَا صِرَاطٌ مُّسْتَقِيمٌ وَإِنَّ اللَّهَ رَبِّي وَرَبُّكُمْ

['Īsā (Jesus) said]: "And verily Allah is my Lord and your Lord. So worship Him (Alone). That is the Straight Path. (Allah's Religion of Islamic Monotheism which He did ordain for all of His Prophets)."

(19:36, Surah Maryam)

مِنَ الْعِلْمِ مَا لَمْ يَأْتِكَ فَاتَّبِعْنِي أَهْدِكَ صِرَاطًا سَوِيًّا يَا أَبَتِ إِنِّي قَدْ جَاءَنِي

"O my father! Verily! There has come to me of knowledge that which came not unto you. So follow me. I will guide you to a Straight Path."

(19:43, Surah Maryam)

Surah al-Anʿām

وَيُونُسَ وَلُوطًا ۚ وَكُلًّا فَضَّلْنَا عَلَى الْعَالَمِينَ وَإِسْمَاعِيلَ وَالْيَسَعَ

وَمِنْ آبَائِهِمْ وَذُرِّيَّاتِهِمْ وَإِخْوَانِهِمْ ۖ وَاجْتَبَيْنَاهُمْ وَهَدَيْنَاهُمْ إِلَىٰ صِرَاطٍ مُّسْتَقِيمٍ

And Ismāʿīl (Ishmael), and Al-Yasaʿ (Elisha), and Yūnus (Jonah) and Lūṭ (Lot), and each one of them We preferred above the ʿĀlamīn (mankind and jinns of their times).

And also some of their fathers and their progeny and their brethren, We chose them, and We guided them to a Straight Path.

(6:86–87, Surah al-Anʿām)

شَرَحْ صَدْرَهُ لِلْإِسْلَامِ ۖ وَمَن يُرِدْ أَن يُضِلَّهُ يَجْعَلْ صَدْرَهُ ضَيِّقًا فَمَن يُرِدِ اللَّهُ أَن يَهْدِيَهُ

حَرَجًا كَأَنَّمَا يَصَّعَّدُ فِي السَّمَاءِ ۚ كَذَٰلِكَ يَجْعَلُ اللَّهُ الرِّجْسَ عَلَى الَّذِينَ لَا يُؤْمِنُونَ

وَهَٰذَا صِرَاطُ رَبِّكَ مُسْتَقِيمًا ۗ قَدْ فَصَّلْنَا الْآيَاتِ لِقَوْمٍ يَذَّكَّرُونَ

And whomsoever Allah wills to guide, He opens his breast to Islam; and whomsoever He wills to send astray, He makes his breast closed and constricted, as if he is climbing up to the sky. Thus Allah puts the wrath on those who believe not.

And this is the Path of your Lord (the Qur'an and Islam) leading Straight. We have detailed Our Revelations for a people who take heed.

(6:125–126, *Surah al-An'ām*)

فَاتَّبِعُوهُ ۖ وَلَا تَتَّبِعُوا السُّبُلَ فَتَفَرَّقَ بِكُمْ عَن سَبِيلِهِ ۚ ذَٰلِكُمْ وَصَّاكُم بِهِ ۚ وَأَنَّ هَٰذَا صِرَاطِي مُسْتَقِيمًا لَعَلَّكُمْ تَتَّقُونَ

"And verily, this (i.e. Allah's Commandments mentioned in the above two Verses 151 and 152) is My Straight Path, so follow it, and follow not (other) paths, for they will separate you away from His Path. This He has ordained for you that you may become Al-Muttaqūn (the pious – see 2:2)."

(6:153, *Surah al-An'ām*)

إِلَىٰ صِرَاطٍ مُّسْتَقِيمٍ دِينًا قِيَمًا مِّلَّةَ إِبْرَاهِيمَ حَنِيفًا ۚ وَمَا كَانَ مِنَ الْمُشْرِكِينَ قُلْ إِنَّنِي هَدَانِي رَبِّي

Say (O Muhammad ﷺ): "Truly, my Lord has guided me to a Straight Path, a right religion, the religion of Ibrāhīm (Abraham), Ḥanīfa [i.e. the true Islamic Monotheism – to believe in One God (Allah, i.e. to worship none but Allah, Alone)] and he was not of Al-Mushrikūn."

(6:161, *Surah al-An'ām*)

Surah Hūd

رَبِّي وَرَبِّكُم ۚ مَّا مِن دَابَّةٍ إِلَّا هُوَ آخِذٌ بِنَاصِيَتِهَا ۚ إِنَّ رَبِّي عَلَىٰ صِرَاطٍ مُّسْتَقِيمٍ إِنِّي تَوَكَّلْتُ عَلَى اللَّهِ

"I put my trust in Allah, my Lord and your Lord! There is not a moving (living) creature but He has grasp of its forelock. Verily, my Lord is on the Straight Path (the truth)."

(11:56, *Surah Hūd*)

Surah al-Nūr

وَاللَّهُ يَهْدِي مَن يَشَاءُ إِلَىٰ صِرَاطٍ مُّسْتَقِيمٍ لَّقَدْ أَنزَلْنَا آيَاتٍ مُّبَيِّنَاتٍ

We have indeed sent down (in this Qur'an) manifest Āyāt (proofs, evidences, verses, lessons, signs, revelations, lawful and unlawful things, and the set boundaries of Islamic religion, etc. that make things clear showing the Right Path of Allah). And Allah guides whom He wills to a Straight Path (i.e. to Allah's religion of Islamic Monotheism).

(24:46, Surah al-Nūr)

Surah Saba'

الَّذِي أُنزِلَ إِلَيْكَ مِن رَّبِّكَ هُوَ الْحَقَّ وَيَهْدِي إِلَىٰ صِرَاطِ الْعَزِيزِ الْحَمِيدِ وَيَرَى الَّذِينَ أُوتُوا الْعِلْمَ

And those who have been given knowledge see that what is revealed to you (O Muhammad ﷺ) from your Lord is the truth, and guides to the Path of the Exalted in Might, Owner of all praise.

(34:6, *Surah Saba'*)

Surah Yā-Sīn

وَالْقُرْآنِ الْحَكِيمِ

إِنَّكَ لَمِنَ الْمُرْسَلِينَ

عَلَىٰ صِرَاطٍ مُّسْتَقِيمٍ

By the Qur'an, full of wisdom (i.e. full of laws, evidences, and proofs),

Truly, you (O Muhammad ﷺ) are one of the Messengers,

On a Straight Path (i.e. on Allah's religion of Islamic Monotheism).

(36:2–4, *Surah Yā-Sīn*)

Surah al-Mu'minūn

إِلَىٰ صِرَاطٍ مُّسْتَقِيمٍ وَإِنَّكَ لَتَدْعُوهُمْ

وَإِنَّ الَّذِينَ لَا يُؤْمِنُونَ بِالْآخِرَةِ عَنِ الصِّرَاطِ لَنَاكِبُونَ

And certainly, you (O Muhammad ﷺ) call them to a Straight Path (true religion – Islamic Monotheism).

And verily, those who believe not in the Hereafter are indeed deviating far astray from the Path (true religion – Islamic Monotheism).

(23:73–74, *Surah al-Mu'minūn*)

Surah al-Mulk

عَلَىٰ وَجْهِهِ أَهْدَىٰ أَمَّن يَمْشِي سَوِيًّا عَلَىٰ صِرَاطٍ مُّسْتَقِيمٍ أَفَمَن يَمْشِي مُكِبًّا

Is he who walks without seeing on his face, more rightly guided, or he who (sees and) walks on a Straight Way (i.e. Islamic Monotheism)?

(67:22, *Surah al-Mulk*)

Surah al-Zukhruf

إِلَيْكَ ۖ إِنَّكَ عَلَىٰ صِرَاطٍ مُّسْتَقِيمٍ فَاسْتَمْسِكْ بِالَّذِي أُوحِيَ

So hold you (O Muhammad ﷺ) fast to that which is inspired in you. Verily, you are on a Straight Path.

(43:43, *Surah al-Zukhruf*)

Surah Ash-Shura

وَكَذَٰلِكَ أَوْحَيْنَا إِلَيْكَ رُوحًا مِّنْ أَمْرِنَا ۚ مَا كُنتَ تَدْرِي مَا الْكِتَابُ وَلَا الْإِيمَانُ وَلَٰكِن جَعَلْنَاهُ نُورًا نَّهْدِي بِهِ مَن نَّشَاءُ مِنْ عِبَادِنَا ۚ وَإِنَّكَ لَتَهْدِي إِلَىٰ صِرَاطٍ مُّسْتَقِيمٍ

صِرَاطِ اللَّهِ الَّذِي لَهُ مَا فِي السَّمَاوَاتِ وَمَا فِي الْأَرْضِ ۗ أَلَا إِلَى اللَّهِ تَصِيرُ الْأُمُورُ

52. And thus We have sent to you (O Muhammad ﷺ) *Ruhan* (an inspiration and a mercy) of Our command. You knew not what the Book was, nor what Faith was, but We have made it (this Qur'an) a light, wherewith We guide whosoever of Our slaves We will. And verily, you (O Muhammad ﷺ) are indeed guiding mankind to the Straight Path (i.e. Allah's religion of Islamic Monotheism).

53. The Path of Allah, to Whom belongs all that is in the heavens and all that is in the earth. Verily, all matters at the end go to Allah (for decision). — *Surah Ash-Shura 42:52–53*

Surah Sad

إِذْ دَخَلُوا عَلَىٰ دَاوُودَ فَفَزِعَ مِنْهُمْ ۖ قَالُوا لَا تَخَفْ ۖ خَصْمَانِ بَغَىٰ بَعْضُنَا عَلَىٰ بَعْضٍ فَاحْكُم بَيْنَنَا بِالْحَقِّ وَلَا تُشْطِطْ وَاهْدِنَا إِلَىٰ سَوَاءِ الصِّرَاطِ

When they entered in upon Dawud (David), he was terrified of them. They said: "Fear not! (We are) two litigants, one of whom has wronged the other. Therefore, judge between us with truth, and treat us not with injustice, and guide us to the Right Way." — ***Surah Sad 38:22***

Surah Al-Fat-h

لِيَغْفِرَ لَكَ اللَّهُ مَا تَقَدَّمَ مِن ذَنبِكَ وَمَا تَأَخَّرَ وَيُتِمَّ نِعْمَتَهُ عَلَيْكَ وَيَهْدِيَكَ صِرَاطًا مُّسْتَقِيمًا

That Allah may forgive you your sins of the past and the future, and complete His favour on you, and guide you on the Straight Path. — *Surah Al-Fat-h 48:2*

Surah Ta-Ha

قُلْ كُلٌّ مُّتَرَبِّصٌ فَتَرَبَّصُوا ۖ فَسَتَعْلَمُونَ مَنْ أَصْحَابُ الصِّرَاطِ السَّوِيِّ وَمَنِ اهْتَدَىٰ

Say (O Muhammad ﷺ): "Each one (believer and disbeliever, etc.) is waiting, so wait you too, and you shall know who they are that are on the Straight and Even Path (i.e. Allah's Religion of Islamic Monotheism), and who are they that have let themselves be guided (on the Right Path)." — *Surah Ta-Ha 20:135*

Surah Al-A'raf

قَالَ فَبِمَا أَغْوَيْتَنِي لَأَقْعُدَنَّ لَهُمْ صِرَاطَكَ الْمُسْتَقِيمَ

(Iblis) said: "Because You have sent me astray, surely I will sit in wait against them (human beings) on Your Straight Path." — *Surah Al-A'raf 20:16*

Surah An-Nisaa

وَلَهَدَيْنَاهُمْ صِرَاطًا مُّسْتَقِيمًا

وَمَن يُطِعِ اللَّهَ وَالرَّسُولَ فَأُولَٰئِكَ مَعَ الَّذِينَ أَنْعَمَ اللَّهُ عَلَيْهِم مِّنَ النَّبِيِّينَ وَالصِّدِّيقِينَ وَالشُّهَدَاءِ وَالصَّالِحِينَ ۚ وَحَسُنَ أُولَٰئِكَ رَفِيقًا

68. And indeed, We should have guided them to a Straight Way.

69. And whoso obeys Allah and the Messenger (Muhammad ﷺ), then they will be in the company of those on whom Allah has bestowed His Grace—of the Prophets, the *Siddiqun* (those followers of the Prophets who were first and foremost to believe in them, like Abu Bakr As-Siddiq), the martyrs, and the righteous. And how excellent these companions are! — *Surah An-Nisaa 4:68–69*

فَأَمَّا الَّذِينَ آمَنُوا بِاللَّهِ وَاعْتَصَمُوا بِهِ فَسَيُدْخِلُهُمْ فِي رَحْمَةٍ مِّنْهُ وَفَضْلٍ وَيَهْدِيهِمْ إِلَيْهِ صِرَاطًا مُّسْتَقِيمًا

175. So, as for those who believed in Allah and held fast to Him, He will admit them to His Mercy and Grace (i.e. Paradise), and guide them to Himself by a Straight Path. — *Surah An-Nisaa 4:175*

Let us now transition to another subject crucial to our practice, one that can guide us along our path.

بِسْمِ ٱللَّهِ ٱلرَّحْمَـٰنِ ٱلرَّحِيمِ

Chapter 7

Religion is very easy and whoever overburdens himself in his religion will not be able to continue in that way. So you should not be extremists, but try to be near to perfection and receive the good tidings that you will be rewarded; and gain strength by worshipping in the mornings, the nights.

Muhammad ﷺ (PBUH)

📖📖📖📖📖📖

Hadith We Follow

بِسْمِ ٱللَّهِ ٱلرَّحْمَـٰنِ ٱلرَّحِيمِ

In the Name of Allah, the Most Gracious, the Most Merciful*****

وَلَا تَلْبِسُوا الْحَقَّ بِالْبَاطِلِ وَتَكْتُمُوا الْحَقَّ وَأَنتُمْ تَعْلَمُونَ

And cover not the Truth with falsehood, nor conceal the Truth when you know (what it is).

2:42 – Surah Al-Baqarah

يَا أَيُّهَا الَّذِينَ آمَنُوا اتَّقُوا اللَّهَ وَكُونُوا مَعَ الصَّادِقِينَ

O you who believe! Fear Allah, and be with those who are true (in word and deed).

9:119 – Surah At-Tawbah

يَا أَيُّهَا الَّذِينَ آمَنُوا اتَّقُوا اللَّهَ وَقُولُوا قَوْلًا سَدِيدًا

O you who believe! Fear Allah, and always speak the truth.

33:70 – Surah Al-Ahzab

As we continue our journey towards embodying virtues essential for navigating the path of righteousness, we confront a pertinent challenge concerning the interplay between *Hadith* and *Sunnah*. The *Sunnah*, revered as an essential practice by every believer in their daily endeavours, holds profound significance in guiding our actions and choices.

247

Just as we rely on manuals for proper operation when acquiring new products, mere instruction manuals do not suffice in all scenarios. For instance, a person cannot navigate an aeroplane's cockpit without the guidance of a skilled instructor. While this analogy is earthly, the divine guidance provided by Allah through scriptures and prophets since the time of Adam serves a similar purpose.

Prophet Muhammad ﷺ, being the final messenger, was entrusted with the Qur'an, which contains comprehensive guidance for humanity's conduct. That entity's guidance—Allah entrusted to His Messenger—was conveyed in the following verse:

بِالْبَيِّنَاتِ وَالزُّبُرِ ۗ وَأَنزَلْنَا إِلَيْكَ الذِّكْرَ لِتُبَيِّنَ لِلنَّاسِ مَا نُزِّلَ إِلَيْهِمْ وَلَعَلَّهُمْ يَتَفَكَّرُونَ

With clear signs and Books (We sent the Messengers). And We have also sent down unto you (O Muhammad ﷺ) the reminder and the advice (the Qur'an), that you may explain clearly to men what is sent down to them, and that they may give thought.

16:44 – Surah An-Nahl

Hence, the teachings, sayings, and actions of Prophet Muhammad ﷺ were meticulously recorded by his companions, forming what Muslims have revered as *Hadith* for centuries. The companions, recognising the profound impact of these narrations on Islam, took great care in preserving them across generations.

Emulating the Prophet's lifestyle to the best of our ability undoubtedly leads to success on our spiritual journey, as Allah says:

لَّقَدْ كَانَ لَكُمْ فِي رَسُولِ اللَّهِ أُسْوَةٌ حَسَنَةٌ لِّمَن كَانَ يَرْجُو اللَّهَ وَالْيَوْمَ الْآخِرَ وَذَكَرَ اللَّهَ كَثِيرًا

Indeed, in the Messenger of Allah (Muhammad ﷺ) you have a good example to follow for him who hopes in (the Meeting with) Allah and the Last Day and remembers Allah much.

33:21 – Surah Al-Ahzab

As we continue along this path, we sense the thrill and challenge of our epic journey. Many of us have already traversed its extremes, each contemplating the future challenges that lie ahead as we prepare for a second journey. This next leg will lead us to the ultimate destination of Heavenly *Darus Salaam* and *Jannatul Ferdows*, while in the interim, we will dwell in the mysterious realm known as *Barzakh*.

Undoubtedly, this upcoming adventure promises to be exhilarating. To prepare for what lies ahead, we must adhere to the teachings laid out in the Qur'an and *Sunnah*. The *Sunnah*, in particular, serves as an indispensable guide for believers in their daily lives.

Although we often rely on scholars and follow their guidance, upon closer observation, it becomes apparent that many of us hold such strong opinions about *Hadith* that we prioritise them over the Qur'an.

Certain scholars emphasise the significance of *Hadith* as a primary source for understanding Islamic law and practice. They argue that the sayings and actions of the Prophet offer valuable insights and clarifications on the teachings of the Qur'an. On the other hand, some adopt a more cautious approach towards *Hadith*, calling for a critical examination of its authentication and interpretation. They place greater emphasis on the Qur'an as the primary source of guidance, considering the *Hadith* a secondary source that should be interpreted and understood in light of the Qur'anic text.

The discourse between these two stances has persisted for centuries, resulting in various methodologies to interpret and implement Islamic teachings. Nevertheless, the consensus among most scholars is that *Hadith* holds paramount importance as a source of guidance for Muslims. It is widely acknowledged that a harmonised approach is indispensable for comprehending and practising the teachings of Islam effectively.

The second point of concern revolves around the varying opinions among Muslim scholars regarding the authenticity and fabrication of *Hadiths*. *Hadiths* are accounts of the Prophet Muhammad's ﷺ sayings, actions, and approval—as well as those of his companions. It has been claimed that Satan utilised *Hadith* as a tool to incite hatred among Muslims immediately after the time of our Prophet Muhammad ﷺ.

Throughout history, Muslim scholars have employed diverse methods to ascertain the reliability and authenticity of *Hadiths*. These methods include examining the chain of transmission (*isnad*) and the content of the *Hadith* itself. Different scholars have adopted varying levels of leniency or strictness in accepting *Hadiths*, leading to discrepancies in opinions regarding their authenticity.

However, it is crucial to note that a majority of Muslim scholars throughout history have agreed upon a set of criteria for evaluating the authenticity of *Hadiths*. These criteria often include scrutinising the chain of narrators and the content of the *Hadith* itself. Disagreements among scholars primarily arise due to differences in interpreting or understanding these evaluation criteria, or due to variations in the strength of evidence supporting or refuting a particular *Hadith*. Such disagreements are a natural aspect of scholarly discourse and should not be perceived as indicative of a lack of consensus or agreement among Muslim scholars as a whole.

Moreover, it is important to acknowledge that there exist numerous *Hadiths* widely accepted and agreed upon by Muslim scholars. These *Hadiths* constitute a fundamental part of Islamic belief and practice. Therefore, while there may be some disagreement among scholars concerning specific *Hadiths*, a significant degree of consensus and agreement exists within the broader Muslim community.

Once, Abu Bakr (RA) said:

"Which sky will cover me and which earth will give me refuge if I say something in this religion which is not true?" *[129]*

Some other scholars also expressed their concern as follows:

• Abu Hurairah (RA) said: The Prophet صلى الله عليه وسلم said, *"It is enough for a man to prove himself a liar when he goes on narrating whatever he hears."* ([Muslim] https://sunnah.com/riyadussaliheen/18/37)

• Anas bin Malik (RA) said: *"Indeed, what prevents me from relating to you a great number of Hadith is that the Messenger* ﷺ *of Allah SWT said: 'Whoever intends to lie upon me, then let him take his seat in the Hellfire.'"*[130]

• Narrated `Abdullah bin Az-Zubair: I said to my father, "I do not hear from you any narration (Hadith) of Allah's Apostle as I hear (his narration) from so-and-so." Az-Zubair replied, "I was always with him (the Prophet), and I heard him saying: *'Whoever tells a lie against me (intentionally), then surely let him occupy his seat in the Hellfire.'"*[131] Many individuals perceive the Qur'an as the sole foundation of their lives and may not place as much importance on evaluating the Hadith. However, it is essential to acknowledge that the Hadith holds a significant position and cannot be replaced in terms of identifying oneself as a believer and seeking guidance. To address the concerns surrounding this matter, we aim to approach the study of Hadith from a unique perspective. By carefully analysing the following questions and seeking answers directly from the divine source, any confusion or queries in our minds will be clarified:

• What is a Hadith?

• Why do we accept Hadith when we follow the Book of Allah?

• Qur'an or Hadith – which should we give more importance to?

• Is it true that the Qur'an is not complete without Hadith?

• And how does a fabricated Hadith affect our daily lives?

---

[129] https://www.academia.edu/34869673/Was_Hadith_Written_200_years_after_the_Prophet
[130] (Bukhari and Muslim https://sunnah.com/bukhari/3/50)
[131] Bukh   (https://sunnah.com/bukhari/3/49)
file:///C:/Users/akmha/Downloads/Was_Hadith_Written_200_years_after_the_P%20(1).pdf

Let us now approach the Hadith from a different angle. What responsibility did Allah (SWT) bestow upon the Prophet Muhammad ﷺ to exemplify and propagate among people in this world? Furthermore, how obligated are we to adhere to his words and teachings? Can we compare his sayings with Qur'anic verses and choose which one to accept? The Qur'an addresses these matters, and although the answers may already be known to many, conducting further analysis can help resolve any lingering confusion.

Muslims generally consider the Hadith to be a vital component of Islamic tradition and rely on it to gain insight into how to practise their faith. The Hadith, which consists of the recorded sayings and actions of the Prophet Muhammad ﷺ, as conveyed by his companions, holds significant value as a source of Islamic teachings and interpretations. It is also regarded as a crucial foundation for Islamic law, ethics, and guidance, enabling Muslims to comprehend and apply the teachings of the Qur'an in their daily lives.

Now, let us revisit the topic of Hadith from a different perspective. What role did Allah assign to the Prophet Muhammad ﷺ in practising and exemplifying the teachings among people in this world? To what extent are we responsible for adhering to his words and teachings? Are we allowed to compare his sayings with the verses of the Qur'an and selectively choose which ones to accept? The Qur'an provides insight into these matters. While the answer is generally understood, any doubts or uncertainties can be clarified through further analysis.

For example:

We often say our Prophet can guide us or use the word *"guide"*, but in a practical sense, the Messenger of Allah cannot guide anyone. It is Allah, and Allah alone, who can guide people. The Qur'anic verse confirming this truth states:

"You (Muhammad) cannot guide the ones you love, but it is Allah who guides whom He wills. He knows best who are the guided ones." (28:56)

In Surah Al-Jinn (72:21), this is further confirmed as it states:

"It is not in my power to cause you harm, or to bring you to right conduct."

The Messenger is a medium between Allah (SWT) and the people, but he cannot change what is in the heart, implant belief, or guide anyone of his own will.

The words and deeds of the Prophet ﷺ were primarily based on revelation from Allah (SWT), and therefore should be considered a fundamental source of direct connection with the Qur'an. In the Qur'an, Allah says about the Prophet ﷺ that he does not speak of his own accord; it is only a revelation that is revealed to him — as found in Surah An-Najm (53:3–4).

We must note that the moment anyone upholds any personal teachings not authorised in the Qur'an, they immediately become guilty of shirk and are promised severe retribution. This will be explored in detail in the appropriate section.

To gain a deeper understanding of the Hadith, let us approach it step by step. Firstly, we can examine specific verses that are connected to the Hadith and emphasise its significance.

In the initial phase, we can identify certain verses that fall into two categories: **Section A** comprises verses that highlight actions governed directly by Allah (SWT), while **Section B** consists of verses that relate to practices entrusted to our Prophet Muhammad ﷺ.

Lastly, in **Part D**, we encounter verses that unequivocally outline our responsibility to follow the Sunnah based on the Hadith. Adhering to this guidance helps us navigate our journey on the straight path with safety and assurance.

At The Beginning:

Allah says to our Prophet in Surah Qaf (50:45):

نَّحْنُ أَعْلَمُ بِمَا يَقُولُونَ ۖ وَمَا أَنتَ عَلَيْهِم بِجَبَّارٍ ۖ فَذَكِّرْ بِالْقُرْآنِ مَن يَخَافُ وَعِيدِ

We know best what they say; and you (O Muhammad ﷺ) are not a tyrant over them (to force them to belief). But warn by the Qur'an, him who fears My Threat.

Allah (SWT) says:

كِتَابٌ فُصِّلَتْ آيَاتُهُ قُرْآنًا عَرَبِيًّا لِّقَوْمٍ يَعْلَمُونَ

A Book, whereof the verses are explained in detail; a Qur'an in Arabic, for people who understand. (41:3 – Surah Ha-Mim Sajdah)

وَتَمَّتْ كَلِمَتُ رَبِّكَ صِدْقًا وَعَدْلًا ۚ لَّا مُبَدِّلَ لِكَلِمَاتِهِ ۚ وَهُوَ السَّمِيعُ الْعَلِيمُ

And the Word of your Lord has been fulfilled in truth and in justice. None can change His Words. And He is the All-Hearer, the All-Knower. (6:115 – Surah Al-An'am)

وَمَا مِن دَابَّةٍ فِي الْأَرْضِ وَلَا طَائِرٍ يَطِيرُ بِجَنَاحَيْهِ إِلَّا أُمَمٌ أَمْثَالُكُم ۚ مَّا فَرَّطْنَا فِي الْكِتَابِ مِن شَيْءٍ ۚ ثُمَّ إِلَىٰ رَبِّهِمْ يُحْشَرُونَ

There is not an animal (that lives) on the earth, nor a being that flies on its wings, but (forms part of) communities like you. Nothing have We omitted from the Book, and they (all) shall be gathered to their Lord in the end. (6:38 – Surah Al-An'am)

لَقَدْ كَانَ فِي قَصَصِهِمْ عِبْرَةٌ لِّأُولِي الْأَلْبَابِ ۗ مَا كَانَ حَدِيثًا يُفْتَرَىٰ وَلَٰكِن تَصْدِيقَ الَّذِي بَيْنَ يَدَيْهِ وَتَفْصِيلَ كُلِّ شَيْءٍ وَهُدًى وَرَحْمَةً لِّقَوْمٍ يُؤْمِنُونَ

Indeed, in their stories there is a lesson for men of understanding. It (the Qur'an) is not a forged statement but a confirmation of the Allah's existing Books [the Taurat (Torah), the Injeel (Gospel), and other Scriptures of Allah], and a detailed explanation of everything – a guide and a mercy for the people who believe. (12:111 – Surah Yusuf)

الر ۚ كِتَابٌ أُحْكِمَتْ آيَاتُهُ ثُمَّ فُصِّلَتْ مِن لَّدُنْ حَكِيمٍ خَبِيرٍ

Alif-Lam-Ra. [These letters are one of the miracles of the Qur'an and none but Allah (Alone) knows their meanings]. (This is) a Book, the verses whereof are perfected (in every sphere of knowledge) and then explained in detail from One (Allah), Who is All-Wise and Well-Acquainted (with all things). (11:1 – Surah Hud)

وَيَوْمَ نَبْعَثُ فِي كُلِّ أُمَّةٍ شَهِيدًا عَلَيْهِم مِّنْ أَنفُسِهِمْ ۖ وَجِئْنَا بِكَ شَهِيدًا عَلَىٰ هَٰؤُلَاءِ ۚ وَنَزَّلْنَا عَلَيْكَ الْكِتَابَ تِبْيَانًا لِّكُلِّ شَيْءٍ وَهُدًى وَرَحْمَةً وَبُشْرَىٰ لِلْمُسْلِمِينَ

And (remember) the Day when We shall raise up from every nation a witness against them from amongst themselves. And We shall bring you (O Muhammad ﷺ) as a witness against these. And We have sent down to you the Book (the Qur'an) as an exposition of everything – a guidance, a mercy, and glad tidings for those who have submitted themselves (to Allah as Muslims). (16:89 – Surah An-Nahl)

وَلَا يَأْتُونَكَ بِمَثَلٍ إِلَّا جِئْنَاكَ بِالْحَقِّ وَأَحْسَنَ تَفْسِيرًا

And no example or similitude do they bring (to oppose or to find fault in you or in this Qur'an), but We reveal to you the truth (against that similitude or example), and the better explanation thereof. (25:33 – Surah Al-Furqan)

Section A

اللَّهُ نَزَّلَ أَحْسَنَ الْحَدِيثِ كِتَابًا مُّتَشَابِهًا مَّثَانِيَ تَقْشَعِرُّ مِنْهُ جُلُودُ الَّذِينَ يَخْشَوْنَ رَبَّهُمْ ثُمَّ تَلِينُ جُلُودُهُمْ وَقُلُوبُهُمْ إِلَىٰ ذِكْرِ اللَّهِ ۚ ذَٰلِكَ هُدَى اللَّهِ يَهْدِي بِهِ مَن يَشَاءُ ۚ وَمَن يُضْلِلِ اللَّهُ فَمَا لَهُ مِنْ هَادٍ

Allah has sent down the best statement – a Book (this Qur'an), its parts resembling each other in goodness and truth, oft-repeated. The skins of those who fear their Lord shiver from it (when they recite it or hear it). Then their skin and their hearts soften to the remembrance of Allah. That is the guidance of Allah. He guides with it whom He pleases; and whomever Allah sends astray, for him there is no guide. (39:23 – Surah Az-Zumar)

مَا لَكُمْ كَيْفَ تَحْكُمُونَ

أَمْ لَكُمْ كِتَابٌ فِيهِ تَدْرُسُونَ

إِنَّ لَكُمْ فِيهِ لَمَا تَخَيَّرُونَ

36. What is the matter with you? How do you judge?

37. Or do you have a Book through which you learn,

38. That you shall have all that you choose? (68:36–38 – Surah Al-Qalam)

أَفَغَيْرَ اللَّهِ أَبْتَغِي حَكَمًا وَهُوَ الَّذِي أَنزَلَ إِلَيْكُمُ الْكِتَابَ مُفَصَّلًا ۚ وَالَّذِينَ آتَيْنَاهُمُ الْكِتَابَ يَعْلَمُونَ أَنَّهُ مُنَزَّلٌ مِّن رَّبِّكَ بِالْحَقِّ ۖ فَلَا تَكُونَنَّ مِنَ الْمُمْتَرِينَ

Say O Muhammad ﷺ*): "Shall I seek a judge other than Allah while it is He who has sent down unto you the Book (the Qur'an), explained in detail?" Those to whom We gave the Scripture [the Taurat (Torah) and the Injeel (Gospel)] know that it is revealed from your Lord in truth. So be not among those who doubt."* (6:114 – Surah Al-An'am)

Then Allah presented this question to us:

فَبِأَيِّ حَدِيثٍ بَعْدَهُ يُؤْمِنُونَ

Then in what statement after this (the Qur'an) will they believe? **(77:50 – Surah Al-Mursalat)**

Then Allah SWT posed the same question to His Messenger ﷺ, which clearly reflects Allah's dismay at our behaviour on this issue. The verse says:

تِلْكَ آيَاتُ اللَّهِ نَتْلُوهَا عَلَيْكَ بِالْحَقِّ ۖ فَبِأَيِّ حَدِيثٍ بَعْدَ اللَّهِ وَآيَاتِهِ يُؤْمِنُونَ

These are the Ayat (proofs, evidences, verses, lessons, revelations, etc.) of Allah, which We recite to you (O Muhammad ﷺ*) with truth. Then in which speech after Allah and His Ayat will they believe?* **(45:6 – Surah Al-Jathiya)**

الرَّحْمَٰنُ

عَلَّمَ الْقُرْآنَ

(Allah) Most Gracious! It is He Who has taught the Qur'an. **(55:1–2 – Surah Ar-Rahman)**

إِنَّ عَلَيْنَا جَمْعَهُ وَقُرْآنَهُ

It is for Us to collect it and to give you (O Muhammad ﷺ*) the ability to recite it (the Qur'an),*

(75:17 – Surah Al-Qiyamah)

ثُمَّ إِنَّ عَلَيْنَا بَيَانَهُ

Then it is for Us (Allah) to make it clear to you,

(75:19 – Surah Al-Qiyamah)

Section B

The Prophet ﷺ's Assignment:

وَأَمَّا بِنِعْمَةِ رَبِّكَ فَحَدِّثْ

And proclaim the Grace of your Lord (i.e. the Prophethood and all other Graces).

(93:11 – Surah Ad-Dhuha)

مَّا عَلَى الرَّسُولِ إِلَّا الْبَلَاغُ ۗ وَاللَّهُ يَعْلَمُ مَا تُبْدُونَ وَمَا تَكْتُمُونَ

The Messenger's duty [i.e. Our Messenger Muhammad ﷺ whom We have sent to you, (O mankind)] is but to convey (the Message). And Allah knows all that you reveal and all that you conceal.

(5:99 – Surah Al-Maidah)

بِالْبَيِّنَاتِ وَالزُّبُرِ ۗ وَأَنزَلْنَا إِلَيْكَ الذِّكْرَ لِتُبَيِّنَ لِلنَّاسِ مَا نُزِّلَ إِلَيْهِمْ وَلَعَلَّهُمْ يَتَفَكَّرُونَ

With clear signs and Books (We sent the Messengers). And We have also sent down unto you (O Muhammad ﷺ) the reminder and the advice (the Qur'an), that you may explain clearly to men what is sent down to them, and that they may give thought.

(16:44 – Surah An-Nahl; Dr. M. Muhsin Khan / Dr. M. Taqi-ud-Din Al-Hilali)

The true meaning of the Qur'an cannot be revealed through translation. However, seeking its translation remains necessary for human understanding, even though it cannot fully reflect the original meaning.

قُلْ إِنِّي لَا أَمْلِكُ لَكُمْ ضَرًّا وَلَا رَشَدًا

Say: "It is not in my power to cause you harm, or to bring you to the Right Path."

(72:21 – Surah Al-Jinn)

... رَبَّنَا وَابْعَثْ فِيهِمْ رَسُولًا مِّنْهُمْ

"Our Lord! Send amongst them a Messenger of their own (and indeed Allah answered their invocation by sending Muhammad, peace be upon him), who shall recite unto them Your Verses and instruct them in the Book (this Qur'an) and Al-Hikmah (full knowledge of the Islamic laws and jurisprudence or wisdom or Prophethood, etc.), and sanctify them. Verily! You are the All-Mighty, the All-Wise."

(2:129 – Surah Al-Baqarah)

... إِنَّكَ لَا تَهْدِي مَنْ أَحْبَبْتَ وَلَٰكِنَّ اللَّهَ يَهْدِي مَن يَشَاءُ

Indeed, [O Muhammad ﷺ], you do not guide whom you like, but Allah guides whom He wills. And He is most knowing of the [rightly] guided.

(28:56 – Surah Al-Qasas; Sahih International)

وَمَا يَنطِقُ عَنِ الْهَوَىٰ

إِنْ هُوَ إِلَّا وَحْيٌ يُوحَىٰ

عَلَّمَهُ شَدِيدُ الْقُوَىٰ

Nor does he speak of (his own) desire.

It is only an Inspiration that is inspired.

He has been taught (this Qur'an) by one mighty in power [Jibreel (Gabriel)].

(53:3–5 – Surah An-Najm)

إِلَّا مَا شَاءَ اللَّهُ ۚ وَلَوْ كُنتُ أَعْلَمُ الْغَيْبَ لَاسْتَكْثَرْتُ مِنَ الْخَيْرِ ۚ قُل لَّا أَمْلِكُ لِنَفْسِي نَفْعًا وَلَا ضَرًّا وَمَا مَسَّنِيَ السُّوءُ ۚ إِنْ أَنَا إِلَّا نَذِيرٌ وَبَشِيرٌ لِّقَوْمٍ يُؤْمِنُونَ

Say (O Muhammad ﷺ): "I possess no power of benefit or harm to myself except as Allah wills. If I had the knowledge of the Ghaib (unseen), I would have secured for myself an abundance of wealth, and no evil would have touched me. I am but a warner, and a bringer of glad tidings to people who believe."

(7:188 – Surah Al-A'raf)

وَلَا أَعْلَمُ الْغَيْبَ وَلَا أَقُولُ لَكُمْ إِنِّي مَلَكٌ ۖ إِنْ أَتَّبِعُ إِلَّا مَا ۚ قُل لَّا أَقُولُ لَكُمْ عِندِي خَزَائِنُ اللَّهِ يُوحَىٰ إِلَيَّ ۚ قُلْ هَلْ يَسْتَوِي الْأَعْمَىٰ وَالْبَصِيرُ ۚ أَفَلَا تَتَفَكَّرُونَ

Say (O Muhammad ﷺ): "I do not tell you that with me are the treasures of Allah, nor (that) I know the unseen; nor do I tell you that I am an angel. I only follow what is revealed to me by inspiration." Say: "Are the blind and the one who sees equal? Will you not then take thought?"

(6:50 – Surah Al-An'am)

إِلَّا اللَّهُ ۚ وَمَا يَشْعُرُونَ أَيَّانَ يُبْعَثُونَ قُل لَّا يَعْلَمُ مَن فِي السَّمَاوَاتِ وَالْأَرْضِ الْغَيْبَ

Say: "None in the heavens and the earth knows the Ghaib (unseen) except Allah, nor can they perceive when they shall be resurrected."

(27:65 – Surah An-Naml)

وَمَا أَدْرِي مَا يُفْعَلُ بِي وَلَا بِكُمْ ۖ إِنْ أَتَّبِعُ إِلَّا مَا يُوحَىٰ إِلَيَّ وَمَا ۚ قُلْ مَا كُنتُ بِدْعًا مِّنَ الرُّسُلِ أَنَا إِلَّا نَذِيرٌ مُّبِينٌ

Say (O Muhammad ﷺ): "I am not a new thing among the Messengers (of Allah) (i.e. I am not the first Messenger), nor do I know what will be done with me or with you. I only follow that which is revealed to me, and I am but a plain warner."

(46:9 – Surah Al-Ahqaf)

Allah SWT also reminds him to be careful not to overstep the boundaries of His authority. This is confirmed in the following verses:

إِنْ عَلَيْكَ إِلَّا الْبَلَاغُ ۗ وَإِنَّا إِذَا أَذَقْنَا الْإِنسَانَ مِنَّا ۚ فَإِنْ أَعْرَضُوا فَمَا أَرْسَلْنَاكَ عَلَيْهِمْ حَفِيظًا رَحْمَةً فَرِحَ بِهَا ۖ وَإِن تُصِبْهُمْ سَيِّئَةٌ بِمَا قَدَّمَتْ أَيْدِيهِمْ فَإِنَّ الْإِنسَانَ كَفُورٌ

But if they turn away (O Muhammad ﷺ from the Islamic Monotheism, which you have brought to them), We have not sent you (O Muhammad ﷺ) as a Hafiz (protector) over them (i.e. to take care of their deeds and to recompense them). Your duty is to convey (the Message). And verily, when We cause man to taste of Mercy from Us, he rejoices therein, but when some ill befalls them because of the deeds which their hands have sent forth, then verily, man becomes ungrateful!

(42:48 – Surah Ash-Shura)

فَذَكِّرْ إِنَّمَا أَنتَ مُذَكِّرٌ

لَّسْتَ عَلَيْهِم بِمُصَيْطِرٍ

So remind them (O Muhammad ﷺ), you are only one who reminds.

You are not a dictator over them.

(88:21–22 – Surah Al-Ghashiyah)

He not only serves as a religious adviser but also exemplifies the utmost standards of character. Through his conduct and deeds, he provides a tangible example for others to emulate, guiding them on a path of righteousness. Allah (SWT) says:

وَإِنَّكَ لَعَلَىٰ خُلُقٍ عَظِيمٍ

And verily, you (O Muhammad ﷺ) are on an exalted standard of character.

[Surah Al-Qalam 68:4]

Section C

Here, Allah (SWT) presents His Messenger and entrusts us to follow his teachings.

The verbal teachings of our Prophet (ﷺ), his actions, and narrations of approved or disapproved matters—recorded by scholars of that period in written form—are collectively known as *Hadith*. Implementing the guidance found in the books of Hadith, where applicable to Muslim life, is referred to as the *Sunnah*.

Righteousness, or the status of a true believer, cannot be attained without following the Sunnah, as the Sunnah is the path to move forward in righteousness. That assurance comes from Allah (SWT), who says:

"Whoever obeys the Messenger obeys Allah. But if anyone turns away, I have not sent you to observe them (evil deeds)."

Allah (SWT) Introduces His Messenger to Us

لَقَدْ جَاءَكُمْ رَسُولٌ مِّنْ أَنفُسِكُمْ عَزِيزٌ عَلَيْهِ مَا عَنِتُّمْ حَرِيصٌ عَلَيْكُم بِالْمُؤْمِنِينَ رَءُوفٌ رَّحِيمٌ

Verily, there has come unto you a Messenger (Muhammad ﷺ) from amongst yourselves (i.e. whom you know well). It grieves him that you should suffer any injury or difficulty. He (Muhammad ﷺ) is anxious over you (to be rightly guided, to repent to Allah, and beg Him to pardon and forgive your sins, so you may enter Paradise and be saved from the punishment of the Hellfire). For the believers, he (ﷺ) is full of pity, kind, and merciful.

[Surah At-Tawbah 9:128]

مَّا كَانَ مُحَمَّدٌ أَبَا أَحَدٍ مِّن رِّجَالِكُمْ وَلَٰكِن رَّسُولَ اللَّهِ وَخَاتَمَ النَّبِيِّينَ ۗ وَكَانَ اللَّهُ بِكُلِّ شَيْءٍ عَلِيمًا

Muhammad (ﷺ) is not the father of any man among you, but he is the Messenger of Allah and the last (end) of the Prophets. And Allah is Ever All-Aware of everything.

[Surah Al-Ahzab 33:40]

وَمَا أَرْسَلْنَاكَ إِلَّا رَحْمَةً لِّلْعَالَمِينَ

And We have not sent you (O Muhammad ﷺ) except as a mercy to the worlds (mankind, jinn, and all that exists).

[Surah Al-Anbiyaa 21:107]

لَقَدْ مَنَّ اللَّهُ عَلَى الْمُؤْمِنِينَ إِذْ بَعَثَ فِيهِمْ رَسُولًا مِّنْ أَنفُسِهِمْ يَتْلُو عَلَيْهِمْ آيَاتِهِ وَيُزَكِّيهِمْ وَيُعَلِّمُهُمُ الْكِتَابَ وَالْحِكْمَةَ وَإِن كَانُوا مِن قَبْلُ لَفِي ضَلَالٍ مُّبِينٍ

Indeed, Allah conferred a great favour upon the believers when He sent among them a Messenger (Muhammad ﷺ) from among themselves, reciting to them His Verses (the Qur'an), purifying them, and instructing them in the Book (the Qur'an) and Al-Hikmah (the wisdom and Sunnah of the Prophet ﷺ), while before that they had been in manifest error.

[Surah Aal-Imran 3:164]

هُوَ الَّذِي بَعَثَ فِي الْأُمِّيِّينَ رَسُولًا مِّنْهُمْ يَتْلُو عَلَيْهِمْ آيَاتِهِ وَيُزَكِّيهِمْ وَيُعَلِّمُهُمُ الْكِتَابَ وَالْحِكْمَةَ وَإِن كَانُوا مِن قَبْلُ لَفِي ضَلَالٍ مُّبِينٍ

He it is Who sent among the unlettered ones a Messenger (Muhammad ﷺ) from among themselves, reciting to them His Verses, purifying them (from the filth of disbelief and polytheism), and teaching them the Book (this Qur'an, Islamic laws, and jurisprudence) and Al-Hikmah (As-Sunnah). Verily, they had been in manifest error.

[Surah Al-Jumu'ah 62:2]

إِنَّ اللَّهَ وَمَلَائِكَتَهُ يُصَلُّونَ عَلَى النَّبِيِّ ۚ يَا أَيُّهَا الَّذِينَ آمَنُوا صَلُّوا عَلَيْهِ وَسَلِّمُوا تَسْلِيمًا

Allah sends His Salat (Graces, Honours, Blessings, Mercy, etc.) on the Prophet (Muhammad ﷺ), and so do His angels. O you who believe! Send your Salat on him (Muhammad ﷺ), and greet him with the Islamic salutation (i.e. As-Salamu 'Alaikum).

[Surah Al-Ahzab 33:56]

Our Obligation as Believers

فَإِن تَنَازَعْتُمْ فِي شَيْءٍ ۖ يَا أَيُّهَا الَّذِينَ آمَنُوا أَطِيعُوا اللَّهَ وَأَطِيعُوا الرَّسُولَ وَأُولِي الْأَمْرِ مِنكُمْ ۖ فَرُدُّوهُ إِلَى اللَّهِ وَالرَّسُولِ إِن كُنتُمْ تُؤْمِنُونَ بِاللَّهِ وَالْيَوْمِ الْآخِرِ ۚ ذَٰلِكَ خَيْرٌ وَأَحْسَنُ تَأْوِيلًا

You who believe! Obey Allah and obey the Messenger (Muhammad ﷺ), and those in authority among you. If you disagree about anything, refer it to Allah and the Messenger, if you believe in Allah and the Last Day. That is better and more suitable for final determination.

[Surah An-Nisaa 4:59]

فَإِن تَوَلَّيْتُمْ فَاعْلَمُوا أَنَّمَا عَلَىٰ رَسُولِنَا الْبَلَاغُ الْمُبِينُ ۝ وَأَطِيعُوا اللَّهَ وَأَطِيعُوا الرَّسُولَ وَاحْذَرُوا

And obey Allah and the Messenger (Muhammad ﷺ), and beware. But if you turn away, then know that Our Messenger's duty is only to convey (the message) clearly.

[Surah Al-Ma'idah 5:92]

وَيَغْفِرْ لَكُمْ ذُنُوبَكُمْ ۚ وَاللَّهُ غَفُورٌ رَّحِيمٌ قُلْ إِن كُنتُمْ تُحِبُّونَ اللَّهَ فَاتَّبِعُونِي يُحْبِبْكُمُ اللَّهُ

Say (O Muhammad ﷺ): "If you (truly) love Allah, then follow me; Allah will love you and forgive you your sins. And Allah is Oft-Forgiving, Most Merciful."

[Surah Aal-Imran 3:31]

مَّا أَفَاءَ اللَّهُ عَلَىٰ رَسُولِهِ مِنْ أَهْلِ الْقُرَىٰ فَلِلَّهِ وَلِلرَّسُولِ وَلِذِي الْقُرْبَىٰ وَالْيَتَامَىٰ وَالْمَسَاكِينِ وَابْنِ السَّبِيلِ كَيْ لَا يَكُونَ دُولَةً بَيْنَ الْأَغْنِيَاءِ مِنكُمْ ۚ وَمَا آتَاكُمُ الرَّسُولُ فَخُذُوهُ وَمَا نَهَاكُمْ عَنْهُ فَانتَهُوا ۚ وَاتَّقُوا اللَّهَ ۖ إِنَّ اللَّهَ شَدِيدُ الْعِقَابِ

What Allah gave as booty to His Messenger (Muhammad ﷺ) from the people of the townships—it is for Allah, His Messenger, the kindred, the orphans, the poor, and the wayfarer—so that it will not become a fortune used only by the rich among you. And whatever the Messenger gives you, take it; and whatever he forbids you, abstain from it. Fear Allah. Verily, Allah is severe in punishment.

[Surah Al-Hashr 59:7] [132]

---

[132] https://www.whyislam.org/hadith/

5.

وَمَا كَانَ لِمُؤْمِنٍ وَلَا مُؤْمِنَةٍ إِذَا قَضَى اللَّهُ وَرَسُولُهُ أَمْرًا أَن يَكُونَ لَهُمُ الْخِيَرَةُ مِنْ أَمْرِهِمْ ¬ وَمَن يَعْصِ اللَّهَ وَرَسُولَهُ فَقَدْ ضَلَّ ضَلَالًا مُبِينًا

It is not for a believer, man or woman, when Allah and His Messenger have decreed a matter, that they should have any option in their decision. And whoever disobeys Allah and His Messenger has indeed strayed in a plain error. (33:36, Surah Al-Ahzab)

SECTION D: The Authenticity of Hadith and Our Caution

The authenticity or potential fabrication of the collected hadith sparks a widespread debate—an issue that cannot be overlooked and may warrant brief discussion in Section 'D'.

Fabrication and Our Caution

1.

إِنَّ الَّذِينَ فَرَّقُوا دِينَهُمْ وَكَانُوا شِيَعًا لَسْتَ مِنْهُمْ فِي شَيْءٍ ۚ إِنَّمَا أَمْرُهُمْ إِلَى اللَّهِ ثُمَّ يُنَبِّئُهُم بِمَا كَانُوا يَفْعَلُونَ

Verily, those who divide their religion and break up into sects (all kinds of religious sects), you (O Muhammad ﷺ) have no concern in them in the least. Their affair is only with Allah, Who then will tell them what they used to do. **(6:159, Surah Al-An'am)**

2.

وَكَذَٰلِكَ جَعَلْنَا لِكُلِّ نَبِيٍّ عَدُوًّا شَيَاطِينَ الْإِنسِ وَالْجِنِّ يُوحِي بَعْضُهُمْ إِلَىٰ بَعْضٍ زُخْرُفَ الْقَوْلِ غُرُورًا ۚ وَلَوْ شَاءَ رَبُّكَ مَا فَعَلُوهُ ۖ فَذَرْهُمْ وَمَا يَفْتَرُونَ

And so We have appointed for every Prophet enemies—Shayatin (devils) among mankind and jinns, inspiring one another with adorned speech as a delusion (or by way of deception). If your Lord had so willed, they would not have done it, so leave them alone with their fabrications. **(6:112, Surah Al-An'am)**

وَمِنَ النَّاسِ مَن يَشْتَرِي لَهْوَ الْحَدِيثِ لِيُضِلَّ عَن سَبِيلِ اللَّهِ بِغَيْرِ عِلْمٍ وَيَتَّخِذَهَا هُزُوًا ۚ ¬ أُولَٰئِكَ لَهُمْ عَذَابٌ مُّهِينٌ

And of mankind is he who purchases idle talk (i.e. music, singing, etc.) to mislead (men) from the Path of Allah without knowledge, and takes it (the Path of Allah, the Verses of the Qur'an) by way of mockery. For such there will be a humiliating torment (in the Hell-fire). **(31:6, Surah Luqman)**

The aforementioned verses of the Qur'an provide us with a clear indication regarding the rules and boundaries of Prophet Muhammad ﷺ in specific matters where he lacks knowledge of the unseen (Ghayb). Despite the existence of numerous hadiths that mention the Prophet's name in relation to various narratives and punishments in the grave, this contradicts the aforementioned verse and hadith. The verse (46:9) can be reiterated here, where Allah SWT says:

$$ قُلْ مَا كُنتُ بِدْعًا مِّنَ الرُّسُلِ وَمَا أَدْرِي مَا يُفْعَلُ بِي وَلَا بِكُمْ ۖ إِنْ أَتَّبِعُ إِلَّا مَا يُوحَىٰ إِلَيَّ وَمَا أَنَا إِلَّا نَذِيرٌ مُّبِينٌ ¬ $$

Say (O Muhammad ﷺ): "I am no bringer of new doctrine among the messengers, nor do I know what will be done with me or with you. I follow but that which is revealed to me by inspiration; I am but a Warner open and clear." **(46:9, Surah Al-Ahqaf)**

The Messenger of Allah himself said:

If there is any personal opinion of mine, do not follow my personal opinion; but when I say to you anything on behalf of Allah, then accept it, for I do not attribute lies to Allah, the Exalted and Glorious. (Narrated by Muslim)

The above verses affirm that our Prophet did not receive any message regarding the fate of our souls after death. This fact becomes even clearer when we examine the Hadiths that accompany the verses revealed by Allah (SWT). Prophet Muhammad ﷺ patiently awaited revelation from Allah SWT in order to address the question:

Abdullah bin Mas'ud reported:

"As I was going along with Allah's Apostle ﷺ in a cultivable land and he—the Prophet—was walking with the support of a wood, a group of Jews happened to meet him. Some of them said to the others: 'Ask him about the soul.' They said: 'What is your doubt about it? There is a possibility that you may ask him about anything (the answer of) which you may not like.' They said: 'Ask him.' So one amongst them asked him about the soul. Allah's messenger ﷺ kept quiet and he gave no reply, and I came to know that revelation was being sent to him. So I stood at my place and thus this revelation descended upon him:

$$ وَيَسْأَلُونَكَ عَنِ الرُّوحِ ۖ قُلِ الرُّوحُ مِنْ أَمْرِ رَبِّي وَمَا أُوتِيتُم مِّنَ الْعِلْمِ إِلَّا قَلِيلًا ¬ $$

And they ask you (O Muhammad ﷺ) concerning the Ruh (the Spirit); Say: "The Ruh (the Spirit): it is one of the things, the knowledge of which is only with my Lord. And of knowledge, you (mankind) have been given only a little." (17:85, Surah Al-Isra)

The verse above distinctly illustrates that humanity has been granted limited insight into the nature of the soul.[133]

---

[133] https://aboutislam.net/counseling/ask-about-islam/prophet-know-unseen

To sidestep Satan's snares, it is imperative that we thoroughly grasp the verse (repeat) in which Allah (SWT) conveyed His message to His Messenger, saying:

1

أَفَغَيْرَ اللَّهِ أَبْتَغِي حَكَمًا وَهُوَ الَّذِي أَنزَلَ إِلَيْكُمُ الْكِتَابَ مُفَصَّلًا ۚ وَالَّذِينَ آتَيْنَاهُمُ الْكِتَابَ يَعْلَمُونَ أَنَّهُ مُنَزَّلٌ مِّن رَّبِّكَ بِالْحَقِّ ۖ فَلَا تَكُونَنَّ مِنَ الْمُمْتَرِينَ

[Say (O Muhammad ﷺ): "Shall I seek a judge other than Allah, while it is He Who has sent down unto you the Book (the Qur'an), explained in detail?" Those unto whom We gave the Scripture [the Taurat (Torah) and the Injeel (Gospel)] know that it is revealed from your Lord in truth. So be not of those who doubt.] **(6:114, Surah Al-An'am)**

2

وَتَمَّتْ كَلِمَتُ رَبِّكَ صِدْقًا وَعَدْلًا ۚ لَّا مُبَدِّلَ لِكَلِمَاتِهِ ۚ وَهُوَ السَّمِيعُ الْعَلِيمُ

[And the Word of your Lord has been fulfilled in truth and in justice. None can change His Words. And He is the All-Hearer, the All-Knower.] **(6:115, Surah Al-An'am)**

3

إِذَا جَاءَكَ الْمُنَافِقُونَ قَالُوا نَشْهَدُ إِنَّكَ لَرَسُولُ اللَّهِ ۗ وَاللَّهُ يَعْلَمُ إِنَّكَ لَرَسُولُهُ وَاللَّهُ يَشْهَدُ إِنَّ الْمُنَافِقِينَ لَكَاذِبُونَ

[When the hypocrites come to you (O Muhammad ﷺ), they say: "We bear witness that you are indeed the Messenger of Allah." Allah knows that you are indeed His Messenger, and Allah bears witness that the hypocrites are liars indeed.] **(63:1, Surah Al-Munafiqun)**

The following verse was bestowed upon us by the Almighty Allah (SWT) when He dispatched a Messenger to compile the teachings of all the prophets, purify them, and unite them under a single religion, calling upon humanity to submit and embrace it:

The Prophet Muhammad ﷺ, as the Messenger of Allah, teaches us with advice rooted in the guidance of the Qur'an. Allah (SWT) says:

وَإِذْ أَخَذَ اللَّهُ مِيثَاقَ النَّبِيِّينَ لَمَا آتَيْتُكُم مِّن كِتَابٍ وَحِكْمَةٍ ثُمَّ جَاءَكُمْ رَسُولٌ مُّصَدِّقٌ لِّمَا مَعَكُمْ لَتُؤْمِنُنَّ بِهِ وَلَتَنصُرُنَّهُ ۚ قَالَ أَأَقْرَرْتُمْ وَأَخَذْتُمْ عَلَىٰ ذَٰلِكُمْ إِصْرِي ۖ قَالُوا أَقْرَرْنَا ۚ قَالَ فَاشْهَدُوا وَأَنَا مَعَكُم مِّنَ الشَّاهِدِينَ

[And (remember) when Allah took the Covenant of the Prophets, saying: "Take whatever I gave you from the Book and Hikmah (understanding of the Laws of Allah, etc.), and afterwards there will come to you a Messenger (Muhammad ﷺ) confirming what is with you; you must then believe in him and help him." Allah said: "Do you agree and will you take up My Covenant (which I conclude with you)?" They said: "We agree." He said: "Then bear witness; and I am with you among the witnesses."] **(3:81, Surah Al-Imran)**

Then Allah (SWT) says:

فَمَن تَوَلَّىٰ بَعْدَ ذَٰلِكَ فَأُولَٰئِكَ هُمُ الْفَاسِقُونَ ¬

[Then whoever turns away after this – they are the Fasiqun (rebellious, those who turn away from Allah's obedience).] **(3:82, Surah Al-Imran)**

Nevertheless, we continue to seek supporting evidence that aligns our adherence to the hadith, which will enable us to strike a harmonious balance between our prayers, our daily lives, and the guidance provided by the Qur'an. It is important for us to avoid adopting an extreme stance on contentious hadiths that exceed the boundaries set by the Qur'an's guidance and the Prophet's teachings.

Allah (SWT) says:

What does Caliph Umar (peace be upon him) say?

"I wanted to write the Sun'an, and I remembered a people who were before you. They wrote other books to follow and abandoned the Book of Allah. And I will never, I swear, replace Allah's Book with anything."

Caliph Umar (RA) refrained from compiling the collections for fear that Muslims might abandon the teachings of the Qur'an in favour of the hadith.

Ali ibn Abu Talib (RA), the fourth Khalifah, said in one of his speeches:

"I urge all those who have writings taken from the Messenger of Allah to go home and erase them. The people before you were annihilated because they followed the hadith of their scholars and left the Book of their Lord."

(Sunan Al-Darimi)

Even in contemporary times, the discourse surrounding hadiths remains fervent within the Muslim community, sometimes making it challenging to adhere comfortably to a selected hadith or one that is logically acceptable.

For example, even scholars are divided over the last sermon of our Prophet Muhammad ﷺ. Some say that the Prophet stated he left nothing but the Qur'an as a guide for Muslims. Others strongly disagree and claim that he said:

"O people, understand the words which I convey to you. I leave behind me two things: the Qur'an and my example, the Sunnah. If you follow these, you will never go astray."

Allah said to His Messenger:

تِلْكَ آيَاتُ اللَّهِ نَتْلُوهَا عَلَيْكَ بِالْحَقِّ ۚ فَبِأَيِّ حَدِيثٍ بَعْدَ اللَّهِ وَآيَاتِهِ يُؤْمِنُونَ ¬

[These are the Ayat (proofs, evidences, verses, lessons, revelations, etc.) of Allah, which We recite to you (O Muhammad ﷺ) with truth. Then in which speech after Allah and His Ayat will they believe?] **(45:6, Surah Al-Jathiya)** [134]

What does the Prophet complain to Allah (SWT)?

لَّقَدْ أَضَلَّنِي عَنِ الذِّكْرِ بَعْدَ إِذْ جَاءَنِي ۗ وَكَانَ الشَّيْطَانُ لِلْإِنسَانِ خَذُولًا

وَقَالَ الرَّسُولُ يَا رَبِّ إِنَّ قَوْمِي اتَّخَذُوا هَٰذَا الْقُرْآنَ مَهْجُورًا

"He indeed led me astray from the Reminder (this Qur'an) after it had come to me. And Shaitan (Satan) is ever a deserter to man in the hour of need." (25:29)

And the Messenger (Muhammad ﷺ) will say:

"O my Lord! Verily, my people deserted this Qur'an (neither listened to it, nor acted on its laws and orders)." (25:30, Surah Al-Furqan)

Conspiracies aimed at distorting and falsifying the sayings, stories, and instructions of our Prophet, and then disseminating them as hadiths within the Muslim community, have the potential to sow confusion and discord—as we witness today. Such actions are in direct opposition to the teachings of Islam, and those who engage in them may face the repercussions of their deeds, just as the Prophet expressed his discontent with such practices.

If we repeat the verse of the Qur'an (6:112, Surah Al-An'am) mentioned earlier:

وَكَذَٰلِكَ جَعَلْنَا لِكُلِّ نَبِيٍّ عَدُوًّا شَيَاطِينَ الْإِنسِ وَالْجِنِّ يُوحِي بَعْضُهُمْ إِلَىٰ بَعْضٍ زُخْرُفَ ¬ الْقَوْلِ غُرُورًا ۚ وَلَوْ شَاءَ رَبُّكَ مَا فَعَلُوهُ ۖ فَذَرْهُمْ وَمَا يَفْتَرُونَ

"And so We have appointed for every Prophet enemies—Shayatin (devils) among mankind and jinns, inspiring one another with adorned speech as a delusion (or by way of deception). If your Lord had so willed, they would not have done it, so leave them alone with their fabrications." *(Tafseer Qurtubi, Vol. 7, Page 67)*

Narrated Abu Hurayrah:

The Prophet صلى الله عليه وسلم said:

"Allah will raise for this Ummah at the end of every hundred years the one who will renovate its religion for it."

(Sunan Abi Dawud 4291)[135]

"Recent research has identified that almost all of the Hadith of the Prophet ﷺ was [sic] written down in the life of the Companions, which stretched to the end of the first century."

---

[134] Index 118 https://theislamtruth.wordpress.com/2015/12/04/examples-of-bad-hadiths/
[135] Index 119 https://sunnah.com/abudawud/39/1

Efforts to corrupt Islam began during the lifetime of Prophet Muhammad ﷺ, when hypocrites started spreading lies and misinformation. These individuals, who invented such fabrications, were the enemies of Allah Almighty and His Messenger. Their false stories were systematically spread among people who had never met or seen the Prophet ﷺ.

The following verse indicates this:

مُحَمَّدٌ رَّسُولُ اللَّهِ ۚ وَالَّذِينَ مَعَهُ أَشِدَّاءُ عَلَى الْكُفَّارِ رُحَمَاءُ بَيْنَهُمْ ۖ تَرَاهُمْ رُكَّعًا سُجَّدًا يَبْتَغُونَ فَضْلًا مِّنَ اللَّهِ وَرِضْوَانًا ۖ سِيمَاهُمْ فِي وُجُوهِهِم مِّنْ أَثَرِ السُّجُودِ ۚ ذَٰلِكَ مَثَلُهُمْ فِي التَّوْرَاةِ ۚ وَمَثَلُهُمْ فِي الْإِنجِيلِ كَزَرْعٍ أَخْرَجَ شَطْأَهُ فَآزَرَهُ فَاسْتَغْلَظَ فَاسْتَوَىٰ عَلَىٰ سُوقِهِ يُعْجِبُ الزُّرَّاعَ لِيَغِيظَ بِهِمُ الْكُفَّارَ ۗ وَعَدَ اللَّهُ الَّذِينَ آمَنُوا وَعَمِلُوا الصَّالِحَاتِ مِنْهُم مَّغْفِرَةً وَأَجْرًا عَظِيمًا

Muhammad (ﷺ) is the Messenger of Allah, and those who are with him are severe against disbelievers, and merciful among themselves. You see them bowing and falling down prostrate (in prayer), seeking Bounty from Allah and (His) Good Pleasure. The mark of them (i.e., of their faith) is on their faces (foreheads) from the traces of (their) prostration (during prayers). This is their description in the Taurat (Torah). But their description in the Injeel (Gospel) is like a (sown) seed which sends forth its shoot, then makes it strong, it then becomes thick, and it stands straight on its stem, delighting the sowers—that He may enrage the disbelievers with them. Allah has promised those among them who believe (i.e., all those who follow Islamic Monotheism, the religion of Prophet Muhammad ﷺ till the Day of Resurrection) and do righteous good deeds, forgiveness and a mighty reward (i.e., Paradise).

(48:29, Surah Al-Fath)

The division of Muslims into sects cannot be solely attributed to hadith writers. Rather, satanic influence and deceit play a significant role in fabricating the narrative surrounding the succession of Prophet Muhammad ﷺ. While numerous examples of such hadiths are recorded in *Sahih al-Bukhari*, it is important to note that many of these stories lack credibility and often contain elements that are demeaning, nonsensical, obscene, or sorrowful. Nevertheless, only Allah (SWT) possesses true knowledge in this matter.

• Prophet Moses beat the stone

Volume 1, Book 5, Number 277 – Narrated Abu Huraira:

The Prophet said, "The (people of) Bani Israel used to take bath naked (all together), looking at each other. The Prophet Moses used to take a bath alone. They said, 'By Allah! Nothing prevents Moses from taking a bath with us except that he has a scrotal hernia.' So once, Moses went out to take a bath and put his clothes over a stone, and then that stone ran away with his clothes. Moses followed that stone saying, 'My clothes, O stone! My clothes, O stone!'—till the people of Bani Israel saw him and said, 'By Allah, Moses has got no defect in his body.' Moses took his clothes and began to beat the stone." Abu Huraira added, "By Allah! There are still six or seven marks present on the stone from that excessive beating."

● Volume 2, Book 23, Number 423 – Narrated Abu Huraira:

The angel of death was sent to Moses. When he went to him, Moses slapped him severely, spoiling one of his eyes. The angel went back to his Lord and said, "You sent me to a slave who does not want to die." Allah restored his eye and said, "Go back and tell him (i.e., Moses) to place his hand over the back of an ox, for he will be allowed to live for a number of years equal to the number of hairs coming under his hand." (So the angel came to him and told him the same.) Then Moses asked, "O my Lord! What will be then?" He said, "Death will be then." He said, "(Let it be) now." He asked Allah that He bring him near the Sacred Land at a distance of a stone's throw. Allah's Apostle (p.b.u.h.) said, "Were I there, I would show you the grave of Moses by the way near the red sand hill."

Numerous hadiths are deemed unacceptable and embarrassing, warranting exclusion from this book. Their inclusion could potentially undermine the credibility of the teachings and guidance of Prophet Muhammad 🕌, as well as the sanctity of hadith literature. Those intrigued by such derogatory hadiths may consult the following reference:

No. 235 – Narrated Abu Qilaba:

Reference:

http://muslimvilla.smfforfree.com/index.php?topic=2483.0;wap2

(Hanbel 6/136,192,213). (Bukhari 4/60,62). (Bukhari 63/27). (Bukhari 8/102; Hanbel 4/86).

(Bukhari, Jihad/146; Abu Dawud 113)

"The parchment that the verse about stoning to death for adultery was written on was eaten and abrogated by a goat."

(Ibni Majah 36/1944; Ibni Hanbal 3/61; 5/131,132,183; 6/269)

However, let us focus on the positive side of the hadith literature, which attempts to follow the Prophet 🕌 directly from the Qur'an. The verse says:

$$\text{إِنَّهُ لَقَوْلُ رَسُولٍ كَرِيمٍ}$$

That this is verily the word of an honoured Messenger [i.e., Jibrael (Gabriel) or Muhammad 🕌 which he has brought from Allah]. (69:40, Surah Al-Haqqa)

The People of the Scripture (Jews) used to recite the Torah in Hebrew and explain it in Arabic to the Muslims. On that, Allah's Apostle said:

266

"Do not believe the People of the Scripture or disbelieve them, but say: 'We believe in Allah and what is revealed to us.'" (2:136)

قُولُوا آمَنَّا بِاللَّهِ وَمَا أُنزِلَ إِلَيْنَا وَمَا أُنزِلَ إِلَىٰ إِبْرَاهِيمَ وَإِسْمَاعِيلَ وَإِسْحَاقَ وَيَعْقُوبَ ﹁ وَالْأَسْبَاطِ وَمَا أُوتِيَ مُوسَىٰ وَعِيسَىٰ وَمَا أُوتِيَ النَّبِيُّونَ مِن رَّبِّهِمْ لَا نُفَرِّقُ بَيْنَ أَحَدٍ مِّنْهُمْ وَنَحْنُ لَهُ مُسْلِمُونَ

Say (O Muslims), "We believe in Allah and that which has been sent down to us, and that which has been sent down to Ibrahim (Abraham), Isma'il (Ishmael), Ishaque (Isaac), Ya'qub (Jacob), and to Al-Asbat [the twelve sons of Ya'qub (Jacob)], and that which has been given to Musa (Moses) and 'Isa (Jesus), and that which has been given to the Prophets from their Lord. We make no distinction between any of them, and to Him we have submitted (in Islam)." (2:136, Surah Al-Baqara)[136]

Faced With Lies

1

إِنَّا أَنزَلْنَا التَّوْرَاةَ فِيهَا هُدًى وَنُورٌ ۚ يَحْكُمُ بِهَا النَّبِيُّونَ الَّذِينَ أَسْلَمُوا لِلَّذِينَ هَادُوا وَالرَّبَّانِيُّونَ وَالْأَحْبَارُ بِمَا اسْتُحْفِظُوا مِن كِتَابِ اللَّهِ وَكَانُوا عَلَيْهِ شُهَدَاءَ ۚ فَلَا تَخْشَوُا النَّاسَ وَاخْشَوْنِ وَلَا تَشْتَرُوا بِآيَاتِي ثَمَنًا قَلِيلًا ۚ وَمَن لَّمْ يَحْكُم بِمَا أَنزَلَ اللَّهُ فَأُولَٰئِكَ هُمُ الْكَافِرُونَ

Verily, We did send down the Taurat (Torah) [to Musa (Moses)], wherein was guidance and light, by which the Prophets, who submitted themselves to Allah's Will, judged the Jews. And the rabbis and the priests [also judged the Jews by the Taurat after those Prophets], for to them was entrusted the protection of Allah's Book, and they were witnesses thereto. Therefore, fear not men but fear Me (O Jews), and sell not My Verses for a miserable price. And whosoever does not judge by what Allah has revealed, such are the Kafirun (i.e., disbelievers – of a lesser degree, as they do not act on Allah's Laws).

[5:44, Surah Al-Ma'idah]

2

وَلْيَحْكُمْ أَهْلُ الْإِنجِيلِ بِمَا أَنزَلَ اللَّهُ فِيهِ ۚ وَمَن لَّمْ يَحْكُم بِمَا أَنزَلَ اللَّهُ فَأُولَٰئِكَ هُمُ الْفَاسِقُونَ

Let the people of the Injeel (Gospel) judge by what Allah has revealed therein. And whosoever does not judge by what Allah has revealed (then) such (people) are the Fasiqun (the rebellious, i.e., disobedient to Allah – of a lesser degree).

[5:47, Surah Al-Ma'idah]

Moses Wrote in Deuteronomy 4:2 (KJV)

---

136 Index 120 http://www.islamicity.com/mosque/sunnah/bukhari/060.sbt.html

"Ye shall not add unto the word which I command you, neither shall ye diminish ought from it, that ye may keep the commandments of the LORD your God which I command you."

King Solomon wrote in Proverbs 30:6 (KJV)

"Add thou not unto his words, lest he reprove thee, and thou be found a liar."

The Apostle John wrote in Revelation 22:18–19 (KJV)

18 For I testify unto every man that heareth the words of the prophecy of this book, If any man shall add unto these things, God shall add unto him the plagues that are written in this book.

19 And if any man shall take away from the words of the book of this prophecy, God shall take away his part out of the book of life, and out of the holy city, and from the things which are written in this book.

Jeremiah wrote in Jeremiah 4:22 (KJV)

"For my people is foolish, they have not known me; they are sottish children, and they have none understanding: they are wise to do evil, but to do good they have no knowledge."

Muslims often appeal to Jeremiah 8:8 as proof that the Torah has been corrupted:

Jeremiah 8:8 (KJV)

"How do ye say, We are wise, and the law of the LORD is with us? Lo, certainly in vain made he it; the pen of the scribes is in vain."

Jeremiah was a prophet of God, which means he was receiving revelation from God. As such, Jeremiah would have been quite capable of restoring the Torah to its true pristine form at the direct order of God. Hence, nothing of the Torah could have been permanently corrupted.

In fact, something similar occurred with Jeremiah's own revelation. If God was capable of restoring the revelation given to Jeremiah after it had been destroyed, then He would also be capable of restoring the original Torah and having His prophets record it.

Furthermore, God promises to write His Law into the hearts of true believers:

"'The time is coming,' declares the LORD, 'when I will make a new covenant with the house of Israel and with the house of Judah. It will not be like the covenant I made with their forefathers when I took them by the hand to lead them out of Egypt, because they broke my covenant, though I was a husband to them,' declares the LORD.

'This is the covenant I will make with the house of Israel after that time,' declares the LORD. 'I will put my law in their minds and write it on their hearts. I will be their God, and they will be my people. No longer will a man teach his neighbour, or a man his brother, saying, "Know the LORD," because they will all know me, from the least of them to the greatest,' declares the LORD. 'For I will forgive their wickedness and will remember their sins no more.'

This is what the LORD says, he who appoints the sun to shine by day, who decrees the moon and stars to shine by night, who stirs up the sea so that its waves roar – the LORD Almighty is his name: 'Only if these decrees vanish from my sight,' declares the LORD, 'will the descendants of Israel ever cease to be a nation before me.'

This is what the LORD says: 'Only if the heavens above can be measured and the foundations of the earth below be searched out will I reject all the descendants of Israel because of all they have done,' declares the LORD."

[Jeremiah 31:31–37]

In light of the foregoing, the only reasonable implication is that the authors of such texts are misleading the public—either by writing their oral traditions or by misinterpreting the Law.

A similar situation existed during the time of Jesus Christ:

"Then certain Pharisees and teachers of the law came to Jesus from Jerusalem, asking, 'Why do your disciples break the tradition of the elders? They do not wash their hands before they eat!'

Jesus answered, 'And why do you break the commandment of God for the sake of your tradition? ... Thus you nullify the word of God for the sake of your tradition. Hypocrites! Isaiah was right when he prophesied about you: "These people honour me with their lips, but their heart is far from me. They worship me in vain; their doctrine is only the law taught by men."'

[Matthew 15:1–3, 6b–9]¹³⁷

So, it is quite plausible that Jeremiah (Jeremiah c. 650 – c. 570 BC, also called Jeremias or the "weeping prophet", was one of the major prophets of the Hebrew Bible) was rebuking the scribes for their traditions that led people astray from God's Word.

---

[137] *Isaiah 61 is the sixty-first chapter of the Book of Isaiah in the Hebrew Bible or the Old Testament of the Christian Bible. This book contains the prophecies attributed to the prophet Isaiah, and is one of the Books of the Prophets. Chapters 56-66 are often referred to as Trito-Isaiah. Wikipedia

That this is a more reasonable interpretation becomes immediately apparent in light of the following:

"The wise shall be ashamed; they shall be disappointed and snared. Because they have rejected the word of the Lord, what kind of knowledge do they have?"[138]

Finally, the Qur'an claims that there were some people who corrupted it. The verse in Surah Al-Hijr says:

كَمَا أَنزَلْنَا عَلَى الْمُقْتَسِمِينَ

الَّذِينَ جَعَلُوا الْقُرْآنَ عِضِينَ

As We have sent down on the dividers (Quraish pagans or Jews and Christians).

Who have made the Qur'an into parts (i.e. believed in a part and disbelieved in the other). — **15:90–91, Surah Al-Hijr**

Satan's scheme extends beyond distorting hadiths or corrupting texts; he also strives to sow confusion in people's minds regarding the authenticity of prophets, whether true or false. People of other sects would not blindly accept that Muhammad ﷺ is a true prophet—that would be foolish and disobedient. Instead, they are commanded to test the prophets to see if they are from God, because the following verses command them to do so:

2 Corinthians 11:14 (KJV)

"And no marvel; for Satan himself is transformed into an angel of light."

Therefore, we must test him to see who he is.

1 John 4:1 (KJV)

"Beloved, believe not every spirit, but try the spirits whether they are of God: because many false prophets are gone out into the world."

Matthew 24:24–25 (KJV)

24 "For there shall arise false Christs, and false prophets, and shall shew great signs and wonders; insomuch that, if it were possible, they shall deceive the very elect.

25 Behold, I have told you before."

1 Thessalonians 5:19–22 (KJV)

19 Quench not the Spirit.

20 Despise not prophesyings.

---

[138] Index 121 Collected from https://www.answering- islam.org/BibleCom/jer8_8_ss.html
http://muslimvilla.smfforfree.com/index.php?topic=2483.0;wap2

21 Prove all things; hold fast that which is good.

22 Abstain from all appearance of evil.

Muhammad ﷺ could be a true prophet, or he could be a false prophet. We must test him to see who he is. Are you ready to test Muhammad as God commanded?

The Qur'an confirms that our Prophet Muhammad ﷺ is a true Messenger of Allah SWT.

1

The verse says:

كَمَا أَرْسَلْنَا فِيكُمْ رَسُولًا مِّنكُمْ يَتْلُو عَلَيْكُمْ آيَاتِنَا وَيُزَكِّيكُمْ وَيُعَلِّمُكُمُ الْكِتَابَ وَالْحِكْمَةَ وَيُعَلِّمُكُم مَّا لَمْ تَكُونُوا تَعْلَمُونَ

Similarly (to complete My blessings on you), We have sent among you a Messenger (Muhammad ﷺ) of your own, reciting to you Our verses (the Qur'an) and sanctifying you, and teaching you the Book (the Qur'an) and the Hikmah (i.e. Sunnah, Islamic laws and fiqh—jurisprudence), and teaching you that which you used not to know. — **2:151, Surah Al-Baqarah**

2

The Qur'an teaches that Islam is the continuing, faithful religion in the same tradition as the prophets before Muhammad ﷺ— the same religion established for you as was commanded to Noah, Abraham, Moses, and Jesus. The verse says:

شَرَعَ لَكُم مِّنَ الدِّينِ مَا وَصَّىٰ بِهِ نُوحًا وَالَّذِي أَوْحَيْنَا إِلَيْكَ وَمَا وَصَّيْنَا بِهِ إِبْرَاهِيمَ وَمُوسَىٰ وَعِيسَىٰ

He (Allah) has ordained for you the same religion (Islam) which He ordained for Nuh (Noah), and that which We have inspired in you (O Muhammad ﷺ), and that which We ordained for Ibrahim (Abraham), Musa (Moses), and 'Isa (Jesus), saying you should establish religion and make no divisions in it. Intolerable to the polytheists is that to which you (O Muhammad ﷺ) call them. Allah chooses for Himself whom He wills, and guides unto Himself those who turn to Him in repentance. — **42:13, Surah Ash-Shura**

3

وَلَا تُجَادِلُوا أَهْلَ الْكِتَابِ إِلَّا بِالَّتِي هِيَ أَحْسَنُ إِلَّا الَّذِينَ ظَلَمُوا مِنْهُمْ ۖ وَقُولُوا آمَنَّا بِالَّذِي أُنزِلَ إِلَيْنَا وَأُنزِلَ إِلَيْكُمْ وَإِلَٰهُنَا وَإِلَٰهُكُمْ وَاحِدٌ وَنَحْنُ لَهُ مُسْلِمُونَ

And argue not with the people of the Scripture (Jews and Christians), unless it be in a way that is better (with good words and in good manner, inviting them to Islamic Monotheism with His verses), except with such of them as do wrong, and say (to them): "We believe in that which has been revealed to us and revealed to you; our Ilah (God) and your Ilah (God) is One (i.e. Allah), and to Him we have submitted (as Muslims)." — **29:46, Surah Al-'Ankabūt**

In the context of interpreting and understanding the Qur'an, it is crucial to evaluate its guidelines based on their intrinsic value, rather than relying solely on hadith. We must consider divine guidance and the teachings of our Prophet ﷺ, while evaluating hadiths on their own merits.

According to our understanding, the following verse should be considered very carefully:

1

وَلَا تَقْفُ مَا لَيْسَ لَكَ بِهِ عِلْمٌ ۚ إِنَّ السَّمْعَ وَالْبَصَرَ وَالْفُؤَادَ كُلُّ أُولَٰئِكَ كَانَ عَنْهُ مَسْئُولًا

And follow not (O man—i.e., do not say, do, or witness) that of which you have no knowledge (e.g., saying: "I have seen," while in fact you have not seen, or "I have heard," while you have not heard). Verily! The hearing, the sight, and the heart—each of those you will be questioned about (by Allah). — **17:36, Surah Al-Isra'**

2

وَيْلٌ يَوْمَئِذٍ لِّلْمُكَذِّبِينَ

فَبِأَيِّ حَدِيثٍ بَعْدَهُ يُؤْمِنُونَ

Woe that Day to the deniers (of the Day of Resurrection)! Then in what statement after this (the Qur'an) will they believe? — **77:49–50, Surah Al-Mursalat**

3

إِنَّا أَنزَلْنَا إِلَيْكَ الْكِتَابَ بِالْحَقِّ لِتَحْكُمَ بَيْنَ النَّاسِ بِمَا أَرَاكَ اللَّهُ ۚ وَلَا تَكُن لِّلْخَائِنِينَ خَصِيمًا

Surely, We have sent down to you (O Muhammad ﷺ) the Book (this Qur'an) in truth that you might judge between people by that which Allah has shown you (i.e., taught through Divine Inspiration), so be not a pleader for the treacherous. — **4:105, Surah An-Nisa'**

4

وَمَا اخْتَلَفْتُمْ فِيهِ مِن شَيْءٍ فَحُكْمُهُ إِلَى اللَّهِ ۚ ذَٰلِكُمُ اللَّهُ رَبِّي عَلَيْهِ تَوَكَّلْتُ وَإِلَيْهِ أُنِيبُ

And in whatsoever you differ, the decision thereof is with Allah (He is the ruling Judge). And say (O Muhammad ﷺ): Such is Allah, my Lord—in Him I put my trust, and to Him I turn in all of my affairs and in repentance. — **42:10, Surah Ash-Shura**

5

اتَّبِعُوا مَا أُنزِلَ إِلَيْكُم مِّن رَّبِّكُمْ وَلَا تَتَّبِعُوا مِن دُونِهِ أَوْلِيَاءَ ۗ قَلِيلًا مَّا تَذَكَّرُونَ

[Say (O Muhammad ﷺ) to these idolaters (pagan Arabs) of your folk:] Follow what has been sent down unto you from your Lord (the Qur'an and the Prophet's Sunnah), and follow not any others besides Him (Allah). Little do you remember!
— **7:3, Surah Al-A'raf**

Travelers Initiative Review

As we approach the culmination of this straight path, it becomes crucial to periodically assess our personal circumstances to ensure that our journey remains on course. In order to regulate ourselves as believers, one of the vital aspects to consider is the practice of the Sunnah. The Sunnah serves as a significant guide for emulating the Prophet's exemplary character, behaviour, and actions. By adhering to the Sunnah, we not only strengthen our connection with Allah but also nurture the development of our spiritual and moral character. This, in turn, leads to an increase in faith and piety, enabling us to receive the abundant blessings and rewards from Allah SWT. Incorporating the Sunnah into our lives is instrumental in successfully completing this phase of the journey and transitioning into the realm of the unknown.

To follow the Sunnah—which refers to the actions and teachings of the Prophet Muhammad ﷺ—Muslims rely on the Hadith, despite ongoing questions regarding their authenticity. The content recorded in the books of Hadith is widely accepted by scholars and incorporated into our daily lives. Nevertheless, there are persistent debates among Muslims concerning the authenticity of many recorded Hadiths, with no clear resolution in sight.

As ordinary Muslims with limited knowledge, it is wise for us to refrain from actively engaging in these debates. Instead, we should focus on self-reflection, self-improvement, and practising the Sunnah that is relevant and applicable to our lives. Our primary concern should be learning how to lead a righteous life and complete our spiritual journey successfully. By dedicating our time and energy to personal growth and adherence to the Sunnah, we can navigate our lives in a way that aligns with our faith.

Today, it is common to use smartphones to receive, forward, and share Hadith (sayings of the Prophet Muhammad ﷺ), Tafsir (interpretations of the Qur'an), and Duas (supplications) in an effort to benefit ourselves and inspire others. However, it is crucial to consider our own knowledge and understanding before engaging in this practice. Furthermore, we often encounter messages warning that failure to forward a particular Hadith, Dua, or piece of advice will result in divine punishment. Such claims should not be taken lightly. Blindly participating in these practices without exercising caution and verifying their authenticity can lead to sin. It is essential for the sender to ensure that the information being shared is legitimate and free from any satanic influence, and to confirm that the recipient is willing to receive it.

We can refer to the following Hadith:

Abu Huraira reported:

The Messenger of Allah ﷺ said:

"Whoever travels a path in search of knowledge, Allah will make easy for him a path to Paradise. People do not gather in the houses of Allah, reciting the Book of Allah and studying it together, but tranquillity will descend upon them, mercy will cover them, angels will surround them, and Allah will mention them to those near Him."

Source: Sunan Abī Dāwūd 3641, Grade: Sahih

Abu Darda reported:

The Messenger of Allah ﷺ said:

"Verily, the angels lower their wings for the seeker of knowledge. The inhabitants of the heavens and earth, even the fish in the depths of the water, seek forgiveness for the scholar. The virtue of the scholar over the worshipper is like the superiority of the moon over the stars. The scholars are the inheritors of the Prophets. They do not leave behind gold or silver coins, but rather they leave behind knowledge. Whoever has taken hold of it has been given an abundant share."

Source: Ṣaḥīḥ al-Bukhārī 3274, Grade: Sahih

Abu Huraira also reported:

The Messenger of Allah ﷺ said:

"When the human being dies, his deeds end except for three: ongoing charity, beneficial knowledge, or a righteous child who prays for him."

As this chapter draws to a close, my role in this endeavour may not be significant enough to greatly benefit the traveller. Instead, I refer these matters to the court of Allah, where His guidance and words reign supreme. Now, it is within your power to determine how much of Allah's wisdom you can embrace, and how deeply you can transform your inner self into that of a true believer.

This chapter concludes with the following verses and the last sermon of our Prophet Muhammad ﷺ, may Allah bless him:

24:51 – Surah An-Nur

إِنَّمَا كَانَ قَوْلَ الْمُؤْمِنِينَ إِذَا دُعُوا إِلَى اللَّهِ وَرَسُولِهِ لِيَحْكُمَ بَيْنَهُمْ أَن يَقُولُوا سَمِعْنَا وَأَطَعْنَا ۚ وَأُولَئِكَ هُمُ الْمُفْلِحُونَ

The only saying of the faithful believers, when they are called to Allah (His Words, the Qur'an) and His Messenger ﷺ to judge between them, is that they say: "We hear and we obey." And such are the prosperous ones (who will live forever in Paradise).

47:33 – Surah Muhammad

يَا أَيُّهَا الَّذِينَ آمَنُوا أَطِيعُوا اللَّهَ وَأَطِيعُوا الرَّسُولَ وَلَا تُبْطِلُوا أَعْمَالَكُمْ

O you who believe! Obey Allah and obey the Messenger (Muhammad ﷺ) and render not vain your deeds.

72:23 – Surah Al-Jinn

إِلَّا بَلَاغًا مِّنَ اللَّهِ وَرِسَالَاتِهِ ۚ وَمَن يَعْصِ اللَّهَ وَرَسُولَهُ فَإِنَّ لَهُ نَارَ جَهَنَّمَ خَالِدِينَ فِيهَا أَبَدًا

"(Mine is) but conveyance (of the truth) from Allah and His Messages (of Islamic Monotheism), and whosoever disobeys Allah and His Messenger, then verily, for him is the Fire of Hell; he shall dwell therein forever."

33:36 – Surah Al-Ahzab

وَمَا كَانَ لِمُؤْمِنٍ وَلَا مُؤْمِنَةٍ إِذَا قَضَى اللَّهُ وَرَسُولُهُ أَمْرًا أَن يَكُونَ لَهُمُ الْخِيَرَةُ مِنْ أَمْرِهِمْ ۗ وَمَن يَعْصِ اللَّهَ وَرَسُولَهُ فَقَدْ ضَلَّ ضَلَالًا مُّبِينًا

It is not for a believer, man or woman, when Allah and His Messenger have decreed a matter, that they should have any option in their decision. And whoever disobeys Allah and His Messenger has indeed strayed into clear error.

Conclusion

This chapter is filled with verses that collectively form an intricate picture—one that is nearly impossible to convey fully through speech or other means. Therefore, it is essential for any seeker to meticulously correlate each verse with its analysis before drawing conclusions or taking action. This is a unique matter, for on the Day of Judgement, only the individual will be accountable to the Almighty.

The Last Sermon of Prophet Muhammad ﷺ

Prophet Muhammad ﷺ delivered his final sermon (Khutbah) on the ninth of Dhul Hijjah (the twelfth and last month of the Islamic year), ten years after the Hijrah (migration from Makkah to Madinah), in the Uranah Valley of Mount Arafat. His words were clear and concise, and they were directed to all of humanity.

After praising and thanking Allah, he said:

"O people, lend me an attentive ear, for I know not whether, after this year, I shall ever be amongst you again. Therefore, listen to what I am saying to you very carefully and take these words to those who could not be present here today.

O people, just as you regard this month, this day, and this city as sacred, so regard the life and property of every Muslim as a sacred trust. Return the goods entrusted to you to their rightful owners. Hurt no one so that no one may hurt you.

Remember that you will indeed meet your Lord, and that He will indeed reckon your deeds. Allah has forbidden you to take usury (interest); therefore, all interest obligations shall henceforth be waived. Your capital, however, is yours to keep. You will neither inflict nor suffer any inequity. Allah has judged that there shall be no interest, and that all the interest due to Abbas ibn Abd Al-Muttalib (the Prophet's uncle) shall henceforth be waived…

Beware of Satan, for the safety of your religion. He has lost all hope that he will ever be able to lead you astray in big things, so beware of following him in small things.

O people, it is true that you have certain rights with regard to your women, but they also have rights over you. Remember that you have taken them as your wives only under Allah's trust and with His permission. If they abide by your rights, then to them belongs the right to be fed and clothed in kindness. Do treat your women well and be kind to them, for they are your partners and committed helpers. And it is your right that they do not make friends with anyone of whom you do not approve, as well as never to be unchaste.

O people, listen to me in earnest. Worship Allah, say your five daily prayers (Salah), fast during the month of Ramadan, and give your wealth in Zakat. Perform Hajj if you can afford to.

All mankind is from Adam and Eve. An Arab has no superiority over a non-Arab, nor does a non-Arab have any superiority over an Arab. Likewise, a white person has no superiority over a black person, nor does a black person have any superiority over a white person—except by piety (taqwa) and good action.

Learn that every Muslim is a brother to every Muslim, and that the Muslims constitute one brotherhood. Nothing shall be legitimate to a Muslim which belongs to a fellow Muslim unless it was given freely and willingly. Do not, therefore, do injustice to yourselves.

Remember, one day you will appear before Allah and answer for your deeds. So beware—do not stray from the path of righteousness after I am gone.

O people, no prophet or apostle will come after me, and no new faith will be born.

Reason well, therefore, O people, and understand the words which I convey to you. I leave behind me two things: the Qur'an and my example, the Sunnah. If you follow these, you will never go astray.

All those who listen to me shall pass on my words to others, and those to others again. And may the last ones understand my words better than those who listen to me directly.

Be my witness, O Allah, that I have conveyed Your message to Your people."[139]

---

[139] Index 122 (Reference: See Al-Bukhari, Hadith 1623, 1626, 6361) Sahih of Imam Muslim also refers to this sermon in Hadith number 98. Imam al-Tirmidhi has mentioned this sermon in Hadith nos. 1628, 2046, 2085. Imam Ahmed bin Hanbal has given us the longest and perhaps the most complete version of this sermon in his Masnud, Hadith no. 19774.)

$$\text{بِسْمِ ٱللَّهِ ٱلرَّحْمَـٰنِ ٱلرَّحِيمِ}$$

Chapter 8

I shall not fear anyone on Earth.

- I shall fear only God.

- I shall not bear ill will toward anyone.

- I shall not submit to injustice from anyone.

- I shall conquer untruth by truth

And in resisting untruth,

I shall put up with all suffering."

— *Mahatma Gandhi*

Justice and Empathy

Travellers have just left the realm of Hadith. Before departing the realm of Hadith, each encounters a pivotal moment for introspection—an opportunity to rectify past errors and carefully imbue the wisdom of Hadith into their possessions as they set forth on the path of righteousness.

Their journey leads them to the vast mountainous region known as the "Fairness, Justice, and Compassion" zone, where daunting trials await, threatening to undermine their moral integrity. Every stride in this domain requires profound self-assessment and accountability.

Here, each traveller faces a crucial opportunity to reflect upon their past actions and rectify any mistakes they may have made, ensuring their reintegration into the group on the righteous path. It is vital to remember that Allah (SWT) eagerly awaits the arrival of the righteous at the gates of Paradise. This simple truth underscores the significance of proving oneself to be a truly righteous individual. All our endeavours will be rendered futile if we fail to demonstrate our righteousness.

Justice is one of the most important moral and political concepts. It occupies centre stage in both ethics and legal and political philosophy. The *Oxford English Dictionary* defines a "just" person as one who generally "does what is morally right" and "gives to each his due", essentially in terms of the most equal freedom of all members.

Rights and Duties. Ethical justification requires equal opportunities and beneficial outcomes for all, including addressing socio-economic disparities in society. Justice in legal terms is not much different from the above definition.

As travellers, we believe in our hearts that we are the believers, and we now seek to understand what Allah (SWT) has told us about the principles of justice that we must implement when necessary.

Allah says in the Qur'an:—

يَا أَيُّهَا الَّذِينَ آمَنُوا كُونُوا قَوَّامِينَ لِلَّهِ شُهَدَاءَ بِالْقِسْطِ ۖ وَلَا يَجْرِمَنَّكُمْ شَنَآنُ قَوْمٍ عَلَىٰ أَلَّا تَعْدِلُوا ۚ اعْدِلُوا هُوَ أَقْرَبُ لِلتَّقْوَىٰ ۖ وَاتَّقُوا اللَّهَ ۚ إِنَّ اللَّهَ خَبِيرٌ بِمَا تَعْمَلُونَ

"You who believe! Stand out firmly for Allah and be just witnesses, and let not the enmity and hatred of others make you avoid justice. Be just: that is nearer to piety, and fear Allah. Verily, Allah is Well-Acquainted with what you do."

Surah Al-Ma'idah 5:8

It is important to recognise that individuals of virtue operate from their innate goodness. They uphold their commitments, find joy in fairness, and abhor wickedness. They remain steadfast in their pursuit of justice, unaffected by the fear of retaliation, guided instead by their inherent sense of right and wrong.

It is crucial to acknowledge that the insidious whispers of Satan can lead us astray, steering us towards a path of damnation. Satan endeavours to corrupt our thoughts, coercing us into acting unjustly and prioritising personal gain over fairness. We must always bear in mind that treating others unjustly ultimately results in the corruption of our own souls.

According to Ali ibn al-Husayn al-Isfahani, a companion and scholar of the tenth century, he says:

"Righteous deeds are not only justice to others but also justice to Allah."

It is important to acknowledge that we bear the responsibility of evaluating our own actions in all aspects of our daily endeavours. Whether it pertains to our treatment of workers, employees, or domestic staff, we must ensure that justice is not withheld from them intentionally.

Assuming the role of a judge over our own triumphant deeds proves to be more challenging than engaging in outward acts of worship or constructing religious structures. When we profess our faith and claim to be on the righteous path, it becomes imperative to demonstrate our commitment by treating all believers as part of a unified brotherhood, without any form of discrimination. Justifying our actions in accordance with this principle is paramount.

Allah (SWT) says:—

إِنَّمَا الْمُؤْمِنُونَ إِخْوَةٌ فَأَصْلِحُوا بَيْنَ أَخَوَيْكُمْ ۚ وَاتَّقُوا اللَّهَ لَعَلَّكُمْ تُرْحَمُونَ

"The believers are nothing else than brothers (in Islamic religion). So make reconciliation between your brothers, and fear Allah, that you may receive mercy."

Surah Al-Hujurat 49:10

We assert that assessing one's actions is more challenging than evaluating their customary prayers. This assertion can be examined by referring to the verses of the Holy Book, wherein Allah (SWT) affirms the following:—

اللَّهُ الَّذِي أَنزَلَ الْكِتَابَ بِالْحَقِّ وَالْمِيزَانَ ۗ وَمَا يُدْرِيكَ لَعَلَّ السَّاعَةَ قَرِيبٌ

"It is Allah Who has sent down the Book (the Qur'an) in truth, and the Balance (i.e. to act justly). And what can make you know that perhaps the Hour is close at hand?"

Surah Ash-Shura 42:17

Now, if we analyse the following verses, it will become clear how far we are from the instructions of Allah (SWT).

Allah says:—

إِنَّ اللَّهَ يَأْمُرُ بِالْعَدْلِ وَالْإِحْسَانِ وَإِيتَاءِ ذِي الْقُرْبَىٰ وَيَنْهَىٰ عَنِ الْفَحْشَاءِ وَالْمُنكَرِ وَالْبَغْيِ ۚ يَعِظُكُمْ لَعَلَّكُمْ تَذَكَّرُونَ

"Verily, Allah enjoins Al-'Adl (i.e. justice and worshipping none but Allah Alone – Islamic Monotheism), and Al-Ihsan [i.e. to be patient in performing your duties to Allah, totally for Allah's sake and in accordance with the Sunnah (legal ways) of the Prophet ﷺ in a perfect manner], and giving (help) to kith and kin (i.e. all that Allah has ordered you to give them — e.g., wealth, visiting, looking after them, or any other kind of help, etc.); and forbids Al-Fahsha' (i.e. all evil deeds, e.g., illegal sexual acts, disobedience of parents, polytheism, telling lies, giving false witness, killing a life without right, etc.), and Al-Munkar (i.e. all that is prohibited by Islamic law: polytheism of every kind, disbelief, and every kind of evil deed, etc.), and Al-Baghy (i.e. all kinds of oppression). He admonishes you, that you may take heed."

Surah An-Nahl 16:90

يَا أَيُّهَا الَّذِينَ آمَنُوا لَا تَأْكُلُوا أَمْوَالَكُم بَيْنَكُم بِالْبَاطِلِ إِلَّا أَن تَكُونَ تِجَارَةً عَن تَرَاضٍ مِّنكُمْ ۚ وَلَا تَقْتُلُوا أَنفُسَكُمْ ۚ إِنَّ اللَّهَ كَانَ بِكُمْ رَحِيمًا

"You who believe! Eat not up your property among yourselves unjustly, except it be a trade amongst you, by mutual consent. And do not kill yourselves (nor kill one another). Surely, Allah is Most Merciful to you."

Surah An-Nisaa 4:29

Greed compels us to unjustly seize the wealth of others, making it the primary catalyst for the injustice we experience, as exemplified in the aforementioned verse:—

وَخَلَقَ اللَّهُ السَّمَاوَاتِ وَالْأَرْضَ بِالْحَقِّ وَلِتُجْزَىٰ كُلُّ نَفْسٍ بِمَا كَسَبَتْ وَهُمْ لَا يُظْلَمُونَ

"And Allah has created the heavens and the earth with truth, in order that each person may be recompensed for what he has earned, and they will not be wronged."

Surah Al-Jathiya 45:22

In Islam, the issue of equitable distribution of justice is concerned with the rules governing the distribution of wealth and resources, as well as the perception of fairness by the recipient.

If an individual is unable to meet their basic needs, it is the responsibility of society or the State to provide assistance. Therefore, the formulation of economic policies—and whether they incorporate guidance from the Qur'an—is left to them. However, this does not absolve us from the obligation to help the less fortunate with our personal wealth and to strive for justice in accordance with Allah's law and guidance.

One of the aims of the Islamic economic distribution system is to ensure the fulfilment of individuals' basic needs. Islam permits the accumulation of honest income and wealth, and it also offers guidelines for the distribution of personal wealth within society. These guidelines aim to address social inequality while maintaining justice, but they do not advocate for the equal distribution of income and wealth in society, because Allah's guidance is clear in the verse below:—

أَهُمْ يَقْسِمُونَ رَحْمَتَ رَبِّكَ ۚ نَحْنُ قَسَمْنَا بَيْنَهُم مَّعِيشَتَهُمْ فِي الْحَيَاةِ الدُّنْيَا ۚ وَرَفَعْنَا بَعْضَهُمْ فَوْقَ بَعْضٍ دَرَجَاتٍ لِّيَتَّخِذَ بَعْضُهُم بَعْضًا سُخْرِيًّا ۗ وَرَحْمَتُ رَبِّكَ خَيْرٌ مِّمَّا يَجْمَعُونَ

"Is it they who would portion out the Mercy of thy Lord? It is We Who portion out between them their livelihood in the life of this world: and We raise some of them above others in ranks, so that some may command work from others. But the Mercy of thy Lord is better than the (wealth) which they amass."

Surah Az-Zukhruf 43:32

However, the justification of interpersonal income and wealth arising from unjust acts—such as exploitative practices or unjust enrichment—is strongly rejected in Islam.

Allah says:—

يَا أَيُّهَا الَّذِينَ آمَنُوا إِنَّ كَثِيرًا مِّنَ الْأَحْبَارِ وَالرُّهْبَانِ لَيَأْكُلُونَ أَمْوَالَ النَّاسِ بِالْبَاطِلِ وَيَصُدُّونَ عَن سَبِيلِ اللَّهِ ۗ وَالَّذِينَ يَكْنِزُونَ الذَّهَبَ وَالْفِضَّةَ وَلَا يُنفِقُونَهَا فِي سَبِيلِ اللَّهِ فَبَشِّرْهُم بِعَذَابٍ أَلِيمٍ

"You who believe! Verily, there are many of the (Jewish) rabbis and the (Christian) monks who devour the wealth of mankind in falsehood, and hinder (them) from the Way of Allah (i.e. Allah's Religion of Islamic Monotheism). And those who hoard up gold and silver [Al-Kanz: the money, the Zakat of which has not been paid], and spend it not in the Way of Allah — announce unto them a painful torment."

Surah At-Tawbah 9:34

أَلَيْسَ اللَّهُ بِأَحْكَمِ الْحَاكِمِينَ

"Is not Allah the Best of judges?"

Surah At-Tin 95:8

Judge and justice are divine principles in the Qur'an. In the Qur'an, justice is both a moral quality and a legal concept. It does not permit discrimination on the basis of race, caste, or gender. The Qur'an nurtures the soul and strengthens individuals with the capacity to uphold justice within society.

It is clearly stated that the purpose of the creation of the universe is, in part, to establish justice and to eliminate cruelty and evil. The supremacy of justice in Islam is one of the highest principles. Allah (SWT) will examine us on the Day of Judgement, but we also find that Allah (SWT) tested His messengers in this world regarding how they implemented justice among their followers.

For example, Allah (SWT) tested His Prophet Dawood (AS) in how he judged the people of his time. The story is as follows:—

Allah (SWT) says:

يَا دَاوُودُ إِنَّا جَعَلْنَاكَ خَلِيفَةً فِي الْأَرْضِ فَاحْكُم بَيْنَ النَّاسِ بِالْحَقِّ وَلَا تَتَّبِعِ الْهَوَىٰ فَيُضِلَّكَ عَن سَبِيلِ اللَّهِ ۚ إِنَّ الَّذِينَ يَضِلُّونَ عَن سَبِيلِ اللَّهِ لَهُمْ عَذَابٌ شَدِيدٌ بِمَا نَسُوا يَوْمَ الْحِسَابِ

Dawood (David), AS:

"Verily, We have placed you as a successor on earth, so judge between men in truth (and justice) and follow not your desire, for it will mislead you from the Path of Allah. Verily, those who wander astray from the Path of Allah shall have a severe torment, because they forgot the Day of Reckoning." (38:26, Surah Sad)

One night, while Dawood was performing in his private sanctuary, something strange happened. Dawood (AS) saw two people climbing the wall and entering the citadel. Dawood (AS) was confused and alarmed by this unusual situation, but the two individuals introduced themselves and reassured him not to fear their presence. They explained that they had come to seek his judgement on a matter they were suffering from.

They said:

"Fear not. [We are] two adversaries, one of whom has wronged the other, so judge between us with truth and do not exceed [it], and guide us to the sound path.

281

Indeed, my brother has ninety-nine sheep, and I have one sheep. He said, 'Leave it to me,' and he overwhelmed me with his speech."

(Dawood) said: "He has undoubtedly wronged you..."

The perplexing conduct and underlying dispute between the two individuals troubled him deeply. It was later recounted that the two men inexplicably vanished from sight. Dawood (AS) realised that these two individuals were, in fact, angels assuming male forms, and they were engaged in a divine test of judgement. Overcome with fear, he swiftly sought repentance, humbling himself before his Lord and earnestly imploring Allah for forgiveness.

There are no authentic reports detailing the specific nature of Dawood's (AS) mistake. Some scholars suggest that Dawood (AS) had erred by judging after hearing only one side of the story. Had Allah (SWT) intended for the details of his wrongdoing to be known to us, He would have disclosed them. By keeping these details hidden, it is evident that what matters is not the specifics of his mistake but rather that Dawood (AS) prostrated in repentance before Allah, and that Allah forgave him.

When the following verse was revealed, our Prophet Muhammad (SAW) also prostrated:

The verses from Surah Sad (38:21-29) are as follows:

"And Dawood became certain that We had tried him, and he asked forgiveness of his Lord and fell down, bowing in prostration, and turned in repentance [to Allah]. So We forgave him that; and indeed, for him is nearness to Us and a good place of return." (38:25)

21. "And has the news of the litigants reached you? When they climbed over the wall into (his) Mihrab (a praying place or a private room),

22. When they entered upon Dawood (David), he was terrified of them. They said: 'Fear not! We are two litigants, one of whom has wronged the other, therefore judge between us with truth, and treat us not with injustice, and guide us to the Right Way.

23. Verily, this my brother (in religion) has ninety-nine ewes, while I have only one ewe, and he says: 'Hand it over to me,' and he overpowered me in speech.'

24. Dawood (David) said: 'He has wronged you in demanding your ewe in addition to his ewes. And verily, many partners oppress one another, except those who believe and do righteous deeds, and they are few.' And Dawood (David) guessed that We had tried him, and he sought forgiveness of his Lord, and he fell down prostrating and turned (to Allah) in repentance.

25. So We forgave him that, and verily, for him is a near access to Us, and a good place of (final) return (Paradise).

26. O Dawood (David)! Verily, We have placed you as a successor on earth, so judge between men in truth (and justice) and follow not your desire, for it will mislead you from the Path of Allah. Verily, those who wander astray from the Path of Allah shall have a severe torment, because they forgot the Day of Reckoning."

27. And We created not the heavens and the earth and all that is between them without purpose! That is the consideration of those who disbelieve. Then woe to those who disbelieve (in Islamic Monotheism) from the Fire!

28. Shall We treat those who believe (in the Oneness of Allah – Islamic Monotheism) and do righteous deeds as Mufsidun (those who associate partners in worship with Allah and commit crimes) on earth? Or shall We treat the Muttaqun (pious ones) as the Fujjar (criminals, disbelievers, wicked, etc)?

29. This is a Book (the Qur'an) which We have sent down to you, full of blessings that they may ponder over its verses, and that men of understanding may remember." (38:21-29, Surah Sad)

Why did Allah reveal this to us in such detail, describing how He tested His messenger's ability to judge? Certainly, Allah's narration of this account is not simply a bedtime story. There is a profound purpose behind revealing this narrative. It serves as a powerful admonition to the people of this world, reminding them of Allah's expectation to uphold impartial justice in every aspect of their lives. It is essential for individuals within the travelling group to reflect on their own personal circumstances in relation to judgment and fairness. They must address any shortcomings in accordance with Allah's guidance, for failing to do so would undermine the entire purpose of their journey.

The challenge lies within ourselves, as inner conflicts arise when our hearts and minds stray from Allah's law in our pursuit of justice. However, through a sincere examination of our actions, we can gauge our compliance with Allah's law. This assessment will be revealed upon the conclusion of this chapter.

Allah (SWT), in His wisdom, has provided a definition of justice that is meant to benefit all people in the world. The teachings of the Qur'an are not confined to any particular community but are intended for all of mankind. This universal message was also conveyed to the ancient Messengers, one such example being the story of Prophet Dawood.

When we look at the verses and events described by the prophets of that time, we witness their deep concern, frustration, and desperation as they sought Allah's mercy for themselves and their people. The Old Testament contains passages that convey a timeless message still relevant today. Despite our outward acts of devotion, such as prayers and religious obligations like Hajj and Zakat, these acts can lose their potency if our actions of justice contradict our prayer or righteousness. Let us recognise that God has bestowed upon every community the same directive: to uphold justice, just as He commanded Prophet Muhammad (SAW), whose teachings are incumbent upon all humanity to heed.

Let us journey back to ancient times and reflect on a few enduring concerns that remain relevant to this day.

1. Of Solomon:

Psalm 72:1–4 (KJV)

1 Give the king thy judgments, O God,

and thy righteousness unto the king's son.

2 He shall judge thy people with righteousness,

and thy poor with judgment.

3 The mountains shall bring peace to the people,

and the little hills, by righteousness.

4 He shall judge the poor of the people,

he shall save the children of the needy,

and shall break in pieces the oppressor.

The psalm is revealed towards the end of David's life, with Solomon becoming the next king. He will judge people in righteousness, defend the afflicted, and save children. The mountains will bring prosperity to the people, and the hills will bear the fruit of righteousness. This psalm is a call to a way of life, a shape of life.

2. Throughout the Old Testament:

God's people are exhorted to "learn to do right and seek justice."

Isaiah 1:15–17 (KJV)

15 And when ye spread forth your hands,

I will hide mine eyes from you:

yea, when ye make many prayers,

I will not hear:

your hands are full of blood.

16 Wash you, make you clean;

put away the evil of your doings from before mine eyes;

cease to do evil;

17 Learn to do well; seek judgment,

relieve the oppressed,

judge the fatherless,

plead for the widow.

Isaiah 1:15 says: "This verse is about the people of Israel who are living sinful, rebellious lives against God. The gesture of stretching out hands is a natural way to ask for help, but the verse continues, 'I will hide mine eyes from you.' This is a gesture of contempt and loathing. The verse also says, 'I will not hear.' This means that God will not answer or fulfil their requests. The verse concludes, 'your hands are full of blood.' Literally, 'bloods,' implying many murderous acts. The words point to the guilt of judges and princes, such as that described in Hosea 4:2. Life was sacrificed to greed, lust, or vindictiveness. To the prophet's eye, those hands, stretched upwards in the Temple by some (at least) of the king's ministers and judges, were red with the blood of the slain."

Comp. *Isaiah 59:3* says: "For *your hands are defiled with blood, and your fingers with iniquity; your lips have spoken lies, your tongue hath muttered perverseness.*" (KJV)[140]

As representatives of God, judges are called to acquit the innocent, condemn the guilty, and expose false accusations and bribery.

2 Chronicles 19:5–7 (KJV)

5 And he set judges in the land throughout all the fenced cities of Judah, city by city,

6 And said to the judges, Take heed what ye do: for ye judge not for man, but for the Lord, who is with you in the judgment.

7 Wherefore now let the fear of the Lord be upon you; take heed and do it: for there is no iniquity with the Lord our God, nor respect of persons, nor taking of gifts. [141]

---

[140] *https://biblehub.com/commentaries/isaiah/1-16.htm*
Note: Isaiah is a popular biblical name significantly shared with the prophet Isaiah. It is the Hebrew r In Islam Isaiah (Arabic: إشَعْيَاء, Romanized: Isha ʿya) is not mentioned by name in the Qur'an or hadith, but appears frequently as a prophet in Muslim sources such as Qisas al-Ambiyya' and various tafsirs. Al-Tabari (310/923) provides the general account for the Islamic tradition about Isaiah. Among the prophets between David and Zakariya are Isaiah (pbuh), Ibn Amoz (Amisiya). According to Muhammad Ibn Ishaq, Isaiah (pbuh) appeared before Zakaria (pbuh) and Yahya (John the Baptist) (pbuh). He was among those who prophesied about Jesus (Jesus) and Muhammad (PBUH). The king in his time was called Hezekiah (Hazekiah). He listened to Isaiah and obeyed him in what he advised him to do and forbid for the good of the state. Matters gathered pace among the Israelites. The king fell ill with an infected foot. While he was ill, Babylonian king Sennacherib (Sennacherib) marched toward Jerusalem with sixty thousand. oot phrase yeshayahu, meaning "God saves."
men.https://www.islamawareness.net/Prophets/isaiah.html
[141] https://www.biblegateway.com/passage

They are not to distort justice by favouring either the poor or the rich (**Exodus 23:3 (KJV)**

> *"Neither shalt thou countenance a poor man in his cause."*

This verse serves as a cautionary tale, advising against favouring a poor person's case solely out of pity or empathy. It underscores the importance of impartiality in dispensing justice, emphasising that decisions should not be influenced by either wealth or poverty. Rather, justice must remain steadfast, uninfluenced by fear of the affluent or sympathy for the disadvantaged.

God also charges kings to act justly and instructs them to look after the weak and defenceless. The psalmist prays:

Leviticus 19:15 (KJV)

Ye shall do no unrighteousness in judgment: thou shalt not respect the person of the poor, nor honour the person of the mighty: but in righteousness shalt thou judge thy neighbour.

Leviticus 19:15 (King James Version)

Ye shall do no unrighteousness in judgment:

thou shalt not respect the person of the poor,

nor honour the person of the mighty:

but in righteousness shalt thou judge thy neighbour.

Psalm 72 serves as a fervent supplication envisioning a time of flawless justice, often categorised as a "royal psalm." Tradition holds that it was recited during the auspicious occasions of coronations, particularly those of the Davidic lineage. This prayer resonates with a plea to bestow blessings upon the kings of Israel, commencing with Solomon, and beseeches for their governance to be marked by equity and their judgments to be righteous in overseeing the affairs of the people.

Similarly, the prophets rail against injustice and insist that the right worship of God cannot exist without loving justice. Prophet Amos threatens judgement on "those who oppress the innocent, take bribes, and deprive the poor of justice in the courts" (Amos 5:12).

Zechariah (PBUH) Note [142]

---

[142] (note)) Zechariah was the son of Berechiah, who was the son of Iddo (see Zechariah 1:1). Iddo was a priest who returned to Jerusalem with Zerubbabel, the first Jewish governor of Jerusalem after the Jews' return from the Babylonian exile (see Nehemiah 12:1–7). Zechariah prophesied from the second to the fourth year of the reign of Darius, about 520 to 518 B.C. (see Zechariah 1:1; 7:1). Along with his contemporary Haggai, Zechariah was instrumental in organizing and inspiring the Jews to finish rebuilding the temple (see Ezra 5:1; 6:14). The prophet Zechariah wrote the book. We do not know precisely when or where the book of Zechariah was written.

Exhorts God's people to "Administer true justice; show mercy and compassion to one another. Do not oppress the widow or the fatherless, the foreigner or the poor." The Psalm says:

Zechariah 7:9–12 (KJV)

9 Thus speaketh the Lord of hosts, saying,

Execute true judgment, and shew mercy and compassions every man to his brother:

10 *And oppress not the widow, nor the fatherless, the stranger, nor the poor;*

and let none of you imagine evil against his brother in your heart.

11 *But they refused to hearken, and pulled away the shoulder,*

and stopped their ears, that they should not hear.

12 *Yea, they made their hearts as an adamant stone,*

lest they should hear the law, and the words which the Lord of hosts hath sent

in his spirit by the former prophets: therefore came a great wrath from the Lord of hosts. [143]

And Micah rhetorically asks:

Micah 6:8 (KJV)

He hath shewed thee, O man, what is good;

and what doth the Lord require of thee,

but to do justly, and to love mercy,

and to walk humbly with thy God?

We humbly seek the Lord's guidance, strength, and wisdom to navigate the challenges ahead. The journey towards reconciliation is fraught with difficulties, yet it is the path that God beckons us to traverse. In Micah 6:8, we are reminded to heed God's voice, to pursue justice tempered with mercy and compassion, all while embodying the humility exemplified by Christ. This verse serves as a guiding light, urging us to walk in righteousness and grace as we strive to build a world reflective of God's love and justice.

Justice in the Old Testament shows up in the book of the prophet Amos:

However, we do know that Zechariah lived in Jerusalem soon after the return of the Jews from their exile in Babylon. He received the visions recorded in this book between the second and fourth years of the reign of Darius, or between 520 and 518 B.C. (see Zechariah 1:1; 7:1). Introduction to the Book of Zechariah, https://www.churchofjesuschrist.org/study/manual/old-testament-seminary-teacher-manual/introduction-to-the-book-of-zechariah?lang=eng

[143] ttps://www.biblegateway.com/passage/?search=Zechariah

287

Amos 5:6–7 (KJV)

6 Seek the Lord, and ye shall live;

lest he break out like fire in the house of Joseph, and devour it,

and there be none to quench it in Bethel.

7 Ye who turn judgment to wormwood,

and leave off righteousness in the earth,

Seeking God is indeed a central theme in the book of Amos. Amos emphasises the importance of seeking God not just in religious rituals or ceremonies, but in everyday life through acts of justice, righteousness, and mercy towards others.

In Amos 5:4-6, for instance, seeking God is equated with seeking good and not evil, which involves establishing justice in the gate—a place of public decision-making. This emphasises the idea that true worship of God involves not just religious rituals but also living in accordance with His principles of justice and righteousness.

Moreover, seeking God also involves listening to and obeying the word of the Lord, as mentioned throughout the book of Amos. This implies a deep commitment to understanding and following God's commands as revealed through His prophets.

So, in essence, for Amos, seeking God encompasses both religious devotion and ethical behaviour, with a strong emphasis on justice, righteousness, and obedience to God's word.

Justice and righteousness here are presented with the presence of God as the life-bestowing force. By calling the evil good (i.e., the so-called "justice" at the gate that had become injustice, and the people's wealth, gained at the expense of the poor and weak) and the good evil (abhorring the one who speaks the truth, 5:10), the Israelites transform what should be sweet (justice) into something bitter (wormwood).

Amos 5:14–15 (KJV)

14 Seek good, and not evil, that ye may live:

and so the Lord, the God of hosts, shall be with you, as ye have spoken.

15 Hate the evil, and love the good,

and establish judgment in the gate:

it may be that the Lord God of hosts will be gracious unto the remnant of Joseph.

When Amos speaks of hating the advocate of the right and abhorring those who speak "the whole truth," he refers to opposition to the court justice system. Such opposition, in God's eyes, leads to death. True life in Israel can only flourish when God's concern for the vulnerable finds embodiment in its social life. Such embodiment requires that the justice at the gate truly be justice, correcting wrongs done.

Concern for such justice goes back to the legal code itself:

Exodus 23:6–8 (KJV)

6 *Thou shalt not wrest the judgment of thy poor in his cause.*

7 *Keep thee far from a false matter; and the innocent and righteous slay thou not: for I will not justify the wicked.*

8 *And thou shalt take no gift: for the gift blindeth the wise, and perverteth the words of the righteous.*

But let justice roll down like waters, and righteousness like an overflowing stream."

Amos 5:21–24 (KJV)

21 *I hate, I despise your feast days, and I will not smell in your solemn assemblies.*

22 *Though ye offer me burnt offerings and your meat offerings, I will not accept them:*

neither will I regard the peace offerings of your fat beasts.

23 *Take thou away from me the noise of thy songs;*

for I will not hear the melody of thy viols.

24 *But let judgment run down as waters,*

and righteousness as a mighty stream.

Once more, Amos intertwines the concept of justice with the essence of life. Just as water is scarce in the desert, justice is indispensable in a community. When Israel fails to uphold justice, the community wilts, and its worship becomes hollow. Life ebbs away from the collective. For vitality to flourish within the community, justice and righteousness must flow abundantly like floods following winter rains, enduring like those rare streams that never run dry, even in the parching summer heat.

Amos 6:12 (KJV)

Shall horses run upon the rock? will one plow there with oxen?

for ye have turned judgment into gall, and the fruit of righteousness into hemlock

Amos's questions were indeed a powerful rhetorical device to highlight the absurdity of the actions of the elite in Israel. By comparing their actions to tasks that would be clearly irrational and futile, he effectively conveyed the gravity of their perversion.

In the context of justice, Amos was condemning the corruption and injustice prevalent among the people of Israel. Just as it would be absurd to expect horses to run on rocks or oxen to plough rocky terrain, it was equally nonsensical for the people to pervert justice, which is meant to uphold righteousness and fairness.

The metaphorical use of these questions underscores the severity of the situation. Instead of promoting righteousness and justice, the elite were causing harm and death through their actions. By equating their perversion of justice to the futile tasks described in his questions, Amos vividly portrayed the destructive consequences of their behaviour.[144] [145]

Major Works: The Book of Amos

In the Hebrew Bible and Christian Old Testament, Amos (/ˈeɪməs/; Hebrew: עָמוֹס – ʿĀmōs) was one of the Twelve Minor Prophets. According to the Bible, Amos was an older contemporary of Hosea and Isaiah, active c. 760–755 BCE during the reign of King Jeroboam II of Israel and King Uzziah of Judah. He is portrayed as being from the southern Kingdom of Judah yet preaching in the northern Kingdom of Israel. The prophet is characterised as speaking against the growing disparity between the very wealthy and the very poor, with themes of justice, God's omnipotence, and divine judgment.

Before becoming a prophet, Amos was a sheep herder and a sycamore fig farmer. His prior professions and his claim, "I am not a prophet nor a son of a prophet" (7:14), suggest that Amos was not from the school of prophets, which he argues would qualify him as a true prophet.

The Book of Amos is attributed to him. In recent years, scholars have grown more sceptical of the Book of Amos' presentation of Amos' biography and background. It's a call to embrace the true worship of God, which should always lead to justice, righteousness, and loving our neighbours. That's what the book of Amos is all about. — *By Ted Grimsrud*

Habakkuk's View of Justice and God's Goodness

The theme of justice indeed presents two formidable challenges. The first is the task of reconciling God's justice and goodness with the existence of injustice. How can a just God tolerate the presence of evil? This question is addressed pointedly in the book of Habakkuk in the Bible.

Habakkuk's lament reflects a timeless struggle with the apparent silence or inaction of a just and righteous God in the face of injustice and suffering. This sentiment resonates with many who grapple with the existence of evil and the apparent absence of divine intervention. It's a profound expression of the tension

---

[144] https://peacetheology.net/restorative-justice/5-old-testament-justice-amos/
[145] https://enterthebible.org/courses/amos/lessons/background-of-amos Amos (prophet) - Wikipedia

between faith and doubt, between the desire for justice and the reality of a world filled with injustice.

In Habakkuk's questioning, we see the anguish of someone trying to reconcile their belief in a just God with the injustice they witness. The prophet's words echo the frustration and confusion that arise when confronted with the prevalence of evil and the seeming impunity of the wicked. It's a cry for understanding, for answers, for a resolution to the apparent contradiction between God's goodness and the existence of evil.

Psalm says (Habakkuk 1:1–4 KJV):

1 The burden which Habakkuk the prophet did see.

Habakkuk's Complaint

2 *O Lord, how long shall I cry, and thou wilt not hear! even cry out unto thee of violence, and thou wilt not save!*

3 *Why dost thou shew me iniquity, and cause me to behold grievance? for spoiling and violence are before me: and there are that raise up strife and contention.*

4 *Therefore the law is slacked, and judgment doth never go forth:*

for the wicked doth compass about the righteous;

therefore wrong judgment proceedeth.

In the book of Habakkuk, the prophet questions how God's justice aligns with the apparent injustices he sees in the world. God responds by indicating that He will use the Babylonians, known for their ruthlessness and impetuosity, as instruments of His justice.

The Lord's Answer Habakkuk 1:5–6 (KJV)

5 *Behold ye among the heathen, and regard, and wonder marvellously:*

for I will work a work in your days, which ye will not believe, though it be told you.

6 *For, lo, I raise up the Chaldeans, that bitter and hasty nation,*

which shall march through the breadth of the land,

to possess the dwellingplaces that are not theirs.

The LORD tells Habakkuk that He will use the Chaldeans as His instrument to carry out His judgement on the people of Judah.

In the previous section, Habakkuk asked the LORD why He allowed him to witness wickedness and injustice that remained unaddressed in his society (vv. 2–4). In the present section, the LORD answers the prophet. In doing so, He uses the second-person plural "you" to indicate that the response was not for Habakkuk alone; it was also for the people of Judah.

Habakkuk, a prophet, stood as a bridge between the LORD and His people, tasked with conveying divine messages. Addressing both Habakkuk and the people of Judah, God acknowledged the issues within Judah and assured them of His awareness and eventual intervention. Divine timing often diverges from our own. Scriptures abound with reminders not to falter in goodness while awaiting the Lord's actions.

1 Peter 5:6–9 (KJV)

6 *Humble yourselves therefore under the mighty hand of God, that he may exalt you in due time:*

7 *Casting all your care upon him; for he careth for you.*

8 *Be sober, be vigilant; because your adversary the devil, as a roaring lion, walketh about, seeking whom he may devour:*

9 *Whom resist stedfast in the faith, knowing that the same afflictions are accomplished in your brethren that are in the world.* [146]

If we look at the book of Habakkuk, we can feel Habakkuk's suffering and his cry to God for the evil and suffering he witnesses:

Habakkuk 1:2–4 (KJV)

2 *O Lord, how long shall I cry, and thou wilt not hear! even cry out unto thee of violence, and thou wilt not save!*

3 *Why dost thou shew me iniquity, and cause me to behold grievance? for spoiling and violence are before me: and there are that raise up strife and contention.*

4 *Therefore the law is slacked, and judgment doth never go forth: for the wicked doth compass about the righteous; therefore wrong judgment proceedeth.*

Now, let me quote the first few verses of the direct context of this verse, which presents a reference to Muhammad ﷺ.

Habakkuk 3:1–8 (KJV)

1 *A prayer of Habakkuk the prophet upon Shigionoth.*

2 *O Lord, I have heard thy speech, and was afraid:*

O Lord, revive thy work in the midst of the years,

in the midst of the years make known;

in wrath remember mercy.

---

[146] https://www.biblegateway.com/passage/?search=1%20Peter%205%3A6-9&version=NIV

3 God came from Teman, and the Holy One from mount Paran. Selah.

His glory covered the heavens, and the earth was full of his praise.

4 And his brightness was as the light; he had horns coming out of his hand:

and there was the hiding of his power.

5 Before him went the pestilence, and burning coals went forth at his feet.

6 He stood, and measured the earth: he beheld, and drove asunder the nations;

and the everlasting mountains were scattered,

the perpetual hills did bow: his ways are everlasting.

7 I saw the tents of Cushan in affliction:

and the curtains of the land of Midian did tremble.

8 Was the Lord displeased against the rivers?

was thine anger against the rivers?

was thy wrath against the sea,

that thou didst ride upon thine horses and thy chariots of salvation?

Prophet Muhammad ﷺ said:

"My case and the prophets before me is that of a man who established a building, beautified and adorned it except for one final missing cornerstone. People kept wandering around it, admiring it, and saying, 'If only this stone was put in its place.' (The Prophet then said): 'Verily, I am this stone, and I am the seal of the prophets.'" [Recorded by Bukhari, Ahmad, An-Nasā'ī, and others].[147] Note

Prophet Jesus' Concern about Justice

During the era of Prophet Isa (peace be upon him), also known as Jesus in the During the era of Prophet Isa (peace be upon him), also known as Jesus in the Qur'an, he stressed the importance of justice, advocating for adherence to truth and righteousness as decreed by God. The Bible similarly assures us of God's ultimate victory over evil and the dispensation of justice. Psalm 12:19 highlights that vengeance belongs to God, guaranteeing that injustices will be rectified.

---

[147] *Note: Habakkuk was spoken (and written down) about 600 B.C., i.e. around 1200 years before Muhammad ﷺ and it was about something that was already then (in 600 B.C.) in the PAST.*
(4) The whole of chapter 3 is one prayer and in verse 1 Habakkuk starts out with "LORD O LORD" [LORD in English representing YHWH, the name of God in Hebrew] and verse 8 we see him still addressing God and saying "O LORD".
Further study can be done on the link with Prophet Mohammad ﷺ
https://www.thenivbible.com/blog/god-of-justice-verses-found-in-the-bible/
https://islamicmethodologiesmadeeasy.wordpress.com/2017/10/27/the-prophecy-of-habakkuk/

Reminiscent of the Old Testament prophets, Jesus confronts the Pharisees for prioritising religious rituals over "justice and the love of God." **Luke 11:42–46 (KJV)**

42 *But woe unto you, Pharisees! for ye tithe mint and rue and all manner of herbs, and pass over judgment and the love of God: these ought ye to have done, and not to leave the other undone.*

43 *Woe unto you, Pharisees! for ye love the uppermost seats in the synagogues, and greetings in the markets.*

44 *Woe unto you, scribes and Pharisees, hypocrites! for ye are as graves which appear not, and the men that walk over them are not aware of them.*

45 *Then answered one of the lawyers, and said unto him, Master, thus saying thou reproachest us also.*

46 *And he said, Woe unto you also, ye lawyers! for ye lade men with burdens grievous to be borne, and ye yourselves touch not the burdens with one of your fingers.* (Index) [148]

Delve deeper into the Bible's teachings on justice through the verses below. May these scriptures provide clarity on the biblical principles of justice and judgment.

The pursuit of justice looms large in our contemporary world. Yet, to achieve true justice on a global scale, we must delve deeper into understanding God's perspective on it. While God is often associated with mercy, Scripture also underscores His role as a just deity who will address injustice and wrongdoing. With an omniscient insight into the hearts and minds of humanity, He will ultimately judge all individuals.

This message highlights the Pharisees' failure to embody love, mercy, and compassion, instead choosing hypocrisy. Unbeknownst to them, God calls for fairness towards others and love for Him. Ezekiel 3:20–21 further elucidates this concept, explaining that even a righteous person who turns from righteousness to commit injustice will face consequences. If one fails to warn them of their wrongdoing, they will bear the weight of their sin, with their righteous deeds forgotten, and their blood required at the hands of those who did not intervene. The Gospel says:

Ezekiel 3:20–21 (KJV)

20 *Again, When a righteous man doth turn from his righteousness, and commit iniquity, and I lay a stumblingblock before him, he shall die:*

because thou hast not given him warning, he shall die in his sin, and his righteousness which he hath done shall not be remembered;

---

[148] https://www.google.com/search?q=Luke+

but his blood will I require at thine hand.

21 *Nevertheless if thou warn the righteous man, that the righteous sin not, and he doth not sin, he shall surely live, because he is warned;*

also thou hast delivered thy soul.

Ecclesiastes 3:17 (KJV)

I said in mine heart, God shall judge the righteous and the wicked: for there is a time there for every purpose and for every work.

Then it continues as Psalms says:

Proverbs 21:15 (KJV)

It is joy to the just to do judgment: but destruction shall be to the workers of iniquity.

This means that true justice is what corresponds to God's will and standards, and that when truth and goodness are enforced, wicked people are rightly afraid.

Micah 6:8 (KJV)

In this psalm, commonly cited to compel people to act in times of injustice, it explains:

He hath shewed thee, O man, what is good; and what doth the Lord require of thee,

But to do justly, and to love mercy, and to walk humbly with thy God?

This is why Westmont chose this verse as the name of our site, referencing our work of justice, reconciliation, and diversity.

Romans 12:19 (KJV)

Dearly beloved, avenge not yourselves, but rather give place unto wrath: for it is written, Vengeance is mine; I will repay, saith the Lord.

This verse expands on Paul's previous statement that believers should not repay evil for evil. It also makes it clear that those who follow righteousness should never avenge themselves, whether the hurt comes from fellow believers or from unbelievers. It continues in **Romans 12:21**:

"On the contrary:

If your enemy is hungry, feed him; if he is thirsty, give him something to drink. In doing this, you will heap burning coals on his head. Do not be overcome by evil, but overcome evil with good."

Isaiah 1:17–18 (KJV)

17 *Learn to do well; seek judgment, relieve the oppressed, judge the fatherless, plead for the widow.*

18 Come now, and let us reason together, saith the Lord: though your sins be as scarlet, they shall be as white as snow; though they be red like crimson, they shall be as wool.

Micah 6:8–9 (KJV)

8 He hath shewed thee, O man, what is good; and what doth the Lord require of thee, but to do justly, and to love mercy, and to walk humbly with thy God?

9 The Lord's voice crieth unto the city, and the man of wisdom shall see thy name: hear ye the rod, and who hath appointed it. (Index) [149]

Micah 6:8 (KJV)

He hath shewed thee, O man, what is good; and what doth the Lord require of thee, but to do justly, and to love mercy, and to walk humbly with thy God?

God also charges kings to act justly and instructs them to look after the weak and defenceless. The psalmist prays,

Psalm 72:1–2 (KJV)

1 Give the king thy judgments, O God, and thy righteousness unto the king's son.

2 He shall judge thy people with righteousness, and thy poor with judgment.

Psalm 72:12–14 expresses the compassionate nature of divine intervention, promising to hear the cries of the poor and to aid the oppressed, who often lack advocates. It emphasises God's empathy for the vulnerable, pledging deliverance from affliction and violence, and declaring that the lives of the needy are precious in His sight.

Psalm 72, categorised as a "royal psalm", beseeches God to bless the kings of Israel with a just rule, ensuring righteous governance over the people's affairs. In verses 13–14, Solomon's prayer extends beyond national borders, envisioning global leadership that attends to the needs of the impoverished and oppressed on a universal scale.

(There was a story behind this psalm.)

Job 29:14–16 (KJV):

14 I put on righteousness, and it clothed me: my judgment was as a robe and a diadem.

15 I was eyes to the blind, and feet was I to the lame.

16 I was a father to the poor: and the cause which I knew not I searched out.

Job adorned himself with righteousness, and it became his attire; his justice was a garment and a crown. He became the eyes for the blind and the feet for the

---

[149] https://www.biblestudytools.com/topical-verses/bible-verses-about-justice/

lame. He assumed the role of a father to the poor and diligently sought out causes he did not initially understand.

Job experienced blessings when he intervened against injustice and oppression. He praised God for enabling him to use his influence to serve as an instrument of divine justice for the downtrodden.[150] Note

Romans 3:10–12 (KJV)

10 As it is written, There is none righteous, no, not one:

11 There is none that understandeth, there is none that seeketh after God.

12 They are all gone out of the way, they are together become unprofitable; there is none that doeth good, no, not one.[151] Index

6 Finally

Both the Old Testament and the New Testament agree: "No one living is righteous before [God]" (Psalms 143:2).

1 Lord, hear my prayer, listen to my cry for mercy;

in your faithfulness and righteousness come to my relief.

2 Do not bring your servant into judgment, for no one living is righteous before you.

Now we return to our time and seek the guidance of our Prophet Muhammad ﷺ regarding justice. The Prophet ﷺ prayed for pardon for his people and received the following reply:

---

[150] *NOTE The story of Job is a famous tale which shows how devotion to God can sustain a person through any adversity. The character of Job from the Bible is now virtually synonymous with suffering, as he becomes the focus of a wager between God and Satan as to how much someone can suffer and still remain loyal to God.*
Job remains patient and grateful, and seeks help from Allah by reciting the dua in Surah Al-Anbiyaa (21:83). The dua reads, "My Lord. Indeed, adversity has touched me. And you are the Most Merciful of the merciful".
Ayūb (Job) is first mentioned in the Quran in the following verse: Indeed, We have revealed to you, [O Muhammad], as We revealed to Noah and the prophets after him. And we revealed to Abraham, Ishmael, Isaac, Jacob, the Descendants, Jesus, Job, Jonah, Aaron, and Solomon, and to David We gave the book [of Zabur].
[151] *The phrase not even one (v 12) corresponds well with the Apostle Paul's statement about himself, that he is no better than those hypocritical slanderers of his gospel message; we are all under sin (Romans 3:9). That is why grace is so essential, because without the grace of God all of humanity is lost. Continuing the quote from Psalms and Isaiah from verse 10–18, Paul makes the point using Scripture that not only is no one righteous on his own, but also no one understands, and no one seeks God. There is none righteous, not even one; there is none who understands, there is none who seeks for God (v 11–12). Scholars attribute seven books of the New Testament to Paul; he was an influential teacher and a missionary to much of Asia Minor and present-day Greece.*
https://thebiblesays.com/commentary/rom/rom-3/romans-310-12/

The narrator, Abbas ibn Mirdas, describes the prayer and the reply as follows:

Allah's Messenger ﷺ prayed for pardon for his people on the late evening of Arafah and received the reply:

"I have forgiven them all except for acts of oppression,

for I shall exact recompense for the one who is wronged, from his oppressor."

He said:

"O my Lord, if Thou wilt,

Thou mayest give the oppressed some of Paradise and forgive the oppressor,"

—but he did not receive a reply that evening. So he repeated the supplication at al-Muzdalifah in the morning and was given an answer to what he asked, whereupon he laughed (or it is said that he smiled).

Abu Bakr and Umar (PBUT) then said to him:

"You, for whom we would give our fathers and mothers as ransom—what has made you laugh? For this is not a time at which you are accustomed to laugh. May Allah give you cause for laughter all your life!"

He replied:

"When Allah's enemy, Iblis, knew that Allah—Who is Great and Glorious—had answered my supplication and forgiven my people, he took some earth and began to throw it on his head, crying out,

'Woe and destruction!' The sight of his distress made me laugh."

Al-Tirmidhi Hadith 818[152] *Index 124*

It has been narrated on the authority of 'Abdullah ibn 'Umar that the Messenger of Allah (ﷺ) said:

Behold! The dispensers of justice will be seated on pulpits of light beside God, on the right side of the Merciful, Exalted and Glorious. Either side of the Being is the right side, both being equally meritorious.

(The dispensers of justice are) those who do justice in their rulings, in matters relating to their families, and in all that they do. [153] *Index*

Ibn Buraidah narrated from his father that the Prophet (ﷺ) said:

"The judges are three: two judges that are in the Fire, and one judge that is in Paradise. A man who judges without the truth, and he knows that—this one is in the Fire. One who judges while not knowing, thereby ruining the rights of the

---

[152] *Index 124   https://www.alim.org/hadith/tirmidi/818/*
[153] *Collection Sahih Muslim In-book reference Book 33, Hadith 21*
Reference Hadith 1827
USC-MSA web (English) reference Book 20, Hadith 4493

people—so he is in the Fire. A judge who judges with the truth—that is the one in Paradise.”

(Da‘if – Collection: Jāmi‘ at-Tirmidhi)

Narrated ‘Ā’ishah (may Allah be pleased with her):

Who is ‘Ā’ishah (may Allah be pleased with her)? She was the daughter of one of the Prophet's earliest and strongest followers, Abū Bakr, and she became the Prophet's third wife. She was also one of the Prophet's most devoted companions. Her influence resonates through the annals of Islamic history, as she played a crucial role in the formative years of Islam, spanning from the time of Muhammad to the aftermath of his passing. She excelled as a stateswoman, scholar, muftī, and judge—blending spirituality, activism, and profound knowledge. ‘Ā’ishah (may Allah be pleased with her)'s legacy endures as an inspiration for countless Muslim women, embodying the essence of leadership and wisdom.

A man came and sat in front of the Messenger (ﷺ) of Allah and said:

“O Messenger of Allah! I have two slaves who lie to me, deceive me, and disobey me, and I scold them and hit them. So what is my case because of them?”

He said:

“The extent to which they betrayed you, disobeyed you, and lied to you will be measured against how much you punish them. If your punishing them is equal to their sins, then the two will be the same—nothing for you and nothing against you. If your punishing them is beyond their sin, some of your rewards will be taken from you and given to them.”

So the man left and began weeping and crying aloud. The Messenger (ﷺ) of Allah said:

A verse revealed in the Qur’an says...

وَنَضَعُ الْمَوَازِينَ الْقِسْطَ لِيَوْمِ الْقِيَامَةِ فَلَا تُظْلَمُ نَفْسٌ شَيْئًا ۖ وَإِن كَانَ مِثْقَالَ حَبَّةٍ مِّنْ خَرْدَلٍ أَتَيْنَا بِهَا ۗ وَكَفَىٰ بِنَا حَاسِبِينَ

“And We shall set up balances of justice on the Day of Resurrection, then none will be dealt with unjustly in anything. And if there be the weight of a mustard seed, We will bring it. And Sufficient are We as Reckoners.” (Surah Al-Anbiyā’, 21:47)

So the man said:

“By Allah, O Messenger of Allah! I see nothing better for myself than to part with them. Bear witness that they are all free.”[154] *Index*

---

[154] *Collection Jami‘ at-Tirmidhi Dar-us-Salam reference Volume 5, Book 44, Hadith 3165 In-book reference Book 47, Hadith 3462 Reference Hadith 3165 Related Qur'an verses 21.47 Index 125*
Index 125 https://quranx.com/Search?Q=JUSTICE+&Context=hadith-Tirmidhi

Hammam b. Munabbih reported that this is among the Hadith which Abu Huraira narrated to us from Muhammad, the Messenger of Allah (ﷺ). While mentioning one such Hadith reported from Allah's Messenger (ﷺ), he said:

"Sadaqa is due on every joint of a person, every day the sun rises. Administering justice between two men is also a Sadaqa. Assisting a man to ride upon his beast, or helping him load his luggage upon it, is a Sadaqa; and a good word is a Sadaqa; and every step that you take towards prayer is a Sadaqa; and removing harmful things from the pathway is a Sadaqa."

(In-book reference: Book 12, Hadith 72; Reference: Hadith 1009)

Hadith No. 67

Allah's Messenger (ﷺ) said:

"Allah's Hand is full, and (its fullness) is not affected by continuous spending, day and night."

He also said:

"Do you see what He has spent since He created the Heavens and the Earth? Yet all that has not decreased what is in His Hand."

He further said:

"His Throne is over the water and in His other Hand is the balance (of justice), and He raises and lowers (whomever He wills)."

(See Hadith No. 206, Vol. 6 — Collection: Sahih Bukhari; Dar-us-Salam reference: Hadith 7411; In-book reference: Book 97, Hadith 40; USC-MSA web reference: Volume 9, Book 93, Hadith 508)

Muslims should never be blind followers of any leader who commits injustice, but rather should stand for justice even when it is difficult.

Hudhaifa reported: The Messenger of Allah (ﷺ) said:

"Do not let yourselves become blind followers, saying: 'If the people are good, then we will be good; and if they are unjust, then we will be unjust.'

Rather, make up your own minds. If the people are good, then be good, but if they are evil, do not be unjust."

(Source: Sunan At-Tirmidhi 2007; Grade: Hasan)

Oppression will come on the Day of Judgement in the form of darkness and punishment.

Jabir ibn Abdullah reported: The Messenger of Allah (peace and blessings be upon him) said:

"Guard yourself from oppression, for oppression will be darkness on the Day of Resurrection.

Guard yourself from greed, for greed destroyed those before you. It caused them to shed blood and to make lawful what was unlawful."[155] *Index*

Justice encompasses both an inherent aspect of one's soul and an outward manifestation of virtue. To truly embody justice, our actions must originate from profound inner nobility. When our actions are tainted by external factors such as materialistic pursuits or fear, they undoubtedly forfeit their righteous nature.

Moreover, the notion of justice is unbiased and extends to all individuals, irrespective of their communal, social, political, religious, or judicial affiliations. It is universally applicable and relevant to the contextual values of each person.

It is also a well-known Hadith that the Prophet ﷺ refused to pardon a crime and expressed displeasure, saying:

"Many a community ruined itself in the past as they only punished the poor and ignored the offences of the exalted.

By Allah, if Muhammad's (my) daughter Fatimah had committed theft, her hand would have been severed."

(Bukhari)

Allah (SWT) has commanded His messengers to establish justice and spoke to them in an affirmative tone, as quoted in Hadith:

"O My slaves, I have forbidden injustice for Myself and have also forbidden it for you. So avoid being unjust to one another."

(Sahih Muslim)

Al-Mīzān describes justice in terms of *scale* or *balance*, because weighing is one of its most evident forms.

The Prophet Muhammad ﷺ also said:

"The heavens and the earth have been established through justice."

That is why the perfect order of the world stems from the necessity of the Earth's existence and its fundamental principles. This intricate balance and justice, manifested in every aspect and being in the universe, are deliberate creations of Allah. They form an essential component of the divine principle or law that governs the harmonious and rational nature observable in the universe.[156] **Note**

---

[155] *Source: Sahih Muslim 2578, Grade: Sahih*

[156] *Note: Al-Mizan fi Tafsir al-Qur'an, "The balance in Interpretation of Quran", more commonly known as Tafsir al-Mizan (تفسير الميزان) or simply Al-Mizan (الميزان),[1] is a tafsir (exegesis of the Quran) written by the Shia Muslim scholar and philosopher Allamah Sayyid Muhammad Husayn Tabataba'i shiaonlinelibrary.com. Retrieved 2020-04-20. From Wikipedia, the free encyclopedia*

The Qur'an speaks of measure, precision, and balance in every aspect of the universe. The following few verses further clarify the truth that our lives are governed by balance—and that balance is a divine law.

1

الَّذِي لَهُ مُلْكُ السَّمَاوَاتِ وَالْأَرْضِ وَلَمْ يَتَّخِذْ وَلَدًا وَلَمْ يَكُن لَّهُ شَرِيكٌ فِي الْمُلْكِ وَخَلَقَ كُلَّ شَيْءٍ فَقَدَّرَهُ تَقْدِيرًا

He to Whom belongs the dominion of the heavens and the earth, and Who has begotten no son (children or offspring), and Who has no partner in the dominion. He has created everything and measured it precisely according to its due proportion. — Surah Al-Furqan 25:22

2

وَالْأَرْضَ مَدَدْنَاهَا وَأَلْقَيْنَا فِيهَا رَوَاسِيَ وَأَنبَتْنَا فِيهَا مِن كُلِّ شَيْءٍ مَّوْزُونٍ

And the earth—We have spread it out like a carpet, set thereon mountains firm and immovable, and produced therein all things in due balance. — Surah Al-Hijr 15:19

3

وَأَنزَلْنَا مِنَ السَّمَاءِ مَاءً بِقَدَرٍ فَأَسْكَنَّاهُ فِي الْأَرْضِ ۖ وَإِنَّا عَلَىٰ ذَهَابٍ بِهِ لَقَادِرُونَ

And We send down water from the sky according to due measure, and We cause it to soak into the soil; and We are certainly able to drain it off with ease. — Surah Al-Mu'minun 23:18

4

وَالَّذِي نَزَّلَ مِنَ السَّمَاءِ مَاءً بِقَدَرٍ فَأَنشَرْنَا بِهِ بَلْدَةً مَّيْتًا ۚ كَذَٰلِكَ تُخْرَجُونَ

That sends down rain from time to time in due measure; and We raise to life thereby a land that is dead; even so will you be raised from the dead. — Surah Az-Zukhruf 43:11

5

كَذَٰلِكَ جَعَلْنَاكُمْ أُمَّةً وَسَطًا لِّتَكُونُوا شُهَدَاءَ عَلَى النَّاسِ وَيَكُونَ الرَّسُولُ عَلَيْكُمْ شَهِيدًا ۗ وَمَا جَعَلْنَا الْقِبْلَةَ الَّتِي كُنتَ عَلَيْهَا إِلَّا لِنَعْلَمَ مَن يَتَّبِعُ الرَّسُولَ مِمَّن يَنقَلِبُ عَلَىٰ عَقِبَيْهِ ۚ وَإِن كَانَتْ لَكَبِيرَةً إِلَّا عَلَى الَّذِينَ هَدَى اللَّهُ ۗ وَمَا كَانَ اللَّهُ لِيُضِيعَ إِيمَانَكُمْ ۚ إِنَّ اللَّهَ بِالنَّاسِ لَرَءُوفٌ رَّحِيمٌ

Thus, We have made you [true Muslims – real believers of Islamic Monotheism, true followers of Prophet Muhammad and his Sunnah (legal ways)], a Wasat (just) (and the best) nation, that you be witnesses over mankind and the Messenger (Muhammad) be a witness over you. And We made the Qiblah (prayer direction towards Jerusalem), which you used to face, only to test those who followed the Messenger (Muhammad) from those who would turn on their heels (i.e., disobey the Messenger). Indeed, it was great (heavy), except for those whom

Allah guided. And Allah would never make your faith (prayers) to be lost (i.e., your prayers offered towards Jerusalem). Truly, Allah is full of kindness, the Most Merciful towards mankind.

— Surah al-Baqarah 2:143

Now, let us reflect upon our current circumstances. Allah (SWT) presents us with a profound question:

Is one who lacks the ability to govern their own soul truly capable of governing others?

In light of this, Allah admonishes those who aspire to rule over others while neglecting the need for self-improvement. Allah (SWT) says:

أَتَأْمُرُونَ النَّاسَ بِالْبِرِّ وَتَنسَوْنَ أَنفُسَكُمْ وَأَنتُمْ تَتْلُونَ الْكِتَابَ ۚ أَفَلَا تَعْقِلُونَ

Enjoin you Al-Birr (piety and righteousness and every act of obedience to Allah) on the people, and forget to practise it yourselves, while you recite the Scripture [the Taurat (Torah)]! Have you then no sense?

— *Surah Al-Baqarah 2:44*

The initial phase of this significant and vital path zone is nearing its completion. Soon, travellers will embark on the realm of compassion and social justice. However, before entering, each individual must pause and take a moment to assess their moral standing through a concise test.

This examination has the potential to reflect one's true self, invoking the sobering apprehension of Judgement Day. Nevertheless, it also presents an opportunity to summon the courage to abandon all immoral actions and unjust gains.

In such circumstances, Allah (SWT) will undoubtedly honour one's decision, absolving their transgressions and welcoming them as a cherished righteous individual. As Allah (SWT) assures us:

وَمَن يَعْمَلْ سُوءًا أَوْ يَظْلِمْ نَفْسَهُ ثُمَّ يَسْتَغْفِرِ اللَّهَ يَجِدِ اللَّهَ غَفُورًا رَّحِيمًا

And whoever does evil or wrongs himself but afterwards seeks Allah's forgiveness, he will find Allah Oft-Forgiving, Most Merciful.

— *Surah An-Nisaa 4:110*

فَاسْتَقِمْ كَمَا أُمِرْتَ وَمَن تَابَ مَعَكَ وَلَا تَطْغَوْا ۚ إِنَّهُ بِمَا تَعْمَلُونَ بَصِيرٌ

So stand (ask Allah to make) you (Muhammad ﷺ) firm and straight (on the religion of Islamic Monotheism) as you are commanded, and those (your companions) who turn in repentance (unto Allah) with you, and transgress not (Allah's legal limits). Verily, He is All-Seer of what you do.

— *Surah Hud 11:112*

Action

From the following verses, Allah instructs us to uphold justice in every facet of our lives, regardless of scale.

Self-assess the situation in light of these verses, and act according to the conclusions you reach.

Self Test

- If obeying all or part of the verse, mark in the box: ✓ or ✓✓

- If you do not understand the verse or do not have knowledge of it, mark in the box: 0

- If you knowingly ignore the content of the verse, mark in the box: ✗ (or "mix")

"We are now approaching a moment of personal judgment, where we must reflect on how faithfully we have followed Allah's commands that were given to us."

Surah An-Nahl 16:90

إِنَّ اللَّهَ يَأْمُرُ بِالْعَدْلِ وَالْإِحْسَانِ وَإِيتَاءِ ذِي الْقُرْبَىٰ وَيَنْهَىٰ عَنِ الْفَحْشَاءِ وَالْمُنكَرِ وَالْبَغْيِ ۚ يَعِظُكُمْ
لَعَلَّكُمْ تَذَكَّرُونَ ☐

Verily, Allah enjoins Al-'Adl (i.e. justice and worshipping none but Allah Alone – Islamic Monotheism) and Al-Ihsan [i.e. to be patient in performing your duties to Allah, totally for Allah's sake and in accordance with the Sunnah (legal ways) of the Prophet ﷺ, in a perfect manner], and giving (help) to kith and kin (i.e. all that Allah has ordered you to give them – e.g. wealth, visiting, looking after them, or any other kind of help, etc.); and forbids Al-Fahsha' (i.e. all evil deeds, e.g. illegal sexual acts, disobedience to parents, polytheism, lying, giving false witness, killing a life without right, etc.), and Al-Munkar (i.e. all that is prohibited by Islamic law: every kind of disbelief, polytheism, and evil deeds), and Al-Baghy (i.e. all kinds of oppression).

He admonishes you, that you may take heed.

— *Surah An-Nahl 16:90*

Allah commands justice:

The doing of good, and liberality to kith and kin:

And He forbids all shameful deeds, injustice, and rebellion:

He instructs you, that you may receive admonition.

Surah An-Nisaa 4:135

304

يَا أَيُّهَا الَّذِينَ آمَنُوا كُونُوا قَوَّامِينَ بِالْقِسْطِ شُهَدَاءَ لِلَّهِ وَلَوْ عَلَىٰ أَنفُسِكُمْ أَوِ الْوَالِدَيْنِ وَالْأَقْرَبِينَ ۚ إِن يَكُنْ غَنِيًّا أَوْ فَقِيرًا فَاللَّهُ أَوْلَىٰ بِهِمَا ۖ فَلَا تَتَّبِعُوا الْهَوَىٰ أَن تَعْدِلُوا ۚ وَإِن تَلْوُوا أَوْ تُعْرِضُوا فَإِنَّ اللَّهَ كَانَ بِمَا تَعْمَلُونَ خَبِيرًا ☐

O you who believe! *Stand out firmly for justice, as witnesses to Allah, even though it be against yourselves, or your parents, or your kin—be he rich or poor, Allah is a Better Protector to both (than you). So follow not the lusts (of your hearts), lest you avoid justice. And if you distort your witness or refuse to give it, verily, Allah is Ever Well-Acquainted with what you do.*

O ye who believe!

Stand out firmly for justice:

As witnesses to Allah, even as against yourselves, or your parents, or your kin:

And whether it be (against) rich or poor, for Allah can best protect both.

Follow not the lusts (of your hearts), lest ye swerve; and if ye distort (justice) or decline to do justice:

Verily, Allah is well-acquainted with all that ye do.

Surah Al-An'am 6:152

وَلَا تَقْرَبُوا مَالَ الْيَتِيمِ إِلَّا بِالَّتِي هِيَ أَحْسَنُ حَتَّىٰ يَبْلُغَ أَشُدَّهُ ۖ وَأَوْفُوا الْكَيْلَ وَالْمِيزَانَ بِالْقِسْطِ ۖ لَا نُكَلِّفُ نَفْسًا إِلَّا وُسْعَهَا ۖ وَإِذَا قُلْتُمْ فَاعْدِلُوا وَلَوْ كَانَ ذَا قُرْبَىٰ ۖ وَبِعَهْدِ اللَّهِ أَوْفُوا ۚ ذَٰلِكُمْ وَصَّاكُم بِهِ لَعَلَّكُمْ تَذَكَّرُونَ ☐

And come not near to the orphan's property, except to improve it, until he (or she) attains the age of full strength; and give full measure and full weight with justice. We burden not any person beyond what he can bear. And whenever you give your word (i.e. judge between men or give evidence, etc.), say the truth—even if a near relative is concerned. And fulfil the Covenant of Allah. This He commands you, that you may remember.

And come not nigh to the orphan's property, except to improve it, until he attains the age of full strength:

Give measure and weight with (full) justice:

No burden do We place on any soul,

But that which it can bear:

Whenever ye speak, speak justly—even if a near relative is concerned:

And fulfil the Covenant of Allah. Thus doth He command you, that ye may remember:

Surah At-Taubah 9:34

يَا أَيُّهَا الَّذِينَ آمَنُوا إِنَّ كَثِيرًا مِّنَ الْأَحْبَارِ وَالرُّهْبَانِ لَيَأْكُلُونَ أَمْوَالَ النَّاسِ بِالْبَاطِلِ وَيَصُدُّونَ عَن سَبِيلِ اللَّهِ ۗ وَالَّذِينَ يَكْنِزُونَ الذَّهَبَ وَالْفِضَّةَ وَلَا يُنفِقُونَهَا فِي سَبِيلِ اللَّهِ فَبَشِّرْهُم بِعَذَابٍ أَلِيمٍ ☐

You who believe! Verily, there are many among the (Jewish) rabbis and the (Christian) monks who devour the wealth of mankind in falsehood and hinder them from the Way of Allah (i.e. Allah's Religion of Islamic Monotheism). And those who hoard up gold and silver [Al-Kanz: the money, the Zakat of which has not been paid], and spend it not in the Way of Allah—announce unto them a painful torment.

O ye who believe! There are indeed many among the priests and anchorites who, in falsehood, devour the substance of men:

And hinder them from the Way of Allah.

And there are those who bury gold and silver, and spend it not in the Way of Allah:

Announce unto them a most grievous penalty:

Surah An-Nisaa 4:58

إِنَّ اللَّهَ يَأْمُرُكُمْ أَن تُؤَدُّوا الْأَمَانَاتِ إِلَىٰ أَهْلِهَا وَإِذَا حَكَمْتُم بَيْنَ النَّاسِ أَن تَحْكُمُوا بِالْعَدْلِ ۚ إِنَّ اللَّهَ نِعِمَّا يَعِظُكُم بِهِ ۗ إِنَّ اللَّهَ كَانَ سَمِيعًا بَصِيرًا ☐

Verily! Allah commands that you should render back the trusts to those to whom they are due; and that when you judge between men, you judge with justice. Verily, how excellent is the teaching which He (Allah) gives you! Truly, Allah is Ever All-Hearer, All-Seer.

Allah doth command you to render back your trusts to those to whom they are due:

And when ye judge between man and man, that ye judge with justice:

Verily, how excellent is the teaching which He giveth you! For Allah is He Who heareth and seeth all things.

Surah An-Nisaa 4:29

يَا أَيُّهَا الَّذِينَ آمَنُوا لَا تَأْكُلُوا أَمْوَالَكُم بَيْنَكُم بِالْبَاطِلِ إِلَّا أَن تَكُونَ تِجَارَةً عَن تَرَاضٍ مِّنكُمْ ۚ وَلَا تَقْتُلُوا أَنفُسَكُمْ ۚ إِنَّ اللَّهَ كَانَ بِكُمْ رَحِيمًا ☐

You who believe! Eat not up your property among yourselves unjustly, except it be a trade amongst you, by mutual consent. And do not kill yourselves (nor kill one another). Surely, Allah is Most Merciful to you.

O ye who believe! Eat not up your property among yourselves in vanities:

But let there be amongst you traffic and trade by mutual good-will:

Nor kill (or destroy) yourselves:

For verily Allah hath been to you Most Merciful!

Surah Al-Hujurat 49:10

إِنَّمَا الْمُؤْمِنُونَ إِخْوَةٌ فَأَصْلِحُوا بَيْنَ أَخَوَيْكُمْ ۚ وَاتَّقُوا اللَّهَ لَعَلَّكُمْ تُرْحَمُونَ ☐

The believers are nothing else but brothers *(in Islamic religion). So make reconciliation between your brothers, and fear Allah, that you may receive mercy.*

The Believers are but a single Brotherhood:

So make peace and reconciliation between your two (contending) brothers;

And fear Allah, that ye may receive Mercy.

Surah Al-Ma'idah 5:8

يَا أَيُّهَا الَّذِينَ آمَنُوا كُونُوا قَوَّامِينَ لِلَّهِ شُهَدَاءَ بِالْقِسْطِ ۖ وَلَا يَجْرِمَنَّكُمْ شَنَآنُ قَوْمٍ عَلَىٰ أَلَّا تَعْدِلُوا ۚ
اعْدِلُوا هُوَ أَقْرَبُ لِلتَّقْوَىٰ ۖ وَاتَّقُوا اللَّهَ ۚ إِنَّ اللَّهَ خَبِيرٌ بِمَا تَعْمَلُونَ ☐

O ye who believe! Stand out firmly for Allah *and be just witnesses, and let not the enmity and hatred of others make you avoid justice. Be just: that is nearer to piety, and fear Allah. Verily, Allah is Well-Acquainted with what you do.*

O ye who believe! Stand out firmly for Allah,

As witnesses to fair dealing,

And let not the hatred of others towards you make you swerve

To wrong and depart from justice.

Be just: that is next to piety; and fear Allah.

For Allah is well-acquainted with all that ye do.

Surah An-Nisa 4:10

إِنَّ الَّذِينَ يَأْكُلُونَ أَمْوَالَ الْيَتَامَىٰ ظُلْمًا إِنَّمَا يَأْكُلُونَ فِي بُطُونِهِمْ نَارًا ۖ وَسَيَصْلَوْنَ سَعِيرًا ☐

Verily, those who unjustly eat up the property of orphans,

They eat up a Fire into their own bodies:

They will soon be enduring a Blazing Fire!

Surah Al-A'raf 7:29

☐ قُلْ أَمَرَ رَبِّي بِالْقِسْطِ ۖ وَأَقِيمُوا وُجُوهَكُمْ عِندَ كُلِّ مَسْجِدٍ وَادْعُوهُ مُخْلِصِينَ لَهُ الدِّينَ ۚ كَمَا بَدَأَكُمْ تَعُودُونَ

Say (O Muhammad ﷺ): My Lord has commanded justice and (said) that you should face Him only (i.e. worship none but Allah and face the Qiblah, i.e. the Ka'bah at Makkah during prayers) in each and every place of worship, in prayers (and not to face other false deities and idols). Invoke Him only, making your religion sincere to Him by not joining any partner in worship and with the intention that you are doing your deeds solely for Allah's sake. As He brought you (into being) in the beginning, so shall you be brought into being (on the Day of Resurrection) [in two groups, one as a blessed one (believers), and the other as a wretched one (disbelievers)].

Say: "My Lord has commanded justice;

and that you set your whole selves (to Him) at every time

and place of prayer,

and call upon Him, making your devotion sincere in His sight.

As He created you in the beginning, so shall you return."

2/177 Surah Al-Baqara

لَيْسَ الْبِرَّ أَن تُوَلُّوا وُجُوهَكُمْ قِبَلَ الْمَشْرِقِ وَالْمَغْرِبِ وَلَٰكِنَّ الْبِرَّ مَنْ آمَنَ بِاللَّهِ وَالْيَوْمِ الْآخِرِ وَالْمَلَائِكَةِ وَالْكِتَابِ وَالنَّبِيِّينَ وَآتَى الْمَالَ عَلَىٰ حُبِّهِ ذَوِي الْقُرْبَىٰ وَالْيَتَامَىٰ وَالْمَسَاكِينَ وَابْنَ السَّبِيلِ وَالسَّائِلِينَ وَفِي الرِّقَابِ وَأَقَامَ الصَّلَاةَ وَآتَى الزَّكَاةَ وَالْمُوفُونَ بِعَهْدِهِمْ إِذَا عَاهَدُوا ۖ وَالصَّابِرِينَ فِي الْبَأْسَاءِ وَالضَّرَّاءِ وَحِينَ الْبَأْسِ ۗ أُولَٰئِكَ الَّذِينَ صَدَقُوا ۖ وَأُولَٰئِكَ هُمُ الْمُتَّقُونَ ☐

It is not righteousness that you turn your faces towards the east or west (in prayers); but righteousness is the one who believes in Allah, the Last Day, the Angels, the Book, and the Prophets, and gives his wealth, in spite of love for it, to kinsfolk, to orphans, to Al-Masakin (the poor), to the wayfarer, to those who ask, and to set slaves free. He performs As-Salat (Iqamat-as-Salat), gives the Zakat, fulfils their covenant when they make it, and is among the As-Sabirin (the patient ones) in extreme poverty, ailment (disease), and during battles. Such are the people of the truth, and they are Al-Muttaqun (the pious – see V.2:2).

It is not righteousness that you turn your faces towards the east or west;

but righteousness is to believe in Allah

and the Last Day,

and the Angels,

and the Book,

and the Messengers;

to spend of your substance, out of love for Him, for your

kin, for orphans, for the needy, for the wayfarer,

for those who ask, and for the ransom of slaves;

to be steadfast in prayer, and practice regular charity;

to fulfil the contracts which you have made;

and to be firm and patient in pain (or suffering)

and adversity, and throughout all periods of panic.

Such are the people of truth, the Allah-fearing.

2/215 Surah Al-Baqarah

يَسْأَلُونَكَ مَاذَا يُنفِقُونَ ۖ قُلْ مَا أَنفَقْتُم مِّنْ خَيْرٍ فَلِلْوَالِدَيْنِ وَالْأَقْرَبِينَ وَالْيَتَامَىٰ وَالْمَسَاكِينِ وَابْنِ السَّبِيلِ ۖ وَمَا تَفْعَلُوا مِنْ خَيْرٍ فَإِنَّ اللَّهَ بِهِ عَلِيمٌ ☐

They ask you (O Muhammad ﷺ) what they should spend. Say: Whatever you spend of good must be for parents, kindred, orphans, Al-Masakin (the poor), and the wayfarers. And whatever good deeds you do, truly, Allah knows them well.

They ask you what they should spend (in charity).

Say: Whatever you spend that is good, is for parents,

kindred, orphans,

those in need, and for wayfarers.

And whatever good you do, Allah knows it well.

11/113 Surah Hud

☐ وَلَا تَرْكَنُوا إِلَى الَّذِينَ ظَلَمُوا فَتَمَسَّكُمُ النَّارُ وَمَا لَكُم مِّن دُونِ اللَّهِ مِنْ أَوْلِيَاءَ ثُمَّ لَا تُنصَرُونَ ☐

And incline not toward those who do wrong, lest the Fire should touch you, and you have no protectors other than Allah, nor will you then be helped.

And incline not to those who do wrong,

or the Fire will seize you;

and you have no protectors other than Allah, nor shall you be helped.

7/199 Surah Al-A'raf

خُذِ الْعَفْوَ وَأْمُرْ بِالْعُرْفِ وَأَعْرِضْ عَنِ الْجَاهِلِينَ ☐

Show forgiveness, enjoin what is good, and turn away from the foolish (i.e. don't punish them).

Hold to forgiveness; command what is right;

But turn away from the ignorant.

❖ ❖ ❖ ❖ ❖ ❖ ❖ ❖ ❖ ❖ ❖

Therefore,

Allah SWT has given His assurance in Surah An-Noor, verse (24):

يَوْمَئِذٍ يُوَفِّيهِمُ اللَّهُ دِينَهُمُ الْحَقَّ وَيَعْلَمُونَ أَنَّ اللَّهَ هُوَ الْحَقُّ الْمُبِينُ ☐

On that Day, Allah will repay them in full for their deeds, and they will realise that Allah is the ultimate Truth, who makes all things manifest.

309

Part II

Empathy And Social Justice

We have discussed the significance of absolute prudence, justice, and compassion, along with their interrelated qualities, which Allah may weigh when assessing the essence of the soul on the Day of Judgment. At this juncture of our journey, the recitation of comprehensive verses, divine decrees, and the impassioned pleas of prophets may unsettle many travellers. Yet, beneath this discomfort lies a fundamental question: Am I truly worthy of traversing this path to victory?

Now, as a continuous measure of the success of our journey, we are redirecting our attention to empathy—an aspect we might have previously overlooked.

As believers, we cannot disregard this crucial principle, particularly when Allah (SWT) has provided verses urging us to follow it closely. Allah says:

لَقَدْ جَاءَكُمْ رَسُولٌ مِّنْ أَنفُسِكُمْ عَزِيزٌ عَلَيْهِ مَا عَنِتُّمْ حَرِيصٌ عَلَيْكُم بِالْمُؤْمِنِينَ رَءُوفٌ رَّحِيمٌ

Verily, there has come unto you a Messenger (Muhammad ﷺ) from amongst yourselves (i.e. whom you know well). It grieves him that you should receive any injury or difficulty. He (Muhammad ﷺ) is anxious over you (to be rightly guided, to repent to Allah, and beg Him to pardon and forgive your sins, in order that you may enter Paradise and be saved from the punishment of the Hell-fire). For the believers, he ﷺ is full of pity, kind, and merciful. (9:128, Surah At-Taubah)

Empathy is acknowledging and feeling someone else's pain and striving with them to help alleviate it. A true Muslim is one who sincerely practises compassion. Without compassion, your faith in Allah is flawed. The Hadith teaches us that:

"None of you will have faith till he wishes for his brother what he likes for himself." — Al-Bukhari

The word empathy comes from the German word "Einfühlung," which first appeared (in print) in German philosopher Robert Vischer's 1873 Ph.D. dissertation and might broadly translate as "feeling into."

The large-scale immoral actions of the Nazis, such as the mass killing of Jews, are a dehumanisation historically associated with the loss of sympathy for the suffering of inhumane individuals and groups. This includes the psychological and legal denial of their human rights and the extreme violence against them.

A true Muslim is one who sincerely practises compassion. Without compassion, your faith in Allah (SWT) is flawed. This can be found in the Golden Rule of Islam as described in this hadith.

We can describe empathy as "the cry of one's heart beats in the heart of others." The philosopher Susanne Langer once called empathy an "involuntary breach of individual separateness"—and this seems to apply particularly when we observe someone suffering, such as a loved one. Empathy is a suppressed cry of a person's

310

heart when they understand and feel another person's pain, suffering, emotions, sorrow, anxiety, and worry. It can also be defined as being humiliated by someone but feeling the inability to protest, rather feeling helpless. In such situations, when someone comes forward and stands by the victims and expresses their feelings, it is called sympathy.

As mentioned earlier, we acknowledged that embarking on this journey would be arduous, requiring perseverance at every step. As we traverse the path ahead, the burdens we carry will inevitably increase, but it is crucial that we implement the newfound knowledge we acquire and persist until we reach our ultimate destination. Presently, we have discovered the profound significance of empathy, and in this regard, we faithfully adhere to the commandments of Allah (SWT) and seek guidance from the teachings of our revered Prophet Muhammad ﷺ.

Allah says:

لِلْفُقَرَاءِ الَّذِينَ أُحْصِرُوا فِي سَبِيلِ اللَّهِ لَا يَسْتَطِيعُونَ ضَرْبًا فِي الْأَرْضِ يَحْسَبُهُمُ الْجَاهِلُ أَغْنِيَاءَ مِنَ التَّعَفُّفِ تَعْرِفُهُم بِسِيمَاهُمْ لَا يَسْأَلُونَ النَّاسَ إِلْحَافًا ۗ وَمَا تُنفِقُوا مِنْ خَيْرٍ فَإِنَّ اللَّهَ بِهِ عَلِيمٌ

*(Charity is) for **Fuqara** (the poor), who, in Allah's Cause, are restricted (from travel) and cannot move about in the land (for trade or work). The one who knows them not thinks that they are rich because of their modesty. You may know them by their mark; they do not beg of people at all. And whatever you spend in good, surely Allah knows it well. (2:273)*

*Allah (SWT) says again in Surah **Al-Balad** (90):*

وَمَا أَدْرَاكَ مَا الْعَقَبَةُ

فَكُّ رَقَبَةٍ

أَوْ إِطْعَامٌ فِي يَوْمٍ ذِي مَسْغَبَةٍ

يَتِيمًا ذَا مَقْرَبَةٍ

أَوْ مِسْكِينًا ذَا مَتْرَبَةٍ

ثُمَّ كَانَ مِنَ الَّذِينَ آمَنُوا وَتَوَاصَوْا بِالصَّبْرِ وَتَوَاصَوْا بِالْمَرْحَمَةِ

12. And what will make you know the path that is steep?

13. (It is) freeing a neck (slave, etc.),

14. Or giving food on a day of hunger (famine),

15. To an orphan near of kin,

16. Or to a Miskin (poor) afflicted with misery.

17. Then he became one of those who believed, and recommended one another to perseverance and patience, and (also) recommended one another to pity and compassion.

311

90:12-17 Surah Al-Balad

The preceding verses underscore the significance of aiding those in need and supporting our impoverished relatives. We must view these directives as our obligatory responsibilities and endeavour to assist others wholeheartedly, to the best of our abilities. However, it is imperative to recognise that our discourse isn't solely about "sympathy." As adherents to a religious faith, we cannot disregard the profound guidance of Allah (SWT) and Prophet Muhammad ﷺ, who have fervently urged all Muslims to approach this matter with utmost reverence. Let us delve into how we can fulfil Allah's commandment of "compassion" in our lives.

Empathy is the ability to recognise, understand, and share the thoughts and feelings of another person, animal, or fictional character. The terms **empathy** and **apathy** are often confused because of the similarities between the two words. Apathy is, in fact, the absence of emotion or a lack of caring. This can refer to not caring about what is going on around you, or it can relate to someone's feelings. It is also a symptom of a number of different mental health conditions, including depression.

Empathy and sympathy carry different concepts and themes, but at one point, both are similar: as victims of suffering, they share in pain and emotion, needing compassion, love, and altruistic help by acknowledging the suffering in others' hearts. Yet, these areas are largely absent within ourselves, despite the command of Allah and the teachings of our Prophet Muhammad ﷺ. This is reflected in the verse **9:128 Surah At-Taubah**, quoted at the beginning of this section.

As devoted followers, it is our duty to fulfil our obligations whenever we encounter the distress of any person, regardless of their faith or background, whether caused by human actions, natural calamities, or any other circumstances.

As devout believers, it is incumbent upon us to fulfil our obligations whenever we encounter the distress of any individual, irrespective of their faith or background, whether caused by human actions, natural calamities, or any other circumstances. Allah (SWT) says:

يَا أَيُّهَا النَّاسُ إِنَّا خَلَقْنَاكُم مِّن ذَكَرٍ وَأُنثَىٰ وَجَعَلْنَاكُمْ شُعُوبًا وَقَبَائِلَ لِتَعَارَفُوا ۚ إِنَّ أَكْرَمَكُمْ عِندَ اللَّهِ أَتْقَاكُمْ ۚ إِنَّ اللَّهَ عَلِيمٌ خَبِيرٌ

Mankind! We have created you from a male and a female, and made you into nations and tribes, that you may know one another. Verily, the most honourable of you with Allah is the one who has At-Taqwa (i.e. one of the Muttaqun – pious [see V.2:2]). Verily, Allah is All-Knowing, All-Aware.

49:13 Surah Al-Hujurat

And also, our Prophet ﷺ says in his khutbah (sermon) that:

"O people, your Lord is One, and your father (Ādam) is one. Verily, there is no superiority of an Arab over a non-Arab, nor a non-Arab over an Arab. There is no

superiority of a white over a black, nor a black over a white. Only piety causes one to excel." — ***Musnad Aḥmad: no. 22978***

Mahatma Gandhi says:

"I call him religious who understands the suffering of others." — ***Az Quotes***

If any individual becomes aware that their actions, whether directly or indirectly, are causing emotional distress, sorrow, anxiety, grief, or depression to their child, spouse, housekeeper, or any other person, it is crucial to prioritise identifying the underlying reasons and promptly taking corrective measures. It is essential to seek forgiveness from Allah (SWT) for these wrongdoings.

In the broadest sense, empathy and human suffering are inherently connected to the concept of social justice. However, the unfortunate reality is that social justice remains largely elusive in our world, particularly in impoverished nations. The struggle for survival is a constant burden for the impoverished, who find themselves trapped within a corrupt and unjust society. In this oppressive system, a privileged few exploit and take advantage of the vulnerable under the guise of providing assistance. The term "social justice" holds great appeal for these marginalised individuals, yet they seldom experience its true essence, perceiving it as nothing more than an empty and deceptive mask.

When addressing the correlation between social justice and poverty, hunger, disease, and the struggle for survival, it is imperative to acknowledge the significant impact that moral values and religious teachings have lost over time, leading society to engage in immoral activities. The integrity of our actions is challenged in such circumstances. The prevailing power dynamics of influential elites have gradually hijacked the principles of social justice, which is evident for all to see. This perversion of justice stands as the root cause of widespread suffering and despair among the global population, making it increasingly challenging to uphold one's faith amidst this ongoing struggle. This issue becomes even more apparent when observing the continuous influx of refugees and the resulting crisis, with countless individuals facing unimaginable hardships.

The world bears witness to the heart-wrenching tragedies of children, mothers, fathers, and young people succumbing to the depths of the sea. As I write this, the latest reports highlight Indonesia's refusal to grant entry to stranded Rohingya refugees. Officials pledged to give food and water to a group of about 120 Rohingya stranded on a damaged wooden boat in Indonesian waters. However, they said they would not take them in as refugees.

A group of about 120 Rohingya people, including dozens of children, will not be allowed to disembark on Indonesian territory, Indonesian officials said.

"The Rohingya are not Indonesian citizens; we can't just bring them in, even as refugees," Navy official Dian Suryansyah was quoted as saying by the Reuters news agency. "This is in line with government policy."[157] Index 126

This instance is merely a fraction of the immense challenges confronting the vulnerable in our global community, as they bravely navigate their way to uphold their livelihoods and cling to their beliefs amidst moral and social injustices. Regrettably, society has yet to implement effective policies to mitigate these heart-wrenching occurrences, which repeatedly play out before us, from our morning routines to our television screens.

Nick Dearden, the director of Global Justice, said:

"What we call a 'migrant crisis' is actually a crisis of global injustice caused by war, poverty, and inequality. To demonise those making a rational choice on behalf of themselves, their family, and their community, obscures the truth. Migration is bringing those of us in Europe face to face with the reality of the brutal and unjust world our leaders have constructed.

We cannot build a decent society on fear and hatred. We are told that the principles of free movement, solidarity between members, and respect for human rights are at the foundation of the EU. But the value of these principles is dramatically undermined if they are only extended to a privileged minority who arbitrarily hold a particular passport."

Alex Scrivener, the author of the briefing and policy officer at Global Justice Now, said:

"It's unacceptable that people from rich countries are free to go almost anywhere in the world, while people from the global south are denied freedom of movement, even when they are fleeing war and extreme poverty. A right that only exists for the rich is not a right at all. There's one rule for 'expat' Europeans and North Americans, and another for the rest of the world. This is apartheid on a global scale. We need to move towards free movement for everyone." [158] *Index 127*

The International Institute for Sustainable Development (IISD) commits that:

The world's richest 1% own 44% of the world's wealth, while almost half the world's people get by on less than USD 5.50 a day. The average person's consumption of oil and other resources is up to 30 times higher in rich countries compared to poor ones. Among the poor, women are more likely to be in low-paid or unpaid work roles, while female-headed households are among the world's poorest. In developing countries, a child born to poor parents is twice as likely to die before the age of five as a child born into a wealthy family.

---

[157] Index 126 https://www.dw.com/en/indonesia-denies-entry-to-rohingya-stranded-at-sea/a-60279486

[158] *Index 127 https://www.globaljustice.org.uk/news/not-migrant-crisis-its-crisis-inequality-and-war/*

The Right Honourable Brian Mulroney, the former Prime Minister of Canada, reminded world leaders that:

"Mankind is not destined to destroy itself; war is not inevitable; poverty can be alleviated; the environment can be preserved; injustices can be made right."

Social justice is now a "meaningless word", but IISD has taken a remarkable step to restore justice, which we appreciate. Following are some quotes that carry great meaning and which we can analyse:

"When I feed the poor, they call me a saint. When I ask why so many people are poor, they call me a communist."

— Dom Hélder Câmara, Brazil's "Archbishop of the Poor"

"Overcoming poverty is not a task of charity, it is an act of justice."

— Nelson Mandela

"We know that a peaceful world cannot exist one-third rich and two-thirds hungry."

— President Jimmy Carter

"You pray for the hungry. Then you feed them. This is how prayer works."

— Pope Francis

"If you can't feed a hundred people, then feed just one."

— Mother Teresa

"We cannot confront the massive challenges of poverty, hunger, disease, and environmental destruction unless we address issues of population and reproductive health."

— Thoraya Ahmed Obaid, UN Under-Secretary-General 2000-2010

"Giving women farmers more resources could bring the number of hungry people in the world down by 100-150 million."**— World Food Programme.** [159]Note

The conclusive part of the article "Social Justice, Food Loss, and the Sustainable Development Goals in the Era of COVID-19" written by Janet Fleetwood states:

Problems of avoidable FLW (Food Loss and Waste) and hunger have long been subjects for debate and scrutiny, but never has global waste—from farm to fork—been so visible and so urgent. As we consider social justice, sustainability, and the

[159] Note: *The United Nations' Sustainable Development Goals (SDGs). Department of Community Health & Prevention, Dornsife School of Public Health, Drexel University, Philadelphia, PA 19104, USA; janet.fleetwood@drexel.edu Received: 3 June 2020; Accepted: 16 June 2020; Published: 19 June 2020*

SDGs, we can see how the most fundamental values—equality, protection of opportunity, and our shared humanity—underlie our global goals. Even without an explicitly stated human right to food in the SDGs, our notions of social justice and the need for environmental sustainability are widely shared. What remains to be seen, however, is how we will move through today's global crisis of hunger and sustainability caused by COVID-19, and whether our commitment to the SDGs and the values they uphold will be sufficient to guide our decision-making.[160] *Index 128*

The above discourse highlights the broader issue of injustice surrounding the allocation of natural resources, a global dilemma fuelled by human greed and myriad sinful practices. Factors such as ineffective governance, war, corruption, and exploitation by powerful entities contribute to these systemic imbalances. Deliberate actions, such as risking millions of lives to floods, demonstrate a callous disregard for human welfare in pursuit of personal or collective gain.

Dictators and oppressive regimes wield authority through coercion, enriching themselves while their citizens suffer. This erosion of public trust is further compounded by financial fraud and deception, depriving nations of their hard-earned savings and impeding progress. Collaboration between multinational corporations and corrupt officials leads to the exploitation of resources and the destruction of local ecosystems, all in the pursuit of profit.

This injustice will persist until the end of time. No force can usher in justice and divine direction against this trajectory, as the influence of malevolent power is already entrenched within the system we have grown accustomed to.

To escape such predicaments, individuals must embrace righteousness, shun the temptations of material gain, and resist the sway of evil. They should commit to walking the path of virtue under divine guidance, actively seeking understanding in all their endeavours. This includes fulfilling social responsibilities to their neighbours and utilising their influence to stand up against injustice and oppression.

As we mentioned the name of the prophet Amos earlier, we recall his concern about the fate of the people of that time, which will help those who are now truly worried about their ultimate fate, because economic injustice is the extraction of wealth. By exploiting others, it was a story from ancient Israel. Many of the people of Israel became rich by unrighteous means, ignoring the advice of their prophets. Amos says, in Psalm 2:6, what the Lord says:

"For three sins of Israel, even for four, I will not relent. They sell the innocent for silver, and the needy for a pair of sandals."

This means judgment comes to Israel: "Because they sell the righteous for silver and the needy for a pair of sandals" (Amos 2:6b). Such condemnation is an inevitable consequence of the nation of Israel's failure to be faithful to its

---

[160] Index 128 file:///C:/Users/akmha/Downloads/sustainability-12-05027.pdf

covenantal responsibilities. For God's trademarks are His steadfast love, justice, and righteousness.

In response, Amos 5:2 says:

The prophet Amos pleads, "Almighty God, many of Your children are ashamed today of the unrighteousness in our world and our nations. Please use us to lead a rebirth of character. As we seek to live holy lives, please keep our eyes on Your righteous character, gracious compassion, and faithful love-based justice."

In the Bible, 1 Timothy 6:9–10 says:

"But those who want to be rich fall into temptation and a trap and many foolish and harmful desires, which plunge those people into ruin and destruction. For the love of money is a root of all evil, by which some, because they desire it, have gone astray from the faith and have pierced themselves with many pains." (1 Timothy 6:9–10)

The consequences of such greed are often more than just damage to our own spiritual state and the deprivation of others economically. Greed can also result in the degradation of the environment, leading to significant damage to the earth, which ultimately affects the capacity of others to live well and reduces future productivity for everyone. [161] **Index**

Although, in our time, believers know who has created this kind of suffering in the world, when Allah has given everything for the benefit of His creation. We must look to the Holy Quran because, when Allah speaks in His source, who are we to tell you what to do or not to do?

Allah says:

1

أَلَمْ تَرَوْا أَنَّ اللَّهَ سَخَّرَ لَكُم مَّا فِي السَّمَاوَاتِ وَمَا فِي الْأَرْضِ وَأَسْبَغَ عَلَيْكُمْ نِعَمَهُ ظَاهِرَةً وَبَاطِنَةً ۗ وَمِنَ النَّاسِ مَن يُجَادِلُ فِي اللَّهِ بِغَيْرِ عِلْمٍ وَلَا هُدًى وَلَا كِتَابٍ مُّنِيرٍ

See you not (O men) that Allah has subjected for you whatsoever is in the heavens and whatsoever is in the earth, and has completed and perfected His Graces upon you, both apparent (i.e., Islamic Monotheism, and the lawful pleasures of this world, including health, good looks, etc.) and hidden (i.e., One's Faith in Allah (of Islamic Monotheism), knowledge, wisdom, guidance for doing righteous deeds, and also the pleasures and delights of the Hereafter in Paradise, etc.)? Yet, of mankind, there is he who disputes about Allah without knowledge, or guidance, or a Book giving light!

31:20, Surah Luqman

---

[161] *Note https://www.theologyofwork.org/key-topics/provision-wealth*

2

أَهُمْ يَقْسِمُونَ رَحْمَتَ رَبِّكَ ۚ نَحْنُ قَسَمْنَا بَيْنَهُم مَّعِيشَتَهُمْ فِي الْحَيَاةِ الدُّنْيَا ۚ وَرَفَعْنَا بَعْضَهُمْ فَوْقَ بَعْضٍ دَرَجَاتٍ لِّيَتَّخِذَ بَعْضُهُم بَعْضًا سُخْرِيًّا ۗ وَرَحْمَتُ رَبِّكَ خَيْرٌ مِّمَّا يَجْمَعُونَ

Is it they who would portion out the Mercy of your Lord? It is We Who portion out between them their livelihood in this world, and We raised some of them above others in ranks, so that some may employ others in their work. But the Mercy (Paradise) of your Lord (O Muhammad ﷺ) is better than the (wealth of this world) which they amass.

Surah At-Tafsir – 43:32, Az-Zukhruf

3

مَّثَلُ الَّذِينَ يُنفِقُونَ أَمْوَالَهُمْ فِي سَبِيلِ اللَّهِ كَمَثَلِ حَبَّةٍ أَنبَتَتْ سَبْعَ سَنَابِلَ فِي كُلِّ سُنبُلَةٍ مِّائَةُ حَبَّةٍ ۗ وَاللَّهُ يُضَاعِفُ لِمَن يَشَاءُ ۚ وَاللَّهُ وَاسِعٌ عَلِيمٌ

The parable of those who spend their substance in the way of Allah is that of a grain of corn: it groweth seven ears, and each ear hath a hundred grains. Allah giveth manifold increase to whom He pleaseth: And Allah careth for all, and He knoweth all things.

2:261, Surah Al-Baqara

Justice

In our society, the pursuit of justice for the less privileged is often a formidable challenge. Across various faiths, there is a shared belief in life's trials and tribulations. Sacred texts unequivocally denounce injustice, yet in practice, everyday individuals encounter a harsh reality marked by unfairness, self-interest, and callousness, leaving them disillusioned with the prospect of a brighter tomorrow.

A US judge expressed concern about access to justice for the poor, saying:

"Equal justice for the poor, too. Far too often, money—or the lack of it—can be the deciding factor in the courtroom," says Justice Goldberg, who calls for a program to ensure justice for all Americans." [162] **Index129**

As Muslims, we believe that we should treat one another as brothers and sisters with common values. In Islam, brotherhood means tolerance, humanity, unity, and working together to uphold our divine values of maintaining justice, regardless of dignity.

Allah says:

إِنَّمَا الْمُؤْمِنُونَ إِخْوَةٌ فَأَصْلِحُوا بَيْنَ أَخَوَيْكُمْ ۚ وَاتَّقُوا اللَّهَ لَعَلَّكُمْ تُرْحَمُونَ

---

[162] *Index 129 https://www.nytimes.com/1964/03/15/archives/equal-justice-for-the-poor-too-far-too-often-moneyor-the-lack-of.html*

The believers are nothing else than brothers (in the Islamic religion). So make reconciliation between your brothers, and fear Allah, that you may receive mercy. 49/10 Surah Al-Hujurat

Allah also sent down the verses:-

وَالْمُؤْمِنُونَ وَالْمُؤْمِنَاتُ بَعْضُهُمْ أَوْلِيَاءُ بَعْضٍ ۚ يَأْمُرُونَ بِالْمَعْرُوفِ وَيَنْهَوْنَ عَنِ الْمُنكَرِ وَيُقِيمُونَ الصَّلَاةَ وَيُؤْتُونَ الزَّكَاةَ وَيُطِيعُونَ اللَّهَ وَرَسُولَهُ ۚ أُولَٰئِكَ سَيَرْحَمُهُمُ اللَّهُ ۗ إِنَّ اللَّهَ عَزِيزٌ حَكِيمٌ

The believers, men and women, are Auliya' (helpers, supporters, friends, protectors) of one another. They enjoin (on the people) Al-Ma'ruf (i.e. Islamic Monotheism and all that Islam orders one to do) and forbid (people) from Al-Munkar (i.e. polytheism and disbelief of all kinds, and all that Islam has forbidden). They perform As-Salat (Iqamat-as-Salat), give the Zakat, and obey Allah and His Messenger. Allah will have His Mercy on them. Surely, Allah is All-Mighty, All-Wise. 9/71 Surah At-Taubah

Then Allah tells us a story about the oppressor of Prophet Moses in verse 17 of Surah Al-Qasas that:

قَالَ رَبِّ بِمَا أَنْعَمْتَ عَلَيَّ فَلَنْ أَكُونَ ظَهِيرًا لِّلْمُجْرِمِينَ

He said: "My Lord! For that with which You have favoured me, I will never more be a helper for the Mujrimun (criminals, disobedient to Allah, polytheists, sinners, etc.)!" 28/17 Al-Qasas.

The above verse was uttered by Prophet Moses (Musa) when he apologised for the unintentional death of a person while intervening in a conflict. History tells us that one day, in the town of Egypt, he saw two men fighting—one an Israelite (his follower) and one Egyptian. When the Israelite asked for help, Moses became involved in the dispute, and in a moment of rage, he hit the Egyptian with such force that the Egyptian was killed on the spot. Upon realising that he had killed a human being, Moses's heart was filled with deep sorrow, and immediately he begged Allah for forgiveness. He had not intended to kill the man. He pleaded with Almighty Allah to forgive him, and a sense of peace filled his whole being. He said in his prayer, "Never shall I be a help to those who sin!"

The following day, when he saw the same Israelite involved in another fight, Moses approached him and said, "You seem to be a quarrelsome fellow. You have a new quarrel with one person or another each day." Fearing that Moses might strike him, the Israelite warned Moses: "Would you kill me as you killed that miscreant yesterday?" Moses believed he was a sinner.

The Egyptian, with whom the Israelites were at war, overheard this remark and reported Moses to the authorities. Soon after, when Musa was passing through the city, a man came and warned him: "O Musa, the chiefs have conspired against you. You will be judged and killed. I advise you to flee." However, that is a different story. We have taken a small part for an example.

319

As travellers, it is crucial to reassess our commitment to honouring Allah's commands, particularly in terms of mercy, compassion, aggression, cruelty, and social justice. Our personal judgement serves as a valuable tool to evaluate whether we are following the right path and truly embodying these principles. It is an opportunity for self-reflection and self-affirmation.

As we engage in the act of self-evaluation, it is crucial to provide additional evidence that exemplifies the conduct of a Muslim within their family or even at a broader societal level, demonstrating the implementation of Allah's instructions. A comprehensive assessment must encompass these elements for a trial to be truly comprehensive.

The reason we emphasise individual assessment is to remind ourselves of the personal accountability we hold before Allah on the Day of Judgment. Each of us will be answerable to Him, and it is through introspection and self-reflection that we can strive to avoid His displeasure.

The global community has been exposed to distressing accounts of the harsh treatment endured by domestic workers in affluent Muslim nations. These countries often employ workers from less privileged nations, but when these individuals face mistreatment from their employers, their hopes and aspirations crumble, and they become desperate to escape or return to their home countries. Newspapers in the Western world and various survey reports shed light on these heart-wrenching narratives, revealing the cruelty inflicted upon these vulnerable workers.

We possess the noble Qur'an as our guiding scripture, and Prophet Muhammad ﷺ serves as our ultimate teacher. We believe that these sources provide us with comprehensive guidance, leaving no need for additional sources. However, in practice, we often tend to forget the teachings contained within them and behave in a manner inconsistent with their principles.

It is disheartening to observe instances where fellow Muslims mistreat their workers to such an extent that they are considered hypocritical rather than true followers of Islam. In such cases, secular organisations like the International Labour Organisation (ILO) and International Maritime Organization (IMO) intervene to support these workers and enforce their recommendations to address the mistreatment perpetuated by some Muslims.

These organisations play a vital role in safeguarding the rights and well-being of workers who find themselves in such situations. By implementing their recommendations, they strive to regulate the behaviour of individuals who claim to adhere to Islamic principles but fail to reflect them in their actions. It is important to acknowledge and rectify these inconsistencies, striving to align our behaviour with the guidance of the Qur'an and the teachings of Prophet Muhammad ﷺ in order to truly exemplify the values of Islam.

To gain clarity on the matter, we can examine the analytical reports of two prominent organisations: the International Labour Organization (ILO) and the International Organization for Migration (IOM). While their effectiveness may differ, they share common objectives such as promoting labour welfare, safeguarding migrant workers from exploitation in the Middle East and North Africa, and advocating for government policies to enhance the conditions of female migrant domestic workers in Arab states. Additionally, they engage in activities such as monitoring, conducting research, and driving institutional policy reforms across various regions worldwide.

Muslims may question why certain organisations dedicate their efforts to establishing policies aimed at safeguarding vulnerable workers from mistreatment by Muslim employers. After all, the principles needed to address such issues are already enshrined in the Qur'an, known to every Muslim anywhere in the world. It may seem hypocritical if a Muslim disregards the Qur'an's teachings and instead follows different principles. To gain insight into this matter, we can turn to the factual statements recorded in IMO reports and press statements that state this.

The Report States:

...Female migrant domestic workers (FMDWs) continue to be vulnerable to specific exploitative practices and abuse, and face the double discrimination threat of being both female and a migrant. Many FMDWs report serious physical and psychological abuse, including threats of and actual beatings, burning with hot iron, food deprivation, sexual harassment and rape, and being confined or locked in a room as punishment. Most victims interviewed for this study highlighted that it was daily derogatory and demeaning comments, repetitive belittling, lack of respect, and constant criticism of their work that was most difficult to accept. One participant noted:

"The madam called me names. [She] followed me around the apartment 'Work faster. Work faster!' She made me clean high windows. I was afraid to fall. She yelled at me 'Lazy! Lazy!' The madam's son, a little boy only 7 [years old], began to hit me each day. I could not touch him. I asked the madam to tell him to stop but she did not care. I wanted to tell her I am also a mother. My children would not hit an elder. Why does she not respect me? Why does she not teach her child respect?"

...Working conditions go unchecked despite these concerning reports of systemic abuse. Victims interviewed for this study reported excessive working hours (sometimes up to 17 hours per day), no rest for days, physical isolation, and being forced to sleep on balconies, in the kitchen, or the laundry. Several participants described the all-consuming nature of their roles:

"On my day off, if I stayed in my room, she would come searching for me. I could never rest. I worked the whole time; there were no set hours. I had to finish my work before I could rest, but the work never ended. I did everything – the cooking, cleaning, laundry, I cared for both the lady and her husband and they were both old. I took them to the shops to buy stuff, I brought them home, I did everything. I worked in the two houses. The lady had five daughters and all of them had kids. So when they came to visit, I worked for 18 people. I was exhausted. I ran away because the lady was not good to me. She used to make me work many

321

hours. She used to scream at me and verbally abuse me. I used to go to sleep at 12 at night, then had to start work at 6:30 a.m. Even if I slept for 5 minutes more, she used to scream at me. The lady was not good."

"I was told my employer was Egyptian. I was told I had a contract for four years. But for two years, I was not paid any money. In the contract, it said I would get a salary increase after six months. Not only did she not increase my money, I never got any salary. I told her to send me back to Ethiopia or give me my money or send me back to the recruitment office. But the lady didn't want any of the three options. So I told her I would no longer work in the house. I stopped doing any work and sat there because we were having this fight. Usually, when the lady goes out of the house, she locks the door. But one day she left the door open, and I ran away. I had worked there for two years with no money. I was getting abused in the house. One day, the lady took me to the supermarket to get some stuff. And I took this chance to run away. I didn't have time to take my salary. In comparison with the second lady, the first lady was a saint. The second lady verbally abused me; she used to scream at me. I only had USD 400 after working for her for one year and two months..."[163] *Index*

Investigation: African Migrants 'Left to Die' in Saudi Arabia's Hellish Covid Detention Centres

"The guards just throw the bodies out back as if they were trash," said one detainee. Another detainee said, "My only crime is leaving my country in search of a better life. But they beat us with whips and electric cords as if we were murderers."

One more individual recounted, "We eat a tiny piece of bread in the day and rice in the evening. There's almost no water, and the toilets are overflowing. It spills over to where we eat. The smell, we grow accustomed to. But there's over a hundred of us in a room, and the heat is killing us," said another young Ethiopian man.

A short video clip smuggled out shows several rooms covered with filth from an overflowing squat toilet. One Ethiopian man can be heard shouting out: "The toilets are clogged. We tried unblocking them, but we're unable to. So we live in this filth, we sleep in it too."

The newspaper also reported, "Oil-rich Saudi Arabia has long exploited migrant labour from Africa and Asia. In June 2019, an estimated 6.6 million foreign workers made up about 20 per cent of the Gulf nation's population, most occupying low-paid and often physically arduous jobs."[164] *Index 130*

---

[163] *Page 32,33 & 71 /111 other_migrant_crisis.pdf*
https://publications.iom.int/system/files/pdf/other_migrant_crisis.pdf
[164] *Index 130   https://www.telegraph.co.uk/global-health/climate-and-people/investigation-african-migrants-left-die-saudi-arabias-hellish*

Now let us see what our Prophet ﷺ says:

Ali is reported to have said that:

"God has made it obligatory on the rich to meet the economic needs of the poor, up to the extent of their absolute necessities. If they are hungry, naked, or involved in other financial difficulties, it will be merely because the rich are not doing their duty. Therefore, God will question them about it on the Day of Judgement and will give them due punishment."

Do not hate each other, do not envy each other, do not turn away from each other, but rather be servants of Allah as brothers. It is not lawful for a Muslim to boycott his brother for more than three days.

Source: Ṣaḥīḥ al-Bukhārī 5718, Grade: Muttafaqun Alayhi

The Messenger of Allah ﷺ said:

The government is the guardian of anyone who has no guardian. – (Abu Dawood, Tirmidhī)

The Prophet of Islam ﷺ is reported to have said:

If anyone spends a night in a town and remains hungry until morning, the promise of Allah's protection for that town comes to an end. – (Musnad Ahmad)

The Messenger of Allah ﷺ said:

No one's faith amongst you is reliable until he likes for his brother (in Islam) what he likes for himself. – (Bukhārī)

An-Nu'man ibn Basheer reported:

The Messenger of Allah ﷺ, peace and blessings be upon him, said:

مَثَلُ الْمُؤْمِنِينَ فِي تَوَادِّهِمْ وَتَرَاحُمِهِمْ وَتَعَاطُفِهِمْ مَثَلُ الْجَسَدِ إِذَا اشْتَكَى مِنْهُ عُضْوٌ تَدَاعَى لَهُ سَائِرُ الْجَسَدِ بِالسَّهَرِ وَالْحُمَّى

The parable of the believers in their affection, mercy, and compassion for each other is that of a body. When any limb aches, the whole body reacts with sleeplessness and fever.

Source: Ṣaḥīḥ al-Bukhārī 5665, Grade: Muttafaqun Alayhi

When we help our brothers and sisters in Islam, in reality, we are helping ourselves. When we pray for them, the angels pray for us. Fulfilling the rights of brotherhood in Islam is a means for Allah to support us and reward us in the Hereafter. Failing our brothers and sisters in Islam results in Allah withdrawing this support.

Abu Huraira reported:

The Messenger of Allah ﷺ, peace and blessings be upon him, said:

مَنْ نَفَّسَ عَنْ مُؤْمِنٍ كُرْبَةً مِنْ كُرَبِ الدُّنْيَا نَفَّسَ اللَّهُ عَنْهُ كُرْبَةً مِنْ كُرَبِ يَوْمِ الْقِيَامَةِ وَمَنْ يَسَّرَ عَلَى مُعْسِرٍ يَسَّرَ اللَّهُ عَلَيْهِ فِي الدُّنْيَا وَالآخِرَةِ وَمَنْ سَتَرَ مُسْلِمًا سَتَرَهُ اللَّهُ فِي الدُّنْيَا وَالآخِرَةِ وَاللَّهُ فِي عَوْنِ الْعَبْدِ مَا كَانَ الْعَبْدُ فِي عَوْنِ أَخِيهِ

Whoever relieves the hardship of a believer in this world, Allah will relieve his hardship on the Day of Resurrection. Whoever helps ease one in difficulty, Allah will make it easy for him in this world and the Hereafter. Whoever conceals the faults of a Muslim, Allah will conceal his faults in this world and the Hereafter. Allah helps the servant as long as he helps his brother.[165]

As brothers and sisters, Muslims are entitled to rights that are specific to the religious community, including the right to be treated with proper manners and etiquette, to be prayed for, to be greeted with peace, to be visited when sick, and to enjoy friendly companionship.

Ali ibn Abi Talib reported: The Messenger of Allah ﷺ, peace and blessings be upon him, said:

A Muslim has six rights over another Muslim in good conduct: to greet him with peace when he meets him, to respond to his invitation, to respond to his sneeze, to visit him when he is sick, to follow his funeral prayer when he dies, and to love for him what he loves for himself. [166]*Index 131,132*

What Does The Bible Say About Empathy?

Hebrews 4

We have a High Priest who fully understands our struggles and weaknesses—He is not distant or disconnected from our human experience.

1 Corinthians 12:25–26

God designed the body of believers to care for one another in unity. When one person suffers, all feel the pain; when one is honoured, everyone shares in the joy.

Romans 12:5

Though we are many, we form one body in Christ, and each person belongs to all the others as essential members of that body.

---

[165] Source: Ṣaḥīḥ Muslim 2699, Grade: Sahih
[166] *Index 131 Source: Sunan al-Tirmidhī 2736, Grade: Hasan*
Index 132 https://www.ilo.org/wcmsp5/groups/public/---arabstates/---ro-beirut/documents/projectdocumentation/wcms_236688.pdf

Matthew 22:37–40

Jesus taught that the greatest commandment is to love God with all your heart, soul, and mind. The second is just as vital: love others as you love yourself. These two principles are the foundation of all that God's law and the prophets have taught.[167]***Index 133***

Finally,

All of you, have unity of mind, sympathy, brotherly love, a tender heart, and a humble mind. Do not repay evil for evil or reviling for reviling, but, on the contrary, bless, for to this you were called, that you may obtain a blessing. [168](Index 134)

Radiance and peace are attained when the virtues of justice, equality, and dignity become inherent in the core of a Muslim's soul. It is through embodying these principles that one can tread the righteous path. Merely relying on prayer is insufficient to attain true righteousness.

Winston Churchill says:

"All the great things are simple, and many can be expressed in a single word: freedom, justice, honour, duty, mercy, hope."

"Never, never, never give up."

The adventure persists, leading us down unfamiliar, challenging paths, where we'll discover uncharted territories and embrace fresh encounters. These experiences will uplift our spirits, ensuring a seamless journey ahead.

---

[167] *Index 133 https://biblereasons.com/empathy/*
[168] *Index 134 ttps://www.bible.com/bible/59/1PE.3.8-12.ESV*

بِسْمِ ٱللَّهِ ٱلرَّحْمَـٰنِ ٱلرَّحِيمِ

Chapter 9

"Peace unto you for that ye persevered in patience! Now how excellent is the final home!"

13:24 – Surah Ar-Ra'd

"For I say unto you, That except your righteousness shall exceed the righteousness of the scribes and Pharisees, ye shall in no case enter into the kingdom of heaven."

Matthew 5:20 – King James Version

📖📖📖📖📖📖📖

Key to My Home: Kingdom of Heaven

Once the travellers have evaluated their strengths and weaknesses concerning justice and compassion, they embark on a captivating journey of inquiry: What actions are necessary to unlock the gates of their celestial home? What standards does Allah set for us to prove ourselves deserving of the honour of being entrusted as custodians of the keys?

To begin with, it's vital for me to comprehend why the gate to my heavenly abode remains closed. The reason lies in our earthly actions possibly diverging from the intentions of the Divine, as our hearts cling to desires that stray from the teachings of God. This is a pivotal moment to introspect—to gauge the misalignment between God's directives and our conduct. Through this introspection, we'll uncover the causes behind the shut gate to Paradise and identify the requisite measures to open it.

Both the Qur'an and the Bible summarise this point by saying that the key to entering heaven or attaining eternal salvation is faith in Allah and living righteously according to His commandments. According to the Qur'an, belief in the Oneness of Allah (*Tawheed*) and following His guidance, as revealed in the Qur'an and through the teachings of the Prophet Muhammad ﷺ, is essential for attaining Paradise.

As discussed earlier, travellers are reminded again that the Qur'an emphasises the importance of sincere faith, good deeds, repentance for sins, and submission to Allah's will as basic messages to obtain the keys to refuge. This includes practising the five pillars of Islam, which we can define as both external and internal prayer.

During this expedition, we take on the responsibility of guiding ourselves and ensuring the protection and control of our inner selves—shielding them from any

326

hindrances that might obstruct our advancement. It's crucial to remind ourselves constantly: if we finish our journey with a corrupted soul, all our efforts will be in vain and lack significance.

What To Do Now

Let's reflect on the moment we commenced this book's journey, solemnly declaring:

"La ilaha illa Allah, Muhammad ar-rasul Allah"

"There is no god but Allah, and Muhammad is His Messenger."

As we journey through its pages, our pursuit now centres on unlocking the gates of heaven. Yet, it's vital to recognise that the essence of this celestial key already resides within us. So long as we genuinely embrace and internalise that oath within our hearts and adhere to its principles, we hold the key.

For those who may have overlooked this opportunity, there's a chance to revisit that initial pledge, reaffirm that dedication, and continue the journey from this point onward.

The Holy Qur'an is our only source of pure soul acquisition and enlightenment with knowledge. For this reason, we combine all the relevant verses that tell us what to do to retain the essence of the key. However, the declaration of faith holds the key to Paradise—yet, like any key, it requires specific ridges that align with the lock on the door; otherwise, it remains ineffective.

Similarly, the testimony of faith encompasses particular conditions that must be fulfilled to guide us towards Paradise. Let us set a few messages before we return to our course:

Al-Bukhari reported: It was said to Wahb,

"Is not the key to Paradise the declaration that there is no God but Allah?"

Wahb said:

"Of course, but rather every key has ridges. If you come with the correct key, the door will be opened for you. Otherwise, it will never be opened." [169]

Ibn Al-Qayyim writes:

"The first matter concerns sincerity, and the second concerns following the Messenger ﷺ. Allah SWT does not accept any action until both of these conditions are met.

The method of absolution from the first question is to purify one's sincerity such that it is for Allah alone.

---

[169] Source: Sahih Bukhari 1180, Grade: Sahih

The method of absolution from the second question is to actualise the following of the Messenger ﷺ, and by securing the heart from any intent that would impair its sincerity and any base desire that would impair its following of the Messenger."

Source: Ighathatul Lahfan fi Masayid ash-Shaytan 1/7

Ibn Abi Al-'Izz writes:

Monotheism is the beginning of the matter and its end. What is meant by this is the belief in the unity of God, for monotheism has three dimensions:

First, matters concerning the attributes of Allah;

Second, the Oneness of Lordship, which states that Allah alone created everything;

Third, the Oneness of Godship, which states that Allah alone should be worshipped without associating any partners with Him.

(Pay special attention to understand the underlined section from any qualified scholar.)

Source: Sharh Aqidah At-Tahawi 24

These three elements originate from multiple references found in the Qur'an and Sunnah. In fact, all three of them are encompassed in a concise statement from Allah SWT:

رَّبُّ السَّمَاوَاتِ وَالْأَرْضِ وَمَا بَيْنَهُمَا فَاعْبُدْهُ وَاصْطَبِرْ لِعِبَادَتِهِ ۚ هَلْ تَعْلَمُ لَهُ سَمِيًّا

Lord of the heavens and the earth, and all that is between them, so worship Him (alone) and be constant and patient in His worship. Do you know of any who is similar to Him?

(Of course, none is similar or coequal or comparable to Him, and He has none as partner with Him. There is nothing like unto Him, and He is the All-Hearer, the All-Seer.)

— *19:65 Surat Maryam*

Abu, رضي الله عنه, reported:

The Messenger ﷺ of Allah SWT said:

Gabriel, upon him be peace, came to me with the good news that anyone from my nation who dies without associating partners with Allah will enter Paradise.

I said, *"Even if he commits adultery and theft?"*

The Prophet ﷺ said:

"Even if he commits adultery and theft."[170]

---

[170] Source: Sahih Bukhari 1180, Grade: Muttafaqun Alayhi

328

Nevertheless, it is important to note that believers are not exempt from the consequences of their actions and may not be entirely spared from Hell. If believers engage in significant transgressions, they will face punishment in Hell until they have received fair retribution for their wrongdoing.

An-Nawawi comments on this tradition, saying:

This is a proof for the people of the Sunnah, that those who commit major sins will not remain in the Hellfire forever. If they enter it, they will be taken out and eventually admitted into Paradise.[171]

Allah SWT Said:

وَاعْبُدُوا اللَّهَ وَلَا تُشْرِكُوا بِهِ شَيْئًا ۖ وَبِالْوَالِدَيْنِ إِحْسَانًا وَبِذِي الْقُرْبَىٰ وَالْيَتَامَىٰ وَالْمَسَاكِينِ وَالْجَارِ ذِي الْقُرْبَىٰ وَالْجَارِ الْجُنُبِ وَالصَّاحِبِ بِالْجَنبِ وَابْنِ السَّبِيلِ وَمَا مَلَكَتْ أَيْمَانُكُمْ ۗ إِنَّ اللَّهَ لَا يُحِبُّ مَن كَانَ مُخْتَالًا فَخُورًا

Worship Allah and associate nothing with Him, and be kind to parents, relatives, orphans, the poor, the neighbour who is near of kin, the neighbour who is a stranger, the companion at your side, the traveller, and those whom your right hands possess. Verily, Allah does not love those who are arrogant and boastful.

— 4:36 *Surat An-Nisa*[172]

By considering all of these conditions collectively, we can determine that success can be attained through cautiousness and focusing on the following areas:

- Jihad of the soul against desires
- Lawful combat (jihad) against evil
- Obedience to Allah SWT in all areas of life
- Good deeds

The following 98 verses provide guidance on how to attain the necessary qualifications for preserving the harmonious nature of the key, enabling it to function seamlessly as you journey towards your heavenly destination. A person who fulfils the conditions can enter any of the eight gates as he wishes (Hadith).

Allah SWT says in Surah Az-Zumar:

لَّهُ مَقَالِيدُ السَّمَاوَاتِ وَالْأَرْضِ ۗ وَالَّذِينَ كَفَرُوا بِآيَاتِ اللَّهِ أُولَٰئِكَ هُمُ الْخَاسِرُونَ

---

[171] Source: Sharh Sahih Muslim 94

[172] https://www.siasat.com/key-paradise-1780477/

To Him belong the keys of the heavens and the earth. And those who disbelieve in the Ayat (proofs, evidences, verses, signs, revelations, etc.) of Allah, such are they who will be the losers. (39:63, Surah Az-Zumar)

This indicates that all things within and beyond our world are subject to the dominion of a supreme authority. All admiration is duly directed towards this entity, as He alone holds the power to achieve all things.

The word "key" in Arabic is *miftaah* (plural: *mafātih*). In Surah al-An'am, Allah says:

وَعِندَهُ مَفَاتِحُ الْغَيْبِ لَا يَعْلَمُهَا إِلَّا هُوَ ۚ وَيَعْلَمُ مَا فِي الْبَرِّ وَالْبَحْرِ ۚ وَمَا تَسْقُطُ مِن وَرَقَةٍ إِلَّا يَعْلَمُهَا وَلَا حَبَّةٍ فِي ظُلُمَاتِ الْأَرْضِ وَلَا رَطْبٍ وَلَا يَابِسٍ إِلَّا فِي كِتَابٍ مُّبِينٍ

And with Him are the keys of the unseen; none knows them but He. And He knows whatever is in the land and in the sea; not a leaf falls but He knows it. There is not a grain in the darkness of the earth nor anything fresh or dry, but it is written in a clear record. (6:59, Surah al-An'am)

The Old Testament also says:

"And I will give unto thee the keys of the kingdom of heaven: and whatsoever thou shalt bind on earth shall be bound in heaven: and whatsoever thou shalt loose on earth shall be loosed in heaven." (Matthew 16:19, KJV)

Search For Your Key

Exploring this lucrative realm reveals crucial clues that lie within its depths. These insights unveil themselves as one navigates this delicate path with utmost care, encountering verse upon verse along the way. By aligning inner intentions with outward actions, seekers may unlock the key to success. Even if initially unrecognised, these verses possess the potential to awaken an inner power, guiding one towards the elusive key. So proceed with caution, ensuring harmony between action and guidance in order to unveil the path to prosperity.

95 Verses

1 - 17:09 – Al-Isra

إِنَّ هَٰذَا الْقُرْآنَ يَهْدِي لِلَّتِي هِيَ أَقْوَمُ وَيُبَشِّرُ الْمُؤْمِنِينَ الَّذِينَ يَعْمَلُونَ الصَّالِحَاتِ أَنَّ لَهُمْ أَجْرًا كَبِيرًا

Verily, this Qur'an guides to that which is most just and right, and gives glad tidings to the believers who do righteous deeds, that they shall have a great reward (Paradise).

2 - 84:06 – Al-Inshiqaq

يَا أَيُّهَا الْإِنسَانُ إِنَّكَ كَادِحٌ إِلَىٰ رَبِّكَ كَدْحًا فَمُلَاقِيهِ

O man! Verily, you are returning towards your Lord with your deeds and actions (good or bad), a sure returning, and you will meet (the results thereof).

3 - 35:06 – Fatir

إِنَّ الشَّيْطَانَ لَكُمْ عَدُوٌّ فَاتَّخِذُوهُ عَدُوًّا ۚ إِنَّمَا يَدْعُو حِزْبَهُ لِيَكُونُوا مِنْ أَصْحَابِ السَّعِيرِ

Surely, Shaitan (Satan) is an enemy to you, so take him as an enemy. He only invites his followers that they may become dwellers of the blazing Fire.

4 - 2:62 – Al-Baqarah

إِنَّ الَّذِينَ آمَنُوا وَالَّذِينَ هَادُوا وَالنَّصَارَىٰ وَالصَّابِئِينَ مَنْ آمَنَ بِاللَّهِ وَالْيَوْمِ الْآخِرِ وَعَمِلَ صَالِحًا فَلَهُمْ أَجْرُهُمْ عِندَ رَبِّهِمْ وَلَا خَوْفٌ عَلَيْهِمْ وَلَا هُمْ يَحْزَنُونَ

Verily! Those who believe, and those who are Jews and Christians, and Sabians—whoever believes in Allah and the Last Day and does righteous good deeds—shall have their reward with their Lord. On them shall be no fear, nor shall they grieve.

5 - 35:07 – Fatir

الَّذِينَ كَفَرُوا لَهُمْ عَذَابٌ شَدِيدٌ ۖ وَالَّذِينَ آمَنُوا وَعَمِلُوا الصَّالِحَاتِ لَهُم مَّغْفِرَةٌ وَأَجْرٌ كَبِيرٌ

Those who disbelieve will face a severe punishment; while those who believe and do righteous good deeds will have forgiveness and a great reward.

6 - 6:82 – Al-An'am

الَّذِينَ آمَنُوا وَلَمْ يَلْبِسُوا إِيمَانَهُم بِظُلْمٍ أُولَٰئِكَ لَهُمُ الْأَمْنُ وَهُم مُّهْتَدُونَ

It is those who believe and do not mix their belief with wrongdoing—for them there is security, and they are the guided ones.

7 - 32:19 – As-Sajdah

إِنَّ الَّذِينَ آمَنُوا وَعَمِلُوا الصَّالِحَاتِ فَلَهُمْ جَنَّاتُ الْمَأْوَىٰ نُزُلًا بِمَا كَانُوا يَعْمَلُونَ

As for those who believe and do righteous good deeds, for them are Gardens (Paradise) as an entertainment for what they used to do.

8 - 29:02 – Al-Ankabut

أَحَسِبَ النَّاسُ أَن يُتْرَكُوا أَن يَقُولُوا آمَنَّا وَهُمْ لَا يُفْتَنُونَ

Do people think that they will be left alone just because they say: "We believe," and will not be tested?

❖ Do men think that they will be left alone on saying "We believe"

❖ And will not be tested?

9 - 14:27 – Ibrahim

يُثَبِّتُ اللَّهُ الَّذِينَ آمَنُوا بِالْقَوْلِ الثَّابِتِ فِي الْحَيَاةِ الدُّنْيَا وَفِي الْآخِرَةِ ۖ وَيُضِلُّ اللَّهُ الظَّالِمِينَ ۚ وَيَفْعَلُ اللَّهُ مَا يَشَاءُ

Allah will keep firm those who believe, with the word that stands firm in this world and in the Hereafter. And Allah leads the wrongdoers astray. And Allah does what He wills.

10 - 3:118 – Al-i-Imran

يَا أَيُّهَا الَّذِينَ آمَنُوا لَا تَتَّخِذُوا بِطَانَةً مِّن دُونِكُمْ لَا يَأْلُونَكُمْ خَبَالًا وَدُّوا مَا عَنِتُّمْ قَدْ بَدَتِ الْبَغْضَاءُ مِنْ أَفْوَاهِهِمْ وَمَا تُخْفِي صُدُورُهُمْ أَكْبَرُ ۚ قَدْ بَيَّنَّا لَكُمُ الْآيَاتِ ۖ إِن كُنتُمْ تَعْقِلُونَ

O you who believe! Take not as your advisors or close associates those outside your faith. They will spare no effort to corrupt you. Hatred has already appeared from their mouths, but what their hearts conceal is far worse. Indeed, We have made clear to you the verses, if you understand.

11 – 48:04 Al-Fath

هُوَ الَّذِي أَنزَلَ السَّكِينَةَ فِي قُلُوبِ الْمُؤْمِنِينَ لِيَزْدَادُوا إِيمَانًا مَّعَ إِيمَانِهِمْ ۗ وَلِلَّهِ جُنُودُ السَّمَاوَاتِ وَالْأَرْضِ ۚ وَكَانَ اللَّهُ عَلِيمًا حَكِيمًا

He it is Who sent down *As-Sakinah* (calmness and tranquillity) into the hearts of the believers, that they may grow more in faith along with their present faith. And to Allah belong the hosts of the heavens and the earth, and Allah is Ever All-Knowing, All-Wise.

12 – 66:06 At-Tahrim

يَا أَيُّهَا الَّذِينَ آمَنُوا قُوا أَنفُسَكُمْ وَأَهْلِيكُمْ نَارًا وَقُودُهَا النَّاسُ وَالْحِجَارَةُ عَلَيْهَا مَلَائِكَةٌ غِلَاظٌ شِدَادٌ لَّا يَعْصُونَ اللَّهَ مَا أَمَرَهُمْ وَيَفْعَلُونَ مَا يُؤْمَرُونَ

O you who believe! Ward off from yourselves and your families a Fire (Hell), whose fuel is men and stones, over which are angels stern and severe, who disobey not the commands of Allah, but do that which they are commanded.

13 – 4:111 An-Nisaa

وَمَن يَكْسِبْ إِثْمًا فَإِنَّمَا يَكْسِبُهُ عَلَىٰ نَفْسِهِ ۚ وَكَانَ اللَّهُ عَلِيمًا حَكِيمًا

Whosoever earns sin, he earns it only against himself. And Allah is Ever All-Knowing, All-Wise.

14 – 3:131 Aal-E-Imran

وَاتَّقُوا النَّارَ الَّتِي أُعِدَّتْ لِلْكَافِرِينَ

And fear the Fire which is prepared for the disbelievers.

15 – 67:12 Al-Mulk

إِنَّ الَّذِينَ يَخْشَوْنَ رَبَّهُم بِالْغَيْبِ لَهُم مَّغْفِرَةٌ وَأَجْرٌ كَبِيرٌ

Verily, those who fear their Lord unseen—for them is forgiveness and a great reward.

16 – 16:128 An-Nahl

إِنَّ اللَّهَ مَعَ الَّذِينَ اتَّقَوا وَّالَّذِينَ هُم مُّحْسِنُونَ

Truly, Allah is with those who fear Him, and those who are *Muhsinun* (good-doers).

17 – 16:30 An-Nahl

وَقِيلَ لِلَّذِينَ اتَّقَوْا مَاذَا أَنزَلَ رَبُّكُمْ قَالُوا خَيْرًا لِّلَّذِينَ أَحْسَنُوا فِي هَذِهِ الدُّنْيَا حَسَنَةٌ وَلَدَارُ الْآخِرَةِ خَيْرٌ وَلَنِعْمَ دَارُ الْمُتَّقِينَ

And when it is said to those who fear Allah, "What has your Lord revealed?" They say, "That which is good." For those who do good in this world, there is good, and the home of the Hereafter is better. And excellent indeed is the home of the *Muttaqun* (the pious).

18 – 28:60 Al-Qasas

وَمَا أُوتِيتُم مِّن شَيْءٍ فَمَتَاعُ الْحَيَاةِ الدُّنْيَا وَزِينَتُهَا وَمَا عِندَ اللَّهِ خَيْرٌ وَأَبْقَى أَفَلَا تَعْقِلُونَ

And whatever you have been given is (only) a provision for the life of this world and its adornment; but that which is with Allah is better and more lasting. Will you not then understand?

19 – 35:10 Fatir

مَن كَانَ يُرِيدُ الْعِزَّةَ فَلِلَّهِ الْعِزَّةُ جَمِيعًا إِلَيْهِ يَصْعَدُ الْكَلِمُ الطَّيِّبُ وَالْعَمَلُ الصَّالِحُ يَرْفَعُهُ وَالَّذِينَ يَمْكُرُونَ السَّيِّئَاتِ لَهُمْ عَذَابٌ شَدِيدٌ وَمَكْرُ أُولَئِكَ هُوَ يَبُورُ

Whosoever desires honour, then all honour belongs to Allah. To Him ascend the good words, and the righteous deeds raise them up. But those who plot evil—upon them is a severe torment, and the plotting of such will perish.

20 – 29:64 Al-Ankabut

وَمَا هَٰذِهِ الْحَيَاةُ الدُّنْيَا إِلَّا لَهْوٌ وَلَعِبٌ ۚ وَإِنَّ الدَّارَ الْآخِرَةَ لَهِيَ الْحَيَوَانُ ۚ لَوْ كَانُوا يَعْلَمُونَ

And this life of the world is only amusement and play. Verily, the home of the Hereafter—that is the true life, if only they knew.

21 – 2:83 Al-Baqara

وَإِذْ أَخَذْنَا مِيثَاقَ بَنِي إِسْرَائِيلَ لَا تَعْبُدُونَ إِلَّا اللَّهَ وَبِالْوَالِدَيْنِ إِحْسَانًا وَذِي الْقُرْبَىٰ وَالْيَتَامَىٰ وَالْمَسَاكِينِ وَقُولُوا لِلنَّاسِ حُسْنًا وَأَقِيمُوا الصَّلَاةَ وَآتُوا الزَّكَاةَ ثُمَّ تَوَلَّيْتُمْ إِلَّا قَلِيلًا مِنكُمْ وَأَنتُم مُّعْرِضُونَ

And (remember) when We took a covenant from the Children of Israel: Worship none but Allah; be kind to parents, and to kindred, orphans, and the poor; and speak kindly to people. Establish prayer, and give charity (Zakat). Then you turned away, except a few among you, and you were backsliders.

22 – 2:220 Al-Baqara

فِي الدُّنْيَا وَالْآخِرَةِ ۗ وَيَسْأَلُونَكَ عَنِ الْيَتَامَىٰ ۖ قُلْ إِصْلَاحٌ لَهُمْ خَيْرٌ ۖ وَإِن تُخَالِطُوهُمْ فَإِخْوَانُكُمْ ۚ وَاللَّهُ يَعْلَمُ الْمُفْسِدَ مِنَ الْمُصْلِحِ ۚ وَلَوْ شَاءَ اللَّهُ لَأَعْنَتَكُمْ ۚ إِنَّ اللَّهَ عَزِيزٌ حَكِيمٌ

In this world and the Hereafter. And they ask you concerning orphans. Say: "Improving their condition is best. And if you mix your affairs with theirs, then they are your brothers." Allah knows him who means mischief from him who means good. And if Allah had willed, He could have put you into hardship. Truly, Allah is Almighty, All-Wise.

23 – 41:49 Ha-Mim

لَا يَسْأَمُ الْإِنسَانُ مِن دُعَاءِ الْخَيْرِ وَإِن مَّسَّهُ الشَّرُّ فَيَئُوسٌ قَنُوطٌ

Man does not tire of asking for good, but if evil touches him, he gives up hope and falls into despair.

24 – 65:05 At-Talaq

ذَٰلِكَ أَمْرُ اللَّهِ أَنزَلَهُ إِلَيْكُمْ ۚ وَمَن يَتَّقِ اللَّهَ يُكَفِّرْ عَنْهُ سَيِّئَاتِهِ وَيُعْظِمْ لَهُ أَجْرًا

That is the Command of Allah, which He has sent down to you. And whosoever fears Allah and keeps his duty to Him, He will remove his sins from him and will enlarge his reward.

25 – 5:89 Al-Maidah

لَا يُؤَاخِذُكُمُ اللَّهُ بِاللَّغْوِ فِي أَيْمَانِكُمْ وَلَٰكِن يُؤَاخِذُكُم بِمَا عَقَّدتُّمُ الْأَيْمَانَ ۖ فَكَفَّارَتُهُ إِطْعَامُ عَشَرَةِ مَسَاكِينَ مِنْ أَوْسَطِ مَا تُطْعِمُونَ أَهْلِيكُمْ أَوْ كِسْوَتُهُمْ أَوْ تَحْرِيرُ رَقَبَةٍ ۖ فَمَن لَّمْ يَجِدْ فَصِيَامُ ثَلَاثَةِ أَيَّامٍ ۚ ذَٰلِكَ كَفَّارَةُ أَيْمَانِكُمْ إِذَا حَلَفْتُمْ ۚ وَاحْفَظُوا أَيْمَانَكُمْ ۚ كَذَٰلِكَ يُبَيِّنُ اللَّهُ لَكُمْ آيَاتِهِ لَعَلَّكُمْ تَشْكُرُونَ

Allah will not hold you accountable for unintentional oaths, but He will hold you accountable for deliberate oaths. The expiation for it is to feed ten poor people from the average of what you feed your families, or to clothe them, or to free a slave. But whoever cannot afford it must fast for three days. That is the expiation for your oaths when you have sworn. And guard your oaths. Thus does Allah make His signs clear to you, that you may give thanks.

26 - 40:39 Al-Mu'min

يَا قَوْمِ إِنَّمَا هَٰذِهِ الْحَيَاةُ الدُّنْيَا مَتَاعٌ وَإِنَّ الْآخِرَةَ هِيَ دَارُ الْقَرَارِ

"O my people! Truly, this life of the world is nothing but a (quick passing) enjoyment, and verily, the Hereafter—that is the home that shall remain for ever."

27 - 72:4 Al-Jinn

وَأَنَّهُ كَانَ يَقُولُ سَفِيهُنَا عَلَى اللَّهِ شَطَطًا

And that the foolish among us [i.e., Iblis (Satan) or the polytheists among the jinns] used to utter against Allah that which was wrong and not right.

28 - 35:18 Fatir

لَا تَزِرُ وَازِرَةٌ وِزْرَ أُخْرَىٰ ۚ وَإِن تَدْعُ مُثْقَلَةٌ إِلَىٰ حِمْلِهَا لَا يُحْمَلْ مِنْهُ شَيْءٌ وَلَوْ كَانَ ذَا قُرْبَىٰ ۗ إِنَّمَا تُنذِرُ الَّذِينَ يَخْشَوْنَ رَبَّهُم بِالْغَيْبِ وَأَقَامُوا الصَّلَاةَ ۚ وَمَن تَزَكَّىٰ فَإِنَّمَا يَتَزَكَّىٰ لِنَفْسِهِ ۚ وَإِلَى اللَّهِ الْمَصِيرُ

And none shall bear the burden of another; and if one that is laden calls another to bear his load, not aught of it shall be borne, though he be near of kin. Thou canst but warn such as fear their Lord unseen and establish prayer. And whoso purifieth himself, purifieth himself only for the benefit of his own soul. And unto Allah is the return.

29 - 2:150 Al-Baqara

وَمِنْ حَيْثُ خَرَجْتَ فَوَلِّ وَجْهَكَ شَطْرَ الْمَسْجِدِ الْحَرَامِ ۚ وَحَيْثُ مَا كُنتُمْ فَوَلُّوا وُجُوهَكُمْ شَطْرَهُ لِئَلَّا يَكُونَ لِلنَّاسِ عَلَيْكُمْ حُجَّةٌ إِلَّا الَّذِينَ ظَلَمُوا مِنْهُمْ فَلَا تَخْشَوْهُمْ وَاخْشَوْنِي وَلِأُتِمَّ نِعْمَتِي عَلَيْكُمْ وَلَعَلَّكُمْ تَهْتَدُونَ

And from wheresoever thou comest forth (for prayer), turn thy face towards Al-Masjid-al-Haram (in Makkah); and wherever ye be, turn your faces thither: that there be no cause of dispute against you among men, save those of them that are unjust. So fear them not, but fear Me; that I may perfect My favour upon you, and that ye may be guided.

30 - 6:17 Al-An'am

فَلَا كَاشِفَ لَهُ إِلَّا هُوَ ۖ وَإِن يَمْسَسْكَ بِخَيْرٍ فَهُوَ عَلَىٰ كُلِّ شَيْءٍ قَدِيرٌ وَإِن يَمْسَسْكَ اللَّهُ بِضُرٍّ

If Allah touch thee with hurt, there is none that can remove it but He; and if He touch thee with good, He is able to do all things.

31 - 39:7 Az-Zumar

وَلَا يَرْضَىٰ لِعِبَادِهِ الْكُفْرَ ۖ وَإِن تَشْكُرُوا يَرْضَهُ لَكُمْ ۚ وَلَا تَزِرُ وَازِرَةٌ وِزْرَ ۚ إِن تَكْفُرُوا فَإِنَّ اللَّهَ غَنِيٌّ عَنكُمْ أُخْرَىٰ ۚ ثُمَّ إِلَىٰ رَبِّكُم مَّرْجِعُكُمْ فَيُنَبِّئُكُم بِمَا كُنتُمْ تَعْمَلُونَ ۚ إِنَّهُ عَلِيمٌ بِذَاتِ الصُّدُورِ

If ye be ungrateful, verily Allah is free of all need of you; and He liketh not ingratitude from His servants. But if ye be thankful, He is pleased therewith for you. And none shall bear the burden of another. Then unto your Lord shall ye return, and He shall declare unto you what ye used to do. Verily, He knoweth well the secrets of the hearts.

32 - 52:21 At-Tur

بِإِيمَانٍ أَلْحَقْنَا بِهِمْ ذُرِّيَّتَهُمْ وَمَا أَلَتْنَاهُم مِّنْ عَمَلِهِم مِّن شَيْءٍ ۚ كُلُّ امْرِئٍ بِمَا وَالَّذِينَ آمَنُوا وَاتَّبَعَتْهُمْ ذُرِّيَّتُهُم كَسَبَ رَهِينٌ

And those who believe and whose offspring follow them in faith—to them shall We join their offspring, and We shall not lessen anything of their deeds. Every soul is pledged for what it has earned.

33 - 39:52 Az-Zumar

لِمَن يَشَاءُ وَيَقْدِرُ ۚ إِنَّ فِي ذَٰلِكَ لَآيَاتٍ لِّقَوْمٍ يُؤْمِنُونَ أَوَلَمْ يَعْلَمُوا أَنَّ اللَّهَ يَبْسُطُ الرِّزْقَ

Know they not that Allah enlargeth the provision for whom He willeth and straiteneth it for whom He willeth? Verily, in this are signs for a people that believe.

34 - 2:149 Al-Baqara

شَطْرَ الْمَسْجِدِ الْحَرَامِ ۖ وَإِنَّهُ لَلْحَقُّ مِن رَّبِّكَ ۗ وَمَا اللَّهُ بِغَافِلٍ عَمَّا تَعْمَلُونَ وَمِنْ حَيْثُ خَرَجْتَ فَوَلِّ وَجْهَكَ

And from wheresoever thou comest forth, turn thy face toward Al-Masjid-al-Haram; for that is indeed the truth from thy Lord. And Allah is not unmindful of what ye do.

35 - 2:214 Al-Baqara

وَلَمَّا يَأْتِكُم مَّثَلُ الَّذِينَ خَلَوْا مِن قَبْلِكُم ۖ مَّسَّتْهُمُ الْبَأْسَاءُ وَالضَّرَّاءُ وَزُلْزِلُوا حَتَّىٰ أَمْ حَسِبْتُمْ أَن تَدْخُلُوا الْجَنَّةَ يَقُولَ الرَّسُولُ وَالَّذِينَ آمَنُوا مَعَهُ مَتَىٰ نَصْرُ اللَّهِ ۗ أَلَا إِنَّ نَصْرَ اللَّهِ قَرِيبٌ

Or think ye that ye shall enter Paradise without such trials as came to those who passed away before you? They were afflicted with severe poverty and hardship and were so shaken that even the Messenger and those who believed with him said, *"When will the help of Allah come?"* Verily, the help of Allah is nigh.

36 - 2:261 Al-Baqara

فِي سَبِيلِ اللَّهِ كَمَثَلِ حَبَّةٍ أَنبَتَتْ سَبْعَ سَنَابِلَ فِي كُلِّ سُنبُلَةٍ مِّائَةُ حَبَّةٍ ۗ وَاللَّهُ يُضَاعِفُ مَّثَلُ الَّذِينَ يُنفِقُونَ أَمْوَالَهُمْ لِمَن يَشَاءُ ۚ وَاللَّهُ وَاسِعٌ عَلِيمٌ

The likeness of those who spend their wealth in the cause of Allah is as the likeness of a grain of corn: it groweth seven ears, in every ear a hundred grains. And Allah giveth manifold increase to whom He will; and Allah is All-Sufficient, All-Knowing.

37 - 65:3 Talaq (Divorce)

وَمَن يَتَوَكَّلْ عَلَى اللَّهِ فَهُوَ حَسْبُهُ ۚ إِنَّ اللَّهَ بَالِغُ أَمْرِهِ ۚ قَدْ جَعَلَ اللَّهُ لِكُلِّ شَيْءٍ وَيَرْزُقْهُ مِنْ حَيْثُ لَا يَحْتَسِبُ قَدْرًا

And He shall provide for him from where he reckoneth not. And whoso putteth his trust in Allah, He shall be sufficient for him. Verily, Allah bringeth His command to pass. Allah hath appointed a measure for all things.

38 - 3:31 Aal-i-Imran

فَاتَّبِعُونِي يُحْبِبْكُمُ اللَّهُ وَيَغْفِرْ لَكُمْ ذُنُوبَكُمْ ۚ وَاللَّهُ غَفُورٌ رَّحِيمٌ قُلْ إِن كُنتُمْ تُحِبُّونَ اللَّهَ

Say: "If ye love Allah, follow me: so Allah shall love you, and forgive you your sins. For Allah is Oft-Forgiving, Most Merciful."

39 - 72:22 Al-Jinn

أَحَدٌ وَلَنْ أَجِدَ مِن دُونِهِ مُلْتَحَدًا ۞ قُلْ إِنِّي لَن يُجِيرَنِي مِنَ اللَّهِ

Say: "None can protect me from Allah, nor can I find refuge beside Him."

40 - 22:67 Al-Hajj

هُمْ نَاسِكُوهُ ۖ فَلَا يُنَازِعُنَّكَ فِي الْأَمْرِ ۚ وَادْعُ إِلَىٰ رَبِّكَ ۖ إِنَّكَ لَعَلَىٰ هُدًى مُّسْتَقِيمٍ لِّكُلِّ أُمَّةٍ جَعَلْنَا مَنسَكًا

For every nation We have ordained religious rites which they must observe. So let them not dispute with thee concerning the matter; but do thou invite them to thy Lord. Verily, thou art indeed upon straight guidance.

For every nation We have ordained religious ceremonies which they must follow—

– e.g., the sacrifice of cattle during the days of Mina (Makkah) during Hajj;

– so let not the disbelievers dispute with thee concerning this matter (e.g., what is lawful to eat);

– but invite them to thy Lord;

– verily, thou, O Muhammad ﷺ, art upon the true and straight path (i.e., Islamic Monotheism).

41 — 50:16 (Qaf)

وَلَقَدْ خَلَقْنَا الْإِنسَانَ وَنَعْلَمُ مَا تُوَسْوِسُ بِهِ نَفْسُهُ ۖ وَنَحْنُ أَقْرَبُ إِلَيْهِ مِنْ حَبْلِ الْوَرِيدِ

And verily, We have created man, and We know what his soul whispers to him. And We are nearer to him than his jugular vein.

42 — 40:18 (Al-Mu'min)

وَأَنذِرْهُمْ يَوْمَ الْآزِفَةِ إِذِ الْقُلُوبُ لَدَى الْحَنَاجِرِ كَاظِمِينَ ۚ مَا لِلظَّالِمِينَ مِنْ حَمِيمٍ وَلَا شَفِيعٍ يُطَاعُ

And warn them of the Day that draweth nigh, when hearts shall rise up to the throats, choked with anguish. The wrongdoers shall have neither a friend nor an intercessor who shall be heard.

43 — 39:53 (Az-Zumar)

قُلْ يَا عِبَادِيَ الَّذِينَ أَسْرَفُوا عَلَىٰ أَنفُسِهِمْ لَا تَقْنَطُوا مِن رَّحْمَةِ اللَّهِ ۚ إِنَّ اللَّهَ يَغْفِرُ الذُّنُوبَ جَمِيعًا ۚ إِنَّهُ هُوَ الْغَفُورُ الرَّحِيمُ

Say: O My servants who have transgressed against their own souls, despair not of the mercy of Allah. Verily, Allah forgiveth all sins: for He is Oft-Forgiving, Most Merciful.

44 — 24:35 (An-Nur)

اللَّهُ نُورُ السَّمَاوَاتِ وَالْأَرْضِ ۚ مَثَلُ نُورِهِ كَمِشْكَاةٍ فِيهَا مِصْبَاحٌ ۖ الْمِصْبَاحُ فِي زُجَاجَةٍ ۖ الزُّجَاجَةُ كَأَنَّهَا كَوْكَبٌ دُرِّيٌّ يُوقَدُ مِن شَجَرَةٍ مُّبَارَكَةٍ زَيْتُونَةٍ لَّا شَرْقِيَّةٍ وَلَا غَرْبِيَّةٍ يَكَادُ زَيْتُهَا يُضِيءُ وَلَوْ لَمْ تَمْسَسْهُ نَارٌ ۚ نُّورٌ عَلَىٰ نُورٍ ۗ يَهْدِي اللَّهُ لِنُورِهِ مَن يَشَاءُ ۚ وَيَضْرِبُ اللَّهُ الْأَمْثَالَ لِلنَّاسِ ۗ وَاللَّهُ بِكُلِّ شَيْءٍ عَلِيمٌ

Allah is the Light of the heavens and the earth. The parable of His Light is as a niche wherein is a lamp: the lamp is in a glass, the glass as it were a brilliant star, lit from a blessed tree—an olive—neither of the east nor of the west, whose oil would well-nigh shine, even though no fire touched it. Light upon Light! Allah guideth whom He will to His Light. And Allah setteth forth parables for mankind: and Allah is All-Knowing of everything.

45 — 35:5 (Fatir)

يَا أَيُّهَا النَّاسُ إِنَّ وَعْدَ اللَّهِ حَقٌّ ۖ فَلَا تَغُرَّنَّكُمُ الْحَيَاةُ الدُّنْيَا ۖ وَلَا يَغُرَّنَّكُم بِاللَّهِ الْغَرُورُ

O mankind! Verily, the promise of Allah is true. So let not the life of this world deceive you, nor let the deceiver deceive you concerning Allah.

46 — 39:8 (Az-Zumar)

وَإِذَا مَسَّ الْإِنسَانَ ضُرٌّ دَعَا رَبَّهُ مُنِيبًا إِلَيْهِ ثُمَّ إِذَا خَوَّلَهُ نِعْمَةً مِّنْهُ نَسِيَ مَا كَانَ يَدْعُو إِلَيْهِ مِن قَبْلُ وَجَعَلَ لِلَّهِ أَندَادًا لِّيُضِلَّ عَن سَبِيلِهِ ۚ قُلْ تَمَتَّعْ بِكُفْرِكَ قَلِيلًا ۖ إِنَّكَ مِنْ أَصْحَابِ النَّارِ

When harm toucheth a man, he calleth upon his Lord, turning unto Him; but when He bestoweth a favour upon him from Himself, he forgetteth that for which he called unto Him before, and setteth up rivals unto Allah, to mislead others from His way. Say: *Enjoy thy disbelief a little: verily, thou art of the companions of the Fire.*

47 — 39:33 (Az-Zumar)

وَالَّذِي جَاءَ بِالصِّدْقِ وَصَدَّقَ بِهِ أُولَٰئِكَ هُمُ الْمُتَّقُونَ

And he that bringeth the truth and believeth therein, they are the righteous (Al-Muttaqun).

48 — 47:1 (Muhammad)

...الَّذِينَ كَفَرُوا وَصَدُّوا عَن سَبِيلِ اللَّهِ

Those who disbelieve and turn others from the way of Allah—He maketh their deeds vain.

49 — 3:134 (Āl-'Imrān)

الَّذِينَ يُنفِقُونَ فِي السَّرَّاءِ وَالضَّرَّاءِ وَالْكَاظِمِينَ الْغَيْظَ وَالْعَافِينَ عَنِ النَّاسِ وَاللَّهُ يُحِبُّ الْمُحْسِنِينَ

Those who spend (in charity) in prosperity and adversity, who restrain anger, and pardon men—verily Allah loveth the good-doers.

50 — 30:36 (Ar-Rum)

وَإِذَا أَذَقْنَا النَّاسَ رَحْمَةً فَرِحُوا بِهَا وَإِن تُصِبْهُمْ سَيِّئَةٌ بِمَا قَدَّمَتْ أَيْدِيهِمْ إِذَا هُمْ يَقْنَطُونَ

When We cause mankind to taste mercy, they rejoice therein, but when evil afflicteth them because of what their own hands have sent forth, lo! they fall into despair.

51 — 3:135–136 (Āl-'Imrān)

وَالَّذِينَ إِذَا فَعَلُوا فَاحِشَةً أَوْ ظَلَمُوا أَنفُسَهُمْ ذَكَرُوا اللَّهَ فَاسْتَغْفَرُوا لِذُنُوبِهِمْ وَمَن يَغْفِرُ الذُّنُوبَ إِلَّا اللَّهُ وَلَمْ يُصِرُّوا عَلَىٰ مَا فَعَلُوا وَهُمْ يَعْلَمُونَ

أُولَٰئِكَ جَزَاؤُهُم مَّغْفِرَةٌ مِّن رَّبِّهِمْ وَجَنَّاتٌ تَجْرِي مِن تَحْتِهَا الْأَنْهَارُ خَالِدِينَ فِيهَا وَنِعْمَ أَجْرُ الْعَامِلِينَ

Those who, when they have committed a shameful deed or wronged their own souls, remember Allah and seek forgiveness for their sins—and who can forgive sins but Allah?—and do not persist in what they did, knowingly.

*136. For such, the*Their reward is forgiveness from their Lord, and gardens beneath which rivers flow, wherein they shall dwell forever. What a blessed reward for those who labour righteousness.

52 — 2:123 (Al-Baqarah)

وَاتَّقُوا يَوْمًا لَّا تَجْزِي نَفْسٌ عَن نَّفْسٍ شَيْئًا وَلَا يُقْبَلُ مِنْهَا عَدْلٌ وَلَا تَنفَعُهَا شَفَاعَةٌ وَلَا هُمْ يُنصَرُونَ

And fear the Day when no soul shall avail another, nor shall compensation be accepted from it, nor shall intercession profit it, nor shall they be helped.

53 — 72:18 (Al-Jinn)

وَأَنَّ الْمَسَاجِدَ لِلَّهِ فَلَا تَدْعُوا مَعَ اللَّهِ أَحَدًا

And verily, the mosques are for Allah alone, so call not upon anyone along with Allah.

54 — 50:17 (Qaf)

إِذْ يَتَلَقَّى الْمُتَلَقِّيَانِ عَنِ الْيَمِينِ وَعَنِ الشِّمَالِ قَعِيدٌ

When the two receivers (angels), sitting one on the right and one on the left, receive (every word and deed).

55 — 65:6 (At-Talaq)

سْكِنُوهُنَّ مِنْ حَيْثُ سَكَنتُم مِّن وُجْدِكُمْ وَلَا تُضَارُّوهُنَّ لِتُضَيِّقُوا عَلَيْهِنَّ ۚ وَإِن كُنَّ أُولَاتِ حَمْلٍ فَأَنفِقُوا عَلَيْهِنَّ حَتَّىٰ يَضَعْنَ حَمْلَهُنَّ ۚ فَإِنْ أَرْضَعْنَ لَكُمْ فَآتُوهُنَّ أُجُورَهُنَّ ۖ وَأْتَمِرُوا بَيْنَكُم بِمَعْرُوفٍ ۖ وَإِن تَعَاسَرْتُمْ فَسَتُرْضِعُ لَهُ أُخْرَىٰ

Lodge them (divorced women) where you dwell, according to your means, and do not harm them so as to distress them. And if they are pregnant, spend on them until they give birth. And if they suckle the child for you, give them their due payment, and consult with each other in kindness. But if you make difficulties for one another, then let another woman suckle the child.

56 — 64:11 (At-Taghabun)

مَا أَصَابَ مِن مُّصِيبَةٍ إِلَّا بِإِذْنِ اللَّهِ ۗ وَمَن يُؤْمِن بِاللَّهِ يَهْدِ قَلْبَهُ ۚ وَاللَّهُ بِكُلِّ شَيْءٍ عَلِيمٌ

No calamity befalleth but by the leave of Allah, and whosoever believeth in Allah, He guideth his heart. And Allah is Knower of all things.

57 — 29:69 (Al-'Ankabut)

وَالَّذِينَ جَاهَدُوا فِينَا لَنَهْدِيَنَّهُمْ سُبُلَنَا ۚ وَإِنَّ اللَّهَ لَمَعَ الْمُحْسِنِينَ

And as for those who strive in Our cause—verily, We shall surely guide them to Our paths; and lo! Allah is with the doers of good.

58 - 23:62 – Al-Mu'minun

وَلَا نُكَلِّفُ نَفْسًا إِلَّا وُسْعَهَا ۖ وَلَدَيْنَا كِتَابٌ يَنطِقُ بِالْحَقِّ ۚ وَهُمْ لَا يُظْلَمُونَ

And We tax not any person except according to his capacity. And with Us is a Record which speaketh the truth, and they shall not be wronged.

59 - 60:6 – Al-Mumtahina

لَقَدْ كَانَ لَكُمْ فِيهِمْ أُسْوَةٌ حَسَنَةٌ لِّمَن كَانَ يَرْجُو اللَّهَ وَالْيَوْمَ الْآخِرَ ۚ وَمَن يَتَوَلَّ فَإِنَّ اللَّهَ هُوَ الْغَنِيُّ الْحَمِيدُ

Certainly, there has been in them an excellent example for you to follow—for those who hope in Allah and the Last Day. And whosoever turneth away, then verily Allah is Self-Sufficient, Worthy of all Praise.

60 - 8:38 – Al-Anfal

قُل لِّلَّذِينَ كَفَرُوا إِن يَنتَهُوا يُغْفَرْ لَهُم مَّا قَدْ سَلَفَ وَإِن يَعُودُوا فَقَدْ مَضَتْ سُنَّتُ الْأَوَّلِينَ

Say to those who disbelieve: If they desist, their past shall be forgiven. But if they return, then the example of those before them hath already passed.

61 - 48:17 – Al-Fath

وَمَن يُطِعِ اللَّهَ لَّيْسَ عَلَى الْأَعْمَىٰ حَرَجٌ وَلَا عَلَى الْأَعْرَجِ حَرَجٌ وَلَا عَلَى الْمَرِيضِ حَرَجٌ وَرَسُولَهُ يُدْخِلْهُ جَنَّاتٍ تَجْرِي مِن تَحْتِهَا الْأَنْهَارُ ۖ وَمَن يَتَوَلَّ يُعَذِّبْهُ عَذَابًا أَلِيمًا

There is no blame on the blind, nor on the lame, nor on the sick. But whosoever obeyeth Allah and His Messenger, He will cause him to enter Gardens beneath which rivers flow. But whosoever turneth away, He will punish him with a painful punishment.

62 - 9:36 – At-Tawbah

إِنَّ عِدَّةَ الشُّهُورِ عِندَ اللَّهِ اثْنَا عَشَرَ شَهْرًا فِي كِتَابِ اللَّهِ يَوْمَ خَلَقَ السَّمَاوَاتِ وَالْأَرْضَ مِنْهَا أَرْبَعَةٌ حُرُمٌ ۚ ذَٰلِكَ الدِّينُ الْقَيِّمُ ۚ فَلَا تَظْلِمُوا فِيهِنَّ أَنفُسَكُمْ ۚ وَقَاتِلُوا الْمُشْرِكِينَ كَافَّةً كَمَا يُقَاتِلُونَكُمْ كَافَّةً ۚ وَاعْلَمُوا أَنَّ اللَّهَ مَعَ الْمُتَّقِينَ

. Verily, the number of months with Allah is twelve, as written in the Book of Allah the day He created the heavens and the earth. Of them, four are Sacred. That is the right religion, so wrong not yourselves therein, and fight against the polytheists collectively, as they fight against you collectively. And know that Allah is with the righteous.

63 - 29:45 – Al-'Ankabut

اتْلُ مَا أُوحِيَ إِلَيْكَ مِنَ الْكِتَابِ وَأَقِمِ الصَّلَاةَ إِنَّ الصَّلَاةَ تَنْهَى عَنِ الْفَحْشَاءِ وَالْمُنكَرِ وَلَذِكْرُ اللَّهِ أَكْبَرُ وَاللَّهُ يَعْلَمُ مَا تَصْنَعُونَ

Recite that which hath been revealed unto thee of the Book, and establish prayer. Verily, prayer restraineth from lewdness and iniquity, and the remembrance of Allah is greater. And Allah knoweth what ye do.

64 - 2:155 – Al-Baqarah

وَلَنَبْلُوَنَّكُم بِشَيْءٍ مِّنَ الْخَوْفِ وَالْجُوعِ وَنَقْصٍ مِنَ الْأَمْوَالِ وَالْأَنفُسِ وَالثَّمَرَاتِ وَبَشِّرِ الصَّابِرِينَ

And surely, We will test you with something of fear, and hunger, and loss of wealth, lives and fruits—but give glad tidings unto the patient.

65 - 22:8 – Al-Hajj

وَمِنَ النَّاسِ مَن يُجَادِلُ فِي اللَّهِ بِغَيْرِ عِلْمٍ وَلَا هُدًى وَلَا كِتَابٍ مُّنِيرٍ

And of mankind is he who disputeth concerning Allah without knowledge or guidance or a Book that giveth light.

66 - 7:158 – Al-A'raf

قُلْ يَا أَيُّهَا النَّاسُ إِنِّي رَسُولُ اللَّهِ إِلَيْكُمْ جَمِيعًا الَّذِي لَهُ مُلْكُ السَّمَاوَاتِ وَالْأَرْضِ لَا إِلَهَ إِلَّا هُوَ يُحْيِي وَيُمِيتُ فَآمِنُوا بِاللَّهِ وَرَسُولِهِ النَّبِيِّ الْأُمِّيِّ الَّذِي يُؤْمِنُ بِاللَّهِ وَكَلِمَاتِهِ وَاتَّبِعُوهُ لَعَلَّكُمْ تَهْتَدُونَ

Say: O mankind, verily I am the Messenger of Allah unto you all—He unto Whom belongeth the dominion of the heavens and the earth. There is no god but He. He giveth life and causeth death. So believe in Allah and His Messenger, the unlettered Prophet, who believeth in Allah and His Words, and follow him that ye may be guided.

67 - 2:207 – Al-Baqarah

وَمِنَ النَّاسِ مَن يَشْرِي نَفْسَهُ ابْتِغَاءَ مَرْضَاتِ اللَّهِ وَاللَّهُ رَؤُوفٌ بِالْعِبَادِ

And of mankind is he who selleth himself, seeking the pleasure of Allah. And Allah is full of kindness to His servants.

68 - 8:28 – Al-Anfal

وَاعْلَمُوا أَنَّمَا أَمْوَالُكُمْ وَأَوْلَادُكُمْ فِتْنَةٌ وَأَنَّ اللَّهَ عِنْدَهُ أَجْرٌ عَظِيمٌ

And know that your wealth and your children are but a trial, and that with Allah is a mighty reward.

69 - 18:46 – Al-Kahf

الْمَالُ وَالْبَنُونَ زِينَةُ الْحَيَاةِ الدُّنْيَا وَالْبَاقِيَاتُ الصَّالِحَاتُ خَيْرٌ عِنْدَ رَبِّكَ ثَوَابًا وَخَيْرٌ أَمَلًا

Wealth and children are the adornment of the life of this world, but the good deeds that endure are better in the sight of thy Lord for reward and better for hope.

70 - 2:219 – Al-Baqarah

يَسْأَلُونَكَ عَنِ الْخَمْرِ وَالْمَيْسِرِ قُلْ فِيهِمَا إِثْمٌ كَبِيرٌ وَمَنَافِعُ لِلنَّاسِ وَإِثْمُهُمَا أَكْبَرُ مِن نَّفْعِهِمَا وَيَسْأَلُونَكَ مَاذَا يُنْفِقُونَ قُلِ الْعَفْوَ كَذَٰلِكَ يُبَيِّنُ اللَّهُ لَكُمُ الْآيَاتِ لَعَلَّكُمْ تَتَفَكَّرُونَ

They ask thee concerning wine and gambling. Say: In them is great sin and some benefit for men, but the sin is greater than the benefit. And they ask thee what they should spend. Say: That which is beyond your needs. Thus doth Allah make His signs clear to you, that ye may reflect.

71 - 6:59–61 – Al-An'am

وَعِنْدَهُ مَفَاتِحُ الْغَيْبِ لَا يَعْلَمُهَا إِلَّا هُوَ وَيَعْلَمُ مَا فِي الْبَرِّ وَالْبَحْرِ وَمَا تَسْقُطُ مِن وَرَقَةٍ إِلَّا يَعْلَمُهَا وَلَا حَبَّةٍ فِي ظُلُمَاتِ الْأَرْضِ وَلَا رَطْبٍ وَلَا يَابِسٍ إِلَّا فِي كِتَابٍ مُبِينٍ

وَهُوَ الَّذِي يَتَوَفَّاكُم بِاللَّيْلِ وَيَعْلَمُ مَا جَرَحْتُم بِالنَّهَارِ ثُمَّ يَبْعَثُكُمْ فِيهِ لِيُقْضَىٰ أَجَلٌ مُسَمًّى ثُمَّ إِلَيْهِ مَرْجِعُكُمْ ثُمَّ يُنَبِّئُكُم بِمَا كُنتُمْ تَعْمَلُونَ

وَهُوَ الْقَاهِرُ فَوْقَ عِبَادِهِ وَيُرْسِلُ عَلَيْكُمْ حَفَظَةً حَتَّىٰ إِذَا جَاءَ أَحَدَكُمُ الْمَوْتُ تَوَفَّتْهُ رُسُلُنَا وَهُمْ لَا يُفَرِّطُونَ

59. And with Him are the keys of the unseen; none knoweth them but He. He knoweth what is in the land and the sea. Not a leaf falleth but He knoweth it, nor a grain in the darkness of the earth, nor anything fresh or dry, but it is in a clear Book.

60. It is He who taketh your souls by night and knoweth what ye have done by day. Then He raiseth you up therein, that a term appointed may be fulfilled. Then unto Him is your return, and He will inform you of what ye used to do.

61. He is the Irresistible over His slaves. And He sendeth over you guardian angels, until, when death cometh to one of you, Our messengers take him, and they fail not.

72 — 16:61 An-Nahl

وَلَوْ يُؤَاخِذُ اللَّهُ النَّاسَ بِظُلْمِهِم مَّا تَرَكَ عَلَيْهَا مِن دَابَّةٍ وَلَكِن يُؤَخِّرُهُمْ إِلَىٰ أَجَلٍ مُّسَمًّى ۖ فَإِذَا جَاءَ أَجَلُهُمْ لَا يَسْتَأْخِرُونَ سَاعَةً ۖ وَلَا يَسْتَقْدِمُونَ

And if Allah were to seize mankind for their wrongdoing, He would not leave on the earth a single living creature. But He postpones them for an appointed term, and when their term comes, they can neither delay it nor advance it by an hour (or even a moment).

73 — 40:58 Al-Mu'min

وَمَا يَسْتَوِي الْأَعْمَىٰ وَالْبَصِيرُ وَالَّذِينَ آمَنُوا وَعَمِلُوا الصَّالِحَاتِ وَلَا الْمُسِيءُ ۚ قَلِيلًا مَّا تَتَذَكَّرُونَ

The blind and the one who sees are not equal, nor are those who believe and do righteous deeds and those who do evil. Little do you remember!

74 — 3:120 Al Imran

إِن تَمْسَسْكُمْ حَسَنَةٌ تَسُؤْهُمْ وَإِن تُصِبْكُمْ سَيِّئَةٌ يَفْرَحُوا بِهَا ۖ وَإِن تَصْبِرُوا وَتَتَّقُوا لَا يَضُرُّكُمْ كَيْدُهُمْ شَيْئًا ۗ إِنَّ اللَّهَ بِمَا يَعْمَلُونَ مُحِيطٌ

If a good befalls you, it grieves them; but if evil overtakes you, they rejoice in it. But if you are patient and fear Allah, their plotting will not harm you in the least. Surely, Allah encompasses all that they do.

75 — 21:1 Al-Anbiyaa

اقْتَرَبَ لِلنَّاسِ حِسَابُهُمْ وَهُمْ فِي غَفْلَةٍ مُّعْرِضُونَ

The time of their reckoning has drawn near for mankind, yet they turn away in heedlessness.

76 — 2:112 Al-Baqara

بَلَىٰ مَنْ أَسْلَمَ وَجْهَهُ لِلَّهِ وَهُوَ مُحْسِنٌ فَلَهُ أَجْرُهُ عِندَ رَبِّهِ وَلَا خَوْفٌ عَلَيْهِمْ وَلَا هُمْ يَحْزَنُونَ

Indeed, whoever submits himself to Allah and is a doer of good, his reward is with his Lord; on them shall be no fear, nor shall they grieve. [See Tafsir Ibn Kathir, Vol. 1, Page 154.]

77 — 30:45 Ar-Rum

لِيَجْزِيَ الَّذِينَ آمَنُوا وَعَمِلُوا الصَّالِحَاتِ مِن فَضْلِهِ ۚ إِنَّهُ لَا يُحِبُّ الْكَافِرِينَ

That He may reward those who believe and do righteous good deeds, out of His bounty. Indeed, He does not love the disbelievers.

78 — 31:8 Luqman

إِنَّ الَّذِينَ آمَنُوا وَعَمِلُوا الصَّالِحَاتِ لَهُمْ جَنَّاتُ النَّعِيمِ

Indeed, those who believe and do righteous good deeds will have Gardens of Delight (Paradise).

79 — 16:97 An-Nahl

مَنْ عَمِلَ صَالِحًا مِّن ذَكَرٍ أَوْ أُنثَىٰ وَهُوَ مُؤْمِنٌ فَلَنُحْيِيَنَّهُ حَيَاةً طَيِّبَةً ۖ وَلَنَجْزِيَنَّهُمْ أَجْرَهُم بِأَحْسَنِ مَا كَانُوا يَعْمَلُونَ

Whoever does righteous deeds, male or female, while being a believer, We shall give them a good life, and We shall certainly reward them according to the best of what they used to do.

80 — 20:112 Ta-Ha

وَمَن يَعْمَلْ مِنَ الصَّالِحَاتِ وَهُوَ مُؤْمِنٌ فَلَا يَخَافُ ظُلْمًا وَلَا هَضْمًا

And whoever does righteous deeds, while he is a believer, will have no fear of injustice or curtailment (of his reward).

81 — 40:40 Al-Mu'min

مَنْ عَمِلَ سَيِّئَةً فَلَا يُجْزَىٰ إِلَّا مِثْلَهَا ۖ وَمَنْ عَمِلَ صَالِحًا مِّن ذَكَرٍ أَوْ أُنثَىٰ وَهُوَ مُؤْمِنٌ فَأُولَٰئِكَ يَدْخُلُونَ الْجَنَّةَ يُرْزَقُونَ فِيهَا بِغَيْرِ حِسَابٍ

Whoever does an evil deed will be requited only with the like thereof, but whoever does righteous deeds, whether male or female, and is a believer, they shall enter Paradise and be provided therein without reckoning.

82 — 30:30 Ar-Rum

فَأَقِمْ وَجْهَكَ لِلدِّينِ حَنِيفًا ۚ فِطْرَتَ اللَّهِ الَّتِي فَطَرَ النَّاسَ عَلَيْهَا ۚ لَا تَبْدِيلَ لِخَلْقِ اللَّهِ ۚ ذَٰلِكَ الدِّينُ الْقَيِّمُ وَلَٰكِنَّ أَكْثَرَ النَّاسِ لَا يَعْلَمُونَ

So set your face towards the religion uprightly — the nature (framed) by Allah in which He has created mankind. There is no changing the creation of Allah. That is the true religion, but most of mankind do not know.

83 — 39:10 Az-Zumar

قُلْ يَا عِبَادِ الَّذِينَ آمَنُوا اتَّقُوا رَبَّكُمْ ۚ لِلَّذِينَ أَحْسَنُوا فِي هَٰذِهِ الدُّنْيَا حَسَنَةٌ ۗ وَأَرْضُ اللَّهِ وَاسِعَةٌ ۗ إِنَّمَا يُوَفَّى الصَّابِرُونَ أَجْرَهُم بِغَيْرِ حِسَابٍ

Say, "O My servants who believe, fear your Lord. For those who do good in this world is good, and the earth of Allah is spacious. Verily, the patient will be given their reward without reckoning."

84 — 29:58 Al-Ankabut

وَالَّذِينَ آمَنُوا وَعَمِلُوا الصَّالِحَاتِ لَنُبَوِّئَنَّهُم مِّنَ الْجَنَّةِ غُرَفًا تَجْرِي مِن تَحْتِهَا الْأَنْهَارُ خَالِدِينَ فِيهَا ۚ نِعْمَ أَجْرُ الْعَامِلِينَ

And those who believe and do righteous deeds — We shall surely give them lofty dwellings in Paradise beneath which rivers flow, to abide therein forever. Excellent is the reward of the workers.

85 — 40:7 Al-Mu'min

الَّذِينَ يَحْمِلُونَ الْعَرْشَ وَمَنْ حَوْلَهُ يُسَبِّحُونَ بِحَمْدِ رَبِّهِمْ وَيُؤْمِنُونَ بِهِ وَيَسْتَغْفِرُونَ لِلَّذِينَ آمَنُوا رَبَّنَا وَسِعْتَ كُلَّ شَيْءٍ رَّحْمَةً وَعِلْمًا فَاغْفِرْ لِلَّذِينَ تَابُوا وَاتَّبَعُوا سَبِيلَكَ وَقِهِمْ عَذَابَ الْجَحِيمِ

Those (angels) who bear the Throne (of Allah) and those around it glorify the praises of their Lord, believe in Him, and ask forgiveness for those who believe, saying: "Our Lord, You encompass all things in mercy and knowledge, so forgive those who repent and follow Your way, and save them from the torment of the blazing Fire."

86 - 74:31 – Al-Muddaththir

وَمَا جَعَلْنَا أَصْحَابَ النَّارِ إِلَّا مَلَائِكَةً ۚ وَمَا جَعَلْنَا عِدَّتَهُمْ إِلَّا فِتْنَةً لِّلَّذِينَ كَفَرُوا لِيَسْتَيْقِنَ الَّذِينَ أُوتُوا الْكِتَابَ وَيَزْدَادَ الَّذِينَ آمَنُوا إِيمَانًا ۙ وَلَا يَرْتَابَ الَّذِينَ أُوتُوا الْكِتَابَ وَالْمُؤْمِنُونَ ۙ وَلِيَقُولَ

الَّذِينَ فِي قُلُوبِهِم مَّرَضٌ وَالْكَافِرُونَ مَاذَا أَرَادَ اللَّهُ بِهَٰذَا مَثَلًا ۚ كَذَٰلِكَ يُضِلُّ اللَّهُ مَن يَشَاءُ وَيَهْدِي مَن يَشَاءُ ۚ وَمَا يَعْلَمُ جُنُودَ رَبِّكَ إِلَّا هُوَ ۚ وَمَا هِيَ إِلَّا ذِكْرَىٰ لِلْبَشَرِ

And We have set none but angels as guardians of the Fire, and We have fixed their number (nineteen) only as a trial for the disbelievers; that the People of the Book may be certain, and the believers may increase in faith, and that no doubt may be left for the People of the Book and the believers; and that those in whose hearts is a disease and the disbelievers may say, "What meaneth God by this parable?" Thus doth God mislead whom He will, and guide whom He will. And none knoweth the hosts of thy Lord but He. And this is nothing else than a reminder unto mankind.

87 - 4:47 – An-Nisa

يَا أَيُّهَا الَّذِينَ أُوتُوا الْكِتَابَ آمِنُوا بِمَا نَزَّلْنَا مُصَدِّقًا لِّمَا مَعَكُم مِّن قَبْلِ أَن نَّطْمِسَ وُجُوهًا فَنَرُدَّهَا عَلَىٰ أَدْبَارِهَا أَوْ نَلْعَنَهُمْ كَمَا لَعَنَّا أَصْحَابَ السَّبْتِ ۚ وَكَانَ أَمْرُ اللَّهِ مَفْعُولًا

O ye who have been given the Scripture, believe in what We have revealed, confirming that which is with you, before We disfigure faces and turn them backward, or curse them as We cursed the Sabbath-breakers. And the commandment of God is ever fulfilled.

88 - 7:179 – Al-A'raf

وَلَقَدْ ذَرَأْنَا لِجَهَنَّمَ كَثِيرًا مِّنَ الْجِنِّ وَالْإِنسِ ۖ لَهُمْ قُلُوبٌ لَّا يَفْقَهُونَ بِهَا وَلَهُمْ أَعْيُنٌ لَّا يُبْصِرُونَ بِهَا وَلَهُمْ آذَانٌ لَّا يَسْمَعُونَ بِهَا ۚ أُولَٰئِكَ كَالْأَنْعَامِ بَلْ هُمْ أَضَلُّ ۚ أُولَٰئِكَ هُمُ الْغَافِلُونَ

And verily, We have created many of the jinn and mankind for Hell. They have hearts wherewith they understand not, eyes wherewith they see not, and ears wherewith they hear not. They are like cattle—nay, more astray. They are the heedless ones.[173]

89 - 40:59 – Al-Mu'min

إِنَّ السَّاعَةَ لَآتِيَةٌ لَّا رَيْبَ فِيهَا وَلَٰكِنَّ أَكْثَرَ النَّاسِ لَا يُؤْمِنُونَ

Verily, the Hour is surely coming—there is no doubt therein—yet most men believe not.

---

[173] Cf. ii. 18. Though they have apparently all the faculties of reason and perception, they have so deadened them that those faculties do not work, and they go headlong into hell. They are, as it were, made for Hell.   Yusuf Ali Translation Note Number : 1153

90 - 21:35 – Al-Anbiyaa

كُلُّ نَفْسٍ ذَائِقَةُ الْمَوْتِ ۗ وَنَبْلُوكُم بِالشَّرِّ وَالْخَيْرِ فِتْنَةً ۗ وَإِلَيْنَا تُرْجَعُونَ

Every soul shall taste of death. And We try you with evil and with good as a trial, and unto Us shall ye be returned.

91 - 29:57 – Al-Ankabut

كُلُّ نَفْسٍ ذَائِقَةُ الْمَوْتِ ۖ ثُمَّ إِلَيْنَا تُرْجَعُونَ

Every soul shall taste of death. Then unto Us shall ye be returned.

92 - 4:78 – An-Nisa

أَيْنَمَا تَكُونُوا يُدْرِككُّمُ الْمَوْتُ وَلَوْ كُنتُمْ فِي بُرُوجٍ مُّشَيَّدَةٍ ۗ وَإِن تُصِبْهُمْ حَسَنَةٌ يَقُولُوا هَٰذِهِ مِنْ عِندِ اللَّهِ ۖ وَإِن تُصِبْهُمْ سَيِّئَةٌ يَقُولُوا هَٰذِهِ مِنْ عِندِكَ ۚ قُلْ كُلٌّ مِّنْ عِندِ اللَّهِ ۖ فَمَالِ هَٰؤُلَاءِ الْقَوْمِ لَا يَكَادُونَ يَفْقَهُونَ حَدِيثًا

Wheresoever ye may be, death will overtake you—even though ye be in towers built strong and high. If some good befalls them, they say, "This is from Allah," but if evil befalls them, they say, "This is from thee (O Muhammad)." Say: "All things are from Allah." What aileth these people that they fail to understand a word?

93 - 6:61 – Al-An'am

وَهُوَ الْقَاهِرُ فَوْقَ عِبَادِهِ ۖ وَيُرْسِلُ عَلَيْكُمْ حَفَظَةً حَتَّىٰ إِذَا جَاءَ أَحَدَكُمُ الْمَوْتُ تَوَفَّتْهُ رُسُلُنَا وَهُمْ لَا يُفَرِّطُونَ

He is the All-Subduer, above His servants, and He sendeth guardians over you until, when death cometh to one of you, Our messengers take his soul, and they neglect not their duty.

94 16:32 – An-Nahl

الَّذِينَ تَتَوَفَّاهُمُ الْمَلَائِكَةُ طَيِّبِينَ ۙ يَقُولُونَ سَلَامٌ عَلَيْكُمُ ادْخُلُوا الْجَنَّةَ بِمَا كُنتُمْ تَعْمَلُونَ

Those whom the angels take in a state of purity, saying unto them, "Peace be upon you; enter ye into Paradise for that which ye used to do." [174]

95 - 3:103 – Al-i 'Imran

وَاعْتَصِمُوا بِحَبْلِ اللَّهِ جَمِيعًا وَلَا تَفَرَّقُوا ۚ وَاذْكُرُوا نِعْمَتَ اللَّهِ عَلَيْكُمْ إِذْ كُنتُمْ أَعْدَاءً فَأَلَّفَ بَيْنَ قُلُوبِكُمْ فَأَصْبَحْتُم بِنِعْمَتِهِ إِخْوَانًا وَكُنتُمْ عَلَىٰ شَفَا حُفْرَةٍ مِّنَ النَّارِ فَأَنقَذَكُم مِّنْهَا ۗ كَذَٰلِكَ يُبَيِّنُ اللَّهُ لَكُمْ آيَاتِهِ لَعَلَّكُمْ تَهْتَدُونَ

And hold fast, all of you together, to the rope of Allah (i.e. this Qur'an), and be not divided among yourselves. And remember the favour of Allah upon you—for ye were enemies one to another, but He joined your hearts together, so that by His grace, ye became brethren. And ye were upon the brink of a pit of fire, and He delivered you therefrom. Thus doth Allah make clear His signs unto you, that ye may be guided.

Conclusion

In the realm of harmony, where celestial notes reside,

To maintain the key's grace, let wisdom be your guide.

For those who seek qualification to journey toward the divine,

Heed these verses; their instructions intertwine:

First, embrace humility—shed the ego's veil;

In modesty and selflessness, let your spirit prevail.

For harmony thrives in hearts that are humble,

A key to unlock heaven's gate—a treasure untroubled.

Next, cultivate compassion—let empathy bloom;

Extend kindness to all; dispel darkness and gloom.

For harmony resonates through acts of love and care,

A symphony of unity, a melody rare.

Then, foster understanding—let knowledge ignite;

Seek wisdom's light, dispel ignorance's blight.

For harmony flourishes in minds enlightened,

A harmony of thoughts, with melodies heightened.

---

[174] In a state of purity: from the evils of this world, from want of faith and want of grace. Purity from such evil is the mark of true Islam, and those who die in such purity will be received into Felicity with a salutation of Peace. (Yusuf Ali Translation Note Number : 2055)

Embrace forgiveness—release the weight of the past;

Let resentment dissolve; make peace steadfast.

For harmony finds solace in hearts free from strife,

A rhythm of forgiveness, notes interwoven with life.

Nurture gratitude—let thankfulness sing;

In every moment, let gratitude take wing.

For harmony dances with hearts that are grateful,

A harmonious key, a melody most delightful.

Finally, cherish unity—embrace diversity's delight;

For in togetherness, harmony shines bright.

Respect each soul's unique part in the symphony,

A symphony divine, a celestial cacophony.

So, dear traveller, with these instructions, hold them dear:

Qualifications to maintain the key—so crystal clear.

In harmony's embrace, your journey shall unfold,

A key that unlocks heaven's door—a story yet untold.

****

بِسْمِ ٱللَّهِ ٱلرَّحْمَـٰنِ ٱلرَّحِيمِ

Chapter 10

"O you who have believed, fear Allah. And let every soul look to what it has put forth for tomorrow — and fear Allah. Indeed, Allah is Acquainted with what you do."

Qur'an, 59:18

"The fear of the Lord is the beginning of knowledge: but fools despise wisdom and instruction."

Proverbs 1:7 (KJV)

📖📖📖📖📖📖

Fear Allah

قُلْنَا اهْبِطُوا مِنْهَا جَمِيعًا فَإِمَّا يَأْتِيَنَّكُم مِّنِّي هُدًى فَمَن تَبِعَ هُدَايَ فَلَا خَوْفٌ عَلَيْهِمْ وَلَا هُمْ يَحْزَنُونَ

We said: "Get down, all of you, from this place (the Paradise); then whenever there comes to you guidance from Me, whosoever follows My guidance, there shall be no fear upon them, nor shall they grieve."

Surah Al-Baqarah 2:38

Ever since Allah (SWT) sent Adam (AS) to inhabit the earth, a divine solution accompanied him from the Almighty for all his descendants. This verse stands as the ultimate assurance for humanity, promising deliverance from sorrow and hardship if they heed the instructions bestowed upon them.

Embracing the "Fear of Allah" involves adopting a principle that empowers us to confront obstacles, make righteous decisions, and embark on a journey of spiritual development. By living with intention, mindfulness, and a profound bond with our faith, we can pave the way for a more harmonious journey towards eternal fulfilment.

The expression **"Fear Allah"** acts as a potent cue for believers to actively seek forgiveness for their transgressions and commit to a journey of genuine repentance. It underscores the mercy of Allah and the opportunity to correct one's mistakes through sincere regret, seeking pardon, and taking tangible steps to set things right.

352

Embracing this mindset motivates individuals to embark on a path of spiritual evolution and self-improvement.

We do not need to make speeches about fearing Allah, as Allah (SWT) Himself tells us to fear Him and assures us that we will be rewarded for it. One should recite the following words of Allah while travelling and act accordingly:

1.

يَا أَيُّهَا الَّذِينَ آمَنُوا اتَّقُوا اللَّهَ حَقَّ تُقَاتِهِ وَلَا تَمُوتُنَّ إِلَّا وَأَنتُم مُّسْلِمُونَ

O you who believe! Fear Allah (by doing all that He has commanded and by abstaining from all that He has forbidden) as He should be feared. Obey Him, be thankful to Him, and remember Him always; and die not except in a state of Islam (as Muslims) with complete submission to Allah.

Surah Al-'Imran 3:102

2.

يَا أَيُّهَا الَّذِينَ آمَنُوا إِن تَتَّقُوا اللَّهَ يَجْعَل لَّكُمْ فُرْقَانًا وَيُكَفِّرْ عَنكُمْ سَيِّئَاتِكُمْ وَيَغْفِرْ لَكُمْ ۗ وَاللَّهُ ذُو الْفَضْلِ الْعَظِيمِ

O you who believe! If you obey and fear Allah, He will grant you Furqan—a criterion (to judge between right and wrong, or a way out of every difficulty), and He will expiate for you your sins, and forgive you. And Allah is the Owner of Great Bounty.

Surah Al-Anfal 8:29

3.

يَا أَيُّهَا الَّذِينَ آمَنُوا اتَّقُوا اللَّهَ وَكُونُوا مَعَ الصَّادِقِينَ

O you who believe! Fear Allah and be with those who are truthful (in word and deed).

Surah At-Tawbah 9:119

We have encountered three profound verses that awaken us to the realisation that the fear of Allah serves as the most enlightening beacon on our journey. While our previous chapter focused on obtaining the keys to the heavenly abode, it is crucial to comprehend that the order and success of our journey depend on our disciplined actions. Therefore, we must wholeheartedly prioritise understanding how to reach our destination safely.

A comprehensive understanding of the term "fear" within the context of the Qur'an can assist individuals in becoming true believers, aligning with Allah's intended purpose for us. Fear, as a natural and potent emotion, has been ingrained in the human psyche since ancient times. It serves as a primal instinct that alerts us to immediate dangers, which could lead to physical or emotional harm, or even death.

For instance, people experience fear when caught in the crossfire of warring factions, or when a boat faces a violent storm, endangering its passengers with the imminent threat of sinking. Similarly, if a pilot detects engine problems mid-flight, there arises a genuine concern for the safety of those on board. Despite the pilot's ardent efforts to land the plane securely, the passengers may succumb to restlessness and panic, feeling the presence of death looming near.

However, the fear of Allah stands in stark contrast to these experiences of being frightened, panicked, or scared, as they are linked to specific events and their consequential effects. In the case of fearing Allah (SWT), there is no discernible cause or visible effect like the aforementioned situations.

Allah SWT says:

فَإِذَا رَكِبُوا فِي الْفُلْكِ دَعَوُا اللَّهَ مُخْلِصِينَ لَهُ الدِّينَ فَلَمَّا نَجَّاهُمْ إِلَى الْبَرِّ إِذَا هُمْ يُشْرِكُونَ

And when they embark on a ship, they invoke Allah, making their faith pure for Him only, but when He brings them safely to land, behold, they give a share of their worship to others. (29:65 Surah Al-'Ankabut)

In the Bible, we can find psalms where God has revealed:

Happy is the man that feareth alway: but he that hardeneth his heart shall fall into mischief.

— Proverbs 28:14 (KJV)

And I will come near to you to judgment; and I will be a swift witness against the sorcerers, and against the adulterers, and against false swearers, and against those that oppress the hireling in his wages, the widow, and the fatherless, and that turn aside the stranger from his right, and fear not me, saith the Lord of hosts.

— Malachi 3:5 (KJV)

It signifies that Allah (SWT) has provided us with examples, conveyed through verses and messengers, to instil a sense of awe and reverence in the hearts of His creation. The responsibility now lies with us to integrate these teachings and admonitions into our lives.

The Qur'an repeatedly emphasises certain key factors that can guide us. Incorporating the principle of "Fear Allah" can assist us in navigating challenges, making ethical decisions, and striving for spiritual development. By embracing this principle, individuals are encouraged to live purposefully, mindfully, and with a profound connection to their faith. This, in turn, contributes to a more harmonious journey towards eternal salvation.

These are:

- **Taqwa (God-consciousness)**

- **Self-accountability on the Day of Judgement**

- **Divine Guidance, i.e., Fear Allah**

- **Seeking Forgiveness**

- **Upholding Morality and Ethics** — To uphold high moral standards, ethical conduct, and justice in dealings with others, encouraging kindness, compassion, honesty, and fairness, and promoting harmony and unity within society.

- **Avoiding Prohibited Actions** — The principle of "Fear Allah" urges individuals...

- **Developing a Strong Relationship with Allah (SWT)** — "Fear Allah" encourages believers to establish a deep and personal connection with Allah through regular prayer, supplication, and remembrance (inner self *dhikr*). This connection strengthens faith, provides solace, and serves as a source of guidance and support throughout life's journey.

Allah (SWT) has set another example for us to understand the issue of fear more clearly in this verse:

أَفَمَنْ أَسَّسَ بُنْيَانَهُ عَلَىٰ تَقْوَىٰ مِنَ اللَّهِ وَرِضْوَانٍ خَيْرٌ أَم مَّنْ أَسَّسَ بُنْيَانَهُ عَلَىٰ شَفَا جُرُفٍ هَارٍ فَانْهَارَ بِهِ فِي نَارِ جَهَنَّمَ ۗ وَاللَّهُ لَا يَهْدِي الْقَوْمَ الظَّالِمِينَ

Is it then he who laid the foundation of his building on piety to Allah and His good pleasure better, or he who laid the foundation of his building on the brink of a crumbling precipice so that it crumbled to pieces with him into the Fire of Hell? And Allah guides not the people who are the Zalimun (cruel, violent, proud, polytheist, and wrong-doer).

(9:109 Surah At-Tawbah)

During the COVID-19 pandemic, the global mortality rates instilled fear within all of us. It becomes even more distressing when our loved ones are affected. In such circumstances, individuals have the option to seek assistance — whether they choose to ask for help from Allah (SWT) or not. It is important to recognise that the fear we experience during these times is temporary and earthly in nature.

However, the fear of Allah transcends worldly concerns. It is distinct from the fear we feel in relation to mortal matters. The fear of Allah naturally grows within the hearts of those who are conscious of His commands and have faith. These individuals find strength within their hearts and truly understand the significance of fearing Allah. They attain a position of belief and righteousness.

For those who are genuinely committed to building confidence and discovering the path that leads to the ultimate destination, the following verses can provide guidance:

Allah SWT says to us in the Qur'an:

إِنَّ الَّذِينَ اتَّقَوْا إِذَا مَسَّهُمْ طَائِفٌ مِّنَ الشَّيْطَانِ تَذَكَّرُوا فَإِذَا هُم مُّبْصِرُونَ

Verily, those who are Al-Muttaqun (the pious – see V.2:2), when an evil thought comes to them from Shaitan (Satan), they remember (Allah), and (indeed) they then see (aright). — Surah Al-A'raf 7:201

In this context, one might ask, *"Who are the believers?"* The answer is provided by Allah SWT Himself as follows:

إِنَّمَا الْمُؤْمِنُونَ الَّذِينَ إِذَا ذُكِرَ اللَّهُ وَجِلَتْ قُلُوبُهُمْ وَإِذَا تُلِيَتْ عَلَيْهِمْ آيَاتُهُ زَادَتْهُمْ إِيمَانًا وَعَلَىٰ رَبِّهِمْ يَتَوَكَّلُونَ

Believers are those who, when Allah is mentioned, feel a tremor in their hearts; and when His signs are rehearsed to them, it increases them in faith; and they put their trust in their Lord alone. — Surah Al-Anfal 8:2

Reciting the Qur'an gains profound significance when we truly understand Allah's words. Genuine guidance and a deepened sense of reverence emerge only when we comprehend the verses during recitation. Therefore, it is essential to continually remind ourselves to prioritise understanding the Qur'an with full concentration and dedication. Only then can one understand why he must fear Allah.

In the following verses, Allah SWT says:

إِنَّمَا ذَٰلِكُمُ الشَّيْطَانُ يُخَوِّفُ أَوْلِيَاءَهُ فَلَا تَخَافُوهُمْ وَخَافُونِ إِن كُنتُم مُّؤْمِنِينَ

It is only Shaitan (Satan) that suggests to you the fear of his Auliya' [supporters and friends — polytheists, disbelievers in the Oneness of Allah and in His Messenger, Muhammad ﷺ]; so fear them not, but fear Me, if you are (true) believers. — Surah Al-Imran 3:175

Regarding love and fear of Allah, we need to free ourselves from fear of Satan. It is only Satan who intimidates and encourages us to follow his supporters and friends.

وَلَا يَحْزُنكَ الَّذِينَ يُسَارِعُونَ فِي الْكُفْرِ ۚ إِنَّهُمْ لَن يَضُرُّوا اللَّهَ شَيْئًا ۗ يُرِيدُ اللَّهُ أَلَّا يَجْعَلَ لَهُمْ حَظًّا فِي الْآخِرَةِ ۖ وَلَهُمْ عَذَابٌ عَظِيمٌ

And let not those grieve thee (O Muhammad ﷺ) who hasten to disbelief; verily, they shall not harm Allah in the least. It is Allah's Will to give them no portion in the Hereafter. For them is a great torment. — Surah Al-Imran 3:176

إِنَّ الَّذِينَ اشْتَرَوُا الْكُفْرَ بِالْإِيمَانِ لَن يَضُرُّوا اللَّهَ شَيْئًا وَلَهُمْ عَذَابٌ أَلِيمٌ

Verily, those who purchase disbelief at the price of faith will not harm Allah in the least. For them is a painful torment. — Surah Al-Imran 3:177

It can, however, be concluded with the following verses. Allah emphasises that to achieve success, we must engage in righteous actions and maintain a reverential fear of Him.

Surah Az-Zumar (39), Verses 10–14

قُلْ يَا عِبَادِ الَّذِينَ آمَنُوا اتَّقُوا رَبَّكُمْ ۚ لِلَّذِينَ أَحْسَنُوا فِي هَذِهِ الدُّنْيَا حَسَنَةٌ ۗ وَأَرْضُ اللَّهِ وَاسِعَةٌ ۗ
إِنَّمَا يُوَفَّى الصَّابِرُونَ أَجْرَهُم بِغَيْرِ حِسَابٍ
قُلْ إِنِّي أُمِرْتُ أَنْ أَعْبُدَ اللَّهَ مُخْلِصًا لَّهُ الدِّينَ
وَأُمِرْتُ لِأَنْ أَكُونَ أَوَّلَ الْمُسْلِمِينَ
قُلْ إِنِّي أَخَافُ إِنْ عَصَيْتُ رَبِّي عَذَابَ يَوْمٍ عَظِيمٍ
قُلِ اللَّهَ أَعْبُدُ مُخْلِصًا لَّهُ دِينِي

10. Say (O Muhammad ﷺ): "O My servants who believe, fear your Lord. For those who do good in this world, there is good, and Allah's earth is spacious. Verily, the patient will be given their reward without reckoning."

11. Say: "Verily, I am commanded to worship Allah, making the religion sincerely His."

12. "And I am commanded to be the first of those who submit."

13. Say: "Verily, if I disobey my Lord, I fear the punishment of a mighty Day."

14. Say: "It is Allah alone whom I worship, sincerely devoting my religion to Him."

Then, in verse 17 of Surah Muhammad (47), Allah assures us:

وَالَّذِينَ اهْتَدَوْا زَادَهُمْ هُدًى وَآتَاهُمْ تَقْوَاهُمْ

And those who are guided, He increases them in guidance and bestows on them their piety. — Surah Muhammad 47:17

This is **taqwa**, which helps to purify the heart and soul, and it is our great reward from Allah (SWT).

How Can I Overcome My Fear?

"Love is better than fear.

Fear restrains us from sinning,

and love compels us to do what is prescribed

with an open heart."

The above quote is taken from *at-Takhwif min an-Nar* by Ibn Rajab. However, note that some scholars hold that fear is better than love — and Allah SWT knows best.

May Allah grant us what we hope for and protect us from what we fear. And may the blessings of Allah be upon our Prophet Muhammad ﷺ, upon his family, his Companions, and upon all those who follow guidance until the Last Day.

Now, let us head out and do some exploring in the next zone.

بِسْمِ ٱللَّهِ ٱلرَّحْمَـٰنِ ٱلرَّحِيمِ

Chapter 11

"Ignorance is the curse of God;
Knowledge is the wing wherewith
We fly to heaven".
William Shakespeare

📖📖📖📖📖📖

Break The Ice

This chapter provides a concise overview of the various factors that will contribute to our sense of wellbeing on the journey. Now is the opportune moment to reflect, prompting introspection regarding our self-perception and addressing any prevalent yet crucial gaps in our understanding. By doing so, we equip ourselves with the attachments necessary to navigate the ongoing journey with empowerment and clarity.

This will afford us the chance to enhance our comprehension by incorporating aspects we have previously neglected or placed lower priority on, thereby bolstering our advancement through the forthcoming chapters.

The profound Qur'anic verses extracted from different sections of this book—alongside a few additional ones—elicit powerful responses from within, capturing the essence of the impure spirit and its repercussions. They also illuminate the path towards internal purity, external cleanliness, and spiritual enlightenment, guiding one towards a heightened state where closeness to Allah SWT is felt.

Many scholars consider the foundation of spiritual wayfaring (*sulūk*) to be mindfulness over one's own thoughts, as Ibn al-Qayyim mentioned:

Many of the masters of spiritual wayfaring based their journeying upon guarding their thoughts—that they would not enable a thought to enter their hearts until the hearts were ready and accepting for unveiling and the presence of higher realities within it.[175]

---

[175] Source: al-Dā' wal-Dawā' 1/158 https://www.abuaminaelias.com/understanding-the-soul-in-islam/

Let's Continue to Expand One's (Self) Thinking

The heart is that by which a human being comes to know himself. If he comes to know himself, he knows his Lord. It is also that by which a human being is ignorant of himself. If he is ignorant of himself, he is ignorant of his Lord.

Whoever does not know his heart—does not remain mindful of it, watch over it, or observe what shines upon it and through it of heavenly treasures—is among those about whom Allah Almighty said:

وَلَا تَكُونُوا كَالَّذِينَ نَسُوا اللَّهَ فَأَنسَاهُمْ أَنفُسَهُمْ ۚ أُولَـٰئِكَ هُمُ الْفَاسِقُونَ

And be not like those who forgot Allah (i.e. became disobedient to Allah), and He caused them to forget their own selves (i.e. let them forget to do righteous deeds). Those are the Fāsiqūn (rebellious, disobedient to Allah).

— Surah Al-Hashr 59:19

Thus, knowledge of the heart, its realities, and its qualities is the foundation of the religion and the basis of spiritual seeking.

Source: Iḥyā' 'Ulūm al-Dīn 3:2–3

Let us see what Allah SWT says about this matter:

قَدْ أَفْلَحَ مَن زَكَّاهَا

Indeed, he succeeds who purifies his own self (i.e. obeys and performs all that Allah ordered, by following the true faith of Islamic monotheism and by doing righteous good deeds).

— Surah Ash-Shams 91:9

And so, is this not the right time to raise the question: how much do we truly know ourselves?

Sahl ibn 'Abdullah—may Allah SWT have mercy on him—said:

If one knows himself, one knows his status with his Lord. If one knows his mind, one knows his state between him and his Lord.

— Source: Ḥilyat al-Awliyā' 10/201

Allah (SWT) also says:

إِذْ يُغَشِّيكُمُ النُّعَاسَ أَمَنَةً مِّنْهُ وَيُنَزِّلُ عَلَيْكُم مِّنَ السَّمَاءِ مَاءً لِّيُطَهِّرَكُم بِهِ وَيُذْهِبَ عَنكُمْ رِجْزَ الشَّيْطَانِ وَلِيَرْبِطَ عَلَىٰ قُلُوبِكُمْ وَيُثَبِّتَ بِهِ الْأَقْدَامَ

(Remember) when He covered you with a slumber as a security from Him, and He caused water (rain) to descend on you from the sky, to cleanse you thereby, and to remove from you the Rijz (whispering, evil suggestions, etc.) of Shayṭān (Satan), and to strengthen your hearts, and make your feet firm thereby.

— Surah Al-Anfāl 8:11

This journey is a continuous quest for truth and a guide to remain on the righteous path, which will lead us safely to face the court of divine judgement. The following verses should be regarded as key sources for careful study. They will surely help to enlighten our hearts.

Our highest priority must be the cleansing of our spiritual hearts, for none shall inherit the rewards of the Day of Judgement without bearing a heart free from impurity.

وَأَمَّا مَنْ خَافَ مَقَامَ رَبِّهِ وَنَهَى النَّفْسَ عَنِ الْهَوَىٰ

فَإِنَّ الْجَنَّةَ هِيَ الْمَأْوَىٰ

But as for him who feared standing before his Lord, and restrained himself from impure evil desires and lusts—verily, Paradise will be his abode.

— *Surah Al-Nāziʿāt 79:40–41*

يَوْمَ لَا يَنفَعُ مَالٌ وَلَا بَنُونَ

إِلَّا مَنْ أَتَى اللَّهَ بِقَلْبٍ سَلِيمٍ

The Day whereon neither wealth nor sons will avail,

Except him who brings to Allah a clean heart [clean from shirk (polytheism) and nifāq (hypocrisy)].

— *Surah Al-Shuʿarā 26:88–89*[176]

وَسَارِعُوا إِلَىٰ مَغْفِرَةٍ مِّن رَّبِّكُمْ وَجَنَّةٍ عَرْضُهَا السَّمَاوَاتُ وَالْأَرْضُ أُعِدَّتْ لِلْمُتَّقِينَ

And march forth in the way which leads to forgiveness from your Lord, and for Paradise as wide as the heavens and the earth, prepared for Al-Muttaqūn (the pious — see 2:2).

— *Surah Āl ʿImrān 3:133*

On page 8 of the book *Secrets of Secret Secrets*, originally written by Hazrat Abd al-Qadir al-Jilani and translated by Shaykh Tosun Bayrak al-Jarrahi al-Halveti, a very powerful message for travellers is defined as follows:

Enter the path. Join the spiritual caravan to return to your Lord. Soon the road will become impossible, and no travelling companion will be left.

We did not come to this base, mined world to rest; we were not sent here to eat, drink, and defecate.

The spirit of our master, the Prophet ﷺ of Allah SWT, is watching you. He is pained, seeing your state.

---

[176] https://www.abuaminaelias.com/understanding-the-soul-in-islam/

He knew what would come when he said, "My pain is for my beloved people who will come in later times."

Let us now see what the Gospel conveys about the importance of a pure heart:

"Submit yourselves therefore to God. Resist the devil, and he will flee from you.

Draw nigh to God, and he will draw nigh to you.

Cleanse your hands, ye sinners; and purify your hearts, ye double minded."

— *James 4:7–8, KJV*

In Conclusion:

On the Day of Judgement, the Prophet ﷺ stated:

"The first thing a person will have to account for is their record of ritual prayer. If the account stands intact, and according to the prescribed conditions, it will be accepted from them. Their other deeds will be judged in light of their record in ritual worship; and if found deficient, it will be heaved at their faces, alongside their other deeds."

The Prophet ﷺ also said:

"If one purifies well and performs prayer with humility and veneration in the heart, their prayer will ascend, light and bright, towards the Throne. In its flight, the prayer will utter, 'May Allah keep you, as you kept me.'"[177]

It signifies that when the external act of ritual prayer aligns harmoniously with the inner devotion of the heart, the prayer attains completion. This integration constitutes perfect worship, and its resultant reward is immense.

At A Glance

Ahle Kitab refers to the divine holy books given to the Jews and Christians. As believers in a revealed religion, they are called *Ahle Kitab* (People of the Book).

We are simple Muslims, and as travellers, we do not need to delve deeply into this, as it does not significantly contribute to the merit of our journey. However, from a religious standpoint, we must believe in our hearts that:

"The Qur'an is the final scripture, and no other divine book will be revealed upon this earth, and Prophet Muhammad ﷺ is the final Messenger of Allah."

All of mankind must follow his teachings. There is no alternative path to righteousness, regardless of the perceived sanctity of other paths. Only Allah

---

[177] (https://www.imamghazali.org/blog/islamic-prayer)

(SWT) knows best, as our capacity to judge others is limited by our own understanding.

Now let us reflect upon some Qur'anic verses for guidance, along with the historical actions of our Prophet Muhammad ﷺ regarding the issues encountered with infidels, Jews, and Christians.

Allah (SWT) says to our Prophet Muhammad ﷺ in the following verse:

لَتَجِدَنَّ أَشَدَّ النَّاسِ عَدَاوَةً لِّلَّذِينَ آمَنُوا الْيَهُودَ وَالَّذِينَ أَشْرَكُوا ۖ وَلَتَجِدَنَّ أَقْرَبَهُم مَّوَدَّةً لِّلَّذِينَ آمَنُوا الَّذِينَ قَالُوا إِنَّا نَصَارَىٰ ۚ ذَٰلِكَ بِأَنَّ مِنْهُمْ قِسِّيسِينَ وَرُهْبَانًا وَأَنَّهُمْ لَا يَسْتَكْبِرُونَ

Verily, thou shalt find the strongest among men in enmity to the believers to be the Jews and those who are idolaters; and thou shalt find the nearest of them in love to the believers to be those who say, "We are Christians." This is because among them are priests and monks, and they are not proud.

— **Surah Al-Ma'idah 5:82**

Allah (SWT) then says to the righteous:

يَا أَيُّهَا الَّذِينَ آمَنُوا لَا تَتَّخِذُوا الْيَهُودَ وَالنَّصَارَىٰ أَوْلِيَاءَ ۘ بَعْضُهُمْ أَوْلِيَاءُ بَعْضٍ ۚ وَمَن يَتَوَلَّهُم مِّنكُمْ فَإِنَّهُ مِنْهُمْ ۗ إِنَّ اللَّهَ لَا يَهْدِي الْقَوْمَ الظَّالِمِينَ

O ye who believe! Take not the Jews and the Christians for friends and protectors: they are but friends and protectors to each other. And he among you that turneth to them (for friendship) is of them. Verily Allah guideth not a people unjust.

— **Surah Al-Ma'idah 5:51**

In Surah Al-Mumtahina, verses 8 and 9, Allah (SWT) clarifies:

لَّا يَنْهَاكُمُ اللَّهُ عَنِ الَّذِينَ لَمْ يُقَاتِلُوكُمْ فِي الدِّينِ وَلَمْ يُخْرِجُوكُم مِّن دِيَارِكُمْ أَن تَبَرُّوهُمْ وَتُقْسِطُوا إِلَيْهِمْ ۚ إِنَّ اللَّهَ يُحِبُّ الْمُقْسِطِينَ

Allah forbiddeth you not, with regard to those who fought you not for (your) faith nor drove you out of your homes, from dealing kindly and justly with them: for Allah loveth those who are just.

— **Surah Al-Mumtahina 60:8**

إِنَّمَا يَنْهَاكُمُ اللَّهُ عَنِ الَّذِينَ قَاتَلُوكُمْ فِي الدِّينِ وَأَخْرَجُوكُم مِّن دِيَارِكُمْ وَظَاهَرُوا عَلَىٰ إِخْرَاجِكُمْ أَن تَوَلَّوْهُمْ ۚ وَمَن يَتَوَلَّهُمْ فَأُولَٰئِكَ هُمُ الظَّالِمُونَ

It is only as regards those who fought you for (your) faith, and drove you out of your homes, and supported others in driving you out, that Allah forbiddeth you to turn to them (for friendship and protection). And whosoever turneth to them (in such circumstances) are wrong-doers.

— **Surah Al-Mumtahina 60:9**

In Surah Al-Ma'idah 5:68, Allah (SWT) says:

قُلْ يَا أَهْلَ الْكِتَابِ لَسْتُمْ عَلَىٰ شَيْءٍ حَتَّىٰ تُقِيمُوا التَّوْرَاةَ وَالْإِنجِيلَ وَمَا أُنزِلَ إِلَيْكُم مِّن رَّبِّكُمْ وَلَيَزِيدَنَّ كَثِيرًا مِّنْهُم مَّا أُنزِلَ إِلَيْكَ مِن رَّبِّكَ طُغْيَانًا وَكُفْرًا ۖ فَلَا تَأْسَ عَلَى الْقَوْمِ الْكَافِرِينَ

Say: "O People of the Book! Ye have no ground to stand upon unless ye stand fast by the Torah, the Gospel, and all the revelation that has come to you from your Lord." It is the revelation that cometh to thee from thy Lord that increaseth in most of them their obstinate rebellion and blasphemy. But sorrow not over (these) people without faith.

— Surah Al-Ma'idah 5:68

Ahl al-Kitab (People of the Book) includes both believers and unbelievers, as stated in the Qur'an. They are those who received the divine scriptures — the Torah and the Gospel. Jews and Christians are referred to collectively as the *Ahle Kitab*. The term encompasses both those who believe and those who do not, though unbelievers among them do not outright deny the existence of Allah (SWT).

Allah (SWT) then says:

يَا أَهْلَ الْكِتَابِ لِمَ تَكْفُرُونَ بِآيَاتِ اللَّهِ وَأَنتُمْ تَشْهَدُونَ

O People of the Book! Why do ye reject the Signs of Allah, seeing that ye are (yourselves) witnesses (to their truth)?

— Surah Al-'Imran 3:70

And again:

قُلْ يَا أَهْلَ الْكِتَابِ لِمَ تَصُدُّونَ عَن سَبِيلِ اللَّهِ مَنْ آمَنَ تَبْغُونَهَا عِوَجًا وَأَنتُمْ شُهَدَاءُ ۚ وَمَا اللَّهُ بِغَافِلٍ عَمَّا تَعْمَلُونَ

Say: "O People of the Book! Why do ye obstruct those who believe from the path of Allah, seeking to make it crooked, while ye were yourselves witnesses (to the truth)? But Allah is not unaware of what ye do."

— Surah Al-'Imran 3:99

Historical Relations With Ahl Al-Kitab

Ahl al-Kitab were granted freedom of worship. During the early Muslim conquests, Jews and Christians were not compelled to embrace Islam. They were only required to pay a special tax (*jizya*) in return for exemption from military service. Muslim authorities were responsible for their protection and well-being.

In this regard, the Prophet ﷺ signed a document regulating the relationship between the tribes around and within Madinah and the Muslims, granting equal rights. He stated:

"Whoever joins the signatories of this scripture shall be entitled to our help and shall not be subject to injustice, nor shall the Muslims conspire against them. The

children of Ouf are a community of believers. The People of the Scripture shall be allowed to practise their religion just as the Muslims are allowed to practise theirs, and so too their allies—except the one who commits injustice or sin, for he harms only himself...

The signatories of this document are entitled to mutual advice, sincerity, and assistance rather than hostility towards one another..."

This document is considered the first of its kind in the history of religious freedom and a foundational declaration of human rights, for which mankind has struggled across the ages.

The Holy Qur'an also clarifies that Prophet Muhammad ﷺ did not speak from his own desire. He was inspired by Allah (SWT):

رَبَّنَا آمَنَّا بِمَا أَنزَلْتَ وَاتَّبَعْنَا الرَّسُولَ فَاكْتُبْنَا مَعَ الشَّاهِدِينَ

Our Lord! We believe in what Thou hast revealed, and we follow the Messenger; so write us down among those who bear witness.

— **Surah Al-'Imran 3:53**

Thus, the nature of the relationship with Ahl al-Kitab is divinely ordained, as referenced earlier in Surah Al-'Imran 3:64.

The Qur'an also extends hope to sincere believers of other faiths in the following verse:

إِنَّ الَّذِينَ آمَنُوا وَالَّذِينَ هَادُوا وَالصَّابِئُونَ وَالنَّصَارَىٰ مَنْ آمَنَ بِاللَّهِ وَالْيَوْمِ الْآخِرِ وَعَمِلَ صَالِحًا فَلَا خَوْفٌ عَلَيْهِمْ وَلَا هُمْ يَحْزَنُونَ

Verily, those who believe, and those who are Jews, and the Sabians, and the Christians — whosoever believeth in Allah and the Last Day, and worketh righteousness, on them shall be no fear, nor shall they grieve.

— **Surah Al-Ma'idah 5:69**

After the death of Prophet Muhammad ﷺ, his successors sent clear instructions to their generals and governors to respect the rights of Ahl al-Kitab, not to interfere with their worship, and to treat them with full dignity and honour.

Conclusion

Our concise survey suggests that within our community, particularly among common Muslims, there are varying opinions regarding different sects. However, as believers, it is imperative that we adopt a perspective rooted in the teachings of Allah (SWT), as conveyed in the Qur'an.

01

أَلَمْ تَرَ إِلَى الَّذِينَ أُوتُوا نَصِيبًا مِّنَ الْكِتَابِ يُدْعَوْنَ إِلَى كِتَابِ اللهِ لِيَحْكُمَ بَيْنَهُمْ ثُمَّ يَتَوَلَّى ¬ فَرِيقٌ مِّنْهُمْ وَهُم مُّعْرِضُونَ

ذَٰلِكَ بِأَنَّهُمْ قَالُوا لَن تَمَسَّنَا النَّارُ إِلَّا أَيَّامًا مَّعْدُودَاتٍ ۖ وَغَرَّهُمْ فِي دِينِهِم مَّا كَانُوا يَفْتَرُونَ ¬

Have you not seen those who have been given a portion of the Scripture? They are being invited to the Book of Allah to settle their dispute, then a party of them turn away, and they are averse.

Surah Aal Imran 3:23

This is because they say: "The Fire shall not touch us but for a number of days." And that which they used to invent regarding their religion has deceived them.

Surah Aal Imran 3:24

02

لَيْسُوا سَوَاءً ۗ مِّنْ أَهْلِ الْكِتَابِ أُمَّةٌ قَائِمَةٌ يَتْلُونَ آيَاتِ اللهِ آنَاءَ اللَّيْلِ وَهُمْ يَسْجُدُونَ ¬

يُؤْمِنُونَ بِاللهِ وَالْيَوْمِ الْآخِرِ وَيَأْمُرُونَ بِالْمَعْرُوفِ وَيَنْهَوْنَ عَنِ الْمُنكَرِ وَيُسَارِعُونَ فِي ¬ الْخَيْرَاتِ وَأُولَٰئِكَ مِنَ الصَّالِحِينَ

وَمَا يَفْعَلُوا مِنْ خَيْرٍ فَلَن يُكْفَرُوهُ ۗ وَاللهُ عَلِيمٌ بِالْمُتَّقِينَ ¬

Not all of them are alike; a party of the People of the Scripture stand for the right. They recite the verses of Allah during the hours of the night, prostrating themselves in prayer.

Surah Aal Imran 3:113

They believe in Allah and the Last Day; they enjoin Al-Ma'ruf (Islamic monotheism and following the Prophet Muhammad ﷺ), and forbid Al-Munkar (polytheism, disbelief and opposing the Prophet ﷺ); they hasten in good works, and they are among the righteous.

Surah Aal Imran 3:114

And whatever good they do, nothing will be rejected of them; for Allah knows well those who are Al-Muttaqun (the pious).

Surah Aal Imran 3:115

03

وَإِذْ أَخَذَ اللهُ مِيثَاقَ الَّذِينَ أُوتُوا الْكِتَابَ لَتُبَيِّنُنَّهُ لِلنَّاسِ وَلَا تَكْتُمُونَهُ فَنَبَذُوهُ وَرَاءَ ظُهُورِهِمْ وَاشْتَرَوْا بِهِ ثَمَنًا قَلِيلًا ۖ فَبِئْسَ مَا يَشْتَرُونَ

لَا تَحْسَبَنَّ الَّذِينَ يَفْرَحُونَ بِمَا أَتَوا وَّيُحِبُّونَ أَن يُحْمَدُوا بِمَا لَمْ يَفْعَلُوا فَلَا تَحْسَبَنَّهُم بِمَفَازَةٍ مِّنَ الْعَذَابِ ۖ وَلَهُمْ عَذَابٌ أَلِيمٌ

(Remember) when Allah took a covenant from those who were given the Scripture (Jews and Christians) to make it known and clear to mankind and not to hide it, but they threw it away behind their backs and purchased with it some miserable gain! And evil indeed is that which they bought.

Surah Aal Imran 3:187

Think not that those who rejoice in what they have done, and love to be praised for what they have not done—think not they shall escape the punishment. For them is a painful torment.

Surah Aal Imran 3:188

(cf. KJV: "Woe unto you, when all men shall speak well of you! for so did their fathers to the false prophets." — Luke 6:26)

04

وَإِنَّ مِنْ أَهْلِ الْكِتَابِ لَمَن يُؤْمِنُ بِاللَّهِ وَمَا أُنزِلَ إِلَيْكُمْ وَمَا أُنزِلَ إِلَيْهِمْ خَاشِعِينَ لِلَّهِ لَا يَشْتَرُونَ بِآيَاتِ اللَّهِ ثَمَنًا قَلِيلًا ۗ أُولَٰئِكَ لَهُمْ أَجْرُهُمْ عِندَ رَبِّهِمْ ۗ إِنَّ اللَّهَ سَرِيعُ الْحِسَابِ

And certainly, among the People of the Scripture (Jews and Christians), there are those who believe in Allah and in that which has been revealed to you, and in that which has been revealed to them, humbling themselves before Allah. They do not sell the verses of Allah for a small price. For them is a reward with their Lord. Surely, Allah is Swift in account.

Surah Aal Imran 3:199

05

أَلَمْ تَرَ إِلَى الَّذِينَ أُوتُوا نَصِيبًا مِّنَ الْكِتَابِ يَشْتَرُونَ الضَّلَالَةَ وَيُرِيدُونَ أَن تَضِلُّوا السَّبِيلَ

Have you not seen those who were given a portion of the Book (the Jews), purchasing error and wishing that you should go astray from the Right Path?

Surah An-Nisaa 4:44

06

مِّنَ الَّذِينَ هَادُوا يُحَرِّفُونَ الْكَلِمَ عَن مَّوَاضِعِهِ وَيَقُولُونَ سَمِعْنَا وَعَصَيْنَا وَاسْمَعْ غَيْرَ مُسْمَعٍ وَرَاعِنَا لَيًّا بِأَلْسِنَتِهِمْ وَطَعْنًا فِي الدِّينِ ۚ وَلَوْ أَنَّهُمْ قَالُوا سَمِعْنَا وَأَطَعْنَا وَاسْمَعْ وَانظُرْنَا لَكَانَ خَيْرًا لَّهُمْ وَأَقْوَمَ وَلَٰكِن لَّعَنَهُمُ اللَّهُ بِكُفْرِهِمْ فَلَا يُؤْمِنُونَ إِلَّا قَلِيلًا

يَا أَيُّهَا الَّذِينَ أُوتُوا الْكِتَابَ آمِنُوا بِمَا نَزَّلْنَا مُصَدِّقًا لِّمَا مَعَكُم مِّن قَبْلِ أَن نَّطْمِسَ وُجُوهًا فَنَرُدَّهَا عَلَىٰ أَدْبَارِهَا أَوْ نَلْعَنَهُمْ كَمَا لَعَنَّا أَصْحَابَ السَّبْتِ ۚ وَكَانَ أَمْرُ اللَّهِ مَفْعُولًا

Among the Jews are those who distort the words from their proper places and say: "We hear and disobey," and "Hear but be not heard," and "Ra'ina" (with a twist of their tongues) as a mockery of the religion. Had they said, "We hear and we obey," and "Hear us" and "Look upon us," it would have been better and more proper for them. But Allah has cursed them for their disbelief, so they do not believe except a few.

Surah An-Nisaa 4:46

O you who have been given the Scripture (Jews and Christians), believe in what We have sent down (to Muhammad ﷺ), confirming what is with you, before We efface faces (by making them like the back of necks) and turn them backwards, or curse them as We cursed the Sabbath-breakers. And the commandment of Allah is always carried out.

Surah An-Nisaa 4:47

أَلَمْ تَرَ إِلَى الَّذِينَ أُوتُوا نَصِيبًا مِّنَ الْكِتَابِ يُؤْمِنُونَ بِالْجِبْتِ وَالطَّاغُوتِ وَيَقُولُونَ لِلَّذِينَ ¬ كَفَرُوا هَؤُلَاءِ أَهْدَىٰ مِنَ الَّذِينَ آمَنُوا سَبِيلًا

أُولَٰئِكَ الَّذِينَ لَعَنَهُمُ اللَّهُ ۖ وَمَن يَلْعَنِ اللَّهُ فَلَن تَجِدَ لَهُ نَصِيرًا

Have you not seen those who were given a portion of the Scripture? They believe in Jibt and Taghut and say to the disbelievers that they are better guided than the believers.

Surah An-Nisaa 4:51

They are those whom Allah has cursed, and he whom Allah curses—you will not find for him any helper.

Surah An-Nisaa 4:52

07

أَمْ يَحْسُدُونَ النَّاسَ عَلَىٰ مَا آتَاهُمُ اللَّهُ مِن فَضْلِهِ ۖ فَقَدْ آتَيْنَا آلَ إِبْرَاهِيمَ الْكِتَابَ وَالْحِكْمَةَ ¬ وَآتَيْنَاهُم مُّلْكًا عَظِيمًا

فَمِنْهُم مَّنْ آمَنَ بِهِ وَمِنْهُم مَّن صَدَّ عَنْهُ ۚ وَكَفَىٰ بِجَهَنَّمَ سَعِيرًا

Or do they envy men (Muhammad ﷺ and his followers) for what Allah has given them of His bounty? Verily, We gave the family of Ibrahim (Abraham) the Book and wisdom, and We conferred upon them a great kingdom.

Surah An-Nisaa 4:54

Of them were some who believed in him (Muhammad ﷺ), and of them were some who turned away. And Hell is sufficient for burning them.

Surah An-Nisaa 4:55

08

فَبِظُلْمٍ مِّنَ الَّذِينَ هَادُوا حَرَّمْنَا عَلَيْهِمْ طَيِّبَاتٍ أُحِلَّتْ لَهُمْ وَبِصَدِّهِمْ عَن سَبِيلِ اللَّهِ كَثِيرًا ۔

وَأَخْذِهِمُ الرِّبَا وَقَدْ نُهُوا عَنْهُ وَأَكْلِهِمْ أَمْوَالَ النَّاسِ بِالْبَاطِلِ ۚ وَأَعْتَدْنَا لِلْكَافِرِينَ مِنْهُمْ عَذَابًا أَلِيمًا

لَّكِنِ الرَّاسِخُونَ فِي الْعِلْمِ مِنْهُمْ وَالْمُؤْمِنُونَ يُؤْمِنُونَ بِمَا أُنزِلَ إِلَيْكَ وَمَا أُنزِلَ مِن قَبْلِكَ ۚ

وَالْمُقِيمِينَ الصَّلَاةَ ۚ وَالْمُؤْتُونَ الزَّكَاةَ وَالْمُؤْمِنُونَ بِاللَّهِ وَالْيَوْمِ الْآخِرِ أُولَٰئِكَ سَنُؤْتِيهِمْ أَجْرًا

عَظِيمًا

*For*Because of the wrongdoing of the Jews, We made unlawful for them certain good foods which had been lawful, and because of their hindering many from Allah's way.

Surah An-Nisaa 4:160

And their taking of riba (usury), though they were forbidden from taking it, and their devouring of people's wealth wrongfully. We have prepared for the disbelievers among them a painful punishment.

Surah An-Nisaa 4:161

But those among them who are well grounded in knowledge and the believers believe in what has been revealed to you and what was revealed before you. And those who perform prayer and give zakat and believe in Allah and the Last Day— to them We shall give a great reward.

Surah An-Nisaa 4:162

09

يَا أَهْلَ الْكِتَابِ لَا تَغْلُوا فِي دِينِكُمْ وَلَا تَقُولُوا عَلَى اللَّهِ إِلَّا الْحَقَّ ۚ إِنَّمَا الْمَسِيحُ عِيسَى ابْنُ مَرْيَمَ

رَسُولُ اللَّهِ وَكَلِمَتُهُ أَلْقَاهَا إِلَىٰ مَرْيَمَ وَرُوحٌ مِّنْهُ ۖ فَآمِنُوا بِاللَّهِ وَرُسُلِهِ ۖ وَلَا تَقُولُوا ثَلَاثَةٌ ۚ انتَهُوا

خَيْرًا لَّكُمْ ۚ إِنَّمَا اللَّهُ إِلَٰهٌ وَاحِدٌ ۖ سُبْحَانَهُ أَن يَكُونَ لَهُ وَلَدٌ ۘ لَّهُ مَا فِي السَّمَاوَاتِ وَمَا فِي الْأَرْضِ ۗ

وَكَفَىٰ بِاللَّهِ وَكِيلًا

O People of the Scripture (Jews and Christians)! Do not exceed the limits in your religion, nor say anything about Allah but the truth. The Messiah, 'Isa (Jesus), son of Maryam (Mary), was no more than a Messenger of Allah and His Word ("Be!" – and he was), which He bestowed upon Maryam, and a spirit (Ruh) from Him. So believe in Allah and His Messengers.

Do not say: "Three (Trinity)!" Cease – it will be better for you. For Allah is the only One God. Glory be to Him – He is far exalted above having a son. To Him belongs all that is in the heavens and all that is in the earth. And Allah is All-Sufficient as a Disposer of affairs.

Surah An-Nisa 4:171

10

وَمِنَ الَّذِينَ قَالُوا إِنَّا نَصَارَىٰ أَخَذْنَا مِيثَاقَهُمْ فَنَسُوا حَظًّا مِّمَّا ذُكِّرُوا بِهِ فَأَغْرَيْنَا بَيْنَهُمُ الْعَدَاوَةَ وَالْبَغْضَاءَ إِلَىٰ يَوْمِ الْقِيَامَةِ ۚ وَسَوْفَ يُنَبِّئُهُمُ اللَّهُ بِمَا كَانُوا يَصْنَعُونَ

يَا أَهْلَ الْكِتَابِ قَدْ جَاءَكُمْ رَسُولُنَا يُبَيِّنُ لَكُمْ كَثِيرًا مِّمَّا كُنتُمْ تُخْفُونَ مِنَ الْكِتَابِ وَيَعْفُو عَن كَثِيرٍ ۚ قَدْ جَاءَكُم مِّنَ اللَّهِ نُورٌ وَكِتَابٌ مُّبِينٌ

And from those who say, "We are Christians," We took their covenant. But they forgot a good part of the message that was sent to them, so We placed enmity and hatred amongst them until the Day of Resurrection – (because they discarded Allah's Book, disobeyed Allah's Messengers and transgressed). Allah will inform them of what they used to do.

Surah Al-Ma'idah 5:14

O People of the Scripture (Jews and Christians)! There has now come to you Our Messenger (Muhammad ﷺ), making clear to you much of what you used to hide from the Scripture, and overlooking much. Indeed, there has come to you from Allah a light (the Prophet Muhammad ﷺ) and a clear Book (the Qur'an).

Surah Al-Ma'idah 5:15

11

وَقَالَتِ الْيَهُودُ وَالنَّصَارَىٰ نَحْنُ أَبْنَاءُ اللَّهِ وَأَحِبَّاؤُهُ ۚ قُلْ فَلِمَ يُعَذِّبُكُم بِذُنُوبِكُم ۖ بَلْ أَنتُم بَشَرٌ مِّمَّنْ خَلَقَ ۚ يَغْفِرُ لِمَن يَشَاءُ وَيُعَذِّبُ مَن يَشَاءُ ۚ وَلِلَّهِ مُلْكُ السَّمَاوَاتِ وَالْأَرْضِ وَمَا بَيْنَهُمَا ۖ وَإِلَيْهِ الْمَصِيرُ

يَا أَهْلَ الْكِتَابِ قَدْ جَاءَكُمْ رَسُولُنَا يُبَيِّنُ لَكُمْ عَلَىٰ فَتْرَةٍ مِّنَ الرُّسُلِ أَن تَقُولُوا مَا جَاءَنَا مِن بَشِيرٍ وَلَا نَذِيرٍ ۖ فَقَدْ جَاءَكُم بَشِيرٌ وَنَذِيرٌ ۗ وَاللَّهُ عَلَىٰ كُلِّ شَيْءٍ قَدِيرٌ

And the Jews and the Christians say: "We are the children of Allah and His beloved." Say: "Why then does He punish you for your sins?" Nay, you are but human beings among those He has created. He forgives whom He wills and punishes whom He wills. And to Allah belongs the dominion of the heavens and the earth and all that is between them, and to Him is the return.

Surah Al-Ma'idah 5:18

O People of the Scripture! Our Messenger (Muhammad ﷺ) has now come to you, making things clear to you after a break in (the succession of) Messengers, lest you say: "There came to us no bringer of glad tidings and no warner." But now there has come to you a bringer of glad tidings and a warner. And Allah is Able to do all things.

Surah Al-Ma'idah 5:19

12

وَلْيَحْكُمْ أَهْلُ الْإِنجِيلِ بِمَا أَنزَلَ اللَّهُ فِيهِ ۚ وَمَن لَّمْ يَحْكُم بِمَا أَنزَلَ اللَّهُ فَأُولَٰئِكَ هُمُ الْفَاسِقُونَ

Let the people of the Injeel (Gospel) judge by what Allah has revealed therein. And whoever does not judge by what Allah has revealed – they are the rebellious (Fāsiqūn – i.e., those disobedient to Allah).

Surah Al-Ma'idah 5:47

13

وَإِذَا نَادَيْتُمْ إِلَى الصَّلَاةِ اتَّخَذُوهَا هُزُوًا وَلَعِبًا ۚ ذَٰلِكَ بِأَنَّهُمْ قَوْمٌ لَّا يَعْقِلُونَ

قُلْ يَا أَهْلَ الْكِتَابِ هَلْ تَنقِمُونَ مِنَّا إِلَّا أَنْ آمَنَّا بِاللَّهِ وَمَا أُنزِلَ إِلَيْنَا وَمَا أُنزِلَ مِن قَبْلُ وَأَنَّ أَكْثَرَكُمْ فَاسِقُونَ

قُلْ هَلْ أُنَبِّئُكُم بِشَرٍّ مِّن ذَٰلِكَ مَثُوبَةً عِندَ اللَّهِ ۚ مَن لَّعَنَهُ اللَّهُ وَغَضِبَ عَلَيْهِ وَجَعَلَ مِنْهُمُ الْقِرَدَةَ وَالْخَنَازِيرَ وَعَبَدَ الطَّاغُوتَ ۚ أُولَٰئِكَ شَرٌّ مَّكَانًا وَأَضَلُّ عَن سَوَاءِ السَّبِيلِ

وَإِذَا جَاءُوكُمْ قَالُوا آمَنَّا وَقَد دَّخَلُوا بِالْكُفْرِ وَهُمْ قَدْ خَرَجُوا بِهِ ۚ وَاللَّهُ أَعْلَمُ بِمَا كَانُوا يَكْتُمُونَ

وَتَرَىٰ كَثِيرًا مِّنْهُمْ يُسَارِعُونَ فِي الْإِثْمِ وَالْعُدْوَانِ وَأَكْلِهِمُ السُّحْتَ ۚ لَبِئْسَ مَا كَانُوا يَعْمَلُونَ

لَوْلَا يَنْهَاهُمُ الرَّبَّانِيُّونَ وَالْأَحْبَارُ عَن قَوْلِهِمُ الْإِثْمَ وَأَكْلِهِمُ السُّحْتَ ۚ لَبِئْسَ مَا كَانُوا يَصْنَعُونَ

وَقَالَتِ الْيَهُودُ يَدُ اللَّهِ مَغْلُولَةٌ ۚ غُلَّتْ أَيْدِيهِمْ وَلُعِنُوا بِمَا قَالُوا ۘ بَلْ يَدَاهُ مَبْسُوطَتَانِ يُنفِقُ كَيْفَ يَشَاءُ ۚ وَلَيَزِيدَنَّ كَثِيرًا مِّنْهُم مَّا أُنزِلَ إِلَيْكَ مِن رَّبِّكَ طُغْيَانًا وَكُفْرًا ۚ وَأَلْقَيْنَا بَيْنَهُمُ الْعَدَاوَةَ وَالْبَغْضَاءَ إِلَىٰ يَوْمِ الْقِيَامَةِ ۚ كُلَّمَا أَوْقَدُوا نَارًا لِّلْحَرْبِ أَطْفَأَهَا اللَّهُ ۚ وَيَسْعَوْنَ فِي الْأَرْضِ فَسَادًا ۚ وَاللَّهُ لَا يُحِبُّ الْمُفْسِدِينَ

وَلَوْ أَنَّ أَهْلَ الْكِتَابِ آمَنُوا وَاتَّقَوْا لَكَفَّرْنَا عَنْهُمْ سَيِّئَاتِهِمْ وَلَأَدْخَلْنَاهُمْ جَنَّاتِ النَّعِيمِ

وَلَوْ أَنَّهُمْ أَقَامُوا التَّوْرَاةَ وَالْإِنجِيلَ وَمَا أُنزِلَ إِلَيْهِم مِّن رَّبِّهِمْ لَأَكَلُوا مِن فَوْقِهِمْ وَمِن تَحْتِ أَرْجُلِهِم ۚ مِّنْهُمْ أُمَّةٌ مُّقْتَصِدَةٌ ۖ وَكَثِيرٌ مِّنْهُمْ سَاءَ مَا يَعْمَلُونَ

And when you proclaim the call for As-Salat (the call to prayer – Adhan), they take it as a mockery and a joke; that is because they are a people who understand not. **(Surah Al-Ma'idah 5:58)**

Say: "O People of the Scripture (Jews and Christians)! Do you resent us only because we believe in Allah, and in that which has been sent down to us, and in that which was sent down before (us), and that most of you are rebellious and disobedient?" **(5:59)**

Say: "Shall I inform you of something worse than that as a recompense from Allah? Those who incurred the curse of Allah and His wrath, those of whom He transformed into apes and swine, those who worshipped false deities. These are worse in rank and further astray from the Right Path." **(5:60)**

When they come to you, they say: "We believe." But they enter with disbelief and leave with it. And Allah knows well what they conceal. **(5:61)**

And you see many of them hurrying towards sin and transgression, and eating unlawful things (such as bribes and usury). Evil indeed is that which they are doing. **(5:62)**

Why do the rabbis and the religious scholars not forbid them from sinful talk and unlawful earnings? Evil indeed is what they have been doing. **(5:63)**

The Jews say: "Allah's Hand is tied." May their hands be tied and cursed be what they say. Nay! Both His Hands are widely outstretched. He spends as He wills. Verily, what has been sent down to you from your Lord increases many of them in rebellion and disbelief. And We have placed enmity and hatred among them until the Day of Resurrection. Whenever they kindle the fire of war, Allah extinguishes it. They strive to cause corruption on the earth, and Allah does not love the mischief-makers. **(5:64)**

And if only the People of the Scripture had believed and been God-fearing, We would surely have remitted their sins and admitted them to Gardens of Delight. **(5:65)**

And if they had established the Torah, the Gospel, and what has now been sent down to them from their Lord (the Qur'an), they would surely have received provision from above them and beneath their feet. Among them is a just community, but many of them do evil deeds. **(5:66)**

14

قُلْ يَا أَهْلَ الْكِتَابِ لَا تَغْلُوا فِي دِينِكُمْ غَيْرَ الْحَقِّ وَلَا تَتَّبِعُوا أَهْوَاءَ قَوْمٍ قَدْ ضَلُّوا مِن قَبْلُ وَأَضَلُّوا كَثِيرًا وَضَلُّوا عَن سَوَاءِ السَّبِيلِ

Say: "O People of the Scripture! Do not go to extremes in your religion beyond the truth, and do not follow the desires of a people who went astray before and led many astray, and strayed from the Straight Path." **(5:77)**

15

لَتَجِدَنَّ أَشَدَّ النَّاسِ عَدَاوَةً لِّلَّذِينَ آمَنُوا الْيَهُودَ وَالَّذِينَ أَشْرَكُوا ۖ وَلَتَجِدَنَّ أَقْرَبَهُم مَّوَدَّةً لِّلَّذِينَ آمَنُوا الَّذِينَ قَالُوا إِنَّا نَصَارَىٰ ۚ ذَٰلِكَ بِأَنَّ مِنْهُمْ قِسِّيسِينَ وَرُهْبَانًا وَأَنَّهُمْ لَا يَسْتَكْبِرُونَ

وَإِذَا سَمِعُوا مَا أُنزِلَ إِلَى الرَّسُولِ تَرَىٰ أَعْيُنَهُمْ تَفِيضُ مِنَ الدَّمْعِ مِمَّا عَرَفُوا مِنَ الْحَقِّ ۖ يَقُولُونَ رَبَّنَا آمَنَّا فَاكْتُبْنَا مَعَ الشَّاهِدِينَ

وَمَا لَنَا لَا نُؤْمِنُ بِاللَّهِ وَمَا جَاءَنَا مِنَ الْحَقِّ وَنَطْمَعُ أَن يُدْخِلَنَا رَبُّنَا مَعَ الْقَوْمِ الصَّالِحِينَ

فَأَثَابَهُمُ اللَّهُ بِمَا قَالُوا جَنَّاتٍ تَجْرِي مِن تَحْتِهَا الْأَنْهَارُ خَالِدِينَ فِيهَا ۚ وَذَٰلِكَ جَزَاءُ الْمُحْسِنِينَ

Verily, you will find the strongest among mankind in enmity to the believers (Muslims) to be the Jews and those who associate others with Allah. And you will find the nearest among them in love to the believers those who say, "We are Christians." That is because among them are priests and monks, and they are not proud. **(5:82)**

And when they hear what has been revealed to the Messenger, you see their eyes overflowing with tears because of the truth they recognise. They say, "Our Lord! We believe; so write us down among the witnesses." **(5:83)**

"And why should we not believe in Allah and in that which has come to us of the truth? And we hope that our Lord will admit us (to Paradise) with the righteous people." **(5:84)**

So Allah rewarded them for what they said: Gardens beneath which rivers flow, wherein they will abide forever. That is the reward of those who do good. **(5:85)**

16

الَّذِينَ آتَيْنَاهُمُ الْكِتَابَ يَعْرِفُونَهُ كَمَا يَعْرِفُونَ أَبْنَاءَهُمْ ۖ الَّذِينَ خَسِرُوا أَنفُسَهُمْ فَهُمْ لَا يُؤْمِنُونَ

Those to whom We have given the Scripture (Jews and Christians) recognise him (i.e. Muhammad ﷺ as a Messenger of Allah, and they also know that there is no Ilah (God) but Allah, and Islam is Allah's religion), as they recognise their own sons. Those who destroy themselves will not believe. (Tafsir At-Tabari) 6:20, Surah Al-An'am

17

وَعَلَى الَّذِينَ هَادُوا حَرَّمْنَا كُلَّ ذِي ظُفُرٍ ۖ وَمِنَ الْبَقَرِ وَالْغَنَمِ حَرَّمْنَا عَلَيْهِمْ شُحُومَهُمَا إِلَّا مَا حَمَلَتْ ظُهُورُهُمَا أَوِ الْحَوَايَا أَوْ مَا اخْتَلَطَ بِعَظْمٍ ۚ ذَٰلِكَ جَزَيْنَاهُم بِبَغْيِهِمْ ۖ وَإِنَّا لَصَادِقُونَ

فَإِن كَذَّبُوكَ فَقُل رَّبُّكُمْ ذُو رَحْمَةٍ وَاسِعَةٍ وَلَا يُرَدُّ بَأْسُهُ عَنِ الْقَوْمِ الْمُجْرِمِينَ

And unto those who are Jews, We forbade every animal with an undivided hoof, and We forbade them the fat of oxen and sheep, except what adheres to their backs or their entrails, or is mixed with bone. Thus, We recompensed them for their rebellion [committing crimes such as murdering the Prophets, consuming Riba (usury), etc.]. And verily, We are Truthful. 6:146, Surah Al-An'am

If they (the Jews) belie you (Muhammad ﷺ), say: "Your Lord is the Owner of Vast Mercy, but never will His Wrath be turned back from the people who are Mujrimun (criminals, polytheists, sinners, etc.)." **6:147, Surah Al-An'am**

18

وَالَّذِينَ آتَيْنَاهُمُ الْكِتَابَ يَفْرَحُونَ بِمَا أُنزِلَ إِلَيْكَ ۖ وَمِنَ الْأَحْزَابِ مَن يُنكِرُ بَعْضَهُ ۚ قُلْ إِنَّمَا أُمِرْتُ أَنْ أَعْبُدَ اللَّهَ وَلَا أُشْرِكَ بِهِ ۚ إِلَيْهِ أَدْعُو وَإِلَيْهِ مَآبِ

Those to whom We have given the Book (such as 'Abdullah bin Salam and other Jews who embraced Islam) rejoice at what has been revealed to you (i.e. the Qur'an), but among the Confederates (from the Jews and pagans), there are those who reject part of it. Say (O Muhammad ﷺ): "I am commanded only to worship Allah (Alone) and not to join partners with Him. To Him (Alone) I call, and to Him is my return." **13:36, Surah Ar-Ra'd**

19

وَعَلَى الَّذِينَ هَادُوا حَرَّمْنَا مَا قَصَصْنَا عَلَيْكَ مِن قَبْلُ ۖ وَمَا ظَلَمْنَاهُمْ وَلَٰكِن كَانُوا أَنفُسَهُمْ يَظْلِمُونَ

And unto those who are Jews, We have forbidden such things as We have mentioned to you (O Muhammad ﷺ) before [in Surah Al-An'am, see verse 6:146]. And We wronged them not, but they used to wrong themselves. **16:118, Surah An-Nahl**

20

الَّذِينَ آتَيْنَاهُمُ الْكِتَابَ مِن قَبْلِهِ هُم بِهِ يُؤْمِنُونَ

وَإِذَا يُتْلَىٰ عَلَيْهِمْ قَالُوا آمَنَّا بِهِ إِنَّهُ الْحَقُّ مِن رَّبِّنَا إِنَّا كُنَّا مِن قَبْلِهِ مُسْلِمِينَ

Those to whom We gave the Scripture [i.e. the Taurat (Torah) and the Injeel (Gospel), etc.] before it – they believe in it (the Qur'an). **28:52, Surah Al-Qasas**

And when it is recited to them, they say: "We believe in it. Verily, it is the truth from our Lord. Indeed, even before it, we have been among those who submit themselves to Allah in Islam, as Muslims (like 'Abdullah bin Salam and Salman Al-Farisi, etc.)." **28:53, Surah Al-Qasas**

21

وَلَا تُجَادِلُوا أَهْلَ الْكِتَابِ إِلَّا بِالَّتِي هِيَ أَحْسَنُ إِلَّا الَّذِينَ ظَلَمُوا مِنْهُمْ ۖ وَقُولُوا آمَنَّا بِالَّذِي أُنزِلَ إِلَيْنَا وَأُنزِلَ إِلَيْكُمْ وَإِلَٰهُنَا وَإِلَٰهُكُمْ وَاحِدٌ وَنَحْنُ لَهُ مُسْلِمُونَ

And argue not with the People of the Scripture (Jews and Christians), except in a way that is better (with good words and a gentle manner, inviting them to Islamic monotheism with His verses), except with those among them who do wrong. And say (to them): "We believe in that which has been revealed to us and to you; our Ilah (God) and your Ilah is One (i.e. Allah), and to Him we have submitted (as Muslims)." 29:46, Surah Al-Ankabut

مَثَلُ الَّذِينَ حُمِّلُوا التَّوْرَاةَ ثُمَّ لَمْ يَحْمِلُوهَا كَمَثَلِ الْحِمَارِ يَحْمِلُ أَسْفَارًا ۚ بِئْسَ مَثَلُ الْقَوْمِ الَّذِينَ كَذَّبُوا بِآيَاتِ اللَّهِ ۚ وَاللَّهُ لَا يَهْدِي الْقَوْمَ الظَّالِمِينَ

قُلْ يَا أَيُّهَا الَّذِينَ هَادُوا إِن زَعَمْتُمْ أَنَّكُمْ أَوْلِيَاءُ لِلَّهِ مِن دُونِ النَّاسِ فَتَمَنَّوُا الْمَوْتَ إِن كُنتُمْ صَادِقِينَ

The likeness of those who were entrusted with the (obligation of the) Taurat (Torah) (i.e. to obey its commandments and practise its legal laws), but who subsequently failed in those obligations, is like a donkey carrying volumes of books (but understanding nothing from them). What an evil example is that of people who deny the Ayat (proofs, evidences, verses, signs) of Allah. And Allah does not guide the wrongdoing people. **62:5, Surah Al-Jumu'a**

Say (O Muhammad ﷺ): "O you Jews! If you claim that you are friends of Allah, to the exclusion of (all) other mankind, then long for death if you are truthful." **62:6, Surah Al-Jumu'a**

22

لَمْ يَكُنِ الَّذِينَ كَفَرُوا مِنْ أَهْلِ الْكِتَابِ وَالْمُشْرِكِينَ مُنفَكِّينَ حَتَّىٰ تَأْتِيَهُمُ الْبَيِّنَةُ

رَسُولٌ مِّنَ اللَّهِ يَتْلُو صُحُفًا مُّطَهَّرَةً

فِيهَا كُتُبٌ قَيِّمَةٌ

وَمَا تَفَرَّقَ الَّذِينَ أُوتُوا الْكِتَابَ إِلَّا مِن بَعْدِ مَا جَاءَتْهُمُ الْبَيِّنَةُ

وَمَا أُمِرُوا إِلَّا لِيَعْبُدُوا اللَّهَ مُخْلِصِينَ لَهُ الدِّينَ حُنَفَاءَ وَيُقِيمُوا الصَّلَاةَ وَيُؤْتُوا الزَّكَاةَ ۚ وَذَٰلِكَ دِينُ الْقَيِّمَةِ

إِنَّ الَّذِينَ كَفَرُوا مِنْ أَهْلِ الْكِتَابِ وَالْمُشْرِكِينَ فِي نَارِ جَهَنَّمَ خَالِدِينَ فِيهَا ۚ أُولَٰئِكَ هُمْ شَرُّ الْبَرِيَّةِ

نَّ الَّذِينَ آمَنُوا وَعَمِلُوا الصَّالِحَاتِ أُولَٰئِكَ هُمْ خَيْرُ الْبَرِيَّةِ

جَزَاؤُهُمْ عِندَ رَبِّهِمْ جَنَّاتُ عَدْنٍ تَجْرِي مِن تَحْتِهَا الْأَنْهَارُ خَالِدِينَ فِيهَا أَبَدًا ۚ رَّضِيَ اللَّهُ عَنْهُمْ وَرَضُوا عَنْهُ ۚ ذَٰلِكَ لِمَنْ خَشِيَ رَبَّهُ

Those who disbelieve from among the People of the Scripture (Jews and Christians) and the polytheists were not going to cease (their disbelief) until there came to them clear evidence. **98:1, Surah Al-Baiyina**

A Messenger (Muhammad ﷺ) from Allah, reciting purified pages (i.e. the Qur'an), purified from falsehood. **98:2, Surah Al-Baiyina**

Containing correct and straight laws from Allah. **98:3, Surah Al-Baiyina**

And the People of the Scripture did not differ until after there came to them clear evidence. **98:4, Surah Al-Baiyina**

And they were commanded only to worship Allah, and to worship none but Him Alone (abstaining from associating partners with Him), to establish prayer, and give Zakat. That is the right religion. **98:5**

Verily, those who disbelieve (in Islam, the Qur'an and Prophet Muhammad ﷺ) from among the People of the Scripture and the polytheists will abide in the Fire of Hell. They are the worst of creatures. **98:6**

Verily, those who believe (in the Oneness of Allah and His Messenger ﷺ) and do righteous deeds, they are the best of creatures. **98:7**

Their reward with their Lord is 'Adn (Eden) Paradise, underneath which rivers flow. They will abide therein forever. Allah is well pleased with them, and they with Him. That is for those who fear their Lord. **98:8**[178]

The Following Holy Books

Allah Swt Revealed To This World

The following four divine books, along with other scriptures, were revealed by Allah SWT through His messengers (angels). These include:

1. the Qur'an, given to Muhammad ﷺ,
2. the Psalms (Zabur), given to David عليه السلام,
3. the Torah, given to Moses عليه السلام,
4. the Scrolls, given to Abraham عليه السلام, and
5. the Gospel, given to Jesus عليه السلام.

Allah SWT has confirmed this in the verse:

لَقَدْ أَرْسَلْنَا رُسُلَنَا بِالْبَيِّنَاتِ وَأَنزَلْنَا مَعَهُمُ الْكِتَابَ وَالْمِيزَانَ لِيَقُومَ النَّاسُ بِالْقِسْطِ ۖ وَأَنزَلْنَا الْحَدِيدَ فِيهِ بَأْسٌ شَدِيدٌ وَمَنَافِعُ لِلنَّاسِ وَلِيَعْلَمَ اللَّهُ مَن يَنصُرُهُ وَرُسُلَهُ بِالْغَيْبِ ۚ إِنَّ اللَّهَ قَوِيٌّ عَزِيزٌ

Indeed, We have sent Our Messengers with clear proofs, and revealed with them the Scripture and the Balance, that mankind may keep up justice. And We brought forth iron, wherein is mighty power (in matters of war), as well as many benefits for mankind, that Allah may test who it is that will help Him and His Messengers in the unseen. Verily, Allah is All-Strong, Almighty.

Surah Al-Hadid 57:25

1. The Zabur

The Zabur is the book of Allah SWT revealed to Prophet Dawud عليه السلام. The word "Zabur" means "songs" in Arabic, as this revelation came to Prophet Dawud عليه السلام in the form of a series of songs or chants.

In the Holy Qur'an, Allah Almighty says:

"...and to Dawood, We gave the Zaboor."

Qur'an 4:163

إِنَّا أَوْحَيْنَا إِلَيْكَ كَمَا أَوْحَيْنَا إِلَىٰ نُوحٍ وَالنَّبِيِّينَ مِن بَعْدِهِ ۚ وَأَوْحَيْنَا إِلَىٰ إِبْرَاهِيمَ وَإِسْمَاعِيلَ وَإِسْحَاقَ وَيَعْقُوبَ وَالْأَسْبَاطِ وَعِيسَىٰ وَأَيُّوبَ وَيُونُسَ وَهَارُونَ وَسُلَيْمَانَ ۚ وَآتَيْنَا دَاوُودَ زَبُورًا

---

[178] https://www.al-islam.org/alphabetical-index-holy-quran/ahlul-kitab

Surely We have revealed to thee as We revealed to Noah and the prophets after him, and We revealed to Abraham and Ishmael and Isaac and Jacob and the tribes, and Jesus and Job and Jonah and Aaron and Solomon, and We gave to David the Psalms.

Surah An-Nisaa 4:163

2. The Torah

The Torah is the revelation sent down by Almighty Allah to Prophet Musa عليه السلام. In the Qur'an, the word Torah generally refers to "The Law", specifically the Law given to Moses. Many associate the Torah with the Jewish scriptures or the Old Testament in the Christian Bible.

Article adapted from Ahlul'l-Kitab.

Allah SWT says:

إِنَّا أَنزَلْنَا التَّوْرَاةَ فِيهَا هُدًى وَنُورٌ ۚ يَحْكُمُ بِهَا النَّبِيُّونَ الَّذِينَ أَسْلَمُوا لِلَّذِينَ هَادُوا وَالرَّبَّانِيُّونَ وَالْأَحْبَارُ بِمَا اسْتُحْفِظُوا مِن كِتَابِ اللَّهِ وَكَانُوا عَلَيْهِ شُهَدَاءَ ۚ فَلَا تَخْشَوُا النَّاسَ وَاخْشَوْنِ وَلَا تَشْتَرُوا بِآيَاتِي ثَمَنًا قَلِيلًا ۚ وَمَن لَّمْ يَحْكُم بِمَا أَنزَلَ اللَّهُ فَأُولَٰئِكَ هُمُ الْكَافِرُونَ

Indeed, We sent down the Torah [to Moses], wherein was guidance and light. By it, the prophets who submitted themselves to Allah judged the Jews. And the rabbis and the priests [also judged by it], for they were entrusted with the protection of Allah's Book and were witnesses to it. So fear not men, but fear Me, and sell not My verses for a small price. And whosoever does not judge by what Allah has revealed – such are the disbelievers.

Surah Al-Ma'idah 5:44

3. The Scrolls (Given to Abraham عليه السلام)

We do not know much about this scripture, as it is widely accepted that the Abrahamic Scrolls, known as *Suhuf*, were the earliest scriptures containing Allah's revelations to Prophet Ibrahim عليه السلام. These were written by him and his followers but have since been lost.

It is also believed that the scriptures of Jesus, Moses, and David (peace be upon them) were altered or distorted and are no longer in their original form. Although the word of Allah cannot be changed or omitted by anyone—as promised by Allah SWT—Satan's influence cannot be overlooked.

We can assume that the scriptures revealed to Prophet Ibrahim عليه السلام were similar to those given to Musa عليه السلام. This is supported by the clear reference in Surah Al-A'la:

$$\text{وَالْآخِرَةُ خَيْرٌ وَأَبْقَىٰ}$$

$$\text{إِنَّ هَٰذَا لَفِي الصُّحُفِ الْأُولَىٰ}$$

$$\text{صُحُفِ إِبْرَاهِيمَ وَمُوسَىٰ}$$

But the Hereafter is better and more enduring.

Verily! This is in the former scriptures—

The Scriptures of Ibrahim (Abraham) and Musa (Moses).

Surah Al-A'la 87:17–19

And also:

$$\text{أَمْ لَمْ يُنَبَّأْ بِمَا فِي صُحُفِ مُوسَىٰ}$$

$$\text{وَإِبْرَاهِيمَ الَّذِي وَفَّىٰ}$$

Or has he not been informed of what was in the scriptures of Moses,

And of Abraham who fulfilled (his obligations)?

Surah An-Najm 53:36–37

4. The Injeel

The Injeel is the holy book revealed by Allah Almighty to Prophet Eesa (Jesus) عليه السلام. The word *Injeel* means Gospel, and it is often translated simply as *The Gospel*.

Muslims believe that the Injeel was a single, divine book revealed to Jesus عليه السلام. The Bible in its current form exists in many versions due to alterations made over time.

Allah SWT says in the Qur'an:

$$\text{ثُمَّ قَفَّيْنَا عَلَىٰ آثَارِهِمْ بِرُسُلِنَا وَقَفَّيْنَا بِعِيسَى ابْنِ مَرْيَمَ وَآتَيْنَاهُ الْإِنْجِيلَ وَجَعَلْنَا فِي قُلُوبِ الَّذِينَ}$$
$$\text{اتَّبَعُوهُ رَأْفَةً وَرَحْمَةً وَرَهْبَانِيَّةً ابْتَدَعُوهَا مَا كَتَبْنَاهَا عَلَيْهِمْ إِلَّا ابْتِغَاءَ رِضْوَانِ اللَّهِ فَمَا رَعَوْهَا}$$
$$\text{حَقَّ رِعَايَتِهَا ۖ فَآتَيْنَا الَّذِينَ آمَنُوا مِنْهُمْ أَجْرَهُمْ ۖ وَكَثِيرٌ مِنْهُمْ فَاسِقُونَ}$$

Then, We sent after them Our Messengers, and We sent Jesus, the son of Mary, and gave him the Gospel. And We placed in the hearts of those who followed him compassion and mercy. But the monasticism which they invented, We did not prescribe for them. They sought it only to please Allah but did not observe it with right observance. So We rewarded those among them who believed, but many of them are rebellious.

Surah Al-Hadid 57:27

And again:

وَقَفَّيْنَا عَلَىٰ آثَارِهِم بِعِيسَى ابْنِ مَرْيَمَ مُصَدِّقًا لِّمَا بَيْنَ يَدَيْهِ مِنَ التَّوْرَاةِ ۖ وَآتَيْنَاهُ الْإِنجِيلَ فِيهِ
هُدًى وَنُورٌ وَمُصَدِّقًا لِّمَا بَيْنَ يَدَيْهِ مِنَ التَّوْرَاةِ وَهُدًى وَمَوْعِظَةً لِّلْمُتَّقِينَ

And We sent Jesus, son of Mary, following in their footsteps, confirming the Torah that had come before him. We gave him the Gospel, in which there was guidance and light, and confirmation of the Torah before it, a guidance and an admonition for the pious.

Surah Al-Ma'idah 5:46

5 The Holy Qur'an

In the Qur'an, Allah says:

نَزَّلَ عَلَيْكَ الْكِتَابَ بِالْحَقِّ مُصَدِّقًا لِّمَا بَيْنَ يَدَيْهِ وَأَنزَلَ التَّوْرَاةَ وَالْإِنجِيلَ

مِن قَبْلُ هُدًى لِّلنَّاسِ وَأَنزَلَ الْفُرْقَانَ ۗ إِنَّ الَّذِينَ كَفَرُوا بِآيَاتِ اللَّهِ لَهُمْ عَذَابٌ شَدِيدٌ ۗ وَاللَّهُ عَزِيزٌ
ذُو انتِقَامٍ

It is He Who has sent down the Book (the Qur'an) to you (Muhammad ﷺ) with truth, confirming what came before it. And He sent down the Taurat (Torah) and the Injeel (Gospel).

Aforetime, as a guidance to mankind. And He sent down the criterion [of judgement between right and wrong (this Qur'an)]. Truly, those who disbelieve in the Ayat (proofs, evidences, verses, lessons, signs, revelations, etc.) of Allah—for them there is a severe torment; and Allah is All-Mighty, All-Able of Retribution.

[Surah Al-Imran 3:3–4]

The Holy Qur'an is the final sanctified book of Allah Almighty, bearing the title *Kalamullah* (كلام الله), meaning "The Word of Allah," and it is the Last Divine Book. No holy book shall be revealed after the Qur'an. The Qur'an originates from the highest level of all His names, with the title "Lord of the Realms."

The order of its *ayahs* is flawless and profound. Its style possesses a glamorous and marvellous beauty. Its explanation and wording reflect clarity and sublimity. The Qur'an conveys integrity and power in its meanings, with accurate and fluent language. It is a universal book, addressing all humankind and jinn, across past and future generations.

The Qur'an encompasses both positive sciences and religious knowledge in essence and seed form. It is the only book that declares reading to be an act of worship.

Every religion believes that Allah (SWT) revealed the Holy Book, the Qur'an, to Muhammad ﷺ, but in a completely different manner than with other prophets. Whenever a verse was revealed to the illuminated heart of the Prophet ﷺ, he would recite it immediately and store it in his memory. He never forgot it, because his infallibility prevented him from forgetting or making a mistake in it.

Allah (SWT) says:

سَنُقْرِئُكَ فَلَا تَنسَىٰ

We shall make you to recite (the Qur'an), so you (O Muhammad ﷺ) shall not forget it.

[Surah Al-A'la 87:6]

Other revealed books were limited to the period and the people to whom they were sent. They came from specific names of Allah (SWT) to meet the needs of a particular tribe and era. In contrast, Allah (SWT) has promised the protection and preservation of the Qur'an through His verses. To this day, one can find the exact same copy of the Qur'an anywhere in the world.

Allah (SWT) says:

إِنَّا نَحْنُ نَزَّلْنَا الذِّكْرَ وَإِنَّا لَهُ لَحَافِظُونَ

Verily We: It is We Who have sent down the Dhikr (i.e. the Qur'an) and surely, We will guard it (from corruption).

[Surah Al-Hijr 15:9] [179]

We will discuss more about the Qur'an in another chapter.

Is it Haram to Read the Bible?

Reading involves absorbing another person's perspective, ideas, thoughts, or accounts of past or current events, which have the power to captivate the reader's mind. This experience can either enlighten the reader and instil wisdom or evoke excitement, depending on the type of literature they are engaged with.

The decision to read the Bible—or any religious book, as mentioned earlier—rests entirely with the individual reader. Reading such texts can be enlightening and educational, but it is crucial for the reader to possess the necessary maturity to grasp the profound meanings within these holy books. Otherwise, the act of reading them may yield more harm than good.

It is worth noting that many educated Muslims may find themselves unable to read the Qur'an, emphasising the importance of first learning and comprehending the Qur'an before delving into other religious texts. However, understanding the Qur'an is no simple task. Translating the Qur'an into any other language cannot

---

[179] (Habiba Afzal https://prezi.com/is2ju0drvq9d/what-are-the-diffferences-between-quran-and-the-other-books)

capture its essence with 100% accuracy, yet we endeavour to comprehend its teachings with sincerity and heartfelt devotion.

Allah SWT says in one verse:

هُوَ الَّذِي أَنزَلَ عَلَيْكَ الْكِتَابَ مِنْهُ آيَاتٌ مُّحْكَمَاتٌ هُنَّ أُمُّ الْكِتَابِ وَأُخَرُ مُتَشَابِهَاتٌ ۖ فَأَمَّا الَّذِينَ فِي قُلُوبِهِمْ زَيْغٌ فَيَتَّبِعُونَ مَا تَشَابَهَ مِنْهُ ابْتِغَاءَ الْفِتْنَةِ وَابْتِغَاءَ تَأْوِيلِهِ ۖ وَمَا يَعْلَمُ تَأْوِيلَهُ إِلَّا اللَّهُ ۖ وَالرَّاسِخُونَ فِي الْعِلْمِ يَقُولُونَ آمَنَّا بِهِ كُلٌّ مِّنْ عِندِ رَبِّنَا ۖ وَمَا يَذَّكَّرُ إِلَّا أُولُو الْأَلْبَابِ

It is He Who hath sent down unto thee the Book: in it are verses basic or fundamental (of established meaning); they are the foundation of the Book: others are allegorical. But those in whose hearts is perversity follow the part thereof that is allegorical, seeking discord, and searching for its hidden meanings, but no one knows its hidden meanings except Allah. And those who are firmly grounded in knowledge say: "We believe in the Book; the whole of it is from our Lord": and none will grasp the Message except men of understanding.

Surah Ale-Imran 3:7

According to scholars, it is widely acknowledged that various sections of previous religious texts have been revised and adapted to suit the wants and inclinations of human beings. While this is indeed the case, it does not undermine our fundamental understanding. In essence, every sacred scripture encompasses the divine words of Allah SWT, many of which are also found in the Qur'an. An excellent illustration of this is the emphasis placed by the Almighty on the purification of the heart. This profound message is consistently present in all holy books.

In the Qur'an, Allah SWT says:

"He has succeeded who purifies himself, who remembers the name of his Lord and prays."

[Qur'an 87:14–15]

"Indeed, Allah loves those who are constantly repentant and loves those who purify themselves."

[Qur'an 2:222]

"We have sent among you a messenger from yourselves, reciting to you Our verses and purifying you and teaching you the Book and wisdom, and teaching you that which you did not know."

[Qur'an 2:151]

The Torah Says:

Create in me a clean heart, O God; and renew a right spirit within me.

[Psalm 51:10, KJV]

The Gospel Says:

Blessed are the pure in heart: for they shall see God.

[Matthew 5:8, KJV]

Who shall ascend into the hill of the Lord? or who shall stand in his holy place? He that hath clean hands, and a pure heart; who hath not lifted up his soul unto vanity, nor sworn deceitfully.

[Psalm 24:3–4, KJV] [180]

"Blessed are the pure in heart, for they shall see God (Matthew 5:8) Note [181]

Sheikh Ahmad Kutty states:

Prophet Muhammad ﷺ forbade Muslims from reading the Bible at the time of the revelation of the Qur'an. He did so in order to ensure that they did not confuse the two.

This inference can be drawn from the fact that the Qur'an itself tells believers to ask the Jews to produce the Torah and recite it.

Prophet Muhammad ﷺ also instructed Zayd ibn Thabit to learn the languages of the Christian and Jewish scriptures. Zayd complied so that he could understand their communications. The Prophet also consulted experts in these scriptures on various occasions.

Furthermore, it is important for us to understand that the Qur'an categorically states that it has been revealed to confirm the previous scriptures—including the Torah and the Gospel—and to act as a corrective, preserving the pristine truths revealed to the earlier prophets. Thus, the Qur'an refers to itself as a clear book, a

---

[180] *Note: - Shaikh Ahmad Kutty (Wikipedia,) a prominent North American Islamic scholar and senior lecturer at the Islamic Institute taught at Emanuel College of the University of Toronto and over the past 40 years, he has been Director of the Islamic Center of Toronto, Director of the Islamic Foundation, Toronto, Canada, and has served on the Fiqh Council of North America. In response to the question about reading the Bible by Muslims,*

[181] *Note:- Shaikh Ahmad Kutty (Wikipedia,) a prominent North American Islamic scholar and senior lecturer at the Islamic Institute taught at Emanuel College of the University of Toronto and Over the past 40 years, he has been Director of the Islamic Center of Toronto, Director of the Islamic Foundation, Toronto, Canada, and has served on the Fiqh Council of North America. In response to the question about reading the Bible by Muslims*

source of light, and guidance. It sheds light on many issues over which the People of the Book have disagreed and in which they have become divided.

Prophet Muhammad ﷺ said:

"I have brought (the religious message) as crystal clear."

It is worth mentioning that this description of the Qur'anic message has also been confirmed by the impressions of many eminent personalities who reverted to Islam from Judaism and Christianity.[182]

****

بِسْمِ اللَّهِ الرَّحْمَٰنِ الرَّحِيمِ

To alleviate the stress of endless travel, which can exhaust a traveller's mind, let us take a moment to shift our focus to topics of historical significance and religious events. These subjects are sure to delight travellers and inspire them to continue their journeys with renewed enthusiasm.

For example:

In a survey conducted among common Muslims, participants were asked about a specific surah in the Qur'an where "Bismillah" (In the name of Allah) appears twice—once at the beginning and once in the middle. The question was: what is the name of this surah, and what is the story behind the repetition of *Bismillah*?

Responses varied. Many Qur'an reciters admitted they didn't know; some provided incorrect answers, others knew the correct surah but not the story behind it, while many gave both the correct answer and the backstory.

If interested to know more, you may read the details below:

The surah in question is **Surah An-Naml** (*The Ant*). The first *Bismillah* appears at the start, as is the case with most surahs. The second *Bismillah* is found in verse 30, where it is part of a letter sent by Prophet Solomon (Sulaiman عليه السلام) to the Queen of Sheba. The letter begins with: *"In the name of Allah, the Most Gracious, the Most Merciful."*

This unique feature highlights the importance of invoking Allah's name in communication and leadership, emphasising the spiritual and respectful approach of Prophet Solomon عليه السلام.

If interested to know further, you may read the details below:

---

[182] Index 143 https://aboutislamver2.aboutislam.net/counseling/ask-the-scholar/ideologies-movements-religions/is-a-muslim-allowed-to-read-the-bible/What

Surah An-Naml [27:28–32]

The context of the story:

The complete phrase بِسْمِ اللهِ الرَّحْمٰنِ الرَّحِيْمِ appears within only one surah—**An-Naml (27), verse 30**:

$$إِنَّهُ مِن سُلَيْمَانَ وَإِنَّهُ بِسْمِ اللَّهِ الرَّحْمَـٰنِ الرَّحِيمِ$$

"Verily! It is from Sulaiman (Solomon), and verily! It (reads): In the name of Allah, the Most Beneficent, the Most Merciful."

A Story

$$بِسْمِ اللهِ الرَّحْمٰنِ الرَّحِيْمِ$$

'Ali ibn Ibrahim narrates that when Sulayman عليه السلام sat on the throne, the birds specially appointed by Allah SWT used to shadow him and all those who were near his throne. One day, the hoopoe (woodpecker) was absent, and because of its absence, the sun's rays fell upon Sulayman عليه السلام. So he raised his head, looked towards the vacant place, and found the hoopoe missing.

As Allah SWT says in **Surah An-Naml**:

And he reviewed the birds, then said:

"What is the matter that I see not the hoopoe? Or is he among the absentees?

I will surely punish him with a severe torment, or slaughter him, unless he brings me a clear reason."

But the hoopoe stayed not long; he (came up and) said:

"I have grasped (the knowledge of a thing) which you have not grasped, and I have come to you from Saba' (Sheba) with true news.

I found a woman ruling over them, and she has been given all things that could be possessed by any ruler of the earth, and she has a great throne.

I found her and her people worshipping the sun instead of Allah, and Shaitan (Satan) has made their deeds fair-seeming to them, and has barred them from (Allah's) Way, so they have no guidance,

Al-la (this word has two interpretations):

(A) [As Shaitan has barred them from Allah's Way] so that they do not worship (prostrate before) Allah, or

(B) So that they may worship (prostrate before) Allah, Who brings to light what is hidden in the heavens and the earth, and knows what you conceal and what you reveal.

Allah, La ilaha illa Huwa (none has the right to be worshipped but He), the Lord of the Supreme Throne!

[Sulaiman (Solomon)] said: "We shall see whether you speak the truth or you are (one) of the liars.

Go you with this letter of mine, and deliver it to them, then draw back from them, and see what (answer) they return."

(27:20–28)

'Ali ibn Ibrahim narrates that the hoopoe said that Bilquis, the Queen of Saba, was sitting on a grand throne, and he could not reach it. Sulayman said, "Throw this letter from the top of the tomb." The hoopoe returned and, through the chandeliers of Bilquis, dropped the letter on her lap. She became alarmed after reading the letter and called her army chief, saying:

قَالَتْ يَا أَيُّهَا الْمَلَأُ إِنِّي أُلْقِيَ إِلَيَّ كِتَابٌ كَرِيمٌ

"She (the queen) said: 'O chiefs! Verily! Here is delivered to me a noble letter.'"

(Surah An-Naml 27:29)

It is narrated from **Imam as-Sadiq** that the greatness of Sulayman عليه السلام's letter lay in the fact that it always bore his seal. So Bilquis said:

إِنَّهُ مِن سُلَيْمَانَ وَإِنَّهُ بِسْمِ اللَّهِ الرَّحْمَٰنِ الرَّحِيمِ

أَلَّا تَعْلُوا عَلَيَّ وَأْتُونِي مُسْلِمِينَ

قَالَتْ يَا أَيُّهَا الْمَلَأُ أَفْتُونِي فِي أَمْرِي مَا كُنتُ قَاطِعَةً أَمْرًا حَتَّىٰ تَشْهَدُونِ

قَالُوا نَحْنُ أُولُو قُوَّةٍ وَأُولُو بَأْسٍ شَدِيدٍ وَالْأَمْرُ إِلَيْكِ فَانظُرِي مَاذَا تَأْمُرِينَ

قَالَتْ إِنَّ الْمُلُوكَ إِذَا دَخَلُوا قَرْيَةً أَفْسَدُوهَا وَجَعَلُوا أَعِزَّةَ أَهْلِهَا أَذِلَّةً ۖ وَكَذَٰلِكَ يَفْعَلُونَ

وَإِنِّي مُرْسِلَةٌ إِلَيْهِم بِهَدِيَّةٍ فَنَاظِرَةٌ بِمَ يَرْجِعُ الْمُرْسَلُونَ

"Verily! It is from Sulaiman (Solomon), and verily! It (reads): In the name of Allah, the Most Beneficent, the Most Merciful.

Be ye not exalted against me, but come to me as Muslims (those who submit)."

She said: "O chiefs! Advise me in this case of mine. I decide no matter until ye are present with me."

They said: "We are possessors of strength, and possessors of great might in war, but the decision is yours; therefore, consider what thou wilt command."

She said: "Surely, when kings enter a town, they ruin it and make the most honourable of its people the lowest. Thus do they behave.

And lo! I am going to send him a present, and shall see with what (answer) the messengers return."

(Surah An-Naml 27:30–35)

Shaykh al-Tusi narrates that the army chiefs of Bilquis were 312 in number, with each chief commanding a thousand men.

'Ali ibn Ibrahim says that Bilquis said, "I will send a gift to him. If he is a king, he will be inclined towards this world and will accept my gift. Then I will understand that he has no power to conquer me." A small casket was prepared for Sulayman, containing a large pearl and precious stones. Along with it was conveyed the message: "Tell Sulayman to make a hole in these, without the help of iron or fire."

When the gift reached Sulayman and the messenger conveyed the words of Bilquis, Sulayman ordered a worm to take a thread in its mouth and bore a hole through the pearl, drawing the thread out from the other side.

"So when he came to Sulayman, he said, What! wilt thou help me with riches? what God hath given me is better than that which he hath given you: nay, it is ye that rejoice in your gift. Go back to them: verily we shall come unto them with hosts that they shall not be able to resist: and we shall drive them out from thence with shame, and they shall be abased."

— Surah An-Naml 27:36–37

فَلَمَّا جَاءَ سُلَيْمَانَ قَالَ أَتُمِدُّونَنِ بِمَالٍ فَمَا آتَانِيَ اللَّهُ خَيْرٌ مِّمَّا آتَاكُم بَلْ أَنتُم بِهَدِيَّتِكُمْ تَفْرَحُونَ

ارْجِعْ إِلَيْهِمْ فَلَنَأْتِيَنَّهُم بِجُنُودٍ لَّا قِبَلَ لَهُم بِهَا وَلَنُخْرِجَنَّهُم مِّنْهَا أَذِلَّةً وَهُمْ صَاغِرُونَ

'Ali ibn Ibrahim narrates that when the messenger of Bilquis returned and described the majesty and dignity of Sulayman, she realised she had no power to wage war against him. Thus, she submitted to his authority and set out to meet him.

Allah (SWT) informed Sulayman that Bilquis was on her way and would soon reach him. Sulayman said to the jinn and satans who were in his presence, "Before Bilquis arrives, bring me her throne." Allah (SWT) says:

"He said, O chiefs! Which of you can bring to me her throne before they come to me in submission? One audacious among the jinn said, I will bring it to you before you rise from your place; and most surely, I am strong (and) trusty for it. One who had the knowledge of the book said, 'I will bring it to you in the twinkling of an eye.'

Then when he saw it settled beside him, he said, 'This is of the grace of my Lord that He may try me whether I am grateful or ungrateful; and whoever is grateful, he is grateful only for his own soul, and whoever is ungrateful, then surely my Lord is Self-sufficient, Honoured.'

He said, 'Alter her throne for her; we will see whether she follows the right way or is of those who do not go aright.'

So when she came, it was said, 'Is your throne like this?'

She said, 'It is as it were the same, and we were given the knowledge before it, and we were submissive.'

And what she worshipped besides Allah prevented her; surely, she was of an unbelieving people."

— Surah An-Naml 27:38–43

قَالَ يَا أَيُّهَا الْمَلَأُ أَيُّكُمْ يَأْتِينِي بِعَرْشِهَا قَبْلَ أَن يَأْتُونِي مُسْلِمِ

قَالَ عِفْرِيتٌ مِّنَ الْجِنِّ أَنَا آتِيكَ بِهِ قَبْلَ أَن تَقُومَ مِن مَّقَامِكَ ۖ وَإِنِّي عَلَيْهِ لَقَوِيٌّ أَمِينٌ ¬

قَالَ الَّذِي عِندَهُ عِلْمٌ مِّنَ الْكِتَابِ أَنَا آتِيكَ بِهِ قَبْلَ أَن يَرْتَدَّ إِلَيْكَ طَرْفُكَ ۚ فَلَمَّا رَآهُ مُسْتَقِرًّا عِندَهُ قَالَ هَٰذَا مِن فَضْلِ رَبِّي لِيَبْلُوَنِي أَأَشْكُرُ أَمْ أَكْفُرُ ۖ وَمَن شَكَرَ فَإِنَّمَا يَشْكُرُ لِنَفْسِهِ ۖ وَمَن كَفَرَ فَإِنَّ رَبِّي غَنِيٌّ كَرِيمٌ

قَالَ نَكِّرُوا لَهَا عَرْشَهَا نَنظُرْ أَتَهْتَدِي أَمْ تَكُونُ مِنَ الَّذِينَ لَا يَهْتَدُونَ ¬

فَلَمَّا جَاءَتْ قِيلَ أَهَٰكَذَا عَرْشُكِ ۖ قَالَتْ كَأَنَّهُ هُوَ ۚ وَأُوتِينَا الْعِلْمَ مِن قَبْلِهَا وَكُنَّا مُسْلِمِينَ ¬

وَصَدَّهَا مَا كَانَت تَّعْبُدُ مِن دُونِ اللَّهِ ۖ إِنَّهَا كَانَتْ مِن قَوْمٍ كَافِرِينَ ¬

38. He said: "O chiefs! Which of you can bring me her throne before they come to me surrendering themselves in obedience?"

39. An Ifrit (strong one) from the jinn said: "I will bring it to you before you rise from your place (of council). And verily, I am indeed strong and trustworthy for such work."

40. One with whom was knowledge of the Scripture said: "I will bring it to you within the twinkling of an eye!" Then when [Sulaiman (Solomon)] saw it placed before him, he said: "This is by the Grace of my Lord to test me whether I am grateful or ungrateful! And whoever is grateful, truly, his gratitude is for the good of his own self, and whoever is ungrateful, he is ungrateful only for the loss of his own self. Certainly, my Lord is Rich (Free of all wants), Bountiful."

41. He said: "Disguise her throne for her that we may see whether she will be guided (to recognise her throne), or she will be one of those not guided."

42. So when she came, it was said to her: "Is your throne like this?" She said: "It is as though it were the very same." And [Sulaiman (Solomon) said]: "Knowledge was bestowed on us before her, and we were submitted to Allah (in Islam as Muslims before her)."

43. And that which she used to worship besides Allah had prevented her (from Islam), for she was of a disbelieving people.

386

— **Surah An-Naml 27:38–43**

'Ali ibn Ibrahim narrates that, before the arrival of Bilquis, the jinn—on the order of Sulayman—constructed a palace of glass and concealed it with water.

قِيلَ لَهَا ادْخُلِي الصَّرْحَ ۖ فَلَمَّا رَأَتْهُ حَسِبَتْهُ لُجَّةً وَكَشَفَتْ عَن سَاقَيْهَا ۚ قَالَ إِنَّهُ صَرْحٌ مُّمَرَّدٌ ¬
مِّن قَوَارِيرَ ۗ قَالَتْ رَبِّ إِنِّي ظَلَمْتُ نَفْسِي وَأَسْلَمْتُ مَعَ سُلَيْمَانَ لِلَّهِ رَبِّ الْعَالَمِينَ

It was said to her: "Enter As-Sarh" [(a glass surface with water underneath) or a palace], but when she saw it, she thought it was a pool, and she (tucked up her clothes) uncovering her legs. Sulaiman (Solomon) said: "Verily, it is a Sarh [(a glass surface with water underneath) or a palace] paved smooth with slabs of glass."

She said: "My Lord! Verily, I have wronged myself, and I submit (in Islam, together with Sulaiman), to Allah, the Lord of the Worlds."

— **Surah An-Naml 27:44**

'Ali ibn Ibrahim narrates that Sulayman then married Bilquis. She was the daughter of Sarah Jasarya. Sulayman instructed the shaitans to prepare a substance to remove the hair from her legs. Afterwards, a bath was prepared for her.[183]

****

What is the Difference Between a "Nabi" and a "Rasul"?

Allah SWT says in Surah Al-Hajj (22), verse 52:

وَمَا أَرْسَلْنَا مِن قَبْلِكَ مِن رَّسُولٍ وَلَا نَبِيٍّ إِلَّا إِذَا تَمَنَّىٰ أَلْقَى الشَّيْطَانُ فِي أُمْنِيَّتِهِ فَيَنسَخُ اللَّهُ مَا
يُلْقِي الشَّيْطَانُ ثُمَّ يُحْكِمُ اللَّهُ آيَاتِهِ ۗ وَاللَّهُ عَلِيمٌ حَكِيمٌ

"Never did We send a Messenger or a Prophet before you, but when he recited the revelation or narrated or spoke, Satan threw (some falsehood) into it. But Allah abolishes that which Satan throws in; then Allah establishes His revelations. And Allah is All-Knowing, All-Wise."

— **Surah Al-Hajj (22:52)**

Based on the Qur'an and scholars' interpretations, we can define the terms *Rasul* and *Nabi* and distinguish between these two significant positions.

A Rasul is granted a Shari'ah (a code of divine law) by Allah SWT and has the authority to receive divine messages through various means, such as visions during sleep, direct communication with angels, and the ability to see and speak with these divine messengers.

---

[183] Index 144 https://www.islamiclearning.org/Docs/Hayat-Qulub-Alama-Majlisi.pdf Page 597
Index 145 Hayatul Qulub - Vol. 1 Stories of the Prophets.
https://www.islamiclearning.org/Docs/Hayat-Qulub-Alama-Majlisi.pdf

This is confirmed in verse 285 of Surah Al-Baqarah (2). The verse says:

آمَنَ الرَّسُولُ بِمَا أُنزِلَ إِلَيْهِ مِن رَّبِّهِ وَالْمُؤْمِنُونَ ۚ كُلٌّ آمَنَ بِاللَّهِ وَمَلَائِكَتِهِ وَكُتُبِهِ وَرُسُلِهِ لَا نُفَرِّقُ بَيْنَ أَحَدٍ مِّن رُّسُلِهِ ۚ وَقَالُوا سَمِعْنَا وَأَطَعْنَا ۖ غُفْرَانَكَ رَبَّنَا وَإِلَيْكَ الْمَصِيرُ

"The Messenger (Muhammad ﷺ) believeth in what hath been revealed unto him from his Lord, and (so do) the believers. Each one believeth in Allah, and His angels, and His books, and His messengers. We make no distinction between any of His messengers. And they say, We hear, and we obey. (Grant us) Thy forgiveness, our Lord. Unto Thee is the journeying."

— Surah Al-Baqarah (2:285)

A *Nabi* (Prophet), however, differs from a *Rasul* in that he does not see the divine messengers while awake or in sleep. In rank, the *Rasul* is higher than the *Nabi*.

All *Rasuls* were *Nabis*, but not all *Nabis* were *Rasuls*. A Prophet is always a *Nabi* by birth, but he becomes a *Rasul* when he is divinely appointed and declares his mission.

For example, our Prophet Muhammad ﷺ was a *Nabi* by birth but became a *Rasul* when he officially received divine authority and delivered the message of *Risalah* at the age of 40.

Allah SWT has sent a Prophet to every nation, and most of the Prophets were from the nations to which they were sent. They preached the worship of Allah alone and warned against false deities.

Allah SWT says:

وَلَقَدْ بَعَثْنَا فِي كُلِّ أُمَّةٍ رَّسُولًا أَنِ اعْبُدُوا اللَّهَ وَاجْتَنِبُوا الطَّاغُوتَ ۖ فَمِنْهُم مَّنْ هَدَى اللَّهُ وَمِنْهُم مَّنْ حَقَّتْ عَلَيْهِ الضَّلَالَةُ ۚ فَسِيرُوا فِي الْأَرْضِ فَانظُرُوا كَيْفَ كَانَ عَاقِبَةُ الْمُكَذِّبِينَ

"And verily, We have sent among every Ummah (community, nation) a Messenger (proclaiming): 'Worship Allah (Alone), and avoid Taghut (false deities).' Then of them were some whom Allah guided, and of them were some upon whom the straying was justified. So travel through the earth and see what was the end of those who denied (the truth)."

— Surah An-Nahl (16:36)

وَمَا مُحَمَّدٌ إِلَّا رَسُولٌ قَدْ خَلَتْ مِن قَبْلِهِ الرُّسُلُ ۚ أَفَإِن مَّاتَ أَوْ قُتِلَ انقَلَبْتُمْ عَلَىٰ أَعْقَابِكُمْ ۚ وَمَن يَنقَلِبْ عَلَىٰ عَقِبَيْهِ فَلَن يَضُرَّ اللَّهَ شَيْئًا ۗ وَسَيَجْزِي اللَّهُ الشَّاكِرِينَ

"Muhammad ﷺ is no more than a messenger; many were the messengers that passed away before him. If he die or be slain, will ye then turn back on your heels? But he that turneth back on his heels shall not harm Allah in the least. And Allah will reward the grateful."

— Surah Al-Imran (3:144)

Most of Allah's messengers, except Prophet Muhammad ﷺ, were sent to specific nations. However, Prophet Muhammad ﷺ was sent with a universal message for all mankind.

It is the duty of Muslims to send *Salam* (peace and blessings of Allah) when mentioning the name of any Prophet.

إِنَّ اللَّهَ وَمَلَائِكَتَهُ يُصَلُّونَ عَلَى النَّبِيِّ ۚ يَا أَيُّهَا الَّذِينَ آمَنُوا صَلُّوا عَلَيْهِ وَسَلِّمُوا تَسْلِيمًا

"Verily Allah and His angels send blessings on the Prophet: O ye that believe! Send ye blessings on him, and salute him with all respect."

— Surah Al-Ahzab (33:56)

How Many Prophets Are Mentioned in the Qur'an?

There are 25 Prophets of Allah mentioned in the Qur'an:

1. Hazrat Adam (A.S.)
2. Idris (A.S.) — Enoch
3. Nuh (A.S.) — Noah
4. Hud (A.S.)
5. Salih (A.S.) — Saleh
6. Ibrahim (A.S.) — Abraham
7. Lut (A.S.) — Lot
8. Ismail (A.S.) — Ishmael
9. Ishaq (A.S.) — Isaac
10. Yaqub (A.S.) — Jacob
11. Yusuf (A.S.) — Joseph
12. Ayyub (A.S.) — Job
13. Shu'aib (A.S.) — Jethro
14. Musa (A.S.) — Moses
15. Harun (A.S.) — Aaron
16. Dhul-Kifl (A.S.) — Ezekiel
17. Dawud (A.S.) — David
18. Sulaiman (A.S.) — Solomon
19. Ilyas (A.S.) — Elijah
20. Al-Yasa' (A.S.) — Elisha
21. Yunus (A.S.) — Jonah

22. Zakariya (A.S.) — Zechariah

23. Yahya (A.S.) — John

24. Isa (A.S.) — Jesus

25. Muhammad ﷺ — The Final Prophet

The truth is, Allah SWT alone knows the total number and locations of all the Prophets He has sent throughout history for the guidance of mankind. He has chosen Prophet Muhammad ﷺ as the final messenger with a universal message for all of humanity.

The hadith of Abu Dharr al-Ghifari: (*Note*)[184] **The Prophet (ﷺ) was asked about the number of Nabi and Rasul.**

He (ﷺ) replied that there were 124,000 Prophets, among whom 315 were Messengers. This hadith is collected in *Musnad Ahmad* and the collections of *At-Tabarani* and *Ibn Hibban*.

However, we wish to conclude this discussion by referring to the verse where Allah (SWT) says:

وَلَقَدْ أَرْسَلْنَا رُسُلًا مِّن قَبْلِكَ مِنْهُم مَّن قَصَصْنَا عَلَيْكَ وَمِنْهُم مَّن لَّمْ نَقْصُصْ عَلَيْكَ ۗ وَمَا كَانَ لِرَسُولٍ أَن يَأْتِيَ بِآيَةٍ إِلَّا بِإِذْنِ اللَّهِ ۚ فَإِذَا جَاءَ أَمْرُ اللَّهِ قُضِيَ بِالْحَقِّ وَخَسِرَ هُنَالِكَ الْمُبْطِلُونَ

And, indeed We have sent Messengers before you (O Muhammad ﷺ); of some of them We have related to you their story, and of some We have not related to you their story. And it was not for any Messenger to bring a sign except by the Leave of Allah. So, when the Commandment of Allah comes, the matter will be decided with truth, and the followers of falsehood will then be lost.

40:78 – Surah Al-Mu'min (Ghafir)

Do We Know That Circumcision Is Sunnat-e-Ibraheem (عليه السلام)?

Circumcision is **Sunnat-e-Ibraheem** (عليه السلام), as affirmed in the Holy Bible:

Genesis 17:12–14 (KJV)

12 And he that is eight days old shall be circumcised among you, every man child in your generations, he that is born in the house, or bought with money of any stranger, which is not of thy seed.

13 He that is born in thy house, and he that is bought with thy money, must needs be circumcised: and my covenant shall be in your flesh for an everlasting covenant.

---

[184] Abu Dharr Al-Ghifari Al-Kinani (أَبُو ذَرّ ٱلْغِفَارِيّ ٱلْكِنَانِيّ, ' Abū Darr al-Ghifārīy al-Kinānīy), also spelled Abu Zarr, born Jundab ibn Junādah (جُنْدَب ٱبْن جُنَادَة), was the fourth or fifth person converting to Islam, and from the Muhajirun.[1] He belonged to the Banu Ghifar, the Kinanah tribe. No date of birth is known. He died in 652 CE, at Al-Rabadha, in the desert east of Medina.

14 And the uncircumcised man child whose flesh of his foreskin is not circumcised, that soul shall be cut off from his people; he hath broken my covenant.

Amazing Story of Prophet Idris (Enoch) (عليه السلام) and Prophet Dawood (عليه السلام)

1. Idris / Enoch إدريس (عليه السلام)

وَاذْكُرْ فِي الْكِتَابِ إِدْرِيسَ ۚ إِنَّهُ كَانَ صِدِّيقًا نَّبِيًّا

وَرَفَعْنَاهُ مَكَانًا عَلِيًّا

And mention in the Book (the Qur'an) Idris (Enoch). Verily, he was a man of truth, (and) a Prophet. And We raised him to a high station.

19:56–57 – Surah Maryam

Idris (عليه السلام) was a Prophet and Messenger, as confirmed in the Qur'an.

2. Isma'il, Idris, and Dhul-Kifl (عليهم السلام)

وَإِسْمَاعِيلَ وَإِدْرِيسَ وَذَا الْكِفْلِ ۖ كُلٌّ مِّنَ الصَّابِرِينَ

وَأَدْخَلْنَاهُمْ فِي رَحْمَتِنَا ۖ إِنَّهُم مِّنَ الصَّالِحِينَ

And (remember) Isma'il (Ishmael), and Idris (Enoch), and Dhul-Kifl (Isaiah); all were from among As-Sabirin (the patient ones). And We admitted them to Our Mercy. Verily, they were of the righteous.

21:85–86 – Surah Al-Anbiyaa

The Messenger of Allah (SWT) said:

"O Abu Dharr! Four of the Prophets were Syriac…"[185]

Adam, Shith, Akhnu' and Nuh (Prophet Noah), and Akhnu', who is called Idris, was the first person to write with a pen.

عليهم السلام أجمعين

And four of the Prophets were Arabs:

Hud, Salih, Shu'ayb, and your Prophet ﷺ

And the first Prophet of the Israelites was Musa عليه السلام, and the last was 'Isa عليه السلام.

"Between them were six hundred Prophets."

---

[185] (Syriac, also known as Syriac Aramaic or Classical Syriac, is a dialect of Middle Aramaic that is the minority language of Syrian Christians in eastern Turkey, northern Iraq, and northeaster Syria. It is also the liturgical language of several churches.)

However, in other traditions, the number of Israelite Prophets is mentioned as 4,000, though the former tradition is considered more reliable.

Authenticated information about the story of Prophet Idris عليه السلام is limited, whether in the Qur'an, the books of Tafsir, or in historical texts on the prophets. Their findings vary. The Bible also tells the story of the Prophet Idris عليه السلام (known as Enoch), but it differs in some respects from Islamic sources. However, we have been able to gather reliable texts from various works written by Islamic scholars, particularly in relation to the explanation of Surah Maryam, verses 19:56–57, as mentioned earlier.

Prophet Idris عليه السلام (Arabic: سيردا) is one of the apostles, and it is said he was the first of Adam's descendants to be granted Prophethood by Allah (SWT) after Adam himself and Shiyth (known as Seth to Jews and Christians). In the Bible, he is known as Enoch. Prophet Idris is the sixth descendant of Prophet Adam, the son of Yarid, son of Qinan, son of Mihla'iel, son of Anush, son of Shiyth, son of Adam عليه السلام. He became the first prophet sent after Adam and Shiyth.

From authentic sources, it is narrated by Wahab that Idris was a well-built man with a broad chest. He was named Idris because he used to teach about the magnanimity (generosity) of Allah SWT and the excellence of Islam.

When Prophet Idris عليه السلام instructed his people to leave Babylon for a reason, they asked, "Where will we find a place like it?" He replied, "If we emigrate for the sake of Allah SWT, He will provide for us." So the people journeyed with Prophet Idris عليه السلام until they reached the land of Egypt. After migrating to Egypt, the people dispersed throughout North and West Africa. During his lifetime, they built 88 cities—the first cities on Earth. At that time, each city was considered a nation, meaning his people had established early civilisations.

Idris عليه السلام was the first to design and teach his people how to build cities. Every group from his nation built cities in their respective lands. These 88 cities formed one of the earliest known civilisations of mankind.

In Egypt, where he preached and sought to establish the religion of Allah SWT, Prophet Idris عليه السلام taught monotheism and became known for his wisdom. He invited people to the worship of Allah alone. Due to this call, many began to follow him. At first, they were seven in number, then seventy, then seven hundred, and eventually one thousand followers joined him.

Then he said to them, "Let us select one hundred pious individuals." From the thousand, seventy were chosen, then ten from them, and finally, seven were selected. He often contemplated the majesty, grandeur, and glory of Allah SWT—how the sky, the earth, the sun, the moon, the stars, the clouds, and all creation have a Creator who, by His power, formed and arranged them all.

According to a hadith from Abu Dharr, it is narrated that thirty scriptures were revealed to Idris عليه السلام. Other traditions state that he was the first person to write with a pen. He was also the first to stitch garments and wear them, whereas people before him used to cover themselves with leaves. Idris عليه السلام used to sew his clothes and worship Allah SWT.

Reliable traditions narrated from Imam Ja'far as-Sadiq state that Masjid as-Sahlah was the residence of Idris, where he used to sew clothes and worship Allah. Allah SWT fulfils the desires of those who supplicate at that place and will elevate their status on the Day of Judgement, as it was the dwelling place of Prophet Idris عليه السلام.

It is also narrated from Imam Ja'far as-Sadiq that during the early days of Prophet Idris's mission, there lived a tyrant king. One day, while out on a walk, the king passed through a lush, green piece of land owned by a devout believer. This man had rejected all false religions and was deeply disturbed by the actions of transgressors, distancing himself from them.

The king desired that particular land and asked his vizier about its owner. The vizier informed him that it belonged to a certain believer in the kingdom. The king summoned the man and expressed his wish to acquire the land. The believer replied that his family had more need of it than the king. Even when asked to sell it, the believer refused. This angered the king, who returned to his palace in an agitated state.

The king had a beloved wife from Iraq named Barak, with whom he often consulted. When he returned home, she noticed his mood and asked what had upset him. He told her about the incident with the landowner.

She replied, "Only one who lacks the power to take revenge gets angry. If you do not wish to execute or behead him without reason, I will show you a way to kill him such that the land will become yours, and even his family will not blame you."

The king asked what plan she had in mind. She said one of her people (from Azarak) would arrest the believer and falsely testify that he had turned away from the king's religion. "That way, you can kill him and seize the land."

The king agreed. Groups from Iraq who followed the queen's religion—people who did not consider the killing of a believer a sin—were called upon. They testified before the king that the man had abandoned the state religion. Upon hearing this, the king ordered the believer's execution and seized his land.

Allah SWT was angered by this murder and revealed to Idris:

"Was he not satisfied with killing the believer, that he also seized the land belonging to the poor man's family? I swear by My Majesty and Power that I will avenge his murder on the Day of Resurrection. I will bring an end to your rule in this world. I will turn your honour and dignity into disgrace and humiliation. And dogs will eat your wife's flesh. Has My forbearance, which was a test for you, made you arrogant?"

Idris عليه السلام addressed the king and said:

"O tyrant ruler! I am the Messenger of Allah SWT,"

And then narrated to him the divine message. The king ordered Idris to leave his court and warned him that he would not be able to save himself. The king told his wife about his discussion with Idris. She said:

"Do not fear the messengership of Idris's God. I will send someone to kill Idris so that the messengership of his God is nullified."

The king agreed to her suggestion and gave his consent.

Among the friends of Idris, there were some who used to attend the royal court. Idris had informed them of the revelation given to him and of his mission to convey the message to the king. They feared Idris would be killed.

The queen sent forty Iraqi men to kill Idris. They reached the place where Idris used to sit with his companions, but did not find him there, so they returned. When his friends saw that they had come to kill Idris, they dispersed and later met Idris. They informed him that forty men had come to kill him and advised him to be cautious.

Idris علیه السلام prayed to Allah SWT:

"O my Sustainer! You sent me to that tyrant to deliver Your message. He has threatened me and now seeks my life."

Allah revealed to Idris:

"Keep away from the king. I swear by My honour that I will enforce My law on him and prove your word and My messengership to be true."

Idris said:

"O my Nourisher, I have a wish."

Allah said:

"Ask Me, and I shall fulfil it."

Idris said:

"Until I allow it, there should be no rain."

Allah SWT said:

"The country will be ruined and people will starve to death."

Idris said:

"Whatever may happen, this is my wish."

Allah replied:

"All right. I accept it, and until the time you pray, I will not send rain. I am the most truthful in My promise."

Hearing this, Idris informed his companions about his conversation with Allah SWT and said:

"O my friends, leave this country and go to some other place."

There were twenty of them, and they spread out to different areas. The people came to know about the prayer of Idris عليه السلام.

Idris عليه السلام himself sought refuge on a hill. Allah SWT appointed an angel who used to bring food to him every evening. Idris fasted during the day and broke his fast in the evening when the angel brought him food.

Allah SWT destroyed the kingdom of the tyrant king. The king was killed, his kingdom obliterated, and the flesh of his wife was eaten by dogs due to their transgression against a believer.

Another unjust and tyrannical oppressor occupied the throne. Twenty years passed without a drop of rain. The people were in severe hardship and difficulty, and their condition deteriorated. They used to bring food supplies from distant regions.

When their condition became dire, they discussed among themselves that the calamity was due to the prayer of Idris, who had asked Allah SWT that no rain should fall until he allowed it.

"We are not aware of his whereabouts because he has concealed himself from us," they said.

They decided that since Allah SWT is more merciful than Idris, they should pray to Him and repent, so that rain might fall on their land and the surrounding areas. So they wore coarse clothes, applied mud to their heads, and, standing on the earth, they wailed, cried, and repented to Allah.

Allah SWT had mercy on them and revealed to Idris عليه السلام:

"Your people are repenting, wailing, and weeping. I am Allah—the Beneficent, the Merciful, the One who accepts repentance and forgives sins. I have mercy on them and wish to fulfil their desire for rain. I have no obstruction, save that you had requested Me not to send rain until you pray for it. Therefore, O Idris, pray to Me so that I may send them rain."

Idris عليه السلام said:

"O my Nourisher, I will not pray for rain."

Allah once again revealed to Idris to pray for rain. Idris again refused. So Allah recalled the angel who had been appointed to bring food to Idris.

When evening came and the food did not arrive, Idris became restless but waited patiently.

On the second day, when the food again did not arrive, his restlessness increased. On the third day, he lost patience and appealed to Allah SWT:

"O my Nourisher, before taking my soul, have You discontinued my sustenance?"

Allah SWT revealed:

"O Idris! You are complaining after three days, yet you were not concerned about your nation who have suffered for twenty years? I informed you of their suffering, and I had mercy on them. I wished that you pray for rain so I might send it, but you abstained. So I wished for you to know what hunger is—and now, in just three days, you have lost patience and complained. Now come out of the cave and search for your sustenance. I have left you on your own."

Hearing this, Idris عليه السلام came down from the hill to procure food. As he approached the town, he saw smoke rising from a house. An old lady had made two chapatis and was roasting them over a fire. He requested her to give him something to eat, as he was weak and restless from hunger.

She replied that due to the curse of Idris, Allah SWT had left them with nothing to spare, and she swore that apart from the two chapatis, there was nothing else in the house. She told him to leave the city and look elsewhere for food.

Idris requested:

"At least give me one chapati so that I can save my life and walk."

She said:

"I have only these two chapatis—one for me and the other for my son. If I give you mine, I will die, and if I give you my child's, he will die. I don't have anything else to offer."

Idris عليه السلام said,

"Your son is young; half a chapatti will suffice him, and half will help me to live."

The woman ate her share and divided the other one between Idris and her son. When the child saw Idris eating from his portion of the chapatti, he began to cry, and was so distressed that he died. The woman shouted out, "Stranger! You have killed my child!"

Idris said,

"Do not fear. By the order of Allah, I will bring him back to life."

Saying this, he placed his hands on the shoulders of the boy and said:

"O soul who has left the body of this child, by the order of Allah, return to his body again. I am Idris, the Messenger of Allah."

The boy came back to life. When the woman saw this, she exclaimed,

"I witness that you are Prophet Idris (عليه السلام)."

She ran out shouting,

"O people! Congratulations and glad tidings! We will be relieved of our troubles and sufferings—Idris has returned to our city!"

Idris عليه السلام came out and made his way to the palace of the first tyrant king, which stood on a hill. A group of people came to him and complained:

"O Idris! For twenty years, you showed no mercy to us. We endured hardship and misery, and many among us starved to death. We now beseech you—pray to Allah for rain."

Idris replied,

"I will not pray until this tyrant king and the people of your city come to me barefoot, walking, and request it."

When the king heard this, he sent forty men to kill Idris. As they approached him, Idris cursed them, and they all died.

When the king learned of this, he sent five hundred men to arrest him. They came to Idris and said,

"We have come to take you to the king."

Idris replied,

"Look at these forty men who came before you—see how they lie dead. If you do not turn back, you will meet the same fate."

They said,

"O Idris, you have caused us to suffer hunger for twenty years, and now you curse us? Is there no mercy in your heart?"

Idris replied,

"I will neither go to that tyrant nor pray for rain until he and all the people come to me barefoot, walking."

Hearing this, the people returned to the king and repeated Idris's statement. So the king, along with the people, came to Idris عليه السلام. All stood before him, helpless, and humbly requested him to pray for rain.

Idris prayed. At that very moment, clouds gathered in the sky; there was thunder and lightning, and it began to rain. It rained so heavily that they feared they would drown. Eventually, they all returned to their homes.

It is related from Imam Ja'far as-Sadiq [186]that an angel was under the wrath of Allah SWT. His hair and wings were cut off, and he was left lying on an island for

---

[186] Note (Imam Ja'far al Sadiq (as) is the sixth holy Imam of the Shi'a school of Islam and is the direct descendent of the Holy Prophet. Prophet Muhammad is the grandfather of Ja'far al Sadiq.Imam Ja'far al Sadiq (as) is the sixth successor after the Holy Prophet (sawa). He is his direct

a long time. When Allah SWT appointed Idris عليه السلام, that angel came to him and requested that he pray for him, so that Allah SWT might be pleased with him and restore his hair and wings.

Prophet Idris عليه السلام prayed for him, and Allah SWT restored the angel's hair and wings. The angel asked Idris,

"Do you wish anything from me?"

Idris عليه السلام said,

"Yes, I wish that you take me up to the heavens so that I can see the Angel of Death, for thinking of him causes me to live in constant fear."

The angel took the Prophet to the fourth heaven on his wings. There he saw the Angel of Death sitting, moving his head in a peculiar manner. Idris عليه السلام greeted him and asked why he was turning his head in such a way.

The Angel of Death replied,

"Allah has ordered me to take your soul between the fourth and fifth heaven."

Idris عليه السلام pleaded,

"O Allah! How is this possible, when the distance up to the fourth heaven is five hundred years of travel, and the distance between the fourth and fifth heaven is another five hundred years of travel? This is the distance between one heaven and another."

Saying this, the Angel of Death took away his soul. These are the words of Allah SWT, which mean:

$$\text{وَرَفَعْنَاهُ مَكَانًا عَلِيًّا}$$

"And We raised him to a high station."

— Surah Maryam (19:57)

Imam as-Sadiq narrates that he is known as Idris عليه السلام because he used to give abundant teachings from the Book of Allah. In a tradition from Amir al-Mu'minin, it is narrated that after the death of Idris عليه السلام, Allah SWT raised him to an elevated position and sustained him with the bounties of heaven.

In a reliable tradition, it is narrated by Imam Muhammad al-Baqir that the Holy Prophet said:

"An angel was very near to Allah. Due to some laxity or laziness, Allah sent him down to earth. He came to Idris and requested him to intercede with Allah on

---

descendent through the lineage of Fatima al Zahra (sa) the daughter of Prophet Muhammad (sawa) and Imam Ali ibn Abi Talib (as), the cousin and first successor of the Prophet. Imam Ja'far al Sadiq (as) is the son of Imam Muhammad al Baqir (as), son of Imam Ali al Sajjad (as), son of Imam Hussain (as), son of Fatima (sa), daughter of Prophet Muhammad (sawa) https://zahratrust.com/blog/6-facts-about-the-sixth-holy-imam-imam-jafar-al-sadiq-as/).

his behalf. Idris agreed, and fasted for three days without breaking the fast, and spent three nights in worship, due to which he became exhausted and weak. Then he prayed to Allah SWT and interceded for the angel. Allah gave permission for that angel to ascend to the skies.

At that time, the angel said,

'I wish that you would ask something from me in return.'

Idris عليه السلام said,

'I wish to meet the Angel of Death so that I can befriend him, because due to his remembrance, no bounty is worth rejoicing.'

The angel seated him on his wings and took him up to the first heaven. Then he took him higher, until they reached between the fourth and fifth skies, where they met the Angel of Death.

They saw the Angel of Death weeping and asked him the reason for his grief. The Angel of Death replied,

'Just now, when I was beneath the skies, there was an order from Allah SWT to take the soul of Idris between the fourth and fifth heaven.'

When Idris عليه السلام heard this, he fell from the wings of the angel, and immediately his soul was taken away. As Allah says:

"We have mentioned in the Book."

— Quran (19:56)

In another tradition, it is narrated from 'Abdullah Ibn Suhas (Abd-Allāh ibn Jaḥsh (Arabic: عَبْد أَله ابْن جَحْش) (c. 586–625), who was the brother-in-law and companion of the Islamic Prophet Muhammad):

Idris used to travel from city to city and used to fast. At night, he would stop and be provided with sustenance at that very place. The angels used to take his good deeds to the skies, just like they did with others' deeds.

The Angel of Death wished to meet Idris and, after getting permission, came to him and said, "I wish to be in your company." Idris agreed.

They became friends and remained together for a long time. Idris would fast during the day, and at night, when he received sustenance, he would eat. He used to invite the Angel of Death to eat with him, but the angel replied,

"I do not require food," and remained busy in prayers.

Idris would sleep due to fatigue, but the Angel of Death was neither lazy nor tired; nor did he sleep. In this way, several days passed until, one day, they passed by an orchard. The grapes were ripe.

The Angel of Death asked Idris whether they should take some grapes and break their fast. Idris replied,

"Glory be to Allah! I invited you to eat from my share of sustenance, and you refused. Now you are inviting me to eat other people's grapes without their permission. You have repaid my companionship in a fine manner. Tell me, who are you?"

He replied,

"I am the Angel of Death."

Idris said,

"I have one request from you."

The Angel of Death asked what it was. Idris said,

"I wish you to take me up to the skies."

The Angel of Death took Allah's permission, seated him on his wings, and took him up to the skies.

Idris عليه السلام said,

"I have one more desire. I have heard that death is very difficult, so I wish to taste it, so that I may verify whether it is as I have heard."

The Angel of Death took Allah's permission. Then he held Idris's breath for a short time, then released it, and asked Idris how he found it.

Idris replied,

"Very severe—more severe than I had heard."

Then Idris said,

"I have one more request. I want to see the fire of Hell."

The Angel of Death ordered the keeper of Hell to open the door. When Idris saw it, he fainted. Upon regaining consciousness, he said,

"I have one more request. I would like to see Heaven."

The Angel of Death asked the permission of the keepers of Heaven, and Idris entered. Then he said,

"O Angel of Death, now I will not come out of it. Allah has said, *'Every soul shall taste death'*—and I have tasted it. And Allah has said, *'There is none among you but shall come to it (Hell)'*—and I have seen it. And about Heaven, it is said, *'The people of Heaven will remain in it forever.'*" [187]

According to the Bible, only two prophets—**Enoch and Elijah**—appear to have been taken straight to heaven without experiencing death (unless one

---

[187] Index 145 Hayatul Qulub - Vol. 1 Stories of the Prophets.
https://www.islamiclearning.org/Docs/Hayat-Qulub-Alama-Majlisi.pdf

speculates that these two are the witnesses mentioned in the Book of Revelation, who do in fact experience death briefly, as described in Revelation 11:7–12).

The background story is extensive, but the passage in Revelation continues from verses 7 to 12 as follows (KJV):

7 And when they shall have finished their testimony, the beast that ascendeth out of the bottomless pit shall make war against them, and shall overcome them, and kill them.

8 And their dead bodies shall lie in the street of the great city, which spiritually is called Sodom and Egypt, where also our Lord was crucified.

9 And they of the people and kindreds and tongues and nations shall see their dead bodies three days and an half, and shall not suffer their dead bodies to be put in graves.

10 And they that dwell upon the earth shall rejoice over them, and make merry, and shall send gifts one to another; because these two prophets tormented them that dwelt on the earth.

11 And after three days and an half the Spirit of life from God entered into them, and they stood upon their feet; and great fear fell upon them which saw them.

12 And they heard a great voice from heaven saying unto them, Come up hither. And they ascended up to heaven in a cloud; and their enemies beheld them.

The Bible also describes **Elijah**. This renowned prophet was taken up to heaven in a chariot of fire after completing his prophetic mission, leaving **Elisha** to continue the work. As it is written:

2 Kings 2:1 (KJV):

And it came to pass, when the Lord would take up Elijah into heaven by a whirlwind, that Elijah went with Elisha from Gilgal.[188]

Who is Elijah?

In the Qur'an, he is referred to as **"Ilyāsīn"** عليه السلام.

$$سَلَامٌ عَلَىٰ إِلْ يَاسِينَ$$

$$إِنَّا كَذَٰلِكَ نَجْزِي الْمُحْسِنِينَ$$

$$إِنَّهُ مِنْ عِبَادِنَا الْمُؤْمِنِينَ$$

---

[188] Index 146 https://www.christianity.com/wiki/bible/who-was-enoch-in-the-bible.html

130. *Salamun (peace) be upon Ilyasin (Elias)!*

131. *Verily, thus do We reward the Muhsinun (good-doers, who perform good deeds totally for Allah's sake only – see V.2:112).* [189]

132. *Verily, he was one of Our believing slaves.*

[Surah As-Saffat 37:130–132] [190]

What Does the Bible Say About Enoch? (Prophet Idris عليه السلام)

Not much is mentioned in our Islamic texts, but the Bible provides some detail. It states that Enoch was Adam's great-great-great-great grandson (and Noah's great-grandfather), who lived a holy and faithful life before the Lord (Genesis 5). He became the father of Methuselah, the longest-living man, as recorded in Genesis 5:27. Over his 365 years on earth, he had many other offspring.

After 365 years, God "took him" (Genesis 5:24). The verb "took" appears to imply that he was snatched up or carried away—perhaps similar to how Elijah the Prophet was taken by God.

Genesis 5:24 (KJV):

And Enoch walked with God: and he was not; for God took him.

However, after Prophet Idris عليه السلام disappeared or died, ignorance began to spread among the people. There was no prophet among them for nearly a thousand years until Prophet Nuh عليه السلام was sent. During this time, Iblis عليه السلام took advantage of the people's ignorance and appeared to them in the form of a man. He

---

[189] The word "Ilyasin" is also pronounced as "Aal-i Yasin" in some dialects; therefore, it is written in a way that can be pronounced in both ways. Yasin is also one of the names of the Messenger of Allah 5; so, some scholars say what is meant by Aal-i Yasin is the ummah of Muhammad; thus, double entendre is used here; that is, both meanings of a word is used.6 It is also narrated that the pedigree of Hz. Ilyas goes back to Hz. Harun (Aaron).7 Jews and Christians call Ilyas Elijah.8

(5 It is reported by Said bin Jubayr. (Muhammed Hamdi Yazır, ibid, V/4006) 6 see Muhammed Hamdi Yazır, ibid, V/4068 7 Ö.N. Bilmen, ibid, II/916; Muhammed Hamdi Yazır, ibid, III/1972 8 Muhammed Hamdi Yazır, ibid, III/1973) https://questionsonislam.com/article/prophet-ilyas-elijah-peace-be-upon-him

[190] The word "Ilyasin" is also pronounced as "Aal-i Yasin" in some dialects; therefore, it is written in a way that can be pronounced in both ways. Yasin is also one of the names of the Messenger of Allah 5; so, some scholars say what is meant by Aal-i Yasin is the ummah of Muhammad; thus, double entendre is used here; that is, both meanings of a word is used.6 It is also narrated that the pedigree of Hz. Ilyas goes back to Hz. Harun (Aaron).7 Jews and Christians call Ilyas Elijah.8
(5 It is reported by Said bin Jubayr. (Muhammed Hamdi Yazır, ibid, V/4006) 6 see Muhammed Hamdi Yazır, ibid, V/4068 7 Ö.N. Bilmen, ibid, II/916; Muhammed Hamdi Yazır, ibid, III/1972 8 Muhammed Hamdi Yazır, ibid, III/1973) https://questionsonislam.com/article/prophet-ilyas-elijah-peace-be-upon-him

whispered to them, encouraging them to build statues of five pious men who had died, so that they might always remember them.

Some people made these statues and were then encouraged to:

"Worship those five statues."

The people began to worship the statues and, as a result, fell into idol worship. This was not the first act of disbelief (kufr), but it marked the time when humans began worshipping other people as gods.

Ayah 23 of Surah Nuh names the five pious Muslims whose images were turned into idols and worshipped. The verse reads:

$$أَمْ يَقُولُونَ بِهِ جِنَّةٌ ۚ بَلْ جَاءَهُم بِالْحَقِّ وَأَكْثَرُهُمْ لِلْحَقِّ كَارِهُونَ$$

Or say they: "There is madness in him?" Nay, but he brought them the truth [i.e., (A) Tawhid: Worshipping Allah Alone in all aspects, (B) The Qur'an, (C) The religion of Islam], but most of them (the disbelievers) are averse to the truth.

[Surah Nuh 71:70]

The names of those pious Muslims were:

1. Wadd

2. Suwa

3. Yaghuth

4. Ya'uq

5. Nasr

Surah Nuh 71:23:

"And they have said (to each other), 'Abandon not your gods: Abandon neither Wadd nor Suwa', neither Yaghuth nor Ya'uq, nor Nasr'."

After blasphemy and idol worship had spread on earth, Allah sent a prophet named Nuh عليه السلام. He began calling the people to Islam—to worship Allah alone and not to associate any partners with Him.

The Knowledge of Idris عليه السلام

(As collected; source link in index page)

Abu Ma'shar, in his book *The Book of Thousands*, writes:

Abū Ma'shar (PBUH) says:

He was the first to speak of celestial matters, such as the motions of the stars. His grandfather, Adam, taught him the hours of the night and day. He was the first to build sanctuaries and to praise God therein, and the first to think and speak of medicine.

He wrote many books of rhythmic poems in the language of his contemporaries, with rhymes, covering terrestrial and celestial knowledge. He was the first to prophesy the coming of the Flood and foresaw that a heavenly plague by water and fire would threaten the Earth.

His residence was in Upper Egypt (Ṣaʿīd), which he chose for himself. There he built the sanctuaries of the pyramids and the temple towns. Out of fear that wisdom might be lost, he constructed the temples—such as the mountain known as al-Barbā and the temple of Akhmīm (Panopolis). He engraved on their walls drawings of all crafts and their practitioners, pictures of all tools used by craftsmen, and inscriptions that described the essence of various sciences for the benefit of future generations.

In doing so, he was motivated by the desire to preserve knowledge and prevent it from vanishing from the earth. It is narrated from the traditions of the ancestors that Idris was the first to study books and contemplate sciences. Allah revealed to him thirty pages of the Heavenly Book. He was also the first to sew garments and wear them.[191]

Allah (SWT) knows best

Prophet Dawood (عليه السلام)

Allah told our Holy Prophet ﷺ about the story in the Qur'an:

وَرُسُلًا قَدْ قَصَصْنَاهُمْ عَلَيْكَ مِن قَبْلُ وَرُسُلًا لَّمْ نَقْصُصْهُمْ عَلَيْكَ ۚ وَكَلَّمَ اللَّهُ مُوسَىٰ تَكْلِيمًا

And Messengers We have mentioned to you before, and Messengers We have not mentioned to you; and to Musa (Moses) Allah spoke directly. — **Surah An-Nisaa 4:164**

Allah continued the story to our Prophet. Allah says:

وَلَقَدْ أَرْسَلْنَا رُسُلًا مِّن قَبْلِكَ مِنْهُم مَّن قَصَصْنَا عَلَيْكَ وَمِنْهُم مَّن لَّمْ نَقْصُصْ عَلَيْكَ ۚ وَمَا كَانَ لِرَسُولٍ أَن يَأْتِيَ بِآيَةٍ إِلَّا بِإِذْنِ اللَّهِ ۚ فَإِذَا جَاءَ أَمْرُ اللَّهِ قُضِيَ بِالْحَقِّ وَخَسِرَ هُنَالِكَ الْمُبْطِلُونَ

And, indeed We have sent Messengers before you (O Muhammad ﷺ); of some of them We have related to you their story, and of some We have not related to you their story. And it was not given to any Messenger that he should bring a sign except by the leave of Allah. So, when the commandment of Allah comes, the matter will be decided with truth, and the followers of falsehood will then be lost. — **Surah Al-Mu'min 40:78**

According to the above verse, Allah (SWT) tells the stories of certain prophets in the Qur'an, but not all of them. In fact, Allah has told the stories of the most

---

[191] Index 148 http://www.aakkl.helsinki.fi/melammu/database/gen_html/a0000761.php
http://wyec.com.tw/mjmndds/prophet-idris-miracles

prominent prophets, such as Adam, Nuh (Noah), Hud, Salih, Shu'ayb, 'Isa (Jesus), Musa (Moses), Dawood (David), Sulayman (Solomon), Yusuf (Joseph), Ibrahim (Abraham), Muhammad ﷺ, and others. **(Peace be upon them all)**.

The story of Prophet Yusuf, found in Surah Yusuf, is referred to in the Qur'an as the best of stories, because Allah (SWT) says:

لَقَدْ كَانَ فِي قَصَصِهِمْ عِبْرَةٌ لِأُولِي الْأَلْبَابِ ۗ مَا كَانَ حَدِيثًا يُفْتَرَىٰ وَلَٰكِن تَصْدِيقَ الَّذِي بَيْنَ يَدَيْهِ وَتَفْصِيلَ كُلِّ شَيْءٍ وَهُدًى وَرَحْمَةً لِقَوْمٍ يُؤْمِنُونَ

Indeed, in their stories there is a lesson for men of understanding. It (the Qur'an) is not a forged statement but a confirmation of Allah's existing Books [the Tawrat (Torah), the Injil (Gospel) and other Scriptures of Allah], and a detailed explanation of everything, and a guide and a mercy for the people who believe. — ***Surah Yusuf 12:111***

In this section, let us emphasise the prayers, devotion, and sacrifices associated with the Hadith about Hazrat Dawood (عليه السلام). This story can inspire believers and travellers to praise Allah more frequently and seek His mercy through prayer.

This is a short, inspiring account of Prophet Dawood (عليه السلام), based on Qur'anic verses and historical narrations.

Allah (SWT) has spoken about Prophet Dawood (عليه السلام):

وَرَبُّكَ أَعْلَمُ بِمَن فِي السَّمَاوَاتِ وَالْأَرْضِ ۗ وَلَقَدْ فَضَّلْنَا بَعْضَ النَّبِيِّينَ عَلَىٰ بَعْضٍ ۖ وَآتَيْنَا دَاوُودَ زَبُورًا

And thy Lord knoweth best all who are in the heavens and the earth: and We did bestow on some Prophets more and greater gifts than on others; and We gave unto Dawood (David) the Psalms. — ***Surah Al-Isra 17:55***

Prophet Dawood (عليه السلام) recited his scripture and glorified Allah. The mountains joined him in praise, and the birds gathered around him.

His sincerity was not the only reason these miracles occurred. The sick were healed, jinn and humans listened to his recitation, and the wind became calm. The mountains, birds, and other creatures joined in glorifying Allah (SWT). Allah also granted him the understanding of the languages of birds and animals. Some narrations state that Allah placed them under the control of Dawood (عليه السلام), and they would obey his commands.

Allah (SWT) confirmed this in the following verses:

إِنَّا سَخَّرْنَا الْجِبَالَ مَعَهُ يُسَبِّحْنَ بِالْعَشِيِّ وَالْإِشْرَاقِ

وَالطَّيْرَ مَحْشُورَةً ۖ كُلٌّ لَّهُ أَوَّابٌ

*Verily, We made the mountains glorify Our praises with him [Dawood (David)] in the evening and at sunrise. And the birds assembled: all with him [Dawood (David)] turned to Allah in praise. — **Surah Sad 38:18–19***

Allah (SWT) also says:

وَشَدَدْنَا مُلْكَهُ وَآتَيْنَاهُ الْحِكْمَةَ وَفَصْلَ الْخِطَابِ

*We strengthened his kingdom and gave him wisdom and decisive speech and judgement. — **Surah Sad 38:20***

Hadith Narrations

Volume 4, Book 55, Number 628

Narrated by Abu Huraira (رضي الله عنه):

The Prophet ﷺ said:

"The reciting of the Zabur (Psalms) was made easy for David (عليه السلام). He used to order that his riding animals be saddled, and would finish reciting the Zabur before they were saddled. And he would never eat except from the earnings of his manual work."

Volume 4, Book 55, Number 630

Narrated by Abdullah bin Amr bin Al-As (رضي الله عنه):

The Prophet ﷺ said to me:

"I have been informed that you pray all the night and fast all the days; is this true?" I replied, *"Yes."* He said, *"If you do so, your eyes will become weak and you will get bored. So fast three days a month, for this is equal to fasting the whole year."*

I said, "I find myself able to fast more." He said:

"Then fast like the fasting of David (عليه السلام), who used to fast on alternate days and would not flee when facing the enemy."

Volume 4, Book 55, Number 631

Narrated by Abdullah bin Amr (رضي الله عنه):

Allah's Apostle ﷺ said to me:

"The most beloved fasting to Allah was the fasting of David (عليه السلام), who fasted on alternate days. And the most beloved prayer to Allah was the prayer of David, who used to sleep for half the night, pray for one-third of it, and sleep again for one-sixth of it."

Volume 4, Book 55, Number 632

I asked Ibn 'Abbas:

"Should we perform a prostration when reciting Surah Sad?"

He recited the Surah including:

'And among his progeny: Dawood, Sulayman... (up to)... so follow their guidance' — Surah Al-An'am 6:84–88

Then he said:

"Your Prophet is among those who have been commanded to follow them."

The verses in the Qur'an say:

وَوَهَبْنَا لَهُ إِسْحَاقَ وَيَعْقُوبَ ۚ كُلًّا هَدَيْنَا ۚ وَنُوحًا هَدَيْنَا مِن قَبْلُ ۖ وَمِن ذُرِّيَّتِهِ دَاوُودَ وَسُلَيْمَانَ وَأَيُّوبَ وَيُوسُفَ وَمُوسَىٰ وَهَارُونَ ۚ وَكَذَٰلِكَ نَجْزِي الْمُحْسِنِينَ

وَزَكَرِيَّا وَيَحْيَىٰ وَعِيسَىٰ وَإِلْيَاسَ ۖ كُلٌّ مِّنَ الصَّالِحِينَ

وَإِسْمَاعِيلَ وَالْيَسَعَ وَيُونُسَ وَلُوطًا ۚ وَكُلًّا فَضَّلْنَا عَلَى الْعَالَمِينَ

وَمِنْ آبَائِهِمْ وَذُرِّيَّاتِهِمْ وَإِخْوَانِهِمْ ۖ وَاجْتَبَيْنَاهُمْ وَهَدَيْنَاهُمْ إِلَىٰ صِرَاطٍ مُّسْتَقِيمٍ

ذَٰلِكَ هُدَى اللَّهِ يَهْدِي بِهِ مَن يَشَاءُ مِنْ عِبَادِهِ ۚ وَلَوْ أَشْرَكُوا لَحَبِطَ عَنْهُم مَّا كَانُوا يَعْمَلُونَ

84. And We gave him Isaac and Jacob; all of them We guided. And before him, We guided Noah. And among his progeny were David, Solomon, Job, Joseph, Moses, and Aaron. Thus do We reward the good-doers.

85. And Zakariya, and John, and Jesus, and Elias: each one of them was of the righteous.

86. And Ishmael, and Elisha, and Jonah, and Lot: and each one We preferred above the people (of their times).

87. And also some of their fathers, and their progeny, and their brethren: We chose them, and We guided them to the Straight Path.

88. This is the guidance of Allah with which He guides whom He will of His servants. But if they had joined in worship others with Allah, all that they used to do would have been of no benefit to them. — Surah Al-An'am 6:84–88

And then He said:

أُولَٰئِكَ الَّذِينَ آتَيْنَاهُمُ الْكِتَابَ وَالْحُكْمَ وَالنُّبُوَّةَ ۚ فَإِن يَكْفُرْ بِهَا هَٰؤُلَاءِ فَقَدْ وَكَّلْنَا بِهَا قَوْمًا لَّيْسُوا بِهَا بِكَافِرِينَ

أُولَٰئِكَ الَّذِينَ هَدَى اللَّهُ ۖ فَبِهُدَاهُمُ اقْتَدِهْ ۗ قُل لَّا أَسْأَلُكُمْ عَلَيْهِ أَجْرًا ۖ إِنْ هُوَ إِلَّا ذِكْرَىٰ لِلْعَالَمِينَ

They are those to whom We gave the Book, the command, and Prophethood. But if these disbelieve therein, then indeed We have entrusted it to a people who

407

are not disbelievers therein. They are those whom Allah has guided, so follow their guidance. Say: I ask of you no reward for this. It is nothing but a reminder to the worlds. — Surah Al-An'am 6:89–90

Allah SWT has again assured that:

الَّذِينَ جَاهَدُوا فِينَا لَنَهْدِيَنَّهُمْ سُبُلَنَا ۚ وَإِنَّ اللَّهَ لَمَعَ الْمُحْسِنِينَ

As for those who strive hard in Us (Our Cause), We will surely guide them to Our Paths (i.e. Allah's Religion – Islamic Monotheism). And verily, Allah is with the Muhsinun (good-doers).

[Surah Al-Ankabut, 29:69]

This verse contains another hint on how to achieve success. Prophet Dawud (عليه السلام) prayed to Allah (SWT), begging for His mercy. A few lines of his prayer are quoted, in which Prophet Dawud says to Allah:

"Bow down thine ear, O LORD, hear me: for I am poor and needy.

Be merciful unto me, O Lord: for I cry unto thee daily.

Give ear, O LORD, unto my prayer; and attend to the voice of my supplications.

In the day of my trouble I will call upon thee: for thou wilt answer me.

Teach me thy way, O LORD; I will walk in thy truth: unite my heart to fear thy name."

[Psalm 86:1, 3, 6–7, 11 KJV]

Although Allah (SWT) loved and protected all His Prophets from calamities, they were concerned that under the influence of Satan, they might commit deeds displeasing to Allah. That is why they were constantly seeking His mercy.

The Old Testament and the Qur'an Tell the Story of Prophet Dawud (عليه السلام)

In Islam, Prophet Dawud (عليه السلام) is recognised as a Messenger of Allah—a Rasul. According to the Hebrew Bible, he was the second king of the united Kingdom of Israel and Judah, reigning circa 1010–970 BCE for around 40 years. The Prophet and King Dawud (عليه السلام) was known as a great warrior.

His prophethood is vividly described in the Torah and the Old Testament, and his name is mentioned many times in the Qur'an.

David (عليه السلام) was the son of Jesse, belonging to the tribe of Ephraim, and from Bethlehem in Judah. He was the youngest of Jesse's eight sons—though **1 Chronicles 2:13–15** indicates that Jesse had only seven sons. As a youth, David helped tend his father's sheep, and later began his career as an aide in the court of Saul, Israel's first king.

Prophet David (عليه السلام) is a prominent figure in all Abrahamic faiths. He is central in Jewish history, having reigned during the "Golden Age of Israel." During his reign, Israel experienced unprecedented prosperity. Allah (SWT) gave Prophet Dawud (عليه السلام) a divine scripture, the **Zabur** (Psalms).

The word *prophet* means "to speak for." Prophets spoke for Allah (SWT) to the people, receiving divine revelation through visions and dreams. The message varied depending on the needs of the time.

From Prophet Ibrahim (Abraham) to our final Prophet Muhammad (ﷺ), Allah (SWT) revealed four major scriptures as mentioned in the Qur'an:

- The *Tawrat* (Torah) revealed to Musa (Moses عليه السلام),
- The *Zabur* (Psalms) revealed to Dawud (David عليه السلام),
- The *Injil* (Gospel) revealed to Isa (Jesus عليه السلام), and
- The *Qur'an* revealed to Prophet Muhammad (ﷺ).

Prophet Dawud (عليه السلام) was known for his wisdom, strength, and deep devotion to Allah (SWT). He was not only an illustrious prophet but also a just and powerful king.

Allah SWT granted David (عليه السلام) great influence. His people engaged in many wars during his time, but they had a problem: iron armour was too heavy for soldiers to move and fight effectively. It is said that one day, while pondering this issue, Dawud (عليه السلام) was toying with a piece of iron. Suddenly, he found his hand sinking into it—Allah had made it soft for him. As the Qur'an says:

وَلَقَدْ آتَيْنَا دَاوُودَ مِنَّا فَضْلًا ۖ يَا جِبَالُ أَوِّبِي مَعَهُ وَالطَّيْرَ ۖ وَأَلَنَّا لَهُ الْحَدِيدَ

أَنِ اعْمَلْ سَابِغَاتٍ وَقَدِّرْ فِي السَّرْدِ ۖ وَاعْمَلُوا صَالِحًا ۖ إِنِّي بِمَا تَعْمَلُونَ بَصِيرٌ

10. And indeed We bestowed grace on David from Us (saying): "O you mountains! Glorify (Allah) with him! And you birds (also)! And We made the iron soft for him."

11. "Make perfect coats of mail, and balance well the rings of chain armour, and work righteousness. Truly, I am All-Seer of what you do."

[Surah Saba, 34:10–11]

وَلَقَدْ آتَيْنَا دَاوُودَ وَسُلَيْمَانَ عِلْمًا ۖ وَقَالَا الْحَمْدُ لِلَّهِ الَّذِي فَضَّلَنَا عَلَىٰ كَثِيرٍ مِّنْ عِبَادِهِ الْمُؤْمِنِينَ

And indeed We gave knowledge to Dawud (David) and Sulaiman (Solomon), and they both said: "All praise and thanks be to Allah, Who has preferred us above many of His believing slaves!"

[Surah An-Naml, 27:15]

The background of this verse is echoed in the Old Testament. The following verse from the Qur'an also connects to this:

"O Dawud (David)! Verily, We have placed you as a successor on earth. So judge between men in truth (and justice) and follow not your desire, for it will mislead you from the Path of Allah. Verily! Those who go astray from the Path of Allah will have a severe punishment, because they forgot the Day of Reckoning."

[Surah Sad, 38:26]

'Ali ibn Ibrahim narrated that Allah SWT gave Dawud (عليه السلام) and Sulaiman (عليه السلام) miracles that were not granted to any other prophet. Dawud (عليه السلام) was taught the language of birds, and iron and pewter (a form of zinc) were made soft for him without fire. Mountains would sing the praises of Allah with him. He was given the **Zabur**, which contained praises, supplications, and declarations of Tawhid (Oneness of Allah). As Allah says:

وَلَقَدْ كَتَبْنَا فِي الزَّبُورِ مِن بَعْدِ الذِّكْرِ أَنَّ الْأَرْضَ يَرِثُهَا عِبَادِيَ الصَّالِحُونَ

And indeed We have written in the Zabur (Psalms)—after the Reminder—that My righteous slaves shall inherit the earth.

[Surah Al-Anbiyaa, 21:105]

According to authentic narration, Imam as-Sadiq said that whenever he faced a difficult task, he would choose to do it on a Tuesday—the day on which Allah made iron soft for Dawud (عليه السلام).

It is recorded with authentic evidences that Imam as-Sadiq [192] said that one day Dawood عليه السلام said, "Today I will worship my Lord and recite the Zabur in an unprecedented manner." Then he went into his niche and did as he had planned. When he concluded his prayers, a frog appeared suddenly and spoke to him by the command of Allah SWT:

"O Dawood! Are you pleased with this worship and recitation made by you now?"

Dawood عليه السلام replied in the affirmative.

The frog said:

---

[192] Ja'far ibn Muhammad al-Sadiq c. 702–765 CE) was a Shia Muslim scholar, jurist, and theologian, and the sixth imam of the Twelver and Isma'ili branches of Shia Islam.[3] Known by the title al-Sadiq ("The Truthful"), Ja'far was the founder of the Ja'fari school of Islamic jurisprudence. The hadith recorded from al-Sadiq and his predecessor, Muhammad al-Baqir, are said to be more numerous than all the hadith preserved from the Islamic prophet Muhammad صلى الله عليه وسلم and the other Shia imams combined. Among other theological contributions, he elaborated the doctrine of nass (divinely inspired designation of each Imam by the previous Imam) and isma (the infallibility of the Imams), as well as that of taqiya (religious dissimulation under persecution). Al-Sadiq is also revered by Sunni Muslims as a reliable transmitter of hadith and a teacher to the Sunni scholars Abu Hanifa and Malik ibn Anas, the namesakes of the Hanafi and Maliki schools of jurisprudence Al-Sadiq also figures prominently in the initiatic chains of many Sufi orders. A wide range of religious and scientific works were attributed to him, though no works penned by al-Sadiq remain extant (From Wikipedia, the free encyclopaedia)

"You must not feel happy over it. I recite 3,000 *Tasbihs* (praises) of my Lord every night. Out of that, 3,000 *Tasbihs* sprout and spread over me, though I remain at the bottom of the water. When I hear the voice of any bird, I presume that it is hungry. So I come up to the surface to enable that bird to eat me up—even though I have not erred."

We gave (in the past) knowledge to David عليه السلام *and Solomon* عليه السلام: *and they both said:*

"Blessed be the LORD God of Israel, which only doeth wondrous things. And blessed be his glorious name for ever: and let the whole earth be filled with his glory; Amen, and Amen."

— Psalm 72:18–19, KJV

The background of many battles mentioned in the verses of the Qur'an is illustrated in detail in the Old Testament. We summarise the story here for better understanding.

According to the Torah, Saul was in search of a man who could play the harp. As the Prophet Dawood عليه السلام was well versed in this art, he was summoned to Talut and stayed with him. The Prophet Dawood عليه السلام spent most of his time in the companionship of his master and occasionally visited his father. He helped him tend the sheep and, in doing so, gained experience in confronting wild beasts.

The Bible relates an incident that highlights the heroic deeds of Prophet Dawood عليه السلام. Once, a war broke out between the Israelites and the Philistines. At that time, King Saul was fighting against the Philistines, Israel's long-time enemies. The Israelites mustered the courage to fight and were prepared for battle. On the way, King Saul decided to test the loyalty of his soldiers:

"Allah will test you all by a river. Whoever drinks water while crossing the river is not mine, except those who drink only a little with their hands."

It is recorded in the Qur'an as:

فَلَمَّا فَصَلَ طَالُوتُ بِالْجُنُودِ قَالَ إِنَّ اللَّهَ مُبْتَلِيكُم بِنَهَرٍ فَمَن شَرِبَ مِنْهُ فَلَيْسَ مِنِّي وَمَن لَّمْ يَطْعَمْهُ فَإِنَّهُ مِنِّي إِلَّا مَنِ اغْتَرَفَ غُرْفَةً بِيَدِهِ ۚ فَشَرِبُوا مِنْهُ إِلَّا قَلِيلًا مِّنْهُمْ ۚ فَلَمَّا جَاوَزَهُ هُوَ وَالَّذِينَ آمَنُوا مَعَهُ قَالُوا لَا طَاقَةَ لَنَا الْيَوْمَ بِجَالُوتَ وَجُنُودِهِ ۚ قَالَ الَّذِينَ يَظُنُّونَ أَنَّهُم مُّلَاقُو اللَّهِ كَم مِّن فِئَةٍ قَلِيلَةٍ غَلَبَتْ فِئَةً كَثِيرَةً بِإِذْنِ اللَّهِ ۗ وَاللَّهُ مَعَ الصَّابِرِينَ

Then when Talut (Saul) set out with the army, he said: "Verily! Allah will try you by a river. So whoever drinks thereof, he is not of me, and whoever tastes it not, he is of me, except him who takes (thereof) in the hollow of his hand." Yet, they drank thereof, all, except a few of them. So when he had crossed it (the river), he and those who believed with him said: "We have no power this day against Jalut (Goliath) and his hosts." But those who knew with certainty that they would meet their Lord said: "How often a small group has overcome a mighty host by Allah's Leave?" And Allah is with the patient ones.

Saul's leadership qualities now became evident. He commanded an army from a nation that had faced numerous defeats throughout its history and was preparing once again to confront a formidable enemy. To ensure his troops were ready, Saul needed to test their willpower and resilience. He had to be sure of their ability to overcome desires, endure hardship and deprivation, and demonstrate loyalty and responsibility.

On the banks of the river, Saul tested his troops to see who would obey him and who would not. The soldiers revealed their thirst, and this test showed that a weak army could be a liability on the battlefield. However, it also highlighted that military power is not defined by the size of the army, but by the willpower, moral strength, and faith of the soldiers.

Two armies gathered in the Valley of Elah, ready once again for battle. The Philistine army was stronger than King Saul's, and their hero, Goliath—a giant— appeared from the mountains, his voice booming like thunder. He called out to King Saul's army:

"Choose one of your men, Saul's army, and fight against me. If he kills me in battle, we will be your slaves. But if he loses, I will kill him, and you will be our slaves."

The mighty giant issued this challenge morning and evening for forty days, but not a single man from King Saul's Israelite army dared accept it.

Dawood عليه السلام was not initially sent to fight but to assist the army in other ways and report back to his father. This is the story of Hazrat Dawood (David) عليه السلام. The king had announced that he would marry his beautiful daughter to the man who would dare to fight Goliath. Even with this tempting offer, no one came forward to accept the challenge.

Suddenly, Dawood عليه السلام stepped forward, announcing that he would take up the challenge and face Goliath. The king and his commanders were astonished by his courage and admired him, but the king initially discouraged him due to his youth and lack of battlefield experience.

However, Prophet Dawood عليه السلام was determined. He eventually persuaded the king, who said to him:

"My brave soldier, if you are willing, then may Allah guard you and grant you strength!"

The Prophet Dawood عليه السلام surprised everyone further when he refused to wear armour and chose instead to fight in his ordinary clothes. He did not use conventional weapons but advanced towards the enemy with stones, pebbles, a wooden bow, and a sling.

The king and his court were extremely worried upon seeing his battle preparation, but Prophet Dawood عليه السلام reassured them:

"Allah, who saved me from the attack of bears and lions, will surely save me in this battle."

He had once killed wild animals with his bare hands while guarding sheep in the forest.

The monster Goliath threatened David عليه السلام, laughing and insulting him with terrifying words. He mocked David as merely a boy, pitying him and declaring that he would kill him with a single blow. But before attacking Goliath with his arrow, Prophet David عليه السلام prayed to Allah (SWT) as follows:

Allah SWT confirms that Hazrat Dawood prayed to Him before facing his enemy:

وَلَمَّا بَرَزُوا لِجَالُوتَ وَجُنُودِهِ قَالُوا رَبَّنَا أَفْرِغْ عَلَيْنَا صَبْرًا وَثَبِّتْ أَقْدَامَنَا وَانصُرْنَا عَلَى الْقَوْمِ الْكَافِرِينَ

"And when they advanced to meet Jalut (Goliath) and his forces, they invoked: 'Our Lord! Pour forth on us patience, and make our steps firm and make us victorious over the disbelieving people.'"

(Surah Al-Baqarah, 2:250)

With that, he took his slingshot and drew a pebble from his bag. He swung the sling, and the pebble flew with the speed of an arrow, striking Goliath on the head with great force. Goliath collapsed to the ground, lifeless, before he had a chance to draw his sword.

Almighty Allah (SWT) declared:

فَهَزَمُوهُم بِإِذْنِ اللَّهِ وَقَتَلَ دَاوُودُ جَالُوتَ وَآتَاهُ اللَّهُ الْمُلْكَ وَالْحِكْمَةَ وَعَلَّمَهُ مِمَّا يَشَاءُ ۗ وَلَوْلَا دَفْعُ اللَّهِ النَّاسَ بَعْضَهُم بِبَعْضٍ لَّفَسَدَتِ الْأَرْضُ وَلَٰكِنَّ اللَّهَ ذُو فَضْلٍ عَلَى الْعَالَمِينَ

"So they routed them by Allah's leave, and Dawud (David) slew Jalut (Goliath); and Allah gave him the kingdom and wisdom, and taught him of that which He willed. And were it not that Allah checks one set of people by means of another, the earth would indeed be full of mischief. But Allah is full of bounty to the worlds."

(Surah Al-Baqarah, 2:251)

When the Israelites saw their mighty enemy slain, they were filled with fierce resolve. Driven by a longing for revenge after years of oppression, they charged at their enemies and killed every soldier they could find. In this war, the Israelites reclaimed their long-lost glory and honour. David عليه السلام emerged as a hero overnight.

After killing Goliath, David عليه السلام retreated into the desert, surrounded by the beauty of nature. There he glorified Almighty Allah and reflected on His countless blessings. Indeed, Allah caused the mountains to join David in glorifying His praises during the *Ashi* (afternoon until sunset) and *Ishraq* (morning until midday). The birds also gathered with him, all turning to Allah in praise. Allah

413

strengthened David's kingdom, granting him wisdom and sound judgement in both speech and decisions.

David عليه السلام quickly gained King Saul's attention, which led to his appointment to the highest rank in the army. The king admired David not only for his performance in every assigned task but also for his rising popularity among the soldiers and citizens. This admiration intensified after David's continued military victories.

King Saul had earlier promised that whoever killed Goliath would be rewarded by marrying his daughter. So, he proposed this marriage to David عليه السلام. However, the Prophet initially declined, saying he was unworthy of such an honour. Despite his refusal, King Saul insisted and set a challenge: David would have to bring the foreskins of 100 dead Philistines as a bridal price to marry his daughter.

David accepted the challenge. With the help of his men, he killed far more Philistines than required and presented the foreskins to King Saul.

The king had ulterior motives for setting such a dangerous task. David's growing popularity stirred Saul's jealousy and fear that David عليه السلام might one day seize the throne. He secretly hoped that David would die in battle during the mission. But when David returned victorious, the king was forced to keep his word, and David married Saul's daughter, Michal (also spelled Mikel).

Although he permitted the marriage, Saul continued to see David عليه السلام as a threat. Influenced by an evil spirit (Satan), the king lost his sense of judgement. Despite the pleas of his son Jonathan, his daughter Michal, other family members, and even army officials—who all considered David an asset to Israel—Saul remained determined to have him killed.

When David عليه السلام realised that the king was after his life without just cause, he went into hiding. King Saul desperately searched for him and ordered his soldiers to kill David wherever they found him. But Allah (SWT) was always with David.

When his wife alerted him of the danger, David عليه السلام fled the city and sought refuge with the spiritual priest Samuel at Ramah. He shared everything with him. King Saul, upon discovering his location, sent troops to capture David. However, a miraculous event occurred: instead of arresting David, the soldiers were overtaken by the Spirit and began to prophesy. This happened repeatedly with each group sent.

Eventually, King Saul himself went to Ramah. But when he arrived, he too was seized by the Spirit of the Lord and began to prophesy. Under its influence, he stripped off his garments and prophesied before Samuel, lying down all that day and night.

"And he went thither to Naioth in Ramah: and the Spirit of God was upon him also, and he went on, and prophesied, until he came to Naioth in Ramah. And he stripped off his clothes also, and prophesied before Samuel in like

manner, and lay down naked all that day and all that night. Wherefore they say, Is Saul also among the prophets?"

(1 Samuel 19:23–24, *King James Version*)

David عليه السلام then left for a town called Nob.

There, he met a priest named Ahimelech, who was surprised to see David alone and questioned him thoroughly. Concealing the truth, David عليه السلام claimed that the king had sent him on a secret mission and that he would be meeting his men at undisclosed locations.

David asked the priest for food. The priest replied that he had no ordinary bread, only holy bread, which could be eaten only by those who were ceremonially clean and had not been with women. David عليه السلام assured him that he had kept himself clean and had not approached any woman since starting his journey. The priest then gave him the holy bread.

It was a sacred place, and the priests served daily in the presence of the Lord. That day, one of King Saul's servants, Doeg the Edomite, was present and witnessed the interaction.

David عليه السلام then asked Ahimelech if he had a sword. He explained that, due to the urgency of the king's mission, he had left without a weapon. The priest responded that the only sword available was the one David had taken from Goliath after defeating him in the Valley of Elah.

David عليه السلام was pleased and accepted the sword of Goliath.[193]

When David realised that the king was pursuing him without any apparent reason, he hid for his life. The king, desperate to find David, ordered his soldiers to kill him wherever they found him. However, God was always with him. Upon receiving a warning from his wife, David fled the city and sought refuge with the spiritual priest Samuel at Ramah, where he confided everything to him.

King Saul tracked David and sent troops to Ramah to capture him. But instead of arresting David, the soldiers, under the influence of a miraculous power, prophesied. This happened repeatedly, frustrating Saul's efforts. Saul himself went to Ramah to oversee David's arrest, but he too fell under the influence of this spiritual power. He ended up prophesying, stripping off his clothes, and sleeping all day and night without any clothes on.

David then left for the town called Nob, where he met a priest named Ahimelech. The priest was surprised to see David alone and asked him many questions about his visit. David, concealing the facts, claimed that the king had sent

---

[193] (In the Bible (1 Samuel chapters 21 and 22), David fled to the high priest Ahimelech's shrine at Nob, where the Tabernacle was now located. Here he ate the showbread which had been withdrawn from the sanctuary and received the sword of Goliath, which was kept there) The ruins of ancient Shiloh and the site of the Tabernacle can be visited today. Located upon a defensible hilltop, Shiloh is found about 20 miles north of Jerusalem.

him on a special secret mission and that he would meet his companions at undisclosed locations.

David requested something to eat, and although the priest had no ordinary food, he offered David the special holy bread, provided he was ritually clean and had not been with a woman. David confirmed that he was clean and had abstained from relations with women since beginning his journey. So the priest gave him the holy bread. The priests would go to the holy place daily in the presence of the Lord.

On that day, one of King Saul's servants, Doeg, was present and saw David. David asked the priest for a sword, explaining that he had left in such haste that he had no weapon. The priest gave him the sword of Goliath the Philistine, whom David had beheaded in the valley of Elah. David accepted the sword gratefully.

David (عليه السلام) still ran away and hid from King Saul. He left the town of Nob and went to another town called Adullam. He hid himself in a large cave near Adullam. David's brothers and his father's household heard of his location and visited him. Eventually, many people joined him for various reasons. He earned their trust and became a leader of his followers.

He then went to the town called Mizpah, in the country of Moab, where he left his parents in the house of the king of Moab with his permission, and David (عليه السلام) went to hide in a safer place.

But Allah (سُبْحَانَهُ وَتَعَالَى) ordered Prophet David (عليه السلام):

"Do not stay in a safe place; go to the land of Judah."

So Prophet David (عليه السلام) left the safe place and went to the forest at Hereth.

On the other hand, King Saul learned from his servant Doeg that he had seen David (عليه السلام) with the priest Ahimelech in the holy place, and that Ahimelech had helped David (عليه السلام) with food and a sword and had also prayed for him.

The king summoned the priest Ahimelech, son of Ahitub, along with all his brothers and their families. The king wanted to know from the priest why he had decided to go against him—why he had given bread and a sword to David and prayed to God on his behalf when David had disobeyed the king.

He said, "Nobody tells me when my son makes a covenant with the son of Jesse and goes against me."

In reply, Ahimelech said, "David (عليه السلام) is the most loyal servant to you. He is also your son-in-law and the captain of your bodyguard. He is honoured by every member of your household. I have prayed many times in the past for him. I do not know if anything has gone wrong between you and David."

The king, however, ignored the priest's defence and ordered Ahimelech and all his brothers and their families to be killed. But the king's officials refused to kill the priests. So the king ordered Doeg to do it. Doeg killed eighty-five priests who wore the linen ephod. He also killed all the people of Nob—the town of the priests—including men, women, children and infants, as well as cattle, donkeys, and sheep.

However, the king still failed to capture Abiathar, the son of Ahimelech, who escaped and fled to David (عليه السلام). David (عليه السلام) said that he was responsible for this catastrophe and offered Abiathar safety and a place to stay without fear.

At that time, Prophet David (عليه السلام) received news that the Philistines were attacking a town called Keilah in Israel and had looted all the grain just harvested from the fields. Prophet David (عليه السلام) could not sit idly after hearing this terrible news. He sought the Lord's permission to defend the people of Keilah and fight the Philistine intruders. The Lord permitted him and assured him and his followers of victory.

Prophet David (عليه السلام) and his men went to Keilah, fought the Philistines, killed many of them, took their livestock, and saved the people of Keilah.

King Saul learned that David (عليه السلام) was in Keilah and that he had fought the Philistines. The king immediately sent his army to Keilah to capture David and his men. However, David (عليه السلام) received word of the king's plans and left the town. He and his men hid in a secure location called Ziph, in the hills of the desert, with the help of the Lord.

However, a spy for the king had located David (عليه السلام) and reported back. But the Lord did not let Saul capture David (عليه السلام). Eventually, the king was informed that David (عليه السلام) was in the desert of Maon. The king's army determined his location and surrounded the area where David (عليه السلام) was hiding. But at that moment, a message came that the Philistines were invading Israel.

This news troubled the king, and he hurried to prepare for battle against the Philistines. David (عليه السلام) also left that hiding place and lived safely in the city of Engedi.

As soon as King Saul had finished fighting the Philistines, he resumed his pursuit of David (عليه السلام) in the desert of Engedi. This time, the Lord delivered King Saul into David's (عليه السلام) hands. David's men ambushed and captured the king, but instead of killing him, David (عليه السلام) said:

"The Lord forbid that I should do this thing unto my master, the Lord's anointed, to stretch forth mine hand against him, seeing he is the anointed of the Lord."

(1 Samuel 24:6, KJV)

He continued:

"Behold, this day thine eyes have seen how that the Lord had delivered thee to day into mine hand in the cave: and some bade me kill thee: but mine eye spared thee; and I said, I will not put forth mine hand against my lord; for he is the Lord's anointed. Moreover, my father, see, yea, see the skirt of thy

417

robe in my hand... I have not sinned against thee; yet thou huntest my soul to take it. The Lord judge between me and thee... but mine hand shall not be upon thee. As saith the proverb of the ancients, Wickedness proceedeth from the wicked: but mine hand shall not be upon thee."

(1 Samuel 24:10–13, KJV)

David (عليه السلام) added that he would not lift his hand against the king and that the Lord would judge between them. He said:

"The Lord therefore be judge, and judge between me and thee, and see, and plead my cause, and deliver me out of thine hand."

(1 Samuel 24:15, KJV)

The king wept and said:

"Thou art more righteous than I: for thou hast rewarded me good, whereas I have rewarded thee evil... And now, behold, I know well that thou shalt surely be king, and that the kingdom of Israel shall be established in thine hand."

(1 Samuel 24:17, 20, KJV)

David (عليه السلام) then departed safely.

However, Satan's influence once again led King Saul to seek David's (عليه السلام) life. This attempt was again thwarted. David (عليه السلام) respected the Lord's anointing of Saul and said:

"As the Lord liveth, the Lord shall smite him; or his day shall come to die; or he shall descend into battle, and perish. The Lord forbid that I should stretch forth mine hand against the Lord's anointed."

(1 Samuel 26:10–11, KJV)

To escape further danger, David (عليه السلام) decided to join the army of the Philistines. King Achish of the Philistines welcomed David (عليه السلام) and offered him safety for as long as he lived.

During the reign of King Saul and his son, many events took place in Palestine. In another battle with the Philistines, many Israelites were killed on Mount Gilboa. The Philistines pursued Saul and his sons, killing his son Jonathan. In that same battle, King Saul took his own life.

When the news of Saul's death spread, and David (عليه السلام) came into the kingdom of Israel, all the tribes of Israel came to David (عليه السلام) in Hebron, saying:

"Also in time past, when Saul was king over us, thou wast he that leddest out and broughtest in Israel: and the Lord said to thee, *Thou shalt feed my people Israel, and thou shalt be a captain over Israel.*" — 2 Samuel 5:2 (KJV)

The prayer which Allah (SWT) loves the most is the prayer of David (عليه السلام).
The fast which God loves the most is that of David (عليه السلام). He would sleep for
half of the night, stand up in prayer for a third, and then sleep for a sixth. He would
fast every other day… (Al-Bukhari)

Revelations upon Dawud

According to authentic narrations, Imam Ja'far as-Sadiq said that the *Zabur* was
revealed to Dawud (عليه السلام) on the night of the 18th of Ramadhan. It is also
narrated from the Holy Prophet that the *Zabur* was in the form of a compiled book.
[194]

It is mentioned in another hadith of the said Imam that Allah sent a revelation
to Dawud:

"O Dawud! Why have you gone into seclusion?"

He replied, "I remain aloof from others to gain Your pleasure, and people also
remain away from me."

Allah asked, "Why do you remain silent?"

He replied, "My Lord! My fear of You has made me silent."

The Lord asked, "Why do you toil so much in worship?"

His submission was, "Your love has made me toil endlessly in Your worship."

He inquired, "Why do you remain penniless, though I have given you ample
wealth?"

Dawud replied, "The remembrance of the rights of Your bounties upon me has
made me like an ever-needy person."

Allah asked, "Why are you so humble?"

Dawud replied, "Your limitless Grandeur and Might have made me extremely
low before You. Moreover, O my Deity! Only humility is appropriate when I am
facing You."

Allah said, "Greetings to you of increases in My Grace and Bounty. When you
come to Me, everything desired by you will be ready for you. So live among the
populace and be social with them, but keep away from bad deeds, so that you may
be able to gain whatever you wish from Me on the Day of Judgment."

In another authentic hadith, the Imam said:

---

[194] Ja'far ibn Muḥammad (Arabic: جعفر بن محمد الصادق; 700 or 702–765 C.E.), commonly known as
Jafar al-Sadiq or simply as-Sadiq (The Truthful), was the sixth Shī'ah Imam, and a major figure in
the Hanafi and Maliki schools of Sunni jurisprudence. He was a descendant of Ali on the side of
his father, Muhammad al-Baqir, and of Muhammad ibn Abu Bakr on the maternal side of his
family, Umm Farwah bint al-Qasim. Muhammad ibn Abu Bakr was raised by Ali, but was not his
son. (https://www.al-islam.org/person/imam-jafar-al-sadiq)

"Allah sent revelation to Dawud that when a servant of Mine does a good deed solely to please Me, I make Paradise admissible for him."

Dawud asked, "What is that good deed?"

Came the Divine reply: "Any good deed a servant does for My pleasure alone, even if he makes Me happy by merely giving a date to a needy person."

Dawud said, "My Lord! Indeed, this merits even to the one who does not recognise You (has no faith in Your Lordship, Divinity, and Mercy), that he may not cut off his hope (nor despair of Your Mercy)."

According to another reliable tradition, it is mentioned regarding the wisdom of the progeny of Dawud (عليه السلام) that:

O Son of Adam! How do you open your mouth to advise others when you yourself have not awakened from the sleep of negligence?

O Son of Adam! You woke up in the morning with a hardened heart, neglecting the Grandeur of your Lord. Had you been aware of your Lord's Greatness and Grace, you would certainly have feared His anger and believed in His promises.

Woe unto you! Why do you not remember your grave, and the impending loneliness and horror?

According to reliable evidence, the Holy Prophet ﷺ said that the Almighty sent revelation to Dawud:

"Verily, if a servant brings to Me a good deed on the Day of Judgment, I will give him the choice to select any place in Paradise, and it will be granted to him."

Dawud asked, "My Lord! Who will be that person?"

The Lord said, "A faithful one who tries to fulfil the need of another faithful, whether or not that need is fulfilled."

In explanation of the holy verse:

وَلَقَدْ كَتَبْنَا فِي الزَّبُورِ مِن بَعْدِ الذِّكْرِ أَنَّ الْأَرْضَ يَرِثُهَا عِبَادِيَ الصَّالِحُونَ

"And indeed We have written in Zabur (Psalms) [i.e. all the revealed Holy Books: the Taurat (Torah), the Injeel (Gospel), the Qur'an] after (We have already written in) Al-Lauh Al-Mahfuz (the Book that is in the heaven with Allah), that My righteous servants shall inherit the land (i.e. the land of Paradise)." — Surah Al-Anbiya, 21:105

It is written in a reliable tradition that the Almighty says:

"We have written in Zabur, after all that We had written in the scriptures of the earlier Messengers, that the earth will be given in charge of Our deserving servants—who are al-Qa'im (aj), the family of Muhammad ﷺ and his companions—as a heritage. It is said that there is information of forthcoming events in Zabur, and it contains Glory, Hallowing, and Remembrance of the Lord."

In another hadith, it is mentioned that Allah (SWT) revealed to Dawud (عليه السلام):

"Most of My servants maintain mere verbal friendship with one another, but they entertain enmity in their hearts."

It is mentioned in some traditions that there were 150 Surahs (chapters) in the Zabur (Psalms), and it was written therein:

"O Dawud! Listen to what I say, and whatever I say is the Truth. Anyone who comes to Me with love for Me, I will admit him to Paradise.

O Dawud! Hear Me. Whatever I say is Truth. If anyone comes to Me ashamed of his sins, I will blot out his sins from his scroll of deeds."

It is recorded in another tradition that Allah revealed to Dawud (عليه السلام):

"O Dawud! Maintain deep distance from those who indulge in worldly affairs and have embraced material joys and pleasures, for there are barriers upon their intelligence and wisdom, and My Grace and Mercy will not reach them."

And it is written in the 10th Surah of Zabur:

"O men! Do not neglect the Hereafter. Let not this worldly life deceive you with its beauty and attractions.

O Israelites! Reflect upon your return to the Hereafter and remember the Day of Resurrection."

And it is written in the 17th chapter:

"O Dawud! Listen to what I say and command Sulayman to make people understand that:

I will give the earth as inheritance to Muhammad ﷺ and his Ummah (followers), and they will be unlike what you are. Their prayer will not involve musical instruments and songs. So recite My Holiness more and more, and weep profusely when you raise the song in My sanctification.

Dawud (عليه السلام), tell the Israelites:

● Do not hoard illegal wealth; otherwise, I will not accept their prayers.

● Say (O man): If your father disobeys Me, distance yourself from him. Keep aloof even from your brother if he indulges in illegal acts."

"O Dawud! When you see an oppressor who has been granted high status in the world, do not long for his position. Surely and without doubt, he will face one of two fates: either I will impose upon him a tyrant greater than himself who will exact retribution, or I will compel him to give the rights of others on the Day of Judgment."

It is written in the 23rd Surah that:

• Sons of dust and dirty water—and yet the most proud people! You lean towards that which I have prohibited for you.

• Had you known where the forbidden leads, you would certainly abhor it. Had you seen the women of Paradise, fragrant with the heavenly scent and free from human discomforts, you would never pay attention to the world.

• The women of Paradise are always happy and smiling. They never get angry or agitated. They are immortal and will never die. Despite being repeatedly deflowered by their husbands, they remain ever-virgin. They are softer than butter and sweeter than honey. Springs of drink and honey flow before their thrones.

• Woe unto you who do not realise the vastness of the kingdom and the everlasting bounties, the untroubled life and eternal happiness, and the unending affluence that lies with Me. Holy is the Lord, the Creator of Light (Noor).

And it is written in the 31st Surah (of the Psalms):

• People! You are mortgaged to death.

• So do something for your Hereafter and purchase it in exchange for this world.

• Do not be like the group of people who wasted their worldly lives in negligence and play.

• Remember that the one who gives Me a loan shall receive back his capital with great profit, and the one who gives a loan to Satan will find himself near him in Hell.

What has happened to you that you love the world and turn away from Truth? Have your imaginations deceived you? What can be the ambition of one who is created from dust?

In the 27th Surah:

O Dawood! Do you know why I transformed the Israelites into monkeys and pigs?

• It was because they used to ignore the crimes of the rich and take them lightly, but when a poor person erred even slightly, they would punish him harshly.

• Therefore, My curse is upon the one who gains power in the world yet does not deal justly with both the rich and the poor.

• You follow your desires in the world. But where will you escape from Me when you come to Me alone?

How emphatically have I prohibited you from dishonouring the Muslims! Yet your tongues have transgressed against the people. The Creator of the Noor (Light) is Sacred.

Last Moment of Prophet Dawood (عليه السلام):

It is mentioned in a reliable tradition from Imam Ja'far as-Sadiq that Dawood (عليه السلام) passed away on a Sunday. Birds shaded him with their wings.

Allah has said:

"And We made Sulaiman (Solomon) to understand [the case]; and to each of them We gave judgement and knowledge. And We subjected the mountains and the birds to glorify Our praises along with Dawud (David); and it was We who did it."

—Surah Al-Anbiya (21:79)

فَفَهَّمْنَاهَا سُلَيْمَانَ ۚ وَكُلًّا آتَيْنَا حُكْمًا وَعِلْمًا ۚ وَسَخَّرْنَا مَعَ دَاوُودَ الْجِبَالَ يُسَبِّحْنَ وَالطَّيْرَ ۚ وَكُنَّا فَاعِلِينَ

The last moment of Prophet Dawood's (عليه السلام) life was dramatic and miraculous. History tells us that he lived a very simple life, leaving no precedent for luxury among the wealthy. One day, upon returning home from work, he saw a man standing in the middle of his house. His wife looked worried.

When Prophet Dawood (عليه السلام) asked about his identity, the man replied, "I am the one who fears no king and whom no barrier can prevent."

Prophet Dawood (عليه السلام) immediately realised that the man was none other than the Angel of Death. The angel took his soul peacefully.

Dawood (عليه السلام) was so beloved by his community that thousands came to pay their final respects. The day of his burial was oppressively hot and sunny. It was so difficult to complete the burial rites that thousands of birds, at the command of Prophet Sulayman (peace be upon him), shaded the sun with their wings until the burial was completed.

Hayāt al-Qulūb – Volume 1: Stories of the Prophets

What is the Religious Faith of the Ancestors of the Holy Prophet?

The *Noor* (Light) was created when Allah intended to bring creation into existence. The first thing Allah (SWT) created was the Light of Muhammad ﷺ.

According to *Al-Qastalani* (Vol. 1, pp. 5, 9, 10), the Prophet's traditions to this effect have been transmitted through Jabir ibn 'Abdullah al-Ansari and 'Ali (عليه السلام). The well-known historian *al-Mas'udi* also quotes a lengthy tradition from 'Ali (عليه السلام) in his *Muruj adh-Dhahab*, which states that when Allah created, the first creation was the Light of Muhammad ﷺ.

He said to it:

"You are My chosen one and the trustee of My Light and Guidance. It is because of you that I am going to create the earth and the skies, lay down reward and punishment, and bring into being the Garden and the Fire."[195]

Then the tradition goes on to speak about the Family of the Prophet ﷺ, the creation of the angels, of the souls, of the world, and of the covenant taken from the souls, which combined the belief in the One God with acceptance of Muhammad's ﷺ Prophethood.

This is why Ibn 'Abbas narrates that the Prophet said:

"I was a Prophet when Adam was between soul and body" (i.e. when Adam's creation was in its preliminary stages)

(*at-Tabarani, Al-Mu'jjam al-Kabir; Al Khasa'is al-Kubra, vol. 1, p. 4*).

Muhammad's ﷺ Light adorned the 'Arsh (Throne) of Allah. When, eons later, Adam was created, that Light was placed in his forehead. It continued its journey, generation after generation, through numerous prophets and their successors, until it came to Prophet Ibrahim (a.s.). From Ibrahim (a.s.), it passed to his eldest son, Prophet Isma'il (a.s.).

The Holy Prophet (s.a.w.w.) said:

"Verily Allah chose Isma'il from the progeny of Ibrahim, and chose Banu Kinanah from the progeny of Isma'il, and chose Quraish from the Banu Kinanah, and chose Banu Hashim from Quraish, and chose me from Banu Hashim."

At-Tirmidhi has narrated this tradition from Wathilah ibn al-Asqa' and has said that this tradition is sahih (authentic).

In the Qur'an, Allah says:

وَإِذْ قَالَ عِيسَى ابْنُ مَرْيَمَ يَا بَنِي إِسْرَائِيلَ إِنِّي رَسُولُ اللَّهِ إِلَيْكُم مُّصَدِّقًا لِّمَا بَيْنَ يَدَيَّ مِنَ التَّوْرَاةِ وَمُبَشِّرًا بِرَسُولٍ يَأْتِي مِن بَعْدِي اسْمُهُ أَحْمَدُ ۖ فَلَمَّا جَاءَهُم بِالْبَيِّنَاتِ قَالُوا هَٰذَا سِحْرٌ مُّبِينٌ

And (remember) when Jesus, the son of Mary, said:

"O children of Israel, I am the messenger of Allah unto you, confirming that which was before me of the Torah, and bringing glad tidings of a Messenger to come after me, whose name shall be Ahmad." But when he came unto them with clear proofs, they said:

"This is plain magic." (Surah As-Saff 61:6)

---

[195] Shihāb al-Dīn Abu'l-'Abbās Aḥmad ibn Muḥammad ibn Abī Bakr al-Qasṭallānī al-Qutaybī al-Shāfi'ī, also known as Al-Qasṭallānī was a Sunni Islamic scholar who specialized in hadith and theology. Wikipedia

The majority of Sunni Muslims, and some Shi'as, believe that Muhammad ﷺ was born on the 12th of Rabi' al-Awwal, while many Twelver Shia Muslims assert that Muhammad ﷺ was born on the 17th of Rabi' al-Awwal.

He was born approximately in 570 CE in Mecca, a mountain town on the high desert plateau of western Arabia. He was the first and only son of Abdullah ibn al-Muttalib and Amina bint Wahb. Abdullah died before Muhammad's birth, and Muhammad was raised by his mother Amina, who, in keeping with Meccan tradition, entrusted her son at an early age to a wet nurse named Halima from the nomadic tribe of Sa'd ibn Bakr.

He grew up in the hill country, learning their pure Arabic. At around five or six years of age, his mother took him to Yathrib, an oasis town a few hundred miles north of Mecca, to stay with relatives and to visit his father's grave there. On the return journey, Amina fell ill and died.

After that incident, his nurse returned to Mecca with the orphaned boy and placed him in the protection of his paternal grandfather, Abdul al-Muttalib, who was one of the most respected leaders in Mecca. Mecca was an important place of pilgrimage, and Abdul al-Muttalib often presided over the Council of Elders.[196]

Upon his grandfather's death in 578 CE, Muhammad ﷺ, aged about eight, passed into the care of a paternal uncle, Abu Talib عليه السلام. Muhammad ﷺ grew up in the older man's home and remained under Abu Talib's protection for many years.

Historians underscore Muhammad's ﷺ difficult childhood. So does the Qur'an:

$$أَلَمْ يَجِدْكَ يَتِيمًا فَآوَىٰ$$

$$وَوَجَدَكَ ضَالًّا فَهَدَىٰ$$

$$وَوَجَدَكَ عَائِلًا فَأَغْنَىٰ$$

Did He not find thee an orphan, and gave thee shelter? And He found thee wandering, and gave thee guidance? And He found thee in need, and made thee self-sufficient? (93:6–8)

It is the accepted belief of the Shi'a Ithna Ashari, the Hanafis, and the Shafi'is that the ancestors of the Holy Prophet ﷺ — from 'Abdullah to Qidar ibn Isma'il عليه السلام and from there right up to Adam عليه السلام — were true believers. They believed in the One and Only God and faithfully followed the Divine religion of their times. From Qidar to 'Abdullah, all of them followed the Shari'ah of Prophet Ibrahim (a.s.), which was the religion prescribed for them by Allah.

---

[196] (The Quraysh were a grouping of Arab clans that historically inhabited and controlled the city of Mecca and its Kaaba. The Islamic prophet Muhammad was born into the Hashim clan of the tribe)

The famous Sunni scholar, Imam Jalaluddin as-Suyuti, has written nine books on this subject and has proved beyond doubt that all the ancestors of the Holy Prophet ﷺ were true believers. Shaykh 'Abdul-Haqq Muhaddith Dehlawi wrote:

"All the ancestors of the Holy Prophet from Adam up to 'Abdullah were pure and clean from the uncleanness of disbelief and paganism. It was not possible for Allah SWT to put that Holy Light (of the Holy Prophet) into dark and dirty places, i.e., the loins of a pagan man or the womb of a pagan woman. Also, how could it be possible for Allah SWT to punish the ancestors of the Holy Prophet on the Day of Judgement and thus humiliate him in the eyes of the world?"

Allamah al-Majlisi has written:

"It is the unanimous belief of Shi'a scholars that the father, mother, and all ancestors of the Holy Prophet followed the true religion, and his Light never entered into the loins of any pagan man or the womb of any pagan woman. Also, the accepted traditions say that all his ancestors were *Siddiqun* (Truthful Ones); they were either prophets or successors of prophets."

Amirul-Mu'minin 'Ali ibn Abi Talib (a.s.) said:

"By Allah, neither my father ever worshipped the idols, nor my grandfather 'Abdul-Muttalib, nor his father Hashim, nor his father 'Abd Manaf. They prayed facing towards the Ka'bah and followed the religion of Ibrahim."

The Holy Prophet ﷺ said:

"Jibril (Gabriel) said to me: 'I searched the east and the west of the earth, but I did not find anyone superior to Muhammad ﷺ; and I searched the east and the west of the earth, but I did not find the children of any father better than the children of Hashim.'"

In the Qur'an, Allah again says:

إِنَّا أَرْسَلْنَاكَ بِالْحَقِّ بَشِيرًا وَنَذِيرًا ۖ وَلَا تُسْأَلُ عَنْ أَصْحَابِ الْجَحِيمِ

Verily, We have sent thee (O Muhammad ﷺ) with the truth (Islam), a bearer of glad tidings and a warner. And thou shalt not be asked about the companions of the blazing Fire. (2:119, Surah Al-Baqarah)

رَبَّنَا وَابْعَثْ فِيهِمْ رَسُولًا مِّنْهُمْ يَتْلُو عَلَيْهِمْ آيَاتِكَ وَيُعَلِّمُهُمُ الْكِتَابَ وَالْحِكْمَةَ وَيُزَكِّيهِمْ ۚ إِنَّكَ أَنتَ الْعَزِيزُ الْحَكِيمُ

Our Lord! Send among them a Messenger of their own, who shall recite unto them Thy Verses and instruct them in the Book and wisdom, and purify them. Verily, Thou art the Almighty, the All-Wise. (2:129, Surah Al-Baqarah)

وَمَن يَرْغَبُ عَن مِّلَّةِ إِبْرَاهِيمَ إِلَّا مَن سَفِهَ نَفْسَهُ ۚ وَلَقَدِ اصْطَفَيْنَاهُ فِي الدُّنْيَا ۖ وَإِنَّهُ فِي الْآخِرَةِ لَمِنَ الصَّالِحِينَ

And who turns away from the religion of Ibrahim (Abraham) except one who makes a fool of himself? Verily, We chose him in this world, and verily, in the Hereafter he will be among the righteous. (2:130, Surah Al-Baqarah)

In Conclusion

We can say that they were among the true believers — the Hanif community — who were practising the faith and traditions passed down from their grandfather, Hazrat Ibrahim عليه السلام.

Allah knows best. [197]

---

[197] Index 149 https://www.imamreza.net/old/eng/imamreza.php?id=209 (1)

بِسْمِ ٱللَّهِ ٱلرَّحْمَـٰنِ ٱلرَّحِيمِ

Chapter 12

The Constitution of This Earth

In Islamic theology, it is our belief that Allah SWT sent down divine books to guide humanity. These books are seen as the ultimate sources of guidance, containing the laws and principles that mankind should follow. The concept likens these books to a constitution—a supreme legal document that dictates how people should live their lives.

The messengers (prophets) are viewed as individuals chosen by Allah SWT to receive His messages and demonstrate how to live according to divine guidance. Each messenger came with specific instructions on how to implement the teachings of the divine books, such as:

- **The Torah (Tawrat):** Given to Moses (Musa), it contains the laws and commandments for the Israelites.
- **The Psalms (Zabur):** Given to David (Dawud), it includes songs of praise and guidance.
- **The Gospel (Injil):** Given to Jesus (Isa), it provides guidance and good news to the people.
- **The Qur'an:** The final revelation given to Muhammad ﷺ, intended for all of humanity.

The Qur'an is considered the final and most comprehensive revelation. It is believed to be an update to all previous scriptures, meant for the entire human race—not just a specific sect or group. It provides guidance on all aspects of life, including spiritual, moral, legal, and social matters.

The finality of Prophet Muhammad ﷺ is central; he is regarded as the last prophet, who came to teach and implement the Qur'anic guidance. His role was not only to convey the Qur'an but also to explain and demonstrate its implementation through his sayings (Hadith) and actions (Sunnah). The Qur'an and Sunnah together form the basis of Islamic law (Sharia).

The verses in the Qur'an serve as an introduction to Allah's divine decrees. Allah SWT says:

نَزَّلَ عَلَيْكَ الْكِتَابَ بِالْحَقِّ مُصَدِّقًا لِّمَا بَيْنَ يَدَيْهِ وَأَنزَلَ التَّوْرَاةَ وَالْإِنجِيلَ

مِن قَبْلُ هُدًى لِّلنَّاسِ وَأَنزَلَ الْفُرْقَانَ ۗ إِنَّ الَّذِينَ كَفَرُوا بِآيَاتِ اللَّهِ لَهُمْ عَذَابٌ شَدِيدٌ ۗ وَاللَّهُ عَزِيزٌ ذُو انتِقَامٍ

It is He who hath sent down the Book (the Qur'an) to thee with truth, confirming that which was before it; and He sent down the Torah and the Gospel, aforetime, for a guidance to mankind; and He sent down the criterion (of judgment between right and wrong). Verily, those who reject the signs of Allah, for them is a severe punishment; and Allah is exalted in might, Lord of Retribution. — Surah Aal-E-Imran 3:3–4

Allah SWT also says:

مَّا كَانَ مُحَمَّدٌ أَبَا أَحَدٍ مِّن رِّجَالِكُمْ وَلَكِن رَّسُولَ اللَّهِ وَخَاتَمَ النَّبِيِّينَ ۗ وَكَانَ اللَّهُ بِكُلِّ شَيْءٍ عَلِيمًا

Muhammad ﷺ is not the father of any man among you, but (he is) the Messenger of Allah, and the Seal of the Prophets: and Allah has full knowledge of all things. — **Surah Al-Ahzab 33:40**

And in the Hadith:

"I have left among you two things, which if you hold fast to them you will never go astray: the Book of Allah and my Sunnah." *(Muwatta Malik, Book 46, Hadith 3)*

These references highlight that the Qur'an is the final and complete guidance for humanity, with Prophet Muhammad ﷺ serving as the ultimate model for its implementation. The following verses should be considered a preface to the works of the Divine Constitution, serving as a reminder and guiding us to conform ourselves to its truth.

Part 1

وَإِذْ أَخَذَ رَبُّكَ مِن بَنِي آدَمَ مِن ظُهُورِهِمْ ذُرِّيَّتَهُمْ وَأَشْهَدَهُمْ عَلَىٰ أَنفُسِهِمْ أَلَسْتُ بِرَبِّكُمْ ۗ قَالُوا بَلَىٰ ۛ شَهِدْنَا ۛ أَن تَقُولُوا يَوْمَ الْقِيَامَةِ إِنَّا كُنَّا عَنْ هَذَا غَافِلِينَ

And (remember) when thy Lord brought forth from the Children of Adam, from their loins, their seed, and made them testify concerning themselves, (saying): Am I not your Lord? They said: Yea! We do testify—lest ye should say on the Day of Resurrection: Verily, of this we were unaware. — Surah Al-A'raf 7:172

إِنَّ رَبَّكُمُ اللَّهُ الَّذِي خَلَقَ السَّمَاوَاتِ وَالْأَرْضَ فِي سِتَّةِ أَيَّامٍ ثُمَّ اسْتَوَىٰ عَلَى الْعَرْشِ يُغْشِي اللَّيْلَ النَّهَارَ يَطْلُبُهُ حَثِيثًا وَالشَّمْسَ وَالْقَمَرَ وَالنُّجُومَ مُسَخَّرَاتٍ بِأَمْرِهِ ۗ أَلَا لَهُ الْخَلْقُ وَالْأَمْرُ ۗ تَبَارَكَ اللَّهُ رَبُّ الْعَالَمِينَ

*IndeedVerily your Lord is Allah who created the heavens and the earth in six days, then mounted the Throne. He draweth the night as a veil over the day, each seeking the other in rapid succession. He created the sun, the moon, and the stars, (all) governed by His command. Surely, His is the creation and the command. Blessed be Allah, the Lord of the Worlds. — **Surah Al-A'raf 7:54***

429

قُلْ إِنَّ صَلَاتِي وَنُسُكِي وَمَحْيَايَ وَمَمَاتِي لِلَّهِ رَبِّ الْعَالَمِينَ

لَا شَرِيكَ لَهُ ۖ وَبِذَٰلِكَ أُمِرْتُ وَأَنَا أَوَّلُ الْمُسْلِمِينَ

Say: Verily, my prayer, and my sacrifice, and my life and my death, are all for Allah, the Lord of the Worlds.

He hath no partner. This I am commanded, and I am the first of those who submit. — ***Surah Al-An'am 6:162–163***

وَمَا مِن دَابَّةٍ فِي الْأَرْضِ وَلَا طَائِرٍ يَطِيرُ بِجَنَاحَيْهِ إِلَّا أُمَمٌ أَمْثَالُكُم ۚ مَّا فَرَّطْنَا فِي الْكِتَابِ مِن شَيْءٍ ۚ ثُمَّ إِلَىٰ رَبِّهِمْ يُحْشَرُونَ

There is not a beast on the earth, nor a bird that flieth with its wings, but they are communities like unto you. We have left nothing out of the Book. Then to their Lord shall they be gathered. — ***Surah Al-An'am 6:38***

These verses serve as the introduction to Allah's divine decrees.

As human beings, we have created constitutions that serve a vital role in providing nations with foundational legal principles. These documents guide citizens' rights and responsibilities and establish the framework for governance.

Every country on Earth has its own constitution, and every citizen is expected to uphold and defend its prescribed rules, regardless of their religious beliefs. Globally, people have respected and integrated God's teachings into their constitutions. This is evident when examining the preambles of several populous countries, such as the USA, the United Kingdom, India, China, and Saudi Arabia.

Preamble To The Constitution

United States Of America

We the People of the United States, in Order to form a more perfect Union, establish Justice, ensure domestic Tranquillity, provide for the common defence, promote the general Welfare, and secure the Blessings of Liberty to ourselves and our Posterity, do ordain and establish this Constitution for the United States of America.

United Kingdom

United, we stand in celebration of the diverse voices that make up the great chorus of the nation. Confident in our individuality, and steadfast in our shared values and common purpose, we—the citizens of the United Kingdom of Great Britain and Northern Ireland—have come together in the spirit of self-determination in order to establish the principles of our law and governance.

- To recognise every citizen as an equal partner in government—at a local, regional, and national level.

- To affirm that each citizen is entitled to fair and equitable treatment under the law.
- To establish the principle of equality of opportunity for all citizens.
- To eradicate poverty and want throughout the nation.
- To protect and cultivate community identities within the four great countries of the Union: England, Scotland, Wales, and Northern Ireland.
- To preserve our common environment, and to hold it in trust for future generations.
- To safeguard freedom of thought, conscience, and assembly; and to facilitate peaceable dissent.
- And to protect these fundamental rights against the encroachment of tyranny and the abdication of reason.[198]

India

WE, THE PEOPLE OF INDIA, having solemnly resolved to constitute India into a **SOVEREIGN SOCIALIST SECULAR DEMOCRATIC REPUBLIC** and to secure to all its citizens:

- **JUSTICE**: social, economic and political;
- **LIBERTY**: of thought, expression, belief, faith and worship;
- **EQUALITY**: of status and of opportunity;
- and to promote among them all **FRATERNITY**, assuring the dignity of the individual and the unity and integrity of the Nation;

IN OUR CONSTITUENT ASSEMBLY, this twenty-sixth day of November, 1949, **DO HEREBY ADOPT, ENACT AND GIVE TO OURSELVES THIS CONSTITUTION.**[199]

The People's Republic of China

General Principles

Article 1

The People's Republic of China is a socialist state governed by a people's democratic dictatorship that is led by the working class and based on an alliance of workers and peasants.

---

[198] Index 150 https://www.parliament.uk/globalassets/documents/commons-committees/political-and-constitutional-reform/The-UK-Constitution.pdf
[199] 151 https://www.constitutionofindia.net/constitution_of_india/preamble

The socialist system is the fundamental system of the People's Republic of China. Leadership by the Communist Party of China is the defining feature of socialism with Chinese characteristics.

- It is prohibited for any organisation or individual to damage the socialist system.
- "China consistently opposes imperialism, hegemonism, and colonialism; works to strengthen its solidarity with the people of all other countries; supports oppressed peoples and other developing countries in their just struggles to win and safeguard their independence and develop their economies; and strives to safeguard world peace and promote the cause of human progress."[200]

Saudi Arabia

Part 2. System of Government

Article 5

a. The system of government in Saudi Arabia shall be monarchical.

b. The dynastic right shall be confined to the sons of the Founder, King Abdul Aziz bin Abdul Rahman Al Saud (Ibn Saud), and their sons. The most eligible among them shall be invited, through the process of *bai'ah*, to rule in accordance with the Book of God and the Prophet's Sunnah.

c. The King names the Crown Prince and may relieve him of his duties by Royal Order.

d. The Crown Prince shall devote full time to his office and to any other duties which may be assigned to him by the King.

e. The Crown Prince shall assume the powers of the King upon the latter's death, pending the outcome of the *bai'ah*.

Article 6

Citizens shall pledge allegiance to the King on the basis of the Book of God and the Prophet's Sunnah, as well as on the principle of "hearing is obeying," both in prosperity and adversity, in situations pleasant and unpleasant.

Article 7

The regime derives its power from the Holy Qur'an and the Prophet's Sunnah, which rule over this and all other State Laws.

---

[200] https://english.www.gov.cn/archive/lawsregulations/201911/20/content_WS5ed8856ec6d0b3f0e9499913.html

Article 8

The system of government in the Kingdom of Saudi Arabia is established on the foundation of justice, *Shoura*, and equality in compliance with the Islamic Shari'ah (the revealed law of Islam).[201]

The Constitution serves as a powerful emblem of a nation's identity, and it is crucial that the laws formulated for its safeguarding and effective governance are actually upheld. Legislators and leaders play a significant role in establishing justice and fairness within the country. However, when the commitment to loyalty and the guidance of those who create laws vanishes, and is replaced by corruption, hypocrisy, tyranny, lack of accountability, insincerity, dishonesty, discrimination, physical abuse, and sexual exploitation, it leads to widespread emigration.

The consequences of such a situation are detrimental to the very essence of humanity within that community, and its effects are evident in various manifestations throughout the world.

Allah SWT says:

كُنتُمْ خَيْرَ أُمَّةٍ أُخْرِجَتْ لِلنَّاسِ تَأْمُرُونَ بِالْمَعْرُوفِ وَتَنْهَوْنَ عَنِ الْمُنكَرِ وَتُؤْمِنُونَ بِاللَّهِ ۗ وَلَوْ
آمَنَ أَهْلُ الْكِتَابِ لَكَانَ خَيْرًا لَّهُم ۚ مِّنْهُمُ الْمُؤْمِنُونَ وَأَكْثَرُهُمُ الْفَاسِقُونَ

"Ye are the best nation brought forth unto mankind: ye enjoin what is right, and forbid what is wrong, and believe in Allah. And if the People of the Book had believed, it had been better for them: among them are believers, but most of them are rebellious."

—Surah Al-Imran 3:110

The laws established by Allah encompass every aspect of creation, surpassing human understanding. They govern the souls of individuals, the formation and regulation of the universe, celestial bodies, the Earth, seas, rivers, rain, the sun, the moon, the wind, the jinn, the angels, the ultimate judgement, refuge, Hell, and countless other realms beyond our knowledge. Allah deliberately conceals the unseen from us according to His will.

Nevertheless, Allah assures us that all of these matters are meticulously recorded in the Book of فِي لَوْح مَّحْفُوظ (*al-Lawh al-Mahfuz*). This sacred scripture remains unchanged and inaccessible, protected from any alterations. Within its pages lies everything, even the smallest occurrence—like a leaf falling from a tree. Every event, whether from the past, present, or future, is inscribed within its divine contents.

It is the notebook of *Qadar* (destiny) and the programme of the universe. It is also referred to as:

---

[201] https://www.constituteproject.org/constitution/Saudi_Arabia_2005.pdf

- *Ummul-Kitab* (Mother of the Book, Main Book)

- *Kitabun Hafiz* (Preserving Book)

- *Kitabun Mubin* (Clear Book)

- *Kitabun Maknun* (Hidden Book)

- *Imamun Mubin* (Clear Guide)

- *Al-Kitab* (The Book) in the Qur'an

- It is also called *Kitabul-Qadar* (The Book of Qadar) since it includes the things that will happen to people.

The pen that wrote it was created 50,000 years before the heavens and the earth, as mentioned in the book. [202]

Allah SWT says in the Qur'an:

يَوْمَ نَطْوِي السَّمَاءَ كَطَيِّ السِّجِلِّ لِلْكُتُبِ ۚ كَمَا بَدَأْنَا أَوَّلَ خَلْقٍ نُّعِيدُهُ ۚ وَعْدًا عَلَيْنَا ۚ إِنَّا كُنَّا فَاعِلِينَ

وَلَقَدْ كَتَبْنَا فِي الزَّبُورِ مِن بَعْدِ الذِّكْرِ أَنَّ الْأَرْضَ يَرِثُهَا عِبَادِيَ الصَّالِحُونَ

إِنَّ فِي هَٰذَا لَبَلَاغًا لِّقَوْمٍ عَابِدِينَ

104. And (remember) the Day when We shall roll up the heavens like a scroll rolled up for books. As We began the first creation, We shall repeat it. (It is) a promise binding upon Us. Truly, We shall do it.

105. And indeed We have written in the Zabur (Psalms) – [i.e., all the revealed Holy Books: the Taurat (Torah), the Injeel (Gospel), the Qur'an] – after (We had already written in) Al-Lauh Al-Mahfuz (the Preserved Tablet in the heavens with Allah), that My righteous servants shall inherit the earth (i.e., the land of Paradise).

106. Verily, in this (the Qur'an), there is a plain message for a people who worship Allah (i.e., true believers in Islamic Monotheism who act according to the Qur'an and the Sunnah).

---

[202] " 46 The Book of Destiny" 2)Chapter: The Debate Between Adam And Musa (Peace And Blessings Of Allah Be Upon Them) Abdullah b. 'Amr b. al-'As reported:I heard Allah's Messenger (ﷺ) as saying: Allah ordained the measures (of quality) of the creation fifty thousand years before He created the heavens and the earth, as His Throne was upon water. Reference :SahihMuslim 2653b https://sunnah.com/muslim:2653b
In-book reference : Book 46, Hadith 27USC-MSA web (English) reference : Book 33, Hadith 6416 (deprecated numbering scheme)

107. *(Surah Al-Anbiya, 21:104–106)*

Lawh Mahfuz (لوح محفوظ), the Preserved Tablet, mentioned in the Qur'an, can be defined as a supreme divine constitutional law and guideline set forth in this Book, which the entire creation of the Almighty follows with consistency. Allah SWT says:

$$يَمْحُو اللَّهُ مَا يَشَاءُ وَيُثْبِتُ ۖ وَعِندَهُ أُمُّ الْكِتَابِ$$

Allah doth blot out or confirm what He pleaseth: with Him is the Mother of the Book.

(Surah Ar-Ra'd, 13:39)

$$۞ وَيَعْلَمُ مَا فِي الْبَرِّ وَالْبَحْرِ ۚ وَمَا تَسْقُطُ مِن وَرَقَةٍ وَعِندَهُ مَفَاتِحُ الْغَيْبِ لَا يَعْلَمُهَا إِلَّا هُوَ ۚ إِلَّا يَعْلَمُهَا وَلَا حَبَّةٍ فِي ظُلُمَاتِ الْأَرْضِ وَلَا رَطْبٍ وَلَا يَابِسٍ إِلَّا فِي كِتَابٍ مُّبِينٍ$$

And with Him are the keys of the unseen; none knows them but He. He knows whatever is in the land and in the sea. Not a leaf falls but He knows it. There is not a grain in the darkness of the earth, nor anything fresh or dry, but it is written in a clear Record.

(Surah Al-An'am, 6:59)

$$النَّبِيُّ أَوْلَىٰ بِالْمُؤْمِنِينَ مِنْ أَنفُسِهِمْ ۖ وَأَزْوَاجُهُ أُمَّهَاتُهُمْ ۗ وَأُولُو الْأَرْحَامِ بَعْضُهُمْ أَوْلَىٰ بِبَعْضٍ فِي كِتَابِ اللَّهِ مِنَ الْمُؤْمِنِينَ وَالْمُهَاجِرِينَ إِلَّا أَن تَفْعَلُوا إِلَىٰ أَوْلِيَائِكُم مَّعْرُوفًا ۚ كَانَ ذَٰلِكَ فِي الْكِتَابِ مَسْطُورًا$$

The Prophet is closer to the believers than their own selves, and his wives are their (believers') mothers. Blood relations among each other have closer personal ties in the Decree of Allah (regarding inheritance) than the brotherhood of the believers and the Muhajirun (emigrants), except that you do kindness to those brothers (whom the Prophet joined in brotherhood). This has been written in the Book of Divine Decrees (Al-Lauh Al-Mahfuz).

$$وَمَا تَكُونُ فِي شَأْنٍ وَمَا تَتْلُو مِنْهُ مِن قُرْآنٍ وَلَا تَعْمَلُونَ مِنْ عَمَلٍ إِلَّا كُنَّا عَلَيْكُمْ شُهُودًا إِذْ تُفِيضُونَ فِيهِ ۚ وَمَا يَعْزُبُ عَن رَّبِّكَ مِن مِّثْقَالِ ذَرَّةٍ فِي الْأَرْضِ وَلَا فِي السَّمَاءِ وَلَا أَصْغَرَ مِن ذَٰلِكَ وَلَا أَكْبَرَ إِلَّا فِي كِتَابٍ مُّبِينٍ$$

(Surah Al-Ahzab, 33:6)

Whatever affair you (O Muhammad ﷺ) may be engaged in, and whatever portion you may be reciting from the Qur'an, and whatever deed you (mankind) may be doing, We are Witness thereof when you are doing it. Nothing is hidden from your Lord, not even the weight of an atom on the earth or in the heavens, nor what is less than that or greater, but it is in a clear Record.

(Surah Yunus, 10:61)

وَمَا مِن دَابَّةٍ فِي الْأَرْضِ إِلَّا عَلَى اللَّهِ رِزْقُهَا وَيَعْلَمُ مُسْتَقَرَّهَا وَمُسْتَوْدَعَهَا ۚ كُلٌّ فِي كِتَابٍ مُّبِينٍ

There is no moving creature on earth whose provision is not due from Allah. He knows its dwelling place and its resting place. All is recorded in a clear Book (Al-Lauh Al-Mahfuz).

(Surah Hud, 11:6)

وَإِن مِّن قَرْيَةٍ إِلَّا نَحْنُ مُهْلِكُوهَا قَبْلَ يَوْمِ الْقِيَامَةِ أَوْ مُعَذِّبُوهَا عَذَابًا شَدِيدًا ۚ كَانَ ذَٰلِكَ فِي الْكِتَابِ مَسْطُورًا

There is not a town but We shall destroy it before the Day of Resurrection, or punish it with a severe torment. That is written in the Book (of Our Decrees).

وَقَالَ الَّذِينَ كَفَرُوا لَا تَأْتِينَا السَّاعَةُ ۖ قُلْ بَلَىٰ وَرَبِّي لَتَأْتِيَنَّكُمْ عَالِمِ الْغَيْبِ ۖ لَا يَعْزُبُ عَنْهُ مِثْقَالُ ذَرَّةٍ فِي السَّمَاوَاتِ وَلَا فِي الْأَرْضِ وَلَا أَصْغَرُ مِن ذَٰلِكَ وَلَا أَكْبَرُ إِلَّا فِي كِتَابٍ مُّبِينٍ

(Surah Al-Isra, 17:58)

Those who disbelieve say: "The Hour will not come to us." Say: "Yes, by my Lord, it will surely come to you." (Allah, He is) the All-Knower of the unseen. Not even the weight of an atom, nor anything smaller or greater, escapes His knowledge in the heavens or in the earth, but it is all in a clear Book.

(Surah Saba, 34:3)

وَاللَّهُ خَلَقَكُم مِّن تُرَابٍ ثُمَّ مِن نُّطْفَةٍ ثُمَّ جَعَلَكُمْ أَزْوَاجًا ۚ وَمَا تَحْمِلُ مِنْ أُنثَىٰ وَلَا تَضَعُ إِلَّا بِعِلْمِهِ ۚ وَمَا يُعَمَّرُ مِن مُّعَمَّرٍ وَلَا يُنقَصُ مِنْ عُمُرِهِ إِلَّا فِي كِتَابٍ ۚ إِنَّ ذَٰلِكَ عَلَى اللَّهِ يَسِيرٌ

And Allah created you from dust, then from a drop of fluid, and then made you in pairs. No female conceives or gives birth but with His Knowledge. No person is granted a longer life, nor is any part of his life shortened, but it is (recorded) in a Book. Verily, that is easy for Allah.

(Surah Fatir, 35:11)

إِنَّا جَعَلْنَاهُ قُرْآنًا عَرَبِيًّا لَّعَلَّكُمْ تَعْقِلُونَ

وَإِنَّهُ فِي أُمِّ الْكِتَابِ لَدَيْنَا لَعَلِيٌّ حَكِيمٌ

Verily, We have made it a Qur'an in Arabic that you may understand. And indeed, it is in the Mother of the Book (Al-Lauh Al-Mahfuz) with Us, exalted and full of wisdom.

(Surah Az-Zukhruf, 43:3–4)

قَدْ عَلِمْنَا مَا تَنقُصُ الْأَرْضُ مِنْهُمْ ۖ وَعِندَنَا كِتَابٌ حَفِيظٌ

We certainly know what the earth consumes of them (their bodies), and with Us is a preserving Book.

(Surah Qaf, 50:4)

...مَا أَصَابَ مِن مُّصِيبَةٍ

No calamity befalls the earth or yourselves but it is inscribed in the Book of Decrees (Al-Lauh Al-Mahfuz), before We bring it into being. Verily, that is easy for Allah.

(Surah Al-Hadid, 57:22)

And therefore:

كَلَّا إِنَّهَا تَذْكِرَةٌ

فَمَن شَاءَ ذَكَرَهُ

فِي صُحُفٍ مُّكَرَّمَةٍ

مَّرْفُوعَةٍ مُّطَهَّرَةٍ

بِأَيْدِي سَفَرَةٍ

11. Nay, indeed it (these verses of the Qur'an) is an admonition.

12. So whoever wills, let him remember it.

13. It is in records held in honour (Al-Lauh Al-Mahfuz),

14. Exalted, purified,

15. In the hands of noble scribes.

In an article by Fethullah Gülen, posted in *Key Concepts in the Practice of Sufism – Volume 4*, he writes:

The scholars of Sufism have usually viewed the Supreme Preserved Tablet as the start, origin, and central point of the sphere of existence, and as the title of what they call "the Universal, Speaking Soul," which was created after the Most Exalted Pen.

It is the first centre for the identification of all creation on the horizon of Knowledge by Knowledge itself. It is a Divine light which was manifested in the same relationship with the Universal Intellect as Eve had with Adam. This light is such an all-encompassing Divine radiance that all the worlds are but an extended shadow of it, dependent on Divine Power. All the Divine religious laws are an illuminating ray of it, issued from Divine Speech, and the Law which Prophet Muhammad ﷺ—upon him be the most perfect blessings—brought is the continuous radiance of it.

These approaches of Sufi scholars mark some of the depths of the Supreme Preserved Tablet.[203]

---

[203] http://fgulen.com/en/fethullah-gulens-works/

Part II

The Qur'an

Allah (SWT), in His benevolence, bestowed His divine law upon humanity to enable them to live a righteous and fulfilling life. This law, guided by unwavering principles free from falsehood or flaws, was instituted among them through the leadership of a devout and pious individual. Allah (SWT), in His infinite wisdom, selected the nation of His Prophet ﷺ to be the exemplar among all nations—calling people towards goodness, advocating for virtuous conduct, and deterring evil. This chosen nation has been entrusted with the responsibility of leading other nations towards actions that bring satisfaction to the Almighty—whose glory is beyond measure. (www.khilafah.com) The verse revealed:

يَا أَيُّهَا النَّاسُ قَدْ جَاءَتْكُم مَّوْعِظَةٌ مِّن رَّبِّكُمْ وَشِفَاءٌ لِّمَا فِي الصُّدُورِ وَهُدًى وَرَحْمَةٌ لِّلْمُؤْمِنِينَ

O mankind! There has come to you a good advice from your Lord (i.e. the Qur'an, ordering all that is good and forbidding all that is evil), and a healing for that (disease of ignorance, doubt, hypocrisy and differences, etc.) in your breasts— a guidance and a mercy (explaining lawful and unlawful things, etc.) for the believers. (10:57, Surah Yunus)

The Qur'an is eternal. It is timeless. We call it the Holy Qur'an, the Noble Qur'an, the Glorious Qur'an, Al-Furqan, Al-Kitab, Al-Zikr, Al-Noor, and Al-Huda. A great book has been sent down from Almighty Allah as the comprehensive constitution of supreme law and guidance, full of wisdom for the humanity of this planet. The people of this world, whether directly or indirectly, adhere to this constitution for their own benefit.

However, it is only the Muslims—the believers—who recognise and accept this book as their exclusive guide. They diligently follow its teachings, seeking rewards in both this life and the Hereafter. This magnificent and divine book is none other than the Qur'an.

The Qur'an, also known as the Furqan, serves as a clear criterion, distinguishing between right and wrong, good and evil. It provides us with guidance on how to lead our lives on this earthly plane.

Allah (SWT) says:

وَلَوْ أَنَّمَا فِي الْأَرْضِ مِن شَجَرَةٍ أَقْلَامٌ وَالْبَحْرُ يَمُدُّهُ مِن بَعْدِهِ سَبْعَةُ أَبْحُرٍ مَّا نَفِدَتْ كَلِمَاتُ اللَّهِ إِنَّ اللَّهَ عَزِيزٌ حَكِيمٌ

And if all the trees on the earth were pens and the sea (were ink wherewith to write), with seven seas behind it to add to its (supply), yet the Words of Allah would not be exhausted. Verily, Allah is All-Mighty, All-Wise. (31:27, Surah Luqman)

Allah (SWT) sent down several divine books for the guidance of mankind, among which we may name the Suhuf given to Noah. These older books are called 'revealed' books or *Kutub*, meaning that Muslims believe they contained essentially

438

the same message as the Qur'an, but that the scriptures lost their originality and were corrupted over time.

However, the revealed verses of the Holy Qur'an are, without doubt, a light to guide the sincere seeker of truth. Allah Himself has preserved this great book, the Qur'an, and thus it has remained unchanged since its revelation and will always continue to be a comprehensive constitution of supreme law and guidance.

At the very beginning, the following verses should be patiently heeded:

ذَٰلِكَ الْكِتَابُ لَا رَيْبَ ۛ فِيهِ ۛ هُدًى لِّلْمُتَّقِينَ

This is the Book (the Qur'an), whereof there is no doubt, a guidance to those who are Al-Muttaqun (the pious and righteous persons who fear Allah and love Him deeply). **(2:2, Surah Al-Baqara)**

قُل لَّئِنِ اجْتَمَعَتِ الْإِنسُ وَالْجِنُّ عَلَىٰ أَن يَأْتُوا بِمِثْلِ هَٰذَا الْقُرْآنِ لَا يَأْتُونَ بِمِثْلِهِ وَلَوْ كَانَ بَعْضُهُمْ لِبَعْضٍ ظَهِيرًا

Say: "If mankind and the jinn were together to produce the like of this Qur'an, they could not produce the like thereof, even if they helped one another." (17:88, Surah Al-Isra)

وَمَا أَنزَلْنَا عَلَيْكَ الْكِتَابَ إِلَّا لِتُبَيِّنَ لَهُمُ الَّذِي اخْتَلَفُوا فِيهِ ۙ وَهُدًى وَرَحْمَةً لِّقَوْمٍ يُؤْمِنُونَ

And We have not sent down the Book (the Qur'an) to you (O Muhammad ﷺ), except that you may explain clearly unto them those things in which they differ, and as a guidance and a mercy for a people who believe. (16:64, Surah An-Nahl)

وَمَا اخْتَلَفْتُمْ فِيهِ مِن شَيْءٍ فَحُكْمُهُ إِلَى اللَّهِ ۚ ذَٰلِكُمُ اللَّهُ رَبِّي عَلَيْهِ تَوَكَّلْتُ وَإِلَيْهِ أُنِيبُ

And in whatsoever you differ, the decision thereof is with Allah. (Say, O Muhammad ﷺ): Such is Allah, my Lord. In Him I put my trust, and to Him I turn in repentance. **(42:10, Surah Ash-Shura)**

وَمَا مِن دَابَّةٍ فِي الْأَرْضِ وَلَا طَائِرٍ يَطِيرُ بِجَنَاحَيْهِ إِلَّا أُمَمٌ أَمْثَالُكُم ۚ مَّا فَرَّطْنَا فِي الْكِتَابِ مِن شَيْءٍ ۚ ثُمَّ إِلَىٰ رَبِّهِمْ يُحْشَرُونَ

There is not a moving creature on earth, nor a bird that flies with its two wings, but are communities like you. We have neglected nothing in the Book. Then unto their Lord they shall be gathered. **(6:38, Surah Al-An'am)**

أَفَلَا يَتَدَبَّرُونَ الْقُرْآنَ أَمْ عَلَىٰ قُلُوبٍ أَقْفَالُهَا

Do they not then ponder over the Qur'an, or are there locks upon their hearts? **(47:24, Surah Muhammad)**

And finally, Allah (SWT) commented:

كُنتُمْ خَيْرَ أُمَّةٍ أُخْرِجَتْ لِلنَّاسِ تَأْمُرُونَ بِالْمَعْرُوفِ وَتَنْهَوْنَ عَنِ الْمُنكَرِ وَتُؤْمِنُونَ بِاللَّهِ ۗ وَلَوْ آمَنَ أَهْلُ الْكِتَابِ لَكَانَ خَيْرًا لَّهُم ۚ مِّنْهُمُ الْمُؤْمِنُونَ وَأَكْثَرُهُمُ الْفَاسِقُونَ

Ye are the best nation brought forth for mankind: ye enjoin what is right, and forbid what is wrong, and believe in Allah. If the People of the Book had believed, it would have been better for them: among them are believers, but most are rebellious. **(3:110, Surah Aal-Imran)**

However, it is not enough for believers to simply appreciate the Qur'an; they must also understand its teachings. Upon examining the Qur'an, we find that it does not refer to itself as a "constitution" for any one group or nation, but as guidance for all of mankind.

In fact, it defines the true purpose of its clear instructions at the very beginning of verses 2–5 in Surah Al-Baqara:

- *This is the Book; in it is sure guidance, without doubt, to those who fear Allah.*

- *Those who believe in the unseen, establish prayer, and spend out of what We have provided for them.*

- *Those who believe in the Revelation sent to thee, and that sent before thee, and are certain of the Hereafter.*

- *They are on true guidance from their Lord, and it is they who will prosper.*

We recite the Qur'an and often attend *Tafsir* classes to comprehend its meaning, but the real question is: how many of us truly understand the interconnected subjects within its verses? Moreover, how many of us are committed to following the teachings of this divine book instead of merely reading it? Ask yourself this question to find the answer.

Due to a lack of understanding of its profound significance, it is not surprising that people sometimes neglect the teachings of the Holy Qur'an.

This was prophesied in Surah Al-Furqan, verse 25:30:

وَقَالَ الرَّسُولُ يَا رَبِّ إِنَّ قَوْمِي اتَّخَذُوا هَـٰذَا الْقُرْآنَ مَهْجُورًا

And the Messenger (Muhammad ﷺ) will say: "O my Lord! Verily, my people deserted this Qur'an (neither listened to it nor acted on its laws and orders)." **(25:30, Surah Al-Furqan)**

Some scholars define the meaning of this verse differently, but our primary concern is how steadfastly we adhere to the commands and instructions of Allah as outlined in the Qur'an and the Sunnah of our Prophet Muhammad ﷺ in our daily lives.

Reciting the Qur'an daily purifies the heart, prevents evil and enmity, fosters a sense of brotherhood and compassion, strengthens the believer's heart, and deepens their connection with Allah.

Allah (SWT) says in Surah Al-Israa':

وَنُنَزِّلُ مِنَ الْقُرْآنِ مَا هُوَ شِفَاءٌ وَرَحْمَةٌ لِّلْمُؤْمِنِينَ ۙ وَلَا يَزِيدُ الظَّالِمِينَ إِلَّا خَسَارًا

And We send down from the Qur'an that which is a healing and a mercy to those who believe (in Islamic Monotheism and act on it), and it increases the Zalimun (polytheists and wrongdoers) in nothing but loss. — Surah Al-Israa' (17:82)

Hence, reciting His words and following His commands regularly brings us closer to Allah and lays a strong foundation for our entrance into Paradise.

Allah (SWT) says:

إِنَّمَا الْمُؤْمِنُونَ الَّذِينَ إِذَا ذُكِرَ اللَّهُ وَجِلَتْ قُلُوبُهُمْ وَإِذَا تُلِيَتْ عَلَيْهِمْ آيَاتُهُ زَادَتْهُمْ إِيمَانًا وَعَلَىٰ رَبِّهِمْ يَتَوَكَّلُونَ

*The believers are only those who, when Allah is mentioned, feel fear in their hearts, and when His verses (this Qur'an) are recited unto them, they increase them in faith; and they put their trust in their Lord (alone). — **Surah Al-Anfal (8:2)***

However, abandoning the Qur'an and its teachings weakens the heart, eventually leaving it dark—an ideal dwelling for Satan, where no light of guidance can penetrate. Even if a person recites the Qur'an, without understanding what they are reading, they remain spiritually vulnerable.

Allah (SWT) confirms this concern in the following verse:

وَمَن يَعْشُ عَن ذِكْرِ الرَّحْمَٰنِ نُقَيِّضْ لَهُ شَيْطَانًا فَهُوَ لَهُ قَرِينٌ

وَإِنَّهُمْ لَيَصُدُّونَهُمْ عَنِ السَّبِيلِ وَيَحْسَبُونَ أَنَّهُم مُّهْتَدُونَ

*And whosoever turns away (blinds himself) from the remembrance of the Most Beneficent (Allah) — We appoint for him a Shaitan (Satan - devil) to be a Qarin (an intimate companion) to him. And verily, they (Satans) hinder them from the Path (of Allah), but they think that they are guided aright! — **Surah Az-Zukhruf (43:36–37)***

A large number of individuals recite the Qur'an sincerely, yet often overlook the importance of understanding its meaning. One may read the Qur'an countless times and still receive rewards, but without comprehension, it will not be reflected in their practical life. Their heart will not align with the teachings of Allah as conveyed in the Qur'an.

Therefore, we must understand that reciting the Qur'an rapidly without grasping its meaning does not exemplify true taqwa (God-consciousness).

Allah (SWT) says:

أَفَلَا يَتَدَبَّرُونَ الْقُرْآنَ أَمْ عَلَىٰ قُلُوبٍ أَقْفَالُهَا

*Do they not then think deeply in the Qur'an, or are their hearts locked up (from understanding it)? — **Surah Muhammad (47:24)***

The true essence of the Qur'an is lost when it is read without comprehension. As a profound guide for humanity, the Qur'an requires our sincere effort to understand its teachings and incorporate them into our lives. Mere recitation is insufficient. It is only through actively engaging with its wisdom that we remain on the straight path.

Allah (SWT) also says:

كِتَابٌ أَنزَلْنَاهُ إِلَيْكَ مُبَارَكٌ لِيَدَّبَّرُوا آيَاتِهِ وَلِيَتَذَكَّرَ أُولُو الْأَلْبَابِ

(This is) a Book (the Qur'an) which We have sent down to you, full of blessings, that they may ponder over its verses, and that men of understanding may remember.
— **Surah Sad (38:29)**

In Surah Al-Baqarah (2:185), a part of the divine constitution reminds us:

شَهْرُ رَمَضَانَ الَّذِي أُنزِلَ فِيهِ الْقُرْآنُ هُدًى لِّلنَّاسِ وَبَيِّنَاتٍ مِّنَ الْهُدَىٰ وَالْفُرْقَانِ ۚ فَمَن شَهِدَ مِنكُمُ الشَّهْرَ فَلْيَصُمْهُ ۖ وَمَن كَانَ مَرِيضًا أَوْ عَلَىٰ سَفَرٍ فَعِدَّةٌ مِّنْ أَيَّامٍ أُخَرَ ۗ يُرِيدُ اللَّهُ بِكُمُ الْيُسْرَ وَلَا يُرِيدُ بِكُمُ الْعُسْرَ وَلِتُكْمِلُوا الْعِدَّةَ وَلِتُكَبِّرُوا اللَّهَ عَلَىٰ مَا هَدَاكُمْ وَلَعَلَّكُمْ تَشْكُرُونَ

The month of Ramadan in which was revealed the Qur'an, a guidance for mankind and clear proofs of the guidance and the criterion (between right and wrong). So whoever of you witnesses the month (of Ramadan), let him fast it, and whoever is ill or on a journey — the same number of days should be made up from other days. Allah intends for you ease and does not intend hardship for you — and that you should complete the period, and that you should magnify Allah for having guided you, so that you may be grateful to Him.

The Importance of Understanding the Qur'an

Understanding the Qur'an is crucial. The following passage from a research article highlights how we can begin to address this issue:

It seems that many Muslims are able to recite the Qur'an, but if asked whether they understand what they recite, many respond with "no." Those who have memorised the Qur'an have certainly achieved something significant.

I recall attending a lecture at the Islamic University of Malaysia by a revert to Islam from America, who was originally from Pakistan. Before his reversion, he described himself as someone who "used to party, be a rapper, and enjoy music." After embracing Islam, he went to Pakistan and memorised the Qur'an in nine months.

After completing his memorisation, he asked his teacher, "Teacher, can you now teach me the meaning of what I memorised?"

His question revealed a critical issue — that he had memorised the Qur'an without understanding it. The teacher responded, "Be patient. Let me teach you a second method of recitation first."

The teacher discouraged his student from immediately learning the meaning of the revelation. This should raise concern. It is not uncommon to meet older Muslims who say, "I know how to recite the Qur'an, but I do not understand it."

How is it possible to "know how to recite" the Qur'an without understanding its content? Can one truly recite without comprehension? If a person simply reproduces the sounds of a language without knowing what they are saying, what kind of knowledge is that?

The mere reproduction of sounds, without knowledge of their meaning, constitutes limited knowledge.

It appears that teachers often place excessive emphasis on recitation and memorisation at the expense of understanding. This needs to be addressed. A proper methodology should integrate formal pronunciation with a clear grasp of meaning, enabling the reader to access the divine message of the Qur'an.[204]

What if you think and contemplate the Qur'an but still don't understand it?

"… Ask the people of the reminder if ye know not." **(Surah Al-Anbiya 21:7)**

وَمَا أَرْسَلْنَا قَبْلَكَ إِلَّا رِجَالًا نُّوحِي إِلَيْهِمْ ۖ فَاسْأَلُوا أَهْلَ الذِّكْرِ إِن كُنتُمْ لَا تَعْلَمُونَ

And We sent not before you (O Muhammad ﷺ) but men to whom We inspired, so ask the People of the Reminder [Scriptures – the Taurat (Torah), the Injeel (Gospel)] if you do not know. **(21:7, Surah Al-Anbiya – The Prophets)**

One commenter said:

The knowledge in interpretation of the Qur'an is limitless, and each commentator can find out some points about a verse, and there are still many points that have not been known. And it is one of the miraculous aspects of the Qur'an; that every individual may understand its points based on his/her conditions of time and place. That is why in Qur'anic interpretations there is always space for growth in understanding the meanings. Hence, do not stick to one interpretation and try to read and listen to different commentaries. Then you can compare them to each other, and at some points, with the help of Allah SWT, you might find some new points about specific verses.

Allah SWT says:

وَمَا أَرْسَلْنَا مِن رَّسُولٍ إِلَّا بِلِسَانِ قَوْمِهِ لِيُبَيِّنَ لَهُمْ ۖ فَيُضِلُّ اللَّهُ مَن يَشَاءُ وَيَهْدِي مَن يَشَاءُ ۚ وَهُوَ الْعَزِيزُ الْحَكِيمُ

204

https://www.researchgate.net/publication/341621397_Retrieving_the_Knowledge_of_Revelation_
Reciting_vs_Knowing_the_Quran_A

And We sent not a Messenger except with the language of his people, in order that he might make (the Message) clear for them. Then Allah misleads whom He wills and guides whom He wills. And He is the All-Mighty, the All-Wise. (14:4, Surah Ibrahim – Abraham) [205]

Allah SWT also says:

إِنَّا أَنزَلْنَاهُ قُرْآنًا عَرَبِيًّا لَّعَلَّكُمْ تَعْقِلُون

Verily, We have sent it down as an Arabic Qur'an in order that you may understand. **(Yusuf 12:2)**

Allah (SWT) sent down the Qur'an in Arabic, known as Classical Arabic, as the Qur'an was written as early as the 6th century AD. This is slightly different from modern Arabic today. Classical Arabic is based on the mediaeval dialects of Arab tribes (Arab Academy). Arabic-speaking people in the Middle East thus have the advantage of understanding the Qur'an without any extra effort. This advantage is not available to non-Arabic speaking nations until they learn the Arabic language.

In this situation, Muslims spend time learning, reciting, or memorising the Qur'an, but less time and effort are dedicated to understanding its meaning. When we enrol our children in madrasas, we apply the same approach, and they also develop the habit of reciting the Qur'an in Arabic rather than focusing on its meaning. We rely entirely on scholars and translators to understand the Qur'an. The translation of the Qur'an has played a major role for the entire Muslim Ummah, apart from Arabic-speaking Muslims. Without the Furqan translation, the Muslim community would fall into darkness, lose the path of guidance, and Satan would exploit that weakness.

Translations and interpretations in native languages are widely recognised by Muslims and Islamic institutions. However, they do not truly capture the original essence and divine meaning of Allah's Word. This means that the essence of the Qur'an is impossible to replicate in any translation. For example, الله has no plural and no feminine form. This unique name itself reflects the fact that He is One and Only, with no partner or equal. The English word "God", however, has a plural form (gods) and a feminine form (goddess). Thus, no translation can replace this divine literary work. Nonetheless, we cannot ignore outright translations of the Qur'an. Before concluding this point, let us again refer to the following verse:

Allah SWT says:

إِنَّمَا الْمُؤْمِنُونَ الَّذِينَ إِذَا ذُكِرَ اللَّهُ وَجِلَتْ قُلُوبُهُمْ وَإِذَا تُلِيَتْ عَلَيْهِمْ آيَاتُهُ زَادَتْهُمْ إِيمَانًا وَعَلَىٰ رَبِّهِمْ يَتَوَكَّلُونَ

---

[205] https://salamislam.com/articles/lifestyle/how-can-i-understand-quran-better

The believers are only those who, when Allah is mentioned, feel a fear in their hearts, and when His verses (this Qur'an) are recited unto them, they increase their faith; and they put their trust in their Lord (alone). **(Al-Anfal 8:2)**

It has become evident that many Muslims play recorded Qur'anic verses in their shops or while driving, yet ignore the teachings of the Qur'an. While bargaining with customers or engrossed in heated personal conversations on the phone, they completely neglect the profound teachings encapsulated within the Qur'an. Such actions are a grave transgression and a clear disgrace, for they fail to embody the genuine reverence and fear of Allah as outlined in the above verse. This behaviour can be considered a serious trial.

Traditionally, Muslims recite the Qur'an at the beginning of significant ceremonies. However, during these recitations, it is disheartening to see that many Muslims continue their conversations, share jokes, and even laugh without showing any respect. These behaviours contradict the divine commandment to listen attentively and silently to every word recited. Consequently, it can be seen as a form of abandoning the Qur'anic teachings. This, too, is a test of faith and devotion.

Allah SWT says:

وَإِذَا قُرِئَ الْقُرْآنُ فَاسْتَمِعُوا لَهُ وَأَنصِتُوا لَعَلَّكُمْ تُرْحَمُونَ

وَاذْكُر رَّبَّكَ فِي نَفْسِكَ تَضَرُّعًا وَخِيفَةً وَدُونَ الْجَهْرِ مِنَ الْقَوْلِ بِالْغُدُوِّ وَالْآصَالِ وَلَا تَكُن مِّنَ الْغَافِلِينَ

When the Qur'an is read, listen to it with attention, and hold your peace: that ye may receive mercy. (Al-A'raf 7:204)

And remember thy Lord in thyself, humbly and with fear, without loudness in words, in the mornings and the evenings; and be not thou of the heedless. (Al-A'raf 7:205)

Some scholars feel that it is permissible to listen to recordings while speaking because it is merely an echo sound. However, generally speaking, it is still the word of Allah. One must pay full attention to its source or stop playing it altogether. It cannot be compared to music played for entertainment.

Part III

Judge One's Strength Of Righteousness

Read All The Verses Patiently And Assess Your Situation Where Applicable.

In this section, let us identify some constitutional mandatory clauses that we must adhere to, understanding that failing to do so will have consequences on the Day of Judgement. If we reflect deeply and ask ourselves what our defence will be on that day, we are reminded of the verse:

445

"You do your will on earth, but where will you flee from Me when you come to Me alone?"

The following selected verses provide ample opportunity to assess one's condition as we continue our journey toward the Day of Judgement:

كُنتُمْ خَيْرَ أُمَّةٍ أُخْرِجَتْ لِلنَّاسِ تَأْمُرُونَ بِالْمَعْرُوفِ وَتَنْهَوْنَ عَنِ الْمُنكَرِ وَتُؤْمِنُونَ بِاللَّهِ ۗ وَلَوْ آمَنَ أَهْلُ الْكِتَابِ لَكَانَ خَيْرًا لَّهُم ۚ مِّنْهُمُ الْمُؤْمِنُونَ وَأَكْثَرُهُمُ الْفَاسِقُونَ

Ye are the best of peoples, evolved for mankind, enjoining what is right, forbidding what is wrong, and believing in Allah.

Had the People of the Book believed, it had been better for them: among them are believers, but most of them are rebellious. **(Aal Imran 3:110)**

QQQ

الَّذِينَ يُؤْمِنُونَ بِالْغَيْبِ وَيُقِيمُونَ الصَّلَاةَ وَمِمَّا رَزَقْنَاهُمْ يُنفِقُونَ

Who believe in the unseen, and establish prayer, and spend out of what We have provided for them. **(Al-Baqarah 2:3)**

QQQ

وَأَقِيمُوا الصَّلَاةَ وَآتُوا الزَّكَاةَ وَارْكَعُوا مَعَ الرَّاكِعِينَ

And establish prayer and give zakat and bow with those who bow [in worship and obedience]. **(Al-Baqarah 2:43)**

QQQ

وَاسْتَعِينُوا بِالصَّبْرِ وَالصَّلَاةِ ۚ وَإِنَّهَا لَكَبِيرَةٌ إِلَّا عَلَى الْخَاشِعِينَ

And seek help through patience and prayer; and truly it is hard save for the humble-minded. **(Al-Baqarah 2:45)**

QQQ

نَّمَا الصَّدَقَاتُ لِلْفُقَرَاءِ وَالْمَسَاكِينِ وَالْعَامِلِينَ عَلَيْهَا وَالْمُؤَلَّفَةِ قُلُوبُهُمْ وَفِي الرِّقَابِ وَالْغَارِمِينَ وَفِي سَبِيلِ اللَّهِ وَابْنِ السَّبِيلِ ۖ فَرِيضَةً مِّنَ اللَّهِ ۗ وَاللَّهُ عَلِيمٌ حَكِيمٌ

The alms are only for the poor and the needy, and those employed to collect them, and those whose hearts are to be reconciled, and to free the captives, and for those in debt, and in the way of Allah, and for the wayfarer; a duty imposed by Allah. And Allah is Knower, Wise. **(At-Tawbah 9:60)**

QQQ

يَا أَيُّهَا الَّذِينَ آمَنُوا لَا تَقْرَبُوا الصَّلَاةَ وَأَنتُمْ سُكَارَىٰ حَتَّىٰ تَعْلَمُوا مَا تَقُولُونَ وَلَا جُنُبًا إِلَّا عَابِرِي سَبِيلٍ حَتَّىٰ تَغْتَسِلُوا ۚ وَإِن كُنتُم مَّرْضَىٰ أَوْ عَلَىٰ سَفَرٍ أَوْ جَاءَ أَحَدٌ مِّنكُم مِّنَ الْغَائِطِ أَوْ لَامَسْتُمُ النِّسَاءَ فَلَمْ تَجِدُوا مَاءً فَتَيَمَّمُوا صَعِيدًا طَيِّبًا فَامْسَحُوا بِوُجُوهِكُمْ وَأَيْدِيكُمْ ۗ إِنَّ اللَّهَ كَانَ عَفُوًّا غَفُورًا

O ye that believe! approach not prayers with a mind befogged, until ye can understand all that ye say; nor in a state of ceremonial impurity, save when travelling on the road, till ye wash your whole body. But if ye are ill, or on a journey, or one of you cometh from the privy, or ye have touched women, and ye find no water, then take for yourselves clean sand or earth, and rub therewith your faces and hands. Lo! Allah is ever Pardoning, Forgiving. **(An-Nisaa 4:43)**

QQQ

أَلَمْ تَرَ إِلَى الَّذِينَ قِيلَ لَهُمْ كُفُّوا أَيْدِيَكُمْ وَأَقِيمُوا الصَّلَاةَ وَآتُوا الزَّكَاةَ فَلَمَّا كُتِبَ عَلَيْهِمُ الْقِتَالُ إِذَا فَرِيقٌ مِّنْهُمْ يَخْشَوْنَ النَّاسَ كَخَشْيَةِ اللَّهِ أَوْ أَشَدَّ خَشْيَةً ۚ وَقَالُوا رَبَّنَا لِمَ كَتَبْتَ عَلَيْنَا الْقِتَالَ لَوْلَا أَخَّرْتَنَا إِلَىٰ أَجَلٍ قَرِيبٍ ۗ قُلْ مَتَاعُ الدُّنْيَا قَلِيلٌ وَالْآخِرَةُ خَيْرٌ لِّمَنِ اتَّقَىٰ وَلَا تُظْلَمُونَ فَتِيلًا

¬ *Hast thou not seen those unto whom it was said, "Withhold your hands (from fighting), and establish prayer, and give Zakat"? But when fighting was ordained for them, behold! A party of them feared men as they ought to have feared Allah, or with greater fear. They said: "Our Lord, wherefore hast Thou ordained for us fighting? Wouldst Thou not grant us respite to a near end?" Say: "The enjoyment of this world is but little, and the Hereafter is better for him that feareth Allah, and ye shall not be wronged, even as much as the thread of a date-stone."*

— **Surah An-Nisa (4:77)**

QQQ

كُنتُمْ خَيْرَ أُمَّةٍ أُخْرِجَتْ لِلنَّاسِ تَأْمُرُونَ بِالْمَعْرُوفِ وَتَنْهَوْنَ عَنِ الْمُنكَرِ وَتُؤْمِنُونَ بِاللَّهِ ۗ وَلَوْ آمَنَ أَهْلُ الْكِتَابِ لَكَانَ خَيْرًا لَّهُم ۚ مِّنْهُمُ الْمُؤْمِنُونَ وَأَكْثَرُهُمُ الْفَاسِقُونَ

¬ *Ye are the best nation brought forth unto mankind, enjoining what is right and forbidding what is wrong, and believing in Allah. And if the People of the Scripture had believed, it had been better for them. Among them are believers, but most of them are rebellious.*

— **Surah Ale-Imran (3:110)**

QQQ

إِنَّ الْمُنَافِقِينَ يُخَادِعُونَ اللَّهَ وَهُوَ خَادِعُهُمْ وَإِذَا قَامُوا إِلَى الصَّلَاةِ قَامُوا كُسَالَىٰ يُرَاءُونَ النَّاسَ وَلَا يَذْكُرُونَ اللَّهَ إِلَّا قَلِيلًا

Verily, the hypocrites seek to deceive Allah, but it is He who deceiveth them. And when they stand up for prayer, they stand with laziness, to be seen of men, and they remember Allah but little.

— **Surah An-Nisa (4:142)**

QQQ

مُّذَبْذَبِينَ بَيْنَ ذَٰلِكَ لَا إِلَىٰ هَٰؤُلَاءِ وَلَا إِلَىٰ هَٰؤُلَاءِ ۚ وَمَن يُضْلِلِ اللَّهُ فَلَن تَجِدَ لَهُ سَبِيلًا

(They are) swaying between this and that, belonging neither to these nor to those. And he whom Allah sends astray, thou shalt not find for him a way (to the truth - Islam).

— **Surah An-Nisa (4:143)**

QQQ

وَمَن يَعْمَلْ سُوءًا أَوْ يَظْلِمْ نَفْسَهُ ثُمَّ يَسْتَغْفِرِ اللَّهَ يَجِدِ اللَّهَ غَفُورًا رَّحِيمًا

And whosoever doeth evil or wrongeth himself but afterward seeketh forgiveness of Allah, he shall find Allah Forgiving, Merciful.

— **Surah An-Nisa (4:110)**

QQQ

لَّٰكِنِ الرَّاسِخُونَ فِي الْعِلْمِ مِنْهُمْ وَالْمُؤْمِنُونَ يُؤْمِنُونَ بِمَا أُنزِلَ إِلَيْكَ وَمَا أُنزِلَ مِن قَبْلِكَ ۚ وَالْمُقِيمِينَ الصَّلَاةَ ۚ وَالْمُؤْتُونَ الزَّكَاةَ وَالْمُؤْمِنُونَ بِاللَّهِ وَالْيَوْمِ الْآخِرِ أُولَٰئِكَ سَنُؤْتِيهِمْ أَجْرًا عَظِيمًا

¬ But those among them that are well-grounded in knowledge, and the believers, believe in what is revealed unto thee and what was revealed before thee. And those who establish regular prayer and give Zakat and believe in Allah and the Last Day — to them shall We soon give a great reward.

— **Surah An-Nisa (4:162)**

QQQ

يَا أَيُّهَا الَّذِينَ آمَنُوا إِذَا قُمْتُمْ إِلَى الصَّلَاةِ فَاغْسِلُوا وُجُوهَكُمْ وَأَيْدِيَكُمْ إِلَى الْمَرَافِقِ وَامْسَحُوا بِرُءُوسِكُمْ وَأَرْجُلَكُمْ إِلَى الْكَعْبَيْنِ ۚ وَإِن كُنتُمْ جُنُبًا فَاطَّهَّرُوا ۚ وَإِن كُنتُم مَّرْضَىٰ أَوْ عَلَىٰ سَفَرٍ أَوْ جَاءَ أَحَدٌ مِّنكُم مِّنَ الْغَائِطِ أَوْ لَامَسْتُمُ النِّسَاءَ فَلَمْ تَجِدُوا مَاءً فَتَيَمَّمُوا صَعِيدًا طَيِّبًا فَامْسَحُوا بِوُجُوهِكُمْ وَأَيْدِيكُم مِّنْهُ ۚ مَا يُرِيدُ اللَّهُ لِيَجْعَلَ عَلَيْكُم مِّنْ حَرَجٍ وَلَٰكِن يُرِيدُ لِيُطَهِّرَكُمْ وَلِيُتِمَّ نِعْمَتَهُ عَلَيْكُمْ لَعَلَّكُمْ تَشْكُرُونَ

¬ O ye who believe! When ye rise up for prayer, wash your faces and your hands up to the elbows, and wipe your heads and your feet up to the ankles. And if ye be in a state of Janabah, purify yourselves. But if ye be ill or on a journey, or one of you cometh from answering the call of nature, or ye have had contact with women and ye find no water — then seek clean earth and wipe your faces and hands. Allah doth not wish to place you in difficulty, but He willeth to purify you and to complete His favour upon you, that ye may be thankful.

— **Surah Al-Ma'idah (5:6)**

QQQ

إِنَّمَا وَلِيُّكُمُ اللَّهُ وَرَسُولُهُ وَالَّذِينَ آمَنُوا الَّذِينَ يُقِيمُونَ الصَّلَاةَ وَيُؤْتُونَ الزَّكَاةَ وَهُمْ رَاكِعُونَ

448

Verily, your protector is Allah, and His Messenger, and the believers — those who establish prayer and give Zakat, and bow down (in submission).

— Surah Al-Ma'idah (5:55)

QQQ

وَلَقَدْ أَخَذَ اللَّهُ مِيثَاقَ بَنِي إِسْرَائِيلَ وَبَعَثْنَا مِنْهُمُ اثْنَيْ عَشَرَ نَقِيبًا ۖ وَقَالَ اللَّهُ إِنِّي مَعَكُمْ ۖ لَئِنْ أَقَمْتُمُ الصَّلَاةَ وَآتَيْتُمُ الزَّكَاةَ وَآمَنتُم بِرُسُلِي وَعَزَّرْتُمُوهُمْ وَأَقْرَضْتُمُ اللَّهَ قَرْضًا حَسَنًا لَّأُكَفِّرَنَّ عَنكُمْ سَيِّئَاتِكُمْ وَلَأُدْخِلَنَّكُمْ جَنَّاتٍ تَجْرِي مِن تَحْتِهَا الْأَنْهَارُ ۚ فَمَن كَفَرَ بَعْدَ ذَٰلِكَ مِنكُمْ فَقَدْ ضَلَّ سَوَاءَ السَّبِيلِ

Indeed, Allah took a covenant with the Children of Israel, and We appointed among them twelve leaders. And Allah said: "Verily, I am with you: if ye perform prayer, give Zakat, believe in My messengers, honour and assist them, and lend unto Allah a goodly loan — verily, I will forgive your sins and admit you into Gardens beneath which rivers flow. But whoso disbelieveth thereafter from among you, he hath verily strayed from the straight path."

— Surah Al-Ma'idah (5:12)

QQQ

وَإِذَا نَادَيْتُمْ إِلَى الصَّلَاةِ اتَّخَذُوهَا هُزُوًا وَلَعِبًا ۚ ذَٰلِكَ بِأَنَّهُمْ قَوْمٌ لَّا يَعْقِلُونَ

And when ye proclaim the call to prayer, they take it as mockery and sport. That is because they are a people who understand not.

— Surah Al-Ma'idah (5:58)

QQQ

إِنَّمَا يُرِيدُ الشَّيْطَانُ أَن يُوقِعَ بَيْنَكُمُ الْعَدَاوَةَ وَالْبَغْضَاءَ فِي الْخَمْرِ وَالْمَيْسِرِ وَيَصُدَّكُمْ عَن ذِكْرِ اللَّهِ وَعَنِ الصَّلَاةِ ۖ فَهَلْ أَنتُم مُّنتَهُونَ

Satan seeketh only to sow enmity and hatred among you through intoxicants and gambling, and to turn you away from the remembrance of Allah and from prayer. Will ye not then abstain?

— Surah Al-Ma'idah (5:91)

QQQ

يَا أَيُّهَا الَّذِينَ آمَنُوا شَهَادَةُ بَيْنِكُمْ إِذَا حَضَرَ أَحَدَكُمُ الْمَوْتُ حِينَ الْوَصِيَّةِ اثْنَانِ ذَوَا عَدْلٍ ¬ مِّنكُمْ أَوْ آخَرَانِ مِنْ غَيْرِكُمْ إِنْ أَنتُمْ ضَرَبْتُمْ فِي الْأَرْضِ فَأَصَابَتْكُم مُّصِيبَةُ الْمَوْتِ ۚ تَحْبِسُونَهُمَا مِن بَعْدِ الصَّلَاةِ فَيُقْسِمَانِ بِاللَّهِ إِنِ ارْتَبْتُمْ لَا نَشْتَرِي بِهِ ثَمَنًا وَلَوْ كَانَ ذَا قُرْبَىٰ ۙ وَلَا نَكْتُمُ شَهَادَةَ اللَّهِ إِنَّا إِذًا لَّمِنَ الْآثِمِينَ

¬ *O you who believe! When death approaches any of you, and you make a bequest, then let the testimony be taken from two just men from among you, or two* others from outside, if you are travelling through the land and the calamity of death befalls you. Detain them both after the prayer; if you doubt (their truthfulness), let them both swear by Allah (saying): "We shall not sell our testimony for any price, even if he be a near relative. And we shall not hide the testimony of Allah, for then indeed we should be among the sinful." **(Surah Al-Ma'idah 5:106)**

QQQ

وَأَنْ أَقِيمُوا الصَّلَاةَ وَاتَّقُوهُ ۚ وَهُوَ الَّذِي إِلَيْهِ تُحْشَرُونَ

"And to establish the prayer and fear Him. And it is He to Whom you shall be gathered." **(Surah Al-An'am 6:72)**

QQQ

وَهَذَا كِتَابٌ أَنزَلْنَاهُ مُبَارَكٌ مُصَدِّقُ الَّذِي بَيْنَ يَدَيْهِ وَلِتُنذِرَ أُمَّ الْقُرَىٰ وَمَنْ حَوْلَهَا ۚ وَالَّذِينَ يُؤْمِنُونَ بِالْآخِرَةِ يُؤْمِنُونَ بِهِ ۖ وَهُمْ عَلَىٰ صَلَاتِهِمْ يُحَافِظُو

And this is a blessed Book which We have sent down, confirming that which came before it, so that you may warn the Mother of Towns (i.e. Makkah) and those around it. Those who believe in the Hereafter believe in it, and they are constant in guarding their prayer. **(Surah Al-An'am 6:92)**

QQQ

قُلْ إِنَّ صَلَاتِي وَنُسُكِي وَمَحْيَايَ وَمَمَاتِي لِلَّهِ رَبِّ الْعَالَمِينَ

Say (O Muhammad ﷺ): "Verily, my prayer, my sacrifice, my life, and my death are for Allah, the Lord of the worlds." **(Surah Al-An'am 6:162)**

QQQ

وَالَّذِينَ يُمَسِّكُونَ بِالْكِتَابِ وَأَقَامُوا الصَّلَاةَ إِنَّا لَا نُضِيعُ أَجْرَ الْمُصْلِحِينَ

And those who hold fast to the Book and establish the prayer – certainly, We shall never waste the reward of those who do righteous deeds. **(Surah Al-A'raf 7:170)**

QQQ

إِنَّمَا الْمُؤْمِنُونَ الَّذِينَ إِذَا ذُكِرَ اللَّهُ وَجِلَتْ قُلُوبُهُمْ وَإِذَا تُلِيَتْ عَلَيْهِمْ آيَاتُهُ زَادَتْهُمْ إِيمَانًا وَعَلَىٰ رَبِّهِمْ يَتَوَكَّلُونَ

الَّذِينَ يُقِيمُونَ الصَّلَاةَ وَمِمَّا رَزَقْنَاهُمْ يُنفِقُونَ

أُولَٰئِكَ هُمُ الْمُؤْمِنُونَ حَقًّا ۚ لَهُمْ دَرَجَاتٌ عِندَ رَبِّهِمْ وَمَغْفِرَةٌ وَرِزْقٌ كَرِيمٌ

The believers are only those who, when Allah is mentioned, feel fear in their hearts, and when His verses are recited unto them, they increase their faith; and they put their trust in their Lord alone.

They establish the prayer and spend out of what We have provided them.

It is they who are the true believers. For them are ranks with their Lord, and forgiveness, and a generous provision. **(Surah Al-Anfal 8:2–4)**

QQQ

إِنَّمَا يَعْمُرُ مَسَاجِدَ اللَّهِ مَنْ آمَنَ بِاللَّهِ وَالْيَوْمِ الْآخِرِ وَأَقَامَ الصَّلَاةَ وَآتَى الزَّكَاةَ وَلَمْ يَخْشَ إِلَّا اللَّهَ ۖ فَعَسَىٰ أُولَٰئِكَ أَن يَكُونُوا مِنَ الْمُهْتَدِينَ

The mosques of Allah are maintained only by those who believe in Allah and the Last Day, establish the prayer, give the Zakat, and fear none but Allah. It is they who are expected to be rightly guided. **(Surah At-Tawbah 9:18)**

QQQ

وَمَا مَنَعَهُمْ أَن تُقْبَلَ مِنْهُمْ نَفَقَاتُهُمْ إِلَّا أَنَّهُمْ كَفَرُوا بِاللَّهِ وَبِرَسُولِهِ وَلَا يَأْتُونَ الصَّلَاةَ إِلَّا وَهُمْ كُسَالَىٰ وَلَا يُنفِقُونَ إِلَّا وَهُمْ كَارِهُونَ

And nothing prevents their contributions from being accepted except that they disbelieved in Allah and His Messenger, and that they come not to prayer except in a lazy state, and that they spend unwillingly. **(Surah At-Tawbah 9:54)**

QQQ

وَالْمُؤْمِنُونَ وَالْمُؤْمِنَاتُ بَعْضُهُمْ أَوْلِيَاءُ بَعْضٍ ۚ يَأْمُرُونَ بِالْمَعْرُوفِ وَيَنْهَوْنَ عَنِ الْمُنكَرِ وَيُقِيمُونَ الصَّلَاةَ وَيُؤْتُونَ الزَّكَاةَ وَيُطِيعُونَ اللَّهَ وَرَسُولَهُ ۚ أُولَٰئِكَ سَيَرْحَمُهُمُ اللَّهُ ۗ إِنَّ اللَّهَ عَزِيزٌ حَكِيمٌ

The believing men and women are allies of one another. They enjoin what is right and forbid what is wrong. They establish the prayer, give the Zakat, and obey Allah and His Messenger. It is they upon whom Allah will have mercy. Surely Allah is All-Mighty, All-Wise. **(Surah At-Tawbah 9:71)**

QQQ

وَأَوْحَيْنَا إِلَىٰ مُوسَىٰ وَأَخِيهِ أَن تَبَوَّآ لِقَوْمِكُمَا بِمِصْرَ بُيُوتًا وَاجْعَلُوا بُيُوتَكُمْ قِبْلَةً وَأَقِيمُوا الصَّلَاةَ ۗ وَبَشِّرِ الْمُؤْمِنِينَ

And We inspired Musa and his brother, saying: "Take dwellings for your people in Egypt and make your dwellings places of worship, and establish the prayer, and give glad tidings to the believers." **(Surah Yunus 10:87)**

QQQ

وَأَقِمِ الصَّلَاةَ طَرَفَيِ النَّهَارِ وَزُلَفًا مِّنَ اللَّيْلِ ۚ إِنَّ الْحَسَنَاتِ يُذْهِبْنَ السَّيِّئَاتِ ۚ ذَٰلِكَ ذِكْرَىٰ لِلذَّاكِرِينَ

وَاصْبِرْ فَإِنَّ اللَّهَ لَا يُضِيعُ أَجْرَ الْمُحْسِنِينَ ¬

"And establish the prayer at the two ends of the day and at the approach of the night. Verily, good deeds remove evil deeds. That is a reminder for those who remember."

"And be patient; for verily Allah does not waste the reward of the doers of good." **(Surah Hud 11:114–115)**

QQQ

وَالَّذِينَ صَبَرُوا ابْتِغَاءَ وَجْهِ رَبِّهِمْ وَأَقَامُوا الصَّلَاةَ وَأَنفَقُوا مِمَّا رَزَقْنَاهُمْ سِرًّا وَعَلَانِيَةً وَيَدْرَءُونَ بِالْحَسَنَةِ السَّيِّئَةَ أُولَئِكَ لَهُمْ عُقْبَى الدَّارِ

And those who remain patient, seeking the Countenance of their Lord, establish the prayer, and spend of what We have provided them, secretly and openly, and repel evil with good — for them is the good end (in the Hereafter). **(Surah Ar-Ra'd 13:22)**

QQQ

قُل لِّعِبَادِيَ الَّذِينَ آمَنُوا يُقِيمُوا الصَّلَاةَ وَيُنفِقُوا مِمَّا رَزَقْنَاهُمْ سِرًّا وَعَلَانِيَةً مِّن قَبْلِ أَن يَأْتِيَ يَوْمٌ لَّا بَيْعٌ فِيهِ وَلَا خِلَالٌ

Say (O Muhammad ﷺ) to My servants who have believed: Establish the prayer and spend from what We have provided them, secretly and openly, before a Day comes in which there will be no exchange nor friendship. **(Surah Ibrahim 14:31)**

QQQ

رَّبَّنَا إِنِّي أَسْكَنتُ مِن ذُرِّيَّتِي بِوَادٍ غَيْرِ ذِي زَرْعٍ عِندَ بَيْتِكَ الْمُحَرَّمِ رَبَّنَا لِيُقِيمُوا الصَّلَاةَ فَاجْعَلْ أَفْئِدَةً مِّنَ النَّاسِ تَهْوِي إِلَيْهِمْ وَارْزُقْهُم مِّنَ الثَّمَرَاتِ لَعَلَّهُمْ يَشْكُرُونَ

"O our Lord! I have made some of my offspring to dwell in an uncultivated valley near Your Sacred House, O our Lord, that they may establish prayer. So make the hearts of some among mankind incline towards them, and provide them with fruits that they may be grateful." **(Surah Ibrahim 14:37)**

QQQ

رَبِّ اجْعَلْنِي مُقِيمَ الصَّلَاةِ وَمِن ذُرِّيَّتِي ۚ رَبَّنَا وَتَقَبَّلْ دُعَاءِ

"O my Lord! Make me one who performs As-Salat (Iqamat-as-Salat), and also from my offspring. Our Lord! Accept my invocation."

Surah Ibrahim 14:40

QQQ

أَقِمِ الصَّلَاةَ لِدُلُوكِ الشَّمْسِ إِلَىٰ غَسَقِ اللَّيْلِ وَقُرْآنَ الْفَجْرِ ۖ إِنَّ قُرْآنَ الْفَجْرِ كَانَ مَشْهُودًا

"Perform As-Salat (Iqamat-as-Salat) from midday till the darkness of the night (i.e. the Zuhr, 'Asr, Maghrib, and 'Isha' prayers), and recite the Qur'an at dawn (i.e.

the Morning Prayer). Verily, the recitation of the Qur'an at dawn is ever witnessed (attended by the angels in charge of mankind during the day and night)."

Surah Al-Isra' (The Journey by Night) 17:78

QQQ

وَمِنَ اللَّيْلِ فَتَهَجَّدْ بِهِ نَافِلَةً لَّكَ عَسَىٰ أَن يَبْعَثَكَ رَبُّكَ مَقَامًا مَّحْمُودًا

"And in some parts of the night, offer the Salat (prayer) with it (i.e. recite the Qur'an in the prayer) as an additional (Tahajjud – optional Nawafil prayer) for you (O Muhammad ﷺ). It may be that your Lord will raise you to Maqaman Mahmuda (a station of praise and glory, i.e. the highest degree in Paradise)."

Surah Al-Isra' (The Journey by Night) 17:79

QQQ

قُلِ ادْعُوا اللَّهَ أَوِ ادْعُوا الرَّحْمَٰنَ ۖ أَيًّا مَّا تَدْعُوا فَلَهُ الْأَسْمَاءُ الْحُسْنَىٰ ۚ وَلَا تَجْهَرْ بِصَلَاتِكَ وَلَا تُخَافِتْ بِهَا وَابْتَغِ بَيْنَ ذَٰلِكَ سَبِيلًا

"Say (O Muhammad ﷺ): 'Invoke Allah or invoke the Most Beneficent (Ar-Rahman), by whatever name you invoke Him (it is the same), for to Him belong the best names. And offer your Salat (prayer) neither aloud nor in a low voice, but follow a way between.'"

Surah Al-Isra' (The Journey by Night) 17:110

QQQ

وَكَانَ يَأْمُرُ أَهْلَهُ بِالصَّلَاةِ وَالزَّكَاةِ وَكَانَ عِندَ رَبِّهِ مَرْضِيًّا

"And he used to enjoin on his family and his people the Salat (prayers) and the Zakat, and his Lord was pleased with him."

Surah Maryam (Mary) 19:55

QQQ

فَخَلَفَ مِن بَعْدِهِمْ خَلْفٌ أَضَاعُوا الصَّلَاةَ وَاتَّبَعُوا الشَّهَوَاتِ ۖ فَسَوْفَ يَلْقَوْنَ غَيًّا

إِلَّا مَن تَابَ وَآمَنَ وَعَمِلَ صَالِحًا فَأُولَٰئِكَ يَدْخُلُونَ الْجَنَّةَ وَلَا يُظْلَمُونَ شَيْئًا

"Then, there succeeded them a generation who gave up As-Salat (the prayers) — either by abandoning them altogether or by neglecting their proper times and conditions — and followed their lusts. So they will be thrown into Hell,

Except those who repent and believe (in the Oneness of Allah and His Messenger Muhammad ﷺ), and do righteous deeds. Such will enter Paradise, and they will not be wronged in the least."

Surah Maryam (Mary) 19:59–60

QQQ

إِنَّنِي أَنَا اللَّهُ لَا إِلَٰهَ إِلَّا أَنَا فَاعْبُدْنِي وَأَقِمِ الصَّلَاةَ لِذِكْرِي

"Verily, I am Allah! There is no god but I. So worship Me, and perform As-Salat (Iqamat-as-Salat) for My remembrance."

Surah Ta-Ha 20:14

QQQ

وَأْمُرْ أَهْلَكَ بِالصَّلَاةِ وَاصْطَبِرْ عَلَيْهَا ۖ لَا نَسْأَلُكَ رِزْقًا ۖ نَحْنُ نَرْزُقُكَ ۗ وَالْعَاقِبَةُ لِلتَّقْوَىٰ

"And enjoin the prayer upon your family, and be patient in offering it. We do not ask you for provision; We provide for you. And the good end (Paradise) is for the righteous (Al-Muttaqun)."

Surah Ta-Ha 20:132

QQQ

إِنَّ الَّذِينَ كَفَرُوا وَيَصُدُّونَ عَن سَبِيلِ اللَّهِ وَالْمَسْجِدِ الْحَرَامِ الَّذِي جَعَلْنَاهُ لِلنَّاسِ سَوَاءً الْعَاكِفُ فِيهِ وَالْبَادِ ۚ وَمَن يُرِدْ فِيهِ بِإِلْحَادٍ بِظُلْمٍ نُذِقْهُ مِنْ عَذَابٍ أَلِيمٍ

"Verily, those who disbelieve and hinder others from the Path of Allah and from Al-Masjid Al-Haram (at Makkah), which We have made open to (all) men — the dweller in it and the visitor from the country are equal there — and whoever intends therein to commit deviation by doing wrong (i.e. associating partners with Allah), We shall cause him to taste a painful punishment."

Surah Al-Hajj (The Pilgrimage) 22:25

QQQ

الَّذِينَ إِن مَّكَّنَّاهُمْ فِي الْأَرْضِ أَقَامُوا الصَّلَاةَ وَآتَوُا الزَّكَاةَ وَأَمَرُوا بِالْمَعْرُوفِ وَنَهَوْا عَنِ الْمُنكَرِ ۗ وَلِلَّهِ عَاقِبَةُ الْأُمُورِ

"Those (Muslim rulers) who, if We give them authority in the land, establish the prayer (Iqamat-as-Salat), pay the Zakat, enjoin good (Al-Ma'ruf), and forbid evil (Al-Munkar). And with Allah rests the outcome of all matters."

Surah Al-Hajj (The Pilgrimage) 22:41

QQQ

قَدْ أَفْلَحَ الْمُؤْمِنُونَ

الَّذِينَ هُمْ فِي صَلَاتِهِمْ خَاشِعُونَ

وَالَّذِينَ هُمْ عَنِ اللَّغْوِ مُعْرِضُونَ

وَالَّذِينَ هُمْ لِلزَّكَاةِ فَاعِلُونَ

وَالَّذِينَ هُمْ لِفُرُوجِهِمْ حَافِظُونَ

1. "Successful indeed are the believers.
2. Those who offer their Salat (prayers) with all solemnity and humility.
3. And those who turn away from vain talk.
4. And those who pay the Zakat.
5. And those who guard their chastity."

QQQ

وَجَاهِدُوا فِي اللَّهِ حَقَّ جِهَادِهِ ۚ هُوَ اجْتَبَاكُمْ وَمَا جَعَلَ عَلَيْكُمْ فِي الدِّينِ مِنْ حَرَجٍ ۚ مِّلَّةَ أَبِيكُمْ إِبْرَاهِيمَ ۚ هُوَ سَمَّاكُمُ الْمُسْلِمِينَ مِن قَبْلُ وَفِي هَٰذَا لِيَكُونَ الرَّسُولُ شَهِيدًا عَلَيْكُمْ وَتَكُونُوا شُهَدَاءَ عَلَى النَّاسِ ۚ فَأَقِيمُوا الصَّلَاةَ وَآتُوا الزَّكَاةَ وَاعْتَصِمُوا بِاللَّهِ هُوَ مَوْلَاكُمْ ۖ فَنِعْمَ الْمَوْلَىٰ وَنِعْمَ النَّصِيرُ

"And strive for Allah with the striving due to Him. He has chosen you and has not placed upon you in the religion any difficulty. It is the religion of your father Abraham. He (Allah) named you Muslims before and in this (Revelation), that the Messenger (Muhammad ﷺ) may be a witness over you and you may be witnesses over mankind. So establish the prayer, give Zakat, and hold fast to Allah. He is your protector. What an excellent protector, and what an excellent helper!"

Surah Al-Hajj (The Pilgrimage) 22:78

QQQ

وَلَا تَزِرُ وَازِرَةٌ وِزْرَ أُخْرَىٰ ۚ وَإِن تَدْعُ مُثْقَلَةٌ إِلَىٰ حِمْلِهَا لَا يُحْمَلْ مِنْهُ شَيْءٌ وَلَوْ كَانَ ذَا قُرْبَىٰ ۗ إِنَّمَا تُنذِرُ الَّذِينَ يَخْشَوْنَ رَبَّهُم بِالْغَيْبِ وَأَقَامُوا الصَّلَاةَ ۚ وَمَن تَزَكَّىٰ فَإِنَّمَا يَتَزَكَّىٰ لِنَفْسِهِ ۚ وَإِلَى اللَّهِ الْمَصِيرُ

And no bearer of burdens shall bear another's burden. If one heavily laden calls another to bear his load, nothing of it will be lifted, even though he be near of kin. You (O Muhammad ﷺ) can warn only those who fear their Lord unseen, and perform As-Salat (Iqamat-as-Salat). And he who purifies himself (from all kinds of sins), purifies only for the benefit of his own self. And to Allah is the final return.

35:18 – Surah Al-Fatir (The Originator or The Angels)

QQQ

رِجَالٌ لَّا تُلْهِيهِمْ تِجَارَةٌ وَلَا بَيْعٌ عَن ذِكْرِ اللَّهِ وَإِقَامِ الصَّلَاةِ وَإِيتَاءِ الزَّكَاةِ ۙ يَخَافُونَ يَوْمًا تَتَقَلَّبُ فِيهِ الْقُلُوبُ وَالْأَبْصَارُ

Men whom neither trade nor sale diverts from the remembrance of Allah (with heart and tongue), nor from performing As-Salat (Iqamat-as-Salat), nor from giving the Zakat. They fear a Day when hearts and eyes will be overturned (from the horror of the torment of the Day of Resurrection).

24:37 – Surah An-Nur (The Light)

QQQ

أَلَمْ تَرَ أَنَّ اللَّهَ يُسَبِّحُ لَهُ مَن فِي السَّمَاوَاتِ وَالْأَرْضِ وَالطَّيْرُ صَافَّاتٍ ۖ كُلٌّ قَدْ عَلِمَ صَلَاتَهُ
وَتَسْبِيحَهُ ۗ وَاللَّهُ عَلِيمٌ بِمَا يَفْعَلُونَ

See you not (O Muhammad ﷺ) that Allah – He it is Whom glorify all that are in the heavens and the earth, and the birds with wings outspread? Each one knows its prayer and its glorification. And Allah is All-Aware of what they do.

24:41 – Surah An-Nur (The Light)

QQQ

وَأَقِيمُوا الصَّلَاةَ وَآتُوا الزَّكَاةَ وَأَطِيعُوا الرَّسُولَ لَعَلَّكُمْ تُرْحَمُونَ

And perform As-Salat (Iqamat-as-Salat), and give Zakat, and obey the Messenger (Muhammad ﷺ), that you may receive mercy (from Allah).

24:56 – Surah An-Nur (The Light)

QQQ

الَّذِينَ يُقِيمُونَ الصَّلَاةَ وَيُؤْتُونَ الزَّكَاةَ وَهُم بِالْآخِرَةِ هُمْ يُوقِنُونَ

Those who perform As-Salat (Iqamat-as-Salat) and give Zakat, and they believe with certainty in the Hereafter (resurrection, recompense of good and bad deeds, Paradise and Hell, etc.).

27:3 – Surah An-Naml (The Ants)

QQQ

اتْلُ مَا أُوحِيَ إِلَيْكَ مِنَ الْكِتَابِ وَأَقِمِ الصَّلَاةَ ۖ إِنَّ الصَّلَاةَ تَنْهَىٰ عَنِ الْفَحْشَاءِ وَالْمُنكَرِ ۗ وَلَذِكْرُ اللَّهِ
أَكْبَرُ ۗ وَاللَّهُ يَعْلَمُ مَا تَصْنَعُونَ

Recite (O Muhammad ﷺ) what has been revealed to you of the Book (the Qur'an), and perform As-Salat (Iqamat-as-Salat). Verily, As-Salat (the prayer) prevents from Al-Fahsha' (great sins of every kind, unlawful sexual intercourse, etc.) and Al-Munkar (disbelief, polytheism, and every kind of wicked deed). And the remembrance of Allah is greater indeed. And Allah knows what you do.

29:45 – Surah Al-Ankabut (The Spider)

QQQ

مُنِيبِينَ إِلَيْهِ وَاتَّقُوهُ وَأَقِيمُوا الصَّلَاةَ وَلَا تَكُونُوا مِنَ الْمُشْرِكِينَ

(Always) turning in repentance to Him, and be dutiful to Him; and perform As-Salat (Iqamat-as-Salat), and be not of Al-Mushrikun (the disbelievers in the Oneness of Allah, polytheists, idolaters, etc.).

30:31 – Surah Ar-Rum (The Romans)

QQQ

وَالَّذِينَ يَجْتَنِبُونَ كَبَائِرَ الْإِثْمِ وَالْفَوَاحِشَ وَإِذَا مَا غَضِبُوا هُمْ يَغْفِرُونَ

وَالَّذِينَ اسْتَجَابُوا لِرَبِّهِمْ وَأَقَامُوا الصَّلَاةَ وَأَمْرُهُمْ شُورَىٰ بَيْنَهُمْ وَمِمَّا رَزَقْنَاهُمْ يُنفِقُونَ

And those who avoid greater sins and Al-Fawahish (illegal sexual intercourse, etc.), and when they are angry, they forgive.

And those who answer the call of their Lord, and perform As-Salat (Iqamat-as-Salat), and conduct their affairs by mutual consultation, and spend of what We have bestowed on them.

42:37–38 – Surah Ash-Shura (The Consultation)

QQQ

هُدًى وَرَحْمَةً لِّلْمُحْسِنِينَ

الَّذِينَ يُقِيمُونَ الصَّلَاةَ وَيُؤْتُونَ الزَّكَاةَ وَهُم بِالْآخِرَةِ هُمْ يُوقِنُونَ

أُولَٰئِكَ عَلَىٰ هُدًى مِّن رَّبِّهِمْ ۖ وَأُولَٰئِكَ هُمُ الْمُفْلِحُونَ

3. A guidance and mercy for the Muhsinun (good-doers).

4. Those who perform As-Salat (Iqamat-as-Salat) and give Zakat, and have faith in the Hereafter with certainty.

5. Such are on guidance from their Lord, and such are the successful.

31:3–5 – Surah Luqman

QQQ

أَأَشْفَقْتُمْ أَن تُقَدِّمُوا بَيْنَ يَدَيْ نَجْوَاكُمْ صَدَقَاتٍ ۚ فَإِذْ لَمْ تَفْعَلُوا وَتَابَ اللَّهُ عَلَيْكُمْ فَأَقِيمُوا الصَّلَاةَ
وَآتُوا الزَّكَاةَ وَأَطِيعُوا اللَّهَ وَرَسُولَهُ ۚ وَاللَّهُ خَبِيرٌ بِمَا تَعْمَلُونَ

Are you afraid of spending in charity before your private consultation (with him)? If then you do it not, and Allah has forgiven you, then (at least) perform As-Salat (Iqamat-as-Salat), give Zakat, and obey Allah and His Messenger. And Allah is All-Aware of what you do.

58:13 – Surah Al-Mujadilah (The Woman Who Disputes)

يَا بُنَيَّ أَقِمِ الصَّلَاةَ وَأْمُرْ بِالْمَعْرُوفِ وَانْهَ عَنِ الْمُنكَرِ وَاصْبِرْ عَلَىٰ مَا أَصَابَكَ ۖ إِنَّ ذَٰلِكَ مِنْ
عَزْمِ الْأُمُورِ

"O my son! Perform As-Salat (Iqamat-as-Salat), enjoin what is right, forbid what is wrong, and bear with patience whatever befalls you. Verily! These are some of the important commandments ordered by Allah, with no exemption."

31:17 – Surah Luqman

QQQ

يَا أَيُّهَا الَّذِينَ آمَنُوا إِذَا نُودِيَ لِلصَّلَاةِ مِن يَوْمِ الْجُمُعَةِ فَاسْعَوْا إِلَىٰ ذِكْرِ اللَّهِ وَذَرُوا الْبَيْعَ ۚ ذَٰلِكُمْ خَيْرٌ لَّكُمْ إِن كُنتُمْ تَعْلَمُونَ

O you who believe! When the call is proclaimed for the Salat (prayer) on the day of Friday (Jumu'ah prayer), come to the remembrance of Allah and leave off business. That is better for you if you but knew.

62:9 – Surah Al-Jumu'ah (Friday)

QQQ

وَالَّذِينَ هُمْ عَلَىٰ صَلَاتِهِمْ يُحَافِظُونَ

أُولَٰئِكَ فِي جَنَّاتٍ مُّكْرَمُونَ

34. And those who guard their Salat (prayers) well.

35. Such shall dwell in Gardens (i.e. Paradise), honoured.

70:34–35 – Surah Al-Ma'arij (The Ways of Ascent)

QQQ

...فِي جَنَّاتٍ يَتَسَاءَلُونَ

عَنِ الْمُجْرِمِينَ

مَا سَلَكَكُمْ فِي سَقَرَ

قَالُوا لَمْ نَكُ مِنَ الْمُصَلِّينَ

40. In Gardens (Paradise), they will ask one another,

41. About Al-Mujrimun (polytheists, criminals, disbelievers, etc.):

42. "What has caused you to enter Hell?"

43. They will say: "We were not of those who used to offer Salat (prayers),

44. Nor did we used to feed the poor..."

74:40–44 – Surah Al-Muddathir (The One Enveloped)

QQQ

وَمَا أُمِرُوا إِلَّا لِيَعْبُدُوا اللَّهَ مُخْلِصِينَ لَهُ الدِّينَ حُنَفَاءَ وَيُقِيمُوا الصَّلَاةَ وَيُؤْتُوا الزَّكَاةَ ۚ وَذَٰلِكَ دِينُ الْقَيِّمَةِ

And they were commanded only to worship Allah, with sincere devotion to Him alone (abstaining from ascribing partners to Him), to perform As-Salat (Iqamat-as-Salat), and to give Zakat. That is the right religion.

98:5 – Surah Al-Bayyinah (The Clear Evidence)

سورة الماعون – Surah Al-Maa'oon (The Small Kindnesses)

أَرَأَيْتَ الَّذِي يُكَذِّبُ بِالدِّينِ

فَذَٰلِكَ الَّذِي يَدُعُّ الْيَتِيمَ

وَلَا يَحُضُّ عَلَىٰ طَعَامِ الْمِسْكِينِ

فَوَيْلٌ لِّلْمُصَلِّينَ ¬

الَّذِينَ هُمْ عَن صَلَاتِهِمْ سَاهُونَ

الَّذِينَ هُمْ يُرَاءُونَ

وَيَمْنَعُونَ الْمَاعُونَ

¬ Have you seen him who denies the Recompense?

¬ That is he who repulses the orphan (harshly),

¬ And urges not the feeding of the poor (Al-Miskin),

¬ So woe unto those who pray,

¬ But are heedless of their prayer,

¬ Those who do good only to be seen,

¬ And withhold small kindnesses (Al-Ma'oon, e.g., salt, sugar, water, etc.).

Why is Salat A Vehicle of The Journey?

Because **Salah** is an act of submission to the Supreme Creator, Allah (SWT). It says:

قُلْ إِنَّنِي هَدَانِي رَبِّي إِلَىٰ صِرَاطٍ مُّسْتَقِيمٍ دِينًا قِيَمًا مِّلَّةَ إِبْرَاهِيمَ حَنِيفًا ۚ وَمَا كَانَ مِنَ الْمُشْرِكِينَ

قُلْ إِنَّ صَلَاتِي وَنُسُكِي وَمَحْيَايَ وَمَمَاتِي لِلَّهِ رَبِّ الْعَالَمِينَ

"Say: Verily, my Lord hath guided me to a straight path, a right religion, the faith of Abraham, the upright one; and he was not of the idolaters."

"Say: My prayer, and my sacrifice, and my life, and my death, are for Allah, the Lord of the Worlds."

(Surah Al-An'am 6:161–162)

By carefully evaluating all these signs, we gradually begin to understand how to attain judgement in our favour and become worthy of seeking the Celestial Kingdom. Salah, one of the primary divine ordinances given to humankind long before our Prophet Muhammad ﷺ, is essential as a form of worship that leads to success.

Salah is a specific and well-defined physical act that embodies the spirit. The daily prayer, referred to as *Salah* in the Arabic language, is an act of worship unique to Islam in both form and essence. In English, the word *prayer* conveys a general meaning of supplication or invocation, whereas *Salah* refers to a structured ritual act of devotion.

This form of worship is ordained upon all Muslims as a duty and is the second pillar of faith. The prescribed five daily prayers are mandatory for all individuals who have reached puberty, as commanded in the Holy Book.

"Verily, Salah is an obligation on the believers to be observed at its appointed time."

Allah (SWT) places the highest importance on the performance of Salah by His servants, as emphasised in verse 103 of Surah An-Nisa. We included this verse in our initial list and reiterate it here. Allah (SWT) says:

فَإِذَا قَضَيْتُمُ الصَّلَاةَ فَاذْكُرُوا اللَّهَ قِيَامًا وَقُعُودًا وَعَلَىٰ جُنُوبِكُمْ ۚ فَإِذَا اطْمَأْنَنتُمْ فَأَقِيمُوا الصَّلَاةَ ۚ إِنَّ الصَّلَاةَ كَانَتْ عَلَى الْمُؤْمِنِينَ كِتَابًا مَّوْقُوتًا

"And when ye have completed the prayer, remember Allah standing, sitting, and reclining. But when ye are secure, perform the prayer. Verily, the prayer is enjoined on the believers at fixed hours." (Surah An-Nisa 4:103) [206]

But **Salat** is not valid if one is affected by alcohol or drugs, because the intoxicated person does not realise what he is saying in his prayer. Allah confirmed this in verse 4:43 of Surah An-Nisaa (The Women).

Allah SWT says:

يَا أَيُّهَا الَّذِينَ آمَنُوا لَا تَقْرَبُوا الصَّلَاةَ وَأَنتُمْ سُكَارَىٰ حَتَّىٰ تَعْلَمُوا مَا تَقُولُونَ وَلَا جُنُبًا إِلَّا عَابِرِي سَبِيلٍ حَتَّىٰ تَغْتَسِلُوا ۚ وَإِن كُنتُم مَّرْضَىٰ أَوْ عَلَىٰ سَفَرٍ أَوْ جَاءَ أَحَدٌ مِّنكُم مِّنَ الْغَائِطِ أَوْ لَامَسْتُمُ النِّسَاءَ فَلَمْ تَجِدُوا مَاءً فَتَيَمَّمُوا صَعِيدًا طَيِّبًا فَامْسَحُوا بِوُجُوهِكُمْ وَأَيْدِيكُمْ ۗ إِنَّ اللَّهَ كَانَ عَفُوًّا غَفُورًا

O ye that believe! Approach not to prayer when ye are drunken, until ye know what ye say; nor when ye are polluted, except travelling on the road, until ye have washed your whole body. But if ye be ill, or on a journey, or one of you cometh from the privy, or ye have touched women, and ye find no water—then take for yourselves clean earth and wipe your faces and your hands therewith. Lo! Allah is ever Pardoning, Forgiving.

(4:43 Surah An-Nisaa – The Women)

---

[206] https://www.ncbi.nlm.nih.gov/pmc/articles/PMC3705686/}

Performing ablution before standing for prayer is also a divinely ordained obligation, as prescribed by Allah SWT in the Holy Qur'an, verse 5:6 of Surah Al-Ma'idah.

The verse says:

يَا أَيُّهَا الَّذِينَ آمَنُوا إِذَا قُمْتُمْ إِلَى الصَّلَاةِ فَاغْسِلُوا وُجُوهَكُمْ وَأَيْدِيَكُمْ إِلَى الْمَرَافِقِ وَامْسَحُوا بِرُءُوسِكُمْ وَأَرْجُلَكُمْ إِلَى الْكَعْبَيْنِ ۚ وَإِن كُنتُمْ جُنُبًا فَاطَّهَّرُوا ۚ وَإِن كُنتُم مَّرْضَىٰ أَوْ عَلَىٰ سَفَرٍ أَوْ جَاءَ أَحَدٌ مِّنكُم مِّنَ الْغَائِطِ أَوْ لَامَسْتُمُ النِّسَاءَ فَلَمْ تَجِدُوا مَاءً فَتَيَمَّمُوا صَعِيدًا طَيِّبًا فَامْسَحُوا بِوُجُوهِكُمْ وَأَيْدِيكُم مِّنْهُ ۚ مَا يُرِيدُ اللَّهُ لِيَجْعَلَ عَلَيْكُم مِّنْ حَرَجٍ وَلَٰكِن يُرِيدُ لِيُطَهِّرَكُمْ وَلِيُتِمَّ نِعْمَتَهُ عَلَيْكُمْ لَعَلَّكُمْ تَشْكُرُونَ

Believe! When ye rise up for prayer, wash your faces, and your hands up to the elbows; and wipe your heads and your feet unto the ankles. And if ye be unclean, purify yourselves. But if ye be ill or on a journey, or one of you cometh from the privy, or ye have touched women and ye find no water—then betake yourselves to clean earth and wipe your faces and hands therewith. Allah willeth not to place you in difficulty, but willeth to purify you and complete His favour unto you, that ye may be thankful.

(5:6 Surah Al-Ma'idah – The Table Spread)

Salat Positions

These are: standing, bowing, and prostrating. The standing position is mentioned in the Qur'an in verse 2:238.

Allah SWT says:

حَافِظُوا عَلَى الصَّلَوَاتِ وَالصَّلَاةِ الْوُسْطَىٰ وَقُومُوا لِلَّهِ قَانِتِينَ

Guard strictly the five obligatory prayers, especially the middle prayer; and stand before Allah in devout obedience.

(2:238 Surah Al-Baqarah – The Cow)

فَنَادَتْهُ الْمَلَائِكَةُ وَهُوَ قَائِمٌ يُصَلِّي فِي الْمِحْرَابِ أَنَّ اللَّهَ يُبَشِّرُكَ بِيَحْيَىٰ مُصَدِّقًا بِكَلِمَةٍ مِّنَ اللَّهِ وَسَيِّدًا وَحَصُورًا وَنَبِيًّا مِّنَ الصَّالِحِينَ

Then the angels called unto him, while he stood praying in the sanctuary: "Allah doth give thee glad tidings of John, confirming the Word from Allah, and (he shall be) honourable, chaste, and a Prophet from among the righteous."

(3:39 Surah Ale-Imran – The Family of Imran)

وَإِذْ بَوَّأْنَا لِإِبْرَاهِيمَ مَكَانَ الْبَيْتِ أَن لَّا تُشْرِكْ بِي شَيْئًا وَطَهِّرْ بَيْتِيَ لِلطَّائِفِينَ وَالْقَائِمِينَ وَالرُّكَّعِ السُّجُودِ

And (remember) when We prepared for Abraham the place of the House, saying: Associate not anything with Me, and purify My House for those who

461

circumambulate it, and those who stand up for prayer, and those who bow and make prostration.

(22:26 Surah Al-Hajj – The Pilgrimage)

مُحَمَّدٌ رَّسُولُ اللَّهِ ۚ وَالَّذِينَ مَعَهُ أَشِدَّاءُ عَلَى الْكُفَّارِ رُحَمَاءُ بَيْنَهُمْ ۖ تَرَاهُمْ رُكَّعًا سُجَّدًا يَبْتَغُونَ فَضْلًا مِّنَ اللَّهِ وَرِضْوَانًا ۖ سِيمَاهُمْ فِي وُجُوهِهِم مِّنْ أَثَرِ السُّجُودِ ۚ ذَٰلِكَ مَثَلُهُمْ فِي التَّوْرَاةِ ۚ وَمَثَلُهُمْ فِي الْإِنجِيلِ كَزَرْعٍ أَخْرَجَ شَطْأَهُ فَآزَرَهُ فَاسْتَغْلَظَ فَاسْتَوَىٰ عَلَىٰ سُوقِهِ يُعْجِبُ الزُّرَّاعَ لِيَغِيظَ بِهِمُ الْكُفَّارَ ۗ وَعَدَ اللَّهُ الَّذِينَ آمَنُوا وَعَمِلُوا الصَّالِحَاتِ مِنْهُم مَّغْفِرَةً وَأَجْرًا عَظِيمًا

Muhammad is the Messenger of Allah, and those who are with him are severe against disbelievers, and merciful among themselves. Thou seest them bowing and prostrating (in prayer), seeking bounty from Allah and His good pleasure. The mark of them is on their faces from the traces of prostration. This is their description in the Torah. And their description in the Gospel is like unto a seed which sendeth forth its sprout, then strengtheneth it, and it riseth firm upon its stalk, delighting the sowers—that He may enrage the disbelievers with them. Allah hath promised such of them as believe and do good works forgiveness and a great reward.

(48:29 Surah Al-Fath – The Victory)

To clarify further, another verse in Surah Al-Baqarah (2:239) states that there is no need for physical movements such as standing, bowing, or prostrating when riding or in emergencies and unusual situations.

Allah says:

فَإِنْ خِفْتُمْ فَرِجَالًا أَوْ رُكْبَانًا ۖ فَإِذَا أَمِنتُمْ فَاذْكُرُوا اللَّهَ كَمَا عَلَّمَكُم مَّا لَمْ تَكُونُوا تَعْلَمُونَ

And if ye fear (danger), then (pray) on foot or riding. But when ye are in safety, then remember Allah as He hath taught you that which ye knew not.

(2:239 Surah Al-Baqarah – The Cow)

Position of the Head in Prayer

إِن نَّشَأْ نُنَزِّلْ عَلَيْهِم مِّنَ السَّمَاءِ آيَةً فَظَلَّتْ أَعْنَاقُهُمْ لَهَا خَاضِعِينَ

If We will, We could send down upon them from heaven a sign, to which their necks would remain bowed in humility.

(26:4 Surah Ash-Shu'araa – The Poets)

سَبِّحِ اسْمَ رَبِّكَ الْأَعْلَى

Glorify the name of thy Lord, the Most High.

(87:1 Surah Al-A'la – The Most High)[207]

---

[207] https://www.quran-islam.org/main_topics/islam/pillars/salat_words_(P1199).html

462

Daily Prayers

Salat In The Biblical Period

The Concept Of Jewish Prayer

Biblical References On Daily Prayers/Salat

It should be noted that *Salat* is not mentioned by name in the Old Testament or the New Testament, but there are references to regular prayers and ablutions (washing before prayers, known as *wudu* in Islam).

Jewish people to this day observe three daily prayer services, or *tefillah*. The word *tefillah* comes from the Hebrew root פ.ל.ל (p-l-l), which does not mean "to beg" but rather "to judge." In fact, the verb "to pray" is *lehitpallel*, the reflexive form of the verb, meaning "to judge oneself." The focus of *tefillah*, then, is not merely on presenting one's concerns to God, but on a special form of self-assessment.

Tefillah consists of three main daily prayers:

- The morning prayer, *Shacharit*

- The afternoon prayer, *Minchah*

- [The evening prayer, which you may wish to mention for completeness, is *Ma'ariv* or *Arvit*]

(Psalms 69:14 in the King James Version reads: "Deliver me out of the mire, and let me not sink: let me be delivered from them that hate me, and out of the deep waters.")[208] Note: and the evening prayer, or *Maariv*. The background and philosophy of the three daily prayers are found in the *Talmud*.[209] Note And the references can be found in the Hebrew Bible and are traced back to the patriarchs: Abraham عليه السلام, Isaac عليه السلام, and Jacob (Yaqub) عليه السلام.

Ablution/Washing Before Prayers:

The Torah describes Moses عليه السلام, Aaron عليه السلام, and the priests washing their hands and feet before entering the altar:

"And he set the laver between the tent of the congregation and the altar, and put water there, to wash withal.

And Moses and Aaron and his sons washed their hands and their feet thereat:

---

[208] (According to the first opinion, the Mincha prayer was originated by Isaac, who "went out to converse in the field", (according to this view) with God. According to the second opinion, the Mincha prayer is based on the afternoon tamid (daily) offering which was offered in the Temple each afternoon. Mincha - Wikipediahttps://en.wikipedia.org › wiki › Mincha)

[209] *(The Talmud is a record of the rabbinic debates in the 2nd-5th century on the teachings of the Torah)*

When they went into the tent of the congregation, and when they came near unto the altar, they washed; as the Lord commanded Moses."

— Exodus 40:30–32, KJV

Not only were they commanded to wash; it was made a permanent law for their descendants:

"And the Lord spake unto Moses, saying,

Thou shalt also make a laver of brass, and his foot also of brass, to wash withal: and thou shalt put it between the tabernacle of the congregation and the altar, and thou shalt put water therein.

For Aaron and his sons shall wash their hands and their feet threat:

When they go into the tabernacle of the congregation, they shall wash with water, that they die not; or when they come near to the altar to minister, to burn offering made by fire unto the Lord:

So they shall wash their hands and their feet, that they die not: and it shall be a statute for ever to them, even to him and to his seed throughout their generations."

— Exodus 30:17–21, KJV

Kneeling (*Ruku*) and Prostration (*Sujud*):

These are considered signs of humility before God and are part of the rituals of Muslim prayer. They have been mentioned many times in the Bible, though not using the same specific terms. The following examples are not necessarily in the context of formal prayer but show expressions of humility before God:

"And Moses and Aaron went from the presence of the assembly unto the door of the tabernacle of the congregation, and they fell upon their faces: and the glory of the Lord appeared unto them."

— Numbers 20:6, KJV

"Then cometh Jesus with them unto a place called Gethsemane, and saith unto the disciples, 'Sit ye here, while I go and pray yonder.'

And he took with him Peter and the two sons of Zebedee, and began to be sorrowful and very heavy.

Then saith he unto them, 'My soul is exceeding sorrowful, even unto death: tarry ye here, and watch with me.'

And he went a little further, and fell on his face, and prayed..."

— Matthew 26:36–39, KJV

Praying Regularly / Prayer Times:

Though praying five times a day is not a standard Christian practice today, there are references in the New Testament to daily prayers performed at specific hours:

"There was a certain man in Caesarea called Cornelius, a centurion of the band called the Italian band,

A devout man, and one that feared God with all his house, which gave much alms to the people, and prayed to God alway.

He saw in a vision evidently about the ninth hour of the day an angel of God coming in to him..."

— *Acts 10:1–3*, KJV

The *Qiblah* or Direction of Prayer:

In the early days of Muhammad ﷺ, the first *Qiblah* was the Al-Quds Mosque in Jerusalem. The *Qiblah* was later changed to the Ka'bah in Mecca, as described in Qur'anic verses 2:142–144. Similarly, the Bible refers to the practice of facing the temple in Jerusalem during prayer:

"That thine eyes may be open toward this house night and day, even toward the place of which thou hast said, 'My name shall be there': that thou mayest hearken unto the prayer which thy servant shall make toward this place.

And hearken thou to the supplication of thy servant, and of thy people Israel, when they shall pray toward this place: and hear thou in heaven thy dwelling place: and when thou hearest, forgive."

— *1 Kings 8:29–30*, KJV

Daniel عليه السلام, another Jewish prophet, also prayed regularly, three times a day, facing Jerusalem:

"Now when Daniel knew that the writing was signed, he went into his house; and his windows being open in his chamber toward Jerusalem, he kneeled upon his knees three times a day, and prayed, and gave thanks before his God, as he did aforetime."

— *Daniel 6:10*, KJV

Conclusion:

Though the ritualistic forms may differ, the essential element of daily prayers—consistent communication with God, sincere supplication, reverence, and a sense of awe—remains central. These acts serve as a continual reminder of our duties to God and as a way to reflect upon His creation.[210]

In summary, it is important to reiterate the significance of a verse from the Qur'an that serves as a reminder for us to seek guidance solely from its profound teachings. Within its verses, nothing is overlooked or disregarded; rather, everything is meticulously elucidated and truthfully unveiled to us by our Lord, Allah (SWT). The verse says:

أَفَغَيْرَ اللَّهِ أَبْتَغِي حَكَمًا وَهُوَ الَّذِي أَنزَلَ إِلَيْكُمُ الْكِتَابَ مُفَصَّلًا ۚ وَالَّذِينَ آتَيْنَاهُمُ الْكِتَابَ يَعْلَمُونَ أَنَّهُ مُنَزَّلٌ مِّن رَّبِّكَ بِالْحَقِّ ۖ فَلَا تَكُونَنَّ مِنَ الْمُمْتَرِينَ

[Say (O Muhammad ﷺ)]: "Shall I seek a judge other than Allah, while it is He who hath sent down unto you the Book (the Qur'an), explained in detail?" Those unto whom We gave the Scripture [the Taurat (Torah) and the Injeel (Gospel)] know that it is revealed from thy Lord in truth. Be not then of those who doubt.

— *Surah Al-An'am (The Cattle), 6:114*

Conclusion

The Qur'an serves as the ultimate constitution for life, providing guidance for peaceful and righteous living. While scholars may define it in different ways, people of all faiths can recognise its role as a universal guide—helping believers navigate life and ultimately succeed in the trial of the Day of Judgment.

While I reference the Psalms and other books in both the Old and New Testaments, their value is superseded by the arrival of the final Scripture, the Qur'an, which is intended as guidance for all humanity from the same Divine Author.

Many people in the world have yet to read or understand the message our Lord has given in the Qur'an for their benefit, despite their pursuit of truth and self-purification. For example, Garry Wills, a Pulitzer Prize-winning author and professor emeritus of history at Northwestern University, explores the Qur'an in his book *What the Qur'an Meant and Why It Matters*. Wills, who studied for the priesthood and taught ancient and New Testament Greek at Johns Hopkins University, invites readers to join him in a timely and necessary reconsideration of the Qur'an. As a non-Muslim with an open mind, he approaches the Qur'an with both sympathy and rigour, seeking to understand why other non-Muslims—like Pope Francis—find it inspiring and worthy of guiding people through the centuries.

The selected verses from the Qur'an offer individuals an opportunity for self-examination, helping them identify deficiencies they need to address to maintain their status as believers while continuing on the straight path. This guidance is

---

[210] Adapted from my book, The Three Abrahamic Testaments.
https://www.patheos.com/blogs/askamuslim/2018/09/salat-or-daily-prayers-were-not-ordained-for-muslims-only/2/ Index 159

valuable not only for those seeking to become believers but also for Muslims who are unfamiliar with the teachings they claim to follow. Such reading may prompt introspection and a deeper concern about the Day of Judgment and the fulfilment of the requirements outlined in the verses.

As we continue our journey, we aim to uncover and address any remaining challenges that hinder our progress—illuminating the path ahead to ensure the steadfastness of our way.

****

« O Allah, forgive our living and our dead, those present and those absent, our young and our old, our males and our females. O Allah, whom amongst us You keep alive, then let such a life be upon Islam, and whom amongst us You take unto Yourself, then let such a death be upon faith. O Allah, do not deprive us of his reward and do not let us go astray after him. »

— *Abu Dawud (3/211)*

بِسْمِ ٱللَّهِ ٱلرَّحْمَـٰنِ ٱلرَّحِيمِ

Chapter 13

When the son of Adam (i.e. human beings) recites a verse of prostration and prostrates himself, Satan withdraws, weeping and saying:

'Woe to me... the son of Adam was commanded to prostrate and he prostrated, so Paradise will be his; I was commanded to prostrate and I refused, so Hell is mine.'

Ṣaḥīḥ Muslim 81

Grade: *Sahih (authentic) according to Muslim*

Hear it from Scripture:

"He hath not dealt with us after our sins; nor rewarded us according to our iniquities.

For as the heaven is high above the earth, so great is his mercy toward them that fear him.

As far as the east is from the west, so far hath he removed our transgressions from us."

— Psalm 103:10–12, KJV

📖📖📖📖📖📖📖

Allah's Clemency

We are rapidly approaching the culmination of our earthly journey, where we will face our ultimate test, transcend our physical bodies, and venture into the unfamiliar realm. Our destination awaits us in the city of Barzak, and our standing in Barzak life will be determined by the outcome of our examinations when the soul departs from the body. The final phase of this new expedition will commence when the call from the Almighty beckons.

In the previous chapter, we focused on the importance of *Salat*, as emphasised in the Divine Constitution, where Allah Most High (SWT) highlights its significance. We should assess our own shortcomings, work towards rectifying them, and seek Allah's forgiveness throughout our journey. It is evident that individuals like ourselves, who are ordinary in nature, continually search for the appropriate supplication to beseech Allah's mercy and seek relief from immediate difficulties and sins.

Moreover, we observe that many of us diligently engage in the recitation of *Tasbeeh* throughout the day and night, yet occasionally become disheartened when the desired outcomes do not materialise, despite Allah's promises. Allah says:

وَقَالَ رَبُّكُمُ ادْعُونِي أَسْتَجِبْ لَكُمْ ۚ إِنَّ الَّذِينَ يَسْتَكْبِرُونَ عَنْ عِبَادَتِي سَيَدْخُلُونَ جَهَنَّمَ دَاخِرِينَ

"Call upon Me; I will answer you." (40:60, Surah Al-Mu'min)

To remove these frustrations and regain full confidence that our *Du'a* prayers will not be in vain, we must search for the elements that need attention. So at the outset, let us find out what sin is, and how our sins and other elements affect our *Du'as*.

Sin

Sin is described in various religious texts as actions that defy the commands of the Supreme Authority, Almighty Allah, and contradict the teachings of the chosen prophets, including the final Prophet Muhammad ﷺ. Engaging in such actions constitutes a sin. It is essential to comprehend the profound significance of sin and its ramifications before seeking forgiveness and mercy from Allah SWT, for doing so without this understanding would be futile.

Let us reflect upon the teachings of Prophet Moses عليه السلام and other messengers, as well as the scholars of their time, who sought forgiveness for their sins. By carefully examining certain aspects of the Old Testament, we come to understand that sin poses a significant barrier for believers of all religions—and humanity as a whole—in attaining Allah's grace.

Our Holy Qur'an echoes this same message, emphasising that a corrupted heart will obstruct our success in this world and the Hereafter, regardless of outward piety. To unlock success, we must seek Allah's mercy and sincerely ask for forgiveness to cleanse ourselves of sins.

Allah (SWT) granted wisdom to Adam عليه السلام and eventually revealed the Holy Book, appointing prophets on Earth with knowledge. They warned us about the consequences of sins such as idolatry, adultery, and murder—both in this world and on the Day of Judgment. It is only when Satan invades and takes complete control of one's soul that a person truly sins.

The first human sin was committed in Heaven through Satan's conspiracy, and the first human sin on Earth occurred when one of Adam's sons committed murder—Cain killed his brother Abel.

In the Bible (Hebrew Bible or Old Testament), Cain, the firstborn son of Adam and Eve, murdered his brother Abel (Genesis 4:1–16). The first murder is also mentioned in the Qur'an.

469

Allah the Almighty revealed:

And (O Muhammad ﷺ) recite to them the truth of the story of the two sons of Adam. Behold! They each presented a sacrifice to Allah. It was accepted from one, but not from the other. Said the latter:

وَاتْلُ عَلَيْهِمْ نَبَأَ ابْنَيْ آدَمَ بِالْحَقِّ إِذْ قَرَّبَا قُرْبَانًا فَتُقُبِّلَ مِنْ أَحَدِهِمَا وَلَمْ يُتَقَبَّلْ مِنَ الْآخَرِ قَالَ لَأَقْتُلَنَّكَ ۖ قَالَ إِنَّمَا يَتَقَبَّلُ اللهُ مِنَ الْمُتَّقِينَ

"And (O Muhammad ﷺ) recite to them (the Jews) the story of the two sons of Adam [Habil (Abel) and Qabil (Cain)] in truth; when each offered a sacrifice (to Allah), it was accepted from the one but not from the other. The latter said to the former: 'I will surely kill you.' The former said: 'Verily, Allah accepts only from those who are Al-Muttaqun (the pious).'"

(5:27, Surah Al-Ma'idah – *The Table Spread with Food*)

Sin is an inherent aspect of human existence, stemming from our imperfect nature and inclination towards wrongdoing. Although individuals are born free from sin, no one can claim to be entirely faultless. It is our human instincts that give rise to sin, rather than any inherited transgressions of our ancestors.

Allah SWT says:

قُلْ أَغَيْرَ اللهِ أَبْغِي رَبًّا وَهُوَ رَبُّ كُلِّ شَيْءٍ ۚ وَلَا تَكْسِبُ كُلُّ نَفْسٍ إِلَّا عَلَيْهَا ۚ وَلَا تَزِرُ وَازِرَةٌ وِزْرَ أُخْرَىٰ ۚ ثُمَّ إِلَىٰ رَبِّكُم مَّرْجِعُكُمْ فَيُنَبِّئُكُم بِمَا كُنتُمْ فِيهِ تَخْتَلِفُونَ

"Say: 'Shall I seek a lord other than Allah, while He is the Lord of all things? No person earns any (sin) except against himself (only), and no bearer of burdens shall bear the burden of another. Then unto your Lord is your return, so He will tell you that wherein you have been differing.'"

(6:164, Surah Al-An'am – *The Cattle*)

A similar message is found in the previous scripture:

"The fathers shall not be put to death for the children, neither shall the children be put to death for the fathers: every man shall be put to death for his own sin."

— *Deuteronomy 24:16, KJV*

By examining the following verses, we can gain a clearer understanding of the critical importance of being diligent and prompt in saving our souls from sin. Allah SWT says:

1.

هُوَ الَّذِي خَلَقَ السَّمَاوَاتِ وَالْأَرْضَ فِي سِتَّةِ أَيَّامٍ ثُمَّ اسْتَوَىٰ عَلَى الْعَرْشِ ۚ يَعْلَمُ مَا يَلِجُ فِي الْأَرْضِ وَمَا يَخْرُجُ مِنْهَا وَمَا يَنزِلُ مِنَ السَّمَاءِ وَمَا يَعْرُجُ فِيهَا ۖ وَهُوَ مَعَكُمْ أَيْنَ مَا كُنتُمْ ۚ وَاللَّهُ بِمَا تَعْمَلُونَ بَصِيرٌ

"He it is Who created the heavens and the earth in six Days and then Istawa (rose over) the Throne (in a manner that suits His Majesty). He knows what goes into the earth and what comes forth from it, what descends from the heaven and what ascends thereto. And He is with you (by His Knowledge) wheresoever you may be. And Allah is the All-Seer of what you do."

(57:4, Surah Al-Hadid – *Iron*)

2.

وَلَقَدْ خَلَقْنَا الْإِنسَانَ وَنَعْلَمُ مَا تُوَسْوِسُ بِهِ نَفْسُهُۥ ۖ وَنَحْنُ أَقْرَبُ إِلَيْهِ مِنْ حَبْلِ الْوَرِيدِ

"And indeed We have created man, and We know what his own self whispers to him. And We are nearer to him than his jugular vein (by Our Knowledge)."

(50:16, Surah Qaf)

If we search the Bible, we find the same message:

"Behold, the LORD's hand is not shortened, that it cannot save; neither his ear heavy, that it cannot hear:

But your iniquities have separated between you and your God, and your sins have hid his face from you, that he will not hear."

— *Isaiah 59:1–2, KJV*

Now, surely the question may arise in someone's mind: how can we confess our sins?

Our Prophet ﷺ said:

"All the sons of Adam are sinners, but the best of sinners are those who repent often."

From the records of At-Tirmidhi and Ibn Majah—both of whom had strong chains of narration—this hadith is reported as Hadith no. 1477. It was also reported by Abu Huraira that the Messenger of Allah ﷺ said:

"By Him in whose hand is my soul, if you did not sin, Allah would replace you with people who would sin and they would seek forgiveness from Allah, and He would forgive them."

Source: Ṣaḥīḥ Muslim 2749

From the two hadiths mentioned, it is evident that as human beings, we are inherently prone to sin—a reality that Allah is fully aware of. In fact, if we were incapable of sinning, we would not truly be human. Therefore, we should not dwell excessively on our past sins. Allah (SWT) assures us that if we sincerely seek His forgiveness, He will forgive all our sins.

This is confirmed in Surah Ash-Shura, verse 37, where Allah (SWT) said:

وَالَّذِينَ يَجْتَنِبُونَ كَبَائِرَ الْإِثْمِ وَالْفَوَاحِشَ وَإِذَا مَا غَضِبُوا هُمْ يَغْفِرُونَ

471

Those who avoid the greater crimes and shameful deeds, and, when they are angry even then forgive.

(Surah Ash-Shura 42:37)

As we concern ourselves with the future, these verses can offer great hope as we move forward to face judgement.

1.

وَهُوَ الَّذِي يَقْبَلُ التَّوْبَةَ عَنْ عِبَادِهِ وَيَعْفُو عَنِ السَّيِّئَاتِ وَيَعْلَمُ مَا تَفْعَلُونَ

And He it is Who accepteth repentance from His servants, and pardoneth sins, and He knoweth what ye do.

(Surah Ash-Shura 42:25)

2.

وَيَا قَوْمِ اسْتَغْفِرُوا رَبَّكُمْ ثُمَّ تُوبُوا إِلَيْهِ يُرْسِلِ السَّمَاءَ عَلَيْكُم مِّدْرَارًا وَيَزِدْكُمْ قُوَّةً إِلَىٰ قُوَّتِكُمْ وَلَا تَتَوَلَّوْا مُجْرِمِينَ

And now, O my people, repent and turn to the Lord, and He shall send you rain in abundance from heaven, and add strength to your strength; but turn not away as guilty ones.

(Surah Hud 11:52)

3.

قُلْ يَا عِبَادِيَ الَّذِينَ أَسْرَفُوا عَلَىٰ أَنفُسِهِمْ لَا تَقْنَطُوا مِن رَّحْمَةِ اللَّهِ ۚ إِنَّ اللَّهَ يَغْفِرُ الذُّنُوبَ جَمِيعًا ۚ إِنَّهُ هُوَ الْغَفُورُ الرَّحِيمُ

Say, O my servants which have transgressed against their own souls, despair not of the mercy of Allah; verily, Allah forgiveth all sins: for He is Oft-Forgiving, Most Merciful.

(Surah Az-Zumar 39:53)

4.

وَالَّذِينَ لَا يَدْعُونَ مَعَ اللَّهِ إِلَٰهًا آخَرَ وَلَا يَقْتُلُونَ النَّفْسَ الَّتِي حَرَّمَ اللَّهُ إِلَّا بِالْحَقِّ وَلَا يَزْنُونَ ۚ وَمَن يَفْعَلْ ذَٰلِكَ يَلْقَ أَثَامًا

يُضَاعَفْ لَهُ الْعَذَابُ يَوْمَ الْقِيَامَةِ وَيَخْلُدْ فِيهِ مُهَانًا

إِلَّا مَن تَابَ وَآمَنَ وَعَمِلَ عَمَلًا صَالِحًا فَأُولَٰئِكَ يُبَدِّلُ اللَّهُ سَيِّئَاتِهِمْ حَسَنَاتٍ ۗ وَكَانَ اللَّهُ غَفُورًا رَّحِيمًا

And those who call not upon any other god with Allah, nor kill such life as Allah hath forbidden, save in justice, nor commit fornication—and whoso doeth this shall meet the penalty.

His punishment shall be doubled on the Day of Judgement, and he shall dwell therein in disgrace.

Except him that repenteth, and believeth, and doeth righteous deeds; for them Allah will change their evil deeds into good ones. Verily Allah is Oft-Forgiving, Most Merciful.

(Surah Al-Furqan 25:68–70)

Now Let's Classify The Nature Of Sins:

Many Small Sins Vs. One Big Sin

Two Jews came to a Chassidic Rabbi to ask for advice about sins they had committed. One had committed a great sin for which he was certain God would never forgive him. The other was less worried, because he had never been guilty of anything so grave, only of a collection of lesser sins.

The Rabbi told them to go to a field and select stones corresponding to the size and number of their sins, and later to return and scatter them. After doing so, they came back to the Rabbi.

"Now go to the field once more," he told them, "pick up the stones you scattered, and bring them to me."

He who had committed the one great sin knew at once which was his stone and brought it back to the Rabbi. The other, however, had scattered so many little stones that he could not identify them. He had a most difficult time finding and returning them.

The Rabbi then said:

"Your deeds are like your stones. You who brought one large stone committed a grave sin. But you were conscious of what you had done, and with a determined effort at repentance, you could be forgiven by God. But you, whose sins were many and small—like those of most human beings—have found how hard it is to catch up with one's minor lapses. And no repentance of yours can possibly be effective until you realise that small things matter."

Christian view of sin

In Christian theology, mortal sins—severe and intentional actions that directly disobey God—are often confused with the seven deadly sins:

1. Pride
2. Envy
3. Wrath
4. Sloth
5. Greed

6. Gluttony

7. Lust

These are called "deadly" because they lead to further sin.

Another group of grave offences identified by the Church are the **"sins that cry to heaven"**, including:

- Murder

- Sodomy

- Oppression of the weak

- Defrauding labourers of their wages

The catechetical tradition recalls further that these sins cry to heaven: the blood of Abel, the sin of the Sodomites, the cry of the oppressed in Egypt, and the cry of the widow, the orphan, and the displaced.

Judaism's view of sin

Judaism describes three levels of sin or *avera*:

1. **B'mezid** – A sin committed intentionally. This is the most serious.

2. **B'shogeg** – A sin committed accidentally. While the person is still responsible, it is considered less severe.

3. **Tinok shenishba** – A person raised in a non-observant or assimilated environment, unaware of halachah (Jewish law). Such a person is not held accountable.

Judaism teaches that no human being is perfect; everyone has sinned many times.

The Talmud says:

"Everyone is responsible to be as great as Moses."

Then the Torah tells us in **Deuteronomy 34:10 (KJV):**

"And there arose not a prophet since in Israel like unto Moses, whom the Lord knew face to face."

Thirteen Attributes of Mercy

According to Rabbeinu Tam in the Babylonian Talmud (Tractate Rosh Hashanah 17b), the Thirteen Attributes of Mercy include:

1. God is merciful before a person sins, even knowing their capability to sin.

2. God is merciful to the sinner after the sin.

3. God's mercy extends even where humans would not expect it.

4. God is compassionate and reduces punishment.

5. God is gracious even to the undeserving.

6. God is slow to anger.

7. God is abundant in kindness.

8. God is truthful and trustworthy in His promises to forgive.

9. God extends kindness to future generations, honouring the deeds of the patriarchs.

10. God forgives intentional sins if one repents.

11. God forgives acts committed in deliberate defiance if one repents.

12. God forgives sins committed in error.

13. God erases the sins of those who sincerely repent.

Allah (SWT) wants us to recognise our major sins from our hearts before asking for His forgiveness. Even those who are not involved in major sins such as hypocrisy, murder, or adultery will be found guilty of lying or worshipping false idols such as wealth or power. We must remember that Allah (SWT) does not decide whether we will sin — it is entirely in our hands. This means that all our activities are linked to Satan's actions, and it is up to us to be determined to abandon Satan's influence.

Praying without determination holds no value in receiving Allah's mercy. However, praying for matters beyond our control, such as health and livelihood, can be highly beneficial because these things are entirely dependent on Divine Providence.

Hadith and the Four Types of Deeds

Now let us search the Hadith to find the valuable advice of our Prophet Muhammad (ﷺ).

A very important hadith was reported by Ibn Abbas: The Messenger of Allah (ﷺ) said:

"Verily, Allah has recorded good and bad deeds and He made them clear."

Source: Sahih Bukhari 6126, Grade: Muttafaqun Alayhi

A scholar has beautifully explained this valuable hadith, which will benefit us all. People are of four types when it comes to good deeds and sins:

- Someone who thought about doing a good deed but didn't do it

- Someone who thought about doing a good deed and did it

- Someone who thought about committing a sin but didn't do it

- Someone who thought about committing a sin and did it

The Prophet (ﷺ) said:

"Allah has overlooked for my nation what their souls contemplate over, so long as they do not act on it or speak of it."

[Reported by Bukhari & Muslim]

(They): Intend to do the action and take initial steps in doing so, though with some hesitation. This is what is being referred to in this hadith.

(Determination): You are 100% sure you want to do it, and what is stopping you is an external impediment — e.g., someone forcing you not to do it, or you are unable to do it for any reason. This too is what is being referred to in this hadith with regards to good deeds only.

Some scholars say that for you to be rewarded for your intention, there must be an impediment stopping you from carrying out the action. Others say that merely intending to do good and not doing so — even without an impediment — will still bring reward.

Our Tongue vs Our Duʿāʾ

Allah has confirmed His disappointment in our behaviour, even though He has given us numerous comforts and taught us many things. We must feel Allah's complaint in our hearts and seriously consider how to act if we want our prayers to benefit us.

In *Surah Ibrahim*, Allah says:

وَآتَاكُم مِّن كُلِّ مَا سَأَلْتُمُوهُ ۚ وَإِن تَعُدُّوا نِعْمَتَ اللَّهِ لَا تُحْصُوهَا ۗ إِنَّ الْإِنسَانَ لَظَلُومٌ كَفَّارٌ

"And He gave you of all that you asked for. And if ye count the blessings of Allah, never will ye be able to number them. Verily man is most unjust and ungrateful."

Surah Ibrahim 14:34

Then Allah (SWT) says in *Surah An-Nahl*:

وَلَا تَقُولُوا لِمَا تَصِفُ أَلْسِنَتُكُمُ الْكَذِبَ هَٰذَا حَلَالٌ وَهَٰذَا حَرَامٌ لِّتَفْتَرُوا عَلَى اللَّهِ الْكَذِبَ ۚ إِنَّ الَّذِينَ يَفْتَرُونَ عَلَى اللَّهِ الْكَذِبَ لَا يُفْلِحُونَ

"And say not concerning that which your tongues put forth falsely: 'This is lawful and this is forbidden,' so as to invent lies against Allah. Verily, those who invent lies against Allah will never prosper."

Surah An-Nahl 16:116

Since we have already identified verses on how to earn Allah's mercy for our sins, we can now explore the verses where Allah instructs us on how to be tactful while keeping our promise to remain under His mercy.

Allah says:

وَإِذَا سَأَلَكَ عِبَادِي عَنِّي فَإِنِّي قَرِيبٌ ۖ أُجِيبُ دَعْوَةَ الدَّاعِ إِذَا دَعَانِ ۖ فَلْيَسْتَجِيبُوا لِي وَلْيُؤْمِنُوا بِي لَعَلَّهُمْ يَرْشُدُونَ

"And when My servants ask thee concerning Me, surely I am nigh. I answer the prayer of the supplicant when he calleth on Me. So let them hearken unto Me and believe in Me, that they may walk in the right way."

Surah Al-Baqarah 2:186

Our personal circumstances, lack of knowledge, and greed often lead us down paths where our prayers become unacceptable to Allah — much like how prayer without ablution is invalid. We must also be mindful of Satan, an evil force that seeks to undermine our efforts.

To overcome these challenges, let us reflect on the verses of *Surah Ar-Rahman*:

الرَّحْمَـٰنُ

عَلَّمَ الْقُرْآنَ

خَلَقَ الْإِنسَانَ

عَلَّمَهُ الْبَيَانَ

"The Most Gracious. Taught the Qur'an. He created man. He taught him eloquent speech."

Surah Ar-Rahman 55:1–4

In *Surah Ar-Rum*, Allah says:

وَمِنْ آيَاتِهِ خَلْقُ السَّمَاوَاتِ وَالْأَرْضِ وَاخْتِلَافُ أَلْسِنَتِكُمْ وَأَلْوَانِكُمْ ۚ إِنَّ فِي ذَٰلِكَ لَآيَاتٍ لِّلْعَالِمِينَ

"And of His signs is the creation of the heavens and the earth, and the differences of your languages and your colours. Verily in that are signs for those who know."

Surah Ar-Rum 30:22

Allah (SWT) then expresses His displeasure with our actions in the following verse:

إِذْ تَلَقَّوْنَهُ بِأَلْسِنَتِكُمْ وَتَقُولُونَ بِأَفْوَاهِكُم مَّا لَيْسَ لَكُم بِهِ عِلْمٌ وَتَحْسَبُونَهُ هَيِّنًا وَهُوَ عِندَ اللَّهِ عَظِيمٌ

"When ye received it with your tongues, and said out of your mouths that whereof ye had no knowledge; and ye thought it a light matter, while it was most serious in the sight of Allah."

Surah An-Nur 24:15

This verse reminds us to be cautious in using our mouth and tongue, especially when commenting without knowledge. We often speak carelessly — for example, in anger, someone might label another as a "Kafir", but this comment can cause immense harm both in this world and the Hereafter.

The Power And Danger Of The Tongue

The tongue is a dangerous beast — "an unruly evil, full of deadly poison" (James 3:8, KJV). No matter what form it takes in our minds or what features it may reveal, it often seems impossible to defend ourselves against its harm. We know there is little good in it when misused — and it can destroy us.

Imam Ali (RA) said of the tongue:

جِرْمُهُ صَغيرٌ وَجُرمُهُ ثَقِيلٌ

"Its mass is small, but its sin is great."

Our small tongue can lead to great sins. Each of the body parts Allah has given us has a specific characteristic and purpose. The human mouth is an organ with the blessed ability to speak — a gift beyond measure. However, this noble faculty becomes a harmful instrument leading man to ruin if misused for swearing, disbelief, or spreading falsehood.

Thus, the Messenger of Allah (ﷺ) utters only one word:-

."استخدم فمك (تونجي) بشكل شرعي وأضمن لك الجنة"

"Use your mouth (tongue) legitimately and I will guarantee Paradise for you."

As an individual, I continue to stay committed to my journey, gathering the necessary resources for the next phase, where my fate will be judged and I may be granted entry to the land of my dreams. We must realise that without Allah's clemency, succeeding on the Day of Judgment and in this world is very difficult. Allah has provided numerous guidelines on how to live a good life in this world and prepare for the Day of Judgment. We must pay close attention to the advice that every believer should follow. Our mouth and tongue—our words and actions—are part of this guidance, and we must continuously review and improve our behaviour accordingly.

Before we focus on our duʿāʾs, we want to broaden our inquiries about the role of the mouth and tongue, along with our hearts and souls, because without properly recognising the importance of, and correctly handling, the mouth and tongue—our only tools that reflect our true selves—all effort towards our destiny in this life and the hereafter will be doomed. A person's character and his inner purity or wickedness are reflected in his speech.

Imam al-Bāqir said:

"A man is hidden under his tongue."

The tongue will unveil the curtain and display our real character.

The tongue is a great endowment of Allah. When used to praise and thank Him, it earns reward. Allah says:

$$\text{مْ نَجْعَل لَّهُ عَيْنَيْنِ}$$

$$\text{وَلِسَانًا وَشَفَتَيْنِ}$$

Have We not made for him a pair of eyes? And a tongue, and a pair of lips?

(Surah Al-Balad, 90:8–9)

So, whoever wishes to speak should reflect before saying anything.

As has been said, the tongue reflects what is in the heart. It expresses one's inner feelings and thoughts. It portrays one's character and personality. There are also potential harms that arise from its misuse.

Al-Barā' ibn 'Āzib narrated that an Arab came to the Prophet ﷺ and asked him to teach him something that would enable him to go to Heaven. The Prophet ﷺ said:

"Feed the hungry. Quench the thirst of the thirsty. Advise the people to do good deeds and admonish them against evil deeds. If you are not able to do that, then just guard your tongue from whatever is not good."

(*Ibid.*, p. 195)

Our Prophet Muhammad ﷺ also said:

"A believer's tongue is located behind his heart. Whenever he wants to talk, he first presents his words to his heart. If the heart approves of what he wants to say, it issues an order to the tongue to utter the words. However, if the heart does not issue a permit, then the lips stay sealed. But a hypocrite's tongue is in front of his heart. Whenever he intends to say something, he utters it without the approval of his heart."

(*Ibid.*)

Our noble Prophet ﷺ also said:

"Heaven is forbidden to whoever is used to swearing. He cannot enter it."

(*Al-Maḥajjah al-Bayḍā'*, vol. 5, p. 215).[211]

Now, let's explore the Torah and the Bible and find out what message they give about the tongue and the mouth.

---

[211] *Index 161 https://www.al-islam.org/a-divine-perspective-on-rights-a-commentary-of-imam-sajjads-treatise-of-rights/right-n-3-right*

"Sticks and stones may break my bones, but words will never hurt me." Maybe you've said it, but do you believe it? Someone revised this to: **"Sticks and stones may break our bones, but words will break our hearts."**

"Death and life are in the power of the tongue: and they that love it shall eat the fruit thereof." (Proverbs 18:21, KJV)

The tongue can be used as a weapon to harm and destroy, or as a tool to build and heal. What kind of impact do your words have?

Judgment on the Last Day will proceed according to a man's words:

"For by thy words thou shalt be justified, and by thy words thou shalt be condemned." (Matthew 12:37, KJV)

The tongue is the instrument of either a great deal of good or a great deal of evil.

Jesus said:

"O generation of vipers, how can ye, being evil, speak good things? For out of the abundance of the heart the mouth speaketh. A good man out of the good treasure of the heart bringeth forth good things: and an evil man out of the evil treasure bringeth forth evil things." (Matthew 12:34–35, KJV)

Regarding evil-fuelled words: Scripture says a tongue not under the control of the Holy Spirit is a restless evil set on fire by hell and controlled by the evil one:

"And the tongue is a fire, a world of iniquity: so is the tongue among our members, that it defileth the whole body, and setteth on fire the course of nature; and it is set on fire of hell. ... But the tongue can no man tame; it is an unruly evil, full of deadly poison." (James 3:6, 8, KJV)

"But I say unto you, That every idle word that men shall speak, they shall give account thereof in the day of judgment. For by thy words thou shalt be justified, and by thy words thou shalt be condemned." (Matthew 12:36–37, KJV)

"But those things which proceed out of the mouth come forth from the heart; and they defile the man." (Matthew 15:18, KJV)

"Thou givest thy mouth to evil, and thy tongue frameth deceit. Thou sittest and speakest against thy brother; thou slanderest thine own mother's son. These things hast thou done, and I kept silence; thou thoughtest that I was altogether such an one as thyself: but I will reprove thee, and set them in order before thine eyes." (Psalm 50:19–21, KJV)

A Prayer For Power Over The Tongue

The tongue is small but powerful. Unbridled, it dispenses deadly poison; bridled by the Holy Spirit, it blesses, refreshes, and gives life. Is your tongue heaven's tool or hell's weapon?

"Set a watch, O LORD, before my mouth; keep the door of my lips." (Psalm 141:3, KJV)

Lord, I know my tongue often gets ahead of my mind and heart. I am quick to speak, and I repent of the many thoughtless things I have spoken. I am sorry for words spoken in anger or in gossip. Please help me to recognise when I am about to speak without thinking, and to check my heart. Help me to be slow to speak. Help me, Lord, to be a person full of loving words, full of Your Spirit— overflowing with love, joy, peace, patience, kindness, gentleness, and self-control. Amen.[212]

Let us return to the Qur'an:

فَإِنَّمَا يَسَّرْنَاهُ بِلِسَانِكَ لِتُبَشِّرَ بِهِ الْمُتَّقِينَ وَتُنذِرَ بِهِ قَوْمًا لُّدًّا

So We have made this (the Qur'an) easy in your own tongue (O Muhammad ﷺ), only that you may give glad tidings to the Muttaqun (pious and righteous persons – see 2:2), and warn with it the Ludda (most quarrelsome) people. (Surah Maryam, 19:97)

رَبِّ هَبْ لِي حُكْمًا وَأَلْحِقْنِي بِالصَّالِحِينَ

وَاجْعَل لِّي لِسَانَ صِدْقٍ فِي الْآخِرِينَ

"O my Lord! Bestow wisdom on me, and join me with the righteous." (Ash-Shu'ara, 26:83)

"Grant me honourable mention on the tongue of truth among the latest generations." (Ash-Shu'ara, 26:84)

وَإِنَّ مِنْهُمْ لَفَرِيقًا يَلْوُونَ أَلْسِنَتَهُم بِالْكِتَابِ لِتَحْسَبُوهُ مِنَ الْكِتَابِ وَمَا هُوَ مِنَ الْكِتَابِ وَيَقُولُونَ هُوَ مِنْ عِندِ اللَّهِ وَمَا هُوَ مِنْ عِندِ اللَّهِ وَيَقُولُونَ عَلَى اللَّهِ الْكَذِبَ وَهُمْ يَعْلَمُونَ

And verily, among them is a party who distort the Book with their tongues (as they read), so that you may think it is from the Book, but it is not from the Book; and they say, "This is from Allah," but it is not from Allah; and they speak a lie against Allah while they know it. (Surah Aal-Imran, 3:78)

---

[212] *Index 162 https://www.biblestudytools.com/bible-study/topical-studies/what-does-life-and-death-are-in-the-power-of-the-tongue-mean-in-the-bible.html*

Undoubtedly, the tongue and the ability to speak are among the greatest blessings that Allah has bestowed on mankind in His creation.

"Even so the tongue is a little member, and boasteth great things. Behold, how great a matter a little fire kindleth!" (James 3:5, KJV) [213]

The tongue possesses a fiery nature, and indeed, it is a destructive flame that can incinerate even the most harmonious endeavours of peace. However, let us not misunderstand this truth as a call to remain silent and retreat from society. Rather, it implores us to employ our speech in a righteous manner. The tongue, residing within our very beings, has the potential to contaminate the entire body. Thus, we must treat it with the utmost reverence.

To use the tongue rightfully means recognising its nobility, refraining from vulgarity, cultivating virtuous speech, and directing it towards politeness. We should only employ it when necessary for religious and worldly benefit, avoiding unnecessary meddling that yields little gain. The tongue's small advantages are accompanied by potential harm, and it is difficult to find complete security from its detrimental effects.

The tongue serves as a witness to and a manifestation of our intellect. The mark of an intelligent individual lies in their ability to engage in meaningful discourse. Ultimately, all power resides solely with Allah, the Supreme, the Magnificent.

Undoubtedly, the tongue and the gift of speech are among the greatest blessings bestowed upon humanity by Allah in His magnificent creation. Our prayers may fail to reach the desired outcome due to the weakness of our tongues. Thus, we must strive to use this gift wisely and refrain from misuse, allowing our supplications to receive the anticipated response from Allah (SWT).

It is crucial to exercise caution and mindfulness in utilising our mouth, tongue, and lips throughout our daily endeavours, particularly when engaging in du'a (prayers). Failing to do so may render all our efforts futile. Nonetheless, in all fairness, if we employ our mouth, tongue, and lips in spreading slander, leading others astray, practising hypocrisy, engaging in forbidden transactions, breaking oaths, and similar actions, while simultaneously beseeching the Almighty for favours using the same tongue, it raises an important question: should one not receive a response from Allah, would it be justifiable to feel disappointed in Him? I leave it to your judgement to decide and deliver your verdict.

Tawbah

Before embarking on the du'a prayer with the intention of seeking its credibility, it is important to ensure that we have fulfilled all the necessary prerequisites. One crucial step in this process is to commence with the tawbah prayer, which serves as a preparation for du'a.

---

[213] Index 163 *https://questionsonislam.com/Source:https://bible.knowing-jesus.com/topics/Tongu*

The Messenger of Allah (ﷺ) said:

"Allah, the Exalted, has said: 'I have prepared for My righteous servants what no eye hath seen, nor ear heard, neither hath entered into the heart of man.' If you wish, recite:

فَلَا تَعْلَمُ نَفْسٌ مَّا أُخْفِيَ لَهُم مِّن قُرَّةِ أَعْيُنٍ جَزَاءً بِمَا كَانُوا يَعْمَلُونَ

No person knows what is kept hidden for them of joy as a reward for what they used to do. (Surah As-Sajda 32:17)

[Al-Bukhari and Muslim, Hadith 1881]

إِنَّ اللَّهَ يُحِبُّ التَّوَّابِينَ وَيُحِبُّ الْمُتَطَهِّرِينَ

Allah says: *Indeed, Allah loves those who are constantly repentant and loves those who purify themselves.* (Surah Al-Baqarah 2:222)

'Abdullah bin Busr said that the Prophet (ﷺ) said:

"Glad tidings to those who find much seeking forgiveness in the record of their deeds." (Sunan Ibn Majah 38:18)

Allah SWT says:

وَإِنِّي لَغَفَّارٌ لِّمَن تَابَ وَآمَنَ وَعَمِلَ صَالِحًا ثُمَّ اهْتَدَىٰ

And verily, I am indeed Forgiving to him who repents, believes (in My Oneness, and associates none in worship with Me), and does righteous good deeds, and then remains constant in doing them (till his death). (Surah Ta-Ha 20:82)

فَقُلْتُ اسْتَغْفِرُوا رَبَّكُمْ إِنَّهُ كَانَ غَفَّارًا

I said (to them): 'Ask forgiveness from your Lord; verily, He is Oft-Forgiving. (Surah Nuh 71:10)

For several years now, the world has been grappling with the escalating COVID-19 pandemic, which shows no signs of abating. Initially, numerous Muslim countries took the difficult decision to close down mosques and other public facilities as a preventive measure. This crisis has served to reinforce the faith of Muslims across the globe, leading us to fervently seek forgiveness from Allah with a pure tongue, employing sincere prayers and supplications. Our collective plea is for divine protection, urging for the well-being and safety of all individuals worldwide, as we confront this formidable adversary.

Finally, we read this verse. Allah SWT says:

يَا أَيُّهَا الَّذِينَ آمَنُوا تُوبُوا إِلَى اللَّهِ تَوْبَةً نَّصُوحًا عَسَىٰ رَبُّكُمْ أَن يُكَفِّرَ عَنكُمْ سَيِّئَاتِكُمْ وَيُدْخِلَكُمْ جَنَّاتٍ تَجْرِي مِن تَحْتِهَا الْأَنْهَارُ يَوْمَ لَا يُخْزِي اللَّهُ النَّبِيَّ وَالَّذِينَ آمَنُوا مَعَهُ نُورُهُمْ يَسْعَىٰ بَيْنَ أَيْدِيهِمْ وَبِأَيْمَانِهِمْ يَقُولُونَ رَبَّنَا أَتْمِمْ لَنَا نُورَنَا وَاغْفِرْ لَنَا إِنَّكَ عَلَىٰ كُلِّ شَيْءٍ قَدِيرٌ

O ye who believe! Turn to Allah with sincere repentance! It may be that your Lord will remit from you your sins and admit you into gardens under which rivers flow, the day that Allah will not disgrace the Prophet and those who believe with him. Their light will run before them and in their right hands. They will say, "Our Lord! Perfect our light for us and forgive us. Verily, Thou art able to do all things." (Surah At-Tahrim 66:8)

قَالَا رَبَّنَا ظَلَمْنَا أَنفُسَنَا وَإِن لَّمْ تَغْفِرْ لَنَا وَتَرْحَمْنَا لَنَكُونَنَّ مِنَ الْخَاسِرِينَ

Our Lord! We have wronged our own souls: if Thou forgive us not, and bestow not upon us Thy mercy, we shall certainly be of the losers. (Surah Al-A'raf 7:23)

Allah SWT says: *Indeed, I am the Perpetual Forgiver of whoever...*

1.

وَإِنِّي لَغَفَّارٌ لِّمَن تَابَ وَآمَنَ وَعَمِلَ صَالِحًا ثُمَّ اهْتَدَىٰ

And verily, I am indeed Forgiving to him who repents, believes (in My Oneness), and does righteous good deeds, and then remains constant in doing them (till his death). (Surah Ta-Ha 20:82)

2.

ثُمَّ إِنَّ رَبَّكَ لِلَّذِينَ عَمِلُوا السُّوءَ بِجَهَالَةٍ ثُمَّ تَابُوا مِن بَعْدِ ذَٰلِكَ وَأَصْلَحُوا إِنَّ رَبَّكَ مِن بَعْدِهَا لَغَفُورٌ رَّحِيمٌ

Then, verily! Your Lord is for those who do evil in ignorance and afterward repent and do righteous deeds. Verily, your Lord thereafter (to such) is Oft-Forgiving, Most Merciful. (Surah An-Nahl 16:119)

3.

وَقُل رَّبِّ اغْفِرْ وَارْحَمْ وَأَنتَ خَيْرُ الرَّاحِمِينَ

And say (O Muhammad ﷺ): "My Lord! Forgive and have mercy, for Thou art the Best of those who show mercy." (Surah Al-Mu'minun 23:118)

It is now clear to us that obtaining the true result of a du'a depends on how we have educated ourselves and prepared our hearts and souls to be humble and ready to "call upon" our Creator, the Almighty.

Prophet Muhammad (ﷺ) said, "Dua is worship itself." Then the Prophet Muhammad (ﷺ) recited this verse:

"Your Lord says:-

وَقَالَ رَبُّكُمُ ادْعُونِي أَسْتَجِبْ لَكُمْ ۚ إِنَّ الَّذِينَ يَسْتَكْبِرُونَ عَنْ عِبَادَتِي سَيَدْخُلُونَ جَهَنَّمَ دَاخِرِينَ

And your Lord said: 'Invoke Me, [i.e. believe in My Oneness (Islamic Monotheism)] and ask Me for anything; I will respond to your invocation. Verily! Those who scorn My worship [i.e. do not invoke Me, and do not believe in My Oneness] will surely enter Hell in humiliation.'"

(Surah Al-Mu'min 40:60 – Tirmidhi)

It is important to acknowledge that the true essence of dua can be realised when we adhere to the specified prerequisites. Prior to engaging in dua, it is recommended to purify our hearts and souls by reciting Al-Tawbah (التوبة) and Istighfar, as these acts will cleanse us of any accumulated negativity. Then begin with:

رَبَّنَا لَا تُزِغْ قُلُوبَنَا بَعْدَ إِذْ هَدَيْتَنَا وَهَبْ لَنَا مِن لَّدُنكَ رَحْمَةً ۚ إِنَّكَ أَنتَ الْوَهَّابُ

رَبَّنَا إِنَّكَ جَامِعُ النَّاسِ لِيَوْمٍ لَّا رَيْبَ فِيهِ ۚ إِنَّ اللَّهَ لَا يُخْلِفُ الْمِيعَادَ

"Our Lord! Let not our hearts deviate (from the truth) after You have guided us, and grant us mercy from You. Truly, You are the Bestower.

Our Lord! Verily, it is You Who will gather mankind together on the Day about which there is no doubt. Verily, Allah never breaks His Promise."

(Surah Al-Imran 3:8–9)

Dua and Dhikr

Prayer and Dhikr hold great significance among Muslims as they seek forgiveness for their sins. Traditionally, these prayers are offered in Arabic, beseeching Allah for His forgiveness. However, reciting prayers without comprehending their meaning may not yield the desired outcomes, as the lack of understanding may hinder the genuine emotions necessary to touch the heart.

Dua, or Dhikr, is a personal and intimate act of surrendering to the Almighty, where one implores in their own language for forgiveness and relief from the challenges they currently face. This practice is believed to be more impactful, as it allows individuals to express their heartfelt words from the depths of their being.

Allah (SWT) also says in the Qur'an:

وَإِذَا سَأَلَكَ عِبَادِي عَنِّي فَإِنِّي قَرِيبٌ ۖ أُجِيبُ دَعْوَةَ الدَّاعِ إِذَا دَعَانِ ۖ فَلْيَسْتَجِيبُوا لِي وَلْيُؤْمِنُوا بِي لَعَلَّهُمْ يَرْشُدُونَ

"And when My slaves ask you (O Muhammad ﷺ) concerning Me, then (answer them), I am indeed near (to them by My Knowledge). I respond to the invocation of the supplicant when he calls on Me (without any mediator or intercessor). So let them obey Me and believe in Me, so that they may be led aright."

(Surah Al-Baqarah 2:186)

The Qur'an also permits calling upon Allah at any time and in any posture— lying, sitting, standing, or even running—as confirmed in the verse:

الَّذِينَ يَذْكُرُونَ اللَّهَ قِيَامًا وَقُعُودًا وَعَلَىٰ جُنُوبِهِمْ وَيَتَفَكَّرُونَ فِي خَلْقِ السَّمَاوَاتِ وَالْأَرْضِ رَبَّنَا مَا خَلَقْتَ هَٰذَا بَاطِلًا سُبْحَانَكَ فَقِنَا عَذَابَ النَّارِ

"Those who remember Allah (always, and in prayers) standing, sitting, and lying down on their sides, and think deeply about the creation of the heavens and the earth (saying): 'Our Lord! You have not created (all) this without purpose, glory to You! Save us from the torment of the Fire.'"

(Surah Al-Imran 3:191)

The practice of preparing for prayer through ablution and facing the Qibla in humility before Allah is a fundamental aspect of Muslim worship. Muslims may recite duas before, during, or after formal prayers, or at various times throughout the day. Typically, dua is recited silently within one's heart.

Numerous supplications in the Qur'an and Hadith are associated with specific benefits. While it is essential to recite them in Arabic, understanding their meanings is equally important.

Many people tirelessly search for the right dua without verifying its authenticity or suitability, often losing hope when they see no results. This approach can be counterproductive, leading to confusion and weakening of faith. In such situations, Satan may exploit our doubts, urging us to seek solutions in ways that undermine our belief.

Instead, we should focus on the powerful, authentic duas available to us and adhere to them confidently.

Dua is a personal supplication, and one's heart will guide them on how to humble themselves before Allah and seek His help. No specific dua, not even those of the prophets, can surpass the heartfelt cries and submission to Allah for His guidance and assistance. Each individual has different problems, and their prayers will differ from others. Therefore, it is essential to pray sincerely from the heart in one's own words with a pure tongue, trusting that Allah (SWT) will respond, insha'Allah.

It is also important to pay attention to the "Rabbana" prayers revealed in the Qur'an, along with these personal supplications. These powerful and effective duas can provide solutions to our problems if we analyse them correctly. For convenience, this chapter has serialised these prayers.

Additionally, the significance of **Tasbih** and other duas cannot be overstated, as they are vital for maintaining a spiritually vibrant heart. Without them, our hearts may become susceptible to the influence of Satan.

To avoid this and benefit from the spiritual strength of dua and tasbih, we should seek out those that are widely recommended within the Muslim faith. For example, certain tasbih are commonly used and valued within the Muslim community:

Subhanallah, Alhamdulillah, La ilaha illallah, Allahu Akbar

Hadith on Dhikr

Narrated Abdullah ibn Abu Awfa:

A man came to the Prophet (ﷺ) and said: "I cannot memorise anything from the Qur'an, so teach me something which is sufficient for me."

He said: "Say: Glory be to Allah, and praise be to Allah, and there is no god but Allah, and Allah is most great, and there is no might and no strength but in Allah."

The man said: "Messenger of Allah, this is for Allah, but what is for me?"

He said: "Say: O Allah, have mercy on me, and sustain me, and keep me well, and guide me."

When the man stood up, he made a sign with his hand (indicating that he had earned a lot). The Messenger of Allah (ﷺ) said: "He filled up his hand with virtues."

(Sunan Abi Dawud 832, Hasan – Al-Albani)

Dhikr / Du'a – Day of Arafat (Hajj)

SubhanAllah, Walhamdulillah, Wala ilaha illallah, Wallahu Akbar

The Prophet (ﷺ) said:

"When I say 'SubhanAllah Walhamdulillah Wala ilaha illallah Wallahu Akbar', this is more beloved to me than all that the sun rises upon."

(Narrated by Muslim)

These words are the most beloved to Allah, the best of words, and they weigh heavily in the balance of good deeds, as was narrated in authentic ahadith.

Personal Daily Duas

أَسْتَغْفِرُ اللهَ رَبِي مِنْ كُلِ ذَنبٍ وَأتُوبُ إِلَيِهِ

Astaghfirullah Rabbi min kulli zambiyon wa atoobu ilaih

"I ask forgiveness of my sins from Allah, who is my Lord, and I turn towards Him."

I invest this dua for my heart and recite it frequently, especially after each of the five daily prayers.

Benefits of Reading:

لا حَوْلَ وَلا قُوَّةَ إِلا بِالله عليِيل عظيم

La hawla wa la quwwata illa billahil 'Aliyyil 'Azim

"There is no might nor power except with Allah, the Most High, the Most Great."

The meaning of this phrase is a person's admission that they are unable to do anything without the help and support of Allah. No matter how great one's strength or power may be, they remain powerless without Allah. Every strong person is weak compared to Allah. Every great person is insignificant in the face of His Might.

This phrase is often uttered when facing difficulties that are beyond one's capacity.

Mafhoom al-Hadith (Meaning of Hadith):

Sayyiduna Abdullah bin Abbas (RA) narrates:

The Messenger of Allah (ﷺ) said:

"Whoever faces hardship or stress in life should seek Allah's help with the dhikr:

Laa hawla wa la quwwata illa billahil 'Aliyyil 'Azim."

Also narrated by Abdullah Ibn Abbas (RA):

"The Prophet (ﷺ) said:

'Laa hawla wa la quwwata illa billahil 'Aliyyil 'Azim' is from the treasures of Paradise."

(Bukhari & Muslim)

The following may suggest the translation of the Hadith (mafhoom ul hadith):

The Prophet ﷺ said:

Laa howla wala quwwata illa billa hil 'Aliyyil 'Azeem is a door from among the doors of Paradise. Whoever recites *laa howla wala quwwata illa billah*, an angel descends to bring healing/cure for that person. (Tirmidhi)

The following may suggest the translation of the Hadith (mafhoom ul hadith):

Anas bin Malik (RA) narrates that the Prophet ﷺ said:

Whoever recites **"Bismillaahi wala howla wala quwwata illa billa hil 'Aliyyil 'Azeem"** ten times will be purified from past sins like a newborn baby.

The following may suggest the translation of the Hadith (mafhoom ul hadith):

The Prophet ﷺ said:

Whoever recites **"Bismillaahi wala howla wala quwwata illa billa hil 'Aliyyil 'Azeem"** ten times will be protected from seventy afflictions, hardships, or difficulties in life which descend from the heavens. Even from illnesses such as insanity or madness, one will be protected from these forms of punishment or trials.

The following may suggest the translation of the Hadith (mafhoom ul hadith):

Abu Huraira (RA) narrates that the Prophet ﷺ said:

Recite **la howla wala quwwata illa billa hil 'Aliyyil 'Azeem** frequently, for it is a treasure from Jannah. (Tirmidhi)

The following may suggest the translation of the Hadith (mafhoom ul hadith):

Abu Huraira (RA) narrates that the Prophet ﷺ said:

Whoever recites **la howla wala quwwata illa billa hil 'Aliyyil 'Azeem**, it is a cure for ninety-nine diseases, and the least of them is stress. Recite it at least 100 times daily.

The following may suggest the translation of the Hadith (mafhoom ul hadith):

Abu Musa (RA) narrates that the Prophet ﷺ said:

Whoever recites **la howla wala quwwata illa billa hil 'Aliyyil 'Azeem** 100 times daily will never be dependent on the creation of Allah.

Sayyidul Istighfar is also one of the most beloved forms of dhikr/du'a.

It is the best du'a for seeking forgiveness. If recited in the morning and evening, you will be a resident of Paradise (Bukhari).

اَللّٰهُمَّ أَنْتَ رَبِّي، لَا إِلٰهَ إِلَّا أَنْتَ، خَلَقْتَنِيْ وَأَنَا عَبْدُكَ، وَأَنَا عَلَى عَهْدِكَ وَوَعْدِكَ مَا اسْتَطَعْتُ، أَعُوْذُ بِكَ مِنْ شَرِّ مَا صَنَعْتُ، أَبُوءُ لَكَ بِنِعْمَتِكَ عَلَيَّ وَأَبُوءُ لَكَ بِذَنْبِيْ، فَاغْفِرْ لِيْ، فَإِنَّهُ لَا يَغْفِرُ الذُّنُوْبَ إِلَّاأَنْتَ.

"Allah, You are my Lord. There is no god but You. You created me and I am Your servant, and I am committed to Your covenant and promise as best I can. I seek refuge in You from the evil of what I have done. I acknowledge Your favour upon me and I acknowledge my sin, so forgive me, for no one forgives sins except You."

Shaddad bin Aus (RA) said:

Our Prophet ﷺ said:

"The best supplication for seeking forgiveness is Sayyidul Istighfar."

If anyone recites this du'a in his own language, he may do so without hesitation. The English translation is:

O Allah! You are my Lord. There is no true deity except You. You created me, and I am Your servant. I hold to Your covenant as best as I can. I seek refuge in You from the evil of what I have done. I acknowledge the favours You have bestowed upon me and confess my sins. Forgive me, for none forgives sins except You.

This du'a is so powerful that whoever recites it during the day with firm belief in it and dies on the same day (before evening) will be one of the dwellers of Paradise. And if he recites it sincerely during the night and dies before morning, he will also be among the dwellers of Paradise. [Al-Bukhari]

Another Important Du'a for Regular Zakireen:

La ilaha illa anta subhanaka inni kuntu minaz-zalimin

لَّا إِلَهَ إِلَّا أَنتَ سُبْحَٰنَكَ إِنِّى كُنتُ مِنَ ٱلظَّٰلِمِينَ

"None has the right to be worshipped but You (O Allah), Glorified and Exalted are You. Truly, I have been of the wrongdoers."

This was recited by Prophet Yunus (AS) when he was alone in the darkness inside the belly of the whale. In the Qur'an, it says that because he recited this du'a, he was relieved of his burden.

"O ye that believe! Remember Allah with much remembrance; and glorify Him morning and evening."

— Al-Ahzab 33:41

Ayat al-Kursi

اللَّهُ لَا إِلَٰهَ إِلَّا هُوَ الْحَيُّ الْقَيُّومُ ۚ لَا تَأْخُذُهُ سِنَةٌ وَلَا نَوْمٌ ۚ لَّهُ مَا فِي السَّمَاوَاتِ وَمَا فِي الْأَرْضِ ۗ مَن ذَا الَّذِي يَشْفَعُ عِندَهُ إِلَّا بِإِذْنِهِ ۚ يَعْلَمُ مَا بَيْنَ أَيْدِيهِمْ وَمَا خَلْفَهُمْ ۖ وَلَا يُحِيطُونَ بِشَيْءٍ مِّنْ عِلْمِهِ إِلَّا بِمَا شَاءَ ۚ وَسِعَ كُرْسِيُّهُ السَّمَاوَاتِ وَالْأَرْضَ ۖ وَلَا يَئُودُهُ حِفْظُهُمَا ۚ وَهُوَ الْعَلِيُّ الْعَظِيمُ

"God is our refuge and strength, a very present help in trouble.

Therefore will not we fear, though the earth be removed,

and though the mountains be carried into the midst of the sea."

— Psalm 46:1–2 (KJV)

"Allah! There is no god but He, the Living, the Self-subsisting, Eternal. Slumber does not overtake Him, nor does sleep. To Him belongs all that is in the heavens and the earth. Who is it that can intercede with Him except by His permission? He knows what is before them and what is behind them, and they cannot encompass anything of His knowledge except what He wills. His Throne extends over the heavens and the earth, and He feels no fatigue in guarding and preserving them. And He is the Most High, the Supreme."

— Surah Al-Baqarah 2:255

Abu Hurairah (RA) narrated:

In Surah Al-Baqarah, there is an ayah that is the best of all the verses of the Qur'an. It is never recited in a house except that Satan leaves it: Ayat al-Kursi.

Abu Umamah Al-Bahili (RA) reported:

The Prophet ﷺ said:

"The one who recites it after each of the obligatory prayers, death will be the only thing preventing him from entering Paradise." [Ibn Sunni, Ibn Hibban]

Everything has its pinnacle, and the pinnacle of the Qur'an is Surah Al-Baqarah. In it, there is an ayah that is the greatest in the Qur'an: Ayat al-Kursi. [Tirmidhi]

The Prophet ﷺ said:

"By reciting it (Ayat al-Kursi), there will be a guardian appointed over you by Allah who will protect you during the night, and Satan will not be able to come near you until morning." [Al-Bukhari]

Hazrat Ibn Mas'ood (RA) narrated:

A man once asked the Prophet ﷺ to teach him something beneficial. The Prophet ﷺ said:

"Recite Ayat al-Kursi—it will protect you, your children, your home, and even the neighbouring houses."

Abu Huraira (RA) reported:

The Prophet ﷺ assigned me to guard the Zakat revenue of Ramadan. Someone came and started stealing food. I caught him and said, *"I will take you to the Messenger of Allah!"*

He pleaded, *"Please don't take me to the Prophet, and I will teach you something by which Allah will benefit you."*

He said, *"When you go to bed, recite Ayat al-Kursi, for then Allah will appoint a guardian over you and no Satan will approach you till dawn."*

When the Prophet ﷺ heard this, he said,

"He told you the truth, though he is a liar. That was Satan." [Sahih Al-Bukhari]

From the above Hadith, it is clear that the recitation of this verse of the Holy Qur'an protects us from Satan, our worst enemy. Every Muslim should learn and recite this verse to seek the protection of Allah and shield themselves from the tricks of Shaytan.

Ayatul Kursi Benefits

Surely, the Surah which is the leader of the Qur'an and full of benefits is Surah Al-Baqarah. Some of the benefits of the greatest Ayatul Kursi are as follows:

1 – For Protection

Recitation of this verse in the morning will keep you under the protection of Allah until night. Its recitation also keeps your family and wealth safe from Satan.

2 – For Weak Memory

The recitation of this verse is highly beneficial for those with weak memory. To increase your memory, recite this leading verse regularly.

3 – For Loved Ones Who Have Died

Recite this verse for your loved ones who have passed away. It will be a source of light for them in the darkness of their graves.

4 – For the Pain of Death

To be protected from the pain of death, you must recite this powerful verse regularly. Its recitation will ease the experience of dying and make death easier.

5 – When Leaving Home

Always recite this verse when leaving your home. Its recitation will place you under the protection of the angels.

6 – Before Going to Bed

Whoever recites Ayatul Kursi before sleeping is under Allah's protection throughout the night. Allah will also protect not only the person but also their neighbour's home from the devil.

7 – For Any Kind of Fear

If you are uneasy or feel any kind of fear, recite this verse. It will remove all fears and bring calm.

8 – For Acceptance of Du'a

Reciting this verse after prayer becomes a means for the acceptance of your du'a. With this in mind, make it a habit to recite Ayatul Kursi after every prayer.

9 – Equal to the Qur'an

One who recites Ayatul Kursi four times will receive the reward of reading the entire Qur'an.

10 – 70,000 Angels Protect You

Recite this verse when leaving your home, and 70,000 angels will be appointed to protect you.

11 – For Poverty

Whoever recites Ayatul Kursi upon entering their home, poverty will not enter that home.

12 – After Wudu

Whoever recites this verse after performing wudu will be raised seventy times in Allah's ranks.

13 – Protection from the Devil

Whoever recites this verse daily will surely enter Paradise. Regular recitation ensures protection from the devil and his mischief.

Shaykh al-Islam Ibn Taymiyyah (رحمه الله) said:

"It is permissible to make du'a in Arabic and in languages other than Arabic. Allah knows the intention of the supplicant and what he wants, no matter what language he speaks, because He hears all the voices in all different languages, asking for all kinds of needs."

Majmoo' al-Fataawa, 22/488-489

The Virtue of Seeking Forgiveness (Istighfar)

Ibn 'Abbas (رضي الله عنه) said:

The Messenger of Allah (ﷺ) said:

"If anyone constantly seeks pardon (from Allah), Allah will appoint for him a way out of every distress, a relief from every anxiety, and will provide sustenance for him from where he expects not."

[Abu Dawud, Hadith 1873]

Keep seeking forgiveness from Allah sincerely.

Istighfar Provides Sustenance

The Prophet (ﷺ) said:

"If anyone constantly seeks pardon (from Allah), Allah will appoint for him a way out of every distress, a relief from every anxiety, and will provide sustenance for him from where he expects not."

(Abu Dawud, Hadith 1873)

Recite different du'as of forgiveness, even if it is simply saying **'Astaghfirullah'** with pure intention. The solutions to your problems can be found in constant repentance, *insha'Allah*.

The Prophet (ﷺ) termed the following supplication as the best manner of seeking forgiveness:

"O Allah! You are my Lord. There is no true God except You. You created me, and I am Your servant, and I hold to Your covenant as best I can. I seek refuge in You from the evil of what I have done. I acknowledge Your favours upon me, and I confess my sins to You. So forgive me, for surely none forgives sins but You."

(Sahih al-Bukhari, 6306)

Morning and Evening Supplications

Ibn 'Umar (رضي الله عنه) mentioned that the Prophet (ﷺ) prescribed morning and evening supplications.

"O Allah, I ask You for forgiveness and well-being in this world and in the Hereafter. O Allah, I ask You for forgiveness and well-being in my religious and worldly affairs. O Allah, conceal my faults, calm my fears, and protect me from in front of me and behind me, from my right and my left, and from above me. And I seek refuge in You from being taken unaware from beneath me."

(Ibn Majah, 3871)

This supplication was taught by the Prophet (ﷺ) to Abu Bakr al-Siddiq (رضي الله عنه):

"O Allah! I have wronged my soul greatly, and none forgives sins but You. So forgive me with Your forgiveness. Surely, You are the Most Forgiving, Most Merciful."

(Sahih al-Bukhari, 6326)

The Prophet (ﷺ) said:

"Whoever makes Istighfar frequently, Allah (SWT) will provide a way for him out of every distress and provide for him from sources he could never expect."

(Abu Dawud, 1518)

"Istighfar" means to ask Allah for protection from the evil consequences and harmful effects of one's sins and misdeeds, both in this world and the Hereafter. "Astaghfirullah" literally means:

"I seek forgiveness from Allah."

Du'a of Laylat al-Qadr

This is the special du'a the Prophet (ﷺ) taught Aisha (رضي الله عنها) to say on the Night of Qadr:

"O Allah, indeed You are Pardoning and Generous. You love to pardon, so pardon me."

(Al-Tirmidhi, 3513)

Rabbana Duas

1.

رَبَّنَا لَا تُزِغْ قُلُوبَنَا بَعْدَ إِذْ هَدَيْتَنَا وَهَبْ لَنَا مِن لَّدُنكَ رَحْمَةً ۚ إِنَّكَ أَنتَ الْوَهَّابُ

"Our Lord! Let not our hearts deviate (from the truth) after You have guided us, and grant us mercy from You. Truly, You are the Bestower."

2.

مِنَ الْبَيْتِ وَإِسْمَاعِيلُ رَبَّنَا تَقَبَّلْ مِنَّا ۖ إِنَّكَ أَنتَ السَّمِيعُ الْعَلِيمُ وَإِذْ يَرْفَعُ إِبْرَاهِيمُ الْقَوَاعِدَ
رَبَّنَا وَاجْعَلْنَا مُسْلِمَيْنِ لَكَ وَمِن ذُرِّيَّتِنَا أُمَّةً مُسْلِمَةً لَّكَ وَأَرِنَا مَنَاسِكَنَا وَتُبْ عَلَيْنَا ۖ إِنَّكَ أَنتَ
التَّوَّابُ الرَّحِيمُ

"Our Lord! Accept [this service] from us. Verily, You are the All-Hearer, the All-Knower."

"Our Lord! And make us submissive unto You, and of our offspring a nation submissive unto You. Show us our rites [of worship], and turn unto us in mercy. Truly, You are the One Who accepts repentance, the Most Merciful."

(Surah Al-Baqarah 2:127–128)

3.

قَالُوا رَبَّنَا أَفْرِغْ عَلَيْنَا صَبْرًا وَثَبِّتْ أَقْدَامَنَا وَانصُرْنَا عَلَى الْقَوْمِ وَلَمَّا بَرَزُوا لِجَالُوتَ وَجُنُودِهِ
الْكَافِرِينَ

"Our Lord! Pour forth on us patience, make our steps firm, and give us victory over the disbelieving people."

(Surah Al-Baqarah 2:250)

Note: The story of Jalut (Goliath) and the life of Dawood عليه السلام *is detailed in Chapter 11 of* **Icebreake**.

4.

لَا يُكَلِّفُ اللَّهُ نَفْسًا إِلَّا وُسْعَهَا ۚ لَهَا مَا كَسَبَتْ وَعَلَيْهَا مَا اكْتَسَبَتْ ۗ رَبَّنَا لَا تُؤَاخِذْنَا إِن نَّسِينَا أَوْ
أَخْطَأْنَا ۚ رَبَّنَا وَلَا تَحْمِلْ عَلَيْنَا إِصْرًا كَمَا حَمَلْتَهُ عَلَى الَّذِينَ مِن قَبْلِنَا ۚ رَبَّنَا وَلَا تُحَمِّلْنَا مَا لَا
طَاقَةَ لَنَا بِهِ ۖ وَاعْفُ عَنَّا وَاغْفِرْ لَنَا وَارْحَمْنَا ۚ أَنتَ مَوْلَانَا فَانصُرْنَا عَلَى الْقَوْمِ الْكَافِرِينَ

Allah burdens not a person beyond his scope. He gets reward for that (good) which he has earned, and he is punished for that (evil) which he has earned. ""Our Lord! Punish us not if we forget or fall into error. Our Lord! Lay not on us a burden like that which You laid on those before us. Our Lord! Put not on us a burden greater than we have strength to bear. Pardon us, forgive us, and have mercy upon us. You are our Protector, so give us victory over the disbelieving people."

(Surah Al-Baqarah 2:286)

5.

لِيَوْمٍ لَّا رَيْبَ فِيهِ ۚ إِنَّ اللَّهَ لَا يُخْلِفُ الْمِيعَادَ رَبَّنَا إِنَّكَ جَامِعُ النَّاسِ

"Our Lord! Verily, it is You Who will gather mankind together on a Day about which there is no doubt. Verily, Allah never breaks His Promise."

(Surah Ale-Imran 3:09)

6

الَّذِينَ يَقُولُونَ رَبَّنَا إِنَّنَا آمَنَّا فَاغْفِرْ لَنَا ذُنُوبَنَا وَقِنَا عَذَابَ النَّارِ

Those who say: "Our Lord! We have indeed believed, so forgive us our sins and save us from the punishment of the Fire."

(3:16, Surah Ale-Imran)

7

رَبَّنَا آمَنَّا بِمَا أَنزَلْتَ وَاتَّبَعْنَا الرَّسُولَ فَاكْتُبْنَا مَعَ الشَّاهِدِينَ

Our Lord! We believe in what Thou hast sent down, and we follow the Messenger ['Isa (Jesus)]; so write us down among those who bear witness.

(3:53, Surah Ale-Imran)

8

وَمَا كَانَ قَوْلَهُمْ إِلَّا أَن قَالُوا رَبَّنَا اغْفِرْ لَنَا ذُنُوبَنَا وَإِسْرَافَنَا فِي أَمْرِنَا وَثَبِّتْ أَقْدَامَنَا وَانصُرْنَا عَلَى الْقَوْمِ الْكَافِرِينَ

And they said nothing but: "Our Lord! Forgive us our sins and our transgressions in our affairs, make firm our steps, and grant us victory over the disbelieving people."

(3:147, Surah Ale-Imran)

9

الَّذِينَ يَذْكُرُونَ اللَّهَ قِيَامًا وَقُعُودًا وَعَلَىٰ جُنُوبِهِمْ وَيَتَفَكَّرُونَ فِي خَلْقِ السَّمَاوَاتِ وَالْأَرْضِ رَبَّنَا مَا خَلَقْتَ هَٰذَا بَاطِلًا سُبْحَانَكَ فَقِنَا عَذَابَ النَّا

رَبَّنَا إِنَّكَ مَن تُدْخِلِ النَّارَ فَقَدْ أَخْزَيْتَهُ ۖ وَمَا لِلظَّالِمِينَ مِنْ أَنصَارٍ

رَّبَّنَا إِنَّنَا سَمِعْنَا مُنَادِيًا يُنَادِي لِلْإِيمَانِ أَنْ آمِنُوا بِرَبِّكُمْ فَآمَنَّا ۚ رَبَّنَا فَاغْفِرْ لَنَا ذُنُوبَنَا وَكَفِّرْ عَنَّا سَيِّئَاتِنَا وَتَوَفَّنَا مَعَ الْأَبْرَارِ

رَبَّنَا وَآتِنَا مَا وَعَدتَّنَا عَلَىٰ رُسُلِكَ وَلَا تُخْزِنَا يَوْمَ الْقِيَامَةِ ۗ إِنَّكَ لَا تُخْلِفُ الْمِيعَادَ

Those who remember Allah while standing, sitting, and lying on their sides, and reflect on the creation of the heavens and the earth, (saying): "Our Lord! Thou hast not created this in vain. Glory be to Thee; save us from the punishment of the Fire.

Our Lord! Verily, whom Thou causest to enter the Fire, him hast Thou indeed brought to disgrace. And the wrongdoers shall have no helpers.

Our Lord! Verily, we have heard the call of one calling to faith, saying, 'Believe in your Lord,' and we have believed. Our Lord! Forgive us our sins, remit from us our evil deeds, and make us die among the righteous.

Our Lord! Grant us what Thou hast promised unto us through Thine Apostles, and disgrace us not on the Day of Resurrection. Verily, Thou breakest not Thy promise."

(3:191–194, Surah Ale-Imran)

10

قَالَ عِيسَى ابْنُ مَرْيَمَ اللَّهُمَّ رَبَّنَا أَنزِلْ عَلَيْنَا مَائِدَةً مِّنَ السَّمَاءِ تَكُونُ لَنَا عِيدًا لِّأَوَّلِنَا وَآخِرِنَا وَآيَةً مِّنكَ ۖ وَارْزُقْنَا وَأَنتَ خَيْرُ الرَّازِقِينَ

'Isa (Jesus), son of Maryam (Mary), said: "O Allah, our Lord! Send down to us a table spread with food from heaven, that it may be a feast for us—for the first and the last of us—and a sign from Thee; and provide for us, for Thou art the Best of providers."

(5:114, Surah Al-Ma'idah)

11

وَإِذَا سَمِعُوا مَا أُنزِلَ إِلَى الرَّسُولِ تَرَىٰ أَعْيُنَهُمْ تَفِيضُ مِنَ الدَّمْعِ مِمَّا عَرَفُوا مِنَ الْحَقِّ ۖ يَقُولُونَ رَبَّنَا آمَنَّا فَاكْتُبْنَا مَعَ الشَّاهِدِينَ

And when they hear what hath been revealed unto the Messenger, thou seest their eyes overflowing with tears for the truth they have recognised. They say: "Our Lord! We believe; write us down among the witnesses."

(5:83, Surah Al-Ma'idah)

12

قَالَا رَبَّنَا ظَلَمْنَا أَنفُسَنَا وَإِن لَّمْ تَغْفِرْ لَنَا وَتَرْحَمْنَا لَنَكُونَنَّ مِنَ الْخَاسِرِينَ

They said: "Our Lord! We have wronged ourselves. If Thou forgive us not and have mercy on us, we shall surely be among the losers."

(7:23, Surah Al-A'raf)

13

وَإِذَا صُرِفَتْ أَبْصَارُهُمْ تِلْقَاءَ أَصْحَابِ النَّارِ قَالُوا رَبَّنَا لَا تَجْعَلْنَا مَعَ الْقَوْمِ الظَّالِمِينَ

And when their eyes are turned towards the dwellers of the Fire, they say: "Our Lord! Place us not with the people who are unjust."

(7:47, Surah Al-A'raf)

14

دِ افْتَرَيْنَا عَلَى اللَّهِ كَذِبًا إِنْ عُدْنَا فِي مِلَّتِكُم بَعْدَ إِذْ نَجَّانَا اللَّهُ مِنْهَا ۚ وَمَا يَكُونُ لَنَا أَن نَّعُودَ فِيهَا إِلَّا أَن يَشَاءَ اللَّهُ رَبُّنَا ۚ وَسِعَ رَبُّنَا كُلَّ شَيْءٍ عِلْمًا ۚ عَلَى اللَّهِ تَوَكَّلْنَا ۚ رَبَّنَا افْتَحْ بَيْنَنَا وَبَيْنَ قَوْمِنَا بِالْحَقِّ وَأَنتَ خَيْرُ الْفَاتِحِينَ

""We should have indeed fabricated a lie against Allah if we returned to your religion after Allah hath delivered us from it. And it is not for us to return to it unless Allah our Lord should so will. Our Lord comprehendeth all things in knowledge. In Allah do we put our trust. Our Lord! Judge between us and our people in truth, for Thou art the Best of judges."

(7:89, Surah Al-A'raf)

15

وَمَا تَنقِمُ مِنَّا إِلَّا أَنْ آمَنَّا بِآيَاتِ رَبِّنَا لَمَّا جَاءَتْنَا ۚ رَبَّنَا أَفْرِغْ عَلَيْنَا صَبْرًا وَتَوَفَّنَا مُسْلِمِينَ

"And you take vengeance on us only because we believed in the signs of our Lord when they came unto us. Our Lord! Pour upon us patience and cause us to die as Muslims."

(7:126, Surah Al-A'raf)

16

فَقَالُوا عَلَى اللَّهِ تَوَكَّلْنَا رَبَّنَا لَا تَجْعَلْنَا فِتْنَةً لِّلْقَوْمِ الظَّالِمِينَ

وَنَجِّنَا بِرَحْمَتِكَ مِنَ الْقَوْمِ الْكَافِرِينَ

They said: "In Allah we put our trust. Our Lord! Make us not a trial for the wrongdoing folk, and save us, through Thy mercy, from the disbelieving people."

(10:85–86, Surah Yunus)

17

رَبَّنَا إِنَّكَ تَعْلَمُ مَا نُخْفِي وَمَا نُعْلِنُ ۗ وَمَا يَخْفَىٰ عَلَى اللَّهِ مِن شَيْءٍ فِي الْأَرْضِ وَلَا فِي السَّمَاءِ

"O our Lord! Verily, Thou knowest what we conceal and what we reveal. And nothing is hidden from Allah in the earth or in the heaven."

(14:38, Surah Ibrahim)

18

رَبِّ اجْعَلْنِي مُقِيمَ الصَّلَاةِ وَمِن ذُرِّيَّتِي ۚ رَبَّنَا وَتَقَبَّلْ دُعَاءِ

بَّنَا اغْفِرْ لِي وَلِوَالِدَيَّ وَلِلْمُؤْمِنِينَ يَوْمَ يَقُومُ الْحِسَابُ

"O my Lord! Make me one who establisheth prayer, and also from my offspring. Our Lord! Accept my supplication.

Our Lord! Forgive me, and my parents, and the believers, on the Day when the account shall be established."

(14:40–41, Surah Ibrahim)

19

إِذْ أَوَى الْفِتْيَةُ إِلَى الْكَهْفِ فَقَالُوا رَبَّنَا آتِنَا مِن لَّدُنكَ رَحْمَةً وَهَيِّئْ لَنَا مِنْ أَمْرِنَا رَشَدًا

(Remember) when the young men took refuge in the Cave, they said: "Our Lord! Bestow upon us mercy from Thyself, and provide for us guidance in our affair."

(18:10, Surah Al-Kahf)

Note: Background of the Cave story can be found in Chapter 15, "Place of Waiting."

20

قَالَا رَبَّنَا إِنَّنَا نَخَافُ أَن يَفْرُطَ عَلَيْنَا أَوْ أَن يَطْغَىٰ

They said: "Our Lord! Verily, we fear lest he should act hastily against us or transgress the bounds."

(20:45, Surah Ta-Ha)

21

إِنَّهُ كَانَ فَرِيقٌ مِّنْ عِبَادِي يَقُولُونَ رَبَّنَا آمَنَّا فَاغْفِرْ لَنَا وَارْحَمْنَا وَأَنتَ خَيْرُ الرَّاحِمِينَ

Verily, there was a party of My servants who used to say: "Our Lord! We believe, so forgive us, and have mercy on us, for Thou art the Best of those who show mercy."

Surah Al-Mu'minun (The Believers) 23:109

22

وَالَّذِينَ يَقُولُونَ رَبَّنَا اصْرِفْ عَنَّا عَذَابَ جَهَنَّمَ ۖ إِنَّ عَذَابَهَا كَانَ غَرَامًا

إِنَّهَا سَاءَتْ مُسْتَقَرًّا وَمُقَامًا

And those who say: "Our Lord! Avert from us the torment of Hell. Verily, its torment is an inseparable, permanent punishment."

"Evil indeed it (Hell) is as a dwelling place and as a place to remain."

Surah Al-Furqan (The Criterion) 25:65–66

23

وَالَّذِينَ يَقُولُونَ رَبَّنَا هَبْ لَنَا مِنْ أَزْوَاجِنَا وَذُرِّيَّاتِنَا قُرَّةَ أَعْيُنٍ وَاجْعَلْنَا لِلْمُتَّقِينَ إِمَامًا

And those who say: "Our Lord! Grant unto us wives and offspring who will be the comfort of our eyes, and make us leaders of the righteous."

Surah Al-Furqan 25:74

24

وَقَالُوا الْحَمْدُ لِلَّهِ الَّذِي أَذْهَبَ عَنَّا الْحَزَنَ ۖ إِنَّ رَبَّنَا لَغَفُورٌ شَكُورٌ

And they shall say: "Praise be to Allah, who hath removed from us (all) sorrow: for our Lord is indeed Oft-Forgiving, Most Appreciative."

Surah Fatir or Al-Mala'ikah (The Originator or The Angels) 35:34

25

الَّذِينَ يَحْمِلُونَ الْعَرْشَ وَمَنْ حَوْلَهُ يُسَبِّحُونَ بِحَمْدِ رَبِّهِمْ وَيُؤْمِنُونَ بِهِ وَيَسْتَغْفِرُونَ لِلَّذِينَ آمَنُوا رَبَّنَا وَسِعْتَ كُلَّ شَيْءٍ رَّحْمَةً وَعِلْمًا فَاغْفِرْ لِلَّذِينَ تَابُوا وَاتَّبَعُوا سَبِيلَكَ وَقِهِمْ عَذَابَ الْجَحِيمِ

رَبَّنَا وَأَدْخِلْهُمْ جَنَّاتِ عَدْنٍ الَّتِي وَعَدتَّهُمْ وَمَن صَلَحَ مِنْ آبَائِهِمْ وَأَزْوَاجِهِمْ وَذُرِّيَّاتِهِمْ ۚ إِنَّكَ أَنتَ الْعَزِيزُ الْحَكِيمُ

وَقِهِمُ السَّيِّئَاتِ ۚ وَمَن تَقِ السَّيِّئَاتِ يَوْمَئِذٍ فَقَدْ رَحِمْتَهُ ۚ وَذَٰلِكَ هُوَ الْفَوْزُ الْعَظِيمُ

Those (angels) who bear the Throne (of Allah) and those around it glorify the praises of their Lord, and believe in Him, and ask forgiveness for those who believe, saying:

"Our Lord! You encompass all things in mercy and knowledge. Forgive those who repent and follow Your way, and protect them from the torment of the blazing Fire.

Our Lord! Admit them into the Gardens of Eternity which You have promised them, and also the righteous among their fathers, their spouses, and their offspring. Verily, You are the Almighty, the All-Wise.

And save them from evil deeds; and whomsoever You save from evil deeds that Day, him verily have You granted mercy. And that is the supreme success."

Surah Ghafir or Al-Mu'min (The Forgiver or The Believer) 40:7–9

26

وَالَّذِينَ جَاءُوا مِن بَعْدِهِمْ يَقُولُونَ رَبَّنَا اغْفِرْ لَنَا وَلِإِخْوَانِنَا الَّذِينَ سَبَقُونَا بِالْإِيمَانِ وَلَا تَجْعَلْ فِي قُلُوبِنَا غِلًّا لِّلَّذِينَ آمَنُوا رَبَّنَا إِنَّكَ رَءُوفٌ رَّحِيمٌ

And those who come after them say: "Our Lord! Forgive us and our brethren who preceded us in faith, and put not in our hearts any hatred against those who have believed. Our Lord! Surely, You are Kind and Merciful."

Surah Al-Hashr (The Gathering) 59:10

27

قَدْ كَانَتْ لَكُمْ أُسْوَةٌ حَسَنَةٌ فِي إِبْرَاهِيمَ وَالَّذِينَ مَعَهُ إِذْ قَالُوا لِقَوْمِهِمْ إِنَّا بُرَآءُ مِنكُمْ وَمِمَّا تَعْبُدُونَ مِن دُونِ اللَّهِ كَفَرْنَا بِكُمْ وَبَدَا بَيْنَنَا وَبَيْنَكُمُ الْعَدَاوَةُ وَالْبَغْضَاءُ أَبَدًا حَتَّىٰ تُؤْمِنُوا بِاللَّهِ وَحْدَهُ إِلَّا قَوْلَ إِبْرَاهِيمَ لِأَبِيهِ لَأَسْتَغْفِرَنَّ لَكَ وَمَا أَمْلِكُ لَكَ مِنَ اللَّهِ مِن شَيْءٍ ۖ رَبَّنَا عَلَيْكَ تَوَكَّلْنَا وَإِلَيْكَ أَنَبْنَا وَإِلَيْكَ الْمَصِيرُ

رَبَّنَا لَا تَجْعَلْنَا فِتْنَةً لِّلَّذِينَ كَفَرُوا وَاغْفِرْ لَنَا رَبَّنَا ۖ إِنَّكَ أَنتَ الْعَزِيزُ الْحَكِيمُ

Indeed, you have an excellent example in Abraham and those with him when they said to their people: "Verily, we are free from you and from whatever you worship besides Allah. We have rejected you, and there has arisen between us and you enmity and hatred for ever – until you believe in Allah alone."

Except the saying of Abraham to his father: "Surely, I will ask forgiveness for you, but I have no power to help you against Allah."

"Our Lord! In You we put our trust, and to You we turn in repentance, and to You is the final return.

Our Lord! Make us not a trial for the disbelievers, and forgive us, our Lord! Verily, You alone are the All-Mighty, the All-Wise."

Surah Al-Mumtahinah (The Woman to be Examined) 60:4–5

28

يَا أَيُّهَا الَّذِينَ آمَنُوا تُوبُوا إِلَى اللَّهِ تَوْبَةً نَّصُوحًا عَسَىٰ رَبُّكُمْ أَن يُكَفِّرَ عَنكُمْ سَيِّئَاتِكُمْ وَيُدْخِلَكُمْ جَنَّاتٍ تَجْرِي مِن تَحْتِهَا الْأَنْهَارُ يَوْمَ لَا يُخْزِي اللَّهُ النَّبِيَّ وَالَّذِينَ آمَنُوا مَعَهُ ۖ نُورُهُمْ يَسْعَىٰ بَيْنَ أَيْدِيهِمْ وَبِأَيْمَانِهِمْ يَقُولُونَ رَبَّنَا أَتْمِمْ لَنَا نُورَنَا وَاغْفِرْ لَنَا ۖ إِنَّكَ عَلَىٰ كُلِّ شَيْءٍ قَدِيرٌ

O ye who believe! Turn to Allah with sincere repentance. It may be that your Lord will remit your sins and admit you into Gardens beneath which rivers flow – the Day that Allah will not disgrace the Prophet and those who believe with him. Their light will run before them and in their right hands, and they shall say:

"Our Lord! Perfect our light for us, and forgive us: for Thou hast power over all things."

Surah At-Tahrim (The Prohibition) 66:8

Conclusion

I hope this chapter encourages us to reassess our situation by considering the consequences we may eventually face. May the prayers mentioned guide you back, set you on the right path, and inspire you to embark on this journey with unwavering determination.

My Prayer

بسم الله الرحمن الرحيم

- O Allah, I seek forgiveness for every sin I have committed. O Allah, You know my inner and outer state, from the beginning until today. O Allah, show Your mercy.

- O Allah, forgive me for not fulfilling the promises I made to myself but did not put into effect.

- O Allah, protect me from evil influences coming from in front of me, from behind, and from above.

- We seek refuge under Your protection. We seek refuge under Your protection. O Allah, we seek Your forgiveness and well-being in this world and the Hereafter.

- O Allah, we seek protection in the perfect words of Allah from every evil that has been created. O Allah, we seek refuge in You from all evil diseases. O Allah, grant us a life of true peace and allow us to enter the House of Peace.

- O Glorious and Beneficent, cleanse my heart—my *qalb*—of everything other than You, and place me in Your hands as a faithful servant. O Allah, to You belongs all praise! I bear witness that there is no god but You.

- Condemn us not if we forget or fall into error. O Allah! Lay not on us a burden greater than we have strength to bear. Have mercy on us. You are our protector. Help us against those who reject faith. *(Adapted from Qur'an 2:286)*

- O Allah, I seek refuge in You from the evil of my hearing, the evil of my sight, the evil of my tongue, the evil of my heart, and the evil of my affairs.

- O Allah! Grant my soul its sense of dutifulness (*taqwaa*) and purify it. You are the One to purify it: You are its Guardian and its Lord. O Allah! I seek refuge in You from knowledge that does not benefit, from a heart that is not humble, from a soul that is never satisfied, and from a supplication that is not answered.

- O Allah, rectify my heart and my actions. O Allah, Turner of the hearts, turn our hearts towards Your obedience. Give light in my heart, light in my sight, light on my right hand, light on my left hand, light in my feelings, light before me, and light behind me.

- O Allah, make firm my intention to obey You. Strengthen my insight in worshipping You. O Allah, grant me success in deeds that will wash away the defilement of my offences.

- O Allah, give us strength for this challenging time. We pray for Your love, compassion, and protection as we walk through this trial. We pray for those who are suffering.

- O Allah, heal those who suffer from long-term chronic illnesses and underlying health concerns. For the children who have been orphaned—O Allah, give them Your shelter and allow them to be established in life.
- O Allah, allow me to listen to others without passing judgment or rushing to fix what I cannot change. Grant me patience, understanding, and grace with my own faults.
- O Allah! Direct me to the Right Path and make me steadfast upon it. Please grant me the ability to do all things in the proper manner.
- O Allah, indeed, You are the Most Merciful of the merciful. Bless our parents, our relatives, our friends, and our children.
- O Allah, keep us healthy in this difficult moment. Protect us from every danger. O Allah, be with those who have passed away due to the virus.
- O Allah, relieve us! O Allah, relieve us! O Allah, relieve us! Grant us blessings from the sky and cause blessings to grow from the earth.
- O Allah, please send Your blessings and grant peace upon our Prophet Muhammad ﷺ, his family, and all his companions. O Allah, be pleased with the Rightly Guided Caliphs—Abu Bakr, Umar, Uthman, and Ali—and all their noble companions.
- Our Lord! Let not our hearts deviate after You have guided us, and grant us mercy from You. Truly, You are the Bestower. *(Adapted from Qur'an 3:8)*
- *My Lord, I seek refuge in Thee from the whisperings of the devils. (King James Version, Psalm 64:2: "Hide me from the secret counsel of the wicked; from the insurrection of the workers of iniquity.")*
- *Our Lord, forgive me and my parents, and the believers, on the Day when the reckoning shall come to pass. (Adapted from Qur'an 14:41)*
- O Allah, we, as a party of Your servants, desire to go to our home in Jannatul Firdaus.
- O Allah, do not despise our pleas—we are being tested by You. O Allah, help us to remain on the straight path during this journey, and allow us to pass Your test at the moment of departure from this stage of life.
- O Allah, do not despise our pleas—we are under Your test—allow us to pass it, O Allah.

اللهم لا تحتقر مناشداتنا ـ نحن في امتحانك ـ اسمح لنا باجتياز امتحانك يا الله.

Allah, protect us.

Amen

بِسْمِ ٱللَّهِ ٱلرَّحْمَـٰنِ ٱلرَّحِيمِ

Chapter 14

"If light is in your heart,
You will find your way home"

When Journey Is Nearing Its End

As humans, our constant fear arises when we venture beyond the boundaries of this beautiful world. However, we can find solace in the existence of other worlds, revealing that there is a single reality with two different paths. One path is materially attractive—where we currently stand—while the other is eternally spiritual, leading us to heaven.

Beliefs about the existence of different worlds and paths are deeply personal. It is up to individuals to explore their own spiritual and philosophical beliefs to find comfort and meaning in the face of such existential concerns.

Muslim beliefs consist of **Faith (Iman)**, **Islam**, and **Ihsan**. All higher-ranking believers, especially those who attain **Ihsan**, follow the same path as common believers. Ihsan is regarded as the highest status in the Islamic faith. Our Prophet Muhammad ﷺ confirmed this when he said:

"To worship Allah as if you see Him, and if you do not see Him, (know that) He sees you."

Another meaning of Ihsan is **Muhsin**, referring to the one who is certain that Allah is watching them in everything they say or do in their life.

The following hadith provides a clear understanding for the gathered crowds at the end of their journey in this material world, eagerly awaiting entry into the next realm. It serves as a guiding light for their continued journey towards their eternal home in the City of Heaven.

The Hadith of Jibril

This hadith was narrated on the authority of Umar (may Allah be pleased with him), who said:

While we were one day sitting with the Messenger of Allah ﷺ, there appeared before us a man dressed in extremely white clothes and with very black hair. No traces of journeying were visible on him, and none of us knew him. He sat down close by the Prophet ﷺ, rested his knees against his thighs, and said:

504

"O Muhammad! Inform me about Islam."

The Messenger of Allah ﷺ said:

"Islam is that you should testify that there is no deity except Allah and that Muhammad is His Messenger; that you should perform salah, pay the zakah, fast during Ramadan, and perform Hajj to the House if you are able to do so."

The man said, "You have spoken truly."

We were astonished at his questioning the Messenger and then confirming that he was right, but he went on to say:

"Inform me about Iman."

He (the Messenger of Allah ﷺ) answered:

"It is that you believe in Allah, His angels, His Books, His Messengers, the Last Day, and in qadar (divine decree), both in its good and evil aspects."

He said, "You have spoken truly."

Then he said:

"Inform me about Ihsan."

He (the Messenger of Allah ﷺ) answered:

"It is that you should serve Allah as though you see Him, for though you do not see Him, surely He sees you."

He said, "Inform me about the Hour."

He (the Messenger of Allah ﷺ) said:

"About that, the one questioned knows no more than the questioner."

So he said: "Well then, inform me about its signs."

He said:

"They are that the slave-girl will give birth to her mistress; that you will see the barefooted, naked, destitute shepherds of sheep competing in constructing lofty buildings."

Thereupon the man left. I waited a while, and then the Messenger of Allah ﷺ said:

"O Umar, do you know who that questioner was?"

I replied, "Allah and His Messenger know best."

He said:

"That was Jibril (the Angel Gabriel). He came to teach you your religion."

Interpretation of "The Hour"

Here, the Prophet ﷺ is explaining that the knowledge of the Hour is something that Allah ﷻ keeps to Himself. It is part of the **ghayb** (the unseen). This is an essential lesson—because it does not matter when the Day of Judgment is. What truly matters is **how** and **what** we are doing to prepare for it.

We should be continuously striving to please Allah and seek His forgiveness..*214*

The second phase of the journey into the unknown world will soon begin—the moment of the final test. This phase involves the behaviour of angels when our souls pass through the trials and exodus of death. It is all part of Allah's divine plan.

The name of the angel **Azrael** is of Jewish origin, but we find no evidence in the Qur'an that the name "Azrael" refers to the angel who takes our souls.

Shaykh al-Albani said in his commentary on the words of al-Tahawi:

"We believe in the Angel of Death who is appointed to take the souls of all creatures."

He continues:

"This (the Angel of Death) is what he is called in the Qur'an. With regard to the name 'Azrail', which is widely known among the people, there is no basis for this. Rather, it comes from the Isra'iliyyat."

We therefore call him **the Angel of Death**, as Allah Himself refers to him. In the following verse, Allah (SWT) says:

قُلْ يَتَوَفَّاكُم مَّلَكُ الْمَوْتِ الَّذِي وُكِّلَ بِكُمْ ثُمَّ إِلَىٰ رَبِّكُمْ تُرْجَعُونَ

Say: "The Angel of Death, who is set over you, will take your souls; then you shall be brought to your Lord."

(Surah As-Sajda 32:11)[215]

Only Allah (SWT) determines and knows the time and manner of every person's death. He has entrusted the responsibility of individual deaths to the Angel of Death, who is reported to have declared:

"I am death, who separates all loved ones!

I am death, who separates man and woman, husband and wife!

I am death, who separates daughters from mothers!

I am death, who separates sons from fathers—and brother from his brother!

I am death, who subdues the power of the sons of Adam.

---

[214] [Muslim] https://40hadithnawawi.com/hadith/2-islam-iman-ihsan/
[215] Index 166 https://islamqa.info/en/answers/40671/name-of-the-angel-of-death-is-it-azrael

I am death, who inhabits the graves.

Not a creature will remain who does not taste me."[216]

Death

Despite our common perception of fear of death, it is considered a beautiful gift from Allah (SWT) for the true believer.

Allah (SWT) says:

يَا أَيَّتُهَا النَّفْسُ الْمُطْمَئِنَّةُ

ارْجِعِي إِلَىٰ رَبِّكِ رَاضِيَةً مَّرْضِيَّةً

فَادْخُلِي فِي عِبَادِي

وَادْخُلِي جَنَّتِي

(It will be said to the pious):

"O (you) the one in (complete) rest and satisfaction!

Come back to your Lord, well-pleased (yourself) and well-pleasing unto Him!

Enter you, then, among My honoured slaves,

And enter you My Paradise!"

— *Qur'an 89:27–30, Surah Al-Fajr (The Break of Day or the Dawn)*

In the hadith narrated by Al-Mughira bin Shu'ba:

The Almighty Allah causes the day to die with its setting and allows the night to take over, which is a time for rest. In this way, He may be showing us that all of us will eventually have to die, just like the day. And when the sun rises in the morning again after our period of rest, it is as if Almighty Allah (SWT) is telling us that we too will be raised to life after we have died.

On the day of Ibrahim's عليه السلام death, the sun eclipsed, and the people said that the eclipse was due to the death of Ibrahim (the son of the Prophet). Allah's Apostle said:

"The sun and the moon are two signs amongst the signs of Allah. They do not eclipse because of someone's death or life. So when you see them, invoke Allah (SWT) and pray till the eclipse is clear."

— *Sahih Al-Bukhari – Book 18, Hadith 168*

(al-islam.org/articles/death-beautiful-gift-believe)

---

[216] *source: Quoted in Jane Idleman Smith and Yvonne Yazbeck Haddad. The Islamic Understanding of Death and Resurrection, p. 35.*

Narrated by Anas bin Malik:

The Prophet (peace be upon him) said:

"None of you should wish for death because of a calamity befalling him; but if he has to wish for death, he should say:

'O Allah! Keep me alive as long as life is better for me, and let me die if death is better for me.'"

— *Sahih Al-Bukhari – Book 70, Hadith 575*

The Holy Qur'an speaks about our two deaths:

The first death took place when we failed to make a stand with Allah's absolute authority. That first death lasted until we were born into this world.

The second death terminates our life in this world.

The Holy Qur'an defines death in the following verses:

كَيْفَ تَكْفُرُونَ بِاللَّهِ وَكُنتُمْ أَمْوَاتًا فَأَحْيَاكُمْ ۖ ثُمَّ يُمِيتُكُمْ ثُمَّ يُحْيِيكُمْ ثُمَّ إِلَيْهِ تُرْجَعُونَ

How can you disbelieve in Allah? Seeing that you were dead and He gave you life. Then He will give you death, then again will bring you to life (on the Day of Resurrection), and then unto Him you will return. — Surah Al-Baqarah 2:28

لَا يَذُوقُونَ فِيهَا الْمَوْتَ إِلَّا الْمَوْتَةَ الْأُولَىٰ ۖ وَوَقَاهُمْ عَذَابَ الْجَحِيمِ

They will never taste death therein except the first death (of this world), and He will save them from the torment of the blazing Fire. — Ad-Dukhan 44:56

وَهُوَ الَّذِي أَحْيَاكُمْ ثُمَّ يُمِيتُكُمْ ثُمَّ يُحْيِيكُمْ ۗ إِنَّ الْإِنسَانَ لَكَفُورٌ

It is He who gave you life, and then will cause you to die, and will again give you life (on the Day of Resurrection). Verily! Man is indeed ungrateful. — Al-Hajj 22:66

قَالُوا رَبَّنَا أَمَتَّنَا اثْنَتَيْنِ وَأَحْيَيْتَنَا اثْنَتَيْنِ فَاعْتَرَفْنَا بِذُنُوبِنَا فَهَلْ إِلَىٰ خُرُوجٍ مِّن سَبِيلٍ

They will say: 'Our Lord! You have made us die twice (i.e., we were dead in the loins of our fathers and dead after our deaths in this world), and You have given us life twice (i.e., life when we were born and life when we are resurrected)! Now we confess our sins, then is there any way to get out (of the Fire)?' — Al-Mu'min (Ghafir) 40:11

Our Second Journey

The second journey between death and resurrection will take a completely different form from our first journey through life on this earth. In Islam, it is believed that when a person dies, the soul enters the state of waiting, also known as *Barzakh*, until the Day of Judgment.

There is a barrier or screen between our material world, and on the other side is the spirit world. Here, a person's body burns to ashes or is consumed by animals, but the life of the soul begins in Barzakh. There is nothing we can do in the life of Barzakh to raise our score or correct the mistakes we have made in this material world.

The second part of the journey will take us to the Day of Resurrection, where our fate will be determined. The Qur'an states:

حَتَّىٰ إِذَا جَاءَ أَحَدَهُمُ الْمَوْتُ قَالَ رَبِّ ارْجِعُونِ

لَعَلِّي أَعْمَلُ صَالِحًا فِيمَا تَرَكْتُ ۚ كَلَّا ۚ إِنَّهَا كَلِمَةٌ هُوَ قَائِلُهَا ۖ وَمِن وَرَائِهِم بَرْزَخٌ إِلَىٰ يَوْمِ يُبْعَثُونَ

Until, when death comes to one of them (those who join partners with Allah), he says: "My Lord! Send me back,

So that I may do good in that which I have left behind!" No! It is but a word that he speaks, and behind them is Barzakh (a barrier) until the Day when they will be resurrected. — Surah Al-Mu'minun 23:99–100

At the Moment of Death

When the moment of death arrives, the union of body and soul will be severed. It is at this precise juncture that individuals come face to face with the outcome of their life's examination, determining whether their soul has been honoured or transgressed during its transition into an unfamiliar realm, where it will remain until the Day of Judgment.

Every person, upon entering this world, is bound to undergo this process. While we may be aware of this fact, we often fail to contemplate the consequences should we falter in our ultimate test.

The Qur'an and the hadith of our Prophet (ﷺ) constantly remind us of matters such as:

أَيْنَمَا تَكُونُوا يُدْرِكْكُمُ الْمَوْتُ وَلَوْ كُنتُمْ فِي بُرُوجٍ مُّشَيَّدَةٍ ۗ وَإِن تُصِبْهُمْ حَسَنَةٌ يَقُولُوا هَٰذِهِ مِنْ عِندِ اللَّهِ ۖ وَإِن تُصِبْهُمْ سَيِّئَةٌ يَقُولُوا هَٰذِهِ مِنْ عِندِكَ ۚ قُلْ كُلٌّ مِّنْ عِندِ اللَّهِ ۖ فَمَالِ هَٰؤُلَاءِ الْقَوْمِ لَا يَكَادُونَ يَفْقَهُونَ حَدِيثًا

"Wheresoever ye be, death will overtake you, even if ye were in lofty towers." And if some good befalls them, they say, "This is from Allah"; but if evil befalls them, they say, "This is from thee (O Muhammad ﷺ)." Say: "All things are from Allah." What is the matter with these people that they understand not a word?"

— Surah An-Nisaa 4:78

كُلُّ نَفْسٍ ذَائِقَةُ الْمَوْتِ ۗ وَنَبْلُوكُم بِالشَّرِّ وَالْخَيْرِ فِتْنَةً ۖ وَإِلَيْنَا تُرْجَعُونَ

"Every soul shall taste of death: and We test you with evil and with good as trial. And unto Us ye shall be returned."

— Surah Al-Anbiyaa' 21:35

كُلُّ نَفْسٍ ذَائِقَةُ الْمَوْتِ ثُمَّ إِلَيْنَا تُرْجَعُونَ

"Every soul shall taste of death. Then unto Us shall ye be brought back."

— Surah Al-'Ankabut 29:57

Even though countless events occur in the unseen realm beyond our knowledge, we can create many fictional stories about them. However, the true events remain unknown to us, except for what Allah reveals through His verses.

Allah SWT says in the Qur'an:

وَهُوَ الْقَاهِرُ فَوْقَ عِبَادِهِ وَيُرْسِلُ عَلَيْكُمْ حَفَظَةً حَتَّىٰ إِذَا جَاءَ أَحَدَكُمُ الْمَوْتُ تَوَفَّتْهُ رُسُلُنَا وَهُمْ لَا يُفَرِّطُونَ

"He is the Irresistible, above His servants, and He sends guardians over you, until when death comes to one of you, Our messengers take his soul, and they neglect not their duty."

— Surah Al-An'am 6:61

According to the hadith of Al-Baraa' ibn 'Aazib, the Angel of Death comes to the believer in a beautiful form and to the disbeliever and hypocrite in a frightening form. This hadith describes how the Messenger ﷺ of Allah SWT said:

Believer

"When the believing slave is about to depart this world and move to the Hereafter, angels come down to him from the heavens with white faces like the sun. They bring with them a shroud from Paradise and aromatics from Paradise. They sit in front of him as far as the eye can see. Then the Angel of Death comes and sits at his head and says: 'O good soul' (according to one report: 'O peaceful soul'), 'Come out to forgiveness from Allah and His pleasure.' Then it comes out like a drop of water from the mouth of a jug, and they take it…"

The Qur'an also confirms the same message for the believers, as Allah says:

إِنَّ الَّذِينَ قَالُوا رَبُّنَا اللَّهُ ثُمَّ اسْتَقَامُوا تَتَنَزَّلُ عَلَيْهِمُ الْمَلَائِكَةُ أَلَّا تَخَافُوا وَلَا تَحْزَنُوا وَأَبْشِرُوا بِالْجَنَّةِ الَّتِي كُنتُمْ تُوعَدُونَ

نَحْنُ أَوْلِيَاؤُكُمْ فِي الْحَيَاةِ الدُّنْيَا وَفِي الْآخِرَةِ وَلَكُمْ فِيهَا مَا تَشْتَهِي أَنفُسُكُمْ وَلَكُمْ فِيهَا مَا تَدَّعُونَ

نُزُلًا مِّنْ غَفُورٍ رَّحِيمٍ

"Verily those who say: 'Our Lord is Allah,' and then remain firm (steadfast), on them the angels descend (saying): 'Fear ye not, nor grieve: but receive the glad tidings of Paradise, which ye were promised.

We are your protectors in this life and in the Hereafter. Therein shall ye have all that your souls shall desire, and therein shall ye have all that ye ask for—

A welcome from the Oft-Forgiving, Most Merciful.'"

— Surah Fussilat (Ha-Mim) 41:30–32

Disbeliever

But when the disbelieving slave (according to one report, the immoral slave) is about to depart this world and move to the Hereafter, angels come down to him from the heavens—harsh and severe, with black faces—bringing sackcloth (a coarse cloth worn for mourning or punishment) from Hell. They sit in front of him as far as the eye can see. Then the Angel of Death comes and sits at his head and says: "O evil soul, come out to the anger and wrath of Allah." Then the soul retreats inside the body and is dragged out like an iron skewer passing through wet wool (cutting veins and nerves).

— [Abu Dawood, Al-Haakim, Ahmad]

We cannot see what happens to the dying person at the point of death, though we may witness its effects. Allah has told us about the state of the dying person:

Allah says:

1.

وَلَوْ تَرَىٰ إِذْ يَتَوَفَّى الَّذِينَ كَفَرُوا ۙ الْمَلَائِكَةُ يَضْرِبُونَ وُجُوهَهُمْ وَأَدْبَارَهُمْ وَذُوقُوا عَذَابَ الْحَرِيقِ

ذَٰلِكَ بِمَا قَدَّمَتْ أَيْدِيكُمْ وَأَنَّ اللَّهَ لَيْسَ بِظَلَّامٍ لِّلْعَبِيدِ

"If thou couldst see when the angels take away the souls of those who disbelieve, they smite their faces and their backs, and (say): 'Taste the punishment of the burning fire!

This is because of what your hands have sent before you, and verily, Allah is not unjust to His servants.'"

— Surah Al-Anfal 8:50–51

2.

فَلَوْلَا إِذَا بَلَغَتِ الْحُلْقُومَ

وَأَنتُمْ حِينَئِذٍ تَنظُرُونَ

وَنَحْنُ أَقْرَبُ إِلَيْهِ مِنكُمْ وَلَٰكِن لَّا تُبْصِرُونَ

"Then why do ye not intervene when the soul reaches the throat?

And ye at that moment are looking on—

But We are nearer to him than you, though ye see not."

— Surah Al-Waqi'ah 56:83–85 [Tafsir At-Tabari, Vol. 27, Page 209]

Allah SWT also says:

3.

$$كَلَّا إِذَا بَلَغَتِ التَّرَاقِيَ$$

$$وَقِيلَ مَنْ ۜ رَاقٍ$$

$$وَظَنَّ أَنَّهُ الْفِرَاقُ$$

$$وَالْتَفَّتِ السَّاقُ بِالسَّاقِ$$

$$إِلَىٰ رَبِّكَ يَوْمَئِذٍ الْمَسَاقُ$$

"Nay, when the soul reaches the collar bone (i.e. the throat),

And it will be said: 'Who can cure him?'

And he will conclude that it is the parting,

And leg will be joined with leg,

That Day the drive will be to thy Lord (Allah)."

— Surah Al-Qiyamah 75:26–30

Allah SWT continues to express His wrath towards certain disgraced people and warns how His punishment will be imposed upon them at the moment of death.

Allah SWT says:

4.

$$وَمَنْ أَظْلَمُ مِمَّنِ افْتَرَىٰ عَلَى اللَّهِ كَذِبًا أَوْ قَالَ أُوحِيَ إِلَيَّ وَلَمْ يُوحَ إِلَيْهِ شَيْءٌ وَمَن قَالَ سَأُنزِلُ مِثْلَ مَا أَنزَلَ اللَّهُ ۗ وَلَوْ تَرَىٰ إِذِ الظَّالِمُونَ فِي غَمَرَاتِ الْمَوْتِ وَالْمَلَائِكَةُ بَاسِطُو أَيْدِيهِمْ أَخْرِجُوا أَنفُسَكُمُ ۖ الْيَوْمَ تُجْزَوْنَ عَذَابَ الْهُونِ بِمَا كُنتُمْ تَقُولُونَ عَلَى اللَّهِ غَيْرَ الْحَقِّ وَكُنتُمْ عَنْ آيَاتِهِ تَسْتَكْبِرُونَ$$

"And who is more unjust than one who invents a lie against Allah, or says, 'I have received inspiration,' whereas he is not inspired in anything; and who says, 'I will reveal the like of what Allah has revealed'?

If thou couldst but see when the wrong-doers are in the agonies of death, and the angels stretch forth their hands, saying, 'Deliver your souls! This day shall ye be recompensed with the torment of degradation, for that ye used to say against Allah other than the truth, and ye were ever proud against His signs!'"

— Surah Al-An'am 6:93

5

The following verse indicates that no excuse will be acceptable for His servants at the time of the soul's departure.

Verse says:

إِنَّ الَّذِينَ تَوَفَّاهُمُ الْمَلَائِكَةُ ظَالِمِي أَنفُسِهِمْ قَالُوا فِيمَ كُنتُمْ ۖ قَالُوا كُنَّا مُسْتَضْعَفِينَ فِي الْأَرْضِ ۚ قَالُوا أَلَمْ تَكُنْ أَرْضُ اللَّهِ وَاسِعَةً فَتُهَاجِرُوا فِيهَا ۚ فَأُولَٰئِكَ مَأْوَاهُمْ جَهَنَّمُ ۖ وَسَاءَتْ مَصِيرًا

Verily, those whom the angels take in death while they wrong themselves—(as they stayed among the disbelievers even though emigration was obligatory for them)—the angels say to them, "In what condition were you?" They reply, "We were weak and oppressed in the land." The angels say, "Was not the earth of Allah spacious enough for you to emigrate therein?" Such men shall find their abode in Hell—and evil is that destination!

(Surah An-Nisaa 4:97)

Ibn Katheer said in his *Tafseer* of this verse:

(This means) if only you could see, O Muhammad ﷺ, *when the angels take the souls of the kuffaar, you would see something tremendously disturbing—when they strike their faces and backs and say, "Taste the punishment of the blazing Fire."* [Ibid.]

The great *mufassir* 'Allaamah Ibn Katheer pointed out that the above verse referred to the Battle of Badr, but it also applies to every *kaafir*. Hence, Allah did not specifically mention the people who died at Badr. Rather, He said:

"And if you could see when the angels take away the souls of those who disbelieve..."

What Ibn Katheer said is correct, and this is indicated by more than one verse in the Qur'an, such as:

فَمَنْ أَظْلَمُ مِمَّنِ افْتَرَىٰ عَلَى اللَّهِ كَذِبًا أَوْ كَذَّبَ بِآيَاتِهِ ۚ أُولَٰئِكَ يَنَالُهُمْ نَصِيبُهُم مِّنَ الْكِتَابِ ۖ حَتَّىٰ إِذَا جَاءَتْهُمْ رُسُلُنَا يَتَوَفَّوْنَهُمْ قَالُوا أَيْنَ مَا كُنتُمْ تَدْعُونَ مِن دُونِ اللَّهِ ۖ قَالُوا ضَلُّوا عَنَّا وَشَهِدُوا عَلَىٰ أَنفُسِهِمْ أَنَّهُمْ كَانُوا كَافِرِينَ

Who is more unjust than he who invents a lie against God, or denies His signs? For such, their appointed portion from the Book shall reach them, until when Our messengers come to take their souls, they will say, "Where are those whom you called upon besides Allah?" They will reply, "They have departed from us," and they will bear witness against themselves that they were disbelievers.

513

(Surah Al-A'raf 7:37)

الَّذِينَ تَتَوَفَّاهُمُ الْمَلَائِكَةُ ظَالِمِي أَنفُسِهِمْ ۖ فَأَلْقَوُا السَّلَمَ مَا كُنَّا نَعْمَلُ مِن سُوءٍ ۚ بَلَىٰ إِنَّ اللَّهَ عَلِيمٌ بِمَا كُنتُمْ تَعْمَلُونَ

Those whose lives the angels take while they wrong themselves (by disbelief and associating partners with Allah and committing all kinds of evil). Then they will make a false submission, saying, "We did no evil." (The angels will reply): "Yea, truly, Allah knoweth well what ye did."

(Surah An-Nahl 16:28)

إِنَّ الَّذِينَ ارْتَدُّوا عَلَىٰ أَدْبَارِهِم مِّن بَعْدِ مَا تَبَيَّنَ لَهُمُ الْهُدَى ۙ الشَّيْطَانُ سَوَّلَ لَهُمْ وَأَمْلَىٰ لَهُمْ ذَٰلِكَ بِأَنَّهُمْ قَالُوا لِلَّذِينَ كَرِهُوا مَا نَزَّلَ اللَّهُ سَنُطِيعُكُمْ فِي بَعْضِ الْأَمْرِ ۖ وَاللَّهُ يَعْلَمُ إِسْرَارَهُمْ فَكَيْفَ إِذَا تَوَفَّتْهُمُ الْمَلَائِكَةُ يَضْرِبُونَ وُجُوهَهُمْ وَأَدْبَارَهُمْ

Lo! Those who turned back after guidance was made clear to them—Satan deceived them and prolonged false hopes for them.

That is because they said to those who hate what Allah has revealed, "We will obey you in part of the matter," but Allah knoweth their secrets.

Then how (will it be) when the angels take their souls in death, striking their faces and their backs?

(Surah Muhammad 47:25–27) [217]

The above verses clearly express the severity of the punishment imposed on the identified persons.

Satan Plays His Final Game at the End of One's Journey

Satan is present at the moment of tribulation when the angel of death comes to take a person's soul and end his earthly life. At this point, Satan plays his final game and works to destroy the person's faith and corrupt the soul—especially if the person is righteous and dear to Allah (SWT).

Satan tries to mislead a person by exploiting his weakness, doubt, or fear, in an effort to lead them astray. He does not concern himself with the soul of the one who lived his earthly life under Satan's command, whom he destroyed long before this final moment. Instead, he rejoices when he sees the angel of death come to that person and sit on his head and say:

"O evil soul, come out to the wrath and anger of Allah."

---

[217] Index 168 https://contemplatequran.wordpress.com/2015/03/26/the-moment-of-death

This is Satan's success. His concern is how he might mislead the soul of a pious person—someone pure from all evil and devoted to the worship of Allah alone.

When the angels of death come to greet the righteous, saying "Salamun 'Alaikum", and are ready to receive his soul, Satan intervenes, trying to confuse the person in this final moment. He knows it is his last chance to divert the believer before he meets Allah (SWT).

However, Satan cannot overpower a person whose faith is strong. The angel will remove the soul with honour and dignity, carrying away that pure and righteous spirit.

Allah (SWT) says:

الَّذِينَ تَتَوَفَّاهُمُ الْمَلَائِكَةُ طَيِّبِينَ ۙ يَقُولُونَ سَلَامٌ عَلَيْكُمُ ادْخُلُوا الْجَنَّةَ بِمَا كُنتُمْ تَعْمَلُونَ

Those whose lives the angels take while they are in a pious state (i.e., pure from all evil and worshipping none but Allah alone), saying (to them): "Salamun 'Alaikum (peace be upon you), enter Paradise for what you used to do."

— *Surah An-Nahl, 16:32*

In this verse, Allah (SWT), glorified be He, declares that the righteous who obey their Lord's commands and avoid what He has forbidden will have their souls taken in a good state. The angels will bring them glad tidings of Paradise and greet them with salutations.

إِنَّ الَّذِينَ قَالُوا رَبُّنَا اللَّهُ ثُمَّ اسْتَقَامُوا تَتَنَزَّلُ عَلَيْهِمُ الْمَلَائِكَةُ أَلَّا تَخَافُوا وَلَا تَحْزَنُوا وَأَبْشِرُوا بِالْجَنَّةِ الَّتِي كُنتُمْ تُوعَدُونَ

Verily, those who say, "Our Lord is Allah," and then remain steadfast, the angels will descend upon them (at the time of death), saying: "Fear not, nor grieve! But receive the glad tidings of Paradise, which you were promised."

— *Surah Fussilat, 41:30*

This moment is truly crucial for all children of Adam. Regardless of their status or righteousness, Satan will attempt to intervene during moments of trial and distress, trying to divert their faith. As mentioned above, this is our fear, and for this reason, we must continually pray to Allah (SWT) to protect us from Satan so we remain firm in faith during our final moments.

The Prophet ﷺ would pray to Allah—may He be exalted—asking Him not to let Satan gain power over him at the time of death. This teaches Muslims the importance of striving to be safe from the *fitnah* of Satan.

It was narrated from Abu'l-Yusr that the Messenger of Allah ﷺ used to say in his supplication:

"O Allah, I seek refuge in You from being crushed. And I seek refuge in You from falling from a height, drowning, burning, and impurity. And I seek refuge in You lest the two slanderers overpower me and confuse me at the time of death. I seek refuge in You lest I die while turning my back in battle for Your sake, and I seek refuge in You lest I die from a bite or a poisonous sting."

The prayer of the Prophet ﷺ serves as a powerful reminder of our vulnerability to Satan. With this in mind, we should turn our hearts to the Protector and recite the following verse to seek His protection:

$$\text{رَبَّنَا لَا تُزِغْ قُلُوبَنَا بَعْدَ إِذْ هَدَيْتَنَا وَهَبْ لَنَا مِن لَّدُنكَ رَحْمَةً ۚ إِنَّكَ أَنتَ الْوَهَّابُ}$$

Our Lord, let not our hearts deviate after Thou hast guided us, and grant us mercy from Thee. Truly, Thou art the Bestower.

— *Surah Aal Imran, 3:8*

Throughout this book, we have consistently emphasised the importance of building a strong spiritual fortress to protect ourselves from the harmful influences of Satan, who relentlessly seeks to undermine our faith and corrupt our hearts.

In Islam, it is not prudent to instil fear in Muslims by suggesting that Satan's presence at the time of death or his incantations during moments of danger can distort their faith. Instead, Islamic teachings should inspire confidence in maintaining a resolute heart—fortified by *duas*—which can help overcome Satan's whispers in one's final moments.

Education should focus on nurturing the understanding that, for true believers in Allah, death is a welcome transition to the next world—our true home.

In any case, we must remember that every soul must pass the test. This is confirmed again in the verse which says:

$$\text{كُلُّ نَفْسٍ ذَائِقَةُ الْمَوْتِ ۗ وَإِنَّمَا تُوَفَّوْنَ أُجُورَكُمْ يَوْمَ الْقِيَامَةِ ۖ فَمَن زُحْزِحَ عَنِ النَّارِ وَأُدْخِلَ الْجَنَّةَ فَقَدْ فَازَ ۗ وَمَا الْحَيَاةُ الدُّنْيَا إِلَّا مَتَاعُ الْغُرُورِ}$$

Everyone shall taste death. Every soul shall taste of death. And only on the Day of Resurrection shall ye be paid your wages in full: and whoso is removed from the Fire and admitted into Paradise, he indeed is successful. And the life of this world is but the enjoyment of deception.

— *Surah Aal Imran, 3:185*

Finally, despite our innate fear surrounding death, we must be convinced that embracing it may be our only true comfort. We will return to Allah (SWT) and be blessed with His good news, Insha'Allah. All we can do is pray for the strength to face our death as Allah's last blessing upon the earth.

Some Golden Tips to Enter Paradise

1. Obeying Allah and His Messenger ﷺ

All who obey Allah and the Apostle are in the company of those upon whom is the Grace of Allah. This verse is good news for us because Allah (SWT) includes that even the *Mu'min* of the lowest rank will be qualified to accompany those of higher rank.

Reflect on this verse:

وَمَن يُطِعِ اللَّهَ وَالرَّسُولَ فَأُولَٰئِكَ مَعَ الَّذِينَ أَنْعَمَ اللَّهُ عَلَيْهِم مِّنَ النَّبِيِّينَ وَالصِّدِّيقِينَ وَالشُّهَدَاءِ وَالصَّالِحِينَ ۚ وَحَسُنَ أُولَٰئِكَ رَفِيقًا

And whoso obeyeth Allah and the Messenger (Muhammad ﷺ), they shall be with those unto whom Allah hath shown favour—of the Prophets, the steadfast affirmers of truth, the martyrs, and the righteous. How excellent a fellowship are they!

— *Surah An-Nisaa, 4:69*

Allah's message in this verse is very clear:

Those who obey Allah and the Apostle

Will be in the company of:

The Prophets (those who teach – *Nabi*)

The sincere (*Siddiq*)

The witnesses/testifiers (*Shuhada*)

The righteous who do good (*Mu'minun*)

Ah! What a beautiful fellowship. Can company with the Prophet ﷺ on the Day of Judgment be anything but the ultimate reward?

2. Kindness in Conduct

The Prophet ﷺ was once asked:

"O Messenger of Allah, such and such a woman spends her nights in prayer, fasts during the day, gives charity, but offends her neighbours with her sharp tongue."

The Prophet ﷺ said: "Her good deeds will be of no avail. She is among the people of Hell."

They said: "And so-and-so prays only the obligatory prayers, gives charity in the form of leftover curds, but does not offend anyone."

The Prophet ﷺ said: "She is among the people of Paradise." *(Bukhari)* [218]

3. Breaking Ties and Reconciling Between Disputing Parties

Carefully notice the verses where Allah (SWT) guides us and says:

إِنَّمَا الْمُؤْمِنُونَ إِخْوَةٌ فَأَصْلِحُوا بَيْنَ أَخَوَيْكُمْ ۚ وَاتَّقُوا اللَّهَ لَعَلَّكُمْ تُرْحَمُونَ

يَا أَيُّهَا الَّذِينَ آمَنُوا لَا يَسْخَرْ قَوْمٌ مِّن قَوْمٍ عَسَىٰ أَن يَكُونُوا خَيْرًا مِّنْهُمْ وَلَا نِسَاءٌ مِّن نِّسَاءٍ عَسَىٰ أَن يَكُنَّ خَيْرًا مِّنْهُنَّ ۖ وَلَا تَلْمِزُوا أَنفُسَكُمْ وَلَا تَنَابَزُوا بِالْأَلْقَابِ ۖ بِئْسَ الِاسْمُ الْفُسُوقُ بَعْدَ الْإِيمَانِ ۚ وَمَن لَّمْ يَتُبْ فَأُولَٰئِكَ هُمُ الظَّالِمُونَ

يَا أَيُّهَا الَّذِينَ آمَنُوا اجْتَنِبُوا كَثِيرًا مِّنَ الظَّنِّ إِنَّ بَعْضَ الظَّنِّ إِثْمٌ ۖ وَلَا تَجَسَّسُوا وَلَا يَغْتَب بَّعْضُكُم بَعْضًا ۚ أَيُحِبُّ أَحَدُكُمْ أَن يَأْكُلَ لَحْمَ أَخِيهِ مَيْتًا فَكَرِهْتُمُوهُ ۚ وَاتَّقُوا اللَّهَ ۚ إِنَّ اللَّهَ تَوَّابٌ رَّحِيمٌ

"The believers are nothing else than brothers: therefore make peace between your brethren, and fear Allah, that ye may obtain mercy." — Surah Al-Hujurat (49:10)

"O ye who believe! Let not a people deride another people, haply they may be better than they; neither let women deride other women, it may be they are better than they. Neither defame yourselves, nor call one another by nicknames: ill-seeming is a name connoting wickedness after faith. And whoso repenteth not, such are the wrongdoers." — Surah Al-Hujurat (49:11)

"O ye who believe! Avoid much suspicion: verily, some suspicion is sin. And spy not, neither backbite one another. Would any of you love to eat the flesh of his dead brother? Nay, ye would abhor it! And fear Allah: for Allah is Oft-Returning, Most Merciful." — Surah Al-Hujurat (49:12)

4. Hadith

Abu Umamah said:

"Walk a mile to visit a sick person, walk two miles to visit your brother for the sake of Allah, and walk three miles to make peace between two."

A Muslim should avoid dissension and discord for the sake of peace and should shun all forms of *fitnah*. This hadith encourages Muslims to reconcile with one another and reduce enmity, which is among the virtues of a true believer.

Our Prophet (ﷺ) said:

"Do not boycott one another, do not turn away from one another, do not hate one another, and do not envy one another. Be slaves of Allah, brothers. And it is

---

[218] Index169) https://www.iuhk.org/index.php/fruits-for-the-week/1081-bad-neighbours-5-june-2020

not lawful for a Muslim to avoid his brother for more than three days." — Al-Bukhari, Muslim

And: *"Whoever forsakes his brother for a year, it is as if he has shed his blood."* — Abu Dawood, authenticated by Al-Albani

Our Prophet Muhammad (ﷺ) also said:

"Anyone who goes to make peace between two persons, the angels of Allah send blessings upon him until he returns, and he will be given the reward of the Night of Destiny (Laylat al-Qadr)."[219]

5 BEWARE: They May Lose the Status of Believers

Consider carefully the powerful verses described below. These serve as a clear warning to us: we may lose our status as believers, even if we perform regular obligatory prayers.

Reflect on verses 2:11, 2:161–162, and 9:84 respectively.

وَإِذَا قِيلَ لَهُمْ لَا تُفْسِدُوا فِي الْأَرْضِ قَالُوا إِنَّمَا نَحْنُ مُصْلِحُونَ

"And when it is said unto them, 'Make not mischief in the earth,' they say, 'We are peacemakers only.'" — Surah Al-Baqara (2:11)

إِنَّ الَّذِينَ كَفَرُوا وَمَاتُوا وَهُمْ كُفَّارٌ أُولَـٰئِكَ عَلَيْهِمْ لَعْنَةُ اللَّهِ وَالْمَلَائِكَةِ وَالنَّاسِ أَجْمَعِينَ

"Verily, those who disbelieve and die while they are disbelievers, upon them is the curse of Allah, and of angels, and of all mankind." — Surah Al-Baqara (2:161)

"They shall abide therein: their punishment shall not be lightened, neither shall they be reprieved." — Surah Al-Baqara (2:162)

وَلَا تُصَلِّ عَلَىٰ أَحَدٍ مِّنْهُم مَّاتَ أَبَدًا وَلَا تَقُمْ عَلَىٰ قَبْرِهِ ۖ إِنَّهُمْ كَفَرُوا بِاللَّهِ وَرَسُولِهِ وَمَاتُوا وَهُمْ فَاسِقُونَ

"And pray thou not over any of them that die, nor stand at his grave; for they believed not in Allah and His Messenger, and died in rebellion." — Surah At-Tawbah (9:84)

A Gift for Your Loved One

It has also been narrated that the Holy Prophet ﷺ said:

"Whatever Sadaqa is given on behalf of the deceased person, the blessed angels adorn it on an illuminated tray whose light spreads across the seven heavens. They take it to the head of the grave and say: 'Peace be upon you, O inhabitant of the grave (Barzakh). This gift has been sent to you by your relatives.' The deceased

---

[219] Index 170 https://www.al-islam.org/living-right-way-jawad-tehrani/peace-and-reconciliation
Index 171 https://www.farhathashmi.com/articles-section/motivational/make-peace

person takes the tray into his grave, and thereafter the entire grave is illuminated and expands in length."

The Prophet ﷺ then continued:

"Those who favour their departed relatives by giving Sadaqa on their behalf will receive a reward as great as the mountain of Uhud in the sight of Allah. On the Day of Judgment, Allah will grant that person shelter under His Throne—when there will be no other shelter except this. Hence, this Sadaqa proves beneficial both for the living and the deceased."— Ma'ad, Index 172[220]

In the next chapter, we will explore the mysterious Kingdom of Barzakh—the transitional realm where souls linger, awaiting their appearance before the Divine Court of Judgment to learn their ultimate fate.

---

[220] Index 172 https://www.islamicinsights.com/religion/the-journey-continues-barzakh-and-beyond.html

بِسْمِ ٱللَّهِ ٱلرَّحْمَـٰنِ ٱلرَّحِيمِ

Chapter 15

"I am the resurrection, and the life: he that believeth in me, though he were dead, yet shall he live:

And whosoever liveth and believeth in me shall never die. Believest thou this?"

— John 11:25–26, King James Version

"When a man dies, his good deeds come to an end, except three: ongoing charity, beneficial knowledge, and a righteous child who will pray for him."

— Hadith | Sahih Muslim

📖📖📖📖📖📖

Place Of Waiting

Once the physical journey concludes, the subsequent stage of the eternal inner exploration commences. In this transformative journey, our earned righteousness becomes the guiding light, supporting us at every step as we strive to encounter Allah (SWT). Time will cease to govern this everlasting expanse—no ticking clocks or yearly calendars. Centuries will lose their significance. Eventually, we shall reunite with the physical forms we left behind, standing as flawless beings in the Court of Judgement before embarking on our entry into Paradise.

However, right now we are entering a strange, unknown world called the Realm of *Barzakh*. This is the second phase of the journey.

Every human being must complete their journey through three main stages. While we are on earth, birth, worship, trials, and death make up the first stage. This is followed by the second stage, which begins after death in the strange, unknown world called *Barzakh*, where our souls remain. This is the place of waiting, or the long sleep of the soul, until the third stage of the journey begins.

This is all we know from our studies, but anything beyond this lies within the realm of the divine, known only to Allah (SWT). Even our Prophet ﷺ affirmed that he knows nothing of the unseen except what Allah reveals. Nevertheless, we will include the opinions and explanations of renowned scholars, widely accepted by believers as established facts. In this quest, we will quote Qur'anic verses in which

Allah has spoken on this issue, leaving it to you to judge and draw your own conclusions.

The physical remains of a human body within a grave hold no intrinsic value and do not represent anything in a tangible manner. Such bodies may be consumed by wild animals, reduced to ashes through cremation, or in some cases, proper burial may not be possible. However, following death, life commences anew as the soul transitions to *Barzakh*. The soul is eternal and persists beyond death, eventually reuniting with a new body in the next cycle, as per the Qur'an.

Determining the fate of our souls in distant lands remains an absolute enigma. Numerous scholars and philosophers from various sects have presented conflicting narratives based on Hadith, yet many of these accounts are speculative and lack substantial value.

Instead, it would be more prudent to turn to the Qur'an and explore its stance on this matter. Within its verses, we find insights into what will occur in the realm of *Barzakh* prior to resurrection. It also likens death to slumber, wherein dreams fill the void between demise and rebirth—resembling a night's sleep.

It is important to remember that Allah (SWT) explicitly emphasises in the Qur'an that neither our Prophet ﷺ nor anyone else possesses knowledge of the *ghayb*—a realm exclusive to Allah (SWT).

We find in the Hadith where it is narrated that the Prophet ﷺ—may God bless him and grant him peace—looked at the well into which the corpses of the disbelievers killed in the Battle of Badr were thrown and said:

"Have you found true what your Lord promised you?"

`Umar (RA) asked, "You are addressing dead people?"

The Prophet ﷺ replied:

"They hear better than you do, but they cannot reply."

(Reported by Al-Bukhari)

These narrations refer to the period closely following the death of a person. After that, however, the deceased moves completely into a different world, where he or she will no longer be aware of what happens in this life. This is confirmed by the following verse:

وَمَا يَسْتَوِي الْأَحْيَاءُ وَلَا الْأَمْوَاتُ ۚ إِنَّ اللَّهَ يُسْمِعُ مَن يَشَاءُ ۖ وَمَا أَنتَ بِمُسْمِعٍ مَّن فِي الْقُبُورِ

إِنْ أَنتَ إِلَّا نَذِيرٌ

إِنَّا أَرْسَلْنَاكَ بِالْحَقِّ بَشِيرًا وَنَذِيرًا ۚ وَإِن مِّنْ أُمَّةٍ إِلَّا خَلَا فِيهَا نَذِيرٌ

522

"Nor are the living and the dead alike. Verily Allah can make whom He will to hear, but thou canst not make those to hear that are in the graves.

Thou art but a warner.

Verily We have sent thee with the truth, a bearer of glad tidings and a warner. And there is not a nation, but a warner hath passed among them."

(Surah Fatir 35:22–24)

Let us explore the insights given by Allah (SWT) about *Barzakh*, as well as the views shared by scholars and philosophers about this possible realm beyond our earthly existence. The following verses provide clear indications of the realm of *Barzakh*, which is mentioned three times in the Qur'an:

1.

بَيْنَهُمَا بَرْزَخٌ لَّا يَبْغِيَانِ

"Between them is a barrier which none of them can transgress."

(Surah Ar-Rahman 55:20)

2.

وَهُوَ الَّذِي مَرَجَ الْبَحْرَيْنِ هَٰذَا عَذْبٌ فُرَاتٌ وَهَٰذَا مِلْحٌ أُجَاجٌ وَجَعَلَ بَيْنَهُمَا بَرْزَخًا وَحِجْرًا مَّحْجُورًا

"And it is He who has let free the two seas, one palatable and sweet, and the other salt and bitter, and He has set a barrier and a complete partition between them."

(Surah Al-Furqan 25:53)

3.

لَعَلِّي أَعْمَلُ صَالِحًا فِيمَا تَرَكْتُ ۚ كَلَّا ۚ إِنَّهَا كَلِمَةٌ هُوَ قَائِلُهَا ۖ وَمِن وَرَائِهِم بَرْزَخٌ إِلَىٰ يَوْمِ يُبْعَثُونَ

"'So that I may do good in that which I have left behind!' No! It is but a word that he speaks, and behind them is *Barzakh* (a barrier) until the Day when they will be resurrected."

(Surah Al-Mu'minun 23:100)

At the end of our earthly journey, we must relinquish everything we possess. However, the only tangible asset we can retain is the good deeds we have accumulated in this lifetime—deeds we can carry with us and utilise in the next phase of our journey. In this diverse world, there is no room for accumulating shortfalls, as these would prove detrimental in avoiding punishment.

Allah confirms this in the following verse:

وَلَيْسَتِ التَّوْبَةُ لِلَّذِينَ يَعْمَلُونَ السَّيِّئَاتِ حَتَّى إِذَا حَضَرَ أَحَدَهُمُ الْمَوْتُ قَالَ إِنِّي تُبْتُ الْآنَ وَلَا الَّذِينَ يَمُوتُونَ وَهُمْ كُفَّارٌ ۚ أُولَٰئِكَ أَعْتَدْنَا لَهُمْ عَذَابًا أَلِيمًا

"And repentance is not for those who continue to do evil deeds until death faces one of them and he says: 'Now I repent;' nor for those who die while they are disbelievers. For them We have prepared a painful torment."

(Surah An-Nisaa 4:18)

In the state of *Barzakh*, the Qur'an explicitly affirms that the souls of Pharaoh and his followers are subjected to punishment from the moment of death until the Day of Judgment. Allah says:

النَّارُ يُعْرَضُونَ عَلَيْهَا غُدُوًّا وَعَشِيًّا ۖ وَيَوْمَ تَقُومُ السَّاعَةُ أَدْخِلُوا آلَ فِرْعَوْنَ أَشَدَّ الْعَذَابِ

"The Fire; they are exposed to it, morning and evening. And on the Day when the Hour shall be established (it will be said): 'Cause the people of Pharaoh to enter the severest torment!'"

(Surah Ghafir 40:46)

01

According to the Qur'an, unless otherwise specified, all souls will remain in a state of slumber until the designated time arrives for the commencement of the third phase of their journey towards the Court of Justice, where our ultimate destiny will be decided. This pivotal moment will occur with the blowing of the trumpet, awakening every soul to face the subsequent stage of their journey. The following verse also illustrates how our souls will be treated differently after death, based on our individual levels of righteousness.

Verse in the Qur'an says:

كُلُّ نَفْسٍ ذَائِقَةُ الْمَوْتِ ۗ وَإِنَّمَا تُوَفَّوْنَ أُجُورَكُمْ يَوْمَ الْقِيَامَةِ ۖ فَمَن زُحْزِحَ عَنِ النَّارِ وَأُدْخِلَ الْجَنَّةَ فَقَدْ فَازَ ۗ وَمَا الْحَيَاةُ الدُّنْيَا إِلَّا مَتَاعُ الْغُرُورِ

And only on the Day of Resurrection shall ye be paid your wages in full: and whoso is removed from the Fire and admitted into Paradise, he indeed is successful. The life of this world is but the enjoyment of deception.

[Surah Al-Imran 3:185]

وَاعْبُدْ رَبَّكَ حَتَّى يَأْتِيَكَ الْيَقِينُ

And worship thy Lord until there cometh unto thee the certainty (i.e. death).

[Surah Al-Hijr 15:99]

يَا أَيَّتُهَا النَّفْسُ الْمُطْمَئِنَّةُ

ارْجِعِي إِلَى رَبِّكِ رَاضِيَةً مَّرْضِيَّةً

524

فَادْخُلِي فِي عِبَادِي

O thou soul that art at rest,

Return unto thy Lord, well pleased and well pleasing unto Him.

Enter thou among My honoured servants.

[Surah Al-Fajr 89:27–29]

The Qur'an does not explicitly state that the soul will undergo interrogation or the torture of the grave upon returning to the body. Instead, it teaches that the Angel of Death honourably welcomes the souls of the righteous to the Paradise of Barzakh, while condemning evil spirits. The moment of death serves as a test, and the Angel of Death guides the soul to the next stage of its journey.

Allah SWT says:

وَنَضَعُ الْمَوَازِينَ الْقِسْطَ لِيَوْمِ الْقِيَامَةِ فَلَا تُظْلَمُ نَفْسٌ شَيْئًا ۖ وَإِن كَانَ مِثْقَالَ حَبَّةٍ مِّنْ خَرْدَلٍ أَتَيْنَا بِهَا ۗ وَكَفَىٰ بِنَا حَاسِبِينَ

And We shall set the balances of justice for the Day of Resurrection, so that no soul shall be wronged in aught. And though it be but the weight of a grain of mustard seed, We will bring it forth. And sufficient are We as accountants.

[Surah Al-Anbiyaa 21:47]

We will set the scales of justice for the Day of Judgment.

The verses in the Qur'an also provide clear indications of the occurrence of interrogation on the Day of Judgment. Allah explicitly mentions in the following verses:

فَلَنَسْأَلَنَّ الَّذِينَ أُرْسِلَ إِلَيْهِمْ وَلَنَسْأَلَنَّ الْمُرْسَلِينَ

فَلَنَقُصَّنَّ عَلَيْهِم بِعِلْمٍ ۖ وَمَا كُنَّا غَائِبِينَ

وَالْوَزْنُ يَوْمَئِذٍ الْحَقُّ ۚ فَمَن ثَقُلَتْ مَوَازِينُهُ فَأُولَٰئِكَ هُمُ الْمُفْلِحُونَ

Then verily We shall question those unto whom (the Message) was sent, and verily We shall question the Messengers.

Then verily We shall narrate unto them (their story) with knowledge, and lo! We were not absent.

And the weighing on that Day is the true (weighing). As for those whose scale (of good deeds) is heavy, they are the successful.

[Surah Al-A'raf 7:6–8]

Again, Allah says that people shall be questioned that Day about the joy— meaning on the Day of Judgment. The verse says:

أَلْهَاكُمُ التَّكَاثُرُ

حَتَّىٰ زُرْتُمُ الْمَقَابِرَ

كَلَّا سَوْفَ تَعْلَمُونَ

ثُمَّ كَلَّا سَوْفَ تَعْلَمُونَ

كَلَّا لَوْ تَعْلَمُونَ عِلْمَ الْيَقِينِ

لَتَرَوُنَّ الْجَحِيمَ

ثُمَّ لَتَرَوُنَّهَا عَيْنَ الْيَقِينِ

ثُمَّ لَتُسْأَلُنَّ يَوْمَئِذٍ عَنِ النَّعِيمِ

The mutual rivalry (for piling up worldly things) distracteth you,

Until ye visit the graves.

Nay, ye shall know!

Again, Nay! ye shall know!

Nay, would ye but know with the knowledge of certainty!

Ye shall surely see Hellfire!

Again, ye shall surely see it with the eye of certainty!

Then shall ye be questioned that Day concerning delight (worldly pleasures).

[Surah At-Takathur 102:1–8]

The above verses confirm that on the Day of Judgment, we will be questioned in the divine court, and our fate will be determined based on the verdict. The Qur'an specifically mentions many events including punishments that can happen in the life of Barzakh, but the questioning and punishment for ordinary souls will occur after the judgment—not before. However, many scholars interpret these verses differently based on their philosophical views.

It is established that Barzakh, and everything beyond it, are divine secrets (Ghayb) that we may speculate about, but cannot fully understand unless Allah reveals them in the Qur'an. Given our limited knowledge, it is crucial not to react hastily to scholars' interpretations but to listen patiently and gather knowledge. This approach will help you stay on the right path.

As an example:

In *Surah Yasin* (36:26), it says:

قِيلَ ادْخُلِ الْجَنَّةَ ۖ قَالَ يَا لَيْتَ قَوْمِي يَعْلَمُونَ

It was said (to him when the disbelievers slew him): Enter thou into Paradise. He said: Would that my people knew!

526

[Surah Yasin 36:26]

Scholars typically interpret "Jannah" (جَنَّة) in this verse to refer to the temporary, honourable accommodations of a heavenly garden granted to the highest-ranking believing prophets in the realm of Barzakh. This interpretation does not imply that this Jannah or Paradise is the final settlement before *Qiyamah* (Judgment Day).

Barzakh refers to the state of existence from the moment of death until the Day of Judgment. It is a realm we know little about beyond what the Qur'an reveals. While we might speculate and imagine various aspects of this intermediary world, its true nature remains largely unknown to us.

Allah SWT says:

لَعَلِّي أَعْمَلُ صَالِحًا فِيمَا تَرَكْتُ ۚ كَلَّا ۚ إِنَّهَا كَلِمَةٌ هُوَ قَائِلُهَا ۖ وَمِن وَرَائِهِم بَرْزَخٌ إِلَىٰ يَوْمِ يُبْعَثُونَ

That I may do good in that which I have left! No! It is but a word that he speaketh. And behind them is a barrier (Barzakh) until the day when they shall be raised again.

[Surah Al-Mu'minun 23:100]

Sleeping in Barzakh

In *Surah Yasin* (36:52), Allah SWT says:

قَالُوا يَا وَيْلَنَا مَن بَعَثَنَا مِن مَّرْقَدِنَا ۜ هَٰذَا مَا وَعَدَ الرَّحْمَٰنُ وَصَدَقَ الْمُرْسَلُونَ

They shall say: Woe unto us! Who hath raised us up from our place of sleep? (It will be said unto them): This is what the Beneficent did promise, and the messengers spoke truth.

[Surah Yasin 36:52]

This verse serves as a reminder to the followers of Allah SWT that when we pass away, regardless of whether we lived a righteous or sinful life, we enter a state of sleep until the Day of Judgment. Upon awakening, some may perceive the resurrection as a frightful event, prompting reflection on the teachings of Allah's messengers. Nevertheless, it is also logical for believers to understand this awakening not as resurrection per se, but as the transition into a new existence following death..[221]

This interpretation gains further support when we consider *Surah Taha* (20:103):

يَتَخَافَتُونَ بَيْنَهُمْ إِن لَّبِثْتُمْ إِلَّا عَشْرًا

They shall whisper among themselves: Ye tarried but ten (days).

[Surah Taha 20:103] *Index 173*

---

[221] Index 173 https://myislam.org/surah-yaseen/ayat-52/

Many scholars still believe that the torment of the grave befalls both the soul and the body. It will be like the dreams we see in this life, where a person feels joy or pain while asleep. In effect, after the soul departs from the body, it continues to be either blessed or punished, and it remains connected to the body from time to time.[222]

However, my findings—based on verses in the Qur'an—articulate the procedure of interrogation, presentation of evidence, and the final judgement in a trial, determining the destiny of the individual, whether they will be rewarded or punished. This is the established process ordained by Allah SWT, as conveyed in the Qur'an. Any alternative method of punishment prior to the Day of Judgement lacks credibility and raises numerous questions that may contradict the verses of Almighty Allah.

However, there are still some verses that may leave more room for discussion. Allah SWT says:

قِيلَ ادْخُلِ الْجَنَّةَ ۖ قَالَ يَا لَيْتَ قَوْمِي يَعْلَمُونَ

بِمَا غَفَرَ لِي رَبِّي وَجَعَلَنِي مِنَ الْمُكْرَمِينَ

26. *It was said (to him, when the disbelievers killed him): "Enter Paradise."* He said: *"Would that my people knew!"* — Surah Ya-Sin 36:26

27. *"That my Lord (Allah) has forgiven me, and made me of the honoured ones!"* — Surah Ya-Sin 36:27

Let us analyse those verses:

Here comes the Divine Word: *"It was said to him: Enter Paradise."* Imam (a.s.) said: Jannat here means the Jannat of Barzakh (interim measures till the Day of Judgement). (As discussed earlier.) Another narration mentions that it refers to the earthly paradise, which is lower than the Paradise of the Hereafter. This holy verse refers to **Habib Najjar**, who remained faithful despite belonging to the sect of Fir'awn.

Divine Declaration

لا أحد في السماء والأرض يعلم أخبار الغيب إلا الله

No one in Heaven and Earth knows the news of the unseen except Allah SWT

Allah (SWT) declared:

قُل لَّا يَعْلَمُ مَن فِي السَّمَاوَاتِ وَالْأَرْضِ الْغَيْبَ إِلَّا اللَّهُ ۚ وَمَا يَشْعُرُونَ أَيَّانَ يُبْعَثُونَ

Say: "None in the heavens and the earth knoweth the unseen, but Allah; neither know they when they shall be raised up." — Surah An-Naml 27:65

---

[222] Index 174 https://studentsofknowledge.org/quran-including-sciences-and-tafseer/question-278-tafseer-of-ayah-52-of-soorah-yaseen-and-punishment-in-grave/

Along with the above verse, the following verse also confirms this:

قُلْ مَا كُنتُ بِدْعًا مِّنَ الرُّسُلِ وَمَا أَدْرِي مَا يُفْعَلُ بِي وَلَا بِكُمْ ۖ إِنْ أَتَّبِعُ إِلَّا مَا يُوحَىٰ إِلَيَّ وَمَا أَنَا إِلَّا نَذِيرٌ مُّبِينٌ

Say (O Muhammad ﷺ): "I am not a new thing among the messengers, nor know I what shall be done with me or with you: I but follow that which is revealed unto me, and I am but a plain warner." — Surah Al-Ahqaf 46:9

These verses convey two important messages:

● Firstly, no one other than Allah SWT knows when the sleeping soul will be raised for judgement.

● Secondly, even our beloved Prophet ﷺ has limitations regarding knowledge of the unseen. He knows nothing about what will happen to him or anyone else.

This message is confirmed in another verse where Allah SWT says:

قُل لَّا أَقُولُ لَكُمْ عِندِي خَزَائِنُ اللَّهِ وَلَا أَعْلَمُ الْغَيْبَ وَلَا أَقُولُ لَكُمْ إِنِّي مَلَكٌ ۖ إِنْ أَتَّبِعُ إِلَّا مَا يُوحَىٰ إِلَيَّ ۚ قُلْ هَلْ يَسْتَوِي الْأَعْمَىٰ وَالْبَصِيرُ ۚ أَفَلَا تَتَفَكَّرُونَ

Say (O Muhammad ﷺ): "I say not unto you, I have the treasures of Allah, nor know I the unseen, nor say I unto you, I am an angel. I but follow that which is revealed unto me." Say: "Are the blind and the one who sees equal? Will ye not then consider?" — Surah Al-An'am 6:50

The above verses dispel confusion caused by many hadiths that are firmly associated with matters of the unseen.

Barzakh Sleep

Now we want to know more about what Allah SWT has said concerning the long sleep in the Barzakh state. To help us understand, Allah SWT gives an example in the Qur'an of how He kept a small group of people in a long sleep, demonstrating His power to preserve life even for hundreds of years. As mentioned earlier in Surah An-Naml 27:65:

قُل لَّا يَعْلَمُ مَن فِي السَّمَاوَاتِ وَالْأَرْضِ الْغَيْبَ إِلَّا اللَّهُ ۚ وَمَا يَشْعُرُونَ أَيَّانَ يُبْعَثُونَ

"None in the heavens and the earth knoweth the unseen, but Allah; neither know they when they shall be raised up."

This thrilling story of a long sleep is revealed in the Qur'an, especially in **Surah Al-Baqarah** and **Surah Al-Kahf**. While we often recite these verses, we tend to overlook the background and deeper significance of the "sleep" they describe, which could symbolise the Barzakh sleep.

We should now analyse this story and the commentary surrounding those verses so that the concept of the long sleep in Barzakh, lasting until the Day of Resurrection, becomes more meaningful. This is a research-based narrative compiled from various historians and religious scholars who have explored the topic and provided different interpretations. While its historical accuracy may differ, only Allah SWT knows the full truth.

Development, History, and Writing — Index 175

The following story, based on research, provides a strong indication of how the **Divine Architect** disciplines every element of His creation. The long sleep of souls in Barzakh also falls under that divine order.[223]

In 249 AD, Trajan Decius was proclaimed Emperor of Rome by his troops after suppressing a rebellion by the Thracian tribe in Moesia. [224] which in our time is the southeastern Balkans, now Serbia, part of Macedonia, and part of Bulgaria. Before Decius's reign, persecution of the Christians in the empire had been sporadic and local. But when Decius became Emperor of the Roman Empire, his ambition to strengthen his rule and the state religion led to the persecution of Christians under what is now known as the Decian Persecution. He issued an edict ordering all citizens to perform a religious sacrifice in the presence of Roman commissioners, to be confirmed by a signed and witnessed certificate from the magistrate. Although the text of the edict has been lost, many examples of the certificates have survived.

A large number of Christians defied the government, for which the bishops of Rome, Jerusalem, and Antioch lost their lives, and many others were arrested. The suppression strengthened rather than weakened the Christian movement, for public opinion condemned the government's violence and applauded the passive resistance of the martyrs. Decius wanted to wipe out Christianity from his state, so he persecuted prominent Christian scholars and learned men. Among them was Pope Fabian, who was put to death on January 20, 250, due to his steadfastness in his faith that there is no one but God. According to tradition, he was the first person killed in the savage onslaught, which was the first persecution to include the entire Roman Empire. The bishop is said to have died bravely in his faith, setting an example for his entire flock.

History has given a strange and intriguing story of Bishop Fabian. Historians describe that when Bishop Anteras died in 236, Fabian was a farmer who came to Rome to observe the choice of a successor. Needless to say, no one in the assembly gave a thought to this layman—until a surprising event took place. The early church historian Eusebius, writing about a hundred years after Fabian's death, reported that suddenly a dove (pigeon) flew into the room and landed on the farmer's head. The

---

[223] Index 175 (https://heylink.me/Israrkhan)https://israrkhan1112 and https://bit.ly/3iaAioK
[224] Note : From Wikipedia, the free encyclopedia
(Moesia was an ancient region and later Roman province situated in the Balkans south of the Danube River. Moesian Province was first administered by governor of Noricum as 'Civitates of Moesia and Triballia'.[1] It included most of the territory of modern eastern Serbia, Kosovo, north-eastern Albania, northern parts of North Macedonia (Moesia Superior), Northern Bulgaria, Romanian Dobruja and small parts of Southern Ukraine (Moesia Inferior).
1 (p. 581) ISBN 9780521264303 Bowman, Alan K.; Champlin, Edward; Lintott, Andrew (8 February 1996). The Cambridge Ancient History, Том 10. Cambridge University Press. ISBN 978-0-521-26430-3.)

assembly took this as a sign from God; had not a dove also descended on Christ at His baptism? Fabian was immediately chosen for the vacant position.

In Rome, a Greek-worn letter is still visible on an old stone slab. Translated, it reads: **"Fabian, Bishop, Martyr."**

After executing the Pope, the Emperor Decius commanded that temples be erected in the centre of the city, so that all should come with him to offer sacrifice to idols. He sought out all Christians and bound them, forcing them to sacrifice or else be put to death. In such terror, every man was so afraid that the friend abandoned his friend, the son denied his father, and the father his son.

The pagan (infidel) Romans would not tolerate the Christians and their new faith. The emperor persecuted Christians, threatening them to renounce their faith or face horrific punishments and death. However, the believers remained firm and willingly accepted death and persecution instead of recanting their religion.

The term *pagan*, which originated toward the end of the Roman Empire, referred to those who worshipped multiple deities. Polytheism is the belief in and veneration of multiple gods or goddesses, both male and female, who have various associations—those who practised a religion other than Christianity, Judaism, or Islam. But Christians questioned their belief. They questioned the authority of the emperor and his polytheistic religion. A few young men also asked the people to stop worshipping many deities, as the pagans believed in many gods, while Christianity taught the oneness of God and worship of the true Creator—the only God.

This made them the centre of the emperor's wrath, so he sent soldiers after them to arrest them and put them to death. When they discovered their lives were at stake, they decided to hide somewhere away from society. Therefore, they headed towards an unknown cave where they took shelter.

According to some legends, they didn't know each other before coming to the cave. Each of them was alone, but they had many similarities—they were all young, true believers, brave, and openly questioned the polytheistic beliefs of the Romans. Thus, God brought them to one place. However, some sources are of the view that they knew each other right from the start.

Qur'an mentioned them in this way:

Therefore, they headed towards an unknown path, seeking shelter. They prayed to their God and asked their Creator Allah (SWT) to show them the right path and to save them. God showed them the way to the cave, as described in verse 18:10 of Surah Al-Kahf:

إِذْ أَوَى الْفِتْيَةُ إِلَى الْكَهْفِ فَقَالُوا رَبَّنَا آتِنَا مِن لَّدُنكَ رَحْمَةً وَهَيِّئْ لَنَا مِنْ أَمْرِنَا رَشَدًا

"Behold, the youths betook themselves to the Cave: they said, 'Our Lord! Bestow on us mercy from Thyself, and dispose of our affair for us in the right way!'"

When they were found, the emperor ordered the disbelievers to seal the mouth of the cave so as to kill them by starvation. But they prayed to God for help.

In my opinion, this prayer is a treasure for finding the direction of life, if we recite it with a clean tongue.

Christian sources also narrate the same story: that these youths did not obey the emperor's orders to recant their belief or to bow before pagan idols. This enraged the emperor, so he ordered them to be put to death. Before going into hiding, they gave up their worldly possessions to the poor.

Allah (SWT) was pleased with their faith and accepted their prayer, as mentioned in verse 18:14 of Surah Al-Kahf:

وَرَبَطْنَا عَلَىٰ قُلُوبِهِمْ إِذْ قَامُوا فَقَالُوا رَبُّنَا رَبُّ السَّمَاوَاتِ وَالْأَرْضِ لَن نَّدْعُوَ مِن دُونِهِ إِلَـٰهًا ۖ لَّقَدْ قُلْنَا إِذًا شَطَطًا

"And We made their hearts firm and strong (with the light of Faith in Allah and bestowed upon them patience to bear the separation of their kith and kin and dwellings, etc.) when they stood up and said: 'Our Lord is the Lord of the heavens and the earth, never shall we call upon any ilah (god) other than Him; if we did, we should indeed have uttered an enormity in disbelief.'"

— Al-Kahf 18:14

So Allah (SWT) guided them to the cave, and all of them went to it. There they saw each other and prayed to God. Then Allah put them to sleep, as He says in verse 18:16:

وَإِذِ اعْتَزَلْتُمُوهُمْ وَمَا يَعْبُدُونَ إِلَّا اللَّهَ فَأْوُوا إِلَى الْكَهْفِ يَنشُرْ لَكُمْ رَبُّكُم مِّن رَّحْمَتِهِ وَيُهَيِّئْ لَكُم مِّنْ أَمْرِكُم مِّرْفَقًا

"(The young men said to one another): 'And when you withdraw from them, and that which they worship, except Allah, then seek refuge in the Cave, your Lord will open a way for you from His Mercy and will make easy for you your affair (i.e. will give you what you will need of provision, dwelling, etc.).'"

— Al-Kahf 18:16

Upon arriving at the cave, they rested and fell asleep due to the exhaustion from their journey. God extended their slumber, and they remained asleep for 300 years. When they awoke, they were astonished by the changes in the world around them. Allah (SWT) confirms this in verse 18:25 of the same Surah:

1

وَلَبِثُوا فِي كَهْفِهِمْ ثَلَاثَ مِائَةٍ سِنِينَ وَازْدَادُوا تِسْعًا

And they stayed in their Cave three hundred (solar) years, and add nine (for lunar years).

Surah Al-Kahf (The Cave), 18:25

When the Jews of Medina asked the Prophet Muhammad ﷺ numerous irrelevant questions—such as details about their sleeping arrangements, the location of each person and their dog, and the dog's position—Allah revealed this Surah to the Prophet Muhammad ﷺ, providing all the answers.

How Did They Sleep In The Cave?

2

وَتَرَى الشَّمْسَ إِذَا طَلَعَت تَّزَاوَرُ عَن كَهْفِهِمْ ذَاتَ الْيَمِينِ وَإِذَا غَرَبَت تَّقْرِضُهُمْ ذَاتَ الشِّمَالِ وَهُمْ فِي فَجْوَةٍ مِّنْهُ ۚ ذَٰلِكَ مِنْ آيَاتِ اللَّهِ ۗ مَن يَهْدِ اللَّهُ فَهُوَ الْمُهْتَدِ ۖ وَمَن يُضْلِلْ فَلَن تَجِدَ لَهُ وَلِيًّا مُّرْشِدًا

And you might have seen the sun, when it rose, declining to the right from their Cave, and when it set, turning away from them to the left, while they lay in the midst of the Cave. That is one of the signs of Allah. He whom Allah guides is rightly guided; but he whom He sends astray—for him, you will find no guardian to lead him to the right path.

Surah Al-Kahf, 18:17

3

وَتَحْسَبُهُمْ أَيْقَاظًا وَهُمْ رُقُودٌ ۚ وَنُقَلِّبُهُمْ ذَاتَ الْيَمِينِ وَذَاتَ الشِّمَالِ ۖ وَكَلْبُهُم بَاسِطٌ ذِرَاعَيْهِ بِالْوَصِيدِ ۚ لَوِ اطَّلَعْتَ عَلَيْهِمْ لَوَلَّيْتَ مِنْهُمْ فِرَارًا وَلَمُلِئْتَ مِنْهُمْ رُعْبًا

And you would have thought them awake, while they were asleep. And We turned them on their right and on their left sides, and their dog stretching forth his two forelegs at the entrance. Had you looked at them, you would certainly have turned back from them in flight and would certainly have been filled with awe of them.

Surah Al-Kahf, 18:18

4

وَكَذَٰلِكَ بَعَثْنَاهُمْ لِيَتَسَاءَلُوا بَيْنَهُمْ ۚ قَالَ قَائِلٌ مِّنْهُمْ كَمْ لَبِثْتُمْ ۖ قَالُوا لَبِثْنَا يَوْمًا أَوْ بَعْضَ يَوْمٍ ۚ قَالُوا رَبُّكُمْ أَعْلَمُ بِمَا لَبِثْتُمْ فَابْعَثُوا أَحَدَكُم بِوَرِقِكُمْ هَٰذِهِ إِلَى الْمَدِينَةِ فَلْيَنظُرْ أَيُّهَا أَزْكَىٰ طَعَامًا فَلْيَأْتِكُم بِرِزْقٍ مِّنْهُ وَلْيَتَلَطَّفْ وَلَا يُشْعِرَنَّ بِكُمْ أَحَدًا

Likewise, We awakened them (from their long deep sleep) that they might question one another. A speaker from among them said, "How long have you stayed (here)?" They said, "We have stayed (perhaps) a day or part of a day." They said, "Your Lord (alone) knows best how long you have stayed. So send one of you with this silver coin of yours to the town, and let him find out which

is the best lawful food, and bring some of that to you. And let him be careful and let no one know of you."

Surah Al-Kahf, 18:19

And similarly (when the trumpet is blown), We will awaken them that they might question one another.

A speaker from among them will say:

"How long have you remained [here]?"

They will say:

"We have remained a day or part of a day."

(Just as they said in the cave, so too shall we say when we awake from the long sleep of Barzakh.)

They will say:

"Your Lord is most knowing of how long you remained. So send one of you with this silver coin of yours to the city and let him look to which is the best food and bring you provision from it. And let him be cautious, and let no one be aware of you."

Here we find compelling evidence of how Allah (SWT) preserves and sustains our souls for as long as He wills—even for billions of years. When the time comes, it is effortless for Him to awaken us for questioning on the Day of Judgment.

The narrative centres on our waiting period in Barzakh, illustrated by how Allah awakened the sleepers in the cave and they questioned one another, as described in verse 19 and further elaborated in verse 20:

5

إِنَّهُمْ إِن يَظْهَرُوا عَلَيْكُمْ يَرْجُمُوكُمْ أَوْ يُعِيدُوكُمْ فِي مِلَّتِهِمْ وَلَن تُفْلِحُوا إِذًا أَبَدًا

"For if they come to know of you, they will stone you (to death or abuse and harm you), or turn you back to their religion, and in that case you will never be successful."

Surah Al-Kahf, 18:20

6

وَكَذَٰلِكَ أَعْثَرْنَا عَلَيْهِمْ لِيَعْلَمُوا أَنَّ وَعْدَ اللَّهِ حَقٌّ وَأَنَّ السَّاعَةَ لَا رَيْبَ فِيهَا إِذْ يَتَنَازَعُونَ بَيْنَهُمْ أَمْرَهُمْ ۖ فَقَالُوا ابْنُوا عَلَيْهِم بُنْيَانًا ۖ رَّبُّهُمْ أَعْلَمُ بِهِمْ ۚ قَالَ الَّذِينَ غَلَبُوا عَلَىٰ أَمْرِهِمْ لَنَتَّخِذَنَّ عَلَيْهِم مَّسْجِدًا

And thus We made their case known to the people, that they might know that the promise of Allah is true and that there can be no doubt about the Hour. (Remember) when they (the people of the city) disputed among

themselves about their case, they said: "Construct a building over them; their Lord knows best about them." Then those who prevailed in their matter said: "We verily shall build a place of worship over them."*Surah Al-Kahf, 18:21*[225]

Who were they ?

The curious researcher is still seeking answers which only Allah (SWT) knows. No one knows exactly who the People of the Cave were or what their origin was. Were they from Rome, Palestine, Syria, Jordan, or some other country? We do not know, as it was either not recorded or the true sources have been lost to history.

However, it is generally accepted that they were Roman citizens who embraced Christianity and worshipped their Creator, remaining steadfast in their belief even in the face of death. Almost every source agrees on this.

Where did they go to the cave?

Although it is still disputed, many sources agree that it was the Cave of Ephesus — located in modern-day Turkey. This was an old city built in the 11th century BC by the Ionian prince Androcles. Since then, the city has fallen to various conquerors and invaders, yet the remains of the city have survived.

How many were they?

Only Allah (SWT) knows.

Historians are uncertain about the exact number. While various historians and scholars continue to debate this, the precise figure remains unknown. According to Gregory of Tours and the list by Bartłomiej Grysa, there were seven, whereas Michael the Syrian states there were six. Other claims suggest different numbers: 10, 9, 8, and even one legend asserts there were as many as 80.

How long did they sleep in the cave?

The Qur'an reveals the truth, so we should encourage everyone to reflect and correct themselves, despite disputes among historians. Many historians claim that the sleepers stayed in the cave for 300 solar years. However, Gregory of Tours asserted they slept for 373 years. According to Jacobus de Varagine, the sleepers were in the cave from 252 to 448, which totals 196 years. He steadfastly believed in his calculations throughout his life.

Allah (SWT) states in the Qur'an:

"And they remained in their cave three hundred years, and add nine."

— *Surah Al-Kahf, 18:25*

---

[225] Index 176 https://www.britannica.com/topic/Seven-Sleepers-of-Ephesus

These years mentioned in the Qur'an are lunar years, which convert to 300 solar years.

People asked about the number of the sleepers, the colour of their dog, the number of years they slept, and similar details. However, most of these questions are irrelevant. Allah (SWT) states in the Qur'an that it is a Book of Guidance, not a collection of aimless stories.

Allah (SWT) revealed to us a powerful message and said:

Surah Al-Kahf, 18:26

قُلِ اللَّهُ أَعْلَمُ بِمَا لَبِثُوا لَهُ غَيْبُ السَّمَاوَاتِ وَالْأَرْضِ أَبْصِرْ بِهِ وَأَسْمِعْ مَا لَهُم مِّن دُونِهِ مِن وَلِيٍّ وَلَا يُشْرِكُ فِي حُكْمِهِ أَحَدً

Say: "Allah knoweth best how long they stayed: with Him is the knowledge of the secrets of the heavens and the earth. How clearly He sees, and hears (everything)! They have no protector other than Him; nor doth He share His command with any person whatsoever."

Surah Al-Kahf, 18:26

And thus We made their case known to the people, that they might know that the promise of Allah is true, and that there can be no doubt about the Hour. (Remember) when they (the people of the city) disputed among themselves about their case, they said: "Construct a building over them; their Lord knows best about them." Then those who prevailed in the matter said (most probably the disbelievers): "We verily shall build a place of worship over them."

— Surah Al-Kahf, 18:21

Allah (SWT) summed up the whole incident in this Surah and gave us a message on how He will deal with our souls after death.

Our travelling party, along with every believer sincerely seeking a clear path to the world of dreams, can find numerous answers in this Surah. It will alleviate their fears and guide them to progress as true believers.

The following verses of the same Surah are also crucial to consider in your quest for truth:

Verses 9–14 of Surah Al-Kahf:

أَمْ حَسِبْتَ أَنَّ أَصْحَابَ الْكَهْفِ وَالرَّقِيمِ كَانُوا مِنْ آيَاتِنَا عَجَبًا

Do you think that the People of the Cave and the Inscription were a wonder among Our Signs? — 18:9

(Remember) when the young men fled for refuge to the Cave, they said: "Our Lord! Bestow on us mercy from Yourself, and facilitate for us our affair in the right way!" — 18:10

فَضَرَبْنَا عَلَىٰ آذَانِهِمْ فِي الْكَهْفِ سِنِينَ عَدَدًا

Therefore We covered up their hearing in the Cave for a number of years. — 18:11

ثُمَّ بَعَثْنَاهُمْ لِنَعْلَمَ أَيُّ الْحِزْبَيْنِ أَحْصَىٰ لِمَا لَبِثُوا أَمَدًا

Then We raised them up (from their sleep), that We might test which of the two parties was best at calculating the time period that they had tarried. — 18:12

نَّحْنُ نَقُصُّ عَلَيْكَ نَبَأَهُم بِالْحَقِّ ۚ إِنَّهُمْ فِتْيَةٌ آمَنُوا بِرَبِّهِمْ وَزِدْنَاهُمْ هُدًى

We narrate unto you (O Muhammad ﷺ) their story with truth: Truly! They were young men who believed in their Lord (Allah), and We increased them in guidance. — 18:13

وَرَبَطْنَا عَلَىٰ قُلُوبِهِمْ إِذْ قَامُوا فَقَالُوا رَبُّنَا رَبُّ السَّمَاوَاتِ وَالْأَرْضِ لَن نَّدْعُوَ مِن دُونِهِ إِلَـٰهًا ۖ لَّقَدْ قُلْنَا إِذًا شَطَطًا

And We made their hearts firm and strong when they stood up and said: "Our Lord is the Lord of the heavens and the earth. Never shall we call upon any god other than Him; if we did, we should indeed have uttered an enormity in disbelief." — 18:14

Claimants of the Location of the Sleepers

The true location of the legendary Seven Sleepers is still uncertain, as multiple sites claim to be the exact location. Below are pictures of two of the seven known sites. The claimants are:

1. Tuyuq Khojam Mazar, Turpan, China
2. Cave of the Seven Sleepers, Amman, Jordan
3. Eshab-ı Kehf Cave, Ephesus, Turkey
4. Mosquée des Sept Dormants, Chenini, Tunisia
5. Mar Musa, Syria
6. Grotto of the Seven Sleepers, İzmir, Turkey
7. Eshab-ı Kehf Cave, Kahramanmaraş, Turkey

Eshab-ı Kehf Kulliye

Eshab-ı Kehf Külliye is a historical building complex in Kahramanmaraş Province, Turkey. The complex is located next to a cave on a hill named Bencilus, 7 kilometres (4.3 mi) from the Afşin district in Kahramanmaraş Province. It is 130 kilometres (81 mi) away from the Kahramanmaraş city centre. Due to its importance, the 18th chapter of the Qur'an is called Kahf, and it recounts the events that occurred there. Christians revere the "Seven Sleepers" as saints, while Muslims consider them miracles. The Eshab-ı Kehf Complex was registered on UNESCO's World Heritage Tentative List in 2015.

https://turkisharchaeonews.net/object/grotto-seven-sleepers-ephesus

https://www.tripadvisor.com/Attraction_Review-g754058-d3630897-Reviews-Eshab_i_Kehf_Cave_Mosque-Tarsus_Mersin_Icel_Turkish_Mediterranean_Coast.html

Let us now turn our attention to the kingdom of Barzakh, where we began this chapter. We know that we will remain there until the Day of Judgment. Our loved ones who have departed are all waiting in that mysterious realm. Some members of our travelling party have already crossed the hurdles of this part of their journey and entered Barzakh, a place unfamiliar to us.

It is our prayer and hope that they receive the mercy of Almighty Allah for their sins and achieve a dignified status by His grace as they rest until the command of Allah comes again, continuing the journey to the court of justice.

Although Prophet Muhammad (ﷺ) serves as our teacher and guide, when it comes to matters of the unseen, Allah alone has declared His dominion over the heavens and the earth. No one possesses the power to interfere with the unseen, and thus, we can only speculate and conjecture on such matters.

We can reflect on the verses from Surah Al-Ahqaf (46:9) and Surah An-Naml (27:65) to remind ourselves that we do not have the authority to fabricate unseen matters in the name of our Prophet or Hadith. We can only analyse and establish the veracity of these matters if we find any clues in the verses.

Allah (SWT) says:

As mentioned at the beginning, the world of Barzakh is different from our world. This is confirmed by Allah (SWT) in Surah Ar-Rahman verse 55:20 and Al-Mu'minun verse 23:100, repeated again:

بَيْنَهُمَا بَرْزَخٌ لَّا يَبْغِيَانِ

"Between them is a barrier which none of them can transgress."

لَعَلِّي أَعْمَلُ صَالِحًا فِيمَا تَرَكْتُ ۚ كَلَّا ۚ إِنَّهَا كَلِمَةٌ هُوَ قَائِلُهَا ۖ وَمِن وَرَائِهِم بَرْزَخٌ إِلَىٰ يَوْمِ يُبْعَثُونَ

538

"So that I may do good in that which I have left behind!" No! It is but a word that he speaks, and behind them is Barzakh (a barrier) until the Day when they will be resurrected."

At the designated time, all souls will be summoned, and their ultimate fate will be declared: darkness for sinners and light for believers.

However, Allah (SWT) has declared in the Qur'an that the souls of a certain group of people will be punished continuously in Barzakh until the Day of Judgment. He has also described the severity of this punishment. Additionally, it is confirmed that they will be cast into Hell on the Day of Judgment.

In the Qur'an, Allah (SWT) says:

النَّارُ يُعْرَضُونَ عَلَيْهَا غُدُوًّا وَعَشِيًّا ۚ وَيَوْمَ تَقُومُ السَّاعَةُ أَدْخِلُوا آلَ فِرْعَوْنَ أَشَدَّ الْعَذَابِ

"The fire; they are exposed to it morning and evening: and in the day when the Hour shall be established, (it shall be said), 'Cause Pharaoh's people to enter the severest torment.'" — Surah Ghafir (40:46)

This verse suggests that the realm of Barzakh experiences days and nights similar to those on Earth. It also states that the angels of Hell bring the fire of Hell to torment the people of Pharaoh every morning and evening until the Day of Judgment.

In another verse, Allah (SWT) speaks of two punishments: the first being inflicted in this world, and the ultimate punishment to be decided on the Day of Judgment. Allah (SWT) says:

وَمِمَّنْ حَوْلَكُم مِّنَ الْأَعْرَابِ مُنَافِقُونَ ۖ وَمِنْ أَهْلِ الْمَدِينَةِ ۖ مَرَدُوا عَلَى النِّفَاقِ لَا تَعْلَمُهُمْ ۖ نَحْنُ نَعْلَمُهُمْ ۚ سَنُعَذِّبُهُم مَّرَّتَيْنِ ثُمَّ يُرَدُّونَ إِلَىٰ عَذَابٍ عَظِيمٍ

"And of the folk of the desert around you there are hypocrites, and among the people of Al-Madinah (too); they persist in hypocrisy whom thou (O Muhammad) knowest not. We, We know them. We shall chastise them twice; then they will be relegated to a painful doom." — Surah At-Tawbah (9:101)

Dr. Mustafa Khattab,

translator of The Clear Quran, explains this verse as follows:

"Some of the nomads around you are hypocrites, like some people from Medina. They have mastered hypocrisy. They are not known to you, O Prophet (ﷺ); they are familiar to Us. We will punish them twice in this world, and then they will be returned to their Lord for a severe punishment (on the Day of Judgment)."

(Note: Mustafa Khattab is a Canadian-Egyptian authority on interpreting the Qur'an.)

Another verse confirms the concept of no intermediate suffering but a final punishment on the Day of Judgment. The verse states:

وَلَنُذِيقَنَّهُم مِّنَ الْعَذَابِ الْأَدْنَىٰ دُونَ الْعَذَابِ الْأَكْبَرِ لَعَلَّهُمْ يَرْجِعُونَ

"And verily We will make them taste the lower punishment before the greater punishment, in order that they may return (to Us)." — Surah As-Sajda (32:21)

These verses indicate that Allah (SWT) punishes sinners in this world to instil awareness in their hearts, giving them the opportunity to return to the right path before death.

Allah's Decree For Punishment in Barzakh

As previously mentioned, certain individuals have their punishment in Barzakh predestined. Allah (SWT) reveals verses to remind His servants about the impending punishment these individuals will face before the Day of Judgment.

Allah (SWT) says in Surah Al-Mu'min (40):

فَوَقَاهُ اللَّهُ سَيِّئَاتِ مَا مَكَرُوا ۖ وَحَاقَ بِآلِ فِرْعَوْنَ سُوءُ الْعَذَابِ

النَّارُ يُعْرَضُونَ عَلَيْهَا غُدُوًّا وَعَشِيًّا ۖ وَيَوْمَ تَقُومُ السَّاعَةُ أَدْخِلُوا آلَ فِرْعَوْنَ أَشَدَّ الْعَذَابِ

وَإِذْ يَتَحَاجُّونَ فِي النَّارِ فَيَقُولُ الضُّعَفَاءُ لِلَّذِينَ اسْتَكْبَرُوا إِنَّا كُنَّا لَكُمْ تَبَعًا فَهَلْ أَنتُم مُّغْنُونَ عَنَّا نَصِيبًا مِّنَ النَّارِ

45. So Allah saved him from the evils that they plotted (against him), while an evil torment encompassed Pharaoh's people.

46. The Fire: they are exposed to it, morning and afternoon, and on the Day when the Hour is established (it will be said to the angels), "Cause Pharaoh's people to enter the severest torment."

47. And when they will dispute in the Fire, the weak will say to those who were arrogant, "Verily! We followed you, can you then take from us some portion of the Fire?" — *Surah Al-Mu'min (40:45–47)*

This is a matter of divine decree by Allah (SWT) regarding the punishment of Pharaoh and his followers in Barzakh. Allah (SWT) has revealed verses describing how the angels will inflict punishment upon Pharaoh and his people, ultimately casting them into the fire of Hell on the Day of Judgment.

Allah SWT, the Most Merciful, forgives the sins of His servants at His discretion. However, there is a unique situation where an individual declares themselves to be "Allah" and persists in this false claim despite receiving numerous opportunities to repent. In such a case, it raises the question: how will Allah, the Almighty, forgive such a person?

The punishment bestowed upon Pharaoh and his followers serves as a perfect and just example, leaving no doubt about the righteousness of Allah's judgment.

It is important to note that, aside from this specific example, there is no explicit mention of a Barzakh punishment applying to any other common individual, regardless of their sins. Allah SWT has made it clear that when the time of Judgement arrives, He will judge His creation with absolute justice. As Muslims, we trust that Allah will manage these matters with wisdom and fairness.

Allah SWT says:

وَنَضَعُ الْمَوَازِينَ الْقِسْطَ لِيَوْمِ الْقِيَامَةِ فَلَا تُظْلَمُ نَفْسٌ شَيْئًا ۖ وَإِن كَانَ مِثْقَالَ حَبَّةٍ مِّنْ خَرْدَلٍ أَتَيْنَا بِهَا ۗ وَكَفَىٰ بِنَا حَاسِبِينَ

And We shall set up balances of justice on the Day of Resurrection, then none shall be wronged in anything. And if there be (no more than) the weight of a mustard seed, We will bring it forth (to account). And sufficient are We as Reckoners. — *Surah Al-Anbiya (21:47)*

Who Is Fir'aun or Pharaoh?

In the Bible, Pharaoh is believed to be:

Died 1225 B.C., king of ancient Egypt, of the 19th Dynasty. The son of Seti I, Ramses was not originally the heir to the throne but usurped it from his brother. He reigned for 67 years (1292–1225 B.C.).

In Islam, Pharaoh is referred to as "Fir'aun" (فرعون in Arabic), the ruler of Egypt between approximately 1279 BC and 1213 BC.

The early life of Fir'aun remains largely unknown, but it is established that he rose to power in Egypt before the birth of Musa (peace be upon him). As the religious leader of the Egyptians, the Pharaoh was seen as a divine intermediary between their numerous gods and the people. Ensuring religious harmony and performing ceremonial duties were among his responsibilities as the head of religion.

Many scholars believe that the first Pharaoh of Egypt was Narmer.[226]

He was the successor to the Predynastic king Ka, also called Menes.

The Pharaoh was a heinous, cold, arrogant, and power-hungry tyrant, ranking among the most evil villains in history. He believed himself to be a god—superior to the Children of Israel—and dismissed any claims of other deities, even pagan idols, as falsehoods. Despite witnessing divine miracles, his arrogance prevented him from acknowledging any higher power.

---

[226] ENCYCLOPEDIC ENTRY VOCABULARY
Narmer was an ancient Egyptian pharaoh of the Early Dynastic Period.// Narmer (c. 3150 BCE) was the first king of Egypt who unified the country peacefully at the beginning of the First Dynastic Period (c. 3150 - 2613 BCE).)

His extreme hubris led him to kill his own wife for supporting the Children of Israel and to brutally murder anyone who believed in God, including the magicians, whose faith infuriated him. He proclaimed:

وَقَالَ فِرْعَوْنُ يَا أَيُّهَا الْمَلَأُ مَا عَلِمْتُ لَكُم مِّنْ إِلَهٍ غَيْرِي فَأَوْقِدْ لِي يَا هَامَانُ عَلَى الطِّينِ فَاجْعَل لِّي صَرْحًا لَّعَلِّي أَطَّلِعُ إِلَى إِلَهِ مُوسَى وَإِنِّي لَأَظُنُّهُ مِنَ الْكَاذِبِينَ

Pharaoh said:

"And Pharaoh said, O ye chiefs, I know not that ye have a god other than me: therefore, O Haman, light me a fire upon the clay, and make me a lofty tower, that I may look upon the God of Moses: and verily, I think he is one of the liars." — *Surah Al-Qasas (28:38)* [227]

It appeared that Pharaoh would never believe in Moses's message, nor would he stop the torture of the Children of Israel. Therefore, the Prophet Moses عليه السلام prayed:

وَقَالَ مُوسَى رَبَّنَا إِنَّكَ آتَيْتَ فِرْعَوْنَ وَمَلَأَهُ زِينَةً وَأَمْوَالًا فِي الْحَيَاةِ الدُّنْيَا رَبَّنَا لِيُضِلُّوا عَن سَبِيلِكَ ۖ رَبَّنَا اطْمِسْ عَلَى أَمْوَالِهِمْ وَاشْدُدْ عَلَى قُلُوبِهِمْ فَلَا يُؤْمِنُوا حَتَّى يَرَوُا الْعَذَابَ الْأَلِيمَ

"And Moses said, Our Lord, Thou hast indeed bestowed Pharaoh and his chiefs with splendour and riches in the life of this world, that they may lead men astray from Thy way. Our Lord, destroy their riches, and harden their hearts, that they may not believe until they see the grievous punishment." (Surah Yunus 10:88)

Allah SWT answered:

قَالَ قَدْ أُجِيبَت دَّعْوَتُكُمَا فَاسْتَقِيمَا وَلَا تَتَّبِعَانِّ سَبِيلَ الَّذِينَ لَا يَعْلَمُونَ

"He said, The prayer of you both is accepted: therefore stand ye upright, and follow not the path of those who know not." (Surah Yunus 10:89)

Afterwards, when Moses stood before Pharaoh and commanded the Children of Israel to follow the path of Allah, Pharaoh responded with arrogance. He asserted his own divinity and warned Moses of severe punishment if he did not comply. This story is recounted in detail by Allah SWT in the Qur'an.

End of Barzakh Life

Our Barzakh life will end when the trumpet is blown. Our material bodies will ascend to this earth and merge with the spirit, and our body and soul will become one. This will be the end of the long sleep of all souls and the beginning of the third path, which means we will move forward towards the court of justice.

---

[227] Index 178 https://villains.fandom.com/wiki/Pharaoh_(theology)#Biography
Firon - Pharaoh – Encyclopedia//https:// encyclopedia2.thefreedictionary.com › Firon

Verse 52 of Surah 36 confirms what has already been mentioned. Allah SWT has given us a clear description of what we will do and what will happen after a long sleep in Barzakh. Allah SWT says:

وَنُفِخَ فِي الصُّورِ فَإِذَا هُم مِّنَ الْأَجْدَاثِ إِلَىٰ رَبِّهِمْ يَنسِلُونَ

"And the trumpet shall be blown, and, behold, they shall come forth from the graves unto their Lord with speed." (Surah Ya-Sin 36:51)

قَالُوا يَا وَيْلَنَا مَن بَعَثَنَا مِن مَّرْقَدِنَا ۗ هَٰذَا مَا وَعَدَ الرَّحْمَٰنُ وَصَدَقَ الْمُرْسَلُونَ

"They shall say, Woe unto us! Who hath raised us from our sleeping place? This is what the Most Gracious had promised, and the messengers spake truth." (Surah Ya-Sin 36:52)

إِن كَانَتْ إِلَّا صَيْحَةً وَاحِدَةً فَإِذَا هُمْ جَمِيعٌ لَّدَيْنَا مُحْضَرُونَ

"It shall be but one shout, and, behold, they shall all be brought before Us." (Surah Ya-Sin 36:53)

Here, Allah SWT makes it clear that the matter of resurrection is not difficult for Him. It is only one shout which will be given by Israfeel عليه السلام, and with that, everyone will be gathered before Him.

According to the commentators, the 'shout' mentioned in the verse refers to the statement of Israfeel عليه السلام which he will utter to the dead bodies. He will address the bodies and say, "O rotten bones; disconnected joints; separated parts and shredded hairs, your Lord has ordered you to gather for the decision of His decree." Upon this, he will then blow the trumpet, and with it, all will be gathered on the plain of Reckoning.

When the trumpet blows, conversation will take place between people in Barzakh on the Day of Resurrection. Allah SWT says:

1

وَاسْتَمِعْ يَوْمَ يُنَادِ الْمُنَادِ مِن مَّكَانٍ قَرِيبٍ

يَوْمَ يَسْمَعُونَ الصَّيْحَةَ بِالْحَقِّ ۚ ذَٰلِكَ يَوْمُ الْخُرُوجِ

إِنَّا نَحْنُ نُحْيِي وَنُمِيتُ وَإِلَيْنَا الْمَصِيرُ

يَوْمَ تَشَقَّقُ الْأَرْضُ عَنْهُمْ سِرَاعًا ۚ ذَٰلِكَ حَشْرٌ عَلَيْنَا يَسِيرٌ

41. "And hearken thou unto the day when the caller shall call from a place near,

42. The day when they shall hear the cry in truth: that is the day of coming forth.

43. Verily We give life and cause death, and unto Us is the final return.

44. On the day when the earth shall be cleft asunder from them, and they come forth with speed. That gathering will be easy for Us." (Surah Qaf 50:41–44)

2

Again, in Surah Ta-Ha, Allah SWT says:

نَّحْنُ أَعْلَمُ بِمَا يَقُولُونَ إِذْ يَقُولُ أَمْثَلُهُمْ طَرِيقَةً إِن لَّبِثْتُمْ إِلَّا يَوْمًا

"We know best what they will say, when the most upright among them shall say, Ye tarried not but a day." (Surah Ta-Ha 20:104) [228]

Olam Ha-Ba

How Does The Old Testament Define Next World

Where Does The Soul Go After Death

The term *olam ha-ba* (literally, "the coming world") refers to the Hereafter, which begins with the termination of man's earthly life. This meaning of the expression is clearly implied in the statement of Rabbi Jacob, quoted in *Avot* (4:17):

"One moment of repentance and good deeds in this world is better than the entire life of the world to come."

This was also, according to Akavyah ben Mahalalel (*Avot* 3:1), man's destiny after the termination of his life on earth.

"The dead do not praise the Lord," said *Avot* (4:17),

"neither any that go down into silence." (Psalm 115:17, KJV)

Job entertained no hope of revivification. He remarked gloomily:

"But man dieth, and wasteth away: yea, man giveth up the ghost, and where is he?

As the waters fail from the sea, and the flood decayeth and drieth up:

So man lieth down, and riseth not: till the heavens be no more, they shall not awake, nor be raised out of their sleep." (Job 14:10–12, KJV)

As for the nature of human existence in the world to come, the Babylonian Amora Rav, who lived at the beginning of the third century BCE, thought that it was completely different from life in this world.

"There is there," he said, "neither eating, nor drinking, nor any begetting of children, no bargaining or jealousy or hatred or strife. All that the righteous do is to sit with their crowns on their heads and enjoy the effulgence of the [divine] Presence." (*Berakhot* 17a)

The question was also asked where the souls of human beings were kept between the time of their death and the resurrection, which is supposed to take place prior to the Last Judgement. The answer given by Rabbi Yose ha-Gelili was that

---

[228] Index 179 https://www.islamweb.net/en/fatwa/83719/life-in-barzakh.

there were special store chambers where the souls of the righteous were deposited, as it is stated:

"Yet a man is risen to pursue thee, and to seek thy soul: but the soul of my lord shall be bound in the bundle of life with the Lord thy God; and the souls of thine enemies, them shall he sling out, as out of the middle of a sling." (1 Samuel 25:29, KJV)

The souls of the wicked, on the other hand, would—according to the interpretation in *Shabbat* 152b—be "slung away in the hollow of the sling".[229]
Index 180

The God of heaven and earth has said,

"All souls are mine." (Ezekiel 18:4, KJV)

Where does your soul go until Judgement Day?

In the Bible, we find many passages dealing with this subject. One commonly referenced verse is:

"His breath goeth forth, he returneth to his earth; in that very day his thoughts perish."

—Psalm 146:4 (KJV)

This verse tells us that when our spirit leaves our body, we return to the dust. This is further confirmed in Genesis:

"In the sweat of thy face shalt thou eat bread, till thou return unto the ground;

for out of it wast thou taken: for dust thou art, and unto dust shalt thou return."

—Genesis 3:19 (KJV)

And the following verse continues:

"And Adam called his wife's name Eve; because she was the mother of all living."

—Genesis 3:20 (KJV)

Yet we also find hope in the promise of resurrection. The prophet Isaiah declared:

"Thy dead men shall live, together with my dead body shall they arise.

Awake and sing, ye that dwell in dust: for thy dew is as the dew of herbs,

and the earth shall cast out the dead."

---

[229] Index 180 https://www.jewishvirtuallibrary.org/olam-ha-ba

—Isaiah 26:19 (KJV) [230]

Bible Verses About the Resurrection of the Dead

Passages concerning the resurrection of the dead can be found throughout Scripture, particularly in relation to the End Times.

In the Book of Daniel, we read:

"And many of them that sleep in the dust of the earth shall awake,

some to everlasting life, and some to shame and everlasting contempt.

And they that be wise shall shine as the brightness of the firmament;

and they that turn many to righteousness as the stars for ever and ever.

But thou, O Daniel, shut up the words, and seal the book,

even to the time of the end: many shall run to and fro, and knowledge shall be increased."

—Daniel 12:2–4 (KJV)

Likewise, the prophet Isaiah proclaimed hope for the resurrection:

"Thy dead men shall live, together with my dead body shall they arise.

Awake and sing, ye that dwell in dust: for thy dew is as the dew of herbs,

and the earth shall cast out the dead."

—Isaiah 26:19 (KJV)[231]

The Valley of Dry Bones

Ezekiel 37:1–14

The hand of the Lord was upon me, and carried me out in the Spirit of the Lord, and set me down in the midst of the valley which was full of bones,

And caused me to pass by them round about: and, behold, there were very many in the open valley; and, lo, they were very dry.

And he said unto me, Son of man, can these bones live?

And I answered, O Lord God, thou knowest.

---

[230] Index 181 https://www.jewishvirtuallibrary.org/afterlife

[231] Holy Bible New International Version®, NIV® Copyright © 1973, 1978, 1984, 2011 by Biblica, Inc.® Used by permission. All rights reserved worldwide.
New International Version (NIV) Holy Bible, New International Version®, NIV® Copyright ©1973, 1978, 1984, 2011 by Biblica, Inc.® Used by permission. All rights reserved worldwide.
Holy Bible, New International Version®, NIV® Copyright ©1973, 1978, 1984, 2011 by Biblica, Inc.® Used by permission. All rights reserved worldwide.

Again he said unto me, Prophesy upon these bones, and say unto them, O ye dry bones, hear the word of the Lord.

Thus saith the Lord God unto these bones; Behold, I will cause breath to enter into you, and ye shall live:

And I will lay sinews upon you, and will bring up flesh upon you, and cover you with skin, and put breath in you, and ye shall live; and ye shall know that I am the Lord.

In 1 Corinthians 15:51–52, the Apostle Paul proclaims:

Behold, I shew you a mystery; We shall not all sleep, but we shall all be changed,

In a moment, in the twinkling of an eye, at the last trump:

for the trumpet shall sound, and the dead shall be raised incorruptible, and we shall be changed.

This passage tells us that, at the final trumpet—when Jesus returns to earth (cf. Revelation 11:15)—our bodies will be instantly transformed into incorruptible bodies.

Somewhere in the hereafter, your soul—the real you—will face the deeds done while your body was alive in this life, whether good or bad. Refer to Hebrews 9:27:

And as it is appointed unto men once to die, but after this the judgment.

God, in the Holy Bible, warns of the impending Final Judgment of all the earth. The Scriptures prophesy that, before that notable Day of Judgment, there will be clear and undeniable signs. There will be no turning back or salvation after death.

Then shall he say also unto them on the left hand, Depart from me, ye cursed, into everlasting fire, prepared for the devil and his angels.

—Matthew 25:41

And cast ye the unprofitable servant into outer darkness: there shall be weeping and gnashing of teeth.

—Matthew 25:30

Let us remember that our just and great Judge will not be influenced by our present wealth or poverty, fame or disgrace, or by our colour, race, caste, or creed.

One day we will all stand before our great Creator and Lord to be judged according to our deeds.

And before him shall be gathered all nations: and he shall separate them one from another,

as a shepherd divideth his sheep from the goats:

And he shall set the sheep on his right hand, but the goats on the left.

—Matthew 25:32–33

At the end shall come the world to come, when the righteous will sit in glory and enjoy the splendour of the Divine Presence in a realm of purely spiritual bliss (Ber. 17). [232]

Conclusion

The question of what happens after we die is a subject that has fascinated and perplexed humanity for centuries. Across various cultures and religions, people have debated the nature of the afterlife, trying to reconcile the unknown with their beliefs and experiences. Scholars and thinkers have delved deeply into these mysteries, offering interpretations and insights based on their profound knowledge and wisdom. Their contributions are invaluable, as they often uncover subtle clues and connections that may not be immediately apparent to the average person.

However, when it comes to matters of faith and the afterlife, it is essential to return to the core texts and teachings of one's religion for ultimate guidance. For Muslims, the **Qur'an** and **Hadith** provide the primary sources of divine instruction. Almighty **Allah (SWT)** has given clear guidance on many aspects of the afterlife—from the nature of Paradise and Hell to the criteria for judgement.

It is crucial to study these verses and teachings carefully, giving them the attention and respect they deserve. By doing so, believers can better understand the expectations and requirements set forth by their faith. This understanding helps in identifying and rectifying actions and behaviours that might jeopardise one's standing on the Day of Judgment.

Therefore, while the wisdom of scholars is significant, it must be balanced with a direct and personal engagement with the sacred texts. This dual approach ensures that one's beliefs and actions are firmly rooted in divine guidance, reducing the risk of errors that could have severe consequences in the hereafter.

Now, as we enter the final stage, we can expect a culmination of the lessons learned and challenges faced in the previous stages. It is an opportunity to showcase personal growth, reflect on the journey thus far, and make a final push towards the ultimate objective.

During this stage, it is important to maintain a sense of focus and determination. The challenges may be more intense, and the stakes could be higher. However, armed with the knowledge and experience gained in the earlier stages, we can approach these obstacles with confidence and resilience—qualities that will lead us to **Darus Salam** and **Jannatul Ferdous**.

---

[232] Index 182 https://www.gospeltractandbible.org/tract/after-death?

بِسْمِ ٱللَّهِ ٱلرَّحْمَـٰنِ ٱلرَّحِيمِ

Chapter 16

The Last Hour (Before the Day of Judgement)

The Last Hour will not come until the land of Arabia becomes meadows and rivers.

Abu Huraira (RadhiAllahu 'anhu) reported:

"And many of them that sleep in the dust of the earth shall awake, some to everlasting life, and some to shame and everlasting contempt."

Daniel 12:2 (KJV)

📖📖📖📖📖📖

Resurrection

فعل القيامة من الأموات

The Greek word *anastasis*, meaning "rise up from sleep or from the dead," is translated as Resurrection.

"And I, behold, I establish my covenant with you, and with your seed after you."

Genesis 9:9 (KJV)

In the Peshitta, a 5th-century Aramaic New Testament, the word used for "resurrection" is קימתא(*Q'yam'ta*).

In the Modern Hebrew Bible, the word for "resurrection" is תקומה(*tequmah*), a term related to the same concept found in the Peshitta.

Another example appears in:

"And they shall stumble one upon another, as it were before a sword, when none pursueth: and ye shall have no power to stand before your enemies."

Leviticus 26:37 (KJV)

From all of this, we can gather that the ancient understanding of the "Resurrection of the Dead" is essentially the rising up or more literally, the standing up of the dead.[233]

Resurrection generally implies a return to life after death, involving both physical and spiritual dimensions, and is a key theme in many religious traditions. Muslims believe in the Day of Judgment, when the dead will be resurrected to be judged by Allah.

Allah (SWT) revealed a verse in the Qur'an confirming resurrection, saying:

كَيْفَ تَكْفُرُونَ بِاللَّهِ وَكُنتُمْ أَمْوَاتًا فَأَحْيَاكُمْ ۖ ثُمَّ يُمِيتُكُمْ ثُمَّ يُحْيِيكُمْ ثُمَّ إِلَيْهِ تُرْجَعُونَ

"How can ye disbelieve in Allah? Seeing that ye were dead, and He gave you life. Then He will give you death, then again will bring you to life (on the Day of Resurrection), and then unto Him ye shall return."

Surah Al-Baqara 2:28

Allah (SWT) confirms in this verse that we will rise and face judgement. It also serves as a reminder to re-evaluate the solidity of our faith and commitment to righteousness.

In **Surah Yasin 36:79**, Allah (SWT) says:

قُلْ يُحْيِيهَا الَّذِي أَنشَأَهَا أَوَّلَ مَرَّةٍ ۖ وَهُوَ بِكُلِّ خَلْقٍ عَلِيمٌ

"He Who created them the first time will give them life again, and He is the All-Knower of every creation."

Surah Yasin 36:79

The truth of the resurrection is affirmed in the Qur'an as part of Allah's divine plan, revealed to our Prophet Muhammad ﷺ, the final messenger of Allah (SWT). This plan has been disclosed to His prophets since the time of Adam عليه السلام.

It is natural to be curious about the verses revealed to previous prophets and the views of medieval scholars on resurrection and judgement. Reflecting on these teachings and the wisdom of past scholars can fortify our faith and help ensure that we remain steadfast in our belief in Allah's (SWT) ultimate plan, including resurrection and judgement.

Resurrection in Judaism

In Judaism, the concept of resurrection (*Techiyat HaMetim* – the revival of the dead) is less explicitly described in the Torah but is found in later texts and rabbinic literature. Key references include:

---

[233] https://www.ancient-hebrew.org/studies-nt/greek-aramaic-and-hebrew-words-for-resurrection.htm

Daniel 12:2 (KJV):

"And many of them that sleep in the dust of the earth shall awake, some to everlasting life, and some to shame and everlasting contempt."

This verse is part of the prophetic vision of the end times given to Daniel. Here's a breakdown of its meaning:

1. **"And many of them that sleep in the dust of the earth shall awake"**: This phrase refers to the resurrection of the dead. "Sleep in the dust" is a metaphor for being dead and buried. The verse predicts a resurrection at the end of times.

2. **"Some to everlasting life"**: This indicates that some of the resurrected will be granted eternal life. In Christian theology, this is often interpreted as the righteous being rewarded with Heaven.

3. **"And some to shame and everlasting contempt"**: Conversely, others will be resurrected to face eternal shame and contempt. In Christian interpretation, this is often understood as the fate of the wicked or unrighteous, who face eternal punishment.

Overall, **Daniel 12:2** is a key verse in biblical eschatology (the study of the end times), emphasising the final resurrection and the eternal destinies of the righteous and the wicked.

Isaiah 26:19 (KJV):

"Thy dead men shall live, together with my dead body shall they arise. Awake and sing, ye that dwell in dust: for thy dew is as the dew of herbs, and the earth shall cast out the dead."

Importance in Jewish Thought

Resurrection as a Fundamental Belief

The resurrection of the dead is not only a theological concept but a crucial part of Jewish eschatology—the area of theology concerned with the final events of history and the ultimate destiny of humanity. It represents the final redemption and the fulfilment of God's promises to the Jewish people.

Maimonides' Thirteen Principles of Faith

The great Jewish philosopher and legal codifier **Maimonides (Rambam)** included the belief in the resurrection of the dead as the thirteenth of his Thirteen Principles of Faith. These principles are considered foundational beliefs required of a Jew. The last principle states:

"I believe with perfect faith that there will be a resurrection of the dead at a time that will please the Creator, blessed be His name and exalted be His mention forever and ever."

Christian Thought: Philosophers and Theologians

Thomas Aquinas and Augustine on Resurrection

Thomas Aquinas, a renowned medieval philosopher and theologian, articulated a detailed concept of resurrection in his magnum opus, *Summa Theologica*.

A proper understanding of Aquinas's psychology is essential to grasp his beliefs about the afterlife and resurrection. Following church doctrine, he accepted that the soul continues to exist after the body's death. His views are deeply rooted in Christian theology and Aristotelian philosophy.

Here is a summary of **Aquinas's concept of resurrection**:

- The resurrected body will be numerically the same as the earthly body—meaning the same body that lived, died, and decayed will be restored.

- The body will be entirely subject to the soul: it will be perfectly obedient to the soul's will, able to move effortlessly and swiftly.

- The body will shine with a brilliance reflecting the soul's perfection.

- Aquinas believed that the **soul is the form of the body**, giving it structure and nature. Upon resurrection, the same soul will reinhabit the resurrected body and, having attained its ultimate state of perfection, will also perfect the body—making it incorruptible and glorified.

- Despite physical death and decay, continuity exists between the earthly and resurrected body because **the same soul animates both**. This continuity preserves **personal identity**.

Aquinas used **Aristotelian metaphysics** to argue that form (soul) and matter (body) together constitute a human being. The resurrection restores this unity. He asserted that resurrection is a **manifestation of divine justice and goodness**: the righteous are rewarded with a glorified body, while the wicked are resurrected for final judgement.

Both **Aquinas and Augustine** allow for a Heaven and Hell as described in scripture, with eternal consequences based on divine justice.[234]

---

[234] *Thomas Aquinas (1225–1274) was an Italian Dominican friar, Catholic priest, and influential philosopher and theologian of the medieval period. He is best known for his integration of Aristotelian philosophy with Christian theology, forming a comprehensive theological framework that has had a lasting impact on Western thought His Philosophical Contributions such as :*
Summa Theologica, Five Ways: Arguments for the existence of God, which include the argu-ments from motion, causation, contingency, perfection, and teleological ar-gument (design).
Summa Theologica: His most famous work, a comprehensive compendium of Christian theology that addresses fundamental theological questions.

Another philosopher, Augustine's theology of the resurrection, is a crucial aspect of his broader theological framework, emphasising the transformative power of divine grace and the ultimate restoration of human nature. Augustine believed that the resurrection was both a physical and spiritual event, in which the body and soul are reunited and glorified. He argued that the resurrection is not merely a return to our earthly state but an elevation to a higher, perfected existence—free from corruption and mortality.

As a major theologian of the resurrection, Augustine emphasised the resurrection of the flesh, maintaining that the same bodies we have now will be raised and transformed into incorruptible and glorified bodies. This underscores the continuity between our current existence and our future state. In the resurrection, believers will be transformed, with their bodies being perfected and freed from the effects of sin and death. This glorification signifies the completion of salvation and the full realisation of God's redemptive work.

Augustine also highlighted the importance of the unity between body and soul. He believed that human beings are incomplete without both, and thus, the resurrection restores the full human nature as God intended. The ultimate purpose of the resurrection, according to Augustine, is to enable believers to enjoy eternal life in the presence of God, experiencing the beatific vision—the direct and unmediated vision of God, which is the fulfilment of all human desires and the ultimate end of human existence.

Augustine's theology of the resurrection offers a hopeful and profound vision of the future, where the effects of sin and death are completely overcome, and believers are fully restored and united with God in eternal glory.

Augustine of Hippo, an ancient philosopher commonly known as Saint Augustine, was a significant early Christian theologian and philosopher. He was born on 13 November 354 in Thagaste, a Roman province in present-day Algeria, and died on 28 August 430 in Hippo Regius (modern-day Annaba, Algeria).

Bishop of Hippo: Augustine became the Bishop of Hippo in 396 and served in that role until his death. He developed the doctrine of original sin, which asserts that humanity inherits a fallen nature and a propensity to sin through Adam. Augustine's thought continues to be studied and respected in both religious and philosophical contexts, making him one of the most influential figures in Western thought.

Five Ways: Arguments for the existence of God, which include the arguments from motion, causation, contingency, perfection, and teleological argument (design).
Thomas Aquinas' taught at various universities, including the University of Paris and the University of Naples His synthesis of faith and reason and his detailed exploration of theological and philosophical issues continue to be foundational in Christian theology and Western philosophical traditions.

When The Trumpet Shall Sound

"Doomsday Will Begin."

The End of the World

Allah SWT says:

وَنُفِخَ فِي الصُّورِ فَصَعِقَ مَن فِي السَّمَاوَاتِ وَمَن فِي الْأَرْضِ إِلَّا مَن شَاءَ اللَّهُ ۖ ثُمَّ نُفِخَ فِيهِ أُخْرَىٰ فَإِذَا هُم قِيَامٌ يَنظُرُونَ

And the Trumpet will be blown, and all who are in the heavens and all who are on the earth will swoon away, except him whom Allah And the Trumpet will be blown, and all who are in the heavens and all who are on the earth will swoon away, except him whom Allah will. Then it will be blown a second time and behold, they will be standing, looking on (waiting). (39:68, Surah Az-Zumar)

The Bible describes this event as:

For the Lord himself shall descend from heaven with a shout, with the voice of the archangel, and with the trump of God: and the dead in Christ shall rise first:

Then we which are alive and remain shall be caught up together with them in the clouds, to meet the Lord in the air: and so shall we ever be with the Lord.

— 1 Thessalonians 4:16–17 (KJV)[235]

13 O how great the plan of our God! For, on the other hand, the paradise of God must deliver up the spirits of the righteous, and the grave must deliver up the body of the righteous; and the spirit and the body shall be restored to itself again. All men shall become incorruptible and immortal, and they shall be living souls, having a perfect knowledge like unto us in the flesh, save it be that our knowledge shall be perfect.

14 Wherefore, we shall have a perfect knowledge of all our guilt, and our uncleanness, and our nakedness; and the righteous shall have a perfect knowledge of their enjoyment and their righteousness, being clothed with purity, yea, even with the robe of righteousness.

15 And it shall come to pass that when all men shall have passed from this first death unto life, insomuch as they have become immortal, they must appear before the judgement seat of the Holy One of Israel; and then cometh the judgement, and they must be judged according to the holy judgement of God.

Resurrected bodies have size, weight, shape, and occupy space. They have every limb, joint, hair, and body part that is natural to the physical body, and they enjoy never-ending youth without sickness or pain. They are dynamic; they eat, drink, and digest food, along with other functions including metabolism and bodily

---

[235] Index 183 https://www.churchofjesuschrist.org/study/scriptures/bofm/2-ne/9?lang=eng

warmth. They have spirit fluid in their veins instead of red blood and do not require sleep.

How Can This Be Possible?

Many feeble-minded believers seek the truth within themselves. In the Qur'an, there is an allusion to the miracles behind Allah's will and how He can reassemble the human body into a beautiful new form, even though the earth consumed the corpse billions of years ago.

Allah (SWT) has confirmed its authenticity in the Qur'an. He says:

رِّزْقًا لِّلْعِبَادِ ۖ وَأَحْيَيْنَا بِهِ بَلْدَةً مَّيْتًا ۚ كَذَٰلِكَ الْخُرُوجُ

A provision for (Allah's) slaves. And We give life therewith to a dead land. Thus will be the resurrection (of the dead). — 50:11, Surah Qaf

To better understand this complex matter, Allah (SWT) has set an example for His servants. The verse describes:

وَفِي الْأَرْضِ قِطَعٌ مُّتَجَاوِرَاتٌ وَجَنَّاتٌ مِّنْ أَعْنَابٍ وَزَرْعٌ وَنَخِيلٌ صِنْوَانٌ وَغَيْرُ صِنْوَانٍ يُسْقَىٰ بِمَاءٍ وَاحِدٍ وَنُفَضِّلُ بَعْضَهَا عَلَىٰ بَعْضٍ فِي الْأُكُلِ ۚ إِنَّ فِي ذَٰلِكَ لَآيَاتٍ لِّقَوْمٍ يَعْقِلُونَ

And in the earth are neighbouring tracts, and gardens of vines, and green crops (fields etc.), and date-palms, growing out two or three from a single stem root, or otherwise (one stem root for every palm), watered with the same water, yet some of them We make more excellent than others to eat. Verily, in these things, there are Ayat (proofs, evidences, lessons, signs) for the people who understand. — 13:4, Surah Ar-Ra'd

Then in the following verse of the same Surah, Allah (SWT) says:

وَإِن تَعْجَبْ فَعَجَبٌ قَوْلُهُمْ أَإِذَا كُنَّا تُرَابًا أَإِنَّا لَفِي خَلْقٍ جَدِيدٍ ۗ أُولَٰئِكَ الَّذِينَ كَفَرُوا بِرَبِّهِمْ ۖ وَأُولَٰئِكَ الْأَغْلَالُ فِي أَعْنَاقِهِمْ ۖ وَأُولَٰئِكَ أَصْحَابُ النَّارِ ۖ هُمْ فِيهَا خَالِدُونَ

And if you (O Muhammad ﷺ) wonder (at these polytheists who deny your message of Islamic Monotheism and have taken besides Allah others for worship who can neither harm nor benefit), then wondrous is their saying: "When we are dust, shall we indeed then be (raised) in a new creation?" They are those who disbelieve in their Lord! They are those who will have iron chains tying their hands to their necks. They will be dwellers of the Fire to abide therein. — 13:5, Surah Ar-Ra'd

From this, we understand that when Allah decreed the death of all living things, the Messenger of Allah ﷺ informed us that the one assigned to blow the horn has been ready to fulfil this task since the moment Allah created him.

555

Abu Huraira (RA), on the authority of al-Mustadrak, said:

The Messenger ﷺ of Allah (SWT) said:

"The gaze of the one who will blow the Trumpet has been fixed since he was entrusted with it, looking towards the throne, ready (to blow it), in case he will be commanded to do so before he blinks, as if his eyes are two shining stars."

Classed as saheeh by al-Albaani in al-Silsilah al-Saheehah, 1078.

Then they will remain like that for as long as Allah decrees, which is described as forty—without specifying whether that is years, months, or days. Allah knows best how long it is. Their bodies will decay within this period until there is nothing left but the bone from the base of the coccyx. This bone, also known as the tailbone, is a small, triangular bone resembling a shortened tail located at the bottom of the spine. It is composed of three to five coccygeal vertebrae or spinal bones.

Then Allah will send a cloud that will release rain, and when the water reaches this bone, the body will grow from it like a plant grows. They will be recreated from this bone, just as Allah created them the first time—for He is able to do all things.

Then He will blow the Trumpet to signal the Resurrection, and the souls will return to their bodies. They will come forth from their graves and hasten to the place of gathering.

We ask Allah for His mercy and kindness..[236]

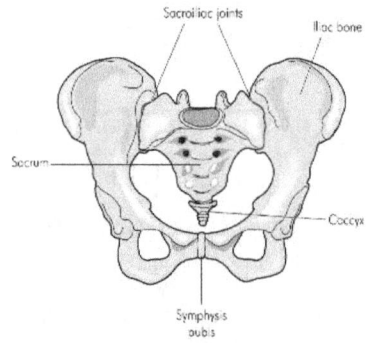

(The coccyx is the triangular bony structure located at the bottom of the vertebral column. It is composed of three to five bony segments held in place by joints and ligaments.)

Allah does not make it incumbent upon us to investigate these matters, but our curiosity continues to explore as far as our knowledge extends, based on the revealed verses. Our responsibility is to believe in the resurrection and in all stages of the process described in the Qur'an until our destiny is determined on the Day of Judgement. Human knowledge, experimentation, or any method of verification is incapable of uncovering the unseen divine science.

---

[236] Index 184 https://islamqa.info/en/answers/96306/gender-of-angels-and-do-they-die

Allah SWT says:

1

$$قُلْ يُحْيِيهَا الَّذِي أَنشَأَهَا أَوَّلَ مَرَّةٍ ۖ وَهُوَ بِكُلِّ خَلْقٍ عَلِيمٌ$$

Say, "He will give them life Who created them the first time! For He is well-versed in every kind of creation." — Surah Ya-Sin 36:79

And then Allah SWT says:

2

$$وَضَرَبَ لَنَا مَثَلًا وَنَسِيَ خَلْقَهُ ۖ قَالَ مَن يُحْيِي الْعِظَامَ وَهِيَ رَمِيمٌ$$

And he puts forth for Us a parable and forgets his own creation. He says: "Who will give life to these bones when they have rotted away and become dust?" — Surah Ya-Sin 36:78

3

$$بَلَىٰ قَادِرِينَ عَلَىٰ أَن نُّسَوِّيَ بَنَانَهُ$$

Yes, We are able to put together in perfect order the tips of his fingers. — Surah Al-Qiyamah 75:4

The majority of scholars are of the view that the Trumpet will be blown twice: the first time, all creatures will swoon; the second time, the resurrection will take place.

Al-Bukhari (4651) and Muslim (2955) narrated that Abu Hurayrah (RA) said:

The Messenger ﷺ of Allah SWT said:

"Between the two blowings of the Trumpet there will be forty."

The people said, "O Abu Hurayrah! Forty days?"

I said: "I am not sure."

They said, "Forty years?"

I said: "I am not sure."

They said, "Forty months?"

I said: "I am not sure."

"Then Allah will send down rain from the sky and they will grow like herbs grow. There is no part of a man which does not decay except a single bone at the base of the coccyx, from which he will be recreated on the Day of Resurrection."

The Last Day of the World's Existence

The "Day of Resurrection"

At a glance through the verses Allah has revealed:

وَنُفِخَ فِي الصُّورِ فَإِذَا هُم مِّنَ الْأَجْدَاثِ إِلَىٰ رَبِّهِمْ يَنسِلُونَ

And the Trumpet will be blown (i.e. the second blowing), and behold! From the graves they will come out quickly to their Lord. — Surah Ya-Sin 36:51

وَيَوْمَ يُنفَخُ فِي الصُّورِ فَفَزِعَ مَن فِي السَّمَاوَاتِ وَمَن فِي الْأَرْضِ إِلَّا مَن شَاءَ اللَّهُ ۚ وَكُلٌّ أَتَوْهُ دَاخِرِينَ

And (remember) the Day on which the Trumpet will be blown, and all who are in the heavens and all who are on the earth will be terrified, except whom Allah will (exempt). And all shall come to Him humbled. — Surah An-Naml 27:87

يَوْمَ يُنفَخُ فِي الصُّورِ فَتَأْتُونَ أَفْوَاجًا

وَفُتِحَتِ السَّمَاءُ فَكَانَتْ أَبْوَابًا

وَسُيِّرَتِ الْجِبَالُ فَكَانَتْ سَرَابًا

18. The Day when the Trumpet will be blown, and you shall come forth in crowds (groups);

19. And the heaven shall be opened, and it will become as gates;

20. And the mountains shall be moved away from their places, and they will be as if they were a mirage. — Surah An-Naba' 78:18–20

يَوْمَ يَقُومُ الرُّوحُ وَالْمَلَائِكَةُ صَفًّا ۖ لَّا يَتَكَلَّمُونَ إِلَّا مَنْ أَذِنَ لَهُ الرَّحْمَٰنُ وَقَالَ صَوَابًا

The Day that Ar-Ruh [Jibrael (Gabriel)] and the angels will stand forth in rows, none shall speak except him whom the Most Beneficent (Allah) allows, and he will speak what is right. — Surah An-Naba' 78:38

وَتَرَكْنَا بَعْضَهُمْ يَوْمَئِذٍ يَمُوجُ فِي بَعْضٍ ۖ وَنُفِخَ فِي الصُّورِ فَجَمَعْنَاهُمْ جَمْعًا

وَعَرَضْنَا جَهَنَّمَ يَوْمَئِذٍ لِّلْكَافِرِينَ عَرْضًا

And on that Day [i.e. the Day Ya'juj and Ma'juj (Gog and Magog) will come out], We shall leave them to surge like waves on one another. And the Trumpet will be blown, and We shall gather them all together.

And on that Day We shall present Hell to the disbelievers, plain to view. — Surah Al-Kahf 18:99–100

Our Destiny On The Day The Trumpet Will Sound

ALLAH SWT SAYS:

That Day, We shall gather the sinful, bleary-eyed (with terror). In whispers will they consult each other:

"Yet tarried not longer than ten days."

يَوْمَ يُنفَخُ فِي الصُّورِ ۚ وَنَحْشُرُ الْمُجْرِمِينَ يَوْمَئِذٍ زُرْقًا

يَتَخَافَتُونَ بَيْنَهُمْ إِن لَّبِثْتُمْ إِلَّا عَشْرًا

The Day when the Trumpet will be blown (the second blowing): that Day, We shall gather the Mujrimun (criminals, polythesists, sinners, disbelievers in the Oneness of Allah, etc.), Zurqa: (blue or blind-eyed with black faces).

In whispers will they speak to each other, saying: "You stayed not longer than ten (days)." — Surah Ta-Ha 20:102–103

وَيَوْمَ تَقُومُ السَّاعَةُ يُقْسِمُ الْمُجْرِمُونَ مَا لَبِثُوا غَيْرَ سَاعَةٍ ۚ كَذَٰلِكَ كَانُوا يُؤْفَكُونَ

وَقَالَ الَّذِينَ أُوتُوا الْعِلْمَ وَالْإِيمَانَ لَقَدْ لَبِثْتُمْ فِي كِتَابِ اللَّهِ إِلَىٰ يَوْمِ الْبَعْثِ ۖ فَهَٰذَا يَوْمُ الْبَعْثِ وَلَٰكِنَّكُمْ كُنْتُمْ لَا تَعْلَمُونَ

55. And on the Day that the Hour will be established, the Mujrimun (criminals, disbelievers, polythesists, sinners, etc.) will swear that they stayed not but an hour; thus were they deluded (away from the truth).

56. And those who have been bestowed with knowledge and faith will say: "Indeed, you have stayed according to the Decree of Allah until the Day of Resurrection. So this is the Day of Resurrection, but you knew not." — Surah Ar-Rum 30:55–56

وَلَا تَدْعُ مَعَ اللَّهِ إِلَٰهًا آخَرَ ۘ لَا إِلَٰهَ إِلَّا هُوَ ۚ كُلُّ شَيْءٍ هَالِكٌ إِلَّا وَجْهَهُ ۚ لَهُ الْحُكْمُ وَإِلَيْهِ تُرْجَعُونَ

And call not, besides Allah, upon another god. There is no god but He. Everything will perish except His own Face. To Him belongs the Command, and to Him shall ye all be brought back. — Surah Al-Qasas 28:88

There is no need to introduce any additional information on this subject, as the preceding verses already give us a comprehensive understanding of the resurrection process and our fate. Allah SWT explicitly advises against seeking further knowledge beyond what He has provided, as human understanding is limited and cannot comprehend beyond the extent of His descriptions.

What Will Happen To The Angels?

Will They Die?

Index 184

Allah (SWT) says:

Shaykh al-Islam Ibn Taymiyah (may Allah have mercy on him) was asked:

Will all of creation, even the angels, die?

He replied:

What most people believe is that all of creation will die—even the angels, and even the Angel of Death. There is a hadeeth concerning this that is *marfoo'*—that is, attributed to the Prophet (ﷺ).

Al-Suyuti (may Allah have mercy on him) said:

I was asked:

Will the angels die when the Trumpet is blown, and will they come to life when the Trumpet blast for resurrection is sounded?

Note – The answer is: Yes.

Allah says:

وَنُفِخَ فِي الصُّورِ فَصَعِقَ مَن فِي السَّمَاوَاتِ وَمَن فِي الْأَرْضِ إِلَّا مَن شَاءَ اللَّهُ ۖ ثُمَّ نُفِخَ فِيهِ أُخْرَىٰ فَإِذَا هُم قِيَامٌ يَنظُرُونَ

wills. Then it will be blown a second time, and behold, they will be standing, looking on (waiting). — 39:68, Surah Az-Zumar[237]

When the first Trumpet is blown, everything in the heavens and the earth will cease to exist.

This is referred to as the **Blow of Destruction**. It will destroy everything except that which Allah wills. These will include the four angels:

Israfil (A.S)

Mikail (A.S)

Jibril (A.S)

The Angel of Death (A.S),

as well as the angels who carry the Throne of Allah (SWT).

It was narrated from Wahb that these four angels were the first creatures to be created by Allah, and they will be the last to die, and the first to be brought back to life.

The Almighty Allah (SWT) will command the Angel of Death to take the souls of Israfil (A.S), Mikail (A.S), and Jibril (A.S). Then, the Almighty Allah (SWT) will ask the Angel of Death, **"Who is left?"** The Angel of Death will reply,

"It is only me."

Allah (SWT) will then command him to take his own life. The Angel of Death will go to a land between the heavens and the earth to take his own soul. He will then say:

"If I had known death was so painful, I would have been more merciful to the souls of the believers."

---

[237] Note: Al-Suyuti; aka Jalaluddin; was an Egyptian polymath, scholar, historian, sufi and jurist. From a family of Persian origin, he was described as one of the most prolific writers of the Middle Ages. Wikipedia

However, we have no definitive information about what will happen to these two angels:

Raqeeb

'Ateed

Even though the other angels die as described above, only Allah (SWT) knows their fate.

Index 185

Now let's consider where our traveller team stands.

We do not know where exactly we will stand on that Day. The place where all will gather is known as the **Place of Qiyamah**. It is a place filled with worry and panic about one's fate, where even concern for one's family will fade away. The next step is to stand trial and have one's destiny decided in the final judgment—with no provision for appeal or review.

Allah has already informed us about the conditions of the arena of Qiyamah. Therefore, a believer who successfully overcomes the tests of this material world will surely receive benefits in addition to the final judgment.

I hope our group falls into this blessed category. The following verses give us hope and we must reflect upon them for our own survival:

Allah (SWT) says about Qiyamah:

وَمَن يُطِعِ اللَّهَ وَالرَّسُولَ فَأُولَٰئِكَ مَعَ الَّذِينَ أَنْعَمَ اللَّهُ عَلَيْهِم مِّنَ النَّبِيِّينَ وَالصِّدِّيقِينَ وَالشُّهَدَاءِ وَالصَّالِحِينَ ۚ وَحَسُنَ أُولَٰئِكَ رَفِيقًا

And whoso obeyeth Allah and His Messenger, they shall be with those upon whom Allah hath bestowed His grace—of the Prophets, the truthful, the martyrs, and the righteous. And how excellent a company are they!

— *Surah An-Nisa (4:69)*

نَحْنُ أَوْلِيَاؤُكُمْ فِي الْحَيَاةِ الدُّنْيَا وَفِي الْآخِرَةِ ۖ وَلَكُمْ فِيهَا مَا تَشْتَهِي أَنفُسُكُمْ وَلَكُمْ فِيهَا مَا تَدَّعُونَ

We are your protectors in this life and in the Hereafter. Therein shall ye have all that your souls shall desire, and therein shall ye have all that ye ask for.

— *Surah Fussilat (41:31)*

وَاتَّقُوا يَوْمًا لَّا تَجْزِي نَفْسٌ عَن نَّفْسٍ شَيْئًا وَلَا يُقْبَلُ مِنْهَا شَفَاعَةٌ وَلَا يُؤْخَذُ مِنْهَا عَدْلٌ وَلَا هُمْ يُنصَرُونَ

And fear the Day when no soul shall avail another, nor shall intercession be accepted from it, nor shall compensation be taken, nor shall they be helped.

— *Surah Al-Baqarah (2:48)*

561

يَا أَيُّهَا النَّاسُ اتَّقُوا رَبَّكُمْ ۚ إِنَّ زَلْزَلَةَ السَّاعَةِ شَيْءٌ عَظِيمٌ

يَوْمَ تَرَوْنَهَا تَذْهَلُ كُلُّ مُرْضِعَةٍ عَمَّا أَرْضَعَتْ وَتَضَعُ كُلُّ ذَاتِ حَمْلٍ حَمْلَهَا وَتَرَى النَّاسَ سُكَارَىٰ وَمَا هُم بِسُكَارَىٰ وَلَٰكِنَّ عَذَابَ اللَّهِ شَدِيدٌ

O mankind! Fear your Lord! Verily, the convulsion of the Hour is a terrible thing.

The Day ye shall see it, every nursing mother shall forget her child, every pregnant woman shall cast her burden, and thou shalt see mankind as if drunken, though they be not drunken: but the punishment of Allah is severe.

— Surah Al-Hajj (22:1–2)

As believers, we understand that none of Allah's (SWT) creations will escape judgement and its consequences. These matters are part of the unseen, so we must rely on what Allah has revealed in the Holy Book. Any additional descriptions are the interpretations of scholars, the authenticity of which lies with Allah alone.

The verse describing the pre-judgement condition is indeed very frightening. To overcome those difficult days, we must seek guidance from Allah's Word, wherein He assures us of ease. Let us reflect on these verses deeply and strive to transform ourselves into true believers. Examine your faith and evaluate the strength of your standing as a true servant of Allah.

Let us now pray for ourselves and for all those still on their journey toward the final abode—Paradise.

We humbly seek Allah's mercy:

O Allah! We seek refuge with You from the punishment of the grave.

O Allah! Help us to live and die as Muslims and help us to understand the true purpose of this life.

O Allah! Grant us good in this life and good in the Hereafter, and save us from the torment of the Hellfire.

"We hear and we obey."

Counting Time

What does Allah (SWT) say about the mechanism of time in this world and the eternal world?

Allah has appointed a set time for reckoning on this earth and has set an appointed time for the events of gathering and judgement.

Allah (SWT) says:

إِنَّ عِدَّةَ الشُّهُورِ عِندَ اللَّهِ اثْنَا عَشَرَ شَهْرًا فِي كِتَابِ اللَّهِ يَوْمَ خَلَقَ السَّمَاوَاتِ وَالْأَرْضَ مِنْهَا أَرْبَعَةٌ حُرُمٌ ۚ ذَٰلِكَ الدِّينُ الْقَيِّمُ ۚ فَلَا تَظْلِمُوا فِيهِنَّ أَنفُسَكُمْ ۚ وَقَاتِلُوا الْمُشْرِكِينَ كَافَّةً كَمَا يُقَاتِلُونَكُمْ كَافَّةً ۚ وَاعْلَمُوا أَنَّ اللَّهَ مَعَ الْمُتَّقِينَ

Verily, the number of months with Allah is twelve (in a year), so was it ordained by Allah on the Day He created the heavens and the earth. Of them, four are Sacred. That is the right religion, so wrong not yourselves therein. And fight against the polytheists collectively as they fight against you collectively. But know that Allah is with those who fear Him.

— Surah At-Tawbah (9:36)

But in the eternal world, time is completely different from our world. After the trumpet is blown, all creation will wait to appear before Allah (SWT), but how long will it take?

We know very little about the mechanism of the other side of the world. We only know what Allah (SWT) tells us. So only He knows how long the wait will be for the judgement of His creation.

Allah (SWT) speaks about His appointed time to end all our affairs, on which our destinies will depend. Allah (SWT) says:

تَعْرُجُ الْمَلَائِكَةُ وَالرُّوحُ إِلَيْهِ فِي يَوْمٍ كَانَ مِقْدَارُهُ خَمْسِينَ أَلْفَ سَنَةٍ

The angels and the Ruh [Jibra'il (Gabriel)] ascend to Him in a Day the measure whereof is fifty thousand years.

70:4, Surah Al-Ma'arij (The Ways of Ascent)

يُدَبِّرُ الْأَمْرَ مِنَ السَّمَاءِ إِلَى الْأَرْضِ ثُمَّ يَعْرُجُ إِلَيْهِ فِي يَوْمٍ كَانَ مِقْدَارُهُ أَلْفَ سَنَةٍ مِّمَّا تَعُدُّونَ

He arranges every affair from the heavens to the earth, then it will ascend to Him in a Day, the measure of which is a thousand years of your reckoning (i.e., reckoning of the present world's time).

32:5, Surah As-Sajda

وَيَسْتَعْجِلُونَكَ بِالْعَذَابِ وَلَن يُخْلِفَ اللَّهُ وَعْدَهُ ۚ وَإِنَّ يَوْمًا عِندَ رَبِّكَ كَأَلْفِ سَنَةٍ مِّمَّا تَعُدُّونَ

And they ask you to hasten on the torment! But Allah will never fail His promise. And verily, a Day with your Lord is as a thousand years of what you reckon.

22:47, Surah Al-Hajj [238]

---

[238] Index 186 https://www.answering-islam.org/Responses/Abualrub/allahs_days.htm

What the Torah and the Gospel Say About the Trumpet

In a moment, in the twinkling of an eye, at the last trump: for the trumpet shall sound, and the dead shall be raised incorruptible, and we shall be changed.

(1 Corinthians 15:52, KJV)

The righteous dead will also hear the sounding of the shofar. Isaiah says:

"All ye inhabitants of the world, and dwellers on the earth, see ye, when he lifteth up an ensign on the mountains; and when he bloweth a trumpet, hear ye."

(Isaiah 18:3, KJV)

Behold, I shew you a mystery; We shall not all sleep, but we shall all be changed,

In a moment, in the twinkling of an eye, at the last trump: for the trumpet shall sound, and the dead shall be raised incorruptible, and we shall be changed.

(1 Corinthians 15:51–52, KJV)

"Blow ye the trumpet in Zion, and sound an alarm in my holy mountain: let all the inhabitants of the land tremble: for the day of the Lord cometh, for it is nigh at hand."

(Joel 2:1, KJV)

In Matthew 24:4–51, Messiah warns about the Day of the Lord.

Trumpets in Revelation

In the Book of Revelation, we find seven trumpet judgments that unfold during the Tribulation, culminating with the seventh trumpet.

"And the seventh angel sounded; and there were great voices in heaven, saying,

The kingdoms of this world are become the kingdoms of our Lord, and of his Christ;

and he shall reign for ever and ever."

(Revelation 11:15, KJV)

The Seventh Seal and the Golden Censer

"And another angel came and stood at the altar, having a golden censer; and there was given unto him much incense,

that he should offer it with the prayers of all saints upon the golden altar which was before the throne.

And the smoke of the incense, which came with the prayers of the saints, ascended up before God out of the angel's hand.

And the angel took the censer, and filled it with fire of the altar, and cast it into the earth:

and there were voices, and thunderings, and lightnings, and an earthquake."

(Revelation 8:3–5, KJV)

In ancient Scriptures, the sounding of the trumpets by the seven angels marks a series of momentous and transformative events. Each blast from the trumpet initiates significant and often devastating consequences—both natural and supernatural—signifying the unfolding of divine judgement and the culmination of prophetic destiny.

Trumpet 1

"The first angel sounded, and there followed hail and fire mingled with blood,

and they were cast upon the earth: and the third part of trees was burnt up, and all green grass was burnt up."

(Revelation 8:7, KJV)

Trumpet 2

"And the second angel sounded, and as it were a great mountain burning with fire was cast into the sea:

and the third part of the sea became blood;

And the third part of the creatures which were in the sea, and had life, died;

and the third part of the ships were destroyed."

(Revelation 8:8–9, KJV)

Trumpet 3

"And the third angel sounded, and there fell a great star from heaven, burning as it were a lamp,

and it fell upon the third part of the rivers, and upon the fountains of waters;

And the name of the star is called Wormwood: and the third part of the waters became wormwood;

and many men died of the waters, because they were made bitter."

(Revelation 8:10–11, KJV)

Trumpet 4

"And the fourth angel sounded, and the third part of the sun was smitten,

and the third part of the moon, and the third part of the stars;

so as the third part of them was darkened, and the day shone not for a third part of it, and the night likewise.

And I beheld, and heard an angel flying through the midst of heaven, saying with a loud voice,

Woe, woe, woe, to the inhabiters of the earth by reason of the other voices of the trumpet of the three angels, which are yet to sound!"

(Revelation 8:12–13, KJV)

"Neither their silver nor their gold shall be able to deliver them in the day of the Lord's wrath;

but the whole land shall be devoured by the fire of his jealousy:

for he shall make even a speedy riddance of all them that dwell in the land."

(Zephaniah 1:18, KJV)

Trumpet 5

"And the fifth angel sounded, and I saw a star fall from heaven unto the earth:

and to him was given the key of the bottomless pit.

And he opened the bottomless pit; and there arose a smoke out of the pit, as the smoke of a great furnace;

and the sun and the air were darkened by reason of the smoke of the pit."

(Revelation 9:1–2, KJV)

The abyss is symbolically seen as a place of evil and spiritual darkness—a bottomless chasm representing the temporary restraint of Satan and the dwelling of imprisoned fallen angels awaiting judgement **(see 2 Peter 2:4 and Jude 1:6).**

Trumpet 6

"And the sixth angel sounded, and I heard a voice from the four horns of the golden altar which is before God,

Saying to the sixth angel which had the trumpet, Loose the four angels which are bound in the great river Euphrates.

And the four angels were loosed, which were prepared for an hour, and a day, and a month, and a year, for to slay the third part of men."

(Revelation 9:13–15, KJV)

Trumpet 7

"And the nations were angry, and thy wrath is come,

and the time of the dead, that they should be judged,

and that thou shouldest give reward unto thy servants the prophets, and to the saints,

and them that fear thy name, small and great;

and shouldest destroy them which destroy the earth."

(Revelation 11:18, KJV)

This final trumpet is believed to correspond to the "last trump" mentioned in Paul's epistles, at which time the resurrection of the dead in Christ will occur. While the precise timing remains unclear, this trumpet heralds the final transformation and victory.[239] *Index 188*

Cool Drink Before Gathering From The Pond Of Kawthar

When people rush to gather on the Day of Resurrection, they will be thirsty and eager to quench their thirst. In honour of our Prophet Muhammad (ﷺ), the Lord will provide cool drinks from the pond of Kawthar.

Al-Kawthar is a pond in Paradise from which the Ummah of the Prophet (ﷺ) will drink on the Day of Judgement. What is the pond of Al-Kawthar? According to Hadith, it is a river from Paradise. Water flows from there through two channels. Before the judgements, the believers of the Prophet Muhammad (ﷺ) will drink from this river (pond). The water of the pond of Al-Kawthar will be whiter than milk, colder than ice, and sweeter than honey. The soil beneath it will smell more fragrant than musk. Everyone who drinks from it will never be thirsty again.

The Prophet (ﷺ) said:

"It (Kawthar) is a canal which my Lord, the Exalted and Glorious, has promised me, and there is an abundance of good in it. It is a cistern, and my people would come to it on the Day of Resurrection, and tumblers there would be equal to the number of stars. Some people would be turned away from (among the people gathered there). Upon this, I would say: My Lord, they are among my people, and He (the Lord) would say: You do not know what they innovated (in religion) after you."

(Sahih Bukhari and Sahih Muslim)

Please note:

Sura Al-Kawthar 108

$$\text{إِنَّا أَعْطَيْنَاكَ الْكَوْثَرَ}$$

$$\text{فَصَلِّ لِرَبِّكَ وَانْحَرْ}$$

$$\text{إِنَّ شَانِئَكَ هُوَ الْأَبْتَرُ}$$

Verily, We have granted thee (O Muhammad ﷺ) Al-Kawthar (a river in Paradise);

Therefore turn in prayer to thy Lord and sacrifice (to Him only).

---

[239] 188 https://hallel.info/trumpets-2020/#trumpet

For he that hateth thee, he shall be cut off.

Salah (prayer) to your Lord and sacrifice—this Surah tells that the Prophet (ﷺ) has been granted a great bounty in the form of Al-Kawthar. Thus, he should do two things to express gratitude:

1. **Offering Salah and Sacrifice**

   In light of the Holy Qur'an and Hadith, the entire Muslim community believes that the most important act of worship after faith (*Emaan*) is Salah. Therefore, Allah Almighty has spoken the most about Salah in the Holy Qur'an. According to the Prophet (ﷺ), *"Man will be first questioned about Salah on the Day of Judgement."* Even the last will of the Prophet (ﷺ) was related to Salah. A great part of his 23 years of Prophethood was spent in prayer.

2. **Sacrifice**

   Sacrifice is also a great form of worship. The Prophet (ﷺ) offered a sacrifice of one hundred camels, of which he slaughtered sixty-three with his own hand. The remaining thirty-seven were slaughtered by Ali (رضي الله عنه). (Sahih Muslim)

Likewise, the Prophet (ﷺ) said: *"No good deed is more beloved to Allah on the tenth of Dhul-Hijjah than the flowing of blood (sacrifice)."*

In another verse of the Holy Qur'an, Surah Al-An'am says:

قُلْ إِنَّ صَلَاتِي وَنُسُكِي وَمَحْيَايَ وَمَمَاتِي لِلَّهِ رَبِّ الْعَالَمِينَ

Say (O Muhammad ﷺ): "Verily, my prayer, my sacrifice, my living and my dying are for Allah, the Lord of the Worlds."

— *Surah Al-An'am 6:162*

Allah Almighty mentioned sacrifice along with Salah, indicating its significance: *"Say, my prayer, my offering, my life and my death are for Allah, the Lord of all the worlds."* (Index 189)

Gathering

يَوْمَ يَجْمَعُكُمْ لِيَوْمِ الْجَمْعِ ۖ ذَٰلِكَ يَوْمُ التَّغَابُنِ ۗ وَمَن يُؤْمِن بِاللَّهِ وَيَعْمَلْ صَالِحًا يُكَفِّرْ عَنْهُ سَيِّئَاتِهِ وَيُدْخِلْهُ جَنَّاتٍ تَجْرِي مِن تَحْتِهَا الْأَنْهَارُ خَالِدِينَ فِيهَا أَبَدًا ۚ ذَٰلِكَ الْفَوْزُ الْعَظِيمُ

وَالَّذِينَ كَفَرُوا وَكَذَّبُوا بِآيَاتِنَا أُولَٰئِكَ أَصْحَابُ النَّارِ خَالِدِينَ فِيهَا ۖ وَبِئْسَ الْمَصِيرُ

(And remember) the Day when He will gather you all on the Day of Gathering, that will be the Day of mutual loss and gain (i.e. loss for the disbelievers who will enter the Hellfire, and gain for the believers who will enter Paradise). And whosoever believeth in Allah and doeth righteous deeds, He will remit from him his sins and will admit him into Gardens beneath which rivers flow, to dwell therein forever: that is the great success.

But those who disbelieve and deny Our signs, they shall be the dwellers of the Fire, to abide therein: and evil is that destination.

— *Surah At-Taghabun 64:9–10*

What We Will See On The Assembly Day!

1.

وَيَوْمَ نُسَيِّرُ الْجِبَالَ وَتَرَى الْأَرْضَ بَارِزَةً وَحَشَرْنَاهُمْ فَلَمْ نُغَادِرْ مِنْهُمْ أَحَدًا

وَعُرِضُوا عَلَىٰ رَبِّكَ صَفًّا لَّقَدْ جِئْتُمُونَا كَمَا خَلَقْنَاكُمْ أَوَّلَ مَرَّةٍ ۚ بَلْ زَعَمْتُمْ أَلَّن نَّجْعَلَ لَكُم مَّوْعِدًا

And (remember) the Day We shall cause the mountains to pass away (like clouds of dust), and thou shalt see the earth a levelled plain, and We shall gather them all together so as to leave not one of them behind.

And they shall be brought before thy Lord in rows: "Now indeed, ye have come unto Us as We created you the first time. Nay, but ye thought We had appointed no meeting for you."

— *Surah Al-Kahf 18:47–48*

2.

يَوْمَ تُبَدَّلُ الْأَرْضُ غَيْرَ الْأَرْضِ وَالسَّمَاوَاتُ ۖ وَبَرَزُوا لِلَّهِ الْوَاحِدِ الْقَهَّارِ

وَتَرَى الْمُجْرِمِينَ يَوْمَئِذٍ مُّقَرَّنِينَ فِي الْأَصْفَادِ

سَرَابِيلُهُم مِّن قَطِرَانٍ وَتَغْشَىٰ وُجُوهَهُمُ النَّارُ

لِيَجْزِيَ اللَّهُ كُلَّ نَفْسٍ مَّا كَسَبَتْ ۚ إِنَّ اللَّهَ سَرِيعُ الْحِسَابِ

On the Day when the earth shall be changed into another earth, and the heavens also, and they shall come forth unto Allah, the One, the Irresistible.

➢ *And thou shalt see the sinners that Day bound together in fetters;*

➢ *Their garments of pitch, and fire covering their faces,*

➢ *That Allah may recompense every soul according to that which it hath earned: verily, Allah is swift in reckoning.*

— *Surah Ibrahim 14:48–51*

As-Sirat

In our previous discussion, we covered the concept of As-Sirat, an integral part of the straight path. Now, let us delve deeper into the challenges that lie ahead as we progress on our journey towards the Court of Justice.

It is important to remember our fellow group members who have completed the initial phase of this earthly journey and now reside in the city of Barzakh, patiently

569

awaiting the next stage. Rest assured, with the grace of Allah, we will soon join them, reunite, and continue our collective journey towards our ultimate destination.

As we are aware, As-Sirat represents a pathway leading to the realm of judgement and ultimately to the gates of Paradise. However, before reaching the place of judgement, there exists a bridge on this path that all individuals—regardless of their faith—must cross. This bridge is known as As-Sirat.

Its true nature remains hidden from our perception, as our knowledge is limited to what Allah has revealed. Nonetheless, scholars have proposed varying perspectives. Some describe the bridge as wide, while others suggest it is treacherous—featuring slippery surfaces, concealed hooks, grapples, sharp spikes, and thorns.

[Recorded by al-Bukhārī and Muslim]

Other scholars assert it is a very narrow bridge, as mentioned in a hadith narrated by Abū Saʿīd al-Khudrī (رضي الله عنه), in which he said:

بَلَغَنِي أَنَّ الصِّرَاطَ أَحَدُّ مِنَ السَّيْفِ وَأَدَقُّ مِنَ الشَّعْرَة

"I heard that the Sirat is sharper than a sword and finer than a hair." [116][240]

It is perplexing that while scholars claim the authenticity of their findings, they are unable to provide a clear explanation of how a person can physically cross such a bridge. In response to this question, it is often stated that Allah possesses the power to enable people to traverse the bridge in ways beyond our understanding. The exact means by which individuals will cross remains unknown, and it is believed that only Allah (SWT) has full knowledge of this. Consequently, these narratives put forth by scholars are considered to be speculative accounts, akin to disputed hadiths, and are subjects of ongoing debates within the Muslim community.

Allah (SWT) again says:

قُل لَّا يَعْلَمُ مَن فِي السَّمَاوَاتِ وَالْأَرْضِ الْغَيْبَ إِلَّا اللَّهُ ۚ وَمَا يَشْعُرُونَ أَيَّانَ يُبْعَثُونَ

Say: *"None in the heavens and the earth knoweth the unseen, but Allah; neither can they perceive when they shall be raised again."* — Surah An-Naml 27:65

In that case, as travellers, we should focus not on finding a clever way to cross the bridge, but on developing the qualities needed to light up our hearts. This illumination will make it easier to see the path across the bridge. Allah has provided numerous indications in the verses of the Qur'an, guiding us toward these essential qualities.

---

[240] Note (Saʿid ibn Malik ibn Sinan al-Khazraji al-Khudri was an inhabitant of Medina and early ally of the Islamic prophet Muhammad and one of the younger "companions of the prophet". Too young to fight at the Battle of Uhud in 625 where his father Malik ibn Sinan fell, he participated in subsequent campaigns. Wikipedia)

Allah (SWT) says in a verse:

أَوْ كَظُلُمَاتٍ فِي بَحْرٍ لُّجِّيٍّ يَغْشَاهُ مَوْجٌ مِّن فَوْقِهِ مَوْجٌ مِّن فَوْقِهِ سَحَابٌ ۚ ظُلُمَاتٌ بَعْضُهَا فَوْقَ بَعْضٍ إِذَا أَخْرَجَ يَدَهُ لَمْ يَكَدْ يَرَاهَا ۗ وَمَن لَّمْ يَجْعَلِ اللَّهُ لَهُ نُورًا فَمَا لَهُ مِن نُّورٍ

Or [the state of a disbeliever] is like the darkness in a vast deep sea, overwhelmed with a great wave, topped by a great wave, topped by dark clouds— darkness, one above another. If a man stretches out his hand, he can hardly see it! And he for whom Allah hath not appointed light, for him there is no light. — Surah An-Nur 24:40

This means Allah (SWT) guides to His Light whom He wills. As it says in the hadith recorded by Imam Ahmad from Abdullah bin Amr, who said:

"I heard the Messenger ﷺ of Allah (SWT) say:

'Allah created His creation in darkness, then on the same day He sent His Light upon them. Whoever was touched by His Light on that day will be guided, and whoever was missed will be led astray. Hence I say: the pens have dried in accordance with the knowledge of Allah, may He be glorified.'"

Allah (SWT) says:

اللَّهُ نُورُ السَّمَاوَاتِ وَالْأَرْضِ ۚ مَثَلُ نُورِهِ كَمِشْكَاةٍ فِيهَا مِصْبَاحٌ ۖ الْمِصْبَاحُ فِي زُجَاجَةٍ ۖ الزُّجَاجَةُ كَأَنَّهَا كَوْكَبٌ دُرِّيٌّ يُوقَدُ مِن شَجَرَةٍ مُّبَارَكَةٍ زَيْتُونَةٍ لَّا شَرْقِيَّةٍ وَلَا غَرْبِيَّةٍ يَكَادُ زَيْتُهَا يُضِيءُ وَلَوْ لَمْ تَمْسَسْهُ نَارٌ ۚ نُّورٌ عَلَىٰ نُورٍ ۗ يَهْدِي اللَّهُ لِنُورِهِ مَن يَشَاءُ ۚ وَيَضْرِبُ اللَّهُ الْأَمْثَالَ لِلنَّاسِ ۗ وَاللَّهُ بِكُلِّ شَيْءٍ عَلِيمٌ

Allah is the Light of the heavens and of the earth. The parable of His light is as if there were a niche, and within it a lamp: the lamp is in glass, the glass as it were a brilliant star, lit from a blessed tree, an olive tree, neither of the east nor of the west, whose oil would almost glow, even if no fire touched it: light upon light. Allah doth guide whom He will to His light: Allah doth set forth parables for mankind, and Allah doth know all things. — Surah An-Nur 24:35

Having mentioned this parable of the Light of His guidance in the heart of the believer, Allah (SWT) ends this Ayah with the words:

اللَّهُ نُورُ السَّمَاوَاتِ وَالْأَرْضِ ۚ مَثَلُ نُورِهِ كَمِشْكَاةٍ فِيهَا مِصْبَاحٌ ۖ الْمِصْبَاحُ فِي زُجَاجَةٍ ۖ الزُّجَاجَةُ كَأَنَّهَا كَوْكَبٌ دُرِّيٌّ يُوقَدُ مِن شَجَرَةٍ مُّبَارَكَةٍ زَيْتُونَةٍ لَّا شَرْقِيَّةٍ وَلَا غَرْبِيَّةٍ يَكَادُ زَيْتُهَا يُضِيءُ وَلَوْ لَمْ تَمْسَسْهُ نَارٌ ۚ نُّورٌ عَلَىٰ نُورٍ ۗ يَهْدِي اللَّهُ لِنُورِهِ مَن يَشَاءُ ۚ وَيَضْرِبُ اللَّهُ الْأَمْثَالَ لِلنَّاسِ ۗ وَاللَّهُ بِكُلِّ شَيْءٍ عَلِيمٌ

And Allah setteth forth parables for men: and Allah is knower of all things. — Surah An-Nur 24:35

This example represents the heart of an unbeliever characterised by simple ignorance. Such a person blindly follows without understanding who he is following or where he is heading. He resembles the ignorant man in the parable who, when asked, "Where are you going?" replied:

"With them."

He was asked, "Where are they going?"

He said, "I do not know."

$$ظُلُمَاتٌ بَعْضُهَا فَوْقَ بَعْضٍ$$

Darkness upon darkness.

Ubayy bin Ka`b said:

"He is enveloped in five types of darkness:

– his speech is darkness,

– his deeds are darkness,

– his coming in is darkness,

– his going out is darkness,

– and his destiny on the Day of Resurrection will be darkness in the fire of Hell."

Other scholars stated similarly. As-Suddi and Ar-Rabi` bin Anas also echoed these sentiments.

$$وَمَن لَّمْ يَجْعَلِ اللَّهُ لَهُ نُورًا فَمَا لَهُ مِن نُّورٍ$$

And he for whom Allah hath not appointed light, for him there is no light. — Surah An-Nur 24:40

One whom Allah does not guide is ignorant and doomed—an utter loser and disbeliever.[241]

When contemplating the importance of adhering to the *Seerat*, reflect on the message of the following selected verses and relate them to your actions. Then, determine what steps you need to take to align yourself with the path to success:

Take note of what Allah (SWT) says:

$$مَن يُضْلِلِ اللَّهُ فَلَا هَادِيَ لَهُ ۚ وَيَذَرُهُمْ فِي طُغْيَانِهِمْ يَعْمَهُونَ$$

Whomsoever Allah sends astray, none can guide him; and He lets them wander blindly in their transgressions.

— Surah Al-A'raf, 7:186

---

[241] (Abu al-As ibn al-Rabi' (Arabic: أبو العاص بن الربيع, 'Abū al-'Āṣ ibn al-Rabī', died in February, AD 634) was a son-in-law and companion of the Islamic prophet Muhammad. His original name was said to have been Hushaym or Yasser.[1] Ibn Hajar, Al-Isaba vol. 7 #10173, p. 224) https://en.wikipedia.org/wiki/Abu_al-As_ibn_al-Rabi%27

هُوَ الَّذِي أَنزَلَ عَلَيْكَ الْكِتَابَ مِنْهُ آيَاتٌ مُّحْكَمَاتٌ هُنَّ أُمُّ الْكِتَابِ وَأُخَرُ مُتَشَابِهَاتٌ ۖ فَأَمَّا الَّذِينَ
فِي قُلُوبِهِمْ زَيْغٌ فَيَتَّبِعُونَ مَا تَشَابَهَ مِنْهُ ابْتِغَاءَ الْفِتْنَةِ وَابْتِغَاءَ تَأْوِيلِهِ ۗ وَمَا يَعْلَمُ تَأْوِيلَهُ إِلَّا اللَّهُ ۗ
وَالرَّاسِخُونَ فِي الْعِلْمِ يَقُولُونَ آمَنَّا بِهِ كُلٌّ مِّنْ عِندِ رَبِّنَا ۗ وَمَا يَذَّكَّرُ إِلَّا أُولُو الْأَلْبَابِ

It is He who hath sent down to thee the Book: in it are verses basic or fundamental (of established meaning); they are the foundation of the Book: others are allegorical. But those in whose hearts is perversity follow the part thereof that is allegorical, seeking discord, and searching for its hidden meanings, but no one knoweth its hidden meanings except Allah: and those who are firmly grounded in knowledge say: "We believe in the Book; the whole of it is from our Lord": and none will grasp the Message except men of understanding.

— Surah Al-Imran, 3:7

وَأَنَّ هَٰذَا صِرَاطِي مُسْتَقِيمًا فَاتَّبِعُوهُ ۖ وَلَا تَتَّبِعُوا السُّبُلَ فَتَفَرَّقَ بِكُمْ عَن سَبِيلِهِ ۚ ذَٰلِكُمْ وَصَّاكُم بِهِ
لَعَلَّكُمْ تَتَّقُونَ

And verily, this is my straight path, so follow it, and follow not other paths, for they will scatter you from His path. This hath He ordained for you, that ye may become righteous.

— Surah Al-An'am, 6:153

Certificate of Clearance

Allah (Swt) Has Declared That:

وَيُنَجِّي اللَّهُ الَّذِينَ اتَّقَوا بِمَفَازَتِهِمْ لَا يَمَسُّهُمُ السُّوءُ وَلَا هُمْ يَحْزَنُونَ

And Allah will deliver those who are righteous to their place of salvation. Evil shall not touch them, nor shall they grieve.

— Surah Az-Zumar, 39:61

إِنَّ الَّذِينَ سَبَقَتْ لَهُم مِّنَّا الْحُسْنَىٰ أُولَٰئِكَ عَنْهَا مُبْعَدُونَ

لَا يَسْمَعُونَ حَسِيسَهَا ۖ وَهُمْ فِي مَا اشْتَهَتْ أَنفُسُهُمْ خَالِدُونَ

لَا يَحْزُنُهُمُ الْفَزَعُ الْأَكْبَرُ وَتَتَلَقَّاهُمُ الْمَلَائِكَةُ هَٰذَا يَوْمُكُمُ الَّذِي كُنتُمْ تُوعَدُونَ

Surely those for whom the good hath already gone forth from Us, they shall be kept far away from it (Hell).

They shall not hear the slightest sound of it, and they shall abide in that which their souls desire.

The great terror shall not grieve them, and the angels shall meet them, saying, "This is your Day, which ye were promised."

— Surah Al-Anbiyaa, 21:101–103

"Allah (SWT) will deliver the righteous to their place of salvation"—and so, crossing the bridge is not a concern for the pious.[242]

Journey To The Final Path To Heaven Old Testament

The Qur'an assures the Christians and Jews of the resolution of their differences on the Day of Judgment. In the following verse, Allah (SWT) says:

وَقَالَتِ الْيَهُودُ لَيْسَتِ النَّصَارَىٰ عَلَىٰ شَيْءٍ وَقَالَتِ النَّصَارَىٰ لَيْسَتِ الْيَهُودُ عَلَىٰ شَيْءٍ وَهُمْ يَتْلُونَ الْكِتَابَ ۚ كَذَٰلِكَ قَالَ الَّذِينَ لَا يَعْلَمُونَ مِثْلَ قَوْلِهِمْ ۚ فَاللَّهُ يَحْكُمُ بَيْنَهُمْ يَوْمَ الْقِيَامَةِ فِيمَا كَانُوا فِيهِ يَخْتَلِفُونَ

The Jews say the Christians have nothing to stand on, and the Christians say the Jews have nothing to stand on, though both of them recite the Scripture. Those who have no knowledge say the same as they say. But Allah will judge between them on the Day of Resurrection concerning that wherein they differ.

(Surah Al-Baqara 2:113)

Here we quote a few more verses from the scriptures regarding the Sirat path. The nature of the path is illustrated in both the Torah and the Bible.

As stated in the Gospel according to Matthew:

Matthew 7:13–14 (KJV)

Enter ye in at the strait gate: for wide is the gate, and broad is the way, that leadeth to destruction, and many there be which go in thereat:

Because strait is the gate, and narrow is the way, which leadeth unto life, and few there be that find it.

Furthermore, in another passage:

Matthew 7:7–8 (KJV)

Ask, and it shall be given you; seek, and ye shall find; knock, and it shall be opened unto you:

For every one that asketh receiveth; and he that seeketh findeth; and to him that knocketh it shall be opened.

The path to eternal life is open to everyone, irrespective of their social standing. However, the secret lies in knowing how to pursue it. Our faith, salvation, and purity of heart are essential in determining our fate.

Yet, achieving these virtues is challenging, as human nature often seeks comfort, pursues happiness, harbours jealousy, engages in conflict, craves power, and sometimes succumbs to conspiracies. These tendencies frequently distract us from recognising the ultimate truth of Allah (SWT).

Let us quote a few more Psalms and scriptures:

---

[242] 190 https://islamqa.info/en/answers/96306/gender-of-angels-and-do-they-die

Isaiah 42:16 (KJV)

And I will bring the blind by a way that they knew not; I will lead them in paths that they have not known:

I will make darkness light before them, and crooked things straight.

These things will I do unto them, and not forsake them.

Isaiah 30:21 (KJV)

And thine ears shall hear a word behind thee, saying, This is the way, walk ye in it,

when ye turn to the right hand, and when ye turn to the left.

Proverbs 8:18–20 (KJV)

Riches and honour are with me; yea, durable riches and righteousness.

My fruit is better than gold, yea, than fine gold; and my revenue than choice silver.

I lead in the way of righteousness, in the midst of the paths of judgment.

Proverbs 2:20–22 (KJV)

That thou mayest walk in the way of good men, and keep the paths of the righteous.

For the upright shall dwell in the land, and the perfect shall remain in it.

But the wicked shall be cut off from the earth, and the transgressors shall be rooted out of it.

As it is written:

"...narrow is the way, which leadeth unto life, and few there be that find it."

(Matthew 7:14, KJV)

One reason why many people struggle to find a fulfilling life is that they do not put in the effort to search for it. Jesus (peace be upon him) promised that those who seek will find. If you haven't found it yet, it might be worth reflecting on the determination behind your search.

God is not distant from any of us; He hears us clearly, and His teachings are not hidden. The way to God was once completely obstructed by sin.

As stated in Romans:

Romans 5:12–14 (KJV)

Wherefore, as by one man sin entered into the world, and death by sin; and so death passed upon all men, for that all have sinned:

(For until the law sin was in the world: but sin is not imputed when there is no law. Nevertheless death reigned from Adam to Moses, even over them that had not

sinned after the similitude of Adam's transgression, who is the figure of him that was to come.)

No one deserves a second chance. We all deserve to remain on the "wide road that leads to destruction." Yet, God loved us enough to provide a path to eternal life.

Romans 3:11–14 (KJV)

There is none that understandeth, there is none that seeketh after God.

They are all gone out of the way, they are together become unprofitable;

there is none that doeth good, no, not one.

Their throat is an open sepulchre; with their tongues they have used deceit;

the poison of asps is under their lips:

Whose mouth is full of cursing and bitterness.

This passage continues with a call to repentance:

Jeremiah 29:12–14 (KJV)

Then shall ye call upon me, and ye shall go and pray unto me, and I will hearken unto you.

And ye shall seek me, and find me, when ye shall search for me with all your heart.

And I will be found of you, saith the Lord: and I will turn away your captivity,

and I will gather you from all the nations, and from all the places whither I have driven you,

saith the Lord; and I will bring you again into the place whence I caused you to be carried away captive.

However, the problem persists because Satan has paved the highway to hell with fleshly temptations, worldly attractions, and moral compromises. Most people allow their passions and desires to rule their lives, choosing temporary, worldly pleasures rather than eternal rewards after this material life.

Rabbi Ya'akov taught:

"This world is compared to an antechamber that leads to Olam Ha–Ba (the World to Come)."

(Pirkei Avot 4:21)

That is, while a righteous person might suffer in this lifetime, they will certainly be rewarded in the next world — and that reward will be far greater. In fact, some rabbis assert that the righteous are made to suffer in this world so their reward will be multiplied in the next.

(Leviticus Rabbah 27:1)

Pirkei Avot 4:22

He used to say: The ones who are born are destined to die,

and the ones who have died are to be brought to life,

and the ones brought to life are to be judged.

So that one may know, make known, and have the knowledge that the Almighty:

He is God,

He is the Designer,

He is the Creator,

He is the Discerner,

He is the Judge,

He is the Witness,

He is the Complainant,

and He will summon to judgment.

Blessed be He,

before Whom there is no iniquity,

nor forgetting,

nor respect of persons,

nor taking of bribes, for all is His.

And know that all is according to the reckoning.

Let not your impulse assure you that the grave is a place of refuge for you;

for against your will were you formed,

against your will were you born,

against your will you live,

against your will you will die,

and against your will you will give an account and reckoning before

the King of kings of kings, the Holy One, blessed be He.

In this lengthy Mishnah, filled with rhetorical expression, Rabbi Elazar Ha-Kappar teaches about the certainty of the Day of Judgment.[243]

---

[243] Index 191 https://www.sefaria.org/English_Explanation_of_Pirkei_Avot.4.22.1?lang=bi

Finally, it ends with a few more verses about the path to heaven, as defined in the Tanakh—the Hebrew Bible—comprising the Torah (Law), Nevi'im (Prophets), and Ketuvim (Writings)[244]

The subject of death is treated inconsistently in the Bible, though most often it suggests that physical death is the end of life. This is the case with such central figures as Abraham, Moses, and Miriam (peace be upon them).

There are, however, several biblical references to a place called *Sheol* (cf. Numbers 30, 33). It is described as a region "dark and deep," "the Pit," and "the Land of Forgetfulness," where human beings descend after death. The suggestion is that in the netherworld of Sheol, the deceased—although cut off from God and humankind—live on in some shadowy state of existence.

"Death taketh everyone,

the righteous and the unrighteous alike,

and no one returneth from the realm of the dead."

While this vision of Sheol (*Seoul* can be compared with *Barzakh*, as we described earlier) is rather bleak—setting precedents for later Jewish and Christian ideas of an underground hell—there is generally no concept of judgement or reward and punishment attached to it. In fact, the more pessimistic books of the Bible, such as *Ecclesiastes* and *Job*, insist that all the dead go down to Sheol, whether good or evil, rich or poor, slave or free.

Job 3:11–19 (KJV)

11 Why died I not from the womb? why did I not give up the ghost when I came out of the belly?

12 Why did the knees prevent me? or why the breasts that I should suck?

13 For now should I have lain still and been quiet, I should have slept: then had I been at rest,

14 With kings and counsellors of the earth, which built desolate places for themselves;

15 Or with princes that had gold, who filled their houses with silver:

16 Or as an hidden untimely birth I had not been; as infants which never saw light.

17 There the wicked cease from troubling; and there the weary be at rest.

18 There the prisoners rest together; they hear not the voice of the oppressor.

---

[244] [Ketuvim, (Hebrew), English Writings, Greek Hagiographa, the third division of the Hebrew Bible, or Old Testament. ... Thus the Ketuvim are a miscellaneous collection of liturgical poetry, secular love poetry, wisdom literature, history, apocalyptic literature, a short story, and a romantic tale.]

19 The small and great are there; and the servant is free from his master.

Daniel 12:2 (KJV)

And many of them that sleep in the dust of the earth shall awake, some to everlasting life, and some to shame and everlasting contempt.

Nehemiah 9:6 (KJV)

Thou, even thou, art Lord alone; thou hast made heaven, the heaven of heavens, with all their host, the earth, and all things that are therein, the seas, and all that is therein, and thou preservest them all; and the host of heaven worshippeth thee.

The *Torah*—the first five books of the Bible—is the only holy book the Jews are commanded to follow. Their scholars teach the existence of the afterlife, reward and punishment, and that the righteous will be reunited with their loved ones on the other side of this world. We can see that many of these teachings convey nearly the same message that we find in the Qur'an. For example:

Leviticus 26:3–6 (KJV)

3 If ye walk in my statutes, and keep my commandments, and do them;

4 Then I will give you rain in due season, and the land shall yield her increase, and the trees of the field shall yield their fruit.

5 And your threshing shall reach unto the vintage, and the vintage shall reach unto the sowing time: and ye shall eat your bread to the full, and dwell in your land safely.

6 And I will give peace in the land, and ye shall lie down, and none shall make you afraid: and I will rid evil beasts out of the land, neither shall the sword go through your land.

Sheol or Barzakh

The dead who are raised will be judged according to the temporary judgement they experienced in the intermediate state—that is, *Barzakh*—the judgement they experienced through being placed in either the righteous or the unrighteous compartment in Sheol. The righteous will rise to everlasting life in the new heavens and new earth, while the unrighteous will rise to everlasting shame and contempt, being cast out into the lake of fire (cf. Revelation 20:7–15; Daniel 12:2).

The Judgement of Satan

7 And when the thousand years are expired, Satan shall be loosed out of his prison,

8 And shall go out to deceive the nations which are in the four quarters of the earth, Gog and Magog, to gather them together to battle: the number of whom is as the sand of the sea.

9 And they went up on the breadth of the earth, and compassed the camp of the saints about, and the beloved city: and fire came down from God out of heaven, and devoured them.

10 And the devil that deceived them was cast into the lake of fire and brimstone, where the beast and the false prophet are, and shall be tormented day and night for ever and ever.

Conclusion

The belief in the resurrection of the dead, as articulated in *Tractate Sanhedrin*, is a cornerstone of Jewish faith, signifying hope for the future, divine justice, and ultimate redemption. It underscores the continuity of life beyond death and the eventual reward for the righteous. This belief has sustained Jewish thought and faith through the centuries, providing a profound sense of purpose and destiny within the framework of God's plan for the world.

In summary, the belief in the resurrection of the dead underscores a fundamental tenet across major religions, emphasising divine accountability for our earthly actions. This conviction shapes moral and ethical behaviours, assuring that ultimate judgement and the resulting reward or punishment are divinely ordained—offering a powerful incentive for righteous living and spiritual responsibility.

بِسْمِ ٱللَّهِ ٱلرَّحْمَٰنِ ٱلرَّحِيمِ

Chapter 17

"Don't wait for the last judgment – it takes place every day."

— Albert Camus

That the Messenger of Allah said:

"Allah, the Almighty, will say on the Day of Judgment: 'Where are those who loved each other for My glory? Today, I will shelter them under My shade – the day when there is no shade but My shade.'"

Abu Hurayrah (may Allah be pleased with him) reported

Sahih/Authentic – [Muslim]

📖 📖 📖 📖 📖 📖 📖

Judgment Day

In this chapter, we find no space to insert our own interpretations, alter the narrative, or create new stories. Everything that has unfolded in this mysterious world is a divine matter, beyond human understanding. However, by carefully contemplating the messages revealed in the Qur'an, the teachings of Prophet Muhammad ﷺ, and the Old Testament, we can gain a deeper insight into how this grand system will operate flawlessly until His ultimate plan is fulfilled.

We will assemble to join the queue for the Court of the Almighty Allah SWT. This marks the culmination of our journey, acting as the central gathering point for the process of judgment. Here, the rules of judgment will be announced to the assembly, guiding our conduct throughout the court proceedings. These rules have been revealed in every holy book during our time on Earth.

As previously discussed, the belief in resurrection underscores themes of justice, renewal, and the continuity of life beyond death in various faiths. This is evident in religious scholars' interpretations based on divine scriptures, which reflect deep theological, philosophical, and moral considerations. Even when considering Hinduism and Buddhism, we see an acceptance of divine judgment, though not exactly analogous to the Abrahamic concept of a single Day of Judgment.

In Hinduism, the concepts of karma and reincarnation serve as forms of divine justice. Sacred texts like the *Bhagavad Gita* and the *Upanishads* explain that individuals' actions in this life determine their fate in future lives. Yama, the god of death, judges souls and directs them to their appropriate next life based on their karma.

Similarly, Buddhism emphasises karma and rebirth rather than a single Day of Judgment. The law of karma dictates that actions in this life affect future existences, with the ultimate goal being Nirvana—liberation from the cycle of birth and rebirth (*samsara*). Various Buddhist texts, such as the *Pali Canon*, elaborate on these principles.

As true Muslims, the Day of Judgment represents a time when moral accountability is ultimately realised, emphasising the importance of ethical conduct and spiritual integrity. The exact timing of this final hour is unknown to anyone on Earth. As Allah declared in the Qur'an:

يَسْأَلُونَكَ عَنِ السَّاعَةِ أَيَّانَ مُرْسَاهَا ۖ قُلْ إِنَّمَا عِلْمُهَا عِندَ رَبِّي ۖ لَا يُجَلِّيهَا لِوَقْتِهَا إِلَّا هُوَ ۚ ثَقُلَتْ فِي السَّمَاوَاتِ وَالْأَرْضِ ۚ لَا تَأْتِيكُمْ إِلَّا بَغْتَةً ۗ يَسْأَلُونَكَ كَأَنَّكَ حَفِيٌّ عَنْهَا ۖ قُلْ إِنَّمَا عِلْمُهَا عِندَ اللَّهِ وَلَٰكِنَّ أَكْثَرَ النَّاسِ لَا يَعْلَمُونَ

"They ask thee about the (final) hour—when shall be its appointed time? Say: My Lord alone knows. He alone will reveal it at the proper time. It is heavy upon the heavens and the earth. It shall not come upon you but suddenly. They ask thee as though thou wast well acquainted therewith. Say: The knowledge thereof is with Allah only: but most men know not."

— *Surah Al-A'raf 7:187*

The next verse of the same surah advises us to avoid spreading fictitious stories, especially those falsely attributed to our trusted Prophet Muhammad ﷺ regarding secret matters. Although we often cite scholars' names, only Allah has ultimate knowledge. The verse, which we referenced earlier and will mention again, states:

قُل لَّا أَمْلِكُ لِنَفْسِي نَفْعًا وَلَا ضَرًّا إِلَّا مَا شَاءَ اللَّهُ ۚ وَلَوْ كُنتُ أَعْلَمُ الْغَيْبَ لَاسْتَكْثَرْتُ مِنَ الْخَيْرِ وَمَا مَسَّنِيَ السُّوءُ ۚ إِنْ أَنَا إِلَّا نَذِيرٌ وَبَشِيرٌ لِّقَوْمٍ يُؤْمِنُونَ

"Say: I have no power over any good or harm to myself except as Allah willeth. If I had knowledge of the unseen, I should have multiplied all good, and no evil should have touched me: I am but a warner, and a bringer of glad tidings to those who have faith."

— *Surah Al-A'raf 7:188*

Gathering for Judgement and Rules Will Be Announced Before the Trial Begins

1

وَنَضَعُ الْمَوَازِينَ الْقِسْطَ لِيَوْمِ الْقِيَامَةِ فَلَا تُظْلَمُ نَفْسٌ شَيْئًا ۖ وَإِن كَانَ مِثْقَالَ حَبَّةٍ مِّنْ خَرْدَلٍ أَتَيْنَا بِهَا ۗ وَكَفَىٰ بِنَا حَاسِبِينَ

We shall set up scales of justice for the Day of Judgment, so that not a soul will be dealt with unjustly in the least, and if there be (no more than) the weight of a mustard seed, We will bring it (to account): and enough are We to take account.

21:47 Surah Al-Anbiyaa

2

فَأَمَّا مَنْ أُوتِيَ كِتَابَهُ بِيَمِينِهِ

فَسَوْفَ يُحَاسَبُ حِسَابًا يَسِيرًا

وَيَنقَلِبُ إِلَىٰ أَهْلِهِ مَسْرُورًا

وَأَمَّا مَنْ أُوتِيَ كِتَابَهُ وَرَاءَ ظَهْرِهِ

فَسَوْفَ يَدْعُو ثُبُورًا

وَيَصْلَىٰ سَعِيرًا

Then, as for him that shall be given his record in his right hand, 84:7

He shall soon receive an easy reckoning, 84:8

And shall return unto his people rejoicing! 84:9

But as for him that shall be given his record behind his back, 84:10

He shall cry out for perdition, 84:11

And he shall enter a blazing fire. 84:12

Surah Al-Inshiqaq 84:7–12

Surah Al-Inshiqaq (84) confirms that whoever is given his record behind his back will cry out for destruction. He will call for ruin. In contrast, the one who is given his record in his right hand will receive an easy reckoning.

Surah Al-Gāshiyah (88) also describes that those who receive their judgement with the left hand will be humiliated—labouring in exhaustion and weariness. They will enter the hot, blazing Fire, given to drink from a boiling spring. No food will be provided for them except a poisonous, thorny plant—one that neither nourishes nor satisfies hunger.

Another group of people, however, will receive their verdicts with honour. They will be glad for their endeavours and will reside in lofty Paradise, where no harmful or false speech will be heard. The verses go on to describe the honourable provisions awaiting them:

Therein will be a running spring,

Thrones raised high,

Cups ready at hand,

Cushions set in rows,

And rich carpets spread out.

The verses then call on humanity to reflect:

Do they not look at the camels—how they are created?

And the heavens—how they are raised?

And the mountains—how they are rooted and fixed?

And the earth—how it is spread out?

In Surah Ash-Shams (91), it is confirmed that one who truly purifies his own soul will succeed:

"He indeed shall be successful who purifieth it,

And he indeed shall fail who corrupteth it."

This refers to those who obey Allah's commands and avoid polytheism and wicked deeds.

When the Throne Appears

And I saw a great white throne, and him that sat on it, from whose face the earth and the heaven fled away; and there was found no place for them.

And I saw the dead, small and great, stand before God; and the books were opened: and another book was opened, which is the book of life: and the dead were judged out of those things which were written in the books, according to their works.

And the sea gave up the dead which were in it; and death and hell delivered up the dead which were in them: and they were judged every man according to their works.

And death and hell were cast into the lake of fire. This is the second death.

And whosoever was not found written in the book of life was cast into the lake of fire.

Revelation 20:11–15 (KJV)[245]

When the Trial Begins
Questions Will Be Asked

يَصْلَوْنَهَا يَوْمَ الدِّينِ

وَمَا هُمْ عَنْهَا بِغَائِبِينَ

Which they will enter on the Day of Judgment,

And they will not be able to keep away therefrom.

Surah Al-Infitar 82:15–16

وَإِذَا الْقُبُورُ بُعْثِرَتْ

عَلِمَتْ نَفْسٌ مَّا قَدَّمَتْ وَأَخَّرَتْ

And when the graves are turned upside down (and they bring out their contents),

Then a person will know what he has sent forward and what he has left behind (of good or bad deeds).

Surah Al-Infitar 82:4–5

وَإِذَا النُّفُوسُ زُوِّجَتْ

وَإِذَا الْمَوْءُودَةُ سُئِلَتْ

بِأَيِّ ذَنبٍ قُتِلَتْ

وَإِذَا الصُّحُفُ نُشِرَتْ

وَإِذَا السَّمَاءُ كُشِطَتْ

وَإِذَا الْجَحِيمُ سُعِّرَتْ

وَإِذَا الْجَنَّةُ أُزْلِفَتْ

عَلِمَتْ نَفْسٌ مَّا أَحْضَرَتْ

And when the souls shall be joined with their bodies;

And when the female (infant) buried alive (as the pagan Arabs used to do) shall be questioned,

For what sin was she killed?

---

[245] Index193 https://www.biblegateway.com/passage/?search=Revelation%2020%3A7-15&version=NI   https://www.desiringgod.org/articles/what-is-sheol

And when the written pages of deeds (good and bad) of every person shall be laid open;

And when the heaven shall be stripped away from its place;

And when the Hell-fire shall be kindled to fierce ablaze;

And when Paradise shall be brought near,

Then every person will know what he has brought (of good and evil).

Surah At-Takwir 81:7–14

وَيَوْمَ نَبْعَثُ مِن كُلِّ أُمَّةٍ شَهِيدًا ثُمَّ لَا يُؤْذَنُ لِلَّذِينَ كَفَرُوا وَلَا هُمْ يُسْتَعْتَبُونَ

And (remember) the Day when We shall raise up from each nation a witness (their Messenger), then those who have disbelieved will not be given leave to offer excuses, nor will they be allowed to return (to the world) to repent and seek Allah's forgiveness.

Surah An-Nahl 16:84

وَبَرَزُوا لِلَّهِ جَمِيعًا فَقَالَ الضُّعَفَاءُ لِلَّذِينَ اسْتَكْبَرُوا إِنَّا كُنَّا لَكُمْ تَبَعًا فَهَلْ أَنتُم مُّغْنُونَ عَنَّا مِنْ عَذَابِ اللَّهِ مِن شَيْءٍ ۚ قَالُوا لَوْ هَدَانَا اللَّهُ لَهَدَيْنَاكُمْ ۖ سَوَاءٌ عَلَيْنَا أَجَزِعْنَا أَمْ صَبَرْنَا مَا لَنَا مِن مَّحِيصٍ

And they all shall appear before Allah (on the Day of Resurrection). Then the weak will say to those who were arrogant: "Verily, we were following you; can you avail us anything from Allah's torment?"

They will reply: "Had Allah guided us, we would have guided you. It is the same to us whether we rage or endure with patience; there is no place of refuge for us."

Surah Ibrahim 14:21

وَإِذَا رَأَى الَّذِينَ أَشْرَكُوا شُرَكَاءَهُمْ قَالُوا رَبَّنَا هَٰؤُلَاءِ شُرَكَاؤُنَا الَّذِينَ كُنَّا نَدْعُو مِن دُونِكَ ۖ فَأَلْقَوْا إِلَيْهِمُ الْقَوْلَ إِنَّكُمْ لَكَاذِبُونَ

And when those who associated partners with Allah see their (so-called) partners, they will say: "Our Lord! These are our partners whom we used to invoke besides You."

But they will throw back their statement at them and say: "Surely, you are liars!"

Surah An-Nahl 16:86

وَيَوْمَ نَبْعَثُ فِي كُلِّ أُمَّةٍ شَهِيدًا عَلَيْهِم مِّنْ أَنفُسِهِمْ ۖ وَجِئْنَا بِكَ شَهِيدًا عَلَىٰ هَٰؤُلَاءِ ۚ وَنَزَّلْنَا عَلَيْكَ الْكِتَابَ تِبْيَانًا لِّكُلِّ شَيْءٍ وَهُدًى وَرَحْمَةً وَبُشْرَىٰ لِلْمُسْلِمِينَ

And (remember) the Day when We shall raise up from every nation a witness against them from amongst themselves.

And We shall bring you (O Muhammad ﷺ) as a witness against these.

And We have sent down to you the Book (the Qur'an) as a clarification for everything, and as guidance, mercy, and glad tidings for those who have submitted.

Surah An-Nahl 16:89

يَوْمَ تَأْتِي كُلُّ نَفْسٍ تُجَادِلُ عَن نَّفْسِهَا وَتُوَفَّىٰ كُلُّ نَفْسٍ مَّا عَمِلَتْ وَهُمْ لَا يُظْلَمُونَ

(Remember) the Day when every person will come pleading for himself, and every one will be paid in full for what he did (good or evil), and they will not be treated unjustly.

Surah An-Nahl 16:111

وَأَلْقَوْا إِلَى اللَّهِ يَوْمَئِذٍ السَّلَمَ ۖ وَضَلَّ عَنْهُم مَّا كَانُوا يَفْتَرُونَ

And they will submit fully to Allah on that Day, and the false deities they invented will abandon them.

Surah An-Nahl 16:87

وَيَوْمَ نَحْشُرُهُمْ جَمِيعًا ثُمَّ نَقُولُ لِلَّذِينَ أَشْرَكُوا مَكَانَكُمْ أَنتُمْ وَشُرَكَاؤُكُمْ ۚ فَزَيَّلْنَا بَيْنَهُمْ ۖ وَقَالَ شُرَكَاؤُهُم مَّا كُنتُمْ إِيَّانَا تَعْبُدُونَ

And on that Day We shall gather them all together, then We shall say to those who associated others in worship: "Remain at your place, you and your partners!"

Then We shall separate them, and their partners will say: "It was not us that you used to worship."

Surah Yunus (Jonah) 10:28

وَكُلَّ إِنسَانٍ أَلْزَمْنَاهُ طَائِرَهُ فِي عُنُقِهِ ۖ وَنُخْرِجُ لَهُ يَوْمَ الْقِيَامَةِ كِتَابًا يَلْقَاهُ مَنشُورًا
اقْرَأْ كِتَابَكَ كَفَىٰ بِنَفْسِكَ الْيَوْمَ عَلَيْكَ حَسِيبًا

And We have fastened every man's deeds to his neck, and on the Day of Resurrection, We shall bring forth for him a book which he will find wide open.

(It will be said): "Read your book. You yourself are sufficient this Day to take account against yourself."

Surah Al-Isra 17:13–14

يَوْمَ تَجِدُ كُلُّ نَفْسٍ مَّا عَمِلَتْ مِنْ خَيْرٍ مُّحْضَرًا وَمَا عَمِلَتْ مِن سُوءٍ تَوَدُّ لَوْ أَنَّ بَيْنَهَا وَبَيْنَهُ أَمَدًا بَعِيدًا ۗ وَيُحَذِّرُكُمُ اللَّهُ نَفْسَهُ ۗ وَاللَّهُ رَءُوفٌ بِالْعِبَادِ

On the Day when every person will find all the good he has done brought before him, and all the evil he has done, he will wish that there were a great distance between him and his evil.

And Allah warns you against Himself, and Allah is full of kindness to His servants.

Surah Ale-Imran 3:30

يَوْمَ نَدْعُو كُلَّ أُنَاسٍ بِإِمَامِهِمْ ۖ فَمَنْ أُوتِيَ كِتَابَهُ بِيَمِينِهِ فَأُولَٰئِكَ يَقْرَءُونَ كِتَابَهُمْ وَلَا يُظْلَمُونَ فَتِيلًا

And (remember) the Day when We shall call every people with their Imam (their leader, Book, or record of deeds).

So whosoever is given his book in his right hand—such will read their records, and they will not be dealt with unjustly in the least.

Surah Al-Isra 17:71

وَإِذَا قِيلَ لَهُم مَّاذَا أَنزَلَ رَبُّكُمْ ۙ قَالُوا أَسَاطِيرُ الْأَوَّلِي

And when it is said to them: "What has your Lord revealed?" They say: "Tales of the ancients!"

Surah An-Nahl 16:24

وَقِيلَ لِلَّذِينَ اتَّقَوْا مَاذَا أَنزَلَ رَبُّكُمْ ۚ قَالُوا خَيْرًا ۗ لِّلَّذِينَ أَحْسَنُوا فِي هَٰذِهِ الدُّنْيَا حَسَنَةٌ ۚ وَلَدَارُ الْآخِرَةِ خَيْرٌ ۚ وَلَنِعْمَ دَارُ الْمُتَّقِينَ

And it will be said to those who fear Allah: "What has your Lord revealed?"

They will say: "That which is good." For those who do good in this world, there is good, and the home of the Hereafter will be better.

QQQ

وَلَوْ تَرَىٰ إِذْ وُقِفُوا عَلَىٰ رَبِّهِمْ ۚ قَالَ أَلَيْسَ هَٰذَا بِالْحَقِّ ۚ قَالُوا بَلَىٰ وَرَبِّنَا ۚ قَالَ فَذُوقُوا الْعَذَابَ بِمَا كُنتُمْ تَكْفُرُونَ

If you could but see when they will be held (brought and made to stand) in front of their Lord! He will say: "Is not this (Resurrection and the taking of the accounts) the truth?" They will say: "Yes, by our Lord!" He will then say: "So taste you the torment because you used not to believe." 6/30 Surah Al-An'am (The Cattle)

And excellent indeed will be the home of the pious.

Surah An-Nahl 16:30

At The End Of The Trial

The Devil Will Proclaim:

وَقَالَ الشَّيْطَانُ لَمَّا قُضِيَ الْأَمْرُ إِنَّ اللَّهَ وَعَدَكُمْ وَعْدَ الْحَقِّ وَوَعَدتُّكُمْ فَأَخْلَفْتُكُمْ ۖ وَمَا كَانَ لِيَ عَلَيْكُم مِّن سُلْطَانٍ إِلَّا أَن دَعَوْتُكُمْ فَاسْتَجَبْتُمْ لِي ۖ فَلَا تَلُومُونِي وَلُومُوا أَنفُسَكُم ۖ مَّا أَنَا بِمُصْرِخِكُمْ وَمَا أَنتُم بِمُصْرِخِيَّ ۖ إِنِّي كَفَرْتُ بِمَا أَشْرَكْتُمُونِ مِن قَبْلُ ۗ إِنَّ الظَّالِمِينَ لَهُمْ عَذَابٌ أَلِيمٌ

"And Satan shall say when the matter is decided, 'Verily, Allah promised you the promise of truth, and I too promised you, but I betrayed you. I had no authority over you except that I called you and you responded to me. So blame me not, but blame yourselves. I cannot help you, nor can you help me. I disbelieve in your associating me with Allah in times past. Verily, the wrongdoers shall have a painful torment.'"

— *Surah Ibrahim (Abraham) 14:22*

And therefore:

لِيَحْمِلُوا أَوْزَارَهُمْ كَامِلَةً يَوْمَ الْقِيَامَةِ ۙ وَمِنْ أَوْزَارِ الَّذِينَ يُضِلُّونَهُم بِغَيْرِ عِلْمٍ ۗ أَلَا سَاءَ مَا يَزِرُونَ

"That they may bear their own burdens in full on the Day of Judgment, and also the burdens of those whom they misled without knowledge. Evil indeed is that which they shall bear!"

— *Surah An-Nahl 16:25*

People will face the consequences.

When divine law prevails:

وَإِذَا رَأَى الَّذِينَ ظَلَمُوا الْعَذَابَ فَلَا يُخَفَّفُ عَنْهُمْ وَلَا هُمْ يُنظَرُونَ

"And when those who did wrong see the punishment, it will not be lightened for them, nor will they be given respite."

— *Surah An-Nahl 16:85*

الَّذِينَ كَفَرُوا وَصَدُّوا عَن سَبِيلِ اللَّهِ زِدْنَاهُمْ عَذَابًا فَوْقَ الْعَذَابِ بِمَا كَانُوا يُفْسِدُونَ

"As for those who disbelieve and hinder others from the way of Allah, We shall add punishment upon punishment because they spread corruption."

— *Surah An-Nahl 16:88*

وَامْتَازُوا الْيَوْمَ أَيُّهَا الْمُجْرِمُونَ

"(It will be said), 'And O you criminals! Stand apart this Day (from the believers).'"

— *Surah Ya-Sin 36:59*

هَـٰذِهِ جَهَنَّمُ الَّتِي كُنتُمْ تُوعَدُونَ

اصْلَوْهَا الْيَوْمَ بِمَا كُنتُمْ تَكْفُرُونَ

"This is Hell which you were promised. Enter into it this Day because of your disbelief."

— *Surah Ya-Sin 36:63–64*

ثُمَّ يَوْمَ الْقِيَامَةِ يُخْزِيهِمْ وَيَقُولُ أَيْنَ شُرَكَائِيَ الَّذِينَ كُنتُمْ تُشَاقُّونَ فِيهِمْ ۚ قَالَ الَّذِينَ أُوتُوا الْعِلْمَ إِنَّ الْخِزْيَ الْيَوْمَ وَالسُّوءَ عَلَى الْكَافِرِينَ

الَّذِينَ تَتَوَفَّاهُمُ الْمَلَائِكَةُ ظَالِمِي أَنفُسِهِمْ ۖ فَأَلْقَوُا السَّلَمَ مَا كُنَّا نَعْمَلُ مِن سُوءٍ ۚ بَلَىٰ إِنَّ اللَّهَ عَلِيمٌ بِمَا كُنتُمْ تَعْمَلُونَ

فَادْخُلُوا أَبْوَابَ جَهَنَّمَ خَالِدِينَ فِيهَا ۖ فَلَبِئْسَ مَثْوَى الْمُتَكَبِّرِينَ

"Then, on the Day of Resurrection, He will disgrace them and say: 'Where are My partners concerning whom you used to dispute?' Those given knowledge will say: 'Verily, disgrace and misery this Day are upon the disbelievers—those whose souls the angels take while they wrong themselves.' They will offer submission saying, 'We did no evil.' But verily, Allah is All-Knowing of what you did. So enter the gates of Hell, to abide therein. What an evil abode for the arrogant!"

— *Surah An-Nahl 16:27–29*

وَيَوْمَ يَقُولُ نَادُوا شُرَكَائِيَ الَّذِينَ زَعَمْتُمْ فَدَعَوْهُمْ فَلَمْ يَسْتَجِيبُوا لَهُمْ وَجَعَلْنَا بَيْنَهُم مَّوْبِقًا

وَرَأَى الْمُجْرِمُونَ النَّارَ فَظَنُّوا أَنَّهُم مُّوَاقِعُوهَا وَلَمْ يَجِدُوا عَنْهَا مَصْرِفًا

"And (remember) the Day He will say: 'Call those partners of Mine whom you claimed.' Then they will call upon them, but they will not respond. And We shall place a barrier between them. And the sinners will see the Fire and realise they will fall into it, and will find no escape from it."

— *Surah Al-Kahf 18:52–53*

وَيَوْمَ يُعْرَضُ الَّذِينَ كَفَرُوا عَلَى النَّارِ أَلَيْسَ هَـٰذَا بِالْحَقِّ ۖ قَالُوا بَلَىٰ وَرَبِّنَا ۚ قَالَ فَذُوقُوا الْعَذَابَ بِمَا كُنتُمْ تَكْفُرُونَ

فَاصْبِرْ كَمَا صَبَرَ أُولُو الْعَزْمِ مِنَ الرُّسُلِ وَلَا تَسْتَعْجِل لَّهُمْ ۚ كَأَنَّهُمْ يَوْمَ يَرَوْنَ مَا يُوعَدُونَ لَمْ يَلْبَثُوا إِلَّا سَاعَةً مِّن نَّهَارٍ ۚ بَلَاغٌ ۚ فَهَلْ يُهْلَكُ إِلَّا الْقَوْمُ الْفَاسِقُونَ

"And on the Day when the disbelievers are presented to the Fire: 'Is not this the truth?' They will say, 'Yes, by our Lord!' He will say, 'Then taste the punishment, because you disbelieved.' So be patient, as were the Messengers of firm resolve, and do not be in haste regarding them. On the Day they see what they were promised, it will be as if they had not tarried but for an hour of a day. This is a warning. Shall any perish save the transgressors?"

— Surah Al-Ahqaf 46:34–35

وَأُدْخِلَ الَّذِينَ آمَنُوا وَعَمِلُوا الصَّالِحَاتِ جَنَّاتٍ تَجْرِي مِن تَحْتِهَا الْأَنْهَارُ خَالِدِينَ فِيهَا بِإِذْنِ رَبِّهِمْ ۚ تَحِيَّتُهُمْ فِيهَا سَلَامٌ

"And those who believed and did righteous deeds shall be admitted to Gardens beneath which rivers flow, to abide therein forever, by permission of their Lord. Their greeting therein will be: Peace!"

— Surah Ibrahim 14:23

وَقِيلَ لِلَّذِينَ اتَّقَوْا مَاذَا أَنزَلَ رَبُّكُمْ ۚ قَالُوا خَيْرًا ۗ لِّلَّذِينَ أَحْسَنُوا فِي هَٰذِهِ الدُّنْيَا حَسَنَةٌ ۚ وَلَدَارُ الْآخِرَةِ خَيْرٌ ۚ وَلَنِعْمَ دَارُ الْمُتَّقِينَ

جَنَّاتُ عَدْنٍ يَدْخُلُونَهَا تَجْرِي مِن تَحْتِهَا الْأَنْهَارُ ۖ لَهُمْ فِيهَا مَا يَشَاءُونَ ۚ كَذَٰلِكَ يَجْزِي اللَّهُ الْمُتَّقِينَ

الَّذِينَ تَتَوَفَّاهُمُ الْمَلَائِكَةُ طَيِّبِينَ ۙ يَقُولُونَ سَلَامٌ عَلَيْكُمُ ادْخُلُوا الْجَنَّةَ بِمَا كُنتُمْ تَعْمَلُونَ

"And when it is said to those who fear Allah, 'What has your Lord revealed?' They say, 'Good!' For those who do good in this world, there is good, and the home of the Hereafter is even better. And excellent indeed is the home of the righteous— Gardens of Eternity which they shall enter, beneath which rivers flow. They shall have therein all that they wish. Thus Allah rewards the righteous—those whom the angels take in a good state. They say to them, 'Peace be upon you! Enter Paradise because of what you used to do.'"

— Surah An-Nahl 16:30–32

"The punishment of Allah SWT will not be for the believers."

The concept of divine punishment holds no fear for the true believer, as outlined in the Qur'an. Almighty Allah SWT declares that no one, not even the Prophet Muhammad ﷺ, knows the specifics of divine unseen matters. Despite this, humans often imagine scenes of grave divine punishments or a punishment not mentioned in the Qur'an before Judgement, which can contradict the teachings of the Qur'an.

For those who become true Muslims, adhering strictly to the guidance provided in the divine scriptures and following the Prophet Muhammad's ﷺ teachings, there is no reason to fear punishment in the Hereafter or on the Day of Judgment. Allah promises to honour true believers from the moment of their death until the Day of Judgment.

This trial is primarily designed to awaken the dormant spirit of those living in delusion. This metaphorical "judgement trial" stirs the inner soul, creating a sense of standing in a divine court, awaiting one's fate. This practice encourages introspection and a dialogue with the soul, fostering a deeper understanding and leading to solutions for one's spiritual journey.

However, our travelling group triumphantly emerged from this trial and is now moving towards the gates of Heaven. Although many stories will still be revealed on the way to Paradise, eventually they will enter their long-awaited destination of JANNATUL FIRDAUS by the command of Allah SWT.

This journey reflects the honour and reward awaiting those who faithfully adhere to their beliefs and live righteous lives.

Journey Towards The Path Of Heaven

The trial is over. The righteous have now started their journey towards Jannatul Firdaus as promised by Allah SWT. We will be welcomed at the gates of Paradise.

إِنَّ الَّذِينَ آمَنُوا وَعَمِلُوا الصَّالِحَاتِ كَانَتْ لَهُمْ جَنَّاتُ الْفِرْدَوْسِ نُزُلًا

"Verily those who believe, and do righteous works, shall have the gardens of Firdaus for their entertainment."

— Surah Al-Kahf 18:107

Welcome At The Gate Of Eden

Only truly righteous souls ascend directly to the Garden of Eden, say the sages. The average person descends to a place of punishment and/or purification, generally referred to as Gehinnom or وادي الربابة Wadi er-Rababi. **Note[246]**

Prophet Jesus declared that the road to eternal life is "narrow, and only a few find it." [247]

Jesus, in Islam عيسَى ابْنُ مَرْيَم, meaning عليه السلام ʿĪsā, son of Mary, is a messenger of Allah SWT sent to guide the Children of Israel (Banī Isrāʾīl) with a book called the Injīl (Evangel or Gospel). In Matthew 7:13–14, it is recorded that Jesus made a profound statement about the way to eternal life:

---

[246] (Eventually the Hebrew term Gehinnom became a figurative name for the place of spiritual purification for the wicked dead in Judaism. According to most Jewish sources, the period of purification or punishment is limited to only 12 months and every Sabbath day is excluded from punishment.) Its Arabic name is وادي الربابة Wadi er-Rababi. In the Hebrew Bible, Gehenna was initially where some of the kings of Judah sacrificed their children by fire.[4] Thereafter, it was deemed to be cursed (Book of Jeremiah 7:31, 19:2–6) https://www.google.com/search/ From Wikipedia, the free encyclopedia

There is a path that leads to heaven, but like the journey of a thousand miles, so too the journey to heaven – we must take that first step. If we desire to reach the end, at some point we must make a beginning, and each step along the way we must resolve to continue going forward.

Jesus عليه السلام taught concerning the path to heaven and eternal life,
[247] Index 194 (Jonathan McAnulty – Minister)
https://www.mydailytribune.com/opinion/45171/search-the-scriptures-a-path-that-leads-to-heaven.
https://www.biblegateway.com/passage/?search=Luke%209%3A23&version=NIV Prophet Jesus declared that the road to eternal life is "narrow, and only a few find it."
https://www.gotquestions.org/narrow-path.html

"Enter ye in at the strait gate: for wide is the gate, and broad is the way, that leadeth to destruction, and many there be which go in thereat:

Because strait is the gate, and narrow is the way, which leadeth unto life, and few there be that find it." — *Matthew 7:13–14, KJV*

This verse carries a significant indication for us to consider: the qualities necessary to be a *Mu'min*—a true believer worthy of Paradise.

Let us analyse this verse as follows:

The **narrow gate** emphasises the exclusivity and difficulty of attaining eternal life. Unlike the broad road that many take, the path to salvation requires a specific, deliberate choice and effort. This highlights that not all paths lead to eternal life; rather, there is a particular way that must be followed.

The narrow path suggests commitment, discipline, and often, sacrifice. It is not an easy or popular path, as it may require one to go against societal norms, personal desires, or even face persecution. By stating that *few find it*, Jesus implies that genuine discipleship and true adherence to his teachings are not common. Many may profess belief, but few actually live out the demands of the faith fully. True discipleship involves a deep and transformative relationship with God, which not everyone achieves.

The narrow path represents the high moral and ethical standards that Jesus taught. It requires love, forgiveness, humility, and a rejection of sinful behaviours. This way of living is often challenging and countercultural, making it less travelled.

While the path is difficult, it is not impossible. Jesus' teaching also implies the necessity of grace and divine guidance. Believers are encouraged to rely on God's strength and guidance to navigate the narrow path successfully. The contrast between the narrow path leading to life and the broad path leading to destruction underscores the eternal consequences of one's choices. It serves as a warning to be mindful of the path one chooses, as it determines one's eternal destiny.

However, Allah SWT will welcome His righteous—*of course, us*—at the gate of Heaven, saying:

ادْخُلُوا الْجَنَّةَ أَنتُمْ وَأَزْوَاجُكُمْ تُحْبَرُونَ

"Enter Paradise, you and your wives, in happiness."

— Surah Az-Zukhruf 43:70

Allah has confirmed in the following verses:

يَا عِبَادِ لَا خَوْفٌ عَلَيْكُمُ الْيَوْمَ وَلَا أَنتُمْ تَحْزَنُونَ

الَّذِينَ آمَنُوا بِآيَاتِنَا وَكَانُوا مُسْلِمِينَ

68. (It will be said to the true believers of Islamic Monotheism): "My worshippers! No fear shall be on you this Day, nor shall you grieve.

69. (You) who believed in Our Ayat (proofs, verses, lessons, signs, revelations, etc.) and were Muslims (i.e. who submit totally to Allah's Will and believe in the Oneness of Allah – Islamic Monotheism)."

— Surah Az-Zukhruf 43:68–69

دَعْوَاهُمْ فِيهَا سُبْحَانَكَ اللَّهُمَّ وَتَحِيَّتُهُمْ فِيهَا سَلَامٌ ۚ وَآخِرُ دَعْوَاهُمْ أَنِ الْحَمْدُ لِلَّهِ رَبِّ الْعَالَمِينَ

10. Their way of request therein will be: "Subḥānaka Allāhumma" (Glory to You, O Allah!) and "Salām" (peace, safety from evil) will be their greeting therein (Jannah)! And the close of their request will be: "Al-ḥamdu lillāhi Rabbi-l-ʿālamīn" (All praise and thanks are to Allah, the Lord of all creation).

— Surah Yūnus 10:10

The Gatekeepers Of Heaven

As we enter Heaven's gates, the guardians will greet us:

"Peace be upon you."

Allah SWT says:

وَسِيقَ الَّذِينَ اتَّقَوْا رَبَّهُمْ إِلَى الْجَنَّةِ زُمَرًا ۖ حَتَّىٰ إِذَا جَاءُوهَا وَفُتِحَتْ أَبْوَابُهَا وَقَالَ لَهُمْ خَزَنَتُهَا
سَلَامٌ عَلَيْكُمْ طِبْتُمْ فَادْخُلُوهَا خَالِدِينَ

"And those who kept their duty to their Lord will be led to Paradise in groups, till—when they reach it, and its gates will be opened (before their arrival for their reception)—its keepers will say: 'Salāmun ʿAlaykum (peace be upon you)! You have done well, so enter here to abide therein.'"

— Surah Az-Zumar 39:73

And:

وَإِن مِّنكُمْ إِلَّا وَارِدُهَا ۚ كَانَ عَلَىٰ رَبِّكَ حَتْمًا مَّقْضِيًّا

"There is not one of you but will pass over it (Hell); this is with your Lord—a Decree which must be accomplished."

— Surah Maryam 19:71

Here, a Hadith reports that all believers qualified to enter Paradise will be stopped before crossing the gate to settle disagreements, resolve any anger or bad feelings, and clear any remaining affairs in their hearts. This is the final purification of the heart needed to enter Paradise.

Because Allah SWT says:

594

اذْخُلُوهَا بِسَلَامٍ آمِنِينَ

وَنَزَعْنَا مَا فِي صُدُورِهِم مِّنْ غِلٍّ إِخْوَانًا عَلَىٰ سُرُرٍ مُّتَقَابِلِينَ

46. "(It will be said to them): 'Enter therein (Paradise), in peace and security.'

47. And We shall remove from their breasts any sense of injury (that they may have), (so they will be) brothers, facing each other on thrones."

— Surah Al-Ḥijr 15:46–47

It has also been narrated in Hadith that:

Cleanliness (Taharah) is a part of faith. Those who do not take care of cleanliness and purification—especially those men and women who do not perform the ceremonial bath (Ghusl Janabat) correctly or at its prescribed time—will be stopped at this Pass.

The Messenger of Allah, ﷺ said:

"The distance between two shutters in Paradise equals the distance of a forty-year walk. It is impossible to see the end of it, where people are crowded."

It was recorded in Bukhari that our Prophet Muhammad ﷺ will be the first to cross the gate and enter into Heaven. The Hadith reports:

"I and my ummah will be the first to permit it, and no one will speak on that day but the messengers, and the supplication of the messengers will be reproached on that day."

In that context, we will accompany Him—if Allah (SWT) accepts our group of travellers—as we strictly follow the chosen stages according to each person's ability, as guided in verse 4:69 of Surah An-Nisa, which is defined as:

وَمَن يُطِعِ اللَّهَ وَالرَّسُولَ فَأُولَٰئِكَ مَعَ الَّذِينَ أَنْعَمَ اللَّهُ عَلَيْهِم مِّنَ النَّبِيِّينَ وَالصِّدِّيقِينَ وَالشُّهَدَاءِ
وَالصَّالِحِينَ ۚ وَحَسُنَ أُولَٰئِكَ رَفِيقًا

And whoso obeyeth Allah and the Messenger, they shall be with those on whom Allah hath bestowed His grace—of the prophets, the truthful, the martyrs, and the righteous: and excellent are these as companions! (Surah An-Nisa 4:69)

Once we step into Paradise, its gates will never close behind us. They remain perpetually open, allowing us to freely come and go and to reside in eternal bliss. The angels, carrying gifts and blessings from our Lord, frequently visit the dwellers of Paradise, spreading joy and happiness. This symbolism highlights that Paradise is a sanctuary where its inhabitants need not worry about shutting their doors, unlike in our earthly existence.

The Qur'an confirms this in the following verses:

جَنَّاتِ عَدْنٍ مُّفَتَّحَةً لَّهُمُ الْأَبْوَابُ

مُتَّكِئِينَ فِيهَا يَدْعُونَ فِيهَا بِفَاكِهَةٍ كَثِيرَةٍ وَشَرَابٍ

Gardens of perpetual residence, whose doors will be open to them,

Wherein they will recline, calling for abundant fruit and drink. (Surah Sad 38:50–51)

II

Gathering at the Gates of Eden

"Gathering at the gates of Eden" refers to the biblical story of Adam and Eve in the Garden of Eden. According to the Book of Genesis, the Garden of Eden was a paradise created by God, where the first humans, Adam and Eve, lived before they were expelled due to their disobedience. The "gates of Eden" symbolise the entry point to this lost paradise.

In Genesis 3:22–24 (KJV):

And the Lord God said, Behold, the man is become as one of us, to know good and evil: and now, lest he put forth his hand, and take also of the tree of life, and eat, and live for ever:

Therefore the Lord God sent him forth from the garden of Eden, to till the ground from whence he was taken.

So he drove out the man; and he placed at the east of the garden of Eden Cherubims, and a flaming sword which turned every way, to keep the way of the tree of life.

The phrase "gathering at the gates of Eden" evokes a longing to return to a state of innocence and divine presence, or to reclaim a place of spiritual perfection.

Gathering at the Gate of Eden

Therefore I will gather thee unto thy fathers, and thou shalt be gathered into thy grave in peace… (cf. 2 Kings 22:20)

In this context, "gathering at the gate of Eden" also symbolises a peaceful reunion with one's ancestors after death, drawing on biblical references. This phrase echoes God's promise of a tranquil end for the righteous, as illustrated in various passages from Genesis:

- The death of Abraham (Gen. 25:8)
- Ishmael (Gen. 25:17)
- Isaac (Gen. 35:29)
- Jacob (Gen. 49:33)

These verses emphasise a peaceful burial and the assurance that the deceased will not witness impending calamities. This message was conveyed to the king as a divine reassurance of peace in the afterlife for the faithful.

"There on the mountain that you have climbed you will die and be gathered to your people, just as your brother Aaron died on Mount Hor and was gathered to his people. Deut. 32:50 Moses and Aaron"

In Deuteronomy 32:50, the verse is part of God's instructions to Moses towards the end of his life. Let's break down the verse for better understanding: **Context**:

❖ This passage is from the Old Testament, specifically the Book of Deuteronomy, which is the fifth book of the Torah or Pentateuch.

❖ In this chapter, God is speaking to Moses, giving him instructions and prophesying about the future of the Israelites.

Verse Breakdown:

❖ *"There on the mountain that you have climbed": This refers to* **Mount Nebo**, *a mountain in the land of Moab, which Moses climbed as instructed by God.*

❖ *"you will die and be gathered to your people": God tells Moses that he will die on Mount Nebo.* **"Gathered to your people"** *is a Hebrew idiom meaning that Moses will join his ancestors in death.*

❖ *"just as your brother Aaron died on Mount Hor and was gathered to his people": This is a comparison to Aaron, Moses' brother, who also died on a mountain (Mount Hor) and was gathered to his ancestors.*

Key Points:-

1. **Mount Nebo:** Moses was instructed by God to climb Mount Nebo, where he would view the Promised Land before he died, as he was not allowed to enter it due to earlier disobedience.

• **Death and Gathering to Ancestors:** The phrase indicates not just physical death but also a spiritual reunion with forebears.

1. **Comparison to Aaron**: This reinforces the inevitability of Moses' death by drawing a parallel to Aaron's death, emphasising that just as Aaron died at God's appointed time and place, so too will Moses.

❖ **Fulfilment of God's Word:** It highlights the fulfilment of God's words and promises, demonstrating that God's plans and instructions are always fulfilled. In summary, Deuteronomy 32:50 is a poignant reminder of the mortality of even the greatest leaders and the importance of obedience to God's commands, as well as the continuity of God's plans through different generations.

2. *Fulfilment of God's promise*: God's plans remain constant across generations.

Our Dream Home – Heaven

Greetings of "Peace!"

According to the divine revelation of Allah (SWT), it is proclaimed that when faithful believers finally enter Paradise and behold their well-deserved abodes, they will recognise that their perseverance through countless challenges and hardships was the key to attaining the homes of their dreams.

Allah (SWT) says:

دَعْوَاهُمْ فِيهَا سُبْحَانَكَ اللَّهُمَّ وَتَحِيَّتُهُمْ فِيهَا سَلَامٌ ۚ وَآخِرُ دَعْوَاهُمْ أَنِ الْحَمْدُ لِلَّهِ رَبِّ الْعَالَمِينَ

Their way of request therein will be: "Subḥānaka Allāhumma" (Glory to You, O Allah!), and their greeting therein will be "Salām" (Peace). And the close of their request will be: "Al-Ḥamdu lillāhi Rabbil-ʿĀlamīn" (All praise and thanks be to Allah, the Lord of all the worlds). (Surah Yunus 10:10)

Then Allah SWT Says:

3.

وَنَزَعْنَا مَا فِي صُدُورِهِم مِّنْ غِلٍّ تَجْرِي مِن تَحْتِهِمُ الْأَنْهَارُ ۖ وَقَالُوا الْحَمْدُ لِلَّهِ الَّذِي هَدَانَا لِهَٰذَا وَمَا كُنَّا لِنَهْتَدِيَ لَوْلَا أَنْ هَدَانَا اللَّهُ ۖ لَقَدْ جَاءَتْ رُسُلُ رَبِّنَا بِالْحَقِّ ۖ وَنُودُوا أَن تِلْكُمُ الْجَنَّةُ أُورِثْتُمُوهَا بِمَا كُنتُمْ تَعْمَلُونَ

And We shall remove from their breasts any (mutual) hatred or sense of injury (which they had, if at all, in the life of this world); rivers will flow beneath them. And they will say: *"All praise and thanks be to Allah, Who has guided us to this. Never could we have found guidance were it not that Allah had guided us. Indeed, the Messengers of our Lord did come with the truth."* And it will be cried out to them: *"This is the Paradise which you have inherited for what you used to do."* — Surah Al-A'raf (7:43)

إِنَّ الْأَبْرَارَ لَفِي نَعِيمٍ

عَلَى الْأَرَائِكِ يَنظُرُونَ

تَعْرِفُ فِي وُجُوهِهِمْ نَضْرَةَ النَّعِيمِ

يُسْقَوْنَ مِن رَّحِيقٍ مَّخْتُومٍ

خِتَامُهُ مِسْكٌ ۚ وَفِي ذَٰلِكَ فَلْيَتَنَافَسِ الْمُتَنَافِسُونَ

وَمِزَاجُهُ مِن تَسْنِيمٍ

عَيْنًا يَشْرَبُ بِهَا الْمُقَرَّبُونَ

22 Verily, Al-Abrar (the pious who fear Allah and avoid evil) will be in delight (Paradise).

23. On thrones, looking (at all things).

24. You will recognise in their faces the brightness of delight.

25. They will be given to drink pure sealed wine.

26. The last thereof (that wine) will be the smell of musk, and for this let (all) those strive who want to strive (i.e., hasten earnestly to the obedience of Allah).

27. It (that wine) will be mixed with Tasnim—

A spring whereof drink those nearest to Allah. — Surah Al-Mutaffife (83:22–28)

وَسَارِعُوا إِلَىٰ مَغْفِرَةٍ مِّن رَّبِّكُمْ وَجَنَّةٍ عَرْضُهَا السَّمَاوَاتُ وَالْأَرْضُ أُعِدَّتْ لِلْمُتَّقِينَ

And march forth in the way (which leads to) forgiveness from your Lord, and for Paradise as wide as the heavens and the earth, prepared for Al-Muttaqun (the righteous). — Surah Al-Imran (3:133)

Throne of Dignity in Heaven

Then Allah SWT declared that the people of Paradise will experience every comfort. This announcement is revealed in the Holy Qur'an, which can be recited as follows:

مُتَّكِئِينَ عَلَىٰ سُرُرٍ مَّصْفُوفَةٍ ۖ وَزَوَّجْنَاهُم بِحُورٍ عِينٍ

وَالَّذِينَ آمَنُوا وَاتَّبَعَتْهُمْ ذُرِّيَّتُهُم بِإِيمَانٍ أَلْحَقْنَا بِهِمْ ذُرِّيَّتَهُمْ وَمَا أَلَتْنَاهُم مِّنْ عَمَلِهِم مِّن شَيْءٍ ۚ كُلُّ امْرِئٍ بِمَا كَسَبَ رَهِينٌ

وَأَمْدَدْنَاهُم بِفَاكِهَةٍ وَلَحْمٍ مِّمَّا يَشْتَهُونَ

يَتَنَازَعُونَ فِيهَا كَأْسًا لَّا لَغْوٌ فِيهَا وَلَا تَأْثِيمٌ

وَيَطُوفُ عَلَيْهِمْ غِلْمَانٌ لَّهُمْ كَأَنَّهُمْ لُؤْلُؤٌ مَّكْنُونٌ

They will recline (with ease) on thrones arranged in ranks. And We shall marry them to Houris (female, fair ones) with wide lovely eyes.

And those who believe, and whose offspring follow them in faith, to them We shall join their offspring. And We shall not decrease the reward of their deeds in anything. Every person is pledged for what he has earned.

And We shall provide them with fruit and meat, such as they desire.

There they shall pass a wine cup to one another, free from any dirty, false, or evil talk, and free from sin (because it will be lawful for them to drink).

And there will circulate among them boy-servants of theirs, like preserved pearls. — Surah At-Tur (52:20–24)

هُمْ وَأَزْوَاجُهُمْ فِي ظِلَالٍ عَلَى الْأَرَائِكِ مُتَّكِئُونَ

لَهُمْ فِيهَا فَاكِهَةٌ وَلَهُم مَّا يَدَّعُونَ

سَلَامٌ قَوْلًا مِّن رَّبٍّ رَّحِيمٍ

They and their spouses will be in pleasant shade, reclining on thrones.

They will have therein fruits (of all kinds) and all that they desire.

(It will be said to them): *"Peace!"*—a Word from the Lord, Most Merciful. — Surah Ya-Sin (36:56–58)

فِي جَنَّةٍ عَالِيَةٍ

لَّا تَسْمَعُ فِيهَا لَاغِيَةً

فِيهَا عَيْنٌ جَارِيَةٌ

فِيهَا سُرُرٌ مَّرْفُوعَةٌ

وَأَكْوَابٌ مَّوْضُوعَةٌ

وَنَمَارِقُ مَصْفُوفَةٌ

وَزَرَابِيُّ مَبْثُوثَةٌ

In a lofty Paradise—

Wherein they shall hear no harmful speech nor falsehood.

Therein will be a flowing spring.

Therein will be thrones raised high,

And cups set at hand,

And cushions set in rows,

And rich carpets spread out. — Surah Al-Ghashiyah (88:10–16)

قَالَ اللَّهُ هَٰذَا يَوْمُ يَنفَعُ الصَّادِقِينَ صِدْقُهُمْ ۚ لَهُمْ جَنَّاتٌ تَجْرِي مِن تَحْتِهَا الْأَنْهَارُ خَالِدِينَ فِيهَا أَبَدًا ۚ رَّضِيَ اللَّهُ عَنْهُمْ وَرَضُوا عَنْهُ ۚ ذَٰلِكَ الْفَوْزُ الْعَظِيمُ

Allah will say: *"This is a day on which the truthful will profit from their truth: theirs are gardens beneath which rivers flow—wherein they shall abide forever. Allah is pleased with them and they with Him. That is the great success."* — Surah Al-Ma'idah (5:119)

مَّثَلُ الْجَنَّةِ الَّتِي وُعِدَ الْمُتَّقُونَ ۖ فِيهَا أَنْهَارٌ مِّن مَّاءٍ غَيْرِ آسِنٍ وَأَنْهَارٌ مِّن لَّبَنٍ لَّمْ يَتَغَيَّرْ طَعْمُهُ وَأَنْهَارٌ مِّنْ خَمْرٍ لَّذَّةٍ لِّلشَّارِبِينَ وَأَنْهَارٌ مِّنْ عَسَلٍ مُّصَفًّى ۖ وَلَهُمْ فِيهَا مِن كُلِّ الثَّمَرَاتِ وَمَغْفِرَةٌ مِّن رَّبِّهِمْ ۖ كَمَنْ هُوَ خَالِدٌ فِي النَّارِ وَسُقُوا مَاءً حَمِيمًا فَقَطَّعَ أَمْعَاءَهُمْ

The description of Paradise which the Muttaqun (pious) are promised: therein are rivers of water the taste and smell of which are not changed; rivers of milk of which the taste never changes; rivers of wine, delicious to those who drink; and rivers of clarified honey, pure and clear. Therein for them is every kind of fruit and forgiveness from their Lord. Is this like those who will dwell forever in the Fire and be given boiling water to drink so it tears apart their intestines? — Surah Muhammad (47:15)

وَعَدَ اللَّهُ الْمُؤْمِنِينَ وَالْمُؤْمِنَاتِ جَنَّاتٍ تَجْرِي مِن تَحْتِهَا الْأَنْهَارُ خَالِدِينَ فِيهَا وَمَسَاكِنَ طَيِّبَةً فِي جَنَّاتِ عَدْنٍ ۚ وَرِضْوَانٌ مِّنَ اللَّهِ أَكْبَرُ ۚ ذَٰلِكَ هُوَ الْفَوْزُ الْعَظِيمُ

Allah has promised to the believers—men and women—Gardens under which rivers flow, to dwell therein forever, and beautiful mansions in Gardens of Eden (Jannat 'Adn). But the greatest bliss is the pleasure of Allah. That is the supreme success. — Surah At-Tawbah (9:72)

أُولَٰئِكَ لَهُمْ جَنَّاتُ عَدْنٍ تَجْرِي مِن تَحْتِهِمُ الْأَنْهَارُ يُحَلَّوْنَ فِيهَا مِنْ أَسَاوِرَ مِن ذَهَبٍ وَيَلْبَسُونَ ثِيَابًا خُضْرًا مِّن سُندُسٍ وَإِسْتَبْرَقٍ مُّتَّكِئِينَ فِيهَا عَلَى الْأَرَائِكِ ۚ نِعْمَ الثَّوَابُ وَحَسُنَتْ مُرْتَفَقًا

These—for them will be Gardens of Eden (Jannat 'Adn), beneath which rivers flow. Therein they will be adorned with bracelets of gold and wear green garments of fine and thick silk. Reclining therein on raised thrones. What an excellent reward, and what a beautiful resting place! — Surah Al-Kahf (18:31)

فِيهِنَّ قَاصِرَاتُ الطَّرْفِ لَمْ يَطْمِثْهُنَّ إِنسٌ قَبْلَهُمْ وَلَا جَانٌّ

Therein will be maidens restraining their glances, whom no man or jinn has touched before them. — Surah Ar-Rahman (55:56)

إِنَّا أَنشَأْنَاهُنَّ إِنشَاءً

فَجَعَلْنَاهُنَّ أَبْكَارًا

عُرُبًا أَتْرَابًا

لِّأَصْحَابِ الْيَمِينِ

35. *Verily, We have created them (maidens) of special creation.*

36. *And made them virgins.*

37. *Loving (their husbands only), equal in age.*

38. *For those on the Right Hand. — Surah Al-Waqi'ah 56:35–38*

وَعِندَهُمْ قَاصِرَاتُ الطَّرْفِ عِينٌ

And with them will be chaste females, restraining their glances (desiring none except their husbands), with wide and beautiful eyes. — Surah As-Saffat 37:48

أُولَٰئِكَ جَزَاؤُهُم مَّغْفِرَةٌ مِّن رَّبِّهِمْ وَجَنَّاتٌ تَجْرِي مِن تَحْتِهَا الْأَنْهَارُ خَالِدِينَ فِيهَا ۚ وَنِعْمَ أَجْرُ الْعَامِلِينَ

For such, the reward is forgiveness from their Lord, and Gardens with rivers flowing underneath (Paradise), wherein they shall abide forever. How excellent is this reward for the doers (who do righteous deeds according to Allah's Orders). —Surah Al-Imran 3:136

Family/Companions

Jannatul-Firdaus will be the highest level of Heaven, where we will find Prophet Muhammad ﷺ

جَنَّاتُ عَدْنٍ يَدْخُلُونَهَا وَمَن صَلَحَ مِنْ آبَائِهِمْ وَأَزْوَاجِهِمْ وَذُرِّيَّاتِهِمْ ۖ وَالْمَلَائِكَةُ يَدْخُلُونَ عَلَيْهِم مِّن كُلِّ بَابٍ

سَلَامٌ عَلَيْكُم بِمَا صَبَرْتُمْ ۚ فَنِعْمَ عُقْبَى الدَّارِ

23. *'Adn (Eden) Paradise (everlasting Gardens), which they shall enter — and also those who acted righteously from among their fathers, their wives, and their offspring. And angels shall enter unto them from every gate (saying):*

24. *"Salamun 'Alaikum (peace be upon you) for that you persevered in patience! Excellent indeed is the final home!" — Surah Ar-Ra'd 13:23–24*

We say again

The Messenger believeth in what

hath been revealed to him from his Lord,

as do the men of faith.

Each one (of them) believeth in Allah,

His angels, His books, and His apostles.

"We make no distinction (they say)

between one and another of His apostles."

And they say:

"We hear, and we obey."

And finally, we say:

"Forgive us, our Lord!

To You is the journey's end."

— Surah Al-Baqarah 2:285

THE END

QUR'ANIC VERSE INDEX

INTRODUCTION

- Surah Al-Fatihah 1:6–7
- Surah Ibrahim 14:1 (Pickthall)
- Surah An-Nisaa 4:174

CHAPTER 1

- Surah Yunus 10:73
- Surah Nuh 71:28
- Surah Al-Anbiyaa 21:32
- Surah Al-Baqarah 2:30
- Surah Ar-Ra'd 13:28
- Surah An-Nur 24:35
- Surah Al-Qasas 28:88
- Surah Qaf 18:16
- Surah Al-Baqarah 2:269

CHAPTER 2

- Surah Al-An'am 6:127
- Surah Yunus 10:25
- Surah As-Sajda 32:17
- Surah Al-Qiyamah 75:22–23
- Surah Fussilat (Ha-Mim) 41:30
- Surah Aal Imran 3:133
- Surah Al-Baqarah 2:214
- Surah Al-Ankabut 29:2–3
- Surah Az-Zumar 39:9
- Surah Al-Baqarah 2:155
- Surah Al-Anbiyaa 21:35
- Surah Al-Mulk 67:2

- Surah Aal Imran 3:142, 3:186, 3:134
- Surah Al-Ankabut 29:4
- Surah Al-Hajj 22:11
- Surah An-Nisaa 4:74
- Surah Al-Hadid 57:20
- Surah Al-Mulk 67:2

CHAPTER 3

- Surah Al-Mu'min 40:17
- Surah Ash-Shu'ara 26:88–89, 26:89–90
- Surah Al-Qiyamah 75:2
- Surah Al-Fajr 89:28
- Surah Yusuf 12:53
- Surah Al-A'raf 7:205, 7:200
- Surah Al-Israa 17:85
- Surah Ash-Shams 91:9–10, 91:7–10
- Surah Al-A'la 87:14–15
- Surah Ar-Ra'd 13:28
- Surah Al-Baqarah 2:177, 2:10, 2:11, 2:12, 2:8, 2:9
- Surah Al-Ankabut 29:45
- Surah Muhammad 47:24
- Surah Al-Mutaffifeen 83:14
- Surah Aal Imran 3:7–8
- Surah Ash-Sharh 94:1
- Surah Al-Jumu'a 62:2
- Surah Abasa 80:1–11

- Surah Al-Hajj 22:32
- Surah Al-Anfal 8:24
- Surah Al-Kahf 18:28
- Surah Al-An'am 6:52
- Surah Ash-Shu'ara 26:89–90
- Surah An-Nur 24:41

CHAPTER 4

- Surah Fatir 35:6
- Surah Ibrahim 14:22
- Surah Sad 38:82–85
- Surah Al-A'raf 7:16–17, 7:27, 7:12, 7:22, 7:200
- Surah Al-Baqarah 2:268, 2:264, 2:195, 2:116, 2:153, 2:109, 2:45, 2:2, 2:183
- Surah Ha-Mim 41:36
- Surah Qaf 50:16
- Surah Ta-Ha 20:120, 20:117
- Surah Al-Naas 6:114:1–6
- Surah An-Nisaa 4:29, 4:74, 4:119, 4:117–118, 4:87, 4:145, 4:54, 4:142
- Surah Al-Israa 17:53, 17:62, 17:82
- Surah Ya-Sin 36:62
- Surah Al-Hujurat 49:14, 49:12
- Surah Aal Imran 3:134, 3:200, 3:146, 3:120, 3:85
- Surah An-Nahl 16:90, 16:126
- Surah Al-Ahqaf 46:15
- Surah Al-Ma'idah 5:93
- Surah Al-Munafiqun 63:1, 63:4
- Surah Saba 34:21
- Surah Al-Ma'un 107:1–7
- Surah Al-Kahf 18:105, 18:50, 28:80
- Surah Al-Mujadila 58:19
- Surah At-Taubah 9:79
- Surah Al-Humaza 104:1
- Surah Al-Hijr 15:26–27
- Surah Ar-Rahman 55:15
- Surah Al-An'am 6:130
- Surah Al-Muddathir 74:38
- Surah Al-Waqi'ah 56:71
- Surah At-Tin 95:1
- Surah Al-Imran 3:134
- Surah Al-Mu'minun 23:111
- Surah Yusuf 12:90
- Surah Az-Zumar 39:10
- Surah Hud 11:11
- Surah Ash-Shura 42:43
- Surah At-Tur 52:48
- Surah Maryam 19:65
- Surah Ibrahim 14:5
- Surah Ta-Ha verse 148
- Surah Al-A'raf 7:149–151
- Surah Al-Baqarah 2:51, 2:54, 2:92, 2:193
- Surah Al-A'raf 7:150

CHAPTER 5

- Al-Baqarah 2:10, 2:30, 2:31, 2:45, 2:62, 2:64, 2:123, 2:149, 2:168, 2:204, 2:205, 2:208, 2:213, 2:219, 2:220, 2:261, 2:264

- Al-Fatir 35:5, 35:6, 35:42, 35:43

- Al-Hadid 57:9

- Al-Hajj 22:11, 22:45, 22:52, 22:67

- Al-Hujurat 49:6, 49:9, 49:10

- Al-Imran 3:3, 3:92, 3:155, 3:160

- Al-Isra 17:33, 17:35, 17:36, 17:82

- Al-Ma'arij 70:3, 70:4, 70:5

- Al-Maidah 5:27, 5:30, 5:32

- Al-Mujadila 58:19

- Al-Naml 27:55

- Al-Nisaa 4:1, 4:10, 4:36, 4:47, 4:58, 4:69, 4:76, 4:102, 4:112, 4:120

- Al-Qamar 54:31

- Al-Sad 38:44

- Al-Saffaat 37:143, 37:144

- Al-Yasin 36:29

- An-Nahl 16:90

- An-Nur 24:21, 24:37

- An-Nur 24:21

- Anbiyaa 21:68, 21:69, 21:83

- Ar-Rahman 55:15

- Ar-Rum 30:41

- As-Saffaat 37:143, 37:144

- Az-Zukhruf 43:36–39

- Fussilat 41:29

- Ha-Mim 41:29

- Hud 11:3, 11:76, 11:77, 11:82

- Luqman 31:18

- Surah Al-A'raf 7:13, 7:27, 7:80

- Surah Al-An'am 6:68, 6:116

- Surah Al-Anbiyaa 21:68, 21:69, 21:83

- Surah Al-Hijr 15:39

- Surah Al-Isra 17:33, 17:35, 17:36, 17:82

- Surah Al-Naml 27:55

- Surah Hud 11:3, 11:76, 11:77, 11:82

- Surah Luqman 31:18

- Surah Sad 38:44

CHAPTER 6

- Al-An'am 6:153

- Al-Ankabut 29:2, 29:58

- Al-A'raf 7:27, 7:33

- Al-Baqarah 2:2, 2:43, 2:62, 2:123, 2:149, 2:168, 2:188, 2:213, 2:219, 2:238, 2:254, 2:261, 2:264, 2:278

- Al-Burooj 85:10

- Al-Fatir 35:6, 35:10

- Al-Fath 48:4

- Al-Hashr 59:16, 59:19

- Al-Humaza 104:1

- Al-Imran 3:76, 3:77, 3:103, 3:118, 3:130, 3:131, 3:135
- Al-Isra 17:23, 17:26, 17:33, 17:35, 17:36, 17:37
- Al-Kahf 18:30
- Al-Maidah 5:9, 5:100
- Al-Mala'ikah 35:6
- Al-Mu'min 40:7, 40:40
- Al-Nahl 16:30, 16:32, 16:97, 16:128
- Al-Qalam 68:10, 68:11, 68:12
- Al-Rum 30:36, 30:39, 30:45
- Al-Shurah 42:42
- An-Nisaa 4:10, 4:17, 4:36, 4:47, 4:58, 4:69, 4:80, 4:112, 4:138, 4:148
- An-Nur 24:37
- Ar-Rum 30:39, 30:45
- As-Sajda 32:19 (listed twice)
- At-Taghabun 64:11
- At-Tahrim 66:6
- At-Talaq 65:5
- Fatir 35:6, 35:10
- Ha-Mim 41:49
- Ibrahim 14:3, 14:27
- Israel 17:19
- Luqman 31:6, 31:8
- Muhammad 47:1
- Qaf 50:17–18
- Surah Al-Baqara 2:2, 2:43, 2:168, 2:183, 2:188, 2:213, 2:219, 2:238, 2:254, 2:261, 2:264, 2:278
- Surah Al-Fatihah 1:6–7
- Surah Al-Humaza 104:1
- Surah Al-Isra 17:23, 17:26, 17:33, 17:35, 17:36, 17:37
- Surah Al-Kahf 18:30
- Surah Al-Nahl 16:30, 16:32, 16:97, 16:128
- Surah Al-Qalam 68:10, 68:11, 68:12
- Surah Al-Rum 30:36, 30:39, 30:45
- Surah Al-Sajda 32:19 (x2)
- Surah Al-Talaq 65:5
- Surah An-Nisaa 4:10, 4:17, 4:36, 4:47, 4:58, 4:69, 4:80, 4:112, 4:138, 4:148
- Surah An-Nur 24:37
- Surah Ar-Rum 30:36, 30:39, 30:45
- Surah As-Sajda 32:19
- Surah At-Tahrim 66:6
- Surah At-Taghabun 64:11

CHAPTER 7
- Surah Al-Baqara 2:42
- Surah At-Taubah 9:119
- Surah Al-Ahzab 33:70
- Surah An-Nahl 16:44
- Surah Al-Ahzab 33:21
- Surah Qaf 50:45
- Surah Ha-Mim Sajdah 41:3
- Surah Al-An'am 6:115

- Surah Al-An'am 6:38
- Surah Yusuf 12:111
- Surah Hud 11:1
- Surah An-Nahl 16:89
- Surah Al-Furqan 25:33
- Surah Az-Zumar 39:23
- Surah Al-Qalam 68:36–38
- Surah Al-An'am 6:114
- Surah Al-Mursalat 77:50
- Surah Al-Jathiya 45:6
- Surah Ar-Rahman 55:1–2
- Surah Al-Qiyamat 75:17
- Surah Al-Qiyamat 75:19
- Surah Adh-Dhuha 93:11
- Surah Al-Maidah 5:99
- Surah An-Nahl 16:44
- Surah Al-Jinn 72:21
- Surah Al-Baqara 2:129
- Surah Al-Qasas 28:56
- Surah An-Najm 53:3–5
- Surah Al-A'raf 7:188
- Surah Al-An'am 6:50
- Surah An-Naml 27:65
- Surah Al-Ahqaf 46:9
- Surah Ash-Shura 42:48
- Surah Al-Gashiya 88:21–22
- Surah Al-Qalam 68:4
- Surah At-Taubah 9:128
- Surah Al-Ahzab 33:40
- Surah Al-Imran 3:164
- Surah Al-Jumu'a 62:2

- Surah Al-Ahzab 33:56
- Surah An-Nisaa 4:59
- Surah Al-Maidah 5:92
- Surah Al-Imran 3:31
- Surah Al-Hashr 59:7
- Surah Al-An'am 6:159
- Surah Al-An'am 6:112
- Surah Al-Isra 17:85
- Surah Al-An'am 6:114
- Surah Al-An'am 6:115
- Surah Al-Munafiqun 63:1
- Surah Al-Imran 3:81
- Surah Al-Jathiya 45:6
- Surah Al-Furqan 25:29–30
- Surah Al-Haqqa 69:40
- Surah Al-Baqara 2:136
- Surah Al-Maidah 5:44
- Surah Al-Maidah 5:47
- Surah Al-Baqara 2:151
- Surah Ash-Shura 42:13
- Surah Al-Isra 17:36
- Surah Al-Mursalat 77:49–50
- Surah An-Nisaa 4:105
- Surah Ash-Shura 42:10
- Surah Al-A'raf 7:3
- Surah An-Nur 24:51
- Surah Muhammad 47:33
- Surah Al-Jinn 72:23
- Surah Al-Ahzab 33:36

CHAPTER 8

- Surah Al-Maidah 5:8

- Surah Al-Hujurat 49:10
- Surah Ash-Shura 42:17
- Surah An-Nahl 16:90
- Surah An-Nisaa 4:29
- Surah Al-Jathiya 45:22
- Surah Az-Zukhruf 43:32
- Surah At-Taubah 9:34
- Surah At-Tin 95:8
- Surah Sad 38:26
- Surah Sad 38:25
- Surah Al-Anbiyaa 21:47
- Surah Al-Furqan 25:2
- Surah Al-Hijr 15:19
- Surah Al-Muminun 23:18
- Surah Az-Zukhruf 43:11
- Surah Al-Baqara 2:143
- Surah An-Nisaa 4:110
- Surah Hud 11:112
- Surah An-Nahl 16:90
- Surah An-Nisaa 4:135
- Surah Al-An'am 6:152
- Surah At-Taubah 9:34
- Surah An-Nisaa 4:58
- Surah An-Nisaa 4:29
- Surah Al-Hujurat 49:10
- Surah Al-Maidah 5:8
- Surah An-Nisaa 4:10
- Surah Al-A'raf 7:29
- Surah Al-Baqara 2:177
- Surah Al-Baqara 2:215
- Surah Hud 11:113
- Surah Al-A'raf 7:199
- Surah An-Nur 24:25
- Surah Al-Anbiyaa 21:47
- Surah Al-Furqan 25:2
- Surah Al-Hijr 15:19
- Surah Al-Muminun 23:18
- Surah Az-Zukhruf 43:11
- Surah Al-Baqara 2:143
- Surah Al-Baqara 2:44
- Surah An-Nisaa 4:110
- Surah Hud 11:112
- Surah An-Nahl 16:90
- Surah An-Nisaa 4:135
- Surah Al-An'am 6:152
- Surah At-Taubah 9:34
- Surah An-Nisaa 4:58
- Surah An-Nisaa 4:29
- Surah Al-Hujurat 49:10
- Surah Al-Maidah 5:8
- Surah An-Nisaa 4:10
- Surah Al-A'raf 7:29
- Surah Al-Baqara 2:177
- Surah Al-Baqara 2:215
- Surah Hud 11:113
- Surah Al-A'raf 7:199
- Surah An-Nur 24:25
- Surah At-Taubah 9:128
- Surah Al-Baqara 2:273
- Surah Al-Balad 90:12–17
- Surah Al-Hujurat 49:13
- Surah Luqman 31:20

- Surah Az-Zukhruf 43:32
- Surah Al-Baqara 2:261
- Surah Al-Hujurat 49:10
- Surah At-Taubah 9:71
- Surah Al-Qasas 28:17

CHAPTER 9

- Maryam 19:65
- An-Nisa 4:36
- Az-Zumar 39:63
- Al-An'am 6:59
- Al-Isra 17:9
- Al-Inshiqaq 84:6
- Fatir 35:6
- Al-Baqara 2:62
- Fatir 35:7
- Al-An'am 6:82
- As-Sajda 32:19
- Al-Ankabut 29:2
- Ibrahim 14:27
- Al-i'Imran 3:118
- Al-Fath 48:4
- At-Tahrim 66:6
- An-Nisa 4:111
- Al-i'Imran 3:131
- Al-Mulk 67:12
- An-Nahl 16:128
- An-Nahl 16:30
- Al-Qasas 28:60
- Fatir 35:10
- Al-Ankabut 29:64

- Al-Baqara 2:83
- Al-Baqara 2:220
- Fussilat (Ha-Mim) 41:41–49
- At-Talaq 65:5
- Al-Ma'idah 5:89
- Al-Mu'min 40:39–40
- Al-Jinn 72:4
- Fatir 35:18
- Al-Baqara 2:150
- Al-An'am 6:17
- Az-Zumar 39:7
- At-Tur 52:21
- Az-Zumar 39:52
- Al-Baqara 2:149
- Al-Baqara 2:214
- Al-Baqara 2:261
- At-Talaq 65:3
- Al-i'Imran 3:31
- Al-Jinn 72:22
- Al-Hajj 22:67
- Qaf 50:16
- Al-Mu'min 40:18
- Az-Zumar 39:53
- Fatir 35:5
- Az-Zumar 39:8
- Az-Zumar 39:33
- Muhammad 47:1
- Al-i'Imran 3:134
- Ar-Rum 30:36
- Al-i'Imran 3:135–136

- Al-Baqara 2:123
- Al-Jinn 72:18
- Qaf 50:17
- At-Talaq 65:6
- At-Taghabun 64:11
- Al-Ankabut 29:69
- Al-Mu'minun 23:62
- Al-Mumtahina 60:6
- Al-Anfal 8:38
- Al-Fath 48:17
- At-Tawbah 9:36
- Al-Ankabut 29:45
- Al-Baqara 2:155
- Al-Hajj 22:8
- Al-A'raf 7:158
- Al-Baqara 2:207
- Al-Anfal 8:28
- Al-Kahf 18:46
- Al-Baqara 2:219
- Qaf 50:17–18
- An-Nahl 16:61
- Al-Mu'min 40:58
- Al-i'Imran 3:120
- Al-Anbiyaa 21:1
- Al-Baqara 2:112
- Ar-Rum 30:45
- Luqman 31:8
- An-Nahl 16:97
- Ta-Ha 20:112
- Al-Mu'min 40:40
- Ar-Rum 30:15
- Az-Zumar 39:10
- Al-Ankabut 29:58
- Al-Mu'min 40:7
- Al-Muddaththir 74:31
- An-Nisa 4:47
- Al-A'raf 7:179
- Al-Mu'min 40:59
- Al-Anbiyaa 21:35
- Al-Ankabut 29:57
- An-Nisa 4:78
- Al-An'am 6:61
- An-Nahl 16:32
- Al-i'Imran 3:103

CHAPTER 10

- Al-Baqara 2:38
- Al-i'Imran 3:102
- Al-Anfal 8:29
- At-Tawbah 9:119
- Al-Ankabut 29:65
- At-Tawbah 9:109
- Al-A'raf 7:201
- Al-Anfal 8:2
- Al-i'Imran 3:176
- Al-i'Imran 3:177
- Muhammad 47:17

CHAPTER 11

- Al-Hashr 59:19
- Ash-Shams 91:9
- Al-Anfal 8:11

- An-Nazi'at 79:40–41
- Al-Ma'idah 5:82
- Al-Ma'idah 5:51
- Al-Mumtahina 60:8–9
- Al-Ma'idah 5:68
- Al-i'Imran 3:70
- Al-i'Imran 3:99
- Al-i'Imran 3:64
- Al-i'Imran 3:53
- Al-Ma'idah 5:69
- Al-i'Imran 3:23
- Al-i'Imran 3:24
- Al-i'Imran 3:113–115
- Al-i'Imran 3:187
- Al-i'Imran 3:188
- Al-i'Imran 3:199
- An-Nisa 4:44
- An-Nisa 4:46–47
- An-Nisa 4:51–52
- An-Nisa 4:54–55
- An-Nisa 4:160–162
- An-Nisa 4:171
- Al-Ma'idah 5:14–15, 18–19
- Al-Ma'idah 5:47
- Al-Ma'idah 5:58–66
- Al-Ma'idah 5:77
- Al-Ma'idah 5:82–85
- Al-An'am 6:20
- Al-An'am 6:146–147
- Ar-Ra'd 13:36
- An-Nahl 16:118
- Al-Qasas 28:52–53
- Al-Ankabut 29:46
- Al-Jumu'a 62:5–6
- Al-Bayyinah 98:1–8
- Al-Hadid 57:25, 57:27
- An-Nisa 4:163
- Al-Ma'idah 5:44
- Al-A'la 87:17–19
- An-Najm 53:36–37
- Al-Ma'idah 5:46
- Al-i'Imran 3:3–4, 3:7
- Al-A'la 87:6, 87:14–15
- Al-Hijr 15:9
- Al-Baqara 2:222, 2:285, 2:119, 2:129–130, 2:249–250
- An-Naml 27:20–44
- Al-Hajj 22:52
- An-Nahl 16:36
- Al-i'Imran 3:144
- Al-Ahzab 33:56
- Al-Mu'min 40:78
- Maryam 19:56–57
- Al-Anbiyaa 21:85–86, 21:79, 21:105
- Yusuf 12:111
- Al-Isra 17:55
- Sad 38:18–20, 38:26
- Al-An'am 6:84–90
- Saba 34:10–11

- As-Saff 61:6

CHAPTER 12

- Surah Ale-Imran: 3:3–4
- Surah Al-Ahzab: 33:40
- Surah Al-A'raf: 7:172, 7:54
- Surah Al-An'am: 6:162–163, 6:38
- Surah Ale-Imran: 3:110
- Surah Al-Anbiyah: 21:104–106
- Surah Ar-Ra'd: 13:39
- Surah Al-Ahzab: 33:6
- Surah Yunus: 10:61
- Surah Hud: 11:6
- Surah Al-Isra: 17:58
- Surah Saba: 34:3
- Surah Fatir: 35:11
- Surah Az-Zukhruf: 43:3–4
- Surah Qaf: 50:4
- Surah Al-Hadid: 57:22
- Surah Abasa: 80:11–15
- Surah Yunus: 10:57
- Surah Luqman: 31:27
- Surah Al-Baqarah: 2:2
- Surah Al-Isra: 17:88
- Surah An-Nahl: 16:64
- Surah Ash-Shura: 42:10
- Surah Al-An'am: 6:38
- Surah Muhammad: 47:24
- Surah Ale-Imran: 3:110
- Surah Al-Furqan: 25:30
- Surah Al-Isra: 17:82
- Surah Al-Anfal: 8:2
- Surah Az-Zukhruf: 43:36–37
- Surah Muhammad: 47:24
- Surah Sad: 38:29
- Surah Al-Baqarah: 2:185
- Surah Al-Anbiyah: 21:7
- Surah Ibrahim: 14:4
- Surah Yusuf: 12:2
- Surah Al-Anfal: 8:2
- Surah Al-A'raf: 7:204, 7:205
- Surah Al-Baqarah: 2:3, 2:43, 2:45
- Surah At-Taubah: 9:60
- Surah An-Nisa: 4:43, 4:77, 4:110, 4:142, 4:143, 4:162
- Surah Al-Ma'idah: 5:6, 5:12, 5:55, 5:58, 5:91, 5:106
- Surah Al-An'am: 6:72, 6:92, 6:162
- Surah Al-A'raf: 7:170
- Surah Al-Anfal: 8:2–4
- Surah At-Taubah: 9:18, 9:54, 9:71
- Surah Yunus: 10:87
- Surah Hud: 11:114–115
- Surah Ar-Ra'd: 13:22
- Surah Ibrahim: 14:31, 14:37, 14:40
- Surah Al-Isra: 17:78, 17:79, 17:110

- Surah Maryam: 19:55, 19:59–60
- Surah Ta-Ha: 20:14, 20:132
- Surah Al-Hajj: 22:25, 22:41, 22:78
- Surah Al-Mu'minun: 23:1–5
- Surah Fatir: 35:18
- Surah An-Nur: 24:37, 24:41, 24:56
- Surah An-Naml: 27:3
- Surah Al-Ankabut: 29:45
- Surah Ar-Rum: 30:31
- Surah Ash-Shura: 42:37–38
- Surah Luqman: 31:3–5, 31:17
- Surah Al-Mujadilah: 58:13
- Surah Al-Jumu'ah: 62:9
- Surah Al-Ma'arij: 70:34–35
- Surah Al-Muddathir: 74:40–44
- Surah Al-Bayyinah: 98:5
- Surah Al-Ma'un: 107
- Surah Al-An'am: 6:16, 6:162–163
- Surah An-Nisa: 4:103, 4:43
- Surah Al-Ma'idah: 5:6
- Surah Al-Baqarah: 2:238, 2:239
- Surah Ale-Imran: 3:39, 3:110
- Surah Al-Hajj: 22:26
- Surah Al-Fath: 48:29
- Surah Ash-Shu'araa: 26:4
- Surah Al-A'la: 87:1
- Surah Al-An'am: 6:114

CHAPTER 13

- Surah Al-Mu'min: 40:60
- Surah Al-Ma'idah: 5:27
- Surah Al-An'am: 6:164
- Surah Al-Hadid: 57:4
- Surah Qaf: 50:16
- Surah Ash-Shura: 42:37, 42:25
- Surah Hud: 52:11
- Surah Az-Zumar: 39:53
- Surah Al-Furqan: 25:68–70
- Surah Ibrahim: 14:34
- Surah An-Nahl: 16:116
- Surah Al-Baqarah: 2:186
- Surah Ar-Rahman: 55:1–4
- Surah Ar-Rum: 30:22
- Surah An-Nur: 24:15
- Surah Al-Balad: 90:8–9
- Gospel of Matthew: 12:34–35
- Surah Maryam: 19:97
- Surah Ash-Shu'ara: 26:83–84
- Surah Ale-Imran: 3:78
- Surah As-Sajda: 32:17
- Surah Al-Baqarah: 2:222, 2:127–128, 2:250, 2:286
- Surah Ale-Imran: 3:8–9, 3:16, 3:53, 3:147, 3:191–194
- Surah Al-Ma'idah: 5:83, 5:114

- Surah Al-A'raf: 7:23, 7:47, 7:89, 7:126
- Surah Yunus: 10:85–86
- Surah Ibrahim: 14:38, 14:40–41
- Surah Al-Kahf: 18:10
- Surah Ta-Ha: 20:45, 20:82
- Surah Al-Mu'minun: 23:109, 23:118
- Surah Al-Furqan: 25:65–66, 25:74
- Surah Fatir: 35:34
- Surah Al-Mu'min: 40:7–9
- Surah Al-Hashr: 59:10
- Surah Al-Mumtahinah: 60:4–5
- Surah At-Tahrim: 66:8
- Surah Al-A'raf: 7:23
- Surah An-Nahl: 16:119

CHAPTER 14
- Surah As-Sajda: 32:11
- Surah Al-Fajr: 89:27–30
- Surah Al-Baqarah: 2:28
- Surah Ad-Dukhan: 44:56
- Surah Al-Hajj: 22:66
- Surah Al-Mu'min: 40:11
- Surah Al-Mu'minun: 23:99–100
- Surah An-Nisa: 4:78, 4:97
- Surah Al-Anbiyah: 21:35
- Surah Al-Ankabut: 29:57
- Surah Al-An'am: 6:61, 6:93

- Surah Fussilat: 41:30–32
- Surah Al-Anfal: 8:50–51
- Surah Al-Waqi'a: 56:83–85
- Surah Al-Qiyamah: 75:26–30
- Surah Al-A'raf: 7:37
- Surah An-Nahl: 16:28, 16:32
- Surah Muhammad: 47:25–27
- Surah Ale-Imran: 3:8, 3:185
- Surah Al-Hujurat: 49:10–12
- Surah At-Taubah: 9:84

CHAPTER 15
- Surah Fatir: 35:22–24
- Surah Ar-Rahman: 55:20
- Surah Al-Furqan: 25:53
- Surah Al-Mu'minun: 23:100
- Surah An-Nisaa: 4:18
- Surah Al-Mu'min (Ghafir): 40:46
- Surah Al-Imran: 3:185
- Surah Al-Hijr: 15:99
- Surah Al-Fajr: 89:27–29
- Surah Al-Anbiyaa: 21:47
- Surah Al-A'raf: 7:6–9
- Surah At-Takathur: 102:1–8
- Surah Ya-Sin: 36:26
- Surah Al-Mu'minun: 23:100
- Surah Ya-Sin: 36:52
- Surah Ta-Ha: 20:103
- Surah Ya-Sin: 36:26–27
- Surah An-Naml: 27:65
- Surah Al-Ahqaf: 46:9
- Surah Al-An'am: 6:50
- Surah Al-Kahf: 18:10
- Surah Al-Kahf: 18:14
- Surah Al-Kahf: 18:16–21
- Surah Al-Kahf: 18:17–20
- Surah Al-Kahf: 18:25–26
- Surah Al-Kahf: 18:9–14

- Surah Ar-Rahman: 55:20
- Surah Al-Mu'minun: 23:100
- Surah Ghafir: 40:46
- Surah At-Taubah: 9:101
- Surah As-Sajda: 32:21
- Surah Al-Mu'min: 40:45–47
- Surah Al-Anbiyaa: 21:47
- Surah Al-Qasas: 28:38
- Surah Yunus (Jonah): 10:88–89
- Surah Ya-Sin: 36:51–53
- Surah Qaf: 50:41–44
- Surah Ta-Ha: 20:104
- Matthew: 25:30

CHAPTER 16

- Surah Al-Baqara: 2:28
- Surah Ya-Sin: 36:79
- Surah Az-Zumar: 39:68
- Surah Qaf: 50:11
- Surah Ar-Ra'd: 13:4–5
- Surah Ya-Sin: 36:78–79
- Surah Ya-Sin: 36:51
- Surah Al-Qiyamah: 75:4
- Surah An-Naml: 27:87
- Surah An-Naba': 78:18–20
- Surah An-Naba': 78:38
- Surah Al-Kahf: 18:99–100
- Surah Ta-Ha: 20:102–103
- Surah Ar-Rum: 30:55–56
- Surah Al-Qasas: 28:88
- Surah Az-Zumar: 39:68
- Surah An-Nisaa: 4:69
- Surah Fussilat (Ha-Mim): 41:31
- Surah Al-Baqara: 2:48
- Surah Al-Hajj: 22:1–2
- Surah Al-Ma'arij: 70:4
- Surah As-Sajda: 32:5
- Surah Al-Hajj: 22:47
- Surah Al-Kawthar: 108:1

- Surah Al-An'am: 6:162
- Surah At-Taghabun: 64:9–10
- Surah Al-Kahf: 18:47–48
- Surah Al-Kahf: 18:48–51
- Surah Ibrahim: 14:48–51
- Surah An-Naml: 27:65
- Surah An-Nur: 24:35
- Surah An-Nur: 24:35
- Surah Al-A'raf: 7:186
- Surah Al-Imran: 3:7
- Surah Al-An'am: 6:153
- Surah Az-Zumar: 39:61
- Surah Az-Zumar: 39:101–103
- Surah Al-Anbiyaa: 21:101–103
- Surah Al-Baqara: 2:113

CHAPTER 17

- Surah Al-A'raf: 7:187–188
- Surah Al-Anbiyaa: 21:47
- Surah Al-Inshiqaq: 84:7–12
- Surah Al-Infitar: 82:4–5
- Surah Al-Infitar: 82:15–16
- Surah At-Takwir: 81:7–14
- Surah An-Nahl: 16:21
- Surah An-Nahl: 16:24
- Surah An-Nahl: 16:25
- Surah An-Nahl: 16:27–30
- Surah An-Nahl: 16:85–89
- Surah An-Nahl: 16:111
- Surah Ibrahim: 14:21
- Surah Ibrahim: 14:22–23
- Surah Ibrahim: 14:30–32
- Surah Yunus: 10:28
- Surah Al-Isra: 17:13–14
- Surah Al-Isra: 17:71
- Surah Ale-Imran: 3:30
- Surah Al-An'am: 6:30
- Surah Ya-Sin: 36:59
- Surah Ya-Sin: 36:63–64

- Surah Al-Kahf: 18:52–53
- Surah Al-Kahf: 18:107
- Surah Al-Ahqaf: 46:34–35
- Surah Az-Zukhruf: 43:68–70
- Surah Yunus: 10:10
- Surah Az-Zumar: 39:73
- Surah Maryam: 19:71
- Surah Al-Hijr: 15:46–47
- Surah Sad: 38:51
- Surah An-Nisaa: 4:69
- Surah Al-A'raf: 7:43
- Surah Al-Mutaffifin: 83:22–28
- Surah Al-Imran: 3:133
- Surah Al-Imran: 3:136
- Surah At-Tur: 52:20–24
- Surah Ya-Sin: 36:56–58
- Surah Al-Ghashiyah: 88:10–16
- Surah Al-Ma'idah: 5:119
- Surah Muhammad: 47:15
- Surah At-Taubah: 9:72
- Surah Al-Kahf: 18:31
- Surah Al-Kahf: 18:56
- Surah Ar-Rahman: 55:35–38
- Surah Al-Waqi'ah: 56:35–38
- Surah As-Saffat: 37:48

KJV BIBLE VERSE INDEX

INTRODUCTION

2 Corinthians 5:10

Revelation 20:12

Deuteronomy 30:15–16

CHAPTER 1

Matthew 24:39

Matthew 24:38

CHAPTER 3

Romans 14:12

Matthew 3:3

Proverbs 4:26–27

Matthew 5:8

Ezekiel 36:26

Mark 7:21–23

1 John 1:5–10

Proverbs 3:5

CHAPTER 4

Romans 1:28–32

Luke 10:25–28

Matthew 23

Psalms 15:1–3

Song of Solomon 8:6

James 3:14–16

Job 5:2

Proverbs 23:17–18

James 5:7

Psalm 33:20

Psalm 37:7

Proverbs 14:29

Proverbs 15:18

Ecclesiastes 7:8–9

CHAPTER 5

Genesis 1:20–21

Genesis 1:24–25

Genesis 2:7

Genesis 2:18

Isaiah 14:12–14

Luke 10:18

Job 1:7

Colossians 1:13

John 8:32

1 Peter 5:8

Matthew 4:9

2 Corinthians 4:6

Psalm 119

Psalm 105

Psalm 130

Isaiah (various)

Psalm 8:20

Philippians 4:6

Psalms 37:7–9

Ephesians 4:2

Genesis Rabbah 38:11

Psalm 12:3–4, 9

Hebrews 11:6

Exodus 20:16

Genesis 12:18–20

John 8:44

Revelation 21:8

Hebrews 2:14–15

John 14:30

John 12:31

John 16:11

2 Thessalonians 2:9–12

Matthew 13:18–22, 38–39

2 Corinthians 4:4

Ephesians 6:12

Genesis 49:5–7

Isaiah 58:10

Matthew 14:16

Romans 12:20

Exodus 20:12

Leviticus 18:22

Romans 1:26–27

1 Corinthians 6:9–10

Genesis 18:32

Genesis 19:9

Genesis 19:23–29

CHAPTER 6

Proverbs 4:23–27

Deuteronomy 4:2

Revelation 22:18–19

Jeremiah 4:22

Jeremiah 8:8

Jeremiah 31:31–37

Matthew 15:1–3, 6–9

2 Corinthians 11:14

1 John 4:1

Matthew 24:24–25

1 Thessalonians 5:19–22

CHAPTER 8

Psalm 72:1–4

Isaiah 1:15–17

2 Chronicles 19:5–7

Exodus 23:3; 19:15

Leviticus (various)

Psalm 72:1–2

Amos 5:12

Zechariah 7:9–12

Micah 6:8

Amos 5:4–7, 10, 14–15, 21–24

Amos 6:12

Habakkuk 1:1–6

1 Peter 5:6–9

Habakkuk 3:1–8

Luke 11:42–46

Ezekiel 3:20–21

Ecclesiastes 3:17

Proverbs 21:15

Romans 12:19

Romans 12:21

Romans 1:17–18

Psalm 37:8–9

Psalms 72:12–14

Job 29:14–16

Romans 3:12

Psalms 143:2

Psalm 2:6

1 Timothy 6:9–10

CHAPTER 9

Matthew 16:19

CHAPTER 10

Proverbs 28:14

Malachi 3:5

CHAPTER 11

Psalm 51:10

Psalm 24

Psalm 24:3–4

Matthew 5:8

Revelation 11:7–12

2 Kings 2

Genesis 5:24, 27

2 Samuel 5:2

CHAPTER 12

Exodus 40:30–32

Exodus 30:17–22

Matthew 26:36–39

Acts 10:1–3

1 Kings 8:29–30

Daniel 6:10

CHAPTER 13

Deuteronomy 24:16

Isaiah 59:1–2

Deuteronomy 34:10

Proverbs 18:21

Matthew 12:34–37

James 3:6, 8

Psalms 50:19–21

Psalm 141:3

Luke 15:24

Luke 16:24

CHAPTER 15

Avot 4:17

Psalm 146:4

Genesis 3:19

Daniel 12

Isaiah 26:19

Ezekiel 37:1–14

1 Corinthians 15:51–52

Revelation 11:15

Matthew 25:32–41

CHAPTER 16

Genesis 9:9

Leviticus 26:37

Daniel 12:2

Isaiah 18:3

1 Corinthians 15:51–52

Joel 2:1

Matthew 24:4–51

Revelation 11:15

Revelation 8:1–7

Revelation 8:8–9

Revelation 8:12–13

2 Peter 2:4

Jude 1:6

Revelation 9:13–21

Revelation 11:15–18

Genesis 17:12–14

Matthew 7:7–14

Isaiah 42:16

Isaiah 30:21

Proverbs 8:18–20

Romans 5:12–14

Romans 3:11

Jeremiah 29:13

Leviticus Rabbah 27:1

Pirkei Avot 4:22

Job 3:11–19

Nehemiah 9:6

Leviticus 26:3–6

Revelation 20:7–15

Daniel 12:2

Proverbs 2:20–22

CHAPTER 17

Genesis 3:22–24

Genesis 25:8

Genesis 25:17

Genesis 35:29

Genesis 49:33

Deuteronomy 32:50

Deuteronomy 7:13–14

Matthew (various)

CONTENTS SOURCING INDEX

CHAPTERS 1–2: Testing is the First Step on This Journey

1. https://www.wow4u.com/accountable-quotes/

2. https://muslimmatters.org/2010/05/12/eye-opening-words-in-the-quran-describing-the-life-of-this-world/

3. http://www.littlethingsmatter.com/blog/2010/10/07/personal-accountability%E2%80%94a-requirement-for-life-advancement/

4. https://abdurrahman.org/2014/01/08/greater-hardship-greater-reward/

CHAPTER 3: Preparation

5. https://www.al-islam.org/articles

6. http://www.spiritofislam.co.in

7. https://salamislam.com/lifestyle

8. https://www.al-islam.org/articles/merits-soul-patience-sab

9. http://www.quranreading.com/blog/

10. http://al-qiyamah.org/ruh_of_allah_al_isra.htm

Scholarly & Historical Sources

Index 6 – Ibn Kathir

(1301–1373 CE) – Renowned Syrian scholar of tafsir and Islamic history. His works include *Tafsir al-Qur'an al-Azim* and *Al-Bidaya wa'l-Nihaya*.

Source: Wikipedia

Index 7 – Imam Muslim (Muslim ibn al-Hajjaj)

Compiler of *Sahih Muslim*, one of the most authentic hadith collections in Sunni Islam.

Source: Wikipedia

Index 8 – Ibn Abbas (c. 619–687 CE)

Cousin of the Prophet Muhammad (ﷺ), known as the "Interpreter of the Qur'an."

Source: Wikipedia

Index 9 – Treaty of Hudaybiyyah

Historical event between Prophet Muhammad (ﷺ) and the Quraysh of Mecca in 628 CE, leading to a pivotal peace agreement.

Source: Wikipedia

Index 10 – The Human Heart in the Glorious Qur'an

http://quranproject.org/The-human-heart-in-the-glorious-Quran-481-d

Christian Sources

Index 11

- Mark 7:21–23 – Bible Gateway (NIV)

- https://www.compellingtruth.org/what-is-the-heart.html

- http://www.arabnews.com/islam-perspective/news/817556

Index 12 – The Conference of the Birds

1. https://www.gradesaver.com/the-conference-of-the-birds/study-guide/summary

2. http://traditionalhikma.com/wp-content/uploads/2015/06/Conference-of-the-Birds-by-Faridudin-Attar.pdf

3. http://www.poemhunter.com/poem/conference-of-the-birds/

4. https://researchmgt.monash.edu/ws/portalfiles/portal/243002885/24300250 04.pdf

5. https://www.sutori.com/en/story/the-conference-of-the-birds--Myf2V1FLnFEJeU2nW7sgdqdx

CHAPTER 4

SATAN AND OUR DEFENSE

Index 13

Nil Sorsky (Russian: Нил Сорский, also Nilus of Sora and Nil Sorski; birth name: Nikolai Maikov (Russian: Николай Майков) (c. 1433–1508) became a leader of a tendency in the medieval Russian Orthodox Church known as the Non-possessors (nestyazhateli), which opposed ecclesiastic landownership.

The Russian Orthodox Church venerates Nil Sorsky as a saint, marking his feast day on the anniversary of his repose on May 7.

🔗 Wikipedia: Nilus of Sora

Index 14

🔗 Acts 5:3 (ESV)

Index 15

🔗 BibleGateway.com

Index 16

🔗 BibleGateway.com

Index 17

🔗 Isaiah 14:12–14 (NKJV)

Index 18

Abu Abdullah Sufyan ibn Said ibn Masruq al-Thawri was a Tābi' al-Tābi'īn Islamic scholar and jurist, founder of the Thawri madhhab. He was also a great hadith compiler. *(Wikipedia)*

Index 19

Ibn al-Jawzi (d. 597 H / 1201 AD) was a Baghdadi storyteller, preacher, and prolific Islamic scholar associated with the Hanbali school of jurisprudence. He is well known for his exegeses of the Qur'an and Hadith, including his famous compendium *Al-Tahqiq*.

Index 20

🔗 Sources of waswas and accountability – IslamQA

Index 20a

🔗 Passover: History.com

🔗 BBC Bitesize: Passover

Index 20b

🔗 Matthew 28 (NIV) – BibleGateway

🔗 Sabbath Definition – Merriam-Webster

Index 20c

🔗 Al-Aqsa Attacks – Al Araby

🔗 ABC News: Violence ahead of Ramadan

Index 20d

🔗 Al Araby – Al-Aqsa attacks

Index 20e

🔗 France24: IS Group mosque blast

Index 20f

🔗 Quran burning riots – Al Jazeera

Index 20g

🔗 BBC: Asia News

Index 20h

🔗 Afghanistan deaths – Al Jazeera

Index 20k

🔗 Kabul mosque attack – Al Jazeera

Index 21

🔗 Arab News

Index 22

🔗 Practice of Ihsan – Deccan Herald

Index 23

🔲 প্রতিনিধি, বাগমারা, রাজশাহী, প্রকাশ: ২০ অগাস্ট ২০২০, ১৪:১৫

🔗 Prothom Alo

Index 24

Al-Ghazali was a Persian philosopher, one of the most prominent and influential Muslim philosophers, theologians, jurists, and mystics of Sunni Islam.

Died: 19 December 1111, Tous, Iran *(Wikipedia)*

Index 25

🔲 My News / MR

🔗 [Daily Amar Sangbad](https://www.dailyamarsangbad.com/crime/239914/গুরুদাসপুর-নাটোর-প্রতিনিধি-আগস্ট-১৯-২০২০)

Index 26

🔗 Sahih Muslim Hadith 38 – IIUM

Index 27

🔗 Prophet Dawud Story PDF – Islamic Studies Resources

Index 27A

🔗 Hypocrites Commentary – IslamicMobility

Index 28

🔗 Sahih al-Bukhari 34 – Sunnah.com

☞ Internal Destruction – IslamWeb

Index 29

☞ AlQuranBD – Read Qur'an

Index 30

📖 *Jamiu's-Saghir*, Hadith No: 8525

☞ Types of Backbiting – Questions on Islam

Index 31

📖 Webb B. Garrison (2007), *"To Backbite"*, *Why You Say It*, Read Books, p. 166. ISBN 9781406776195

Note: Includes background on distinct development of the Baha'i faith from Islam.

Index 32

☞ CTV News – Babies Get Jealous

Index 33

☞ Islamicity: Satan – His Origin and Purpose

Index 34

☞ Jealousy – GSALAM.net

Index 34a

☞ Reality of Jinn – QuranExplorer Blog

Index 35

Hasan of Basra, Sunni Islamic ulama, known as Abi Sayeed, born during the era of Caliph Umar.

Index 36

From *Wikipedia, the free encyclopedia*

Index 38

☞ Deceitful Women in Arabic Literature – Mount Holyoke

Index 39

Hisham ibn al-Kalbi, Arab historian. Dihyah bin Khalifah al-Kalbi was a companion of the Prophet Muhammad and resembled the angel Jibril in human form. *(Wikipedia)*

Index 40

Rukn al-Dīn Maḥmūd ibn Muḥammad al-Malāḥimī al-Khuwārazmī (d. 1141), Muʿtazilī and Ḥanafī theologian. *(Wikipedia)*

Index 41

Imam Ibn al-Jawzī (c. 1116 – 1201), prominent Hanbali scholar, orator, and historian based in Baghdad. *(Wikipedia)*

Index 42

Further details on Ibn al-Malāḥimī's opposition to metaphysics and works on Muʿtazilī theology.

Index 43

Mujahid ibn Jabr, a renowned Qur'anic exegete, student of Imam Ali and Ibn Abbas.

⊶ Wikipedia: Mujahid ibn Jabr

Index 44

Abd Allah ibn Abbas, cousin of Prophet Muhammad and father of Qur'anic exegesis. *(Wikipedia)*

Index 45

https://quran.com/114 — Sūrat al-Nās: The final chapter of the Qur'an, often recited for protection against the whisperings of Satan (waswas).

Index 46

https://sunnah.com/abudawud:4738 — Reference from Sunan Abi Dawud on seeking protection from Satan before entering the bathroom or during times of vulnerability.

Index 47

Al-Nawawi (1233–1277 CE), a leading Islamic scholar of the Shafi'i school, known for his works such as *Riyadh as-Salihin* and his commentary on *Sahih Muslim*. He emphasized the role of dhikr in repelling satanic influences.

Index 48

https://www.al-islam.org/articles/influence-shaytan — Article detailing Shi'a Islamic perspectives on Satan's influence and human responsibility.

Index 49

https://www.biblestudytools.com/commentaries/matthew-henry-complete/ — Matthew Henry's Complete Commentary on the Bible, offering Protestant theological perspectives on Satan's tactics.

Index 50

Imam Ibn Taymiyyah (1263–1328 CE), a renowned Hanbali scholar, author of *Majmu' al-Fatawa*, addressed Satan's influence in depth, especially regarding thoughts and intentions.

Index 51

https://www.learnreligions.com/what-is-satanism-95814 — Overview of modern Satanism and its divergence from religious texts, illustrating distortions of truth that can serve Satan's narrative.

Index 52

https://www.psychologytoday.com/us/blog/out-the-darkness/202007/how-different-cultures-understand-evil — Discussion on cross-cultural views of evil, including Satanic archetypes.

Index 53

Imam Fakhr al-Din al-Razi (1149–1209 CE), known for *Tafsir al-Kabir*, explored the philosophical and theological aspects of Iblis' rebellion and human susceptibility to deception.

Index 54

https://www.thegospelcoalition.org/essay/satan/ — Evangelical Christian overview of Satan's origin, role, and destiny, drawn from both Old and New Testament texts.

Index 55

https://sunnah.com/muslim:2814 — Hadith from Sahih Muslim about the power of Ayat al-Kursi (Surah al-Baqarah 2:255) in protecting from Satan.

Index 56

Sayyid Qutb (1906–1966), in his *Fi Zilal al-Qur'an* (In the Shade of the Qur'an), provided insight into the Qur'anic narrative of Satan and human struggle, especially in the context of social justice.

Index 57

https://quranx.com/Tafsirs/7.200 — Tafsir on Qur'an 7:200: "And if an evil suggestion comes to you from Satan, then seek refuge in Allah."

Index 58

https://www.blueletterbible.org/lexicon/h7854/kjv/ — Hebrew lexicon entry for "Satan" (שָׂטָן), showing its linguistic roots as "adversary" or "accuser," important for intertextual comparison.

Chapter 5

LIVING IN THE DARK OCCUPIED WORLD

Index 60

- Life on Earth Before Adam – SomaliWave

- Was Adam the First Man? – Islamic Info

- Victory for Abraham Blog – Was Adam the First Man?

- Wikipedia Articles:

    o "Azazil"

    o "Who is Iblis?"

- Referenced Works:

1. Briggs, Constance Victoria (2003). *The Encyclopedia of God*. Hampton Roads Publishing. ISBN 978-1-612-83225-8.

2. Nagawasa, Eiji (1992). *An Introductory Note on Contemporary Arabic Thought*.

3. Welch, Alford T. (2008). *Studies in Qur'an and Tafsir*. Scholars Press.

4. Gauvain, Richard (2013). *Salafi Ritual Purity*. Routledge.

5. Islam Issa. *Milton in the Arab-Muslim World*. Taylor & Francis (2016). ISBN 978-1-317-09592-7.

Index 61

- Women and Deceit – Mount Holyoke Project

Index 62

- Group Bible Study – War in Heaven and on Earth

Index 63

- Colossians 1 – Bible Gateway (NIV)

Index 64

- Facing History – Holocaust, Education, and the Future

Index 65

- Tearfund – Decoding Coronavirus

Index 66

- Arab News – Islamic Perspective

Index 67

- Wikipedia – Abraham in Islam

Index 68

- The Image of Ayyub – BibleInterp

Index 69

- Truth and Lies in Jewish Tradition – My Jewish Learning
- Status of a Liar in Islam – IslamicFinder

Index 70

- RAND Corporation – Monograph MG246

Index 71

- FBI – East African Embassy Bombings

Index 72–73

- AOAV – Suicide Attacks on 9/11 Remembered

Index 74

- PBS Frontline – Bin Laden's Edicts

Index 75

- 9/11 Commission Report (PDF)

Index 76

- Definition of Terrorism – JMVH

Index 77–78

- BBC News – Reality Check: Terrorism

Index 79

- Al Jazeera – 20 Years After 9/11

Index 80

- History.com – Colin Powell's Speech on Iraq Invasion

Index 81

- Satan's Lies – FOLCC

Index 82

- Tony Blair and the Iraq War – Middle East Eye
- *Not the Chilcot Report* by Peter Oborne (Referenced Book)

Index 83–85

- History.com – Iraq War Begins
- CFR – Iraq War Timeline
- The American Conservative – U.S. Lost Iraq War

Index 86–88

- New Yorker – Torture at Abu Ghraib
- Truthout – Corporate Accountability for Abu Ghraib
- Al Jazeera – Abu Ghraib Legacy

Index 89

- Al Jazeera – Iraqis Reject Bush's Abu Ghraib Plan

Index 90

- Amnesty – Arab Spring, Five Years On

Index 91–92

- Military Wikia – Grand Mosque Seizure

Index 93

- History.com – Treaty of Versailles and WWII

Index 94

- Britannica – Biljana Plavsic
- Independent – Karadzic and European Mass Murder
- Atlantic – Bosnian War Photo Essay

Index 95

- LA Times – Bosnia Conflict Coverage (1993)

Index 96

- ReliefWeb – Sudan Civil War Death Toll

Index 97

- DOJ Issues Paper – Chronology of Events 1993–1995 (PDF)

Index 98–99

- UK Government – Same-Sex Marriage Law
- Wikipedia – LGBT Rights by Country

Index 100–101

- Gospel Herald – Bible Verses in Gay Marriage Debate

- Biblia – 1 Corinthians 6:9–10 (ESV)
- Living Out – The Bible and SSA

Index 102–103

- My Islam – Story of Prophet Lut
- Christianity.com – Sin of Sodom and Gomorrah

Index 104

- Britannica – Pompeii
- SunnahOnline – Fate of Pompeii

Index 105

- Politico – Germans Blame China for Pandemic

Index 106

- Express UK – Pope Francis: Devil Is Real
- **Daily Mail – Pope Warns About Satan**

Index 107

- NCBI – Pandemic Research Article

Index 108

- National Geographic – Devil in Medieval Art

Index 109–113

- Wikipedia – Persecution of Jews During Black Death
- BBC – The Black Death
- Ancient Origins – The Black Death
- Ancient.eu – Cats in the Middle Ages

Index 114–117

- BibleHub – Matthew 4:9
- Biblia – Psalm 119:130
- Answering Islam – Satan in Islam

CHAPTERS 6–7: Straight Path / Hadith We Follow

Index 118 – Examples of Bad Hadiths

Index 119 – Sunan Abu Dawud 39/1

Index 120 – Sahih Bukhari, Book 60

631

Index 121 – Collected from:

- **Jeremiah 8:8 Bible Commentary**
- Muslim Villa: Misinterpretation of Hadith
- **Index 122 –** Arab News Article

CHAPTER 8: Justice and Empathy

Index 123 – Prophet Daud (AS) Part II – Hadith of the Day

Index 124 – [Jamiat-Tirmidhi 818](https://www.alim.org/hadith/tirmidi/818/)

Index 125 [Search on Justice Tirmidhi Hadith]

(https://quranx.com/Search?Q=JUSTICE+&Context=hadith-Tirmidhi)

Index 126 [Indonesia Denies Entry to Rohingya]

(https://www.dw.com/en/indonesia-denies-entry-to-rohingya-stranded-at-sea/a-60279486)

Index 127[Global Justice: Crisis of Inequality and War]

(https://www.globaljustice.org.uk/news/not-migrant-crisis-its-crisis-inequality-and-war/)

Index 128 – PDF Source — Local File:sustainability-12-05027.pdf

Index 129 – Equal Justice for the Poor – NYT 1964

Index 130 – African Migrants Left to Die – Telegraph

Index 131 – *Sunan al-Tirmidhi 2736*, **Grade: Hasan**

Index 132 – ILO Report on Arab States

Index 133 – Bible Verses on Empathy – Bible Reasons

Index 134 – 1 Peter 3:8–12 (ESV)

Index 135 – *Not Provided*

CHAPTERS 9–10: My Key to Heaven / Fear Allah

Index 136 – Surah Āl-'Imrān – Quran Shareef

Index 137 – *Not Provided*

CHAPTER 11: Break the Ice

Index 138 – British Muslims – MCB

Index 139 – Religious Inequality in London – Trust for London

Index 140 – *PDF Source* — Local File: 28024844_First_draft_Classical_Tafsir_al-Mathur_a.pdf

Index 141 – <u>Marabout – Britannica</u>

Index 142 – <u>Ahlul Kitab – About Islam</u>

Index 143 – <u>Is a Muslim Allowed to Read the Bible?</u>

Index 144 – <u>Hayatul Qulub PDF – Page 597</u>

Index 145 – *Hayatul Qulub – Vol. 1: Stories of the Prophets*

Index 146 – <u>Enoch in the Bible – Christianity.com</u>

Index 147 –

- <u>Sirr al-Asrar – Jilani</u>

- <u>The Prophet Idris (AS) – Ghayb</u>

- **Index 148 –**

- <u>Prophet Idris – Helsinki Database</u>

- <u>Miracles of Idris – WyeC</u>

- **Index 149 –**

- <u>Imam Reza – Biography of the Prophet</u>

- <u>Faith of the Prophet's Ancestors – Al-Islam</u>

CHAPTER 12: The Constitution of This Earth

Index 150: <u>The UK Constitution (UK Parliament)</u>

Index 151: <u>Preamble – Constitution of India</u>

Index 152: <u>Chinese Laws & Regulations – State Council</u>

Index 153: <u>Saudi Arabia Constitution (2005) – Constitute Project</u>

Index 154:

- <u>Story of Creation – IslamReligion.com</u>

- <u>Lawh al-Mahfuz in the Qur'an – The Last Dialogue</u>

- **Index 155:** <u>Fethullah Gülen's Works</u>

- **Index 156:** <u>Retrieving the Knowledge of Revelation – ResearchGate</u>

- **Index 157:** <u>Understanding the Qur'an – Salam Islam</u>

- **Index 158:** <u>Pillars: Salat Words – Quran-Islam.org</u>

- **Index 159:** <u>Daily Prayers: Not for Muslims Only – Patheos</u>

CHAPTER 13: Allah's Clemency

Index 160: <u>The Depth of Our Sin – Ligonier Ministries</u>

Index 161: <u>A Divine Perspective on Rights – Al-Islam.org</u>

Index 162: <u>Power of the Tongue – Bible Study Tools</u>

Index 163: <u>Tongue in Scripture – Knowing Jesus</u>

Index 164: <u>What is Tawbah – UnderstandQuran.com</u>

Index 165: <u>Tongue in Scripture – Knowing Jesus (duplicate reference)</u>

CHAPTER 14: When My Journey Ends

Index 166: <u>Angel of Death – IslamQA</u>

Index 167: <u>Death: A Beautiful Gift – Al-Islam.org</u>

Index 168: <u>The Moment of Death – Contemplate Qur'an</u>

Index 169: <u>Bad Neighbours – IUHK</u>

Index 170: <u>Peace and Reconciliation – Al-Islam.org</u>

Index 171: <u>Make Peace – Farhat Hashmi</u>

Index 172: <u>The Journey Continues: Barzakh and Beyond – Islamic Insights</u>

CHAPTER 15: Place of Waiting

Index 173: <u>Surah Yaseen: Ayah 52 – MyIslam.org</u>

Index 174: <u>Tafseer of Ayah 52 – StudentsofKnowledge.org</u>

Index 175: <u>Israr Khan – HeyLink</u>

Index 176:

- <u>Seven Sleepers of Ephesus – Britannica</u>
- <u>Grotto of Seven Sleepers – Turkish Archaeology News</u>
- <u>YouTube Video</u>
- <u>Decius – Wikipedia</u>
- <u>Surah al-Kahf – Quran.com</u>
- **Index 177:** <u>Seven Sleepers – Britannica</u>
- **Index 178:** <u>Firon – Encyclopedia & Villains Wiki</u>
- **Index 179:** <u>Life in Barzakh – IslamWeb</u>
- **Index 180:** <u>Olam Ha-Ba – Jewish Virtual Library</u>
- **Index 181:** <u>Afterlife in Judaism – Jewish Virtual Library</u>
- **Index 182:** <u>After Death – Gospel Tract and Bible Society</u>

CHAPTER 16: Resurrection

Index 183: 2 Nephi 9 – Church of Jesus Christ

Index 184: Do Angels Die? – IslamQA

Index 185:

- On Eschatology and the Day of Reckoning – Medium
- **Index 186: Allah's Days – Answering Islam**
- **Index 187:** Who is Apollyon? – StackExchange
- **Index 188:** Feast of Trumpets – Hallel.info
- **Index 189:** Tafseer of Al-Kawthar – Najeeb Qasmi
- **Index 190:** Do Angels Die? – IslamQA (Repeated)
- **Index 191:** Pirkei Avot 4:22 – Sefaria
- **Index 192:** Job 3 – BibleGateway (ESV)

CHAPTER 16–17: Resurrection & Judgment Day

Index 193:

- Revelation 20:7–15 – BibleGateway
- What is Sheol – DesiringGod.org
- **Index 194:**
- Search the Scriptures – MyDailyTribune
- Luke 9:23 – BibleGateway
- Narrow Path – Got Questions
- **Index 195:**
- Cross As-Sirat Safely – Isa and Islam
- Day of Resurrection: Bridge Siraat – AbdurRahman.org
- Hadith: Gates of Heaven – Reddit
- Doors of Jannah – ScienceFaith.com
- An-Nur 24:40 – Qurano.com
- Seven Levels of Heaven – ZamZam Blog

References

General References

1. "Some Misconceptions – Quran's True Light." https://quranstruelight.com/some-history/misconceptions

2. "Saudi Islamic scholar Dr. Al Malki at risk of execution." *MENA Rights Group*. Retrieved June 30, 2020. https://www.menarights.org

3. "Death penalty sought for Islamic researcher Hassan al-Maliki on charges that his religious views contradict Mohammad bin Salman's pledge to destroy extremism." *European-Saudi Organisation for Human Rights*. Retrieved June 30, 2020.

4. "Archived copy." Archived from the original on March 3, 2020. Retrieved March 3, 2020.

5. "Anti-Wahhabi Saudi thinker faces execution: HRW." *PressTV*. Retrieved June 30, 2020.

6. Admin. "Hassan al-Maliki from his jail: Wahhabism arrested me not government." *International Shia News Agency*, October 28, 2014. Retrieved June 30, 2020.

Academic Sources

7. Seliktar, Ofira, and Farhad Rezaei. *Proxies in the Gulf and Beyond: Saudi Arabia, the Gulf Principalities, and Yemen.* In *Iran, Revolution, and Proxy Wars.* Palgrave Macmillan, Cham, 2020. pp. 203–234.

8. El-Ghattis, Nedal. "Deconstructing Islamic Banking – History of Debates, and Steps to an Alternative Future." *Foresight* (2016).

Multimedia Sources

9. Video timestamps:
   - 3:50 – Percentages
   - 6:40 – Terms for Sunnis & Shias
   - YouTube Video

Hadith and Mutʿah Marriage

- ☒ "Exposing Mutah" & "The Quranic Evidence Against Mutah." *Myth Busting About Islam.*

- ☒ Source PDF: Exposing Mutah

- ☒ Qur'anic Reference:

☒ Surah Al-Ma'idah (5:5) – Verse discourages secrecy or private love, which is interpreted as contrary to Mutʿah.

Prayer & Forgiveness

☒ "What is Sin?" AllAboutGod.com

☒ Hadith Commentary:

https://hadithcommentary.com/nawawi/hadith37/

☒ Islamic Phrases: https://myislam.org/subhanallah-walhamdulillah-wala-ilaha-illallah/

☒ Islamic Blog: https://rislyonline.wordpress.com/

☒ Ibn Taymiyyah (Biography from Wikipedia):

Taqī ad-Dīn Aḥmad ibn Abd al-Halim ibn Abd al-Salam al-Numayri al-Ḥarrānī, known as Ibn Taymiyyah, was a Muslim scholar, muhaddith, theologian, judge, and philosopher.

Born: January 22, 1263, Harran, Turkey.

Died: September 26, 1328, Citadel of Damascus.

☒ "Why Pray in Arabic?" Ahmed H. Sheriff – al-Islam.org

☒ "Quranic Arabic vs. Modern Standard Arabic" – Arab Academy

☒ Duas for Forgiveness – Quran Academy

☒ "Five Virtues of Istighfar" – OnePath Network

Sirat al-Mustaqeem (The Straight Path)

1. Ahmad Muhammad Shakir (1892–1958). Prominent Egyptian Hadith scholar. Wikipedia

2. Abdullah ibn Masʿud – Noted for transmitting 848 hadith. Wikipedia

3. "What is the Sirat al-Mustaqeem?" – AFOSA

4. "Lessons from Surah Fatihah: Identifying the Straight Path" – Virtual Mosque

5. "Ranks of Paradise – Some Details" – Verse by Verse Quran Study Circle

6. Imam Ragheeb al-Isfahani (Referenced via the same link above)

7. Al-Nasā'ī (c. 829 – 915 CE) – Author of *As-Sunan*, among the six canonical Sunni hadith collections. Wikipedia

8. Mowlana Syed Aftab Haider – Ramadan Lecture No. 23, Ottery, Cape Town, 17 May 2020.

9. Islam21c Source – www.islam21c.com

Final Notes and Additional Online Sources

"To You is the journey's end. The following websites have helped to write this part of the book."

- ☒ https://www.isaandislam.com/miscellaneous-questions/cross-al-sirat-safely-to-paradise/

- ☒ https://abdurrahman.org/2018/11/30/day-of-resurrection-the-bridge-siraat/

- ☒ Hadith about Gates of Heaven – Reddit

- ☒ Gulf Times – At the Gates of Paradise

- ☒ "Some of the Bounties Allah Has Prepared for the Believers in Paradise" – Sunnah Online

- ☒ "The Angels Present at the Time of Death" – Ideal Muslimah

www.ingramcontent.com/pod-product-compliance
Lightning Source LLC
Chambersburg PA
CBHW080942120626
46546CB00010B/2812